WORKSHOPS IN COMPUTING
Series edited by C. J. van Rijsbergen

Also in this series

Logic Program Synthesis and Transformation
Proceedings of LOPSTR 92, International
Workshop on Logic Program Synthesis and
Transformation, University of Manchester,
2–3 July 1992
Kung-Kiu Lau and Tim Clement (Eds.)

NAPAW 92, Proceedings of the First North
American Process Algebra Workshop, Stony Brook,
New York, USA, 28 August 1992
S. Purushothaman and Amy Zwarico (Eds.)

First International Workshop on Larch
Proceedings of the First International Workshop on
Larch, Dedham, Massachusetts, USA,
13–15 July 1992
Ursula Martin and Jeannette M. Wing (Eds.)

Persistent Object Systems
Proceedings of the Fifth International Workshop on
Persistent Object Systems, San Miniato (Pisa),
Italy, 1–4 September 1992
Antonio Albano and Ron Morrison (Eds.)

**Formal Methods in Databases and Software
Engineering,** Proceedings of the Workshop on
Formal Methods in Databases and Software
Engineering, Montreal, Canada, 15–16 May 1992
V.S. Alagar, Laks V.S. Lakshmanan and
F. Sadri (Eds.)

Modelling Database Dynamics
Selected Papers from the Fourth International
Workshop on Foundations of Models and
Languages for Data and Objects, Volkse, Germany,
19–22 October 1992
Udo W. Lipeck and Bernhard Thalheim (Eds.)

14th Information Retrieval Colloquium
Proceedings of the BCS 14th Information
Retrieval Colloquium, University of Lancaster,
13–14 April 1992
Tony McEnery and Chris Paice (Eds.)

Functional Programming, Glasgow 1992
Proceedings of the 1992 Glasgow Workshop on
Functional Programming, Ayr, Scotland,
6–8 July 1992
John Launchbury and Patrick Sansom (Eds.)

Z User Workshop, London 1992
Proceedings of the Seventh Annual Z User
Meeting, London, 14–15 December 1992
J.P. Bowen and J.E. Nicholls (Eds.)

Interfaces to Database Systems (IDS92)
Proceedings of the First International Workshop
on Interfaces to Database Systems,
Glasgow, 1–3 July 1992
Richard Cooper (Ed.)

AI and Cognitive Science '92
University of Limerick, 10–11 September 1992
Kevin Ryan and Richard F.E. Sutcliffe (Eds.)

Theory and Formal Methods 1993
Proceedings of the First Imperial College
Department of Computing Workshop on Theory
and Formal Methods, Isle of Thorns Conference
Centre, Chelwood Gate, Sussex, UK,
29–31 March 1993
Geoffrey Burn, Simon Gay and Mark Ryan (Eds.)

**Algebraic Methodology and Software
Technology (AMAST'93)**
Proceedings of the Third International Conference
on Algebraic Methodology and Software
Technology, University of Twente, Enschede,
The Netherlands, 21–25 June 1993
M. Nivat, C. Rattray, T. Rus and G. Scollo (Eds.)

Logic Program Synthesis and Transformation
Proceedings of LOPSTR 93, International
Workshop on Logic Program Synthesis and
Transformation, Louvain-la-Neuve, Belgium,
7–9 July 1993
Yves Deville (Ed.)

Database Programming Languages (DBPL-4)
Proceedings of the Fourth International
Workshop on Database Programming Languages
– Object Models and Languages, Manhattan, New
York City, USA, 30 August–1 September 1993
Catriel Beeri, Atsushi Ohori and
Dennis E. Shasha (Eds.)

**Music Education: An Artificial Intelligence
Approach,** Proceedings of a Workshop held as
part of AI-ED 93, World Conference on Artificial
Intelligence in Education, Edinburgh, Scotland,
25 August 1993
Matt Smith, Alan Smaill and
Geraint A. Wiggins (Eds.)

Rules in Database Systems
Proceedings of the 1st International Workshop on
Rules in Database Systems, Edinburgh, Scotland,
30 August–1 September 1993
Norman W. Paton and
M. Howard Williams (Eds.)

continued on back page...

D.J. Andrews, J.F. Groote and C.A. Middelburg (Eds.)

Semantics of Specification Languages (SoSL)

Proceedings of the International
Workshop on Semantics of Specification
Languages, Utrecht, The Netherlands,
25–27 October 1993

Published in collaboration with the
British Computer Society

BCS
FACS

Springer-Verlag
London Berlin Heidelberg New York
Paris Tokyo Hong Kong
Barcelona Budapest

Universiteit
Utrecht

D.J. Andrews
Department of Mathematics and Computer Science
University of Leicester, University Road
Leicester, LE1 7RH, UK

J.F. Groote, dr.ir
C.A. Middelburg, prof.dr.ir

Department of Philosophy
Utrecht University
Heidelberglaan 8, 3584 CS Utrecht
The Netherlands

ISBN-13:978-3-540-19854-3   e-ISBN-13:978-1-4471-3229-5
DOI: 10.1007/978-1-4471-3229-5

British Library Cataloguing in Publication Data
A catalogue record for this book is available from the British Library

Typesetting: Camera ready by contributors

34/3830-543210 Printed on acid-free paper

Preface

SoSL was the first International Workshop on Semantics of Specification Languages, held from 25–27 October 1993 in Utrecht, the Netherlands. The workshop was organized by the Department of Philosophy of Utrecht University with financial support from the Nationale Faciliteit Informatica of the Nederlandse Organisatie voor Wetenschappelijk Onderzoek (NWO), and under the auspices of the British Computer Society's specialist group in Formal Aspects of Computing Science (BCS FACS).

The concern of the workshop was the semantics of specification languages, and the issues closely related to this area, such as type checking and the justification of proof rules and proof obligations. Its aim was the exchange of problems and ideas in this field of formal methods, and the identification of common programs of work for further investigation.

The program of SoSL consisted of 3 invited lectures presenting the developments of the semantics of 3 major specification languages. Furthermore, there were 16 presentations of submitted papers. This volume provides a direct account of the workshop. It contains 3 papers that match the invited lectures and the 16 selected papers.

The editors want to thank all those who have contributed to the workshop; the Program Committee and the referees for selecting the contributed papers, the invited speakers for their interesting talks, the Organizing Committee for all their efforts, and of course the participants. We have the feeling that the workshop was worthwhile and should be repeated.

Utrecht, November 1993   The Editors

Invited Speakers:

Stephen Brien, Oxford University (Z)
Loe Feijs, Philips Research Laboratories Eindhoven (COLD)
Robert Milne, BNR Europe (RSL)

Program Committee:

Derek Andrews, University of Leicester (chair)
Jan Bergstra, University of Amsterdam, Utrecht University

George Leih, PTT Research
Brian Monahan, University of Manchester
Hans Toetenel, Delft University of Technology
Jean Goubault, Bull Corporate Research Centre
Jim Woodcock, Oxford University

Organizing Committee

Annemarie Besselink, Utrecht University
Jan Friso Groote, Utrecht University
Kees Middelburg, PTT Research, Utrecht University (chair)
Rick Thomas, University of Leicester

Contents

The Development of Z

Stephen Brien

Programming Research Group, Oxford University

Abstract

Z is a model-oriented specification language, which originated in the early 1980s. The first description by Abrial included a structuring mechanism called a class, which was very similar to a schema (i.e. a combination of a declaration and a constraining predicate). The Z style has developed as a result of tackling practical examples and adapting the notation to their needs; this has resulted in a style and notation that is widely applicable to the description of certain kinds of computer system, particularly the client-server model.

With the publication of Sufrin's Z Handbook the development and understanding of Z had progressed. A type inference system and rules for reasoning were provided and the notions of schemas and generic types had evolved into their now familiar form. The first formal semantics was given by Spivey using a variety-based denotational semantics where the metalanguage used was Z itself, and included a brief sketch of a possible proof theory.

The standardisation process for Z provided a powerful motivation to attempt this exercise again. The standard semantics uses a relational approach, and attempts a loose definition of the meaning of undefined elements so as to accommodate some of the different possible treatments while ensuring that the logic is two-valued. This paper traces the evolution of the semantics of Z from the early efforts to the definition in the Z standard, comparing the various approaches to defining the model, presenting the semantics and dealing with undefinedness.

1   The Early Days

The origins of the development of Z can be traced back to the Software Engineering Project at the Programming Research Group in Oxford. This project started in 1978 with both Tony Hoare and Bernard Sufrin associated with it from the beginning. It was the first of many projects which supported researchers engaged in work on specification. At around the same time Jean-Raymond Abrial was giving lectures on specification at Queen's University Belfast. The language was based on three principles: a strict formalism, recognition of set theory as a sound basis, and the necessity of a strong structuring mechanism. These course notes were published with Steve Schumann and Bertrand Meyer in a paper simply called "Specification Language"[4].

In late 1979 Abrial moved to Oxford. He presented a seminar course to research staff and students on his specification language. This language included schema-like objects called classes which were a combination of declarations and a constraining predicates:

$$
\begin{array}{ll}
\underline{\text{class}} & \hspace{4cm} (1) \\
\quad a : X; & \\
\quad b : Y & \\
\underline{\text{where}} & \\
\qquad P & \\
\underline{\text{end}} &
\end{array}
$$

Notably, there were no semantics for this language. Rod Burstall observed at the time that the language had a strong flavour of "Bourbaki".

In 1980 Abrial produced two papers on Z [1, 2] a Basic Library and a Syntax and "Semantics". The basic library was a series of chapters of Z specifications of sets, functions, relations and other mathematical structures. This was an early forerunner of the mathematical toolkit which was published in Spivey's Reference Manual [42]. The syntax and semantics paper included an outline proof system for the mathematical sublanguage, which lay somewhat neglected for many years.

Soon afterwards Abrial, Sorensen and Clement started a project suggested by Bernie Cohen, then of STL, to formally specify and implement CAVIAR (Computer Aided Visitor Information and Reception) System [14].

During this project the notation underwent a redesign and the notion of a class conjunction was introduced. The notation that resulted from this reworking was essentially the same as the current mathematical language of Z, however the concrete notation used keywords. For example, the definition of set union was as follows:

$$
\begin{aligned}
\text{op}(\cup) \; = \; & \textit{fn } S1, S2 \to S3 \textit{ then} \hspace{3cm} (2) \\
& S3 \; = \; \textit{set } X \textit{ where} X \in S1 \textit{ or } X \in S2 \textit{ end end};
\end{aligned}
$$

The style reverted to a more familiar notation "under the impact" of Dana Scott's verdict that it was too verbose. Although there was some form of generic definition, there was no formal type system and only an informal semantics.

Impetus for the further development of schemas came from the realisation that the standard mathematical forms of extending states and promoting operations on them were too unwieldy for use in the specification of large scale systems. Experience in VDM[26, 25], influenced by the presence of in the PRG of Cliff Jones, suggested that what was needed was a formalism in which extension and promotion were simply expressible, and for which proof rules could be given directly.

These efforts produced the nucleus of what later became known as the schema calculus. Generated mostly from problems encountered in defining conjunction and providing proof rules for it. Around that time the idea, prevalent in VDM, that the state should contain as little redundancy as possible was rejected. Also nondeterminism (underspecification) was developed as a technique (though excessively so at the early stages).

The work of this period, until the departure in 1981 of Jones and Abrial was reported in separate publications of Abrial and Sorensen on the specification language [3, 38] and on a case study they did jointly on KWIK-index generation [5].

2 CICS and Distributed Computing

The next major developments in Z resulted from work on two projects which started at the PRG in 1982. These were the Distributed Computing Project and the IBM CICS project.

2.1 The IBM Project

CICS is IBM Hursley's Customer Information Control System. It provides a range of services—communications, data access, integrity, security — which are used to support application programs. CICS has been subjected to continuous development for over 20 years. In the early 1980s, the complexity of the CICS structure was becoming a serious problem. Some parts of the code in particular were restricting the developers' ability to enhance the product. In order to redesign the modules, it was necessary to find a more precise way of defining what facilities would be provided.

The desired precision required the use of mathematical techniques that were, at that time, little known outside universities. The manager of CICS, Tony Kenny, and the leader of Oxford's Programming Research Group, Tony Hoare, developed a plan to apply Oxford's ideas to Hursley's problems, and so the Oxford-IBM collaboration started. The PRG advised on how formal mathematical methods could be used for the specification and design of new CICS modules. At the same time, Oxford learned from Hursley how the methods could be adapted to problems on an industrial scale.

Until then, the PRG had only been able to apply them to small and medium sized examples, so this provided an opportunity to see whether the methods would scale up to industrial problems. The first stage involved PRG researchers working on case studies. Specifications of several small program modules and parts of the API were produced with Ib Sørensen collaborating with Pete Collins and John Nicholls at IBM.

2.2 The Distributed Computing Project

At around the same time as the IBM project started, the Distributed Computing Project began with Roger Gimson and Carroll Morgan as research officers. The aim of the distributed computing project was to explore the new possibilities of distributed operating system design which were made possible by the low cost of distributed processing hardware. Mathematical techniques of program specification played a crucial part in this aim because of their abstraction, precision, ease of comprehension and amenity to refinement.

2.3 Schemas

The removal of keywords from the language heralded the introduction of boxes to denote schemas. There were two notations. A vertical schema definition, which was most commonly used; and there was a horizontal schema expression, which was structurally the same as a class:

$$[\,a:X;\; b:Y \mid P\,] \quad . \tag{3}$$

These notations were used by Bernard Sufrin in his early courses in Z for MSc students. Though there was agreement on the notation, there was some debate as to whether schemas/classes should be considered as syntactic macros or whether they represented values in their own right. Sufrin in the defence of the "not" position developed an explanation of the type system and a characterisation of the semantics of classes and class conjunction which was based on databases and database join operator:

$$[\,a:X;\; b:Y \mid P\,] \wedge [\,b:Y;\; c:Z \mid Q\,] = [\,a:X;\; b:Y;\; c:Z \mid P \wedge Q\,]. \tag{4}$$

It was this strong parallel between the database relation as a model for schemas and the tentative semantics of what were still called classes that led to the use of the term schema.

The first schema calculus operator appeared in a paper presented by Tony Hoare at a conference in Strathclyde [20]. The paper was a specification of a dry cleaning system based on work by Carroll Morgan who had recently arrived in the PRG. There is a definition of a schema made by the functional composition of two others. The idea of basing this idea on dry cleaning was Tony's – he thought that it would help Carroll to concentrate on the essentials of the service without getting confused by any computational preconceptions.

This paper also introduced Δ-schemas [1] and led to a shift from describing Z operations as mathematical functions and relations to defining them using schemas. The Δ was originally used as a device to save writing out the before and after states again in operations. However, it soon came to be used as a way of carrying around a "dynamic" invariant:

$$\Delta S = [\,S;\; S' \mid \ldots Inv \ldots\,] \quad . \tag{5}$$

Sufrin produced a further consolidation of this notation with examples in [43].

---

[1] Steve Schumann suggested the name Δ by analogy with δ in differential calculus. The Ξ notation for the no-change operation came from Bernard Sufrin.

2.4   Schema Calculus

The use of delta-schemas gradually adopted by the IBM project where Tim Clement was working on combining functions which were "not quite compatible". Hayes and Morgan worked together to convert the functional CICS specs into ones which used delta-schemas to define operations. This then made it possible to combine operations which were "not quite compatible" by matching the names of schema components.

This work led to the introduction of the schema disjunction operator which was used to separate out error conditions from the functional part of the operator:

$$Total\_Op = Partial\_Op \lor Error\_Condition .   \eqno(6)$$

This separation of concerns was first exploited by Carroll Morgan in his specification of the Cambridge model name service [29]. The combination of the conjunction and disjunction operators led Bernard Sufrin to coin the phrase "schema calculus". Although at the time it wasn't yet a calculus, the potential was later realised when a formal semantics was used to underpin a logic which included rules for manipulating schemas.

Further developments in the notation came from the application of these Oxford-style formal methods to distributed systems. The notation conventionally used for input (?) and output (!) were introduced at this stage. The interaction between the IBM and Distributed Computing projects is illustrated by the way that Hayes took this notation and developed the pipe chaining operator >> for the IBM work. This operator matches the output of one schema with the input of another:

$$[a? : X;\ b! : Y \mid \ldots] >> [b? : Y;\ c! : Z \mid \ldots] = [a? : X;\ c! : Z \mid \ldots] .   \eqno(7)$$

These new features were used by Morgan and Sufrin to give a specification of the Unix filing system [32]. This is widely recognised as the first full use of the schema calculus, in which schemas are used to define operations as well as states and included the first use of what was then called framing (promotion).

3   Consolidation of Notation

The mid-eighties heralded a wider use of Z and the production of more substantial definition of the language. The main result of these efforts was the explanation of schemas to a wider audience. Morgan's working papers on using mathematics in user manuals [30] and on schemas in Z [31] together with Sufrin's Z handbook [6] were the main sources for those learning about Z and its use.

The continued emphasis on worked examples ensured that there were many case studies available. The best known of these was a collection edited by Hayes which was originally published as a PRG monograph [17] and later by Prentice-Hall [18] and is now in its second edition. Other case studies came from the Distributed Computing project [16] and work in data refinement.

The data refinement work resulted from problems that IBM were having using data refinement rules taken directly from VDM. These rules proved to be inadequate. So the Z group met regularly in 1984 and collaborated with Cliff Jones' group in Manchester. These efforts led to work on the completeness of data refinement, using upwards as well as downwards simulation, resulting in a key paper by He Jifeng, Tony Hoare and Jeff Sanders [19].

At the same time Mike Spivey was working on his thesis [39] which included a formal semantics for the language. An interesting feature of his definition was that Z itself was used as a metalanguage for the definition. The semantics include rules for type inference and a comprehensive definition of the meaning of schemas.

In that thesis he contends that "such a mathematical description – a formal semantics of Z – is both feasible and beneficial". This he successfully demonstrated using a variety-based denotational semantics, and included a brief sketch of a possible proof theory: a sequent calculus similar to that described in [46]. A second, informal semantics is outlined in [42], with different meanings for some of the key concepts in Z. In order to compare styles Spivey's semantics with the standard semantics, the definition of the type of schemas is given.

Consider the following example of a simple generic schema:[2]

$$
\begin{array}{|l}
\hline
A[X, Y] \\
\hline
p : X \\
q : X \times Y \\
\hline
\exists\, y : Y \bullet q = (p, y) \\
\hline
\end{array}
$$

The definition of A contains the given-set names X and Y, the variable names p and q, some type information that p has type X and q has type $X \times Y$, and an axiom that constrains the values that p and q may take. The given-set names, variable names, and type information together form the *signature* of the schema A. Spivey formalises the notion of a signature as follows:

$$
\begin{array}{|l}
\hline
SIG \\
\hline
given : \mathbb{F}\, NAME \\
vars : \mathbb{F}\, NAME \\
type : NAME \nrightarrow TYPE \\
\hline
type \in vars \rightarrow Type(given) \\
\hline
\end{array}
$$

Thus, in a signature, we have an alphabet of given-set names, an alphabet of variable names, and a function which ascribes a type in terms of these given-set names for each variable. In fact, in Spivey's semantics, *given* and *vars* contain not simply the generic parameters and component names of our schema, but also the given-sets and global variables in scope at the point of the schema's definition.

---

[2]This example, first appeared in Spivey's thesis.

The signature of A is

$\mu\, SIG \mid$
  $given = \{\,\text{``}X\text{''}, \text{``}Y\text{''}\,\} \wedge$
  $vars = \{\,\text{``}p\text{''}, \text{``}q\text{''}\,\} \wedge$
  $type = \{\,\text{``}p\text{''} \mapsto \text{``}X\text{''}, \text{``}q\text{''} \mapsto \text{``}X\text{''} \times \text{``}Y\text{''}\,\}.$

The draft standard definition of the type of a schema will be given in a later section using the same example.

4 The Development of Applications

4.1 Microprocessors

The use of formal methods in the design of microprocessors has been one of the great successes of Z. Some early papers were written by Geoff Barrett [7] and Jonathan Bowen [9]. Barrett's paper presents a formalisation of the IEEE standard for binary floating-point arithmetic in Z. The procedures presented form the basis for the floating-point unit of the Inmos IMS T800 transputer. This work was done in close collaboration with Inmos who themselves published, in 1988, a specification of the instruction set of the T800 floating-point transputer [24].

Further work was reported in more general article by David Shepherd and Greg Wilson on the development of the floating point unit [37]. Shepherd's article on verified microcode design [36] shows how a high-level program in Occam was transformed to a low level implementation that matched the micromachine functions of the T800 transputer in order to verify its microcode. The high-level specification is first given in Z.

The work on the formalisation of the IEEE standard for floating point arithmetic in Z formed the basis for the floating point unit of the Inmos IMS T800 transputer. It resulted in a joint Queens Award for technological achievement for Inmos Ltd and the Oxford University Computing Laboratory. It was estimated that the approach saved a year in the development time compared to traditional methods.

Bowen has continued this line of research with a formal specification of ProCoS/Safemos instruction set [10]. This article gives a preview of the work of two European government-sponsored projects investigating design methods for 'provable' computer systems. As a common interface both projects use subsets of Occam and the transputer instruction set. A number of transputer instructions are presented using Z.

4.2 Transaction Processing

The CICS project attempted to scale up formal mathematical methods, used so far within a research environment, to large scale software in an industrial environment. This work was concerned with the specification of existing parts of the system. In 1984 a decision was taken to use Z for some of the next release. Z was used to record the specification and high level design decisions. This use of Z superseeded the previous natural language specifications, and hence required extensive training of IBM staff in the reading and writing of Z. Three day courses were taught by Oxford personnel, who were no longer in direct close contact with their IBM counterparts.

The IBM project evolved from research into small case studies to specifying actual code. This work was concerned with the formal specification of existing parts of CICS code [22]. This was used as a first stage in the revision of CICS modules[3]. The first CICS product designed with Z was CICS/ESA, announced in June 1989. Since then, Z has played a part in the development of subsequent CICS products.

A major breakthrough for Z came when IBM published the Z specifications of its CICS application programming interface (API) [8, 12, 23, 21, 27, 33].

In April 1992, the Queen's Award for Technological Achievement was conferred jointly upon IBM United Kingdom Laboratories Limited and Oxford University Computing Laboratory for "the development and use of an advanced programming method that reduces development costs and significantly enhances quality and reliability": namely, Z.

5   Gaining Widespread Appeal

The widespread appeal and knowledge of Z came about as a result of two factors: the publication of text books and the publication of more general research papers on Z in computing journals with a wider readership. The earliest text books were the result of work in the PRG, including Spivey's thesis [40] and Hayes' case studies [18]. Many others have now written books which are widely used to support university courses in Z [47, 34, 13, 48].

The publication of more general papers on Z in journals has been a fruitful method of introducing formal methods, and Z in particular, to others in the field of computing. Some of the most popular have been [41, 35, 44, 45]. The largest forum for such publications has been the annual Z User Meetings, which have been held since 1986. The later proceedings have been published by Springer Verlag in the Workshops in Computing series.

It was at the Z user meeting of 1989 that there was a public call for an agreed formal standardisation of the notation. The first work along the road to standardisation had already been funded by IBM. In 1988 King, Sørensen and Woodcock published [28] as a PRG monograph. This was, to date, the most comprehensive definition of the language barring its omission of any formal semantics, being more complete than Spivey's thesis. However, a year later, Prentice-Hall published Spiveys Reference Manual [42] which rapidly became a de-facto standard. The prospect of an agreed standard was particularly welcomed by tool builders who wanted an agreed definition, so as to justify their investments. One reason for the different versions of the language was that much of the developments were case study driven, so parts of the language in

---

[3]The rest of the development at this stage followed IBM's normal practices.

use were not covered by earlier definitions.

This standardisation work was taken up by the Zip project which was starting in early 1990. A standard review committee was formed and work commenced on the drafting of a standard using Spivey's reference manual and King et. al. as sources. In the Summer of 1991, the committee decided to include a formal semantics as a part of the definition. This has now been fully integrated into the document. The committee has considered many proposals for enhancing the language and has taken a strict approach concerning additions. In general the rules concerning where schemas can be used have been loosened. The other main change, substitution, has been introduced to support the use of logics. The main effort has been to provide a consistent and complete definition of the language as it is used and to provide for some changes where they have been shown to be necessary. The first public version of the standard [11](version 1.0) was produced for the Z user meeting in London, in 1992. Future versions will produced as the committee revises the draft.

6   The New Semantics

One important part of the standard (which had not been considered at the beginning) was a complete semantics for Z. Once again IBM's interest helped to promote the development of a tractable semantics.

Some of the motivation came from Jim Woodcock's work on calculating properties of specifications. He wanted a logic for calculating preconditions proofs using the B-tool. In order to formalise, and prove correct such a logic, he needed a tractable semantics. The task of proving that every rule in a logic is sound is a formidable task; if the semantics had been written with this proof in mind, the task could be much easier. This is a story familiar to those who write and reason about formal specifications: it is the interplay that goes on between modeling and verification. One way to get insight into the appropriateness of a model is to try to reason about it. The simplifications that are needed in order that a proof becomes tractable often lead to specifications that are easier to comprehend.

The standardisation itself also justifies a new look at the semantics as it effort places many more demands on the design of a language. Many design issues must be considered with respect to the languages (proposed) semantics. So the definition must be complete, precise and comprehensible, and easily altered. This effort provides an opportunity to investigate all levels of the semantics, from the metamathematics of the model to the form of presentation of the semantic definitions.

Spivey's semantics serves its primary purpose as a definition of the language; but it is a complex and detailed definition. A soundness proof of a logic would be very difficult using Spivey's semantics without first developing a calculus for his semantic structures. If more familiar and better understood constructs could be used instead such a body of work would be unnecessary.

There seemed to be several simplifications that one could make to the original semantics for Z. It was in this area that the first changes were made.

Though initially, Z was kept as a metalanguage [15], it was eventually dropped, together with his definition of the world of sets, in favour of working within a world of Zermelo-Fraenkel set theory. The structures themselves were also simplified. The type of a schema is still constructed from a signature, but this is much simpler. A signature is a mapping from names to types:

$$SIG = Name \nrightarrow Type \qquad (8)$$

This is a simple type, there are no generic components. The signature of the sample schema used to illustrate Spivey's semantics would, when instantiated by types τ and σ, be:

$$\{'p' \mapsto \tau, 'q' \mapsto (\tau \times \sigma)\} \qquad (9)$$

There has been a separation of concerns within the semantics, treating the generic part of the type separately. The type of a generic schema is considered to be a function from the types of its parameters to the resulting type of the schema:

$$Gen\_Type = Type^* \nrightarrow Type \qquad (10)$$

So the type of the sample generic schema is a function defined as follows:

$$\lambda X, Y : Type \bullet \{'p' \mapsto X, 'q' \mapsto (X \times Y)\} \qquad (11)$$

This simplification of the underlying structure, together with the use of Bird-Meertens style formalisms has enabled the soundness proofs to be undertaken in a calculational style. This has resulted in proofs of between a quarter and a tenth the complexity of the previous attempts.

The other main difference between the standard semantics and 'Spivey's is in the treatment of undefined elements. Spivey's semantics support a very strict logic. The equality and membership relations are strict. If either or both arguments to them are undefined then the relations do not hold and are considered to be false. On the other hand, the semantics in the standard adopts a loose approach to the meaning of undefined elements. Rather than prescribing a particular treatment of undefined elements, it leaves the choice to the user. The meaning of a function application is given for when it is defined, but not when it is not. So one could assume that it is undefined, or that is has some arbitrary value. This is of great benefit for top level proof in a development, as one is not over-concerned about whether particular terms are defined. However, when refining into programming variables, a much more strict approach must be taken, and then care must be taken.

The draft standard, therefore, does not have a prescribed logic. It does however contain one logic $\mathcal{W}$ [46] which conforms to the standard. This is a classical logic, which assumes that all terms denote. Thus there is no need for definedness checking during a proof, making it a suitable logic for high-level reasoning. It is emphasised that this logic is not the only possible one for Z. Indeed, there are many other ones in use, such as the Balzac Logic, and ICL's Proof Power which provides a Z interface to HOL. These logics are different to $\mathcal{W}$, but nonetheless support the standard.

7 The Future

The future developments of Z will include the completion of the International Standard. Further areas of active research are in object oriented techniques applied to specifications. This includes object oriented extensions to Z as well as definitions of objects and classes within Z.

There is a significant use of Z in security areas. Though there are some publications available, the nature of the work, does not lend itself to publicity. This is seen by many as a growth area for Z where both the resources are available and the need for correctness is very great. One of the main factors inhibiting the use of Z and other formal methods has been the lack of people competent in the techniques. The increasing number of universities offering undergraduate courses in formal methods, should provide a critical mass of users in the near future who will be able to both read and write formal specifications with ease. This would then provide the necessary base for the uninhibited use of Z and other methods.

8 Acknowledgements

The author has benefited greatly from the previously collated material of Carroll Morgan, Bernard Sufrin and John Nicholls. Help and advice from Jim Woodcock, Steve King and Mike Spivey was most instructive.

References

[1] J.-R. Abrial. The specification language Z: Basic library. Lecture notes, Programming Research Group, 11 Keble Road, Oxford, UK, 1980.

[2] J.-R. Abrial. The specification language Z: Syntax and "Semantics". Lecture notes, Programming Research Group, 11 Keble Road, Oxford, UK, 1980.

[3] J.-R. Abrial. A course on system specification. Lecture notes, Programming Research Group, 11 Keble Road, Oxford, UK, 1981.

[4] J.-R. Abrial, S.A. Schuman, and B. Meyer. Specification language. In R.M. McKeag and A.M. Macnaghten, editors, *On the Construction of Programs: An Advanced Course*, pages 343–410. Cambridge University Press, UK, 1980.

[5] J.-R. Abrial and Ib H. Sørensen. KWIC-index generation. In J. Staunstrup, editor, *Program Specification: Proceedings of a Workshop*, volume 134 of *Lecture Notes in Computer Science*, pages 88–95. Springer-Verlag, 1981.

[6] B.A. Sufrin. Z handbook, draft 1.1. Technical report, Oxford University Computing Laboratory, 11 Keble Road, Oxford, UK, March 1986.

[7] G. Barrett. Formal methods applied to a floating-point number system. *IEEE Transactions on Software Engineering*, 15(5):611–621, May 1989.

12

[8] D. Blyth. The CICS application programming interface: Temporary storage. IBM Technical Report TR12.301, IBM United Kingdom Laboratories Ltd., Hursley Park, Winchester, Hampshire SO21 2JN, UK, December 1990.

[9] J.P. Bowen. Formal specification and documentation of microprocessor instruction sets. In H. Schumny and J. Mølgaard, editors, *Proc. EUROMICRO'87, Microcomputers: Usage, Methods and Structures*, volume 21, pages 223–230. EUROMICRO, Elsevier Science Publishers B.V. (North-Holland), August 1987.

[10] J.P. Bowen. Formal specification of the ProCoS/safemos instruction set. *Microprocessors and Microsystems*, 14(10):631–643, December 1990.

[11] S.M. Brien and J.E. Nicholls. Z base standard, version 1.0. Technical Monograph PRG-107, Oxford University Computing Laboratory, 11 Keble Road, Oxford, UK, November 1992.

[12] S. Croxall, P. Lupton, and J.B. Wordsworth. A formal specification of the CPI communications. IBM Technical Report TR12.277, IBM United Kingdom Laboratories Ltd., Hursley Park, Winchester, Hampshire SO21 2JN, UK, 1990.

[13] A. Diller. *Z: An Introduction to Formal Methods*. Wiley, Chichester, UK, June 1990.

[14] L.W. Flinn and I.H. Sørensen. CAVIAR: A case study in specification. Technical Monograph PRG-48, Oxford University Computing Laboratory, 11 Keble Road, Oxford, UK, July 1985.

[15] P.H.B. Gardiner, P.J. Lupton, and J.C.P. Woodcock. A simpler semantics for Z. In J.E. Nicholls, editor, *Z User Workshop, Oxford 1990*, Workshops in Computing, pages 3–11. Springer-Verlag, 1991.

[16] R.B. Gimson and C.C. Morgan. The Distributed Computing Software project. Technical Monograph PRG-50, Oxford University Computing Laboratory, 11 Keble Road, Oxford, UK, July 1985.

[17] I.J. Hayes. Specification Case Studies. Technical Monograph PRG-46, Oxford University Computing Laboratory, 11 Keble Road, Oxford, UK, July 1985.

[18] I.J. Hayes, editor. *Specification Case Studies*. International Series in Computer Science. Prentice Hall, Hemel Hempstead, Hertfordshire, UK, 1987.

[19] He Jifeng, C.A.R. Hoare, and J.W. Sanders. Data refinement refined. In B. Robinet and R. Wilhelm, editors, *Proc. ESOP 86*, volume 213 of *Lecture Notes in Computer Science*, pages 187–196. Springer-Verlag, 1986.

[20] C.A.R. Hoare and C.C. Morgan. Specification of distributed computing services. Typescript notes, Oxford University Computing Laboratory, 11 Keble Road, Oxford, UK, June 1982.

[21] I.S.C. Houston. The CICS application programming interface: Automatic transaction initiation. IBM Technical Report TR12.300, IBM United Kingdom Laboratories Ltd., Hursley Park, Winchester, Hampshire SO21 2JN, UK, December 1990.

[22] I.S.C. Houston and S. King. CICS project report: Experiences and results from the use of Z in IBM. In S. Prehn and W.J. Toetenel, editors, *VDM'91: Formal Software Development Methods*, volume 551 of *Lecture Notes in Computer Science*, pages 588–596. Springer-Verlag, 1991.

[23] I.S.C. Houston and J.B. Wordsworth. A Z specification of part of the CICS file control API. IBM Technical Report TR12.272, IBM United Kingdom Laboratories Ltd., Hursley Park, Winchester, Hampshire SO21 2JN, UK, 1990.

[24] Inmos Ltd. Specification of instruction set & Specification of floating point unit instructions. In *Transputer Instruction Set – A compiler writer's guide*, pages 127–161. Prentice Hall, Hemel Hempstead, Hertfordshire, UK, 1988.

[25] C. Jones. *Software Development, a Rigorous Approach*. Prentice-Hall International, London, 1980.

[26] D. Bjørner and C. Jones. *Formal Specification and Software Development*. Prentice-Hall International, London, 1982.

[27] S. King. The CICS application programming interface: Program control. IBM Technical Report TR12.302, IBM United Kingdom Laboratories Ltd., Hursley Park, Winchester, Hampshire SO21 2JN, UK, December 1990.

[28] S. King, I.H. Sørensen, and J.C.P. Woodcock. Z: Grammar and concrete and abstract syntaxes. Technical Monograph PRG-68, Oxford University Computing Laboratory, 11 Keble Road, Oxford, UK, 1988.

[29] C.C. Morgan. Specification of the cambridge model distributed system name service. Distributed computing project working paper, Programming Research Group, 11 Keble Road, Oxford, UK, 1982.

[30] C.C. Morgan. Using mathematics in user manuals. Distributed computing project working paper, Programming Research Group, 11 Keble Road, Oxford, UK, 1983.

[31] C.C. Morgan. Schemas in Z: A preliminary reference manual. Distributed computing project working paper, Programming Research Group, 11 Keble Road, Oxford, UK, 1984.

[32] C.C. Morgan and B.A. Sufrin. Specification of the unix file system. *IEEE Trans. Soft. Eng.*, March 1984.

[33] P. Mundy and J.B. Wordsworth. The CICS application programming interface: Transient data and storage control. IBM Technical Report TR12.299, IBM United Kingdom Laboratories Ltd., Hursley Park, Winchester, Hampshire SO21 2JN, UK, October 1990.

[34] B.F. Potter, J.E. Sinclair, and D. Till. *An Introduction to Formal Specification and Z.* International Series in Computer Science. Prentice Hall, Hemel Hempstead, Hertfordshire, UK, 1990.

[35] Chr.T. Sennett. Formal specification and implementation. In Chr.T. Sennett, editor, *High-Integrity Software.* Pitman, 1989.

[36] D.E. Shepherd. Verified microcode design. *Microprocessors and Microsystems*, 14(10):623–630, December 1990.

[37] D.E. Shepherd and G. Wilson. Making chips that work. *New Scientist*, 1664:61–64, May 1989.

[38] I.H. Sørensen. A specification language. In J. Staunstrup, editor, *Program Specification: Proceedings of a Workshop*, volume 134 of *Lecture Notes in Computer Science*, pages 381–401. Springer-Verlag, 1981.

[39] J.M. Spivey. Towards a formal semantics for the Z notation. Technical Monograph PRG-41, Oxford University Computing Laboratory, 11 Keble Road, Oxford, UK, October 1984.

[40] J.M. Spivey. *Understanding Z: A Specification Language and its Formal Semantics*, volume 3 of *Cambridge Tracts in Theoretical Computer Science*. Cambridge University Press, UK, January 1988.

[41] J.M. Spivey. An introduction to Z and formal specifications. *Software Engineering Journal*, 4(1), January 1989.

[42] J.M. Spivey. *The Z Notation: A Reference Manual.* International Series in Computer Science. Prentice Hall, Hemel Hempstead, Hertfordshire, UK, 1989.

[43] B.A. Sufrin. Formal system specification: Notation and examples. In D. Neel, editor, *Tools and Notations for Program Construction.* Cambridge University Press, UK, 1982.

[44] J.C.P. Woodcock. Teaching how to use mathematics for large-scale software development. *Bull. BCS-FACS*, July 1988.

[45] J.C.P. Woodcock. Structuring specifications in Z. *Software Engineering Journal*, 4(1):51–66, January 1989.

[46] J.C.P. Woodcock and S.M. Brien. $\mathcal{W}$: A logic for Z. In J.E. Nicholls, editor, *Z User Workshop*, Workshops in Computing, pages 77–96. Springer-Verlag, 1991.

[47] J.C.P. Woodcock and M. Loomes. *Software Engineering Mathematics: Formal Methods Demystified.* Pitman Publishing Ltd., London, UK, 1988.

[48] J.B. Wordsworth. *Software Development with Z.* Addison-Wesley, Wokingham, UK, 1992.

An Overview of the Development of COLD

L.M.G. Feijs

Philips Research Laboratories Eindhoven

Abstract

This overview addresses the development of the wide-spectrum design langage COLD. The language unifies algebraic specification techniques and model-oriented state based specification techniques. The main language versions are surveyed, together with some of the semantical problems and their solutions.

1 Introduction

The development of the language COLD began in the early 1980s when Jonkers set out to combine algebraic and state based specification styles. One of the language requirements was that it would support the specification and the transformation of programs manipulating complex data structures. In part this requirement can be traced back to the work on the specification and implementation of garbage collectors [1]. The states of a garbage collector are complex structures in which array-indexing, pointer-dereferencing and address-manipulation functions play a role. This led to the "the states-as-algebras" paradigm that is at the heart of the language.

The work took place in the ESPRIT projects FAST and METEOR in which also purely algebraic approaches like PLUSS [2] and ASL [3] were studied. In this context it became clear that the module composition mechanisms of importing, hiding, and parameterisation were to be included in the language. It also became clear that the initial-algebra approach, based on conditional equations, was convenient for basic data types like Booleans and natural numbers, but from case studies it was concluded that both full predicate logic (in the language) and looseness (in its semantics) were indispensable.

2 COLD-S

This language was devised as a study to demonstrate the feasibility of the abovementioned requirements.

A module was called a 'class' and in the language a class appeared as a pair

$$(I, B)$$

where I was an 'interface' (containing an export signature, an import clause and, remarkably, preconditions) and B a 'body' (containing imports, operation definitions, and a list of modification rights).

Modification rights are related to the principle of "selective updating". This works as follows. Consider a class with variable sorts (dynamic sets) of switches and ports, introduced as TYPE Switch and TYPE Port, with two creation procedures, introduced as PROC create_s and PROC mk_port together with two special procedures PROC connect and PROC disconnect. There is a variable function is_connected which maps triples (s, p, q) to Booleans (s a switch and p, q ports). Then

```
MODIFY create_s   : Switch,
       mk_port    : Port,
       connect,
       disconnect : is_connected(Switch,Port,Port)
```

guarantees that create_s only changes Switch, whereas mk_port only affects the set of ports. Moreover connect and disconnect can change is_connected, but they can not, for example create new switches or ports.

In this language algebraic specifications were allowed too, and e.g. Int was available as syntactic sugar, essentially based upon the axioms:

```
FORALL m,n : Int
  [ m /= succ(m);
    succ(m) = succ(n) => m = n;
    succ(pred(m)) = m ]
```

The no-junk property was built into the language. The informal semantics stipulated that a state of a class is characterised by the mapping which maps the finitely generated terms to their corresponding values. The language was described in [4].

The idea of syntactic sugar, i.e. introducing new language constructs which could essentially be defined within the language (though more clumsy), is a frequently returning theme in the development of the language. It is a relative of the bootstrapping process chosen for the later development: language constructs getting their meaning by definition in or translation to a more fundamental (powerful but clumsy) language or logic.

3 COLD-K

This is a kernel language, designed to contain the essential semantical notions, but with a somewhat unpractical syntax. This work took place in the context of the METEOR project and a cooperation between Philips Research and university logicians, notably C.P.J. Koymans, G.R. Renardel de Lavalette, and P.H. Rodenburg. For an overview, see [5] or [6]. At the syntactic level, there are six sublanguages:

- the name language,
- the expression language,
- the assertion language,

- the definition language,
- the scheme language,
- the design language.

The expression, assertion and definition language include Harel's dynamic logic and elementary programming constructs [7]:

- after X then A, denoted as: $[\,X\,]\,A$,
- and its dual: $<X>A$,
- repetition of X, denoted as: $X\,*$,
- composition: $X\,;\,Y$,
- choice: $X\mid Y$,
- guard: $A\,?$.

At the semantic level, there are three systems of a logical nature, which were developed for the purpose of giving meaning to the kernel language:

- the logic MPL_ω,
- the algebra CA,
- the calculus $\lambda\pi$.

The logic MPL_ω is a many-sorted logic with countably infinite conjunctions. If A_0, A_1, A_2, ... are formulae, then one can form the formula

$$\bigwedge_n A_n$$

with the intended meaning A_0 *and* A_1 *and* A_2 *and* .... Such conjunctions are useful for expressing the closure properties stemming from inductive definitions and iteration. MPL_ω has a built-in notations for (un)definedness. For a term X, the formula $X\downarrow$ says that X is defined; in the model-theory, undefined terms have a special undefined value as their meaning. As in Scott's E-logic, there are strictness principles built into the logic, for example:

$$f(X)\downarrow\;\to\;X\downarrow$$

that is, if $f(X)$ is defined, then so must X. The logic is complete, sound, and satisfies Craig's interpolation property. For details, see [8, 9, 10].

The class algebra CA is closely related to Bergstra's module algebra [11]. As in the latter approach, there are module composition operators + (import), □ (hiding), Σ (taking signature), and • (renaming). Typical laws of class algebra shared with module algebra include:

$$\Sigma(X+Y)=\Sigma(X)+\Sigma(Y)$$

$$\Sigma(\Sigma_1\square X)=\Sigma_1\square\Sigma(X)$$

$$\Sigma(\rho \bullet X) = \rho \bullet \Sigma(X)$$

$$X + Y = Y + X$$

The major addition of CA with respect to module algebra is that symbols (identifiers) in CA are structured objects, containing 'origins' built from origin constants and/or origin variables. There is a special unification operation μ working upon class descriptions with the effect of declaring the origins of symbols with the same name to be equal. The origins are indispensible for treating state-based descriptions where a shared module X can be imported into a composite module named Y_1 and Y_2, say. Now when Y_1 and Y_2 are combined again, there must still be only one instance of each variable in X – not two copies. Furthermore origins can be used to give meaning to the **FREE** definitions in the language, which are essentially a kind of forward declaration. For details, see [12].

The calculus $\lambda\pi$ is a version of lambda calculus with simple types and special parameter restrictions. The parameter restrictions are part of the terms (as in the Church-style typed calculus). The calculus requires a basic implementation relation $\sqsubseteq$. The rules of the calculus then extend this relation to include lambda terms as well. If X and Y are terms, then so is $\lambda x \sqsubseteq X.Y$. Application of P to Q is written as (PQ). The classical rule (β) is adapted to become the rule (π):

$$((\lambda x \sqsubseteq X.Y)Z) = Y[x := Z] \quad \text{provided} \ Z \sqsubseteq X$$

It has the Church-Rosser (confluency) property and the strong normalisation property. The way it is used is as follows: the lambda variables range over modules and each term starting with a λ represents a parameterised module. If Y_s is a module with a sorting algorithm, then X_i must specify the set of items to be sorted and a $<$ or $\leq$-relation to be used; under these assumptions $\lambda x \sqsubseteq X_i.Y_s$ is a generic sorting algorithm. For more information, see [13, 14, 15].

The synthesis of the language and its translation to the underlying logical systems is described in a single document, the formal definition of COLD-K [16]. This is a "translation semantics". The meaning of a specification is defined as a $\lambda\pi$-term, containing expressions from CA, and the latter containing formulae from MPL_ω. There are no built-in data types, but a standard library including number systems, finite sets, sequences, bags and maps emerged soon when the language was used for case studies.

4 COLD-K revisited

In the book [17] the language is explained without reference to MPL_ω. Instead a model-oriented approach is taken. The meaning of a class description is a collection of classes; each class has a set of states and a collection of transition relations (one for each procedure). A procedure which has no parameters denotes a relation on $State \times State$ whereas, for example, a procedure introduced as PROC p : S -> T denotes a relation on $State \times S \times State \times T$. Each state $\in State$ has an algebraic structure associated with it. This turns the states-as-algebra paradigm directly into a definition of 'model' and 'truth' ($\models$).

Amongst the shortcuts achieved when avoiding the translation to logic, going directly from language syntax to models, we mention:

- elimination of the special undefined elements,

- interpretation of hiding as a forgetful mapping, forgetting sorts, functions, predicates and procedures,

- direct existence proof of smallest predicates for Horn-clause style inductive definitions,

- options for reducing the set of states by exploiting an auto-bisimulation relation on this set.

The book explains most of the language in an informal style and adds examples to it.

5 COLD-1

In [18] a user-oriented language is defined. The language constructs get their semantics by means of a translation to COLD-K, which was precisely meant for that purpose. Amongst the advantages of this language over its kernel version, we mention:

- user definable infix and postfix operators,

- helpful patterns for definitions, like

```
PROC p : S -> T
IN   x
OUT  y
PRE  TRUE
SAT  MOD vars
POST etc.
```

- helpful patterns for components, like

```
COMPONENT ABC[Item] SPECIFICATION
ABSTRACT  ...
EXPORT    ...
IMPORT    ...
CLASS
  definitions
END
```

- a variety of mechanisms for naming.

A new version of the standard library was created; the bootstrap process was carried on by using generators for 'virtual components'. E.g. data types like $ENUM_n$ of enumerated sets with n elements cannot conveniently be captured by one parameterised description. But a simple generator tool does the job, and if it happens that ENUM3287 is needed, it is easily made.

6 Related developments

Other languages have been based in part on one of the abovementioned language versions. Notably these are COLD-K^2 [19], CoDDLe [20], PSF_c [21] and VVSL [22, 23]. In [24], a proposal for inheritance in COLD is described.

Inside Philips, the SPRINT method was developed (Specification, Prototyping and Reusability INTegration) [25], with the aim of exploiting formal specifications in an industrial setting. SPRINT includes an execution model for a subset of the language, which is called PROTOCOLD [26]. The execution model, which is based on backtracking, is also investigated in [27] and [28].

References

[1] H.B.M. Jonkers. Abstraction, specification and implementation techniques with an application to garbage collection. Mathematical centre tracts, 166, Mathematical Centre Amsterdam (1982).

[2] M.C. Gaudel. Towards structured algebraic specifications, in: ESPRIT'85: Status Report of Continuing Work, Part 1, North Holland, pp. 439-510 (1986).

[3] M. Wirsing. Structured algebraic specifications: a kernel language, Habilitation thesis, Technische Universität München (1983).

[4] H.B.M. Jonkers. Description of the design language COLD-S, Philips report (1995).

[5] H.B.M. Jonkers. An introduction to COLD-K, in: M. Wirsing, J.A. Bergstra (Eds.), Algebraic Methods: Theory, Tools and Applications, Springer-Verlag LNCS 394, pp. 139-205 (1989).

[6] L.M.G. Feijs, H.B.M. Jonkers, J.H. Obbink, C.P.J. Koymans, G.R. Renardel de Lavalette, P.H. Rodenburg. A survey of the design language COLD, in: ESPRIT '86: Results and Achievements, Elsevier Science Publishers B.V. (North-Holland), pp. 631-644 (1986).

[7] D. Harel. Dynamic logic, in: D. Gabbay, F. Guenther (Eds.), Handbook of philosophical logic, Vol. II, pp. 497-604, D. Reidel Publishing Company, ISBN 90-277-1604-8 (1984).

[8] D.S. Scott. Existence and description in formal logic, in R. Schoenman (Ed.), Bertrand Russell, Philosopher of the Century, Allen & Unwin, London, pp. 181-200 (1967).

[9] C.P.J. Koymans, G.R. Renardel de Lavalette. The logic MPL_ω, in: M. Wirsing, J.A. Bergstra (Eds.), Algebraic Methods: Theory, Tools and Applications, Springer-Verlag LNCS 394, pp. 247-282 (1989).

[10] C.P.J. Koymans, G.R. Renardel de Lavalette. Inductive Definitions in COLD-K. Logic Group reprint series No. 50, Department of Philosophy, University of Utrecht (1989).

[11] J.A. Bergstra, J. Heering, P. Klint. Module algebra, JACM Vol. 37 No. 2, pp. 335-372 (1990).

[12] H.B.M. Jonkers. Description algebra, in: M. Wirsing, J.A. Bergstra (Eds.), Algebraic Methods: Theory, Tools and Applications, Springer-Verlag LNCS 394, pp. 283-305 (1989).

[13] L.M.G. Feijs, A formalisation of design structures, COMPEURO-87, pp. 214-229, IEEE Society Press (1987).

[14] L.M.G. Feijs, A formalisation of design methods: a λ-calculus approach to system design, with an application to text editing. Ellis Horwood Limited (1993).

[15] L.M.G. Feijs. The calculus $\lambda\pi$, in: M. Wirsing, J.A. Bergstra (Eds.), Algebraic Methods: Theory, Tools and Applications, Springer-Verlag LNCS 394, pp. 307-328 (1989).

[16] L.M.G. Feijs, H.B.M. Jonkers, C.P.J. Koymans, G.R. Renardel de Lavalette. Formal definition of the design language COLD-K. Revised Edition, ESPRIT document METEOR/t7/PRLE/7 (Oct. 1987).

[17] L.M.G. Feijs, H.B.M. Jonkers. Formal specification and design, Cambridge Tracts in Theoretical Computer Science 35, Cambridge University Press.

[18] H.B.M. Jonkers. Description of COLD-1, Philips IST Report RWR-513-hj-91020-hj (1991).

[19] G.R. Renardel de Lavalette. COLD-K^2, the static kernel of COLD-K. ESPRIT document METEOR/t9/PRLE/11 (1989).

[20] G.J. Akkerman. CoDDLe: Common Design and Description Language, SERC Report RP/mod-89/9. Software Engineering Research Centre. Utrecht, The Netherlands (1989).

[21] J.C.M. Baeten, J.A. Bergstra, S. Mauw, G.J. Veltink. A process specification formalism based on static COLD, in: J.A. Bergstra, L.M.G. Feijs (Eds.), Algebraic Methods: Theory, Tools and Applications Part II, Springer-Verlag LNCS 490, pp. 303-335 (1991).

[22] C.A. Middelburg. Syntax and semantics of VVSL, Ph. D. Thesis, University of Amsterdam (1990).

[23] C.A. Middelburg. Experiences with combining formalisms in VVSL, in: J.A. Bergstra, L.M.G. Feijs (Eds.), Algebraic Methods: Theory, Tools and Applications Part II, Springer-Verlag LNCS 490, pp. 83-103 (1991).

[24] H.B.M. Jonkers. Inheritance in COLD, in: J.A. Bergstra, L.M.G. Feijs (Eds.), Algebraic Methods: Theory, Tools and Applications Part II, Springer-Verlag LNCS 490, pp. 277-301 (1991).

[25] H.B.M. Jonkers. An overview of the SPRINT method, in: J.C.P. Woodcock, P.G. Larsen (Eds.), FME'93: Industrial-Strength Formal Methods, Springer-Verlag LNCS 670, pp. 403-427 (1993).

[26] H.B.M. Jonkers. PROTOCOLD 1.1 User manual, Philips IST Report RWR-513-hj-91080-hj (1991).

[27] J.A. Bergstra, A. Ponse, J.J. van Wamel. Process algebra with backtracking, University of Amsterdam report P9306 (1993).

[28] S.F.M. van Vlijmen, J.J. van Wamel. A semantic approach to Protocold using process algebra, University of Amsterdam report P9317 (1993).

The formal basis for the
RAISE specification language

Robert Milne*

BNR Europe Limited
London Road
Harlow
Essex
CM17 9NA, UK

Abstract

The RAISE specification language was developed for industrial use on the basis of experience in applying VDM and other approaches to software development. This experience suggested the need to have, in one common framework, some specification concepts besides those of VDM, together with methods and tools to make them easier to use.

The language meets this need by unifying the model oriented and property oriented specification techniques for both applicative and imperative systems. It also provides a unified approach to the development of applicative and imperative systems, based on a proof theoretic view of refinement. All this affects how the semantic foundations and proof theory for the language are formalised.

In this paper, some language design decisions are motivated and the associated effects on the formal basis of the language are discussed. Particular attention is paid to how semantic difficulties are resolved. The design decisions are placed in a wider context by looking at other ways of unifying specification techniques, some of which have been adopted in other projects. Some conclusions are drawn about the completed formal work and the outstanding tasks.

1 Introduction

1.1 Scope

The RAISE Specification Language (RSL) provides an approach to developing systems according to a particular method, and with the aid of some tools, in such a way that implementations comply with specifications. The specifications may be formally expressed and verifiably refined into implementations in the same language. The method and tools both assist with verifying the correctness of the implementations and provide for compiling the implementations into executable code.

---

*This work was partly supported by STC Technology Limited (the predecessor of BNR Europe Limited) and the Commission of the European Communities (CEC) under the ESPRIT programme for software technology, project number 315, "Rigorous Approach to Industrial Software Engineering (RAISE)".

The language allows the user to describe systems either implicitly, in terms of their interfaces, or explicitly, in terms of the details of their operation, and to move between these extremes of descriptive style in a continuous process. The systems concerned may appear applicative or imperative, may operate sequentially or concurrently, and may comprise many modules. The semantic foundations [21] and proof theory [22] for the language accommodate this degree of variation. This paper is mainly a report on what doing this entails in practice; in particular, it indicates how certain difficulties in formalising the language are resolved.

There are many possible approaches to formal development. To users this may appear confusing and counter-productive, but it may be inevitable, given our limited understanding of development processes. To assist with understanding the essential differences between the approaches, the paper contains several comparisons between the characteristics of RAISE and the characteristics of other approaches which affect the formalisation of the language.

The semantic foundations and proof theory for the language themselves constitute large formal descriptions. They therefore suggest several observations about the formal description task and about the design thus described. The paper contains these observations.

1.2 Structure

Some characteristics of the language and method are described in Section 2, which outlines enough of them to illustrate the connections with other formal development approaches. Further details are provided in Section 3; this is by no means a complete account of the language and method, but it should serve to motivate the discussion of the difficulties encountered in the formalisations. How these difficulties affect the semantic foundations is indicated in Section 4. How they affect the proof theory is indicated in Section 5. General conclusions, about the formal description task and about the design thus described, are given in Section 6.

2 General characteristics

2.1 The RAISE project

The RAISE (Rigorous Approach to Industrial Software Engineering) project was set up to provide notations, techniques and tools that would facilitate the industrial use of formal development. It was based on experience with 'model oriented' specifications, especially in VDM [17] and Z [28]. (For instance, using their own tools and version of VDM, STC Submarine Systems specified an underwater cable supervisory system, informally refined the specification into a detailed design in the same language, and manually encoded this design in about 30 000 lines of C.) However, it was also intended to meet a perceived need for 'property oriented' specifications, with a treatment of modularity which allowed information hiding and with the ability to describe concurrency. To support these concepts it aimed to produce a language, a method and tools.

The programme of the project was not flawless. For example, it could have tried to address a broader audience, by considering 'graphical' and 'structured' techniques of analysis and design: entity relationship diagrams, state transition diagrams and data flow diagrams have long been fairly widespread and potentially formalisable, and their users might be more ready than others to proceed to the use of a richer set of concepts. Also, it could have treated formal development as needing application specific support constructed from a simple general framework; then unsynchronised message passing (say) would have been handled by the language, the method and the tools with the same ease as synchronised message passing in the manner of CCS [24] or CSP [15].

Nonetheless, in many respects the project was as ambitious as any such collaborative project could be. Moreover, in its own terms, it was successful, despite having four industrial partners, three of which changed owners during its course. The language met the original requirements (and others too, some of which are mentioned later). The method was developed; a successor project is now endeavouring to ensure that it receives adequate field trials. The tools covered the usual things (such as parsing, structure editing and type checking) well and more unusual things (such as 'justification editing', which combines proof editing with informal reasoning, and compilation into C++) in prototype form.

As with many practical designs, there were compromises: compactness and generality had to vie with expressiveness and familiarity to existing VDM users. The formalisations of the language helped to expose the more unfortunate of these compromises. However, so much effort was devoted to maintaining the cohesiveness of the design that there was too little time to establish properly some relations between the formalisations which are outlined later.

2.2 The specification language

RSL [30], the RAISE specification language, offers uniform and integrated ways of specifying and refining systems. The systems may be applicative or imperative and sequential or concurrent. Specifications may be equational or, in the sequential case, based on post-conditions. This degree of uniformity and integration, when founded in formality, avoids any need for expedients like those sometimes adopted for system developments, in which (say) VDM is adopted for describing one module and CSP is adopted for another, with only hope to ensure that the whole thing holds together.

This sort of uniformity and integration is completely different from just putting different syntaxes and concepts in the same language, as is done, for instance, in recent extensions to SDL [16]. It entails providing a single semantic formalisation for an entire language, not multiple semantic formalisations for multiple language fragments. Doing this is in turn rather different from providing a single semantic formalisation for multiple languages, in the way advocated as a use of institutions [1]; what this semantic approach provides in practice has yet to be explored fully.

The phrase 'based on VDM' can have various interpretations. RSL is indeed based on VDM, in that it provides, among other things, types, sub-types, pre-conditions and post-conditions developed from those of VDM. However, it is not the only way of adapting the VDM treatment of applicative and imperative features. RSL is a unified language covering both specification and implementation (either applicative or imperative); it therefore does not make the user work in more than one language during development or relate interfaces written in different styles, but it does make the user learn quite a large language. Larch [11] is also based on VDM, but it distinguishes between a shared language, to specify equational data types applicatively, and interface languages, one for each programming language, to describe imperative implementations in terms of pre-conditions and post-conditions using these data types.

In being a unified language for specification and implementation, RSL resembles another 'wide spectrum' language, CIP-L [3]. However, RSL differs from CIP in emphasising both applicative and imperative programming. Moreover, it is directed towards developing programs by verifiable refinements as much as by proven transformations.

The stress in RSL on information hiding in imperative specifications, through the use of objects, is found also in COLD-K [8]. Significant differences between the languages arise in the treatments of the logic, sequential imperative specifications (which rely only on post-conditions in COLD-K) and concurrent imperative specifications (which are absent from COLD-K).

Perhaps Extended ML [26], when seen as an extension to Standard ML [25], is the language having the greatest similarity to RSL; for instance, Extended ML signatures, structures and functors are like RSL classes, objects and schemes in several respects (but not in all). However, by contrast with Extended ML, RSL does not have exceptions, pointers or implicit polymorphism, and it supports the specification of sequential and concurrent imperative systems. Hence the semantic problems due to RSL are rather different from those due to Extended ML. In addition, the view of refinement adopted for RSL is rather different from that adopted for initial versions of Extended ML. This topic is considered next.

2.3   The refinement relation

In common with Larch and COLD-K, RSL adopts a 'proof theoretic' view of refinement. According to it:
- a *theory* is a set of assertions which is closed under applications of the rules of inference for the logic;
- a *specification* is a theory;
- refinement involves theory extension, so specification $spec_2$ is a *refinement* of specification $spec_1$ if $spec_2$ includes $spec_1$.

The advantage of this view is that there is no need to resort to model theoretic reasoning to justify refinements. Refinement only works by 'what you see is what you get': if enough assertions to present $spec_2$ can be inferred from the assertions in

$spec_1$ then $spec_2$ is a refinement of $spec_1$. The view is perhaps particularly well suited to 'point and click' interfaces and is exploited in the RAISE tools.

The disadvantage of this view is that handling observational equivalence generally involves introducing explicit interpretation functions and limits the value of equational reasoning for imperative systems. Specifications may be shortened, and observational equivalence can be made available, by making equality non-logical (so that it is interpreted in the course of refinement); however, doing this is not feasible when the state variables are not known (as can be so in RSL).

An alternative, more widespread, view of refinement is 'model theoretic'. This is typically found in algebraic specification languages, such as Act One [7] and OBJ [9], and has been explored well in ASL [27], the forerunner of Extended ML. According to it:
- a *model* of a theory is an interpretation of names in assertions which is compatible with all the assertions in theory;
- a *specification* is the class of models of a theory;
- refining a specification involves restricting the class of models of a theory, so specification $spec_2$ is a *refinement* of specification $spec_1$ if $spec_2$ is included in $spec_1$.

The advantage of this view is that it allows observational equivalence: for certain kinds of specification, if every observation made about $spec_2$ (using the observer functions for $spec_1$) can also be made about $spec_1$ then $spec_2$ is a refinement of $spec_1$.

The disadvantage of this view is that justifications of refinement are sometimes tortuous, unless they can exploit proof theoretic counterparts of the model theoretic arguments. Moreover, there are doubts about whether a semantics for Extended ML can sustain this view [18].

3   Specific features

3.1   Computation and logic

In the interests of syntactic simplicity, among the expressions (or, strictly, the value expressions) of RSL are the imperative commands (which return results having type **Unit**) and the logical assertions (which return results having type **Bool**). Accordingly RSL offers a form of higher order logic, in which an induction axiom for lists, say, may be written as

$\forall\, p : L \rightarrow \textbf{Bool} \cdot$
$(p\,(empty) \wedge (\forall\, l : L \cdot \forall\, e : Elem.E \cdot p\,(l) \Rightarrow p\,(add\,(e , l)))) \Rightarrow$
$(\forall\, l : L \cdot p\,(l))$

As the evaluation of expressions may fail to terminate, in RSL the conventional 'computational' equality = is distinguished from a 'logical' one, $\equiv$. The 'logical' equality is available between any two expressions having compatible types, and returns the 'correct' result even if either evaluation does not terminate or has side effects. When the expressions have side effects, such as assigning to variables or communicating along channels, the assertion of 'logical' equality indicates equality between the side effects as well as the results (for a given state).

The existence of 'logical' equality assists with the evaluation of assertions in the presence of non-termination. Simple syntactic tests indicate whether an expression *value_expr* occurs in a 'computational' context such as

if *value_expr* **then true else false end**

or a 'logical' one, such as

∀ *binding* : *type_expr* · *value_expr*

Where the context is 'logical',

value_expr

can be transformed into

value_expr ≡ **true**

Where the context is not only 'logical' but also intended to be independent of the state (as is so, for example, in axioms),

value_expr

can even be transformed into the corresponding expression which quantifies over all states, which is written as

always *value_expr*

The 'logical' equality can be defined, for sequential expressions, in terms of post-conditions: if the sequential expressions have type t, then

$value\_expr_1 \equiv value\_expr_2$

can be transformed into

∀ p : t → **write any Bool** ·
(*value_expr*$_1$ **as** b **post** p (b)) ⇔ (*value_expr*$_2$ **as** b **post** p (b))

The ordering, ⊑, which induces this equality is not explicitly available in RSL; however, it is such that, for sequential expressions,

$value\_expr_1 \sqsubseteq value\_expr_2$

if and only if

∀ p : t → **write any Bool** ·
(*value_expr*$_1$ **as** b **post** p (b)) ⇒ (*value_expr*$_2$ **as** b **post** p (b))

The example specifications later exhibit the use of **result**, which is also not explicitly available in RSL; for sequential expressions,

result *value_expr*

can be taken to be

⊓ { c | c : t · *value_expr* ≡ (*value_expr* ; c) }

In fact post-conditions in RSL are currently defined in a different way, which uses **let** and ≡ and which does not obey all these transformations when the sequential expressions contain internal choice. However, they could easily be made to accommodate internal choice. Making them accommodate both internal and external choice is less simple for users, so here sequential expressions are restricted to exclude external choice, deadlock and communication, as well as concurrency.

Here the 'computational' choice combinator, ⊓, is used along with set comprehension. In this form it is best regarded as an adaptation of the 'logical' choice quantifier, ε, to possibly non-terminating evaluations of expressions which access the state; ε itself is not available in RSL, by contrast with HOL [10], for example. A 'computational' choice differs from a 'logical' choice in its responses to non-termination and equality: in RSL only bounded non-determinism is present (so choosing from an infinite set produces **chaos**), and an expression such as

$$0 \sqcap 1 = 0 \sqcap 1$$

amounts to

true $\sqcap$ **false**

though, of course,

$$0 \sqcap 1 \equiv 0 \sqcap 1$$

amounts to

true

The laws for evaluation order dictate that 'computational' choice can be distributed out of **let** definitions but not out of λ abstractions. Consequently in expressions like

let $f = \lambda$ n : **Int** · **let** m = $0 \sqcap 1$ **in** m + m **end in** f (2) = f (3) **end**

it offers a reasonable interpretation of the loose definitions found in VDM [19].

3.2 Access

Different procedures have different kinds of side effect. The differences can be exploited, for instance, in laws about concurrent expressions that do not access the same variables. Hence in RSL the notion of procedure type provide information about the kinds of side effect allowed for the procedure; conformance with the (maximal) procedure type can be checked statically. For example, the declarations

    tail"_ : **Unit** → **write Unit** ,

    tail'_ : **Unit** → **write** a **Unit** ,

    tail_ : **Unit** → **write any Unit** ,

make tail"_, tail'_ and tail_ all denote (total) procedures that take parameters of type **Unit** and return results of type **Unit**; however, tail"_ must not write to, or read from, any variable, tail'_ may write to, or read from, the variable a, and tail_ may write to, or read from, any variable declared in the object where the procedure is instantiated. Thus some or all of the variables in particular objects may be included in the access rights of procedure types. (Access rights also indicate which channels can be used.)

A procedure which does not write to any variables can be used instead of one which may write to some variables. There are therefore orderings on access rights and (maximal) types, which must be reflected in the formation rules and semantics.

The RSL counterpart to VDM invariants is provided by sub-types:

    L = {| l : **Unit** → **write any Unit** · is_l (l) |}

defines a sub-type L of **Unit** → **write any Unit** comprising all those members of the type **Unit** → **write any Unit** which satisfy is_l for all states. Distinctions between different sub-types of the same (maximal) type cannot be checked statically, so the ordering of sub-types, as opposed to maximal types, only has dynamic significance.

Procedures may be assigned to variables, communicated along channels, passed as parameters or returned as results. They may also be recursive, and they may contain local declarations of variables and channels (and indeed other names, such as sorts).

3.3 Modularity

An RSL class consists mainly of declarations, axioms and scheme invocations (where a scheme is a class with parameters). A class may be subject to operations for hiding names, renaming names and extending it with other classes; these operations obey laws like those for module algebra [4]. However, hiding variables, channels or sorts in a class could result in exporting values which have types that are not expressible outside the class. The static formation rules should ban such exports.

An RSL object is an instance in a class. It provides instantiated entities corresponding to **any** and to the names declared in the class.

The parameters of schemes are objects, not classes. Sharing between parameters is accomplished either by providing two coincident actual parameters or by including among the formal parameters objects which express the desired sharing by themselves being used to define the classes of the other formal parameters.

There can be arrays of objects, which may be declared or passed as parameters to schemes. For example, a scheme declaration beginning

TABLE (Elem : ELEM , List [**Int**] : LIST (Elem)) = ...

introduces two parameters: an object Elem which has an extension of ELEM as its class and an array of objects each of which has an extension of LIST (Elem) as its class and all of which share the same interpretation for names qualified by Elem.

3.4 Sequencing and concurrency

The use of $\equiv$ extends from sequential systems to concurrent systems: besides equational axioms for sequential systems such as

add_ (e) ; tail_ ( ) $\equiv$ ( ) ,

there are equational axioms for concurrent descriptions, such as

(add_ (e) ; tail_ ( )) ++ 1 ( ) $\equiv$ 1 ( ) ,

in which ++ is an combinator which combines concurrency with concealment. (This particular combinator is not ideal, as it does not obey simple composition laws.)

In RSL there is no effective extension of the use of post-conditions from sequential systems to concurrent ones; constructions similar to the modal μ calculus [29] were rejected as being too intricate for the intended uses of the language.

The concurrency combinator is like that of CCS, except that the use of τ is replaced by suitable uses of the internal choice combinator, $\sqcap$, and the external choice combinator, $\square$; the typical form of an expression which can internally choose to proceed with $value\_expr_2$ but not $value\_expr_1$ is

($value\_expr_1$ $\square$ $value\_expr_2$) $\sqcap$ $value\_expr_2$

The adoption of this hybrid formal system was motivated by a wish to keep both concurrency and choice simple and was justified by earlier work on τ [6]; of course it yields the equality of CSP rather than the more refined equality of CCS.

Input and output are synchronised as in CCS, not according to the 'broadcast' synchronisation of CSP. Doing this allows values to be passed along channels in a way which is equivalent to the passing of parameters to procedures. Treatments based on that in RSL have been given for other, related, value passing systems [14].

Sequencing is like 'serialised' concurrency, in that, when the expressions are deterministic,

$(\ value\_expr_1\ \square\ \textbf{skip}\ )\ ;\ value\_expr_2$

is equivalent with

$(\ (\ value\_expr_1\ ;\ value\_expr_2\ )\ \square\ value\_expr_2\ )\ \sqcap\ value\_expr_2$

not with

$value\_expr_1\ ;\ value\_expr_2$

(in which case **skip** resembles **stop** in how it relates to $\square$) and not with

$(\ value\_expr_1\ ;\ value\_expr_2\ )\ \square\ value\_expr_2$

The second of these alternatives would have led to a slightly less complicated proof system but would not have captured the usual way of modelling sequencing in terms of concurrency.

The examples given next illustrate the sequential expressions of RSL, not the concurrent ones.

3.5 Examples

The examples illustrate some simple list specifications.

In Figure 1 there is a introduction of a class which occurs in almost every general scheme definition. It is used, in particular, to achieve sharing between formal parameters of schemes.

In Figure 2 there is a specification of functions acting on a list type (though in fact lists are available as a pre-defined type in RSL, in the manner of VDM). In Figure 3 there is a specification of procedures acting on a list object which permits the procedures to write to, or read from, any of the variables in the object; this imperative specification can be drawn up by analogy with the applicative one or by exploiting a systematic transformation [23]. In Figure 4 there is an interpretation of the functions needed by a list type in terms of the procedures supplied by a list object; this exploits the higher order nature of RSL, both by introducing an induction axiom and by using a sub-type of a procedure type. In Figure 5 there is a further interpretation, of an abstraction procedure using this list type. (However this interpretation constrains the original procedures for list objects by being total.)

In Figure 6 there is a specification of procedures acting on a list object which permits the procedures to write to, or read from, any of the variables in the object. By contrast with the specification in Figure 4, this deals not with the equality between states but rather with the equality between observations on states, as supplied by an abstraction procedure. Its variant which replaces **result** by **post** is like a Larch interface language specification.

In Figure 7 there is an implementation of procedures acting on a list object which restricts the procedures so that they write to, or read from, one variable. Its variant which replaces $\equiv$ and := by **post** and = is like a VDM imperative specification.

Figure 1: Elements

```
ELEM =
class
  type
    E
end
```

Figure 2: Applicative lists specified in a 'property oriented' style

```
LIST ( Elem : ELEM ) =
 class
  type
   L
  value
    empty : L ,
    add : ( Elem.E × L ) → L ,
    head : L → Elem.E ,
    tail : L → L ,
    is_empty : L → Bool
  axiom forall e : Elem.E , l : L ·
    is_empty ( empty ) = true ,
    head ( add ( e , l ) ) = e ,
    tail ( add ( e , l ) ) = l ,
    is_empty ( add ( e , l ) ) = false
end
```

Figure 3: Imperative lists specified in a 'property oriented' style

```
TRANS_LIST ( Elem : ELEM ) =
class
  value
    empty_ : Unit → write any Unit ,
    add_ : Elem.E → write any Unit ,
    head_ : Unit → write any Elem.E ,
    tail_ : Unit → write any Unit ,
    is_empty_ : Unit → write any Bool
  axiom forall e : Elem.E ·
    result ( empty_ ( ) ; is_empty_ ( ) ) = true ,
    result ( add_ ( e ) ; head_ ( ) ) = e ,
    add_ ( e ) ; tail_ ( ) ≡ ( ) ,
    result ( add_ ( e ) ; is_empty ( ) ) = false
end
```

Figure 4: Applicative lists interpreted in terms of imperative lists

```
EXT_TRANS_LIST ( Elem : ELEM ) =
extend TRANS_LIST ( Elem ) with
class
  type
    L = {| l : Unit → write any Unit · is_l ( l ) |}
  value
    empty : L ,
    add : ( Elem.E × L ) → L ,
    head : L → Elem.E ,
    tail : L → L ,
    is_empty : L → Bool ,
    is_l : ( Unit → write any Unit ) → Bool
  axiom forall e : Elem.E , l : L ·
    empty ( ) ≡ empty_ ( ) ,
    add ( e , l ) ( ) ≡ ( l ( ) ; add_ ( e ) ) ,
    is_empty ( l ) = false ⇒ head ( l ) = result ( l ( ) ; head_ ( ) ) ,
    is_empty ( l ) = false ⇒ tail ( l ) ( ) ≡ ( l ( ) ; tail_ ( ) ) ,
    is_empty ( l ) = result ( l ( ) ; is_empty_ ( ) )
  axiom forall p : L → Bool ·
    ( p ( empty ) ∧ ( ∀ e : Elem.E , l : L · p ( l ) ⇒ p ( add ( e , l ) ) ) ) ⇒
    ( ∀ l : L · p ( l ) )
end
```

Figure 5: Imperative lists limited in terms of applicative lists

```
ABS_EXT_TRANS_LIST ( Elem : ELEM ) =
extend EXT_TRANS_LIST ( Elem ) with
class
  value
    abs_l_ : Unit → write any L
  axiom forall e : Elem.E ·
    abs_l_ ( ) ≡
    if result is_empty_ ( )
    then empty
    else add ( result head_ ( ) , result ( tail_ ( ) ; abs_l_ ( ) ) )
    end
end
```

Figure 6: Imperative lists specified in a 'model oriented' style

```
TRANS_REP_LIST ( Elem : ELEM ) =
extend LIST ( Elem ) with
class
  value
    empty_ : Unit → write any Unit ,
    add_ : Elem.E → write any Unit ,
    head_ : Unit → write any Elem.E ,
    tail_ : Unit → write any Unit ,
    is_empty_ : Unit → write any Bool ,
    abs_l_ : Unit → write any L
  axiom forall e : Elem.E ·
    result ( empty_ ( ) ; abs_l_ ( ) ) = empty ,
    result ( add_ (e) ; abs_l_ ( ) ) = result add ( e, abs_l_ ( ) ) ,
    result is_empty_ ( ) = false ⇒
    result head_ ( ) = result head ( abs_l_ ( ) ) ,
    result is_empty_ ( ) = false ⇒
    result ( tail_ ( ) ; abs_l_ ( ) ) = result tail ( abs_l_ ( ) ) ,
    result is_empty_ ( ) = result is_empty ( abs_l_ ( ) )
end
```

Figure 7: Imperative lists implemented in terms of applicative lists

```
IMP_LIST ( Elem : ELEM ) =
extend LIST ( Elem ) with
class
  value
    empty_ : Unit → write a Unit ,
    add_ : Elem.E → write a Unit ,
    head_ : Unit → write a Elem.E ,
    tail_ : Unit → write a Unit ,
    is_empty_ : Unit → write a Bool ,
    abs_l_ : Unit → write any L
  variable
    a : L
  axiom forall e : Elem.E ·
    empty_ ( ) ≡ ( a := empty ) ,
    add_ ( e ) ≡ ( a := add ( e , a ) ) ,
    is_empty_ ( ) = false ⇒ head_ ( ) ≡ head ( a ) ,
    is_empty_ ( ) = false ⇒ tail_ ( ) ≡ ( a := tail ( a ) ) ,
    is_empty_ ( ) ≡ is_empty ( a ) ,
    abs_l_ ( ) ≡ ( a )
end
```

3.6   The relations between the example specifications

Some of the relations between the applicative lists and the imperative lists specified above are depicted in Figure 8.

ABS_EXT_TRANS_LIST (Elem) is an extension of both TRANS_LIST (Elem) and TRANS_REP_LIST (Elem), but it is not a conservative extension of either. Firstly, it is an extension of TRANS_REP_LIST (Elem) only because it postulates that abs_l_ is total (through its particular choice of function arrow, →); it thereby extends TRANS_LIST (Elem) non-conservatively. Secondly, it inherits a simple use of ≡ from TRANS_LIST (Elem) which excludes observational equivalences that are admitted by abs_l_; it thereby extends TRANS_REP_LIST (Elem) non-conservatively.

IMP_LIST (Elem) is an extension of both TRANS_LIST (Elem) and TRANS_REP_LIST (Elem), but it is not one of ABS_EXT_TRANS_LIST (Elem). The reasons why are largely technical. Firstly, ABS_EXT_TRANS_LIST (Elem) defines L as a sub-type of a bigger type rather than as a sort which is isomorphic to a sub-type of a bigger type; if L were a sort, it could be proved to be isomorphicwith the sort L used in IMP_LIST (Elem). Secondly, ABS_EXT_TRANS_LIST (Elem) requires L to be generated from empty and add, but IMP_LIST (Elem) uses L from LIST (Elem), which omits an induction axiom and which therefore imposes no requirement on how L is generated.

Other specifications, REP_LIST (Elem) and EXT_TRANS_REP_LIST (Elem), are in the same relation to TRANS_REP_LIST (Elem) as LIST (Elem) and EXT_TRANS_LIST (Elem) are in to TRANS_LIST (Elem). Furthermore, REP_LIST (Elem) can be conservatively extended to an extension of LIST (Elem). These specifications can be constructed by analogy with, or transformation from, those above.

Figure 8: Relations between specifications

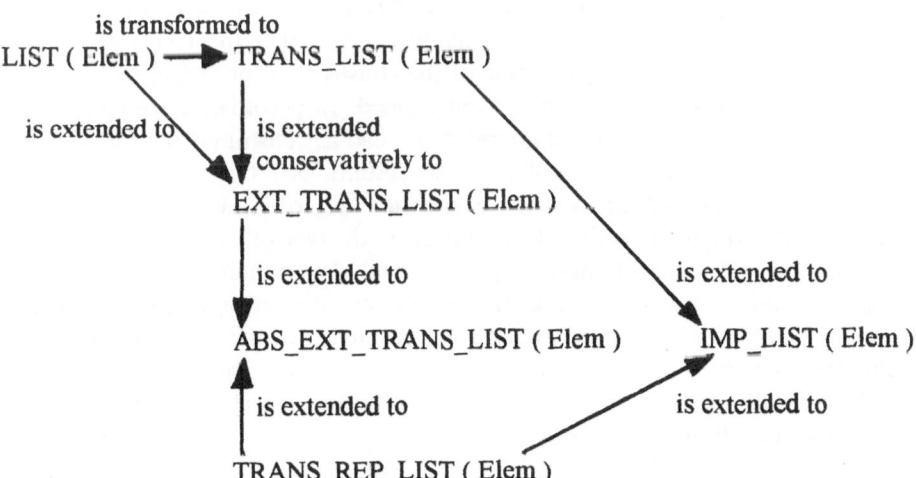

4   The semantic foundations

4.1   Intentions

The purposes of the semantic foundations for RSL [21] are as follows:
- to provide an interpretation for the proof theory;
- to formalise a conceptual model of specification meanings;
- to clarify the meanings of complicated constructs, as an aid to their simplification.

4.2   Forms

The static semantic rules are a version of the context dependent formation rules for the language. The dynamic semantic rules indicate the meanings of constructs.

Most constructs in the language need both a static semantics and a dynamic semantics (though occasionally just one is needed). The value given by the static semantics to a construct typically depends on the values given by the static semantics to the components of the construct, and the value exists only if some context conditions are satisfied. The value given by the dynamic semantics to a construct typically depends on the value given by the static semantics (for reasons that are indicated later).

For convenience, therefore, the static semantic rules and dynamic semantic rules for a given construct are expressed together in the following three part form:

context free side conditions
static applicability conditions

---

constraint on static semantic value of construct

---

constraint on dynamic semantic value of construct

There is one of these forms for each construct. The first part expresses conditions which ensure that the construct is well formed; in doing so, it also introduces names for some of the values used in these conditions. The second part defines the value of the construct according to the static semantics, given that the construct is well formed. The third part defines the value of the construct according to the dynamic semantics, given that the construct is well formed. In accordance with the usual pattern matching style, the parts of the rules are read as constraints on the values of the names that they mention rather than just as definitions of those values.

Because the parts of the rules express constraints rather than just definitions, they can themselves exploit constraints. If, for instance, the type of static environments is subject to an invariant which makes it a proper subset of a more obvious type, then simply mentioning in a constraint a static environment is enough to ensure that if the static environment exists then it satisfies the invariant. Hence constraints that would otherwise appear explicitly in the semantic rules can instead be captured in the definitions of the static semantic domains. Doing this can shorten semantic rules using pattern matching considerably.

The metalanguage used in the rules and in the definitions of the static semantic domains is syntactically almost a subset of the applicative fragment of RSL and has a straightforward interpretation. In particular, type definitions in the metalanguage use the RSL syntax for variant type definitions (which is similar to, but slightly more general than, those in Z, Standard ML and Extended ML). The definitions of the dynamic semantic domains go beyond this subset by introducing dependencies on the static semantic domains. The reasons for this will become apparent in the rest of this section, which addresses some the problems in formalising the semantics.

4.3 Naming

4.3.1 The problem

Variables, channels and sorts can be invisible but accessible. For instance, the following should associate the correct variable v with the procedure g:

> **extend**
> **hide** v **in**
> **class variable** v : **Int value** f : **Unit write any Unit axiom** f ( ) ≡ (v := 1) **end**
> **with**
> **class variable** v : **Int value** g : **Unit write any Unit axiom** g ( ) ≡ f ( ) **end**

Moreover, the variables and channels declared in an object may not be known when declarations forming part of the class of the object are made. For instance, the following should let o.f be regarded as having type **Unit** → **write** o.**any Unit** in the invocation s (o) and should make q.g and q.h have types **Unit** → **write** o.**any Unit** (which allows access to o.v) and **Unit** → **write** q.**any Unit** (which allows access to q.v) respectively:

> **scheme**
> s (p : **class** f : **Unit** → **write any Unit end**) =
> **class value** g : **Unit** → **write** p.**any Unit** , h : **Unit** → **write any Unit end**
> **object**
> o : **class variable** v : **Int value** f : **Unit** → **write** v **Unit end** ,
> q : **extend variable** v : **Int end with** s (o)

Somewhat similar remarks apply to sorts. Different sort names must be treated as corresponding to different types during static type checking; however, they may be refined into the same types. This refinement may take place, for example, when the sorts are supplied as declared names in objects passed as formal scheme parameters and the types are supplied as declared names in objects passed as actual scheme parameters.

In addition names declared in classes or supplied in objects passed as scheme parameters may be renamed. All this suggests that, though the modularity of RSL is static in the absence of object arrays, the names associated with values must be regarded as purely syntactic entities without much part to play in the semantics. Local declarations of variables and channels in recursive procedures present the same problem, at least for the dynamic semantics.

4.3.2 The solution

To overcome the problem, the semantics diminishes the part played by names by introducing a level of indirection. In both the static semantics and the dynamic semantics, variables, channels and sorts are distinguished from their denotations ('static' and 'dynamic' variables, channels and sorts).

There must be enough 'static' variables, channels and sorts to take into account the unconstrained nature of **any**, in particular. Hence:

- each object (or object array) has a set of 'static' variables and channels, which **any** denotes, which is unbounded for every type, and which includes one 'static' variable and channel for each of its variable and channel declarations;
- every object (or object array) has a set of 'static' sorts, which comprises one 'static' sort for each of its sort declarations;
- different objects (or object arrays) have disjoint sets of 'static' variables, channels and sorts;
- each formal scheme parameter has its 'static' variables, channels and sorts fitted (many-one) to the variables, channels and types supplied by the actual scheme parameter.

There must be enough 'dynamic' variables, channels and sorts to allow each 'static' variable, channel or sort to correspond with many 'dynamic' variables, channels or sorts (because of object arrays and recursive procedures). Hence:

- each object (or array component) has a set of 'dynamic' variables and channels for each of its 'static' variables and channels, which is unbounded (to treat recursion);
- each object (or array component) has a 'dynamic' sort for each of its 'static' sorts, which is an interpretation of the sort;
- different objects (or array components) have disjoint sets of 'dynamic' variables, channels and sorts;
- each formal scheme parameter has its 'dynamic' variables, channels and sorts fitted (many-one) to the variables, channels and types supplied by the actual scheme parameter.

To achieve all this, the environment must keep indications of the 'static' variables, channels and sorts already used (in objects and in schemes). Though the principle underlying this is clear, the encodings involved are rather tedious and are not stated quite correctly in the semantic foundations document [21].

4.4 Typing

4.4.1 The problem

Procedures may be stored in variables or passed as parameters. Processes may allow bounded non-determinism by letting an outcome be either a non-terminating computation or a member of a finite set of pairs comprising values and stores. (The additional effects due to communication will be considered later.) This suggests that, when 'dynamic' variables are in Loc, for instance, the dynamic semantics ought to be expressed in terms of domains which satisfy equations like

Store =
  Loc **finmap** Value
Action =
  Value → (Store → Process)
Process =
  Routine $_\perp$
Routine =
  (Value × Store) **finset**
Value =
  Action + ...

Here **finset** signifies finite sets and **finmap** signifies finite maps. (The semantic foundations document [21] also uses the RSL syntax for variant type definitions in a limited way in order to abbreviate axioms about domains.)

Procedures may be discontinuous predicates, such as

$$\lambda\ (\ f:\mathbf{Int}\to\mathbf{Int}\ )\cdot(\ f=\lambda\ n:\mathbf{Int}\cdot n\ )$$

The operator for constructing domains of functions in the semantics, →, must therefore provide a domain containing discontinuous functions. In fact it is taken to contain all the functions from its parameter domain into its result domain (with the effect that infinite sets of values can be treated as such functions). However, there are then no solutions to the domain equations above.

4.4.2 The solution

The dynamic semantic domains actually provided for RSL evade the difficulty described above: they do not try to satisfy such domain equations. Instead, they use strong typing to ensure that no procedure accesses a variable, accesses a channel or accepts a parameter which has a type that might include the type of the procedure.

Specifically, in the static semantics it is necessary to:
- ban variables and channels that have types that mention variables or channels that have types that mention ... the variables or channels;
- ban variables and channels that have **any** in their types;
- ban types that are defined, in effect, to be abbreviations of themselves;
- constrain sorts to have (unknown) types that satisfy these conditions.

Types defined by variant type definitions need not be subject to the same check as types that are abbreviations, because their definitions can be expanded into declarations of sorts, declarations of functions, and axioms, and these expanded declarations cannot be conveniently checked. In particular, a contradictory system specification, not a contradictory language semantics, results from a definition like

big_set == make_int (get_int : **Int**) | make_test (get_test : big_set → **Bool**)

The static semantic values capture constraints on the entities found in a well formed specification; for instance, the domain S_Value comprises the types that the results of expressions may have. The definitions of the static semantic domains should therefore contain invariants which express (among other things) the above conditions on variables, channels and sorts. Ignoring these invariants, the definitions take the form:

$S\_Store =$
 $\{ \ s\_store \mid$
  $s\_store \in S\_Loc \ \textbf{finmap} \ S\_Value \cdot$
   $\forall \ s\_loc \in \textbf{dom} \ s\_store \cdot loc\_s\_value \ (\ s\_loc \ ) = s\_store \ (\ s\_loc \ ) \ \}$
$S\_Action =$
 $S\_Value \times (\ S\_Store \times S\_Process \ )$
$S\_Process =$
 $S\_Routine$
$S\_Routine =$
 $S\_Value \times S\_Store$
$S\_Value =$
 $S\_Action + ...$
$S\_Loc =$
 $D\_Int \times S\_Value$

Here s_loc refers to a 'static' variable and loc_s_value (s_loc) is the maximal type that the values stored in the variable may have. According to the definition of S_Loc, this type can be modelled as the second component of s_loc; the first component is an integer which distinguishes this 'static' variable from any other which can hold the same type of value. (The treatment in the semantic foundations document [21] is slightly different, in order to accommodate object arrays, and does not make all the invariants explicit.)

The definitions of the dynamic semantic domains are now made to depend on the static semantic domains by taking the form:

$D\_Store \ (\ s\_store \ ) =$
 $\Pi \ \{ \ D\_Loc \ (\ s\_loc \ ) \to D\_Value \ (\ s\_store \ (\ s\_loc \ ) \ ) \mid s\_loc \in \textbf{dom} \ s\_store \ \}$
$D\_Action \ (\ s\_value \ , \ (\ s\_store \ , \ s\_process \ ) \ ) =$
 $D\_Value \ (\ s\_value \ ) \to (\ D\_Store \ (\ s\_store \ ) \to D\_Process \ (\ s\_process \ ) \ )$
$D\_Process \ (\ s\_value \ , \ s\_store \ ) =$
 $D\_Routine \ (\ s\_value \ , \ s\_store \ )_\perp$
$D\_Routine \ (\ s\_value \ , \ s\_store \ ) =$
 $(\ D\_Value \ (\ s\_value \ ) \times D\_Store \ (\ s\_store \ ) \ ) \ \textbf{finset}$
$D\_Value \ (\ s\_value \ ) =$
 $D\_Action \ (\ value\_s\_action \ (\ s\_value \ ) \ ) + ...$
$D\_Loc \ (\ s\_loc \ ) =$
 $D\_Int \times \{ \ s\_loc \ \}$

In fact this is not quite good enough, because it does not ensure that the dynamic semantic domains respect the static type ordering: the consistency of the dynamic semantics with the static semantics depends on assertions like

$s\_value_1 \le s\_value_2 \Rightarrow D\_value \ (s\_value_1) \subseteq D\_value \ (\ s\_value_2 \ )$

Such assertions hold up to a natural isomorphism, which in this case is between $D\_value \ (s\_value_1)$ and a subset of $D\_value \ (\ s\_value_2 \ )$.

There is an analogous difficulty created by recursion between the classes of parameters of schemes and classes forming the bodies of the schemes. It is addressed in an analogous way.

The relations between the static semantic domains and the dynamic semantic domains can be wholly systematic (though making them wholly systematic can lead to unnecessarily complicated dynamic domains). The system is outlined in Table 1.

Table 1: Relations between static domains and dynamic domains

Static domain	Dynamic domain
S_Z =	*D_Z* (s_z) =
{ s_int }	D_Int
S_X + S_Y	D_X (z_s_x (s_z)) + D_Y (z_s_y (s_z))
S_X × S_Y	D_X (z_s_x (s_z)) × D_Y (z_s_y (s_z))
S_X × S_Y	D_X (z_s_x (s_z)) → D_Y (z_s_y (s_z))
S_X × S_Y	D_X (z_s_x (s_z)) **finmap** D_Y (z_s_y (s_z))
S_X	D_X (s_x) **finset**
S_X	D_X (s_x) $_\perp$
S_X **finset**	Π { { s_x } → D_X (s_x) | s_x $\in$ s_z }
S_X **finmap** S_Y	Π { D_X (s_x) → D_Y (s_z (s_x)) | s_x $\in$ **dom** s_z }
S_F (S_Z)	D_F (s_f (s_z)) **if** s_z > s_f (s_z)

4.5 The imperative aspects

4.5.1 The problem

The language provides a wide spectrum of imperative features covering:
- sequencing;
- concurrency;
- internal and external choice;
- synchronised communication of values along channels;
- iteration and recursion.

Furthermore, even when the dynamic domains are dependent on the static ones in the manner described above, they remain recursively defined when all these features are provided.

42

4.5.2 The solution

The treatment of sequencing, in conjunction with internal choice, is outlined above. It entails letting an outcome be either a non-terminating computation or a member of a finite set of pairs comprising values and stores. The extension of this treatment to cover concurrency is based on acceptance sets [13] but could be based equivalently on failure sets. It entails changing the notion of processes so that, in the version without dependencies between the static domains and the dynamic domains,

Process =
  Routine $_\perp$
Routine =
  { (r , i , o , a) |
  (r , i , o , a) ∈
  { √ } **finmap** ((Value × Store) **finset**) ×
  Pos **finmap** (Value → Process) ×
  Pos **finmap** (Value **finmap** Process) ×
  ({ √ } **finset** × Pos **finset** × Pos **finset**) **finset** ·
  matching (r , i , o , a) ∧ *saturated* (a) }

The semantic foundations document [21] cuts corners at this point, slightly inaccurately; the version presented here comes from an earlier document [20], which also motivates this choice. A full account of the formal details of the construction of this domain is given elsewhere [5].

The first component of a quadruple in the domain Routine, r, provides a finite set of pairs of values and stores which can result from finitely many choices in a terminating process; an empty set of pairs occurs if there is no possibility of producing a result before a communication along a channel. The second component, i, can map any input channel to a function from values to processes which defines the process that will ensue after a particular value is input on the channel; an empty map occurs if there is no possibility of input on any channel. The third component, o, can map any output channel to values and processes which indicate the process that will ensue after a particular value is output on the channel; an empty map occurs if there is no possibility of output on any channel. The fourth component, a, provides a finite set of triples comprising finite sets of marks in { √ } (to signify that the process can terminate with a result), 'dynamic' input channels in Pos and 'dynamic' output channels in Pos; an empty set of triples occurs if the process must make an internal choice which leads nowhere, and a triple comprising empty sets occurs if the process may make an external choice which leads nowhere. The constraints on the consistency of r, i, o and a are captured by *matching*. The constraints on the acceptance sets, which make internal choice distribute through external choice, are captured by *saturated*. These constraints are defined in Table 2.

This degree of complication is needed to capture the meanings of expressions like
  (v := 0) □ (v := c ?) □ ((c ! 2 ; v :=2) ⊓ (c ! 3 ; v := 3))
Nonetheless the semantics is in fact a direct representation of simple algebraic laws governing choice, assignment and communication. The laws governing sequencing and concurrency use representations involving intricate derived semantic functions.

For this domain Routine, the greatest lower bound operator coincides in effect with the semantic interpretation of the internal choice combinator and produces an upper bound, $\sqcap\varnothing$, for the whole domain. Iteration can be handled by using this greatest lower bound operator and noting that the interpretations of the sequencing, concurrency and other combinators are monotonic; this monotonicity (indeed, continuity) follows from the inductive constructions of the interpretations in terms of processes.

The dynamic domains here are recursively defined when all these features are provided. Moreover, they remain recursively defined even when they are made to depend on the static domains, in the manner outlined above: it is reasonable to demand that a procedure type is not circular, but it is not reasonable to demand that each step in the evolution of a process needs fewer variables and channels than the one before. However, this aspect of the recursive definition of dynamic domains is not problematic, because the definitions of Process and Routine above mention each other only in a covariant way, not in a contravariant way.

Accordingly, for a given set of members of the static domains, there can be recursive definitions of the corresponding dynamic domains which apply the systematic technique given above to formalising the definitions of Process and Routine.

Table 2: Auxiliary process functions

$on\ (\ a\ ) =$
$\quad \cup\{\ x\ |\ (\ x\ ,\ y\ ,\ z\ ) \in a\ \}$

$in\ (\ a\ ) =$
$\quad \cup\{\ y\ |\ (\ x\ ,\ y\ ,\ z\ ) \in a\ \}$

$out\ (\ a\ ) =$
$\quad \cup\{\ z\ |\ (\ x\ ,\ y\ ,\ z\ ) \in a\ \}$

$matching\ (\ r\ ,\ i\ ,\ o\ ,\ a\ ) =$
$\quad (\ \textbf{dom}\ r = on\ (\ a\ ) \wedge \textbf{dom}\ i = in\ (\ a\ ) \wedge \textbf{dom}\ o = out\ (\ a\ ) \wedge$
$\quad (\ \sqrt{} \in \textbf{dom}\ r \Rightarrow r\ (\ \sqrt{}\ ) \neq \varnothing\ ) \wedge$
$\quad (\ \sqrt{} \in \textbf{dom}\ r \Rightarrow (\ \{\ \sqrt{}\ \}\ ,\ \varnothing\ ,\ \varnothing\ ) \in a\ ) \wedge$
$\quad \forall\ p \in \textbf{dom}\ o \cdot \textbf{dom}\ (\ o\ (\ p\ )\ ) \neq \varnothing\ )$

$saturated\ (\ a\ ) =$
$\quad (\ \forall\ (\ x'\ ,\ y'\ ,\ z'\ ) \in a \cdot$
$\quad \forall\ (\ x''\ ,\ y''\ ,\ z''\ ) \in \{\ \sqrt{}\ \}\ \textbf{finset} \times \text{Pos}\ \textbf{finset} \times \text{Pos}\ \textbf{finset} \cdot$
$\quad (\ x' \subseteq x'' \wedge y' \subseteq y'' \wedge z' \subseteq z'' \wedge x'' \subseteq on\ (\ a\ ) \wedge y'' \subseteq in\ (\ a\ ) \wedge z'' \subseteq out\ (\ a\ )\ ) \Rightarrow$
$\quad (\ x''\ ,\ y''\ ,\ z''\ ) \in a\ )$

5 The proof theory

5.1 Intentions

The purposes of the proof theory for RSL [22] are as follows:
- to be the normative formal statement about the language;
- to define the inferences permitted about specifications;
- to provide users with a more convenient reference than the semantics.

5.2 Forms

The static proof rules are a version of the context dependent formation rules for the language. The dynamic proof rules indicate what deductions may be made about constructs; because the logic of RSL is subsumed in the general structure of the language, often these deductions allow one construct to be transformed into another, equivalent, one.

The semantic rules can be presented in a simple syntax directed manner, with one three part rule per construct. The proof rules, however, do not fit this style. Certainly the static proof rules, which ensure that constructs are well formed, can have the same pattern as the static semantic rules and consider one construct at a time. However, the dynamic proof rules often consider not one construct but two constructs, with one nested inside the other, because they often express algebraic laws. Hence the static and dynamic proof rules cannot be combined in the same way as the static and dynamic semantics rules.

The static proof rules are expressed in the following two part form:

context free side conditions
static applicability conditions

---

static consequence

This form resembles the first two parts of the form for semantic rules.

The dynamic proof rules are expressed in the following two part form:

context free side conditions
static applicability conditions
dynamic applicability conditions

---

dynamic consequence

This form may occur several times for each construct. However, the individual rules for each construct typically follow conventional algebraic and logical patterns (typified by laws for idempotence and distributivity) which can be used to order the rules for a construct.

The rules also provide definitions of attributes (like *new* and *free*, which identify declared and used names) and transformations (like name substitutions). These are particularly important because the proof rules rely on renaming to achieve effects like those achieved by 'static' and 'dynamic' variables, channels and sorts in the semantics.

In fact several kinds of rule acting on constructs can be identified, and for any construct the rules are ordered according to this identification. (This is in addition to the ordering within the dynamic proof rules, which results from the algebraic and logical patterns.) The kinds of rules are as follows:
- context free transformations into other constructs that do not change attribute values;
- context free definitions of attribute values;
- context free transformations into other constructs that change attribute values;
- context free combinations with other constructs that change attribute values;
- context dependent transformations into other constructs that change attribute values;
- context dependent combinations with other constructs that change attribute values;
- context dependent assertions about properties that constitute decidable formation rules;
- context dependent assertions about properties that let meanings be inferred;
- context dependent combinations with other constructs that let meanings be inferred.

A brief account of some of these is given in the rest of this section.

5.3 Constructs in the rules but not in the language

Using suitable transformations reduces the number of basic proof rules that is needed to describe the whole language. However, as the classification above indicates, there are several different kinds of transformation. For the different kinds of transformation there are different notions of equivalence between constructs: besides $\equiv$, for instance, there is $\cong$, which is used to indicate that two constructs are equivalent in the very strong sense that even their context free attributes are identical. Some of these equivalences, such as $\equiv$, lie inside RSL itself; others, such as $\cong$, lie outside. Their proliferation may be confusing to users but can be largely hidden by suitable tools.

Similarly, there are several different kinds of combination of construct in the proof rules. These combinations arise because the transformations of some constructs into others need to pass through constructs which are not in RSL, though the beginnings and ends of the transformation sequences are in RSL. These intermediate transformations act on combinations of constructs, not on individual constructs. They, too, can be hidden by tools, which need to make manifest only the transformation sequences acting on individual constructs.

Examples of the rules for combinations of constructs are provided by sequencing and concurrency. The laws relating these to external choice (which have the same purpose as the expansion theorem in CCS) depend on decomposing expressions into combinations of 'externally synchronised' and 'internally synchronised' expressions which interact with other expressions in different ways. These different ways of interacting are not explicitly available in RSL: they depend on extra combinators, resembling the left merge and communication merge of other process algebras [2], which are deliberately omitted from the language. Instead, the equational laws which would govern these extra combinators if they were in the language are included in the proof theory as transformations acting on combinations of expressions.

Other examples of rules for combinations of constructs are provided by:

- variant type definitions, which are expanded into declarations of sorts, declarations of functions, and axioms;
- function definitions, which are expanded into declarations of functions and axioms;
- **case** expressions, which are expanded into **if** expressions.

Terms in the proof rules, therefore, may use equivalences and combinators not in the language. Something similar is true of hypotheses in the proof rules. Essentially, hypotheses in the proof rules introduce names and assert properties; they are therefore like the declarations and axioms in RSL classes. However, they are not just declarations and axioms like those in RSL classes; in particular, the declarations in hypotheses may be non-recursive and they may overwrite (rather than just clash with) declarations of the same names occurring earlier in the hypotheses. Because of this the algebra of contexts uses one or two constants and operators which are not needed by the algebra of classes.

6 Conclusion

6.1 Work still needed

The formal descriptions of RSL described above have various deficiencies and make various deviations from informal descriptions. For the most part these are itemised in the formal documents. With most of them the deficiency or deviation points to revising the language, not changing the formal documents. This is particularly so where difficulties occur in formulating the proof rules: it is harder to encode some contextual information in the proof rules than in the semantics, so if reviewers of specifications are to br able to rely on 'what you see is what you get' then infelicities in the proof rules should be avoided.

The proof theory has yet to be demonstrated to be sound or relatively complete with respect to the semantics. Some fragments of a demonstration would be quite straightforward; for instance, the semantics for sequencing and concurrency are drawn up with a particular set of proof rules and a particular notion of equivalence in mind. Others, however, would be rather tiresome, because the treatments of modularity in the proof theory and the semantics are fairly different from one another.

Moreover, the original intention, to provide a proof theoretic approach to refinement, has not yet been fully achieved. There has long been a result, like the modularization theorem developed elsewhere [31], to the effect that a subset of the language allowed refinement to commute with conservative extension. This result has not been extended to cover RSL schemes as they currently are. There can be sharing between actual scheme parameters which is not present in the corresponding formal scheme parameters, and this may invalidate the result.

Before proofs of such results are attempted for RSL, it might be best to combine the static and dynamic semantics, by providing two part forms for the semantics rules in which the operators have both static and dynamic interpretations. This might shorten the presentation but would require an extra layer of abstraction.

The difficulty, or otherwise, of much of this work is unknown at present: other matters, such as getting formal systems to be better used, are currently more pressing than getting them to be better formalised. Hence this section ends with a discussion of what the formalisation of RSL suggests about development processes.

6.2 Observations so far

The semantic foundations for RSL would be contradictory if they assumed that there were recursively defined dynamic domains which did not depend on the static domains. Yet one early document [12] on the semantics of a large part of the language makes this assumption (knowing that it is incorrect). Paradoxically, this document is perhaps less erroneous than the semantic foundations document [21]: because it is shorter and simpler, straightforward coding errors are easier to discover. The formal invalidity of the document is less important than its comprehensibility.

Of course, it can be argued that the early document is not contradictory but merely operating at a higher level of abstraction. (This argument is exactly the one sometimes advanced for graphical informal system descriptions which have internal conflicts of interpretation over matters like synchronisation.) Formalising the higher level of abstraction involves constructing the machinery employed in the semantic foundations document, so the argument seems to establish nothing.

Incidentally, the semantic foundations document does indicate the value of abstraction (or, more precisely, implicit definition). It exploits implicit definition to shorten the semantics in two ways:
- by using invariants on static semantic domains and assertions of the existence of static semantic values (in the semantic rules), in order to test implicitly that constructs are well formed;
- by postulating the existence of dynamic semantic domains where they can 'reasonably' be assumed to exist without an explicit construction.

Nonetheless, both the semantics and the proof rules remain large formal descriptions, and large formal descriptions have limited appeal. A lot of their meaning is conveyed not by the formality but by the contexts and names chosen. (Evidently a balance must be struck between the brevity, consistency and utility of names, and the semantic foundations document may have become more difficult to understand because long names lengthened it disproportionately.) For purposes of communication, particularly in a small group, explanation is often more effective than formalisation. Where formalisation can be used, a little formality, which may be read, can be better than a lot, which will not.

48

The proof theory document [22] is perhaps more widely used than the semantic foundations document. The reasons for this appear to be as follows:

- it is smaller (for, though it includes many dynamic rules for each construct instead of one, it does not need laborious domain definitions);
- it is better able to display the unity of apparently diverse constructs which satisfy laws that follow shared algebraic and logical patterns;
- it is better suited to application writers and proof editor writers (but not compiler writers), because it describes constructs as they are nested in practice, rather than as individual constructs composed together through the environment.

The RAISE project shows in various ways how appeals to simplicity of formalisation do not always succeed against appeals to familiarity. Some of the ways will be apparent from this paper. (For instance, provided that **any** was retained, the explicit variables and channels could be abolished, with benefit to theorists and practitioners alike.) However, without formality the project would have had nothing to offer, even if with formality it may have had too much.

Acknowledgements

Many people took part in various stages of the RAISE project. This is not the place to mention them all. However, special thanks are due here to Klaus Havelund, Anne Haxthausen and Kim Ritter-Wagner, who all worked on the specification language and early versions of the formal semantics, and to Chris George, who expounded the development method. All these people contributed greatly to the cohesive parts of the final design.

References

[1]   Astesiano, E., and Cerioli, M., Multiparadigm Specification Languages: a First Attempt at Foundations, in this volume.

[2]   Baeten, J.C.M., and Weijland, W.P., *Process Algebra*, Cambridge Tracts in Theoretical Computer Science, 18, Cambridge University Press (1990).

[3]   Bauer, F.L., Moller, B., Parsch, H., and Pepper, P., Programming by formal reasoning: computer-aided intuition-guided programming, *IEEE Transactions on Software Engineering*, 15 (2), 165-180 (1989).

[4]   Bergstra, J.A., Heering, J., and Klint, P., Module Algebra, *Journal of the ACM*, 37 (2), 335-372 (1990).

[5]   Bolignano, D., and Debabi, M., Higher Order Communicating Processes with Value-Passing, Assignment and Return of Results, *Algorithms and Computation*, Lecture Notes in Computer Science, 650, 319-331, Springer-Verlag (1992).

[6]   De Nicola, R., and Hennessy, M., CCS without τs, *TAPSOFT '87. Volume 1,* Lecture Notes in Computer Science, 249, 138-152, Springer-Verlag (1987).

[7]   Ehrig, H., and Mahr, B., *Fundamentals of Algebraic Specification 1, Equations and Initial Semantics,* EATCS Monographs on Theoretical Computer Science, 6, Springer-Verlag (1985).

[8]   Feijs, L.M.G., and Jonkers, H.B.M., *Formal Specification and Design,* Cambridge Tracts in Theoretical Computer Science, 35, Cambridge University Press (1992).

[9]   Goguen, J.A., and Winkler, T., Introducing OBJ3, Report SRI-CSL-88-9, SRI International (1988).

[10]   Gordon, M.J.C., HOL: A Proof Generating System for Higher-Order Logic, *VLSI Specification, Verification and Synthesis,* 73-128, Kluwer (1988).

[11]   Guttag, J.V., Horning, J.J., and Wing, J.M., *Larch in Five Easy Pieces,* Technical Report, 5, DEC SRC (1985).

[12]   Havelund, K., *Semantics of RSL,* RAISE/DDC/KH/43/V1, Computer Resources International (1989).

[13]   Hennessy, M., Acceptance Trees, *Journal of the ACM,* 32 (4), 896-928 (1985).

[14]   Hennessy, M., A Proof System for Communicating Processes with Value-Passing, Formal Aspects of Computing, 3 (4), 346-366 (1991).

[15]   Hoare, C.A.R., *Communicating Sequential Processes,* Prentice-Hall International (1985).

[16]   International Telecommunications Union, *Specification and Description Language SDL,* Recommendation Z.100 (1992).

[17]   Jones, C.B., *Systematic Software Development Using VDM,* Prentice-Hall International (1990).

[18]   Kahrs, S., Sannella, D., and Tarlecki, A., The Semantics of Extended ML: A Gentle Introduction, in this volume.

[19]   Larsen, P.G., Towards Proof Rules for Looseness in Explicit Definitions from VDM-SL, in this volume.

[20]   Milne, R.E., *Concurrency models and axioms,* RAISE/STC/REM/6/V2, STC (1988).

50

[21] Milne, R.E., *The semantic foundations of the RAISE specification language*, RAISE/STC/REM/11/V2, STC (1990).

[22] Milne, R.E., *The proof theory for the RAISE specification language*, RAISE/STC/REM/12/V2, STC (1990).

[23] Milne, R.E., Transforming axioms for data types into sequential programs, *Proceedings of the Fourth Refinement Workshop*, 197-240, Springer-Verlag (1991).

[24] Milner, A.J.R.G., *Communication and Concurrency*, Prentice-Hall International (1989).

[25] Milner, A.J.R.G., Tofte, M., and Harper, R., *The Definition of Standard ML*, MIT Press (1990).

[26] Sannella, D., and Tarlecki, A., Extended ML: an institution-independent framework for formal program development, *Category Theory and Computer Programming*, Lecture Notes in Computer Science, 240, 364-389, Springer Verlag (1986).

[27] Sannella, D., and Tarlecki, A., Towards formal development of programs from algebraic specifications: implementation revisited, *Acta Informatica*, 25, 223-281 (1988).

[28] Spivey, M., *The Z Notation: A Reference Manual*, Prentice-Hall International (1989).

[29] Stirling, C., Modal Logics for Communicating Systems, *Theoretical Computer Science*, 49, 311-347 (1987).

[30] The RAISE Language Group, *The RAISE Specification Language*, Prentice-Hall International (1991).

[31] Turski, W. M., and Maibaum, T.S.E., *The specification of computer programs*, Addison-Wesley (1987).

The Static Part of the Design Language COLD-K

Gerard R. Renardel de Lavalette

Department of Computing Science, University of Groningen,

P.O. box 800, 9700 AV Groningen, the Netherlands

E-mail: grl@cs.rug.nl

Abstract

This paper is about the static fragment of the design language COLD-K, obtained by dropping all dynamic features (procedures and expressions). It contains definitions of syntax and semantics, together with a presentation of the notions used in the definition of the semantics, such as MPL_ω (many-sorted partial infinitary logic), inductive definitions, the algebra of theories (with the operations renaming, import and export) and the type structure defined over this algebra.

1 Introduction

COLD-K is a wide spectrum design language, developed at Philips Research Eindhoven (the Netherlands), mainly in the ESPRIT project METEOR. In this paper we give a survey of several – not all – features of COLD-K with an emphasis on their semantics. These features are:

- algebraic expressions (denoting objects) containing partial functions and descriptions;
- assertions over objects as in first order many-sorted predicate logic with equality;
- both explicit and inductive definitions of functions and predicates;
- the modularisation constructs import, export and renaming;
- parametrisation by lambda abstraction, involving an implementation relation.

The fragment of COLD-K consisting of these features is baptized COLD-K^2. The main features of COLD-K not in COLD-K^2 are:

- multivalued functions;
- overloading;
- dynamic features involving state changes (statements, procedures with side effects, modification of functions and predicates);
- the notions of origin and origin consistency.

1.1 Survey of the rest of this paper

In 2, we present some background information on COLD (some history, design decisions, the status of this paper). 3 is devoted to the syntax and semantics of COLD-K^2 and related theory. Some more technical information is presented in the Appendix, and also a few remarks on wellformedness (sometimes called the static semantics).

1.2 Acknowledgements

The research for this paper was partly performed in close and animated collaboration with Loe Feijs, Hans Jonkers, Karst Koymans and Job Zwiers. Many valuable comments on a draft version were given by Kees Middelburg. Jan Bergstra suggested to consider the static fragment of COLD-K.

2 Background information

2.1 Some history

The main designer of COLD is Hans Jonkers. In 1983, in a joint project of Philips Research and Philips Telecommunication Industry, the idea of a single linguistic framework emerged. This was worked out by Jonkers to a prototype for a design language called COLD, for CHILL-Oriented Language for Design (CHILL is a programming language frequently used for telecommunication applications); following the CHILL-independent development of the language, the meaning of the acronym was changed into Common Object-oriented Language for Design; it is described in [15]. In the ESPRIT pilot project FAST, a simplified version called COLD-S (S for sequential) was developed. FAST has been succeeded by the ESPRIT project METEOR, in which the development of COLD was pursued further, leading to an elaborated and detailed formal definition of COLD-K and its semantics in [11] which forms the basis and main reference for this paper.

Some case studies involving the successive versions of COLD have been published (e.g., [6], [7], [9], [22]). A textbook on formal specification and design based on COLD has recently appeared ([10]). A user-oriented version, COLD-1, is currently under development: see e.g. [14].

COLD-K has served as a model for other specification languages, notably VVSL (the VIP VDM Specification Language, see [17], [18]) and PSF (Process Specification Formalism, see [1]).

2.2 Design decisions in the development of COLD

The main design decisions in the development of COLD-K are:
- the choice for a wide-spectrum language, covering not only formal specification but also design and implementation (this led to the incorporation of imperative programming constructs);
- an important role for the logical semantics during the design of the language;

- algebraic specifications as a starting point, but extending equational logic to full first order predicate logic with equality;
- partial functions combined with two-valued logic, inspired by E-logic [24];
- an assertion language for programs based on a variant of Dynamic Logic [13];
- inductive definitions of functions and predicates;
- modularisation inspired by Module Algebra [4];
- parametrisation by lambda abstraction of free module terms, with an important role for the implementation relation betwen modules;
- language constructs supporting the notion of software components.

2.3 Overview of COLD

The central notion in COLD is the class concept. In COLD-K, a class can be seen as an abstract machine with a collection of states. These states are many-sorted algebras with predicates and (partial) functions, all states of a class having the same signature. States can be modified nondeterministically by procedures: the basic change actions are the creation of a new object and the modification of a function or a predicate. Moreover a procedure can return one or more objects. In COLD-K^2 , however, no dynamic features are present and a class is just a many-sorted algebra.

Classes can be described by giving definitions of the sorts, functions and predicates of its states and of the procedures that can modify the states. These class descriptions can be subjected to modularisation and parametrisation operations, and this results in schemes. Finally schemes can be combined to form components which constitute systems.

2.4 Status of this paper

In the language COLD-K^2 presented in this paper, we have combined language features of COLD-K which have a rather well-understood semantics (see the first part of this Introduction). Most of the material presented here is based on work reported in other publications which we mention here.

- [11], the reference report of COLD-K, containing the full definition of syntax and semantics. The language definition is preceded by chapters on some of the fundamentals behind the semantical domains: the logic MPL$_\omega$ (for the semantics of assertions, expressions and inductive definitions), the Class Algebra (for the semantics of modularisation constructs) and a version of lambda calculus called $\lambda\pi$ (for the semantics of parametrisation).
- [16] about the logic MPL$_\omega$, an adapted version of the corresponding chapter of [11].
- [21] on the algebra of theories, a related alternative for Class Algebra as the semantical domain for the modularisation constructs.
- [23] on the semantics of the implicit inductive definitions used in COLD.

This is a condensed version of [20]. The theory behind some dynamical aspects of COLD-K is studied in [12].

The following parts of this paper contain new material:

- 3.3.5 on the semantics of implicit inductive definitions of functions (only sketched in [23]);
- 3.5.3 on the type structure over the algebra of theories.

3 COLD-K²

3.1 The description of syntax and semantics

The overall structure of COLD-K² can be rendered as follows: the terms refer to sublanguages.

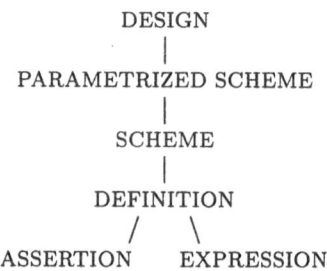

DESIGN
|
PARAMETRIZED SCHEME
|
SCHEME
|
DEFINITION
/ \
ASSERTION   EXPRESSION

In the subsequent subsections, we present these sublanguages. After the definition of the syntax in the form of a BNF-grammar, the semantic domain is discussed and finally the semantics is defined.

!The definition of COLD-K² given here is presented in the form of a BNF-grammar, where | separates alternatives, [X] denotes zero or one occurrence of X, and {X} denotes one or more occurrences of X. We add the following meta-rules:

<xxxxx-list> : :   = [<xxxxx>]
<xxxxx-list '*'> : :   = [<xxxxx> {*<xxxxx>}]
                             where * is some symbol acting as delimiter
<'*'xxxxx-list '**' '***'> : : = [*< xxxxx> {**<xxxxx>}***]
<xxxx-name> : :   = <identifier>
<xxxx-var> : :   = <identifier>

3.2 The expression language and the assertion language

3.2.1 Introduction.

Expressions describe objects in many-sorted algebra's, using variables, (partial) functions and descriptions (THAT xA: the unique object satisfying A).

Expressions may be undefined, due to the use of partial functions or descriptions involving an assertion that is not uniquely satisfied. Moreover, we have the following constructs:

$A?t$ with the same meaning as THAT $x(x = t$ AND $A)$

$s|t$ with the same meaning as THAT $x(x = s$ OR $x = t)$

(assuming x not free in A, s, t). So $A?t$ is equal to t if A holds, otherwise undefined, and $s|t$ acts as the join of s and t, being undefined if both are defined and different.

Assertions are those of many-sorted predicate logic with the expressions as terms; moreover, there is a definedness predicate $t!$, expressing that t is defined.

The semantic domains of the expression and the assertion sublanguage consist of linguistic objects: terms and formulae of the logical language MPL. This is a many-sorted version of Scott's E-logic, a two-valued logic with partial functions. This is in contrast with LPF, the three-valued logic underlying VDM (see [3], [5]; the third truth value is *undefined*). The main reasons for adopting a two-valued logic are simplicity, the desire to adhere to the well-known theory of two-valued logic and the apparent absence of a compelling reason for a third truth value. See [19] for a comparison of LPF and MPL.

3.2.2 Syntax definition

```
<expression> : : = <object-var>
        | <function-name> <'(' expression-list ',' ')' >
        | THAT <varsort> <assertion>
        | LET <assignment-list ','> ; <expression>
        | <assertion> ? <expression>
        | <expression> | <expression>
        | ( <expression> )
```

```
<assertion> : : = TRUE
        | FALSE
        | <expression>!
        | <expression> = <expression>
        | <predicate-name> <'(' expression-list ',' ')'>
        | NOT <assertion>
        | <assertion> AND <assertion>
        | <assertion> OR <assertion>
        | <assertion> => <assertion>
        | <assertion> <=> <assertion>
        | FORALL <varsort-list> <assertion>
        | EXISTS <varsort-list> <assertion>
        | LET <assignment-list ','> ; <assertion>
        | ( <assertion> )
```

```
<varsort> : : = <object-var> : <sortname>
```

<assignment> : : = <object-var> := <expression>

3.2.3 Semantic domain: the logic MPL

The expressions and assertions in COLD-K^2 correspond with the terms and formulae of MPL, many-sorted predicate logic with partial functions. MPL is the finitary fragment of MPL$_\omega$ (introduced below), which is studied extensively in [16], to which we refer for more information. In Appendix B, we indicate how MPL can be reduced to ordinary predicate logic with equality.

MPL has, for every sort S, an equality predicate $=_S$ and a definedness predicate $\downarrow_S$ (postfix notation, so $t \downarrow_S$ means 't is defined', for terms t of sort S). The quantifiers $\forall, \exists$ range over defined objects only, so we have

$$t \downarrow_S \leftrightarrow \exists x : S(x =_S t).$$

For every sort S, there is a constant $\uparrow_S$ denoting the undefined object of sort S, i.e. $\neg(\uparrow_S \downarrow_S)$. Free variables range over possibly undefined objects, i.e. we do not have $x \downarrow_S$ for variables x of sort S. As a consequence, we do not necessarily have $\exists x : S(x \downarrow_S)$, so sorts can be empty. Sort subscripts in $=_S, \downarrow_S$ and $\uparrow_S$ are often omitted.

Functions and predicates are *strict*, i.e. we have

$$f(t_1, \ldots, t_n) \downarrow \rightarrow t_1 \downarrow \wedge \ldots \wedge t_n \downarrow$$
$$P(t_1, \ldots, t_n) \rightarrow t_1 \downarrow \wedge \ldots \wedge t_n \downarrow$$

for all function and predicate symbols. This also holds for the equality predicate, so e.g. $\uparrow = \uparrow$ is false. We define, for every sort S, an equivalence predicate $\simeq_S$ which satisfies $t \simeq_S t$ for *all* terms of sort S. It is defined as the symmetric closure of the relation $\hookrightarrow_S$ with the intended meaning s *rewrites to* t for $s \hookrightarrow t$: whenever t (is defined and) has value x, then s (is defined and) has the value x. So

$$s \hookrightarrow_S t \quad =_{\text{def}} \forall x : S(t =_S x \rightarrow s =_S x)$$
$$s \simeq_S t \quad =_{\text{def}} s \hookrightarrow_S t \wedge t \hookrightarrow_S s$$

Observe that $s \hookrightarrow t$ is equivalent to $(t \downarrow \rightarrow s = t)$. Here (as in the definition of $s \hookrightarrow t$) the logical arrow $\rightarrow$ points from t to s; this can be paraphrased by saying that the 'stream of meaning' is opposite to the rewrite direction.

In MPL we can define terms by *description*. This is done as follows: if A is some formula, then $\iota x : S(A)$ refers either to the unique defined object x of sort S satisfying A, or to the undefined object of sort S if such an x does not exist or is not uniquely characterised by A. The axiom of the description operator ι reads:

$$\forall y : S(y = \iota x : S(A) \leftrightarrow \forall x : S(A \leftrightarrow x = y)) \quad (y \text{ not free in } A)$$

Given a signature $\Sigma \subseteq \text{SORT} \cup \text{FUNC} \cup \text{PRED}$, a model $M = M(\Sigma)$ consists of a non-empty domains S^M for every sort $S \epsilon \Sigma$, total and strict functions f^M for every $f\epsilon\Sigma$ and strict predicates P^M for every $P\epsilon\Sigma$. Every domain S^M contains an object $*_S^M$ which plays the role of undefined object.

The interpretation of terms and formulae in M w.r.t. an assignment a (sending variables to objects of the corresponding domain) is defined as follows:

$$
\begin{aligned}
x^{M,a} &=_{\text{def}} a(x) \\
f(t_1,\ldots,t_n)^{M,a} &=_{\text{def}} f^M(t_1^{M,a},\ldots,t_n^{M,a}) \\
\uparrow S^{M,a} &=_{\text{def}} *_S^M \\
\iota x : S(A)^{M,a} &=_{\text{def}} \text{ the unique } d\epsilon S^M - \{*S^M\} \\
&\qquad\quad \text{ such that } M,a[x \to d] \models A \\
&\qquad\quad \text{ if this } d \text{ exists, otherwise } *_S^M.
\end{aligned}
$$

$$
\begin{aligned}
M,a &\models s = t & &\text{iff } s^{M,a} \neq t^{M,a} \neq *S^M \\
M,a &\models (t \downarrow_S) & &\text{iff } t^{M,a} \neq *S_M \\
M,a &\models P(t_1,...,t_n) & &\text{iff } < t_1^{M,a},\ldots,t_n^{M,a} > \epsilon P^M \\
M,a &\models \neg A & &\text{iff not } M,a \models A \\
M,a &\models A \wedge B & &\text{iff } M,a \models A \text{ and } M,a \models B \\
M,a &\models \forall x : S(A) & &\text{iff for all } d\epsilon S^M - \{*S^M\} M,a[x \to d] \models A \\
M &\models A & &\text{iff } M,a \models A \text{ for all assignments } a \\
\Gamma &\models A & &\text{iff } (M \models B \text{ for all } B\epsilon\Gamma) \text{ implies } M \models A \\
&\models A & &\text{iff } M \models A \text{ for all models } M
\end{aligned}
$$

We list some properties of MPL, referring to [16] for more information (on MPL_ω, but directly applicable to MPL: see also 3.3.3).

Soundness and completeness: we have

$$\Gamma \vdash A \text{ iff } \Gamma \models A$$

Soundness is proved straightforwardly with induction over the length of derivations, the completeness is proved using semantic tableaux.

Elimination of descriptions. It is possible to translate formulae containing descriptions into equivalent formulae without descriptions. This elimination of ι is accomplished by a mapping ι whose behaviour on atomic formulae is suggested by

$$\left(Pt(\iota x.A)\right)^\iota = \exists!x A \wedge \exists x (A \wedge Pt(x)); \tag{ι}$$

ι commutes with the logical operators. We have (see [16, 3.1.3] for more details):

$$
\begin{aligned}
&\text{MPL} \vdash A \leftrightarrow A^\iota, \\
&\text{MPL} \vdash A \Leftrightarrow \text{MPL} -(\iota) \vdash A^\iota.
\end{aligned}
$$

Interpolation. An interpolant for $A \vdash B$ is a formula I with:

$$\text{MPL} \vdash (A \to I) \wedge (I \to B) \quad \text{and} \quad \text{par}(I) \subseteq \text{par}(A) \cap \text{par}(B),$$

where $\text{par}(A)$, the collection of parameters of A, is defined as the collection of free variables and signature elements occurring in A, including the sorts of all terms occurring in A. We have:

If MPL: $A \vdash B$, then there is an interpolant for $A \vdash B$.

The proof is similar to the proof for interpolation in MPL_ω which is given in [16, 3.3]. It is based on the cut-elimination property for MPL^-, i.e. MPL^- minus the non-logical axioms, and this result is extended to full MPL.

3.2.4 *Interpretation of the expression language and the assertion language*

We now give the interpretation of the expression and the assertion language. First we present a list of variables (without possible subscripts) ranging over different collections of COLD-K^2-constructs.

S	sort names
f	function names
P	predicate names
x	object variables
A B	assertions
s t	expressions

We assume a canonical mapping from signature elements and variables of COLD-K^2 to MPL, which in our notation corresponds with going from the Courier font (used for COLD) to the Times font (used for MPL). Moreover we assume that x does not occur in $[A]$, $[s]$ or $[t]$ and that S is the sort of $[t]$.

$[\![\text{x}]\!]$ $=_\text{def} x$

$[\![\text{f(t1}, \ldots, \text{t n)}]\!]$ $=_\text{def} f([\![\text{t1}]\!], \ldots, [\![\text{tn}]\!])$

$[\![\text{THAT x:S A}]\!]$ $=_\text{def} \iota x : S[\![A]\!]$

$[\![\text{LET x1:=t1}, \ldots, \text{xn:=tn; t}]\!]$ $=_\text{def} [x_1 := [\![\text{t1}]\!], \ldots, x_n := [\![\text{tn}]\!]][\![\text{t}]\!]$

$[\![\text{A ? t}]\!]$ $=_\text{def} \iota x : S([\![A]\!] \wedge x = [\![\text{t}]\!])$

$[\![\text{s | t}]\!]$ $=_\text{def} \iota x : S(x = [\![\text{s}]\!] \vee x = [\![\text{t}]\!])$

$[\![\text{(t)}]\!]$ $=_\text{def} [\![\text{t}]\!]$

$[\![\text{TRUE}]\!]$ $=_\text{def} \top$

$[\![\text{FALSE}]\!]$ $=_\text{def} \bot$

$[\![\text{t!}]\!]$ $=_\text{def} [\![\text{t}]\!] \downarrow$

$[\![\text{s = t}]\!]$ $=_\text{def} [\![\text{s}]\!] = [\![\text{t}]\!]$

$[\![\text{P(t1}, \ldots, \text{tn)}]\!]$ $=_\text{def} P([\![\text{t1}]\!], \ldots, [\![\text{tn}]\!])$

$[\![\text{NOT A}]\!]$ $=_\text{def} \neg[\![A]\!]$

$[\![\text{A AND B}]\!]$ $=_\text{def} [\![A]\!] \wedge [\![B]\!]$

$[\![\text{A OR B}]\!]$ $=_\text{def} [\![A]\!] \vee [\![B]\!]$

$[\![\text{A => B}]\!]$ $=_\text{def} [\![A]\!] \rightarrow [\![B]\!]$

$[\![\text{A <=> B}]\!]$ $=_\text{def} [\![A]\!] \leftrightarrow [\![B]\!]$

$[\![\text{FORALL x1: S1} \ldots \text{xn: Sn A}]\!]$ $=_\text{def} \forall x_1 : S_1 \ldots \forall x_n : S_n[\![A]\!]$

$[\![\text{EXISTS x1: S1} \ldots \text{xn:Sn A}]\!]$ $=_\text{def} \exists x_1 : S_1 \ldots \exists x_n : S_n[\![A]\!]$

$[\![\text{LET x1: = t1}, \ldots, \text{xn: =tn; A}]\!]$ $=_\text{def} [x_1 := [\![\text{t1}]\!], \ldots, x_n := [\![\text{tn}]\!]][\![A]\!]$

$[\![\text{(A)}]\!]$ $=_\text{def} [\![A]\!]$

3.3 The definition language

3.3.1 Introduction

The items that are defined in the definition language are sorts, predicates and functions. A definition has in general two aspects, viz. declarative and assertional. A declaration introduces a sort, predicate or function name (the latter two provided with a type); in the assertional part of a definition, the meaning of a sort, predicate and/or function is given directly (by a defining expression or assertion) or indirectly (by an axiom). Looking at the four kinds of definitions, we see:

- sort definitions only have a declarative aspect;
- predicate and function definitions are both declarative and assertional;
- axioms are purely assertional, without a declarative aspect.

The semantics of the declarative aspect of definitions is straightforward. Idem for explicit function and predicate definitions (with keyword DEF) and for axioms. For implicit definitions (keyword IND) the situation is more subtle. The idea is that the meaning of a predicate P defined by IND A is: the smallest P that satisfies A. In order to achieve this in the definition of the semantics it would suffice to extend MPL to full second-order logic, but this logic was considered to be far too strong and not well enough understood to provide the semantics for COLD. Instead the logic MPL_ω has been chosen, an extension of MPL with countably infinite conjunctions and disjunctions. MPL_ω has two important properties:

- the Interpolation Property, desirable for an adequate sementics of modularisation and parametrisation, holds for MPL_ω;
- fixpoints $\mu\Phi$ of continuous predicate functions Φ can be expressed explicitly in MPL_ω as follows: $\mu\Phi = \vee_n A_n$ with $A_0 = \bot, A_{n+1} = \Phi(A_n)$.

In order to make this work, one step has to be taken: transform assertions A (intended to be inductive definitions) into continuous predicate functions whenever possible. This is worked out in [23]; in 3.3.4 an overview is given.

An alternative to this approach, circumventing this last step, is: restrict the use of inductive definitions in COLD to those explicitly denoted as the least fixpoint of continuous predicate functions. However , the disadvantage of this is that such definitions are more difficult to devise and harder to read.

3.3.2 Syntax definition

```
<definition> : : = SORT <sort-name>
        | FUNC <typed function> [ <function body> ]
        | PRED <typed predicate> [ <predicate body> ]
        | AXIOM <assertion>

<typed function> : : = <function-name> <function type>

<typed predicate> : : = <predicate-name> <predicate type>
```

<function type> : : = <sort-name-list '#'> -> <sort-name>

<predicate type> : : = <sort-name-list '#'>

<function body> : : = PAR <object-var-list> DEF <expression>
    | IND <assertion>

<predicate body> : : = PAR <object-var-list> DEF <assertion>
    | IND <assertion>

3.3.3 MPL$_\omega$

Here we shall show how explicit definitions of a large class of inductively defined predicates and functions can be obtained in the infinitary extension MPL$_\omega$ of MPL. More information on MPL$_\omega$ is in [16]; the technique used here to make inductive definitions explicit is also described more generally in [23].

MPL$_\omega$ is obtained from MPL by adding countably infinite conjunctions $\bigwedge_n A_n$ (where $< A_n >_{n<\omega} = < A_0, A_1, \dots >$ are formulae containing only finitely many different free variables).

Infinite disjunctions are definable: $\bigvee_n A_n = \neg \bigwedge_n \neg A_n$. The proof system of MPL$_\omega$ contains the following rules:

$$(\bigwedge L) \quad \frac{\Gamma, A_i \vdash \Delta}{\Gamma, \bigwedge_n A_n \vdash \Delta} \quad \text{for all } i \qquad (\bigwedge R) \quad \frac{< \Gamma \vdash \Delta, A_n >_{n<\omega}}{\Gamma \vdash \Delta, \bigwedge_n A_n}$$

MPL$_\omega$ is a conservative extension of MPL, i.e.

$$\text{MPL}_\omega \vdash A \Leftrightarrow \text{MPL} \vdash A \ (A \text{ in the language of MPL}).$$

$\Leftarrow$ is trivial, $\Rightarrow$ follows from MPL$_\omega$: $\Gamma \vdash \Delta \Rightarrow$ MPL: $\Gamma \vdash \Delta$ for MPL-sequents $\Gamma \vdash \Delta$, and this is proved by induction over a cut-free derivation of MPL$_\omega$: $\Gamma \vdash \Delta$.

MPL$_\omega$ shares the properties mentioned above in 3.2.3 for MPL: Soundness & completeness, Eliminability of descriptions, Interpolation.

Before we can embark on inductive definitions, we have to introduce some notation.

If A is a formula, then $\{x_1 : S_1, \dots, x_n : S_n \mid A\}$, or $\{\mathbf{x} : \mathbf{S} \mid A\}$ or even $\{\mathbf{x} \mid A\}$ for short, is a *defined predicate* of type $\mathbf{S} = S_1, \dots, S_n$. The meaning of $\{\mathbf{x} \mid A\}$ is given by

$$\{\mathbf{x} \mid A\}(\mathbf{t}) =_{\text{def}} [\mathbf{x} := \mathbf{t}]A \wedge \mathbf{t} \downarrow$$

for terms $\mathbf{t}$ of sort $\mathbf{S}$. $\mathbf{t} \downarrow$ has been added in order to make defined predicates strict. Predicate symbols P of type S are identified with the defined predicate $\{x \mid P(x)\}$. Inclusion and extensional equality between defined predicates are defined by

$$\{x \mid A\} \subseteq \{x \mid B\} \quad =_{\text{def}} \quad \forall x : S(A \to B),$$
$$\{x \mid A\} = \{x \mid B\} \quad =_{\text{def}} \quad \forall x : S(A \leftrightarrow B),$$
$$\{x \mid A\} \equiv \{x \mid B\} \quad =_{\text{def}} \quad \vdash \{x \mid A\} = \{x \mid B\}.$$

We also put

$$
\begin{array}{lll}
S & =_{\text{def}} & \{x : S \mid \top\} \\
\emptyset_S & =_{\text{def}} & \{x : S \mid \bot\} \\
x^c & =_{\text{def}} & \{y \mid y \neq x\} \\
\bigcup\{D_n \mid n\epsilon\omega\} & =_{\text{def}} & \{x \mid \bigvee_n A_n\} \text{ if } D_n = \{x \mid A_n\} \\
\bigcap\{\{x \mid A(x,y)\} \mid B(y)\} & =_{\text{def}} & \{x \mid \forall y(B(y) \to A(x,y))\}
\end{array}
$$

As a consequence of this last definition, we have
$$\bigcap \emptyset = \bigcap\{X(y) \mid \bot\} = S.$$

If P is a predicate symbol and D a defined predicate of the same type, then $[P := D]$ is a *predicate substitution*, defined straightforwardly. The following rule is a derived rule in MPL_ω:

$$(\text{psub}) \quad \frac{\Gamma \vdash \Delta}{[P := D]\Gamma \vdash [P := D]\Delta}$$

We also introduce the predicate substitutions $[P^+ := D], [P^- := D]$. They are defined on formulae of MPL_ω not containing descriptions; the intended meaning is that only the positive resp. negative occurrences of P are replaced by D. The clauses of the definitions of $[P^+ := D]A, [P^- := D]A$ are similar to those for $[P := D]A$, with the following modifications:

$$
\begin{array}{lll}
[P^+ := D]P(t) & =_{\text{def}} & D(t) \\
[P^- := D]P(t) & =_{\text{def}} & P(t) \\
[P^+ := D]\neg A & =_{\text{def}} & [P^- := D]A \\
[P^- := D]\neg A & =_{\text{def}} & [P^+ := D]A
\end{array}
$$

Observe that $A \equiv B$ does *not* imply $[P^+ := D]A \equiv [P^+ := D]B$: take $A = (P \to P), B = (Q \to Q)$, then $A \equiv B$ (for $\vdash A$ and $\vdash B$), but $[P^+ := D]A = P \to D$ is not equivalent to $[P^+ := D]B = Q \to Q$. A similar argument holds for $[P^- := D]$. To preserve $\equiv$ under $[P^+ := D]$, $\equiv$ has to be strengthened to $\equiv_P$, *strong equivalence in* P, defined by

$$A \equiv_P B =_{\text{def}} [P^+ := Q]A \equiv [P^+ := Q]B,$$

where Q is a fresh predicate variable of the same type as P. Now we have

$$(SEq) \quad A \equiv_P B \Rightarrow [P^+ := D, P^- := E]A \equiv [P^+ := D, P^- := E]B.$$

If P is a predicate symbol of type S and A is a formula, then $\Gamma = \Lambda P.A$ is a *predicate function* of type S, with the defining equation

$$(\Lambda P.A)D =_{\text{def}} [P := D]A$$

for defined predicates D of type S.

Predicate operators are defined analogously, but with defined predicates instead of formulae: if P is a predicate symbol of type S and $D = \{x \mid A\}$ is a defined predicate of type T, then $\Lambda P.D$ is a predicate operator of type $S \to T$, which satisfies

$$(\Lambda P.\{x \mid A\})E =_{\text{def}} \{x \mid [P := E]A\}$$

for defined predicates E of type S. In order to distinguish them, we use Φ for predicate functions and Γ for predicate operators.

A predicate operator Γ is called *monotonic* if it satisfies $D \subseteq E \Rightarrow \Gamma(D) \subseteq \Gamma(E)$. Γ is called *continuous* if it satisfies

$$D_0 \subseteq D_1 \subseteq D_2 \subseteq \ldots \Rightarrow \Gamma(\cup\{D_n \mid n\epsilon\omega\}) \equiv \cup\{\Gamma(D_n) \mid n\epsilon\omega\}$$

It is clear that continuity implies monotonicity.

$\lambda x.t$ (or $\lambda x : S.t$, or $\lambda x_1 : S_1 \ldots x_n : S_n.t$) is a *defined function*, with the meaning given by

$$s \downarrow \to (\lambda x.t)(s) \simeq [x := s]t.$$

Observe that we do *not* define

$$(\lambda x.t)(s) =_{\text{def}} [x := s]t;$$

this would yield non-strict functions: if c is a constant, then we would have $(\lambda x.c)(\uparrow) = c$. So, generally speaking, we have to consider $(\lambda x.t)(s)$ as an extension of the language, not as a mere abbreviation. However, if t has the form $\iota y.A(x, y)$, then $(\lambda x.t)(s)$ can be defined as an abbreviation:

$$\big(\lambda x.\iota y.A(x, y)\big)(s) =_{\text{def}} \iota y.\big(A(s, y) \wedge s \downarrow\big).$$

Function symbols f are identified with the defined function $\lambda x.f(x)$. We also put

$$\begin{aligned}
\lambda x.s \subseteq \lambda x.t \quad &=_{\text{def}} \forall x(s \downarrow \to s = t)\\
\lambda x.s = \lambda x.t \quad &=_{\text{def}} \forall x(s \simeq t)\\
\lambda x.s \equiv \lambda x.t \quad &=_{\text{def}} \vdash \lambda x.s = \lambda x.t
\end{aligned}$$

A (defined) predicate $F = F(x, y)$ is called *functional* (notation: $\text{Func}(F)$) if

$$\forall xyz\big(F(x, y) \wedge F(x, z) \to y = z\big).$$

3.3.4 Inductive definition of predicates

An inductively defined predicate P is defined as the smallest predicate satisfying some inductive definition $A(P)$. Let us write $\delta P.A$ for the predicate defined inductively by A (using the predicate parameter P), then we have under certain conditions (denoted by $A\epsilon\text{Adm}(P)$ and worked out below):

(I1) $[P := \delta P.A]A$,   ($\delta P.A$ satisfies A);
(I2) $A \rightarrow \delta P.A \subseteq P$, (if P satisfies A, then P extends $\delta P.A$.)

First we consider the easy case: A happens to be of the form $\Gamma(P) \equiv P$ where Γ is continuous. In that case, $Fix(\Gamma) = \cup\{\Gamma^n(\emptyset) \mid n\epsilon\omega\}$ will do for $\delta P.A$, and $Fix(\Gamma)$ has an explicit definition in MPL_ω (using an infinite disjunction):

$$Fix(\Gamma)(t) = \bigvee_n \big(\Gamma^n(\emptyset)\big)(t).$$

or the general case, we use the technique explained in [23] which we paraphrase here as follows. We put

$$\begin{aligned}
\Delta P.A &=_{\mathrm{def}} \Lambda P.\{x \mid \neg[P^+ := x^c]A\}, \\
\delta P.A &=_{\mathrm{def}} Fix(\Delta P.A).
\end{aligned}$$

Now, in order to be able to show that this $\delta P.A$ indeed satisfies (I1) and (I2), we have to define the admissibility condition $\mathrm{Adm}(P)$. This is done as follows. A predicate function Φ is called $\bigcap$-*preserving* iff, for all A, B

$$\forall y\big(B(y) \rightarrow \Phi(\{x \mid A(x,y)\})\big) \rightarrow \Phi\big(\bigcap\{x \mid A(x,y) \mid B(y)\}\big);$$

Now

> $A\epsilon\,\mathrm{Adm}(P)$ iff $\Delta P.A$ is continuous & $\Lambda P.[P^- := Q]A$
> is $\bigcap$−preserving

(Q is a fresh predicate variable of the same type as P). Observe that, for $\bigcap$-preserving Φ, we have $\vdash \Phi(S)$ (for $S = \bigcap\emptyset = \bigcap\{X(y) \mid \bot\}$).

$\mathrm{Adm}(P)$ is not closed under $\equiv$: consider

$$A =_{\mathrm{def}} (Pa \vee Pb) \rightarrow (Pa \vee Pb);$$

$A \equiv T, T\epsilon\mathrm{Adm}(P)$, but $A \notin \mathrm{Adm}(P)$, for $\Lambda P.[P^- := Q]A$ is not $\bigcap$-preserving: we have (taking $X(y) =_{\mathrm{def}} \{z \mid B(y,z)\}$)

$$\begin{aligned}
(\Lambda P.[P^- := Q]A)\,(\cap\{X(y) \mid T\}) &= (Qa \vee Qb) \\
&\rightarrow (\forall y B(y,a) \vee \forall y B(y,b)) \\
\bigcap(\Lambda P.[P^- := Q]A)\{X(y) \mid T\} &= \forall y\big((Qa \vee Qb) \\
&\rightarrow (B(y,a) \vee B(y,b))\big)
\end{aligned}$$

and these two are not equivalent. However, $\mathrm{Adm}(P)$ is closed under $\equiv_P$.

Theorem Let $A\epsilon\mathrm{Adm}(P)$. Then
  i) $\vdash [P := \delta P.A]A$;
  ii) $\vdash A \rightarrow \delta P.A \subseteq P$.
In words: $\delta P.A$ is an explicit definition of the predicate P, inductively defined by A.

Proof.

(i) Let $\Phi =_{\text{def}} \Lambda P.[P^- := \delta P.A]A$. Then Φ is $\cap$-preserving, for $A \epsilon \text{Adm}(P)$. Now we have

$\vdash \forall x \big(\Phi(x^c) \to \Phi(x^c) \big)$

$\vdash \Phi \big(\cap \{ x^c \mid \Phi(x^c) \} \big)$ (Φ preserves $\cap$)

$\vdash \Phi \big(\{ y \mid \forall x (\Phi(x^c) \to y \neq x) \} \big)$

$\vdash \Phi \big(\{ y \mid \forall x (y = x \to \neg \Phi(x^c)) \} \big)$ (contraposition)

$\vdash \Phi (\{ x \mid \neg \Phi(x^c) \})$

$\vdash \Phi (\{ x \mid \neg [P^- := \delta P.A, P^+ := x^c] A \})$ (definition of Φ)

$\vdash \Phi \big((\Delta P.A)(\delta P.A) \big)$ (definition of $\Delta P.A$)

$\vdash \Phi (\delta P.A)$ (continuity of $\Delta P.A$)

$\vdash [P := \delta P.A] A$ (definition of Φ)

(ii). We have

$\vdash A \wedge \neg P(x) \to [P^+ := x^c] A$ (monotonicity of
                                          $\Lambda Q.[P^+ := Q] A)$

$\vdash A \to \forall x \big(\neg [P^+ := x^c] A \to P(x) \big)$ (contraposition)

$\vdash A \to \{ x \mid \neg [P^+ := x^c] A \} \subseteq P$ (definition of $\subseteq$)

$\vdash A \to (\Delta P.A) P \subseteq P$ (definition of $\Delta P.A$)

$\vdash A \to \delta P.A \subseteq P$ (by (2))   □

Observe that only one instance (viz. $\{ x^c \mid \Phi(x^c) \}$) of the $\cap$-preserving property of Φ has been used.

We establish a syntactically defined subset of $\text{Adm}(P)$. We have

$\text{Adm}(P) =_{\text{def}} \{ A \mid \neg [P^+ := x^c] A \epsilon Cts(P, x)$ and

$[P^- := Q] A \epsilon\ Pres(P) \}$

where

$Cts(P, x) \quad =_{\text{def}} \{ A \mid \Lambda P. \{ x \mid A \} \text{ is continuous} \},$
$Pres(P) \quad =_{\text{def}} \{ A \mid \Lambda P.A \text{ is } \cap\text{-preserving} \}.$

The following properties of Cts and $Pres$ are proved easily.

i) $Cts(P, x)$ contains all formulae of the form

$$\bigvee \exists (A \wedge P(..) \wedge \ldots \wedge P(..)) \quad (P \text{ not in } A),$$

i.e. all (finite or infinite) disjunctions of existentially quantified formulae $A_1 \wedge \ldots \wedge A_n$, where A_i is of the form $P(t_1, \ldots, t_k)$ or does not contain P. (Observe that x is not explicitly involved in the definition of this class of formulae.)

ii) $Pres(P)$ contains all formulae of the form

$$\bigwedge \forall (A \wedge t \downarrow P(t)) \quad (P \text{ not negatively in } A),$$

i.e. all (finite or infinite) conjunctions of universally quantified formulae of the form $A \wedge t_1 \downarrow \wedge \ldots \wedge t_n \downarrow \rightarrow P(t_1 \ldots, t_n)$, where A does not contain P negatively.

Now we define: a *Horn formula* in P is a formula of the form

$$\bigwedge \forall (A \wedge P(..) \wedge \ldots \wedge P(..) t \downarrow \rightarrow P(t)) \wedge \quad (P \text{ not in } A),$$

i.e. a (finite or infinite) conjunction of universally quantified formulae of the form $A_1 \wedge \ldots \wedge A_m \wedge t_1 \downarrow \wedge \ldots \wedge t_n \downarrow \rightarrow P(t_1, \ldots, t_n) \quad (m, n \geq 0)$, where A_i is of the form $P(t'_1, \ldots, t'_n)$ or does not contain P. The collection of all Horn formulae in P is denoted $\mathrm{Horn}(p)$. ¿From (i), (ii) it follows that

$$\mathrm{Horn}(P) \subseteq \mathrm{Adm}(P).$$

In the sequel, we shall allow ourselves some sloppiness in the use of the phrase " $\cdots \epsilon \ \mathrm{Horn}(P)$" , in the following sense: whenever $s \downarrow$ always holds in the context under consideration, $\mathrm{Horn}(P)$ is supposed to contain also the formulae of the form

$$\bigwedge \forall (A \wedge P(..) \wedge \ldots \wedge P(..) \wedge t \downarrow \rightarrow P(s, t)),$$

although such formulae are in fact only $\equiv P$-equivalent to elements of $\mathrm{Horn}(P)$, hence in $\mathrm{Adm}(P)$ by the next lemma. Examples of such terms s are: bound variables, and the terms 0 and Sx (x ranging over the natural numbers) in the context of arithmetic.

3.3.5 Inductive definition of functions

The explicit definition of an inductively defined function can be obtained as follows: replace the function f of type $S_1 \times \ldots \times S_n \rightarrow S_{n+1}$ by an associated predicate F of type $S_1 \times \ldots \times S_n \times S_{n+1}$, give an explicit definition of F and put $f(t_1, \ldots, t_n) := \iota x : S_{n+1}.F(t_1, \ldots, t_n, x)$. We describe this in somewhat greater detail.

To replace the function f by the predicate F, the mapping ^{F} is used. Let A be a formula containing f; we assume that all occurrences of f in A are provided with a unique index. We put

$$
\begin{aligned}
\epsilon(t) &=_{\mathrm{def}} T \text{ if } f \text{ not in } t \\
\epsilon\big(f_i(t)\big) &=_{\mathrm{def}} F(t^F, x_i) \\
\epsilon\big(g(t)\big) &=_{\mathrm{def}} \epsilon(t)(= \epsilon(t_1) \wedge \ldots \wedge \epsilon(t_m)) \\
&\qquad \text{if } g \text{ different from } f
\end{aligned}
$$

$$
\begin{aligned}
t^F &=_{\mathrm{def}} t \text{ if } f \text{ not in } t \\
\big(f_i(t)\big)^F &=_{\mathrm{def}} x_i \\
\big(g(t)\big)^F &=_{\mathrm{def}} g(t^F) \text{if } g \text{ different from } f
\end{aligned}
$$

$P(t)^F =_{\text{def}} P(t)$ if f not in t

$P(t)^F =_{\text{def}} \exists x(\epsilon(t) \wedge P(t^F))$ otherwise,

where x is the list of variables x_i occurring in $\epsilon(t)$.

^{F} commutes with the logical operators.

This mapping ^{F} is akin to the elimination translation $^{\iota}$ of descriptions mentioned in 3.2.3. It is straightforward that

$$(f \leftrightarrow F) \qquad \vdash \forall xy\big(f(x) = y \leftrightarrow F(x,y)\big) \rightarrow (A \leftrightarrow A^F)$$

holds. We also put

$$\begin{aligned}
\delta f.A &=_{\text{def}} \lambda x.\iota y.(\delta F.A^F)(x,y). \\
\text{Adm}(f) &=_{\text{def}} \{A \mid A^F \epsilon \text{Adm}(F)\}. \\
A \equiv_f B &=_{\text{def}} A^F \equiv_F B^F.
\end{aligned}$$

Theorem. Let $A \epsilon \text{Adm}(f)$.

Then

i) $\vdash \text{Func}(\delta F.A^F) \rightarrow [f := \delta f.A]A$;

ii) $\vdash \text{Func}(\delta F.A^F) \rightarrow (A \rightarrow \delta f.A \subseteq f)$.

In words: if $\delta F.A^F$ is a functional predicate, then $\delta f.A$ is an explicit definition of the function f, inductively defined by A.

iii) If $A, B \epsilon \text{Adm}(f)$ and $A \equiv B$, then $\delta f.A \equiv \delta f.B$.

Proof. (i) By $(f \leftrightarrow F)$ we have

$$\vdash \forall xy\big(f(x) = y \leftrightarrow F(x,y)\big) \rightarrow (A \leftrightarrow A^F),$$

so, applying the substitution $[F := \delta F.A^F]$ and using
$\vdash [F := \delta F.A^F]A^F$:

$$\vdash \forall xy\big(f(x) = y \leftrightarrow (\delta F.A^F)(x,y)\big) \rightarrow A;$$

now we apply $[f := \delta f.A]$ and get, by the definition of $\delta f.A$:

$$\vdash \forall xy\big(\iota y.(\delta F.A^F)(x,y) = y \leftrightarrow (\delta F.A^F)(x,y)\big)$$
$$\rightarrow [f := \delta f.A]A;$$

since

$$\vdash \text{Func}(\delta F.A^F)$$
$$\rightarrow \forall xy\big(\iota y.(\delta F.A^F)(x,y) = y \leftrightarrow (\delta F.A^F)(x,y)\big),$$

we now get (i).

(ii). By (i) and the substitution $[F := \{(x,y) \mid f(x) = y\}]$, we have

$$\vdash A \leftrightarrow [F := \{(x, y) \mid f(x) = y\}]A^F;$$

combining this with $\vdash A^F \to \delta F.A^F \subseteq F$ and the same substitution, we get

$$\vdash A \to \delta F.A^F \subseteq \{(x, y) \mid f(x) = y\};$$

with

$$\vdash \operatorname{Func}(\delta F.A^F)$$
$$\to (\delta F.A^F \subseteq \{(x, y) \mid f(x) = y\} \leftrightarrow \lambda x.\iota y.(\delta F.A^F)(x, y) \subseteq f)$$

and the definition of $\delta f.A$ this yields (ii).

iii) If $A, B \epsilon \operatorname{Adm}(f)$ then $A^F, B^F \epsilon \operatorname{Adm}(F)$, so $\delta F.A^F \equiv \delta F.B^F$ and this implies $\delta f.A \equiv \delta f.B$. $\qquad\qquad\qquad\qquad\qquad\qquad\qquad\qquad\qquad\qquad\qquad$ $\square$

Before defining the subset $\operatorname{Horn}(f)$ of $\operatorname{Adm}(f)$, we consider an example.

Example: addition. The usual way of writing down an inductive definition of addition is:

$$(+) \qquad \forall x(x + 0 = x) \land \forall xy (x + Sy = S(x + y))$$

Transforming this in the format used in this section yields

$$A =_{\text{def}} \forall x (f(x, 0) = x) \land \forall xy (f(x, Sy) = S(f(x, y))), \text{ so}$$

$$A^F \equiv_F \forall x F(x, 0, x) \land \forall xy \exists uv (F(x, Sy, u) \land F(x, y, v) \land u = Sv)$$
$$\equiv_F \forall x F(x, 0, x) \land \forall xy \exists v (F(x, Sy, Sv) \land F(x, y, v))$$

Now this does not help us much, for $A \notin \operatorname{Adm}(f)$, since $\Lambda F.A^F$ is not $\cap$-preserving; also

$$\Lambda F.A^F \quad = \Lambda F.\{(x, y, z) \mid (x = z \land y = 0)$$
$$\lor \exists w \forall v ((y = Sw \land z = Sv) \lor (y = w \land z = v))\}$$
$$= \Lambda F.\{(x, 0, x) \mid x = x\},$$

and the fixpoint of this constant predicate operator is $\{(x, 0, x) \mid x = x\}$, which is definitely not the graph of the addition function.

In fact this is not surprising, since $(+)$ is ambiguous as a definition: is $x + Sy$ defined in terms of S and $x + y$, or is $x + y$ defined as the inverse of $x + Sy$ under S? The understanding reader knows that the first reading is meant, but here we have to indicate this explicitly in order to obtain an explicit definition of $+$. This can be done by presenting the equations as rewrite rules. We therefore recall the notation $s \hookrightarrow t$ defined in 3.2.3 as an abbreviation of $\forall x(t = x \to s = x)$ (suggestively: if t is defined, then s is defined in the same way). The defining formula of addition can be written as

$$B =_{\text{def}} \forall x(f(x, 0) \hookrightarrow x) \land \forall xy (f(x, Sy) \hookrightarrow S(f(x, y)))$$

and this appears to be an element of $\mathrm{Adm}(f)$ (by the next lemma); also

$$
\begin{aligned}
B^F &= \forall x F(x, 0, x) \land \forall xyz (\exists u (F(x, y, u) \land Su = z) \\
&\quad \to \exists v (F(x, Sy, v) \land v = z)) \\
&\equiv_F \forall x F(x, 0, x) \land \forall xyu (F(x, y, u) \to F(x, Sy, Su)),
\end{aligned}
$$

so

$$
\begin{aligned}
\Delta F.B^F &\equiv \Lambda F. \{(p, q, r) \mid \exists x (p = r = x \land q = 0) \\
&\quad \lor \exists xyu (F(x, y, u) \land p = x \land q = Sy \land r = Su)\} \\
&= \Lambda F. \{(x, 0, x) \mid x = x\} \cup \{(x, Sy, Sz) \mid F(x, y, z)\}.
\end{aligned}
$$

To see that the fixpoint $\delta F.B^F$ of $\Delta F.B^F$ is functional, it suffices (using the fact that $\emptyset$ is functional) to know that $\Delta F.B^F$ preserves functionality, i.e. that $\{(x, 0, x) \mid x = x\} \cup \{(x, Sy, Sz) \mid F(x, y, z)\}$ is functional whenever F is. This does not follow from the syntactic form of B, but is based on the properties $Sx \neq 0$ and $Sx = Sy \to x = y$ of S.

A *Horn formula* in f is a formula of the form

$$
\bigwedge \forall \big(A \land P_1(..f..) \land \ldots \land P_n(..f..) \land s \downarrow \to f(s) \hookrightarrow t(..f..) \big)
$$
$$
(f \text{ not in } A, s)
$$

i.e. a (finite or infinite) conjunction of universally quantified formulae of the form $A_1 \land \ldots \land A_m \land s_1 \downarrow \land \ldots \land s_n \downarrow \to f(s_1, \ldots, s_n) \hookrightarrow t$ $(m, n \leq 0)$, where A_i is an atomic formula or does not contain f, and f does not occur in the terms s_i. The collection of all Horn formulae in f is denoted $\mathrm{Horn}(f)$. We have

$$
\mathrm{Horn}(f) \subseteq \mathrm{Adm}(f).
$$

To see this, consider a typical element of $\mathrm{Horn}(f) : A =_{\mathrm{def}} \forall y (B \land P(f(t_1) \land t_2 \downarrow \to f(t_2) \hookrightarrow g(f(t_3))))$. Now $A^F = \forall y (B \land \exists x_1 (F(t_1, x_1) \land P(x_1)) \land t_2 \downarrow \to \forall z (\exists x_3 (F(t_3, x3) \land z = g(x3)) \to \exists x_2 (F(t_2, x_2) \land z = x_2)))$, so

$$
\begin{aligned}
A^F \equiv_F \quad &\forall x_1 x_3 yz (B \land F(t_1, x_1) \land P(x_1) \land t_2 \downarrow \\
&\land F(t_3, x_3) \land z = g(x_3) \to F(t_2, z));
\end{aligned}
$$

this last formula belongs to $\mathrm{Horn}(F)$, hence to $\mathrm{Adm}(F)$, so $A\epsilon\mathrm{Adm}(f)$.

A useful syntactic characterisation of functionality is not easy to find. We confine ourselves to observing that, in the simple case that

$$
A = \forall x \big(f(x) \hookrightarrow t(f, x) \big),
$$

$A\epsilon\ \mathrm{Horn}(f)$, and also $\mathrm{Func}(\delta F.A^F)$ holds; this corresponds to the inductive definition

$$
f(x) \simeq \iota y.(t(f, x) = y)
$$

which is considered in [16, 4.8]. In the general case, the functionality of the operator $\delta F.A^F$ involved depends on (axiomatically presented) properties of functions and predicates occurring in A, as in the example given above.

3.3.6 Interpretation of the definition language

For the definition language, we give two interpretations: $\{\!\!\{.\}\!\!\}$ for the declarative and $[\![.]\!]$ for the definitional aspect. They will be combined in the definition of the interpretation of classes (3.4.4). Besides those introduced in 3.2.4, we use the following variables:

fbody   for function bodies,
Pbody   for predicate bodies.

$$\{\!\!\{ \text{ SORT S } \}\!\!\} \qquad\qquad\qquad\qquad\qquad\qquad =_{\text{def}} \{S\}$$
$$\{\!\!\{ \text{ FUNC f : } \text{S1 \# \ldots \# Sn -> S fbody}\}\!\!\} \quad =_{\text{def}} \{f : \text{S1}\times\ldots\times\text{Sn}\to S\}$$
$$\{\!\!\{ \text{ PRED P : S1 \#\ldots\# Sn Pbody } \}\!\!\} \quad =_{\text{def}} \{P:\text{S1}\times\ldots\times \text{Sn}\}$$
$$\{\!\!\{ \text{ AXIOM A } \}\!\!\} \qquad\qquad\qquad\qquad\qquad =_{\text{def}} \emptyset$$
$$[\![\text{ SORT S }]\!] \qquad\qquad\qquad\qquad\qquad\qquad =_{\text{def}} \top$$
$$[\![\text{ AXIOM A }]\!] \qquad\qquad\qquad\qquad\qquad\quad =_{\text{def}} [\![A]\!]$$

$$[\![\text{ FUNC f: } \text{S1 \#\ldots\# Sn} \to \text{PAR x1\ldots xn DEF t}]\!]$$
$$=_{\text{def}} \forall x_1 : S_1\ldots\forall x_n : S_n(f(x_1,\ldots,x_n) \simeq [\![t]\!])$$

$$[\![\text{ FUNC f: } \text{S1 \#\ldots\# Sn} \to \text{S IND A}]\!]$$
$$=_{\text{def}} \forall x_1 : S_1\ldots\forall x_n : S_n\big(f(x_1,\ldots,x_n)$$
$$\simeq (\delta f.[\![A]\!])(x_1,\ldots,x_n)\big)$$

$$[\![\text{ PRED P: } \text{S1 \#\ldots\# Sn PAR x1\ldots xn DEF A}]\!]$$
$$=_{\text{def}} \forall x_1 : S_1\ldots\forall x_n : S_n(P(x_1,\ldots,x_n) \leftrightarrow [\![A]\!])$$

$$[\![\text{ PRED P: } \text{S1 \#\ldots\# Sn IND A}]\!]$$
$$=_{\text{def}} \forall x_1 : S_1\ldots\forall x_n : S_n(P(x_1,\ldots,x_n)$$
$$\leftrightarrow (\delta P.[\![A]\!])(x_1,\ldots,x_n))$$

3.4 The scheme language

3.4.1 Introduction

In COLD, scheme is synonymous with module. Flat schemes consist of a collection of definitions; arbitrary schemes are constructed form flat schemes by applying renamings, imports and exports. Import is a binary symmetric operator here, taking in some sense the union of its arguments. The export operator restricts the (visible) signature of a scheme, making hiding and encapsulation possible.

The semantics of a scheme is a theory in MPL_ω: this corresponds to the theory semantics of Module Algebra as described in [4]. Some differences between that approach and the one pursued here are:

- renamings ρ in [4] are involutive (i.e. $\rho \circ \rho$ is the identity); here we have no such restrictions;
- the *good renaming property*, used implicitly in [4], has an explicit formulation here.

3.4.2 Syntax definition

```
<scheme> ::= <scheme-var>
       | CLASS <definition-list> END
       | RENAME <renaming> IN <scheme>
       | IMPORT <scheme> INTO <scheme>
       | EXPORT <signature> FROM <scheme>
       | LET <scheme-var> := <scheme> ; <scheme>

<renaming> ::= <namepair-list ','>
       | <renaming> $ <renaming>

<namepair> ::= <sort-name> TO <sort-name>
       | <predicate-name> TO <predicate-name>
       | <function-name> TO <function-name>

<signature> ::= <item-list ','>
       | <renaming> @ <signature>
       | <signature> + <signature>
       | <item> ∧ ˆsignature>
       | SIG <scheme>

<item> ::= SORT <sort-name>
       | FUNC <typed function>
       | PRED <typed predicate>
```

3.4.3 Semantic domain: the algebra of theories

The algebra of theories we describe here has three sorts: signatures, theories and renamings. We give a short description of this algebra and its properties, based on [21], where more information and references can be found.

Sorts, typed predicates and typed functions are collectively called signature elements. We assume that, for every type, there are infinitely many signature elements with that type available: this will allow us to apply the *fresh signature element principle* (see below). A *signature* is a finite set of signature elements. It is called *closed* if it contains all sorts (if any) occurring in the types of its elements. The closure $c(\Sigma)$ of a signature is the least closed signature containing Σ. If X is a (collection of) logical expression(s) then $SIG(X)$ is the closure of the collection of all signature elements occurring in (elements of) X.

Let Γ be a collection of sentences of L, Σ a signature, then the *closure of* Γ in Σ is defined by

$$Cl(\Sigma, \Gamma) =_{\text{def}} \{A \,|\, \text{MPL}_\omega : \Gamma \vdash A \text{ and } \text{SIG}(A) \subseteq c(\Sigma)\}$$

These closures are called *theories*. TH is defined as the collection of all theories of MPL$_\omega$.

The *union* of two theories is the smallest theory containing them, defined by

$$T + U =_{\text{def}} Cl(SIG(T \cup U), T \cup U).$$

It is obvious that $+$ is commutative, associative and idempotent.

The *restriction* of a theory to a signature is the closure of that theory in that signature:

$$\Sigma \ \square \ T =_{\text{def}} Cl(\Sigma \cap SIG(T), T).$$

Renamings are finitely generated mappings defined on expressions of L, changing only signature elements and commuting with taking types (i.e. the type of a renamed signature element is the renaming of the type of that signature element). Observe that we are liberal in the definition of renamings in the sense that they need not be bijective, so e.g. $[P := R, Q := R]$ is a correct renaming (if P, Q and R have the same type); this is in contrast to [4], where renamings are bijective and even involutive (i.e. if $\rho(P) = Q$ then $\rho(Q) = P$). We define domain and range of a renaming by

$$
\begin{aligned}
dom(\rho) \quad &=_{\text{def}} \{I \mid \rho(I) \neq I\} \\
rg(\rho) \quad &=_{\text{def}} \{\rho(I) \mid \rho(I) \neq I\}
\end{aligned}
$$

All renamings are finitely generated, so domain and range of a renaming are finite and hence signatures. We shall use some injectivity properties of renamings, defined by

$$
\begin{aligned}
inj(\rho, \Sigma, \Pi) \quad &=_{\text{def}} \forall I \epsilon \Sigma \forall J \epsilon \Pi (\rho(I) = \rho(J) \rightarrow I = J) \\
inj(\rho, \Sigma) \quad &=_{\text{def}} inj(\rho, \Sigma, \Sigma) \\
inj(\rho) \quad &=_{\text{def}} inj(\rho, dom(\rho))
\end{aligned}
$$

We also put:

ρ *renames* Σ *outside* Π iff
$dom(\rho) = \Sigma \cap \Pi, rg(\rho) \cap (\Sigma \cup \Pi) = \emptyset$ and $inj(\rho, \Sigma)$.

We shall use the *good renaming property*:

for any signatures Σ, Π there is a renaming $\gamma(\Sigma, \Pi)$
renaming Σ outside Π,

which follows directly from the finiteness of signatures and the fresh signature element principle.

The application of renamings on theories is defined by

$$\rho(T) =_{\text{def}} Cl(\rho(S(T)), \{\rho(A) \mid A \epsilon T\}).$$

It is clear that $\rho(T) = \{\rho(A) \mid A \epsilon T\}$ if $inj(\rho, SIG(T))$.

The operators introduced above satisfy several properties, of which the least trivial read as follows. Let T, U, V range over theories, Σ and Π over signatures, ρ and σ over renamings.

$$
\begin{aligned}
&(\;\square\;\square\;) && \Sigma \;\square\; (\Pi \;\square\; T) = (\Sigma \cap \Pi) \;\square\; T \\
&(\rho \;\square\;) && inj(\rho, SIG(T) - \Sigma, SIG(T) \cup \Sigma) \Rightarrow \rho(\Sigma \;\square\; T) = \rho(\Sigma) \;\square\; \rho(T) \\
&(\;\square\; \rho) && (dom(\rho) \cup rg(\rho)) \cap \Sigma = \emptyset \quad \& \quad inj(\rho, SIG(T)) \Rightarrow \Sigma \;\square\; T \\
& && = \Sigma \;\square\; \rho(T) \\
&(\;\square\; +) && SIG(T) \cap SIG(U) \subseteq \Sigma \Rightarrow \Sigma \;\square\; (T + U) = \Sigma \;\square\; T + \Sigma \;\square\; U \\
&(\gamma) && dom\big(\gamma(\Sigma, \Pi)\big) = \Sigma \cap \Pi \quad \& \quad rg\big(\gamma(\Sigma, \Pi)\big) \cap (\Sigma \cup \Pi) = \emptyset \\
& && \& \; inj(\gamma(\Sigma, \Pi), \Sigma)
\end{aligned}
$$

The condition in $(\rho \;\square\;)$ is required to prevent new identifications of names in $\rho(T)$ and between names in $\rho(\Sigma)$ and $\rho(T)$ not present in $\rho(\Sigma \;\square\; T)$; the condition in $(\;\square\; \rho)$ guarantees that ρ does not affect names in $\Sigma \;\square\; T$, neither introduces new identifications in T.

Most of the properties listed have a straightforward proof; only the proof of $(\;\square\; +)$ is more involved and makes essential use of the Interpolation Property of MPL$_\omega$.

Now define the language TL of *theory terms* by

$$T ::= Th \mid \rho(T) \mid \Sigma \;\square\; T \mid T + T,$$

where Th denotes constants $Th_1, Th_2 \ldots$ referring to specific theories.

We have the following Normal Form Theorem: any expression of TL is equivalent to an normal form expression

$$\Sigma \;\square\; \big(\rho_1(Th_1) + \ldots + \rho_n(Th_n)\big).$$

To prove this, it suffices to show that the collection of normal forms contains the constants T_i and is closed under renamings, $\square$ and $+$. Now $T_i = S(T_i) \;\square\; \rho_{id}(T_i)$ which is in normal form, and closure under $\square$ follows from $(\;\square\; \square\;)$; closure under renamings and $+$ follows from

1) for any Σ, T, ρ there is a σ with $\rho(\Sigma \;\square\; T) = \rho(\Sigma) \;\square\; \sigma(T)$;
2) for any Σ, Π, T, U, there are ρ, σ with $\Sigma \;\square\; T + \Pi \;\square\; U = (\Sigma \cup \Pi) \;\square\; \big(\rho(T) + \sigma(U)\big)$.

(1) relies on (γ), $(\;\square\; \rho)$ and $(\rho \;\square\;)$; (2) on $(\;\square\; \rho)$ and $(\;\square\; +)$. See [17] for more details.

3.4.4 Interpretation of the scheme language

Let a be an assignment mapping scheme variables to elements of TH; if a is such an assignment and $T \epsilon TH$, then $a[X \to T]$ is the assignment wich sends X to T and behaves like a with respect to the other scheme variables.

In the following definition of the semantics of the scheme language, the interpretation of schemes and signatures have an assignment as parameter; the interpretation of renamings and items does not depend on assignments. Besides the variables introduced in 3.2.4 and 3.3.6, we shall use the following variables for COLD-K^2-constructs:

k l   schemes
X   scheme variables
D   definitions
R   renamings
Σ signatures
S   sort names
I J   items

$$[\![\mathtt{X}]\!](a) =_{\mathrm{def}} a(X)$$

$$[\![\mathtt{CLASS}\ \mathtt{D}_1 \ldots \mathtt{Dn}\ \mathtt{END}]\!](a) =_{\mathrm{def}} Cl((\{\!\{\mathtt{D}_1\}\!\} \cup \ldots \cup \{\!\{\mathtt{Dn}\}\!\}),$$
$$\{[\![\mathtt{D}_1]\!], \ldots, [\![\mathtt{Dn}]\!]\})$$

$$[\![\mathtt{RENAME}\ \mathtt{R}\ \ \mathtt{IN}\ \mathtt{k}]\!](a) =_{\mathrm{def}} [\![\mathtt{R}]\!]([\![\mathtt{k}]\!](a))$$
$$[\![\mathtt{IMPORT}\ \mathtt{k}\ \ \mathtt{INTO}\ \mathtt{l}]\!](a) =_{\mathrm{def}} [\![\mathtt{k}]\!](a) + [\![\mathtt{l}]\!](a)$$
$$[\![\mathtt{EXPORT}\ \Sigma\ \ \mathtt{FROM}\ \mathtt{k}]\!](a) =_{\mathrm{def}} [\![\Sigma]\!](a)\ \square\ [\![\mathtt{k}]\!](a)$$
$$[\![\mathtt{LET}\ \mathtt{X}\ \mathtt{:=}\ \mathtt{k}\ \mathtt{;}\ \mathtt{l}]\!](a) =_{\mathrm{def}} [\![\mathtt{l}]\!](a[X \to [\![\mathtt{k}]\!](a)])$$

$$[\![\mathtt{I1}\ \mathtt{TO}\ \mathtt{J1}, \ldots, \mathtt{In}\ \mathtt{TO}\ \mathtt{Jn}]\!] =_{\mathrm{def}} [[\![\mathtt{I1}]\!] := [\![\mathtt{J1}]\!], \ldots,$$
$$[\![\mathtt{In}]\!] := [\![\mathtt{Jn}]\!]]$$

$$[\![\mathtt{R}\ \mathtt{\$}\ \ \mathtt{S}]\!] =_{\mathrm{def}} [\![\mathtt{R}]\!] \circ [\![\mathtt{S}]\!]$$
$$[\![\mathtt{I1}, \ldots, \mathtt{In}]\!](a) =_{\mathrm{def}} \{[\![\mathtt{I1}]\!](a), \ldots, [\![\mathtt{In}]\!](a)\}$$
$$[\![\mathtt{R}\ \mathtt{@}\Sigma]\!](a) =_{\mathrm{def}} [\![\mathtt{R}]\!]([\![\Sigma]\!](a))$$
$$[\![\Sigma_1 + \Sigma_2]\!](a) =_{\mathrm{def}} [\![\Sigma_1]\!](a) \cup [\![\Sigma_2]\!](a)$$
$$[\![\mathtt{I}\ \mathtt{\wedge}\Sigma]\!](a) =_{\mathrm{def}} [\![\Sigma]\!](a) - \{[\![\mathtt{I}]\!](a)\}$$
$$[\![\mathtt{SIG}\ \mathtt{k}]\!](a) =_{\mathrm{def}} SIG([\![\mathtt{k}]\!](a))$$
$$[\![\mathtt{SORT}\ \mathtt{S}]\!](a) =_{\mathrm{def}} S$$
$$[\![\mathtt{FUNC}\ \mathtt{f}\ \mathtt{:}\ \ \mathtt{S1}\ \mathtt{\#} \ldots \mathtt{\#}\ \mathtt{Sn}\ \mathtt{-}\mathtt{>}\ \mathtt{S}]\!](a) =_{\mathrm{def}} f$$
$$[\![\mathtt{PRED}\ \mathtt{P}\ \mathtt{:}\ \mathtt{S1}\ \mathtt{\#} \ldots \mathtt{\#}\ \mathtt{Sn}]\!](a) =_{\mathrm{def}} P$$

3.5   The parametrized scheme language

3.5.1   Introduction

Parametrisation is obtained in COLD by extending the scheme language with (parametrised) scheme variables, a kind of lambda abstraction (over these variables) and application. This leads to a hierarchy of parametrised schemes of arbitrary finite type. An interesting feature is the kind of lambda abstraction used here: $\lambda X : A.B(X)$ application of this parametrised scheme to C (of the right type) only leads to $B(C)$ if C *implements* A. For flat schemes C and A, we have that C implements A iff the meaning of C (a theory in MPL$_\omega$) extends the meaning of A. This relation is extended straightforwardly to parametrised schemes of higher type.

As an illustration, think of $B(X)$ as a specification of a sorting routine for sequences of objects of X w.r.t. some ordering R also present in X. It is natural then to restrict the application of a parametrisation of A to those instances C where the ordering R is linear. This can be done by taking for A the specification of a linear ordering R.

The semantics of the parametrised scheme language is given in a type structure on top of the collection of theories used for the semantics of the scheme language.

3.5.2 Syntax definition

```
<parscheme> ::= <parscheme-var>
         | <scheme>
         | LAMBDA <parscheme-var> : <parscheme> OF <parscheme>
         | APPLY <parscheme> TO <parscheme>
         | LET <parscheme-var> := <parscheme> ; <parscheme>
```

3.5.3 Semantic domain: the type structure over the algebra of theories

The interpretation of the scheme language is given in terms of a type structure $TH^\omega = \{TH^\tau \mid \tau\epsilon \text{ type}\}$ over the collection of theories $TH = TH^0$. Here type is the set of Curry types, containing 0 and closed under $\rightarrow$, and $TH^{\sigma\rightarrow\tau}$ is defined as the collection of functions from TH^σ to TH^τ.

For $\tau\epsilon$type, the ordering $\leq^\tau$ on TH^τ with least element $\perp^\tau$ is defined by

$$
\begin{aligned}
&\leq^0 &&=_{\text{def}} \subseteq\\
&\Phi \leq^{\sigma\rightarrow\tau} \Psi &&\text{iff } \forall T\epsilon TH^\sigma\big(\Phi(T) \leq^\tau \Psi(T)\big)\\
&\perp^0 &&=_{\text{def}} Cl(\emptyset,\emptyset)\\
&\perp^{\sigma\rightarrow\tau} &&=_{\text{def}} \lambda T\epsilon TH^\sigma.\, \perp^\tau
\end{aligned}
$$

We extend the theory language TL of 3.4.3 to TTL, *typed theory language*, containing terms T^τ of type $\tau\epsilon$type:

$$
\begin{aligned}
T^0 &:: &&= Th \mid X^0 \mid \rho(T^0) \mid \Sigma \;\square\; T^0 \mid T^0 + T^0\\
T^t &:: &&= X^\tau \mid T^{\sigma\rightarrow\tau}T^\sigma\\
T^{\sigma\rightarrow\tau} &:: &&= \lambda X^\sigma \geq^\sigma T^\sigma.T^\tau
\end{aligned}
$$

with the restriction that, in $\lambda X^\sigma \geq^\sigma A.B$, X^σ does not occur free in A. Conventions: type subscripts are often omitted, and $\lambda X.T$ abbreviates $\lambda X \geq\perp .T$.

The meaning of terms of type 0 is as in TL; AB denotes function application of A to the argument B, and $\lambda X \geq A.B$ denotes the function sending X to $B = B(X)$ provided $X \geq A$, otherwise to $\perp$.

Substitution $[X := A]B$ is defined with α-conversion, so

$$
\begin{aligned}
[X := A](\lambda Y \geq B.C) \;\; &=_{\text{def}} \lambda Y \geq [X := A]B.[X := A]C\\
&\quad \text{if } Y \text{ not free in } A\\
&=_{\text{def}} \lambda Z \geq [X := A][Y := Z]B.[X := A]\\
&\quad [Y := Z]C \text{ if } Y \text{ free in } A,
\end{aligned}
$$

where Z is a fresh variable not occurring in A, B or C.

Besides the properties listed above, we have here:

$(\leq^\tau po)$ $\leq^\tau$ is a partial order with least element $\bot^\tau$
$(\leq ap)$ $A \leq B \to AC \leq BC$
$(\leq \lambda 1)$ $A \leq B \to (\lambda X \geq A.C) \geq (\lambda X \geq B.C)$
$(\leq \lambda 2)$ $\forall X(X \geq A \to B \leq C) \to (\lambda X \geq A.B) \leq (\lambda X \geq A.C)$
(π) $(C \geq A \to (\lambda X \geq A.B)C = [X := C]B) \land$
        $(C \geq A \lor (\lambda X \geq A.B)C = \bot)$
(η) $\forall X(X \geq A \lor BX = \bot) \to \lambda X \geq A.BX = B$
        (provided X not free in B)

Observe that not all terms of higher type denote monotonic functions: $\lambda X.\lambda Y \geq X.B$ is in general not monotonic, and antimonotonic if X does not occur in B. (π) is the partial version of the β-conversion axiom $(\lambda X.A)B = [X := B]A$ of the λ-calculus, (η) is a variant of the η-conversion axiom $\lambda X.AX = A$ (X not free in A).

Comparison of TTL with $\lambda\pi$-calculus.

In [11] several variants of the so-called $\lambda\pi$-calculus are introduced. The simplest version, untyped $\lambda\pi$-calculus, is just λ-calculus with abstraction terms $\lambda X \geq A.B$; the axiomatics is given in the form of a derivation system with sequents $\Gamma \vdash A \leq B$, where Γ is a collection of inequalities ($A = B$ is defined as the conjunction of $A \leq B$ and $B \leq A$). The rule for reduction reads (in our notation)

$$\frac{\Gamma \vdash C \geq A}{\Gamma \vdash (\lambda X \geq A.B)C = [X := C]B}$$

The corresponding reduction relation $\to$ is defined by: $\Gamma \vdash A \to A'$ iff $\Gamma \vdash B \leq D$ and A' is obtained from A by replacing a subformula $(\lambda X \geq B.C)D$ by $[X := D]C$. The reflexive and transitive closure $\to^*$ satisfies the Diamond Property:

$(\Diamond)$ if $\Gamma \vdash A \to^* B, A \to^* C$, then $\Gamma \vdash B \to^* D, C \to^* D$ for some D.

The proof given in [11, 4.2.5.7] follows the lines of P. Martin-Löf's proof of the corresponding property for the λ-calculus, as given in [2, 3.2].

Applied $\lambda\pi$-calculus is the extension of an algebraic system with preorder with a typed version of $\lambda\pi$-calculus. The corresponding derivation system is obtained by adding all sequents with terms in the algebraic language which are valid in the algebraic system. An instance of an algebraic system considered is class algebra, which is closely related to the theory algebra of Appendix E; the resulting applied $\lambda\pi$-calculus can be compared with TTL.

Applied $\lambda\pi$-calculus inherits the Diamond Property of the untyped $\lambda\pi$-calculus, and also satisfies Strong Normalisation:

(SN) no term of applied $\lambda\pi$-calculus has an infinite reduction path.

As remarked in [11, 4.3.9.8], the easiest way to see this is by an idea first used by Plotkin (in the context of a λ-typed λ-calculus): define an embedding of the applied $\lambda\pi$-calculus into the typed λ-calculus, with the only nontrivial clause $(\lambda X \geq A.B)^* = \lambda Y.(\lambda X.B^*)A^*$; this transfers (infinite) reduction paths from applied $\lambda\pi$-calculus to typed λ-calculus, and (SN) follows from the strong normalisation property of typed $\bigwedge$-calculus.

Reduction in TTL. Let A, B, C be TTL-terms of appropriate type. We call the transitions

$$(\lambda X \geq A.B)C \to \quad [X := C]B$$
$$(\lambda X \geq A.B)C \to \quad \bot$$
$$\lambda X \geq A.BX \to \quad B$$

reductions of the *redex* (the term at the left hand side) to the *reduct* (the term at the right hand side). If $C \geq A$ holds, then the first reduction is called *valid*; if $C \geq A$ is false (or $[X := C]B$ equals $\bot$), then the second reduction is valid; the third reduction is valid if $\forall X(X \geq A \lor BX = \bot)$ holds. The relation $\to$ is extended as follows: if $A \to A'$, then $AB \to A'B, BA \to BA', \lambda X \geq A.B \to \lambda X \geq A'.B$ and $\lambda X \geq B.A \to \lambda X \geq B.A'$.

The relation $\to^*$ is the reflexive and transitive closure of $\to$; $A \to^* B$ is called valid if all intermediate $\to$-steps are valid. By (π) and (η) it is clear that $A = A'$ holds if $A \to^* A'$ is a valid reduction.

Theorem TTL satisfies (SN) and $(\Diamond)$.

Proof

If $A_0 \to A_1 \to \ldots$ is an infinite reduction path in TTL, then $A_0^* \to A_1^* \to \ldots$ (where $*$ is Plotkin's interpretation given above) is an infinite reduction path in typed extensional λ-calculus; but that theory is strongly normalizing, so we have contradiction and conclude that (SN) holds for TTL.

By Newman's lemma (see [2, 3.1.25]), in the presence of (SN) the diamond property is equivalent to the weak diamond property:

$(W\Diamond)$ if $A \to A_1$ and $A \to A_2$, then $A_1 \to^* B$ and $A_2 \to^* B$
        for some B.

The proof of $(W\Diamond)$ for TTL consists of a case analysis on $A \to A_1$ and $A \to A_2$, based on the following observation: if $A \to A'$ is valid, then one of the following holds (here $\equiv$ means literal identity):

(1) $A \equiv BC, A'$ $\equiv B'C, B \to B'$
(2) $A \equiv BC, A'$ $\equiv BC', C \to C'$
(3) $A \equiv \lambda X \geq B.C, A'$ $\equiv \lambda X \geq B'.C, B \to B'$
(4) $A \equiv \lambda X \geq B.C, A'$ $\equiv \lambda X \geq B.C', C \to C'$
(5) $A \equiv (\lambda X \geq B.C)D, A'$ $\equiv [X := D]C, D \geq B$
(6) $A \equiv (\lambda X \geq B.C)D, A'$ $\equiv \bot, D \not\geq B$
(7) $A \equiv \lambda X \geq B.CX, A'$ $\equiv C, \forall X(X \geq B \lor CX = \bot)$

We consider a typical case:

(5,2): $A \equiv (\lambda X \geq B.C)D, A_1 \equiv [X := D]C, D \geq B, A_2 \equiv (\lambda X \geq B.C)D', D \to D'$. Take $A_3 := [X := D']C$, then $A_1 \to^* A_3$ and $A_2 \to^* A_3$, for $D' \geq B$ (since $D' = D \geq B$). The other cases are treated likewise. $\square$

A term N of TTL is a *normal form* if N cannot be reduced, i.e. there is no N' with $N \rightarrow N'$. As a direct consequence of (SN) and $(\Diamond)$, we have:

every term in TTL reduces to a unique normal form.

It is not the case that a normal form contains no redices, even with the restriction to closed normal forms. Consider

$$\lambda X.\lambda Y.((\lambda Z \geq X.A)Y);$$

this is a closed term containing the redex $(\lambda Z \geq X.A)Y$ which cannot be reduced, since $Y \geq X$ can be either true or false.

3.5.4 *Interpretation of the parametrized scheme language*

Now let a be an assignment mapping scheme variables to elements of TH^ω of corresponding type; if a is such an assignment and $T \epsilon TH^\omega$ has the same type as X, then $a[X \rightarrow T]$ is the assignment wich sends X to T and behaves like a on the other scheme variables. We use the following variables for COLD-K^2-constructs:

K L M   parschemes
Y   parscheme variables

We define

$$
\begin{aligned}
&[\![Y]\!](a) &&=_{\text{def}} a(Y) \\
&[\![\text{LAMBDA Y : K OF L}]\!](a) &&=_{\text{def}} \lambda T \geq [\![K]\!](a).[\![L]\!](a[Y \rightarrow T]) \\
&[\![\text{APPLY K TO L}]\!](a) &&=_{\text{def}} [\![K]\!](a)[\![L]\!](a) \\
&[\![\text{ LET Y := K ; L}]\!](a) &&=_{\text{def}} [\![L]\!](a[Y \rightarrow [\![K]\!](a)])
\end{aligned}
$$

3.6 Designs

3.6.1 *Introduction*

Designs are descriptions of systems consisting of parametrised schemes, using components. Components have a name, a specification and (possibly) an implementation. The semantics is straightforward. See [8] for more information of designs.

3.6.2 *Syntax definition*

```
<design> ::= DESIGN <component-list ';' > SYSTEM
        <parscheme-list ','>

<component> ::= COMP <parscheme-var> : <parscheme>
        [:= <parscheme>]| LET <parscheme-var> := <parscheme>
```

3.6.3 Interpretation of the design language

Assignments a are defined as in 3.5.4. for the definition of the semantics of the parametrized scheme language. To the variables introduced in 3.5.4 we add C (possibly with subscript) ranging over components.

$$[\![\text{DESIGN C1};\ldots;\text{Cm SYSTEM M1},\ldots,\text{Mn}]\!](a) =_{\text{def}}$$
$$< [\![\text{DESIGN C1};\ldots;\text{Cm SYSTEM M1}]\!](a),$$
$$\ldots,$$
$$[\![\text{DESIGN C1};\ldots;\text{Cm SYSTEM Mn}]\!](a) >$$

$$[\![\text{DESIGN SYSTEM M}]\!](a) =_{\text{def}} [\![\text{M}]\!](a)$$

$$[\![\text{DESIGN Y : K := L; C1};\ldots;\text{Cm SYSTEM M}]\!](a) =_{\text{def}}$$
$$\big(\lambda T \geq [\![\text{K}]\!](a).[\![\text{DESIGN C1};\ldots;\text{Cm SYSTEM M}]\!]$$
$$(a[Y \rightarrow T])\big)\big([\![\text{L}]\!](a)\big)$$

$$[\![\text{DESIGN Y : K; C1};\ldots;\text{Cm SYSTEM M}]\!] =_{\text{def}}$$
$$\Lambda T \geq [\![\text{K}]\!](a).[\![\text{DESIGN C1};\ldots;\text{Cm SYSTEM M}]\!](a[Y \rightarrow T])$$

$$[\![\text{DESIGN LET Y : K; C1};\ldots;\text{Cm SYSTEM M}]\!] =_{\text{def}}$$
$$[\![\text{DESIGN C1};\ldots;\text{Cm SYSTEM M}]\!](a[Y \rightarrow [\![\text{K}]\!](a)])$$

References

[1] J.C.M. Baeten, J.A. Bergstra, S. Mauw, G.J. Veltink, *A process specification formalism based on static* COLD, in: J.A. Bergstra, L.M.G. Feijs (eds.) *Algebraic methods: Theory, Tools and Applications* (Part II), LNCS, Springer-Verlag, 1991.

[2] H.P. Barendregt, *The lambda calculus, its syntax and semantics* (Revised edition), North-Holland, 1984.

[3] H. Barringer, J.H. Cheng, C.B. Jones, A logic covering undefinedness in program proofs, Acta Informatica 21 (1984) 251–269.

[4] J.A. Bergstra, J. Heering, P. Klint, *Module algebra*, Journal of the ACM 37 (1990) 335–372.

[5] J.H. Cheng, A Logic for Partial Functions, Ph.D. thesis, University of Manchester, Department of Computer Science, 1986 Technical Report UMCS-86-7-1.

[6] M.E.A. Corthout, H.B.M. Jonkers, *The transformational development of a new point containment algorithm*, Philips Journal of Research 41 (1986), 83–174.

[7] M.E.A. Corthout, H.B.M. Jonkers, *A new point containment algorithm for B-regions in the discrete plane*, Proceedings of the Conference on Theoretical Foundations of Computer Graphics and CAD, Italy (1987).

[8] L.M.G. Feijs, A formalisation of design methods, Ph.D. thesis, Technical University Eindhoven, 1990.

[9] L.M.G. Feijs, H.B.M. Jonkers, *Transformational design: an annotated example*, Proceedings of the IFIP TC 2 Working Conference on Program Specification and Transformation, North-Holland (1986).

[10] L.M.G. Feijs, H.B.M. Jonkers, *Formal Specification and Design*, Cambridge Tracts in Theoretical Computer Science 35, Cambridge University Press, 1992.

[11] L.M.G. Feijs, H.B.M. Jonkers, C.P.J. Koymans, G.R. Renardel de Lavalette, *Formal definition of the design language* COLD-K, Technical Report, ESPRIT project 432, Doc.Nr. METEOR/t7/PRLE/7 (1987).

[12] R. Groenboom, G.R. Renardel de Lavalette, *Reasoning over dynamic features in specification languages*, this volume.

[13] D. Harel, *Dynamic Logic*, in: Handbook of Philosophical Logic, vol. II (D. Gabbay, F. Guenthner, eds.) Reidel (1984) 497–604.

[14] H.B.M. Jonkers, *Inheritance in* COLD, in: J.A. Bergstra, L.M.G. Feijs (eds.) Algebraic methods: Theory, Tools and Applications (Part II), LNCS, Springer-Verlag, 1991.

[15] H.B.M. Jonkers, J.H. Obbink, COLD: *a common object-oriented language for design*, Working document, Philips Research Laboratories Eindhoven, 1983.

[16] C.P.J. Koymans, G.R. Renardel de Lavalette, *The logic* MPL$_\omega$, in: Algebraic methods: Theory, Tools and Applications (M. Wirsing, J.A. Bergstra, eds.) Lecture Notes in Computer Science 394, Springer-Verlag, 1989.

[17] C.A. Middelburg, *The* VIP VDM *specification language*, in: VDM'88, VDM – the WAY AHEAD (r. Bloomfield, L. Marshall, R. Jones, eds.), Lecture Notes in Computer Science 328, Springer-Verlag (1989) 187–201.

[18] C.A. Middelburg, VVSL: *a language for structured* VDM *specifications*, Formal aspects of Computing 1 (1989) 115–135.

[19] C.A. Middelburg, G.R. Renardel de Lavalette, LPF *and* MPL$_\omega$ – *a logical comparison of* VDM SL *and* COLD-K, in: S. Prehn, W.J. Toetenel (eds.) VDM'91: Formal Software Development Methods, LNCS551, Springer-Verlag, 279–308.

[20] G.R. Renardel de Lavalette, COLD-K^2, *the static kernel of* COLD-K, Report RP/mod-89/8, Software Engineering Research Centre, Utrecht, the Netherlands, November 1989.

[21] G.R. Renardel de Lavalette, *Logical semantics of modularisation*, in: Computer Science Logic '91 (E. Börger, G. Jäger, H. Kleine Büning, M.M. Richter, eds.), LNCS626, 306–315.

[22] G.R. Renardel de Lavalette, *Formal development of a serial copy management system*, in: VDM'91: Formal Software Development Methods (S. Prehn, W.J. Toetenel, eds.), LNCS551, Springer-Verlag, 477–495.

[23] G.R. Renardel de Lavalette, *From implicit via inductive to explicit definitions*, this volume.

[24] D.S Scott, *Existance and description in Formal Logic*, in: R. Schoenman (Ed.), Bertrand Russell, Philosopher of the Century, Allen & Unwin, London, (1967), 181–200.

Appendix A: well-formedness.

In the previous sections only the context-free part of the syntax definition has been given, which is to be supplemented with well-formedness conditions in order to yield a complete language definition. We do not attempt to give a complete and rigorous definition of well-formedness here, but confine ourselves to presenting an incomplete and informal list of well-formedness conditions.

i) In LET x1:=t1, ... , xn:=tn, the object variables x1, ... xn are mutually different.

ii) In the definitions.

```
FUNC f:   S1 # ... # Sm → S PAR x1 ... xn   DEF t
FUNC f:   S1 #... # Sm → S PAR x1... xn   IND A1
PRED P: S1 #... # Sm PAR x1 ... xn   DEF A2
PRED P: S1 # ... # Sm   PAR x1... xn   IND A3
AXIOM A4
```

we have:
- m equals n and the variables $x_1 \ldots x_n$ are all different;
- the free variables in t, A_1, A_2, A_3 are among $x_1 \ldots x_n$;
- A_4 is closed, i.e. does not contain free variables;
- f does not occur in t, and P not in A_2.

iii) For every function symbol f occurring in CLASS $D_1 \ldots D_n$ END, there is exactly one i $(1 \leq i \leq n)$ such that D_i equals FUNC $f : S_1 \# \ldots \# S_m \rightarrow S$ $f$body, where $f$body may be empty; this D_i is called the definition of f; the same holds for predicate symbols.

iv) all occurrences of function and predicate symbols are correct w.r.t. the type assigned to that symbol by its definition.

v) Renamings of the form

$$I_1 \text{ TO } J_1, \ldots, I_n \text{ TO } J_n$$

are well-formed if:

- the items $I_1, \ldots, I_n$ are all different;
- if I_i $(1 \leq i \leq n)$ denotes a sort, then so does J_i;
- if I_i $(1 \leq i \leq n)$ equals FUNC $f : S_1 \# \ldots \# S_m \to S_{m+1}$, then J_i equals FUNC $g : S_1' \# \ldots \# S_m' \to S_{m+1}'$, satisfying, for all k between 1 and $m+1$: S_k equals S_k' unless for some $l(1 \leq l \leq n)I_l$ equals SORT S_k and J_l equals SORT S_k';
- analogously for predicates.

vi) In LAMBDA $Y : K$ OF L the scheme variable Y does not occur free in K.

Appendix B: reduction of MPL to first-order logic

We indicate briefly how to reduce MPL to L, first-order logic with equality. It suffices to do so for MPL - (ι).

Signatures for L consist of finite subsets of SORT $\cup$ FUNC $\cup$ PRED $\{\uparrow\}$; their elements no longer have a type but do have an arity, indicating the number of arguments. Moreover, the elements of SORT are unary predicates and $\uparrow$ is a constant (i.e. a function with arity 0). The mapping ^{L} : MPL - $(\iota) \to L$ is defined by

$$
\begin{aligned}
(\uparrow s)^L & =_{\text{def}} \uparrow \\
t^L & =_{\text{def}} t \text{ for all other terms } t \\
(s =_S t)^L & =_{\text{def}} (S(s) \wedge s = t) \\
(t \downarrow s)^L & =_{\text{def}} S(t) \\
(P(t))^L & =_{\text{def}} P(t^L) \text{ for all other predicates } P \\
(\neg A)^L & =_{\text{def}} \neg A^L \\
(A \wedge B)^L & =_{\text{def}} A^L \wedge B^L \\
(\forall x : S(A))^L & =_{\text{def}} \forall x(S(x) \to A^L)
\end{aligned}
$$

Abbreviating $S_1(x_1) \wedge \ldots \wedge S_n(x_n)$ by $\mathbf{S}(\mathbf{x})$, we also put

$$
\begin{aligned}
Ax(S) & =_{\text{def}} \neg S(\uparrow) \\
Ax(f) & =_{\text{def}} \forall \mathbf{x}\big(S(f(\mathbf{x})) \to \mathbf{S}(\mathbf{x})\big) \\
& \quad \text{if type}(f) \quad = S_1 \times \ldots \times S_n \to S \\
Ax(P) & =_{\text{def}} \forall \mathbf{x}\big(P(\mathbf{x}) \to \mathbf{S}(\mathbf{x})\big) \\
& \quad \text{if type}(P) \quad = S_1 \times \ldots \times S_n \\
Ax(\Sigma) & =_{\text{def}} \{Ax(I) \mid I \epsilon \Sigma\} \qquad \text{for MPL-signatures } \Sigma.
\end{aligned}
$$

Now we have

$$\text{MPL}(\Sigma) - (\iota) \vdash A \Leftrightarrow L(\Sigma \cup \{\uparrow\}) : Ax(\Sigma) \vdash A^L$$

$\Rightarrow$ is proved by induction over the length of a derivation of $\vdash A$. For $\Leftarrow$, it suffices to see that for every $M = M(\Sigma)$ there is a model M' of L with signature $\Sigma \cup \{\uparrow\}$ such that $M' \models A_x(\Sigma)$ holds, and also $M' \models A^L \Rightarrow M \models A$; then the result follows with the completeness theorem for MPL.

We indicate with an example how M' can be obtained from M. Let $\Sigma = \{S, S', f : S \to S', P : S\}$, then $M = \{S^M, S'^M, f^M, P^M\}$; now $M_A = \{D, \underline{f}, \underline{S}, \underline{S'}, \underline{P}, \underline{*}\}$ is given by

$$
\begin{aligned}
D &=_{\text{def}} \underline{S} \cup \underline{S'} \cup \{\underline{*}\} \\
\underline{f} &=_{\text{def}} f^M \cup \{< d, \underline{*}> \mid d\epsilon\underline{S'} \cup \{\underline{*}\}\} \\
\underline{S} &=_{\text{def}} S^M - \{{}^*S^M\} \\
\underline{S'} &=_{\text{def}} S'^M - \{{}^*S'^M\} \\
\underline{P} &=_{\text{def}} P^M.
\end{aligned}
$$

Generation of Proof Obligations for Type Consistency (Extended Abstract)

Flemming M. Damm

Department of Computer Science, The Technical University of Denmark
Lyngby, Denmark

Bo Stig Hansen

Department of Computer Science, The Technical University of Denmark
Lyngby, Denmark

Abstract

This work concerns a type system for a simple applicative language. The system can be used for generating proof obligations which rule out "dynamic" type errors such as taking the head or tail of an empty list.

The system has been proved sound and complete with respect to a denotational semantics of the language. In this semantics, the head of an empty list is the special element **wrong**, denoting type error, and not $\perp$ which is used only for modelling non-termination.

It turns out that completeness with respect to a "classical" denotational semantics is not easily obtained and the semantics actually used is therefore different in many respects. Included in the work is a discussion of the problems related to obtaining completeness.

1 Introduction

The notion of type plays two important rôles in programming and specification languages.

First of all, types are used as a modelling tool. This use is best supported by expressive notions of type which allow detailed or intricate properties to be described in terms of type definitions. Some examples are: dependent types [2], subtypes described by arbitrary predicates [8, 7] and types which preclude "dynamic type errors" and ensure termination [11].

Secondly, types are used as a basis for automatic type checking in compilers and interpreters. When considering types for this purpose, there has been a tradition for restricting the expressiveness in order to obtain decidability of type checking. (Without decidability, there can be no correct type checking algorithm which is guaranteed to terminate for all inputs.)

So can we have both an expressive notion of types and some notion of type checking which is decidable? In the work reported here, we have investigated the idea of generating proof obligations during type checking; the proof obligations concern those type properties which could not be verified automatically by the type checker. Type consistency may then be ensured by discharging the proof obligations, either using a proof tool or by hand.

Authors' e-mail addresses: fmd@id.dth.dk and bsh@id.dth.dk

1.1 Types and Semantics

The approach presented in this paper was originally motivated by the wish to define type checking algorithms for the kind of model oriented specification languages used with the Vienna Development Method [4, 1, 8].

In this setting, a type expression τ is essentially viewed as denoting a set of values. An expression e denotes a value which either is or is not included in the set; if it is included, we say that e has type τ. We assume that expressions with type errors denote a special value called **wrong** which is not a member of any type.

A type checker will either accept or reject a given expression and the correctness of this behavior may be justified by reference to the semantics of the expression. As a classical example, Milner [9] proves that ML programs which are accepted by ML type checking "will not go wrong", i.e. will not have the semantics **wrong**.

In general, a type checking algorithm must be able to determine not only whether an expression goes wrong but more precisely whether it has a given type or not. If we also allow type checking to generate proof obligations, Milner's soundness property may be reformulated in the following way:

> If type checking accepts that an expression has a given type and the properties expressed by the generated proof obligations hold then the expression actually has that type.

Since no type includes **wrong**, this soundness requirement also ensures that the expression does not go wrong—provided that the proof obligations can be discharged.

Soundness alone does, however, not preclude the generation of proof obligations which are unnecessarily strong. A specification could be semantically type consistent, i.e. not go wrong and yet it might not be possible to establish this if the generated proof obligation is so strong that it cannot be proved. To avoid this situation, one may require a form of completeness:

> If an expression has a given type then type checking accepts this by generating proof obligations which can be satisfied.

The work presented here concerns sound as well as complete generation of proof obligations for type consistency.

It should be noted that classical type systems such as the one for ML [9] will typically not be complete with respect to the semantics: having chosen a "natural", straight-forward definition of the semantics, completeness will usually not be possible when soundness and decidability (strong typing) is also required. With languages such as lisp, based mainly on dynamic type checking, soundness and completeness of a classical type system is possible but then decidability must be sacrificed (weak typing). Considering type checking with generation of proof obligations, however, opens for the possibility of having both soundness, completeness and decidability. This approach, which we will call natural strong typing, is the one pursued here.

1.2 Types Precluding Dynamic Type Errors

As an exponent of the problems related to the generation of proof obligations, we have chosen to consider a notion of type which precludes so-called dynamic type errors. Taking the head or tail of an empty list are typical examples of such errors.

When looking at types as a modelling tool, e.g. in specification languages, it may be argued that preclusion of dynamic type errors is a natural choice: the tail of an empty list is not a list—it is an error much like the sum of an integer and a truth value. The tail of an empty list should therefore not be considered an element of any list type.

Whether the evaluation of an expression eventually will lead to taking the tail of an empty list is, however, a problem which for usual expression languages is undecidable. So with this notion of type, there can be no type checking algorithm which for an arbitrary expression and type will terminate and correctly judge whether the expression has the type or not.

Correct and terminating behavior of a type checking algorithm can be obtained, however, if the algorithm is allowed to make conditional judgements of the form: the expression has the type provided certain conditions (proof obligations) hold. The proof obligations generated could, e.g., regard non-emptiness of lists.

Considering programming languages, the traditional approach has been to accept the tail of an empty list as a valid element of list types; this and similar choices has made type checking decidable. Dynamic type errors are then left for detection at run-time but they may stay undetected for a long time if no input provoking them is supplied to the program.

Types precluding dynamic type errors and type checkers generating proof obligations may constitute an alternative or a supplement to this traditional approach: if the proof obligations generated are actually proved, it is certain that no run-time type errors will occur.

1.3   Overview

For this exposition, we have chosen to consider a "minimal" expression language based on the lambda calculus and also a very simple notion of types.

In the following, we first present the syntax of expressions and type expressions. Then the semantic domains are considered and the semantics of type expressions is defined.

A "traditional" semantics of expressions and proof system for types is then summarized to give a basis for the subsequent discussions. This is followed by a presentation and discussion of a semantics and a proof system oriented towards generation of proof obligations. Finally, soundness and completeness of the proof system with respect to the semantics is considered.

2   Syntax

The considered language is small and not practical for programming or specification but it includes enough type and expression constructs to illustrate essential issues in the generation of proof obligations for type consistency.

Let x range over a set of variables Id, and let b range over built-in constants and ι over basic types, then the language Exp of expressions and $TypeExp$ of type expressions are generated by the grammars:

$$e \quad ::= \quad x \mid b \mid \texttt{if } e \texttt{ then } e \texttt{ else } e \mid$$
$$\texttt{nil} \mid \texttt{cons}(e,e) \mid \texttt{hd } e \mid \texttt{tl } e \mid$$
$$\texttt{lambda } x:\tau . e \mid e(e) \mid \texttt{rec } x:\tau . e$$
$$\tau \quad ::= \quad \iota \mid \tau \texttt{ list} \mid \tau \rightarrow \tau$$

Note that special expressions are introduced for `nil`, `cons`, `hd`, and `tl` in order to avoid the complication of having to consider type polymorphism.

3 Semantic Domains

Expressions are interpreted using the following recursively defined domain $\mathbf{V}$. The domain operators $+$, $\times$ and $\rightarrow$ are respectively coalesced disjoint sum, smashed product and continuous function space.

$$\mathbf{V} = \mathbf{B}_0 + \mathbf{B}_1 + \ldots + \mathbf{S} + \mathbf{F} + \mathbf{W}$$
$$\mathbf{S} = \mathbf{B}_0 + \mathbf{S}_1$$
$$\mathbf{S}_1 = \mathbf{V} \times \mathbf{S}$$
$$\mathbf{F} = \mathbf{V} \rightarrow \mathbf{V}$$
$$\mathbf{W} = \{\mathsf{w}, \perp_{\mathbf{W}}\}$$

The domains $\mathbf{B}_i$ are flat domains of basic values, each with a bottom value $\perp_{\mathbf{B}_i}$. The domain $\mathbf{B}_0$ contains a single element nil besides the bottom value and $\mathbf{B}_1 = \mathbf{T} = \{\mathsf{true}, \mathsf{false}, \perp_{\mathbf{T}}\}$ is the domain of truth values. We let b_{ij} denote the jth element of the basic domain $\mathbf{B}_i$.

The domain $\mathbf{S}$ of sequences is used to give semantics to sequence expressions. Sequences may either be empty (represented by nil) or non-empty in which case they have a first element: the head and a possibly empty tail.

The domain of continuous functions, $\mathbf{F}$, is used to give semantics to `lambda` expressions. The domain $\mathbf{W}$ contains a single element w. It is used to model all type errors, i.e. applications of functions to arguments for which they are not defined. The name **wrong** is used to denote w as member of $\mathbf{V}$ (**wrong** = w in $\mathbf{V}$). The bottom value $\perp_{\mathbf{V}}$ is used only to model non-termination. We shall use $\perp$ (without subscript) as an abbreviation for $\perp_{\mathbf{V}}$.

4 The Meta Language

In order to give semantics to expression and types, the following conventions are introduced:

- If $\mathbf{D} = \mathbf{D}_1 + \ldots + \mathbf{D}_n$ and $d \in \mathbf{D}_i$ $(1 \leq i \leq n)$, then d in $\mathbf{D}$ is the injection of d into $\mathbf{D}$. Note that the individual bottom values of the summands are all mapped to $\perp_{\mathbf{D}}$ by the injection.

- If $\mathbf{D} = \mathbf{D}_1 + \ldots + \mathbf{D}_n$ and $d \in \mathbf{D}$, then $d \in \mathbf{D}_i$ is a function yielding: $\perp_{\mathbf{T}}$ if $v = \perp_{\mathbf{D}}$; true if $d = d_i$ in $\mathbf{D}$ for some $d_i \in \mathbf{D}_i$; false otherwise.

- If $\mathbf{D} = \mathbf{D}_1 + \ldots + \mathbf{D}_n$ and $d \in \mathbf{D}$, then $d \mid \mathbf{D}_i$ is a projection function yielding: d_i if $d = d_i$ in $\mathbf{D}$ for some $d_i \in \mathbf{D}_i$; $\perp_{\mathbf{D}_i}$ otherwise.

- If $x = <x_1, x_2>$ is an element of a product domain $\mathbf{D}$ and $x \neq \perp_{\mathbf{D}}$, then fst $x = x_1$ and snd $x = x_2$.

- $\mathbf{Y} \in (\mathbf{V} \rightarrow \mathbf{V}) \rightarrow \mathbf{V}$ is the least fixed point operator.

- if c then v else v' is syntax for application of a function cond $\in \mathbf{T} \rightarrow \mathbf{V} \rightarrow \mathbf{V} \rightarrow \mathbf{V}$ yielding: $\perp$ if $c = \perp_{\mathbf{T}}$; v if $c =$ true and v' if $c =$ false.

- Let $\mathcal{P}\mathbf{V}$ be the power domain over $\mathbf{V}$. Then the auxiliary functions elems $\in \mathbf{S} \rightarrow \mathcal{P}\mathbf{V}$ and empty $\in \mathbf{V} \rightarrow \mathbf{T}$ are defined by

$$\text{elems } s \; = \; \text{if } s \in \mathbf{B}_0 \text{ in } \mathbf{S} \text{ then } \emptyset \text{ else } \{\text{fst}(s \mid \mathbf{S}_1)\} \cup \text{elems snd}(s \mid \mathbf{S}_1)$$

$$\text{empty } s \; = \; (s = \text{nil in } \mathbf{S} \text{ in } \mathbf{V})$$

5 Semantics of Type Expressions

The semantics of types is defined by a function mapping type expressions to subsets of $\mathbf{V}$.

$$\mathcal{D}[\![\iota_i]\!] \; = \; \mathbf{B}_i \text{ in } \mathbf{V}$$
$$\mathcal{D}[\![\tau \text{ list}]\!] \; = \; \{s \in \mathbf{S} \mid \text{elems } s \subseteq \mathcal{D}[\![\tau]\!]\} \text{ in } \mathbf{V}$$
$$\mathcal{D}[\![\sigma \rightarrow \tau]\!] \; = \; \{f \in \mathbf{F} \mid v \in \mathcal{D}[\![\sigma]\!] \Rightarrow f v \in \mathcal{D}[\![\tau]\!]\} \text{ in } \mathbf{V}$$

In this definition, injection of a set of values is defined by element-wise injection: $\mathbf{D}$ in $\mathbf{V} = \{d \text{ in } \mathbf{V} \mid d \in \mathbf{D}\}$.

Notice that the semantic function $\mathcal{D}$ includes $\perp$ in the result. When used in the definition of type consistency for expressions, this has as consequence that an expression may denote non-termination and still be type consistent.

6 A Traditional Approach

Aiming not only at soundness of type checking but also completeness, gives a new perspective on the issue of defining semantics of expressions. In the following, we will illustrate this by introducing and discussing what we consider a "traditional" semantics for the language *Exp* (figure 1).

The function $\mathcal{E}$ gives semantics to expressions. Its functionality is *Exp* $\rightarrow$ *Env* $\rightarrow \mathbf{V}$, where *Env* is the domain of environments, i.e. functions from *Id* to $\mathbf{V}$. The notation $\rho\{v/x\}$ denotes an environment which is identical to ρ except that $\rho' x = v$. The semantics of basic values is given by $\mathcal{B} \in Exp \rightarrow \mathbf{V}$ which is not further defined.

As a basis for discussing the relationship between the semantics of expressions and the semantics of type expressions, we introduce the following definitions:

Definition 6.1 (Typability of environments) *An environment ρ is typable, if for all x in the domain of ρ there exists a type τ such that $\rho x \in \mathcal{D}[\![\tau]\!]$.*

Definition 6.2 (Model typability) *An expression e is model typable if there exists some type τ and typable environment ρ such that $\mathcal{E}[\![e]\!]\rho \in \mathcal{D}[\![\tau]\!]$.*

$$\mathcal{E}[\![x]\!]\rho = \rho\, x$$

$$\mathcal{E}[\![b_{ij}]\!]\rho = \mathcal{B}[\![b_{ij}]\!]$$

$$\mathcal{E}[\![\text{if } e_0 \text{ then } e_1 \text{ else } e_2]\!]\rho =$$
if $\mathcal{E}[\![e_0]\!]\rho$ E **T**
then if $\mathcal{E}[\![e_0]\!]\rho \mid$ **T**
       then $\mathcal{E}[\![e_1]\!]\rho$
       else $\mathcal{E}[\![e_2]\!]\rho$
else **wrong**

$$\mathcal{E}[\![\text{nil}]\!]\rho = \text{nil in } \mathbf{S} \text{ in } \mathbf{V}$$

$$\mathcal{E}[\![\text{cons}(e_1, e_2)]\!]\rho =$$
$<\mathcal{E}[\![e_1]\!]\rho, \mathcal{E}[\![e_2]\!]\rho \text{ in } \mathbf{S}> \text{ in } \mathbf{S} \text{ in } \mathbf{V}$

$$\mathcal{E}[\![\text{hd } e]\!]\rho =$$
if $\mathcal{E}[\![e]\!]\rho$ E **S**
then if $\neg\text{empty}\, \mathcal{E}[\![e]\!]\rho$
     then $\text{fst}(\mathcal{E}[\![e]\!]\rho \mid \mathbf{S} \mid \mathbf{S}_1)$
     else $\perp$
else **wrong**

$$\mathcal{E}[\![\text{tl } e]\!]\rho =$$
if $\mathcal{E}[\![e]\!]\rho$ E **S**
then if $\neg\text{empty}\, \mathcal{E}[\![e]\!]\rho$
     then $\text{snd}(\mathcal{E}[\![e]\!]\rho \mid \mathbf{S} \mid \mathbf{S}_1)$
     else $\perp$
else **wrong**

$$\mathcal{E}[\![\text{lambda } x : \sigma\, .\, e]\!]\rho =$$
$(\lambda v.\mathcal{E}[\![e]\!]\rho\{v/x\}) \text{ in } \mathbf{V}$

$$\mathcal{E}[\![e_1(e_2)]\!]\rho =$$
if $\mathcal{E}[\![e_1]\!]\rho \notin \mathbf{F} \text{ in } \mathbf{V} \vee$
  $\mathcal{E}[\![e_2]\!]\rho = \textbf{wrong}$
then **wrong**
else if $\mathcal{E}[\![e_1]\!]\rho = \perp \vee \mathcal{E}[\![e_2]\!]\rho = \perp$
    then $\perp$
    else $(\mathcal{E}[\![e_1]\!]\rho \mid \mathbf{F})(\mathcal{E}[\![e_2]\!]\rho)$

$$\mathcal{E}[\![\text{rec } x : \tau\, .\, e]\!]\rho =$$
$\mathbf{Y}(\lambda v\, .\, \mathcal{E}[\![e]\!]\rho\{v/x\})$

Figure 1: A simple semantics for *Exp*

Definition 6.3 (Type consistency) *An expression e is type consistent if there exists some environment ρ such that $\mathcal{E}[\![e]\!]\rho \neq$* **wrong**.

The semantics imposes some of the typing constraints which we would also expect from a type checker. For instance, the condition of an if-then-else expression must be boolean and the argument of hd must be a list. There are, however, also some typing constraints which are not included in the semantics even if we would expect a traditional type checker to impose them.

For instance, the branches of an if-then-else expression are not required to be of the same type. As a consequence of this, the language is not typable with the type expressions presented, i.e., there exist type consistent expressions which are not model typable.

Observe that retrieving the head or tail of an empty list is not considered a type error (**wrong**) because it, in general, is impossible to check statically. Instead the bottom value is returned in these cases. Finally, one may note that the type expressions in lambda and rec expressions do not contribute to the semantics.

6.1 Traditional Type System

In figure 2, we have presented a type system, i.e., a proof system for statements of the form $B \vdash e : \tau$ where e is an expression and τ is a type. The *basis B* is a set of assumptions of the form $x : \tau$ regarding the types of variables; a variable will at most appear once in a basis. The notation $B, x : \tau$ is used for adding the assumption $x : \tau$ to a set of assumptions B. In the following, we will call $e : \tau$ a *typing statement*.

$$[\text{VAR}] \frac{}{B, x:\tau \vdash x:\tau} \quad [\text{BAS}] \frac{}{B \vdash b_{ij}:\iota_i}$$

$$[\text{COND}] \frac{B \vdash e_0:\textbf{bool} \quad B \vdash e_1:\tau \quad B \vdash e_2:\tau}{B \vdash \texttt{if } e_0 \texttt{ then } e_1 \texttt{ else } e_2:\tau}$$

$$[\text{NIL}] \frac{}{B \vdash \texttt{nil}:\tau\,\textbf{list}} \quad [\text{CONS}] \frac{B \vdash e_1:\tau \quad B \vdash e_2:\tau\,\textbf{list}}{B \vdash \texttt{cons}(e_1, e_2):\tau\,\textbf{list}}$$

$$[\text{HD}] \frac{A \vdash e:\tau\,\textbf{list}}{A \vdash \texttt{hd}\,e:\tau} \quad [\text{TL}] \frac{A \vdash e:\tau\,\textbf{list}}{A \vdash \texttt{tl}\,e:\tau\,\textbf{list}} \quad [\text{ABS}] \frac{B, x:\sigma \vdash e:\tau}{B \vdash (\texttt{lambda }x:\sigma\;.\;e):\sigma \to \tau}$$

$$[\text{APPLY}] \frac{B \vdash e_1:\sigma \to \tau \quad B \vdash e_2:\sigma}{B \vdash e_1(e_2):\tau} \quad [\text{REC}] \frac{B, x:\tau \vdash e:\tau}{B \vdash (\texttt{rec }x:\tau\;.\;e):\tau}$$

Figure 2: A traditional type system

Having introduced the type system, we may now consider the proof theoretic counterpart to the notion of model typability:

Definition 6.4 (Proof typability) *An expression e is proof typable if there exists a set of assumptions B and a type τ such that $B \vdash e:\tau$ follows from the type system.*

The type system presented is typical for the traditional approach. It is sound in the sense that all proof typable expression are also type consistent. Soundness is, however, only obtained because retrieving the head and tail of an empty list is not considered a type error (**wrong**). In the traditional setting not including generation of proof obligations, this is a very sensible choice. Otherwise, a sound and decidable type system would have to reject most type consistent expressions using hd and tl.

The system is not complete. Consider for example the two expressions hd cons$(5, \texttt{cons}(\texttt{true}, \texttt{nil}))$ and if $1 > 0$ then 1 else nil which both are type consistent according to the semantics. The latter is even model typable but none of the expressions are proof typable.

Even though such traditional type systems are not complete, they are often used in type checking to reject programs. Consequently, some programs are rejected even if they, in fact, are model typable. In these cases, the rejection cannot be justified formally—it must simply be accepted as a *type discipline* imposed on the programmer. By obeying the discipline, type consistency is, however, guaranteed (when disregarding dynamic type errors).

7 A New Approach: Generating Proof Obligations

There are several issues which must be addressed when trying to move from the traditional semantics and type system above towards the goals stated in the introduction. First of all, the meaning assigned to the head or tail of an empty list should be **wrong** rather than $\bot$.

Secondly, as indicated when presenting the traditional approach, there are potential completeness problems. Some of them are specificly related to the list type while others are of a more general nature. Let us first consider the general ones:

1. Some `if-then-else` expressions are model typable even if one of the branches is not. This could, e.g., be the case if the test always evaluates to the same truth value and thus makes one of the branches "dead code". Here, one might consider restrictions to the semantics requiring the existence of a type which includes the values of both branches. Alternatively, the type system must be altered to reflect that typability of both branches is not always required.

2. Some `if-then-else` expressions may yield results of different types depending on the bindings in the environment. Consider, e.g., the expression: `if b then 1 else true` where b is a variable. Such an expression cannot be typed but still it could be composed with other `if-then-else` expressions to form expressions which are model typable. Like above, restrictions on the semantics or relaxation of the type system may solve the problem.

3. The bodies of `lambda` expressions may denote values of different types depending on the value of the arguments. However, there is no function type which includes such "inhomogeneous" functions. To solve the problem, we may either introduce more descriptive types or make the semantics more restrictive so the meaning of such `lambda` expressions becomes **wrong**.

4. The denotation of `lambda` expressions may be functions which yield model typable results when applied to arguments outside their declared domain type. However, a traditional type system rejects a function application if the argument is not in the domain type of the function. Restricting the semantics of expressions and relaxing the type system are again two possible ways of approaching the problem.

5. Non-termination represented by $\bot$ is a valid value of any type. For example, adding the result of a non-terminating Boolean function to the result of a function over the reals does not yield **wrong** but $\bot$ in the denotational semantics. Again, we could try to make the semantics more restrictive to disallow this situation and, alternatively, we could make the type system more liberal so the expression would become proof typable.

6. A recursive expression `rec` $x : \tau$. e may be type consistent even though the body e is not type consistent for all x in the denotation of τ. Consider, e.g., the following recursively defined function which takes a list of integers

and adds them pairwise to produce another list:

$$\text{rec } addsucc : \textbf{int list} \rightarrow \textbf{int list}.$$
$$\texttt{lambda } l : \textbf{int}.\texttt{if } l = \texttt{nil}$$
$$\texttt{then nil}$$
$$\texttt{else if } addsucc\,(\texttt{tl } l) = \texttt{nil}$$
$$\texttt{then } l$$
$$\texttt{else cons}(\texttt{hd } l + \texttt{hd tl } l, addsucc\,(\texttt{tl tl } l))$$

The problem is that *addsucc* is used recursively in the test of the emptiness of the tail. The body will not be model typable for all functions *addsucc* of type **int list** → **int list**, but it will be for the specific function which is the solution to this recursive definition. The problem may be solved by either restricting the semantics to disallow expressions like the one above, or by modifying the type system to take account of such expressions.

The problems specificly related to the list type are:

1. Expressions denoting inhomogeneous lists (lists with mixed types of elements) are allowed in the denotational semantics. However, there is no type which includes inhomogeneous lists. Like the similar problem regarding inhomogeneous functions, we may either introduce more descriptive types or make the semantics more restrictive so the meaning of such expressions becomes **wrong**.

2. The empty list is a valid value in any list type and, likewise, a list whose elements are all empty lists is a a valid value in any list of lists type. However, an expression like: tl cons(1, nil) will, with a traditional type system, receive a specific list type: **nat list**. This problem is quite similar to the problem regarding ⊥ as a value in all types and it may be solved in similar ways.

Concerning the problem of inhomogeneous lists and functions, we have chosen to restrict the semantics, mapping these to **wrong**. Introducing more expressive types is an interesting alternative but not within the scope of this presentation.

Regarding if-then-else expressions, the only acceptable choice is to define the type system so proof typability of both branches is not always required. Restricting the semantics to require model typability of both branches would rule out many essential uses of if-then-else, e.g., taking the head of a list under the condition that it is not empty.

The completeness problem related to the fact that ⊥ is a value of any type is not easily solved by modifying the semantics. This would for example require that *succ*(*e*) and *not*(*e*) are given different semantics even though *e* is nonterminating. In general, modification of the semantics to solve this problem would require bottom values which were tagged with a type. We have chosen to leave the semantics as it is (in this respect) and instead relax the type system. This is also the solution chosen to solve the similar problem related to polymorphic list values such as the empty list.

$$\mathcal{E}[\![x]\!]\rho = \rho\,x$$

$$\mathcal{E}[\![b_{ij}]\!]\rho = \mathcal{B}[\![b_{ij}]\!]$$

$$\mathcal{E}[\![\text{if } e_0 \text{ then } e_1 \text{ else } e_2]\!]\rho =$$
if $\mathcal{E}[\![e_0]\!]\rho$ E **T**
then if $\mathcal{E}[\![e_0]\!]\rho \mid$ **T**
  then $\mathcal{E}[\![e_1]\!]\rho$
  else $\mathcal{E}[\![e_2]\!]\rho$
else **wrong**

$$\mathcal{E}[\![\text{nil}]\!]\rho = \text{nil in } \mathbf{S} \text{ in } \mathbf{V}$$

$$\mathcal{E}[\![\text{cons}(e_1, e_2)]\!]\rho =$$
if $\mathcal{E}[\![e_1]\!]\rho = \perp \vee \mathcal{E}[\![e_2]\!]\rho = \perp$
then $\perp$
else if $\exists\tau.\mathcal{E}[\![e_1]\!]\rho \in \mathcal{D}[\![\tau]\!] \wedge$
      $\mathcal{E}[\![e_2]\!]\rho \in \mathcal{D}[\![\tau \text{ list}]\!]$
  then $<\mathcal{E}[\![e_1]\!]\rho, \mathcal{E}[\![e_2]\!]\rho$ in **S**$>$
                in **S** in **V**
  else **wrong**

$$\mathcal{E}[\![\text{hd } e]\!]\rho =$$
if $\mathcal{E}[\![e]\!]\rho$ E **S**
then if $\neg$empty $\mathcal{E}[\![e]\!]\rho$
  then fst $(\mathcal{E}[\![e]\!]\rho \mid \mathbf{S} \mid \mathbf{S}_1)$
  else **wrong**
else **wrong**

$$\mathcal{E}[\![\text{tl } e]\!]\rho =$$
if $\mathcal{E}[\![e]\!]\rho$ E **S**
then if $\neg$empty $\mathcal{E}[\![e]\!]\rho$
  then snd $(\mathcal{E}[\![e]\!]\rho \mid \mathbf{S} \mid \mathbf{S}_1)$
  else **wrong**
else **wrong**

$$\mathcal{E}[\![\text{lambda } x : \sigma \,.\, e]\!]\rho =$$
if $\exists\tau.\forall v \in \mathcal{D}[\![\sigma]\!].\mathcal{E}[\![e]\!]\rho\{v/x\} \in \mathcal{D}[\![\tau]\!]$
then $(\lambda v.\text{if } v = \perp$
    then $\perp$
    else if $v \in \mathcal{D}[\![\sigma]\!]$
      then $\mathcal{E}[\![e]\!]\rho\{v/x\}$
      else **wrong**) in **V**
else **wrong**

$$\mathcal{E}[\![e_1(e_2)]\!]\rho =$$
if $\mathcal{E}[\![e_1]\!]\rho = \perp \vee \mathcal{E}[\![e_2]\!]\rho = \perp$
then $\perp$
else if $\mathcal{E}[\![e_1]\!]\rho$ E **F**
  then $(\mathcal{E}[\![e_1]\!]\rho \mid \mathbf{F}) (\mathcal{E}[\![e_2]\!]\rho)$
  else **wrong**

$$\mathcal{E}[\![\text{rec } x : \tau \,.\, e]\!]\rho =$$
if $\forall v \in \mathcal{D}[\![\tau]\!].\mathcal{E}[\![e']\!]\rho\{v/x\} \in \mathcal{D}[\![\tau]\!]$
then $\mathbf{Y}(\lambda v \,.\, \mathcal{E}[\![e]\!]\rho\{v/x\})$
else **wrong**

Figure 3: A refined semantics for *Exp*

The problem of functions which may be defined outside their declared domain is handled by restricting the semantics of lambda expressions so all functions defined in this way will yield **wrong** when applied to an argument outside the domain. The alternative of relaxing the type system is again an an interesting possibility but not within the scope of this presentation.

With respect to recursive definitions there is no simple modification to the type system which makes it complete. In general, knowledge about the specific behavior of the fixed point is necessary to prove type consistency. However, it is still desirable with typing rules covering the most usual sort of definitions like the factorial function:

rec $fac : \text{nat} \to \text{nat}$. lambda $x : \text{nat}$. if $x = 0$ then 1 else $x \times fac(x-1)$

The REC rule of the traditional type system is actually complete for this function, but it does not seem easy to characterize a sufficient large subclass of the recursive definition for which the traditional REC rule is complete. For reason of simplicity we have chosen to restrict the semantics so that a recursive definition rec $x : \tau$. e only is type consistent if the body is type consistent for any x in the denotation in of τ.

The resulting, revised semantics of expressions is presented in figure 3. Note that it is not possible to construct an interpreter which reports all type errors

$$\mathcal{M}[\![\text{true}]\!] = \lambda\rho \; . \; \text{true}$$

$$\mathcal{M}[\![\text{false}]\!] = \lambda\rho \; . \; \text{false}$$

$$\mathcal{M}[\![P_1 \wedge P_2]\!] = \lambda\rho \; . \; \mathcal{M}[\![P_1]\!]\rho \wedge \mathcal{M}[\![P_2]\!]\rho$$

$$\mathcal{M}[\![P_1 \vee P_2]\!] = \lambda\rho \; . \; \mathcal{M}[\![P_1]\!]\rho \vee \mathcal{M}[\![P_2]\!]\rho$$

$$\mathcal{M}[\![P_1 \Rightarrow P_2]\!] = \lambda\rho \; . \; \mathcal{M}[\![P_1]\!]\rho \Rightarrow \mathcal{M}[\![P_2]\!]\rho$$

$$\mathcal{M}[\![\neg P]\!] = \lambda\rho \; . \; \mathcal{M}[\![P]\!]\rho \Rightarrow \text{false}$$

$$\mathcal{M}[\![\forall x \in \tau \cdot P]\!] = \lambda\rho \; . \; \forall v \in \mathcal{D}[\![\tau]\!].\mathcal{M}[\![P]\!]\rho\{v/x\}$$

$$\mathcal{M}[\![\pi(e)]\!] = \lambda\rho \; . \; \Pi[\![\pi]\!]\mathcal{E}[\![e]\!]\rho$$

$$\Pi[\![\text{defined}]\!] = \lambda v \; . \; v \neq \bot$$

$$\Pi[\![\text{istrue}]\!] = \lambda v \; . \; v = \text{true}$$

$$\Pi[\![\text{isfalse}]\!] = \lambda v \; . \; v = \text{false}$$

$$\Pi[\![\text{empty}]\!] = \lambda v \; . \; v = \text{nil}$$

$$\Pi[\![\text{polylist}_1]\!] = \lambda v \; . \; v = \text{nil}$$

$$\Pi[\![\text{polylist}_{n+1}]\!] = \lambda v \; . \; v = \text{nil} \vee \forall v' \in \text{elems}\,(v \mid \mathbf{S}). \; \Pi[\![\text{polylist}_n]\!]v'$$

$$\cdots$$

Figure 4: Semantics of proof obligations

in accordance with this semantics. The problem is the tests in the semantics of **lambda** and **rec** expressions. Thus, the value **wrong** is not a computable value as it would normally be, and it is best interpreted as a completely unspecified (and undesirable) behavior.

7.1 A Type System for Generating Proof Obligations

With the refined semantics presented above, it is now considered a type error (**wrong**) to ask for the tail of an empty list. To obtain decidability of type checking, we therefore introduce a proof system for *conditional* statements:

$$P; B \vdash e : \tau$$

These statements can be read: The expression e has type τ provided that the proof obligation P can be proved and the variables have types as indicated by the basis B. The syntax of proof obligations is as follows:

$$P \quad ::= \quad \text{true} \mid \text{false} \mid P \wedge P \mid P \vee P \mid P \Rightarrow P \mid \neg P \mid \forall x \in \tau \cdot P \mid \pi(e)$$
$$\pi \quad ::= \quad \text{defined} \mid \text{istrue} \mid \text{isfalse} \mid \text{empty} \mid \text{polylist}_n \mid \cdots$$

The semantics is presented in figure 4. Semantically, proof obligations are viewed as denoting functions from environments to truth values. To explain the idea behind this, let us first introduce a notion of *agreement*:

Definition 7.1 (Agreement) *A set of assumptions B regarding types of variables agrees with an environment ρ if for all $x : \tau$ in B, $\rho x \in \mathcal{D}[\![\tau]\!]$. The notation $\rho \lhd B$ is used for agreement of B with ρ.*

Now, consider a conditional statement $P; B \vdash e : \tau$. With the definition of agreement, the proof obligation P can be viewed as selecting some of the environments which the assumptions B agree with. The statement then expresses that evaluating e in these environments will yield values in the type τ.

The type system in figure 5 can be used to prove conditional statements. Taking a brief look at some of the rules, we see that the trivial proof obligation

$$[\text{CASE}] \ \frac{P_1; B \vdash e : \tau \quad P_2; B \vdash e : \tau}{P_1 \lor P_2; B \vdash e : \tau} \qquad [\text{LOOP}] \ \frac{}{\neg\text{defined}(e); B \vdash e : \tau}$$

$$[\text{VAR}] \ \frac{}{\text{true}; B, x : \tau \vdash x : \tau} \qquad [\text{BAS}] \ \frac{}{\text{true}; B \vdash b_{ij} : \iota_i}$$

$$[\text{IFTRUE}] \ \frac{P_0; B \vdash e_0 : \textbf{bool} \quad P_1; B \vdash e_1 : \tau}{P_0 \land P_1 \land \text{istrue}(e_0); B \vdash \textbf{if } e_0 \textbf{ then } e_1 \textbf{ else } e_2 : \tau}$$

$$[\text{IFFALSE}] \ \frac{P_0; B \vdash e_0 : \textbf{bool} \quad P_2; B \vdash e_2 : \tau}{P_0 \land P_2 \land \text{isfalse}(e_0); B \vdash \textbf{if } e_0 \textbf{ then } e_1 \textbf{ else } e_2 : \tau}$$

$$[\text{POLY}] \ \frac{}{\text{polylist}_n(e); B \vdash e : \tau \ \textbf{list}} \qquad n = depth(\tau \ \textbf{list})$$

$$[\text{NIL}] \ \frac{}{\text{true}; B \vdash \texttt{nil} : \tau \ \textbf{list}} \qquad [\text{CONS}] \ \frac{P_1; B \vdash e_1 : \tau \quad P_2; B \vdash e_2 : \tau \ \textbf{list}}{P_1 \land P_2; B \vdash \texttt{cons}(e_1, e_2) : \tau \ \textbf{list}}$$

$$[\text{HD}] \ \frac{P; B \vdash e : \tau \ \textbf{list}}{P \land \neg\text{empty}(e); B \vdash \texttt{hd } e : \tau} \qquad [\text{TL}] \ \frac{P; B \vdash e : \tau \ \textbf{list}}{P \land \neg\text{empty}(e); B \vdash \texttt{tl } e : \tau \ \textbf{list}}$$

$$[\text{ABS}] \ \frac{P; B, x : \sigma \vdash e : \tau}{\forall x \in \sigma \cdot P; B \vdash (\texttt{lambda } x : \sigma \ . \ e) : \sigma \to \tau}$$

$$[\text{APPLY}] \ \frac{P_1; B \vdash e_1 : \sigma \to \tau \quad P_2; B \vdash e_2 : \sigma}{P_1 \land P_2; B \vdash e_1(e_2) : \tau}$$

$$[\text{REC}] \ \frac{P; B, x : \tau \vdash e : \tau}{\forall x \in \tau \cdot P; B \vdash \texttt{rec } x : \tau \ . \ e : \tau}$$

Figure 5: Type system with generation of proof obligations

true is sufficient for establishing that `nil` has a list type. The `hd` and `tl` functions may only be applied to non-empty lists and this is ensured by the proof obligation $\neg\text{empty}(e)$. Also note how the proof obligations of each branch of an `if-then-else` expression is tied to a proof obligation concerning the value of the condition. Concerning the IFTRUE and IFFALSE rules, it may seem strange that there is a proof obligation (P_0) ensuring the condition of the `if-then-else` to have type **bool** when there also is a proof obligation requiring the condition to have a specific truth value ($\text{istrue}(e_0)$ or $\text{isfalse}(e_0)$). From a semantic point of view the proof obligation P_0 is redundant. However, it is left for pragmatic reasons since it gives the user new ways to prove or disprove the overall proof obligation.

When used, the CASE rule will result in a proof obligation expressing a case analysis. Considering, e.g., an `if-then-else` expression with condition e_0, there are three cases to consider: The condition may be either true, false or $\bot$. These cases may be attacked using respectively the IFTRUE, IFFALSE, and LOOP rules. The resulting three proof obligations may be joined using the CASE rule (twice).

As another example, consider the typing statement `tl e : τ list`. Applying only the TL rule and thus requiring e to have type $τ$ **list**, might yield a too restrictive proof obligation since e may be a singleton list of another list type. Performing a case analysis using the CASE rule, we may also take into account that `tl e` might be a polymorphic value. This will yield a necessary proof obligation.

Note that it is necessary to treat non-termination very carefully when wanting a complete type system. In this work, we have chosen to accept non-termination as a possible denotation of model typable expressions. To obtain completeness, it is therefore important to recognize an expression as proof typable if it denotes ⊥—even if it would have been judged ill-typed by a traditional type system. This is reflected in the LOOP rule. The possibility of type consistency by non-termination has also the consequence that a case analysis always is necessary in connection with **cons** expressions and applications. These expressions may be type consistent even though one of the subexpressions is type inconsistent since non-termination of the other subexpression causes non-termination of the whole expression. Thus in connection with application of the CONS and APPLY rule, a case analysis using the LOOP rule as a second alternative is necessary in order to obtain the desired proof obligation.

The POLY rule has a similar motivation as the LOOP rule: to obtain completeness, a polymorphic list value, such as the empty list or a list of empty lists, must be recognized as belonging to any list type. The rule makes use of the auxiliary function *depth* which yields the nesting of list types:

$$
\begin{aligned}
depth(\iota_i) &= 0 \\
depth(\tau\,\textbf{list}) &= 1 + depth(\tau) \\
depth(\sigma \rightarrow \tau) &= 0
\end{aligned}
$$

8 Soundness and Completeness

As mentioned in the preceding sections, we want to generate sufficient and necessary proof obligations. These properties are established by two theorems on respectively soundness and completeness. To prove the theorems some lemmas are needed. We present only the theorems and the most important lemmas. The detailed proofs may be found in a technical report [5].

In section 7, we discussed some potential completeness problems. In the traditional approach, **lambda** expressions may yield model typable results when applied to arguments outside their declared argument type. In the new approach, we solved this problem by restricting the semantics such that **lambda** expressions yield **wrong** whenever they are applied to an argument outside their declared argument type. In the formulation of the lemmas and theorems, this property is important. In order to formalize the property some auxiliary, type related definitions are needed. We let $\sigma \overset{w}{\rightarrow} \tau$ denote the subset of $\sigma \rightarrow \tau$ which maps the values not belonging to the argument type σ into **wrong**. Formally, we have

$$
\mathcal{D}[\![\sigma \overset{w}{\rightarrow} \tau]\!] = \{\bot\} \cup \{f \text{ in } \mathbf{F} \mid v \in \mathcal{D}[\![\sigma]\!] \Rightarrow f(v) \in \mathcal{D}[\![\tau]\!] \land \\
v \notin \mathcal{D}[\![\sigma]\!] \Rightarrow f(v) = \textbf{wrong}\} \text{ in } \mathbf{V}
$$

We call such functions types *rejection function types* since they reject arguments outside their argument type. It turns out that function expressions are strict with respect to values of rejection types, i.e. values of rejections types are mapped into values of rejection types. The following transformation maps types into types with these rejection properties:

$$
\begin{aligned}
\iota_i^w &= \iota_i \\
(\tau\,\text{list})^w &= \tau^w\,\text{list} \\
(\sigma \to \tau)^w &= \sigma \xrightarrow{w} \tau \sqcap \sigma^w \to \tau^w
\end{aligned}
$$

Here $\sigma \sqcap \tau$ denotes the intersection of two types:

$$\mathcal{D}[\![\sigma \sqcap \tau]\!] = \mathcal{D}[\![\sigma]\!] \cap \mathcal{D}[\![\tau]\!]$$

We call types in the range of the above transformation *rejection types*. The transformation extends naturally to sets of assumptions. If B is a set of assumptions, then B^w is the result of applying the transformation to all types in the range of B.

Before turning to the properties of the type system for generation of proof obligations, we present some model theoretic lemmas. The first lemma concerns a limited form of disjointness of types.

Lemma 8.1 (Disjointness of types) *If the bottom value $\bot$ is excluded from the semantics of all types, then all syntactically different rejection types are disjoint except for list types which share polymorphic list values.*

The next lemma concerns model typability. It essentially says that all type consistent expressions are model typable.

Lemma 8.2 (Model typability) *Let e be any expression and ρ any environment typable with rejection types. If $\mathcal{E}[\![e]\!]\rho \neq \textbf{wrong}$ then there exists a type τ such that $\mathcal{E}[\![e]\!]\rho \in \mathcal{D}[\![\tau]\!]$.*

In fact, type consistent expressions are even model typable with rejection types. The next lemma establishes this together with lemma 8.2.

Lemma 8.3 (Typability with rejection types) *Let e be any expression, ρ any environment typable with rejection types, and τ any type. If $\mathcal{E}[\![e]\!]\rho \in \mathcal{D}[\![\tau]\!]$ then $\mathcal{E}[\![e]\!]\rho \in \mathcal{D}[\![\tau^w]\!]$.*

In order to obtain a complete type system, it turned out necessary to introduce the CASE rule which allows for case analysis. We had to treat non-termination and polymorphic values as special cases. Case analysis is, however, also necessary in connection with function application. Considering a typing statement $e_1(e_2):\tau$, the APPLY rule can be used in several different ways. For each potential argument type of e_1 we may use the APPLY rule and get distinct proof obligations. The following lemma says that for all expressions there exist a finite set of types such that whenever the expression is type consistent, its denotation belongs to one of these types. This allows a complete case analysis in connection with applications.

Lemma 8.4 (Possible types) *Let e be an expression and B a set of assumption ranging over the free variables of e. There exist types $\tau_1,\ldots,\tau_n$ such that for all environments $\rho \lhd B^w$: If $\mathcal{E}[\![e]\!]\rho \neq \textbf{wrong}$ then $\mathcal{E}[\![e]\!]\rho \in \mathcal{D}[\![\tau_1]\!] \cup \ldots \cup \mathcal{D}[\![\tau_n]\!]$.*

$$[\text{LOOP}_{pt}] \ \frac{}{B \vdash_{pt} e : \mathbf{empty}} \qquad [\text{VAR}_{pt}] \ \frac{}{B, x:\tau \vdash_{pt} x:\tau} \qquad [\text{BAS}_{pt}] \ \frac{}{B \vdash_{pt} b_{ij} : \iota_i}$$

$$[\text{IFTRUE}_{pt}] \ \frac{B \vdash_{pt} e_1 : \tau}{B \vdash_{pt} \text{if } e_0 \text{ then } e_1 \text{ else } e_2 : \tau}$$

$$[\text{IFFALSE}_{pt}] \ \frac{B \vdash_{pt} e_2 : \tau}{B \vdash_{pt} \text{if } e_0 \text{ then } e_1 \text{ else } e_2 : \tau}$$

$$[\text{NIL}_{pt}] \ \frac{}{B \vdash_{pt} \text{nil} : \mathbf{empty\ list}} \qquad [\text{CONS}_{pt}] \ \frac{B \vdash_{pt} e_1 : \tau}{B \vdash_{pt} \text{cons}(e_1, e_2) : \tau \text{ list}}$$

$$[\text{HD}_{pt}] \ \frac{B \vdash_{pt} e : \tau \text{ list}}{B \vdash_{pt} \text{hd } e : \tau} \quad [\text{TL1}_{pt}] \ \frac{B \vdash_{pt} e : \tau \text{ list}}{B \vdash_{pt} \text{tl } e : \tau \text{ list}} \quad [\text{TL2}_{pt}] \ \frac{}{B \vdash_{pt} \text{tl } e : \mathbf{empty\ list}}$$

$$[\text{ABS}_{pt}] \ \frac{B, x:\sigma \vdash_{pt} e : \tau}{B \vdash_{pt} (\text{lambda } x:\sigma \,.\, e) : \sigma \to \tau} \qquad [\text{APPLY}_{pt}] \ \frac{B \vdash_{pt} e_1 : \sigma \to \tau}{B \vdash_{pt} e_1(e_2) : \tau}$$

$$[\text{REC}_{pt}] \ \frac{}{B \vdash_{pt} (\text{rec } x:\tau \,.\, e) : \tau}$$

Figure 6: Type system for possible types

Figure 6 shows a type system which can be used to infer such a set of possible types. We have introduced a type **empty** which denotes the empty set of computable values, i.e. $\mathcal{D}[\![\mathbf{empty}]\!] = \{\bot\}$. The type system fulfills the following completeness property:

Lemma 8.5 (Completeness of possible typings) *Let e be an expression, let B be a set of assumption ranging over the free variables of e, and let $\rho \lhd B^w$ be an environment. If $\mathcal{E}[\![e]\!]\rho \neq$ **wrong** then there exists a type τ such that $B \vdash_{pt} e : \tau$ and $\mathcal{E}[\![e]\!]\rho \in \mathcal{D}[\![\tau]\!]$.*

Informally speaking, the lemma says that for any expression the type system can accept a set of types which so to speak covers the possible expression values. The type system can only be used to very simple type analyses. We have chosen a simple system since the system is only used to direct the generation of proof obligations by defining cases for a case analysis. However, a more detailed analysis could reduce the set of possible types and thus reduce the generated proof obligation.

With these lemmas we are able to prove the following main theorems which give the semantic soundness and completeness of the type system for generation of proof obligations.

Theorem 8.1 (Semantic soundness) *Let e be any expression, τ any type, B any set of assumptions ranging over the free variables of e, and P any proof obligations such that $P; B \vdash e : \tau$ is derivable. For all environments $\rho \lhd B^w$: If $\mathcal{M}[\![P]\!]\rho = $ **true** then $\mathcal{E}[\![e]\!]\rho \in \mathcal{D}[\![\tau]\!]$.*

Theorem 8.2 (Semantic completeness) *Let e be any expression, τ any type, B any set of assumptions ranging over the free variables of e. There exists a proof obligation P such that $P; B \vdash e : \tau$ is derivable, and for all environments $\rho \lhd B^w$: If $\mathcal{E}[\![e]\!]\rho \in \mathcal{D}[\![\tau]\!]$ then $\mathcal{M}[\![P]\!]\rho = $ true.*

It follows immediately from the completeness theorem that for all expressions e, types τ and sets of assumptions B there exists a proof obligations P such that $P; B \vdash e : \tau$ is derivable. Thus a proof obligation can always be inferred. It will, however, be unsatisfiable if the expression does not denote a value in the type.

In summary, we have a type system which for each typing statement $e : \tau$ can be used to generate necessary and sufficient proof obligations ensuring fulfillment of the typing statement.

9   Algorithmic Aspects

The proof of completeness presented in the technical report [5] is constructive. Hence, it defines an algorithm which for each typing statement $e : \tau$ and set of assumptions B yields a necessary proof obligation ensuring that the value denoted by the expression e is in the set of values denoted by the type τ.

The algorithm which also may be found in [5], is directed by the syntax of the expression argument. For some expression forms, the recursive descend is straightforward. As mentioned in section 7.1, a very carefully treatment of non-termination is, however, necessary. Since $\bot$ is in the denotation of all types, any typing statement $e : \tau$ may be fulfilled by proving non-termination of the expression e. Consequently, the LOOP rule presents an alternative to the syntax directed rules. In some cases LOOP, is the only applicable rule. In many of these cases, the LOOP rule will generate unsatisfiable proof obligation. Automatic recognition of some such unsatisfiable proof obligations may be used to reject "clearly" inconsistent programs. For example, trying to establish $\texttt{cons}(1, \texttt{nil}) : \sigma \to \tau$ will result in the proof obligation $\neg\mathsf{defined}(\texttt{cons}(1, \texttt{nil}))$ which is clearly unsatisfiable.

There are some automatic reductions of the proof obligations which seem to be relevant in any attempt to discharge a proof obligation. In the technical report [5], we have presented some such reductions. Using these it is possible to reduce a proof obligation to a semantically equivalent but syntactically simpler one.

To illustrate which proof obligations can be generated using this approach, consider the following function which yields the length of a list:

> **rec** $len : \tau$ **list** $\to$ **nat**.
>   **lambda** $x : \tau$ **list** . **if** $isempty(x)$ **then** 0 **else** $succ(len(\texttt{tl}\, x))$

Assume we want to show that this expression has type τ **list** $\to$ **nat**. Applying our type checking algorithm leaves us with the following reduced proof obligation:

> $\forall x \in \tau$ **list** $\cdot$ isfalse($isempty(x)$) $\Rightarrow \neg\mathsf{empty}(x)$

This proof obligation expresses exactly that the condition of the **if-then-else** must prevent **tl** from being applied to the empty list.

10   Concluding Remarks

In general, writers of programs and formal specifications face the problem of establishing consistency. As a help, type checking may detect some inconsistencies. At the same time, types play an essential role as a modelling tool.

We have considered a notion of type which excludes dynamic type errors and for which model typability is undecidable. This is seen as a representative of the more expressive notions of type appropriate for specification and modelling. As a main result, we have shown how such notions of type also may be used in automatic type checking. The central idea is to obtain decidability of type checking with such types by generating proof obligations for the "difficult" parts which cause the undecidability (here the dynamic type errors).

The example language considered in this paper is small and its semantics simple in order to achieve simplicity in the presentation. We think, however, that the principles outlined here may be generalized. In a related work [4], we have informally discussed how to treat subtyping and set theoretic union types in connection with generation of proof obligations.

The most natural application of the approach of generating proof obligations is in formal verification of type consistency, but it may, however, also serve other purposes. Proof obligations may be used as pointers to dangerous places in a program or specification. Consider, e.g., a proof obligation which requires some subexpression to non-terminate. This is most likely a programming or specification mistake, and before attacking such a proof obligation, the programmer should check if this is really wanted. In a similar way, proof obligations generated in connection with conditionals may indicate that a program or specification is type consistent only in the presence of "dead code". In other words, some proof obligations could be interpreted as warnings.

Type checking with generation of proof obligations may also be viewed as partial type checking. In the work by Gomard [6], program parts which are not proof typable are marked with annotations. These annotations may be used to insert necessary run-time checks. See also the work by Cartwright and Fagan on soft typing [3].

In general, type systems may be used to many sorts of static analysis of programs and specifications. Type consistency is just a special case. As an example, the approach of generating proof obligations could be used to perform semi-automatic analyses in connection with compiling. A compiler could, e.g., offer correctness of certain optimizations provided that associated proof obligations could be satisfied.

At last, we would like to mention two more references to related work. In the RAISE Specification Language [7] an expressive notion of types is also used for type checking. Here, however, each type is a subtype of some unique maximal type and decidable type checking is obtained by only considering the maximal types. As a separate facility, not part of type checking, proof obligations called "confidence conditions" may be generated; these rule out, e.g., dynamic type errors.

Type checking in PVS [10] also generates proof obligations but there does not seem to be a clear relation to the dynamic semantics.

Acknowledgement

Thanks to Hans Bruun who took part in the discussions motivating this work.

References

[1] D. Bjørner and C.B. Jones, editors. *The Vienna Development Method: The Meta-Language*, volume 61 of *Lecture Notes in Computer Science*. Springer-Verlag, 1978.

[2] Luca Cardelli. Structural subtyping and the notion of power type. In *Conference Record of the Fifteenth Annual ACM Symposium on Principles of Programming Languages (POPL'88)*, pages 70–79, 1988.

[3] Robert Cartwright and Mike Fagan. Soft typing. In *Proceedings of the ACM SIGPLAN'91 Conference on Programming Language Design and Implementation (PLDI'91)*, pages 278–292. ACM Press, 1991.

[4] Flemming Damm, Bo Stig Hansen, and Hans Bruun. On type checking in VDM and related consistency issues. In S. Prehn and W. J. Toetenel, editors, *Proceedings of 4th International Symposium of VDM Europe on Formal Software Development Methods (VDM'91), Noordwijkerhout, The Netherlands, October 1991, Volume 1: Conference Contributions*, volume 551 of *Lecture Notes in Computer Science*, pages 45–62. Springer-Verlag, 1991.

[5] Flemming M. Damm and Bo Stig Hansen. Generation of proof obligations for type consistency. Technical Report ID-TR: 1993-123, Department of Computer Science, The Technical University of Denmark, 1993.

[6] Carsten K. Gomard. Partial type inference for untyped functional programs (extended abstract). In *Proceedings of the 1990 ACM Conference on Lisp and Funtional Programming*, pages 282–287, 1990.

[7] The RAISE Language Group. *The RAISE specification Language*. BCS Practitioner Series. Prentice Hall, 1992.

[8] Cliff B. Jones. *Systematic Software Development using VDM*. Prentice Hall International series in computer science. Prentice Hall, second edition, 1990.

[9] Robin Milner. A theory of type polymorphism in programming. *Journal of Computer and System Sciences*, 17:348–375, 1978.

[10] S. Owre, J. M. Rushby, and N. Shankar. PVS: A prototype verification system. In D. Kapur, editor, *Proceedings of 11th International Conference on Automated Deduction (CADE-11), Saratoga Springs, NY, USA, June 1992*, volume 607 of *Lecture Notes in Artificial Intelligence*, pages 748–752. Springer-Verlag, 1992.

[11] Simon Thompson. *Type Theory and Functional Programming*. International Computer Science Series. Addison-Wesley, 1991.

Experiences in Developing a Proof Theory for VDM Specifications

J. S. Fitzgerald
Dept. of Computing Science *
University of Newcastle upon Tyne
Newcastle upon Tyne
NE1 7RU, UK

R. Moore
Dept. of Computer Science,
University of Manchester
Manchester
M13 9PL, UK

Abstract

This paper records experience in the provision of the necessary theories to support formal reasoning about the contents of specifications written in the VDM Specification Language. The need for an axiomatisation of VDM logic and data types is briefly reviewed and a framework suitable for its expression is introduced. This is illustrated with examples from the predicate Logic of Partial Functions and the theory of finite sets.

The main part of the paper discusses problems of choosing the form of the axiomatisation of specification language constructs. Specifically, we address the use of syntactic versus axiomatic definition and direct versus indirect interpretation of language constructs. Aspects of VDM which have been found difficult to describe, or which complicate proofs, are discussed. These include proliferation of typing hypotheses, finiteness of comprehensions, flatness of data types involving functions, and interpretation of loose expressions.

Particular stress is laid on the repercussions a choice made during axiomatisation may have on the intuitive clarity of the axioms and the ease of construction of proofs.

1 Introduction

While formal specification of computing systems is increasingly viewed as a beneficial activity by commercial systems developers, the exploitation of formal or rigorous proof is not so widespread. One way of improving the viability of proof is by providing machine support, including databases of useful theorems of the logic, data types and type constructors of the specification language. These can be used in deriving properties of the types and operations defined in a specification, including validation conjectures (results expected to hold if the formal specification has indeed captured informal requirements accurately), proof obligations regarding internal consistency of a specification, and obligations to show the faithfulness of a refinement step.

The Vienna Development Method (VDM) [1] uses a model-oriented specification language. In order to reason about the types, functions and operations defined in a VDM specification, two things are required: a logic in which to conduct the proofs and a means of translating the specification into a collection of axioms in the logic. The prover (human or machine) can then discharge obligations and prove conjectures by appealing to the logic. Work on machine-supported specification and proof in mural,

*Work undertaken under the auspices of the British Aerospace Dependable Computing Systems Centre.

described in [2], suggested that the provision of extensive collections of proved results about the VDM logic and data types was essential to the effective conduct of such proofs.

The underlying logic of VDM specifications, the Logic of Partial Functions (LPF), is described in its untyped form in [3] and [4]). Jones, in [1], also gives (comparatively informally) a collection of axioms and theorems for the VDM data types and type constructors. A team including the authors has worked on the provision of a fully formal proof theory for typed LPF and the data types of VDM, to be presented in [5]. In this paper, we discuss some interesting problems encountered and trade-offs made in the course of this work. We concentrate on the axiomatisation of the logic and data types; work on interpreting a VDM specification as a theory is described in [6]. The recent work of Jones and Middelburg [7] also describes a typed form of LPF and some extensions, along with its embedding in a classical infinitary logic.

In parallel with our work, the specification language of VDM is the subject of international standardisation. The standard language, VDM-SL[1], has a denotational model-based semantics [8]. The development of its proof theory will involve extensions to the proof theory discussed here. One of these, involving the interpretation of loose expressions, is discussed in Larsen's work [9].

The logical framework used in the paper is briefly described in Section 2. Section 3 gives a flavour of our overall approach by describing the theory of predicate LPF and part of the theory of finite sets. Section 4 then discusses two areas in which interesting problems have been encountered: the effects of choosing particular axiomatisations on the complexity of proof, and aspects of VDM-SL which are difficult to represent directly in the logical framework we have used.

2   Logical Framework

In this section we review enough of the logical framework underlying our axiomatisation to facilitate an understanding of subsequent sections. This is based on the work of Lindsay in [2].

Axioms and theorems take the form familiar to readers of [1]. Both are treated as inference rules for application in Natural Deduction-style proofs. For example, the rule for elimination of disjunction in propositional LPF is:

$$\boxed{\text{∨-E}} \; \frac{e_1 \lor e_2; \; e_1 \vdash e; \; e_2 \vdash e}{e} \; \text{Ax}$$

The **Ax** to the right indicates that this rule is an axiom; the box to the left contains the rule's name. In this paper, an unnamed rule is introduced for discussion purposes only; named rules appear in our final axiomatisation. Each rule has just one conclusion, but may have a number of hypotheses including (as in this example) sequent hypotheses. Sequent symbols ("⊢") are subscripted by the names of the variables they bind, in this case none. Rules are, in fact, rule schemas. In the above example the symbols e_1, e_2 and e are metavariables, instantiated at the time of use of the rule. See [2] for a more detailed discussion of the syntax of rules and the mechanisms of instantiation.

---

[1]While our work has established a proof theory for the main VDM specification concepts, it has not been aimed specifically at VDM-SL. In this paper, therefore, our specification language differs from that of [8] in a few respects, but not in major issues of principle. Where the text refers to "VDM-SL", it means specifically the language defined in the proto-standard.

Symbols of the logic may be introduced in one of two ways: by *axiomatisation* or by *syntactic definition* in terms of other symbols. Primitives are always introduced axiomatically. For example, in our axiomatisation of propositional LPF, the primitives are disjunction, negation and the value true, and their properties are given via axioms including:

$$\boxed{\text{∨-I-left}} \; \frac{e_2}{e_1 \vee e_2} \; \text{Ax} \qquad \boxed{\neg\neg\text{-I}} \; \frac{e}{\neg\neg e} \; \text{Ax} \qquad \boxed{\text{true-I}} \; \frac{}{\text{true}} \; \text{Ax}$$

Syntactically defined symbols are given definitions in terms of other constructs. In propositional LPF, for example, conjunction is defined thus:

$$e_1 \wedge e_2 \stackrel{def}{=\!=} \neg(\neg e_1 \vee \neg e_2)$$

This definition means that, at any point in a proof, a conjunction can be replaced by its definition or a negated disjunction of negations (matching the right-hand expression of the definition) can be replaced by a conjunction. These transformations are termed "unfolding" and "folding" respectively.

The logical frame distinguishes ordinary expressions and type expressions. Thus, while disjunction above takes two ordinary expressions as its arguments, the type constructor '_-set' for finite sets takes one type expression (e.g. $(\mathbb{N}^*)$-set). All such symbols have a fixed arity, represented as a pair of numbers indicating respectively the numbers of ordinary expressions and type expressions they take as arguments. In the examples above, the arity of disjunction is (2,0), negation (1,0), true (0,0) and _-set (0,1). The logical frame also supports binders which bind a single (typed) variable in an expression.

3 Example Theories from the Axiomatisation

Our axiomatisation work has involved using the logical framework outlined above to give theories of propositional and predicate LPF, and the basic data types and type constructors (union types, finite maps, finite sets, etc.). In this section we present two small parts of the axiomatisation as examples of the approach taken. The first is taken from the theory of LPF, the second from the theory of finite sets.

3.1 Typed Predicate LPF with Equality

A distinguishing feature of LPF is its handling of the possibility that functions may be applied outside their domain of definition. Logical expressions constructed from such mis-applications may yet denote logical values (for example, "0 < 1 ∨ 7 < 1/0" is true irrespective of whether or not "7 < 1/0" is a meaningful expression).

In typed predicate LPF types are ascribed to *denoting* terms only. The type judgement "$x: A$" is used to indicate that the expression x denotes a value from type A, including satisfying any invariants of A. Since VDM invariants may contain arbitrarily complex predicates, this typing relation is in general only partially statically decidable.

Just as propositional LPF is axiomatised in terms of disjunction and negation, so existential quantification (∃) is taken to be primitive in predicate logic. Its properties are therefore defined axiomatically. The quantifier is defined as a binder in the logical framework.

The introduction axiom states that, if a predicate P is known to be true at some witness value a of type A, then the quantification holds:

104

$$\boxed{\text{∃-I}} \; \frac{a\colon A;\; P(a)}{\exists x\colon A \cdot P(x)} \; \textbf{Ax}$$

The elimination axiom is related to the axiom for elimination of disjunction, shown above. If it is known that there is at least one value satisfying the predicate P, and if it is possible to conclude some e for an arbitrary value y satisfying P, then e must hold in general[2]:

$$\boxed{\text{∃-E}} \; \frac{\begin{array}{c} \exists x\colon A \cdot P(x) \\ y\colon A,\; P(y) \vdash_y e \end{array}}{e} \; \textbf{Ax}$$

Other axioms for existential quantification describe its interaction with negation:

$$\boxed{\neg\text{-∃-I}} \; \frac{x\colon A \vdash_x \neg P(x)}{\neg(\exists y\colon A \cdot P(y))} \; \textbf{Ax} \qquad\qquad \boxed{\neg\text{-∃-E}} \; \frac{a\colon A;\; \neg(\exists x\colon A \cdot P(x))}{\neg P(a)} \; \textbf{Ax}$$

Useful derived rules about $\exists$ can then be proved from these axioms.

The universal quantifier ($\forall$, also a binder) is defined syntactically in terms of $\neg$ and $\exists$. A predicate P holds everywhere over a type A if there does not exist a value at which it does not hold:

$$\forall x\colon A \cdot P(x) \; \stackrel{def}{=} \; \neg\,\exists x\colon A \cdot \neg P(x)$$

Using this definition, assertions involving $\forall$ could all be reduced to assertions involving only the existential quantifier, and proofs would then be conducted using the rules defining it introduced above. A better strategy, however, in that work is saved in the long term, is to derive theorems about the universal quantifier itself using the definition. The derived introduction and elimination rules are then:

$$\boxed{\text{∀-I}} \; \frac{y\colon A \vdash_y P(y)}{\forall x\colon A \cdot P(x)} \qquad\qquad \boxed{\text{∀-E}} \; \frac{a\colon A;\; \forall x\colon A \cdot P(x)}{P(a)}$$

In developing a theory for predicate LPF, the definedness of quantified expressions is of particular interest. A distinctive feature of the logic is that the law of the excluded middle does not in general hold. Thus we do not have an axiom of the form

$$\frac{}{e \vee \neg e}\textbf{Ax}$$

Following [3], we introduce the δ symbol to indicate definedness of an expression:

$$\delta e \; \stackrel{def}{=} \; e \vee \neg e$$

Consider now the definedness of the expression $\exists x\colon A \cdot P(x)$. From the rules already given, if a witness value a can be produced to show $P(a)$, then certainly $\exists x\colon A \cdot P(x)$ follows by '∃-I ', and hence $\delta(\exists x\colon A \cdot P(x))$. Conversely, if it can be shown that a witness value does not exist, then $\neg\,\exists x\colon A \cdot P(x)$ follows by '$\neg$-∃-I ' and once again $\delta(\exists x\colon A \cdot P(x))$ is shown. However, there is a third case: the predicate P is known to be defined at every value in the type A, but one has insufficient information to either produce or refute the existence of a witness value at which P is true. In this case, one cannot prove either $\exists x\colon A \cdot P(x)$ or $\neg\,\exists x\colon A \cdot P(x)$, but one does know that one or the other is true, and so $\delta(\exists x\colon A \cdot P(x))$ is known. To cover this third case, the following additional axiom is introduced:

---

[2]When a rule with a sequent hypothesis is applied in a proof, the local variable name must not already be in use. If a variable clash does occur the local variable is renamed in order to distinguish it. We do not therefore need the familiar side-condition that y does not occur free in e. (See [2] for details.)

$$\boxed{\delta\text{-}\exists\text{-inherit}} \quad \frac{x: A \vdash_x \delta P(x)}{\delta(\exists x: A \cdot P(x))} \text{ Ax}$$

Using this and the definition of $\forall$ the corresponding result for $\forall$ can be proved:

$$\boxed{\delta\text{-}\forall\text{-inherit}} \quad \frac{y: A \vdash_y \delta P(y)}{\delta(\forall x: A \cdot P(x))}$$

Our formulation of predicate LPF takes account of equality. Within the logical frame used here, the equality symbol is a binary predicate, taking two expressions as its arguments. Its properties are given by just a few axioms, the simplest of which states that equality is reflexive:

$$\boxed{=\text{-self-I}} \quad \frac{a: A}{a = a} \text{ Ax}$$

The typing hypothesis may seem unusual. In LPF, equality (called *weak equality* in [3]) is defined only over denoting terms.

The value of equality lies in the ability to substitute equal values in predicates. This property is captured by axioms which substitute the expression on one side of an equality for some or all occurrences of the expression on the other in an arbitrary predicate:

$$\boxed{=\text{-subs-right(a)}} \quad \frac{a: A;\ a = b;\ P(a)}{P(b)} \text{ Ax} \qquad \boxed{=\text{-subs-left(b)}} \quad \frac{b: A;\ a = b;\ P(b)}{P(a)} \text{ Ax}$$

The suffix on each axiom's name indicates which expression in the equality has a known type. Note that the familiar rules for symmetry and transitivity of equality can be proved from these axioms.

The last axiom needed asserts that equality is defined when *both* of its operands are defined:

$$\boxed{\delta\text{-}=\text{-I}} \quad \frac{a: A;\ b: A}{\delta(a = b)} \text{ Ax}$$

Note that this axiom says only that two elements of *the same* type are either equal or unequal: it does not give any indication of which, nor does it say anything about the equality of elements of different types. These issues depend on the provision of specific equality axioms for specific types and on the notion of type extension through the construction of union types. They are addressed more fully in Section 4.2.1 below.

The requirement in LPF that the arguments of equality be denoting leads to an abundance of typing hypotheses in rules relating to equality. Such hypotheses are tiresome, but straightforward, to discharge in proofs. A mechanised proof support system should take advantage of static type checking to reduce the need to manually discharge typing assumptions. The use of typing hypotheses in the proof theory presented here is discussed further in Section 4.2.1.

3.2 Finite Sets

As an example of the axiomatisation of a data type constructor, we consider finite sets. They are axiomatised in terms of generators: the empty set { } and an *add* operator which adds an element to a set.

The empty set represents an empty collection of arbitrary type, as defined by the rule '{ }-form ':

$$\boxed{\{\,\}\text{-form}} \quad \frac{}{\{\,\}\colon A\text{-set}} \ \mathbf{Ax}$$

Set membership is expressed by the symbol '$\in$', so that the expression $a \in s$ represents the assertion that some object a is an element of the set s. The negation of this relation, namely that a particular object is not an element of a given set, is denoted by the symbol '$\notin$', defined simply as:

$$a \notin s \ \overset{def}{=\!=} \ \neg (a \in s)$$

The statement that the empty set is empty can be equivalently expressed as the statement that any arbitrary object is not a member of it. This is the form used in the rule '$\{\,\}$-is-empty':

$$\boxed{\{\,\}\text{-is-empty}} \quad \frac{a\colon A}{a \notin \{\,\}} \ \mathbf{Ax}$$

The properties of operators on sets are defined in terms of *formation* and *membership* rules, the former effectively giving the signature of the operator, the latter defining the contents of the appropriate set. For *add*, the formation and membership rules are as follows:

$$\boxed{\text{add-form}} \quad \frac{a\colon A; \ s\colon A\text{-set}}{add(a, s)\colon A\text{-set}} \ \mathbf{Ax}$$

$$\boxed{\in\text{-add-defn}} \quad \frac{a\colon A; \ b\colon A; \ s\colon A\text{-set}}{a \in add(b, s) \Leftrightarrow a = b \lor a \in s} \ \mathbf{Ax}$$

The empty set and the function *add* form a pair of generators for finite sets because any finite set is either empty or can be expressed as a series of applications of *add* to the empty set. This property forms the basis of the induction rule:

$$\boxed{\text{set-indn}} \quad \frac{s\colon A\text{-set}; \ P(\{\,\}) \qquad a\colon A, \ s_1\colon A\text{-set}, \ P(s_1), \ a \notin s_1 \vdash_{a,s_1} P(add(a, s_1))}{P(s)} \ \mathbf{Ax}$$

Set equality is defined using the notion of *subset*. A set s_1 is a subset of a set s_2 (written $s_1 \subseteq s_2$) if any member of the set s_1 is also a member of the set s_2. This property is expressed via the axiom '$\subseteq$-defn':

$$\boxed{\subseteq\text{-defn}} \quad \frac{s_1\colon A\text{-set}; \ s_2\colon A\text{-set}}{s_1 \subseteq s_2 \Leftrightarrow \forall a \in s_1 \cdot a \in s_2} \ \mathbf{Ax}$$

Two sets s_1 and s_2 are then equal if each is a subset of the other. This is stated as the following axiom:

$$\boxed{=\text{-set-defn}} \quad \frac{s_1\colon A\text{-set}; \ s_2\colon A\text{-set}}{s_1 = s_2 \Leftrightarrow s_1 \subseteq s_2 \land s_2 \subseteq s_1} \ \mathbf{Ax}$$

Other operators on sets (for example set union, set intersection and power set) are defined analogously to *add* above, i.e. by giving formation and membership rules for them, and additional properties of them can be proved by induction. For example, the axioms for set union are:

$$\boxed{\cup\text{-form}} \quad \frac{s_1\colon A\text{-set}; \ s_2\colon A\text{-set}}{s_1 \cup s_2 \colon A\text{-set}} \ \mathbf{Ax}$$

$$\boxed{\in\text{-}\cup\text{-defn}} \quad \frac{a\colon A; \ s_1\colon A\text{-set}; \ s_2\colon A\text{-set}}{a \in s_1 \cup s_2 \Leftrightarrow a \in s_1 \lor a \in s_2} \ \mathbf{Ax}$$

However, this approach to axiomatisation runs into difficulties when applied naïvely to set comprehension expressions. These difficulties are discussed in Section 4.2.2 below.

4 Choices and Trade-Offs in the Axiomatisation

The theories described in the preceding sections are only examples drawn from a full axiomatisation of most of the types and operators required for interpretation of VDM specifications. The provision of this axiomatisation has raised a number of interesting issues concerning the representation of certain concepts essential to VDM-SL, such as finiteness of comprehension expressions, "flatness" of data types and interpretation of loose specification. These are discussed in Section 4.2. A number of other issues, discussed in Section 4.1, relate to the choice of how to axiomatise a construct: when to use syntactic definition, and how to deal with constructs such as composite types which do not have a fixed form.

4.1 Choosing the Form of an Axiomatisation

There are normally many alternative ways of axiomatising a theory. In providing axioms for VDM constructs, we have been particularly concerned with the effects of a particular choice of axioms on the difficulty or ease of proof. The following sections describe two choices to be made in dealing with a construct of the specification language: when it is safe to use a syntactic definition, and how to strike a balance between direct support for a construct in the logic and interpretation of a construct which has no direct equivalent in the logic.

4.1.1 Syntactic Definition or Definition by Rules?

Although the mechanism of syntactic definition introduced in Section 2 above is a powerful one, using a polymorphic operator like equality in the definition of some new operator can lead to a situation in which it is possible to prove nonsense from the definition.

Consider, for example, the two subset relations $\subseteq$ and $\subset$. The first of these has been defined axiomatically in Section 3.2 and admits equality of s_1 and s_2. The second requires s_2 to be strictly larger than s_1. It is tempting to simply make a syntactic definition of the *proper subset* relation $\subset$ in terms of the subset relation $\subseteq$ as follows:

$$s_1 \subset s_2 \overset{def}{=\!=} s_1 \subseteq s_2 \land s_1 \neq s_2$$

that is that s_1 is a proper subset of s_2 if it is a subset of it but is not equal to it. However, a direct definition like this does not restrict the values of its parameters in any way, so that it is perfectly reasonable to take both s_1 and s_2 to be the number 19, for example. However, the fact that $19 = 19$ is true means that $19 \neq 19$ is false, and hence, by the properties of LPF, it is possible to deduce

$$\neg\,(19 \subseteq 19 \land 19 \neq 19)$$

But the expression $19 \subseteq 19 \land 19 \neq 19$ is just the definition of $19 \subset 19$ so this amounts to having proved that $19 \subset 19$ is false, contrary to the spirit of LPF which says it should be undefined.

Of course, there was nothing special about the choice of 19 in the above example – any denoting term would have done equally well. This means that, using the syntactic definition of $\subset$ above, we could prove the general rule

$$\frac{a:A}{\neg\,(a \subset a)}$$

for any a of some arbitrary type A. The proof is as follows:

$$
\begin{array}{lll}
 & \text{from } a:A & \\
1 & \quad \neg\,(a \neq a) & \neg\text{-}{\neq}\text{-self-I}\;\; (h1) \\
2 & \quad \neg\,(a \subseteq a \wedge a \neq a) & \neg\text{-}{\wedge}\text{-I-left}\;\; (1) \\
 & \text{infer } \neg\,(a \subset a) & \text{folding}\;\; (2)
\end{array}
$$

The reason for this is that the polymorphic nature of equality means that the term containing it, and hence the whole defining expression, can have a well-defined value outside the intended scope of the definition, thus introducing some degree of polymorphism into the definition. The use of polymorphic terms in syntactic definitions is therefore best restricted to cases where the definition itself is intended to be polymorphic.

This problem suggests a limitation in our logical framework: the syntactic definition mechanism does not accommodate "side conditions" on folding and unfolding. The presence of such conditions (e.g. in typing requirements from the signature restrictions of VDM function definitions) necessitates axiomatic definition with the conditions stated as hypotheses.

4.1.2   Direct Support or Translation?

In the logical framework on which we have built our axiomatisation, each construct has a fixed arity. For example, disjunction and type union are both binary. This means that we cannot give a general theory of VDM-SL constructs which do not have a fixed number of components (e.g. composite types); we must instead devise schemas for translating such constructs into definitions and axioms. Our treatment of composite types illustrates the approach.

Consider the composite type definition

$$
\begin{array}{ll}
D :: & a : A \\
 & b : B
\end{array}
$$

This is translated into a type name D, a constructor $mk\text{-}D$ which takes two arguments, and two selectors a and b each of which takes one argument. These are related by axioms of formation and definition[3]:

$$\boxed{a\text{-form}}\;\; \frac{d:D}{d.a:A}\;\;\text{Ax} \qquad\qquad \boxed{a\text{-defn}}\;\; \frac{mk\text{-}D(x,y):D}{mk\text{-}D(x,y).a = x}\;\;\text{Ax}$$

$$\boxed{b\text{-form}}\;\; \frac{d:D}{d.b:B}\;\;\text{Ax} \qquad\qquad \boxed{b\text{-defn}}\;\; \frac{mk\text{-}D(x,y):D}{mk\text{-}D(x,y).b = y}\;\;\text{Ax}$$

$$\boxed{mk\text{-}D\text{-form}}\;\; \frac{a:A;\;\; b:B}{mk\text{-}D(a,b):D}\;\;\text{Ax} \qquad\qquad \boxed{mk\text{-}D\text{-defn}}\;\; \frac{d:D}{mk\text{-}D(d.a,d.b) = d}\;\;\text{Ax}$$

---

[3]The axioms are slightly different in the presence of an invariant.

Other constructs of arbitrary length can be dealt with in a similar way. For example, simple case statements can be translated to nested conditionals (if..then..else expressions).

Related problems arise when interpreting the VDM-SL μ operator, which modifies some field(s) of an element of a composite type. For example, given the type definition:

$$D :: a : A$$
$$b : B$$
$$c : C$$

inv $mk\text{-}D(a, b, c) \triangleq P(a, b, c)$

the expression $\mu(d, a \mapsto e_1, b \mapsto e_2)$, where $d : D$, corresponds to $mk\text{-}D(e_1, e_2, d.c)$, provided this value satisfies the invariant on D. For example, if both A and B are the natural numbers N and the invariant on D requires that $a < b$ then the expression $\mu(d, b \mapsto 2)$ is not of type D if $d.a \geq 2$.

There are a number of ways one might interpret the μ expression in our logical framework. To begin with, one might attempt to use a μ in the logical framework, with a defining axiom of the following form:

$$\frac{d : D;\ mk\text{-}D(e_1, e_2, d.c) : D}{\mu(d, a \mapsto e_1, b \mapsto e_2) = mk\text{-}D(e_1, e_2, d.c)} \text{Ax}$$

However, this only describes μ on the type D and only deals with modifications to the a and b components thereof. A completely general rule would have to be parameterised over a general composite type and its selectors, requiring a variable number of arguments to μ and some formalisation of the notion of being a selector function of a composite type. One way of avoiding this would be to define a different μ operator for each composite type and for each possible combination of the fields which are to be modified. In the example above, this would lead to the expression $\mu(d, a \mapsto e_1, b \mapsto e_2)$ translating to $\mu_{D,ab}(d, e_1, e_2)$ with $\mu_{D,ab}$, a 3-ary operator, defined via the following axiom:

$$\frac{d : D;\ mk\text{-}D(e_1, e_2, d.c) : D}{\mu_{D,ab}(d, e_1, e_2) = mk\text{-}D(e_1, e_2, d.c)} \text{Ax}$$

Other expressions in which the μ operator was applied to different fields of the type D would be treated similarly, with each different combination of fields yielding a new μ symbol and a corresponding defining axiom. For example, the expression $\mu(d, c \mapsto e_1)$ would translate to an expression using a symbol $\mu_{D,c}$ with defining axiom:

$$\frac{d : D;\ mk\text{-}D(d.a, d.b, e_1) : D}{\mu_{D,c}(d, e_1) = mk\text{-}D(d.a, d.b, e_1)} \text{Ax}$$

Note that this translation requires information which would have to be obtained from static checking of the specification: the type of d and the names of the selectors. An alternative approach, also needing information from static checking, might be to translate $\mu(d, a \mapsto e_1, b \mapsto e_2)$ to $mk\text{-}D(e_1, e_2, d.c)$ directly and make it a proof obligation to show that this satisfies the invariant, although in this case results derived about the expression cannot be regarded as valid until the obligation has been discharged.

The μ example illustrates a range of possible approaches to the axiomatisation of a single language construct. Which approach we will use in our current work has not yet been firmly decided.

4.2 Representation of VDM Concepts

Some VDM concepts (e.g. strong typing, weak equality, finiteness of comprehension expressions, flatness and looseness in expressions) result in complications to the proof theory. We discuss these examples here.

4.2.1 Typing, Polymorphism and Weak Equality

In the axiomatisation of equality given above in Section 3.1, the rule 'δ-=-I ' states that equality between any two elements of a type is either true or false. On its own, this does not give sufficient information to determine which of the alternatives is true for specific elements of a specific type. That additional information must come from equality axiom(s) for the specific type in question. Thus, for example, the equality axiom '=-set-defn ' for set theory given above in Section 3.2 permits us to deduce that the empty set and an arbitrary singleton set are in fact *different*, that is that, for arbitrary (denoting) a:

$$\{\,\} \neq \{a\}$$

However, this axiom requires both arguments to have the same type just as the equality rule 'δ-=-I ' does, so it would seem that there is no provision for comparing elements of different types. This is not entirely the case, in fact, as it is possible to use the notion of a union type to prove a more general form of the rule 'δ-=-I ' in which the expressions on either side of the equality are of different types:

$$\boxed{\delta\text{-=-I-gen}} \quad \frac{a\!:\!A; \;\; b\!:\!B}{\delta(a = b)}$$

The union type $A \mid B$ is the non-disjoint union of the types A and B, defined via the following axioms:

$$\boxed{\text{|-I-left}} \quad \frac{b\!:\!B}{b\!:\!(A \mid B)} \;\text{Ax} \qquad\qquad \begin{array}{c} u\!:\!(A \mid B) \\ a\!:\!A \vdash_a P(a) \end{array}$$

$$\boxed{\text{|-I-right}} \quad \frac{a\!:\!A}{a\!:\!(A \mid B)} \;\text{Ax} \qquad \boxed{\text{|-E}} \quad \frac{b\!:\!B \vdash_b P(b)}{P(u)} \;\text{Ax}$$

The introduction rules above can be used to "extend" each of the types A and B to a common supertype $(A \mid B)$, allowing the application of the like-type rule 'δ-=-I '. The proof of 'δ-=-I-gen ' is therefore:

$$
\begin{array}{lll}
\text{from } a\!:\!A; \; b\!:\!B & & \\
1 \qquad a\!:\!(A \mid B) & & \text{|-I-right (h1)} \\
2 \qquad b\!:\!(A \mid B) & & \text{|-I-left (h2)} \\
\text{infer } \delta(a = b) & & \delta\text{-=-I (1, 2)}
\end{array}
$$

The rule 'δ-=-I-gen ' thus allows us to deduce that two elements of arbitrary types are either equal or unequal, but as in the like-type case provides no means of deciding which. Again, this extra information would have to be embodied in additional axioms relating elements of different specific types explicitly. Without these extra axioms the most we can say about an expression like

$$7 = \text{true}$$

which compares values of disjoint types (in this example the booleans $\mathbb{B}$ and the natural numbers $\mathbb{N}$) is that it is either true or false, even though the first of these possibilities would seem to be ludicrous.

There are a couple of ways we might add these extra axioms. One is to simply give a series of axioms like:

$$\frac{a\colon \mathbb{B};\ b\colon \mathbb{R}}{a \neq b}\text{Ax}$$

which assert directly that elements of different specific types are unequal. Alternatively, we could formalise the notion of disjoint types through a predicate *are-disjoint* on types and introduce a more general axiom stating that elements of arbitrary disjoint types are unequal:

$$\frac{a\colon A;\ b\colon B;\ \textit{are-disjoint}(A,B)}{a \neq b}\text{Ax}$$

together with a collection of axioms defining which types are disjoint, for instance:

$$\frac{}{\textit{are-disjoint}(\mathbb{B},\mathbb{R})}\text{Ax}$$

The problem with both these solutions, however, is that they rapidly get out of hand, as not only do we require "disjoint-types" axioms for all the basic types, we also need them for the constructed types and for the composite types introduced in specifications. Our experience to date is that such axioms are generally not needed, although they may prove to be important in specifications of abstract syntax.

One consequence of the fact that we can compare values of different types at all, however, is that our notion of equality is polymorphic. This has the advantage that it obviates the need to introduce a new equality symbol for every distinct type, along with rules such as:

$$\frac{a =_A b}{a =_{A|B} b}\text{Ax}$$

relating different equality symbols. The disadvantage is that we cannot have rules such as:

$$\frac{a = b}{a \subseteq b}$$

which relate equality and non-polymorphic operators without additional typing hypotheses to remove the polymorphism (because otherwise we could conclude "$3 \subseteq 3$", for example). There is thus a trade-off between introducing separate versions of operators for each type and no typing hypotheses on rules, or having truly polymorphic operators and introducing typing hypotheses to remove unwanted polymorphism. We have chosen the latter course. While this leads to an abundance of typing hypotheses in our axioms and rules, we expect that machine assistance will be of value in discharging them.

4.2.2   *Finiteness and Definedness in Comprehension Expressions*

As indicated in Section 3.2 above, naïvely writing down formation and membership rules for set comprehension expressions leads to problems which might not be obvious at first sight. This section addresses these problems, which are consequences of the fact that the VDM type constructor "$\_$-set" only describes finite sets. Similar problems arise with other forms of comprehension expression (map comprehension and sequence comprehension) for similar reasons.

Consider the set comprehension expression

$$\{x: A \mid P(x)\}$$

This notionally represents the set of all objects x of type A for which the predicate $P(x)$ is true, and it is therefore tempting to write down the following formation and membership rules to describe it:

$$\frac{}{\{x: A \mid P(x)\}: A\text{-set}} \qquad \frac{a: A}{a \in \{x: A \mid P(x)\} \Leftrightarrow P(a)}$$

There are, however, two potential pitfalls here. The first of these becomes clear by taking the type A to be the natural numbers N and the predicate $P(x)$ to be identically true in the first of these rules (the formation rule). This instantiation yields

$$\frac{}{\{x: N \mid \text{true}\}: N\text{-set}}$$

However, the set comprehension expression then reduces simply to the set of all natural numbers, which is not finite and which is therefore not a set in the VDM sense. This means that we should not be able to deduce that it is of type N-set. This suggests that the above rules require an additional "guard" hypothesis to ensure that the set represented is finite (alternatively that there are only a finite number of elements x satisfying the predicate $P(x)$).

One way of doing this might be to introduce the concept of finiteness directly, say via a predicate *exist-finitely-many*, but this is somewhat clumsy. A neater way of proceeding is to make use of the finiteness of sets and say that there must be some set s which contains all the elements x satisfying $P(x)$. This effectively amounts to showing that the set comprehension expression represents a subset of some other set, of course. The appropriate additional hypothesis has the form:

$$\exists s: A\text{-set} \cdot \forall y: A \cdot P(y) \Rightarrow y \in s$$

Adding this hypothesis to the defining rules is not sufficient to avoid the second, more subtle, pitfall, however. Consider what happens in the membership rule if the defining predicate $P(x)$ becomes undefined at some value, say at b. Assuming that the set comprehension expression does now represent a set, the rule would let us deduce

$$b \in \{x: A \mid P(x)\} \Leftrightarrow P(b)$$

However, it is a consequence of the finiteness of sets that set membership is decidable, i.e. it is possible to prove (by induction and the axioms for *add* given in Section 3.2) the rule:

$$\boxed{\delta\text{-}\in} \; \frac{a: A; \; s: A\text{-set}}{\delta(a \in s)}$$

This tells us that the left-hand side of the above equivalence is either true or false, which means that the right-hand side, namely $P(b)$, must also be either true or false and cannot be undefined as postulated. There is thus an inconsistency in the rules.

The simplest way around this problem is to add another hypothesis to the rules to ensure that the set comprehension expression only represents a set if the predicate is defined everywhere. This takes the form

$$\forall x: A \cdot \delta P(x)$$

and the correct versions of the formation and membership rules are therefore

$$\boxed{\text{those-form}}\ \frac{\begin{array}{c}\forall x{:}\,A\cdot\delta P(x)\\ \exists s{:}\,A\text{-set}\cdot\forall y{:}\,A\cdot P(y)\Rightarrow y\in s\end{array}}{\{x{:}\,A\mid P(x)\}{:}\,A\text{-set}}$$

$$\boxed{\in\text{-those-defn}}\ \frac{\begin{array}{c}a{:}\,A\\ \forall x{:}\,A\cdot\delta P(x)\\ \exists s{:}\,A\text{-set}\cdot\forall y{:}\,A\cdot P(y)\Rightarrow y\in s\end{array}}{a\in\{y{:}\,A\mid P(y)\}\Leftrightarrow P(a)}$$

The consequence of needing these extra hypotheses is that reasoning about set (and map and sequence) comprehension expressions becomes tortuous and long-winded since it must be demonstrated that all such expressions have total defining predicates and only finitely many elements. Some relief of this complexity might be achieved through development of specific proof tactics dealing with finiteness and totality.

4.2.3 Flatness and Type Constructors

Besides the finite map type, VDM provides the type of (possibly infinite) total functions, elements of which are constructed using lambda expressions. Thus the lambda expression

$$\lambda n{:}\,\mathbb{N}\cdot n^2$$

is an element of the function type $\mathbb{N}\to\mathbb{N}$. More generally, the function type $A\to B$ represents all total functions from type A to type B.

It is not difficult to give an axiomatisation of lambda expressions and function types. One possible collection of axioms[4] is as follows:

$$\frac{x{:}\,A\vdash_{\!\!x} P(x){:}\,B}{(\lambda x{:}\,A\cdot P(x)){:}\,A\to B}\text{-Ax}$$

$$\frac{x{:}\,A\vdash_{\!\!x} P(x)=Q(x)}{\lambda x{:}\,A\cdot P(x)=\lambda x{:}\,A\cdot Q(x)}\text{-Ax}$$

$$\frac{a{:}\,A;\ \lambda x{:}\,A\cdot P(x){:}\,A\to B}{(\lambda x{:}\,A\cdot P(x))\cdot(a)=P(a)}\text{-Ax}$$

$$\frac{f{:}\,A\to B}{\lambda x{:}\,A\cdot(f\cdot(x))=f}\text{-Ax}$$

$$\frac{a{:}\,A;\ f{:}\,A\to B}{f\cdot(a){:}\,B}\text{-Ax}$$

where $f\cdot(x)$ represents the result of applying the function f to x. However, a problem arises in that VDM imposes restrictions on how function types can be combined with the other type constructors (sets, maps, union types, etc.). Thus, for example, sets of functions are not allowed, nor is it permitted to construct a map whose domain is a function type.

This problem is addressed in VDM by the introduction of the notion of *flatness* of a type, so that the function type and various combinations of it with the other basic type constructors are considered as *non-flat*. The restrictions on the use of function types then translate into restrictions on the use of non-flat types.

Unfortunately, the ramifications of this approach for the proof theory are severe – most of the formation rules for the basic type constructors (sets, maps, etc.) require

---

[4]It is a moot point whether it is meaningful, or indeed necessary, to reason about the equality of functions (the axioms in the right hand column below).

additional hypotheses restricting the values of certain type parameters to flat types. As an example, the familiar polymorphic formation rule for the empty set ('{ }-form ') given above in Section 3.2 is not valid when A is non-flat, and must therefore be replaced by the rule

$$\frac{is\text{-}flat(A)}{\{\}: A\text{-set}}\text{Ax}$$

where the predicate *is-flat* (not defined here) represents the notion of a flat type.

We could devise an axiomatisation of *is-flat*, based on the VDM definitions of type flatness, modifying all the basic formation rules for the type constructors accordingly. However, although one can envisage some sort of mechanical support for dealing with these "flatness" hypotheses, there is a price in doing so: reasoning about familiar constructs like sets becomes more complicated due to the need to show that the type parameters are flat, and the modified axioms for sets etc. lose their intuitive clarity when flatness is introduced.

One point worth noting in conclusion is that it is *only* function types which make complex types non-flat – any type constructed only out of the other basic VDM type constructors is automatically flat. The simplification of the axiomatisations of the other basic type constructors engendered by the absence of function types caused us to omit them from the treatment in [5].

4.2.4   Loose Specification: Let Expressions

The most familiar form of a let expression is:

let $x = y$ in $P(x)$

which means "The value of the expression $P(x)$ with every occurrence of x replaced by y". We would naturally expect this expression to be shorthand for $P(y)$, though again we need to ensure that the substitution actually produces a meaningful expression. For example, the expression

let $x = n^2 + 1$ in $y \in \text{dom}\, x$

is not a valid use of a let expression as $n^2 + 1$ is not a map, and therefore does not have a domain. The let expression will therefore only make sense if the expression $P(y)$ represents a valid expression. This is ensured by a typing hypothesis, and leads to an axiom describing this form of let statement:

$$\frac{P(y): A}{(\text{let } x = y \text{ in } P(x)) = P(y)}\text{Ax}$$

This kind of let expression is straightforward to describe axiomatically because, if the expression denotes a value at all, that value is uniquely determined. However, VDM also supports the use of a different form of let expression whose value is not necessarily uniquely determined (sometimes said to be "loose"), and its axiomatisation is much more problematic.

This looseness is introduced by allowing x to be defined implicitly by giving a predicate which it satisfies instead of giving an explicit definition. This form of let expression is written

let $x: A$ be s.t. $P(x)$ in $Q(x)$

Here, there is no guarantee in general that there will be only one value of x of the correct type which satisfies the predicate $P(x)$. If there is, as in the expression

let $x: \mathsf{N}$ be s.t. $x^2 - x = 6$ in $Q(x)$

then the meaning of the let expression is clear, assuming in this case that $Q(3)$ is well-formed. But if we wrote instead

let $x: \mathsf{Z}$ be s.t. $x^2 - x = 6$ in $Q(x)$

then it is not so obvious what the value of the let expression should be. Indeed, according to the semantics of VDM one *arbitrarily* chooses some value of x of the given type which satisfies the defining predicate and evaluates $Q(x)$ for this value.

On the basis of this interpretation, one might try to formalise these "loose" let expressions in terms of the Hilbert choice operator ε of predicate logic. Of course such a formulation would need to ensure that at least one value of x satisfying the predicate $P(x)$ should exist and that $Q(x)$ should be well-formed for the particular arbitrary value of x chosen. This suggests an axiom of the form

$$\frac{\exists x: A \cdot P(x); \quad Q(\varepsilon x: A \cdot P(x)): B}{(\text{let } x: A \text{ be s.t. } P(x) \text{ in } Q(x)) = Q(\varepsilon x: A \cdot P(x))}\text{Ax}$$

This approach works because the choice operator is deterministic, that is always returns the same arbitrary value, so that both occurrences in the above rule denote the same value.

Unfortunately, even this is not the whole story! If the same loose let expression occurs in two different places in a specification, each different occurrence can have a different value. This situation is not covered by the above axiomatisation as the fact that the choice operator ε is deterministic guarantees that the same value of x satisfying the defining predicate $P(x)$ will be chosen each time. Thus, the let expression as formalised above will always have the same value.

Getting round this problem is impossible with the machinery available so far. One possible approach might be to try to introduce some sort of non-deterministic choice operator which does not necessarily return the same choice of value every time it occurs, but this just shifts the problem to that of ensuring that certain cases where the evaluation of expressions must be deterministic (for example the result of an auxiliary function) actually are. Another possible solution might be to introduce a "parameterised" let expression which records details of the context from which it originated. This seems a more promising line of approach, but is likely to make the manipulation of let expressions exceedingly cumbersome as a large amount of contextual information would appear to be needed. These issues are addressed in Larsen's research [9].

As a final note, however, it is worth recording that it is easy to describe these loose let expressions when there is a unique value satisfying the predicate. In such a restricted case the defining axiom would use the unique existential quantifier $\exists!$ as a guard hypothesis and the unique choice operator ι to select the unique value satisfying the predicate. The appropriate axiom would have the form

$$\frac{\exists! \, x: A \cdot P(x); \quad Q(\iota x: A \cdot P(x)): B}{(\text{let } x: A \text{ be s.t. } P(x) \text{ in } Q(x)) = Q(\iota x: A \cdot P(x))}\text{Ax}$$

5   Conclusions

It is impossible in a short paper to give the full details of our axiomatisation of the logic and data types used in VDM (for full details see [5]). We have instead sought to give a flavour of this by describing the theories of predicate LPF and finite sets. More importantly, we have sought to consider the choices and trade-offs made in the axiomatisation.

A number of aspects of the specification language are problematic in the sense that they have unfortunate consequences for practical proof. Examples here are type flatness and finiteness. In both these cases we had to add extra hypotheses to rules, and these hypotheses must be discharged when the rules are used in proofs. In the case of the flatness hypotheses, the comparative simplicity of the rules governing flatness in VDM-SL means that static checks (implementing the static semantics) on a specification could effectively produce axioms stating the flatness or otherwise of constructed types. A similar process may also alleviate the drudgery of discharging typing hypotheses, though such machine support could not deal with all typing hypotheses because of the arbitrary complexity of data type invariants in VDM. We also expect that discharging the finiteness hypotheses in the comprehension rules will not be particularly susceptible to machine support.

Our axiomatisation covers the logic and the main data types of VDM, but some areas and details remain unexplored. We have only a limited axiomatisation of natural numbers (in terms of zero and the successor function) and have not yet considered real numbers. We have not provided support for the language of VDM *statements*, allowing for relational composition of operation applications, nor have we considered VDM-SL patterns. A number of these areas will be addressed in work following on from the model-based semantics of the standard language VDM-SL.

We have concentrated in this paper on the *difficulties* encountered in our axiomatisation. It would be wrong to ascribe all of these to VDM-SL. Some, such as the inability to represent composite types directly, are primarily limitations of the logical framework. An interesting subject for further work is to determine more precisely which problems are due to the framework and which are due to the specification language.

A consideration of the proof-theoretic semantics of a specification language raises a number of issues which do not necessarily come out of a consideration of the model-based semantics. In particular, constructs which are comparatively easily described in terms of their models may prove to be unintuitive to axiomatise, or result in a surprisingly heavy burden on the prover. We would argue that the complexity of proof is an important factor to be taken into consideration when designing language semantics, especially if we are to increase the use of rigorous or formal argument in practical systems development.

Acknowledgements: We are grateful to our colleagues working on the VDM axiomatisation for many long and detailed discussions on the issues mentioned in this paper: Peter Lindsay, Brian Ritchie, Juan Bicarregui and Peter Gorm Larsen. Thanks also to Peter Gorm Larsen and Stephen Paynter for influential review comments, and to Cliff Jones who has, as always, offered helpful advice and encouragement. JSF acknowledges the support of British Aerospace.

References

[1] C. B. Jones. *Systematic Software Development Using VDM*. Prentice-Hall, second edition, 1990.

[2] C. B. Jones, K. D. Jones, P. A. Lindsay, and R. Moore. *mural: A Formal Development Support System*. Springer-Verlag, 1991.

[3] H. Barringer, J. H. Cheng, and C. B. Jones. A Logic Covering Undefinedness in Program Proofs. *Acta Informatica*, 21:251–269, 1984.

[4] J. H. Cheng. A Logic for Partial Functions (PhD Thesis). Technical Report UMCS-86-7-1, Dept of Computer Science, University of Manchester, January 1986.

[5] J. C. Bicarregui, J. S. Fitzgerald, P. A. Lindsay, R. Moore, and B. Ritchie. *Proof in VDM: A Practitioner's Guide*. FACIT Series. Springer-Verlag, 1993. To appear.

[6] J. C. Bicarregui and B. Ritchie. Reasoning about VDM Developments using the VDM Support Tool in Mural. In S. Prehn and W. J. Toetenel, editors, *Proceedings of VDM'91 Symposium, Delft 1991*, volume 551 of *Lecture Notes in Computer Science*, pages 371–388. Springer-Verlag, 1991.

[7] C. B. Jones and C. A. Middelburg. A Typed Logic of Partial Functions Reconstructed Classically . Technical Report Logic Group Preprint Series No. 89, Dept. of Philosophy, University of Utrecht, The Netherlands, April 1993.

[8] British Standards Institute, Working Group IST/5/19. *VDM Specification Language Proto-Standard*, 1992. Document 246 B, 1 December, 1992.

[9] Peter Gorm Larsen. Towards Proof Rules for Looseness in Explicit Definitions from VDM-SL. March 1993.

Towards Proof Rules for Looseness in Explicit Definitions from VDM-SL

Peter Gorm Larsen

The Institute of Applied Computer Science

Forskerparken 10

DK – 5230 Odense M

Denmark

Abstract

The model-oriented formal method called VDM contains a specification language called VDM-SL. This language existed in a number of different dialects, but now a standard for the language has been prepared, including a dynamic semantics defined from a model-theoretic point of view. Thus, it is not at all clear that the defined semantics is appropriate for deriving proof rules which reflect the semantics. This paper focus on the possible ways of defining proof rules which reflect the semantics of explicit definitions which contain looseness.

The model-theoretic view which has been chosen for the definition of the semantics for VDM-SL, incorporates looseness by denoting the semantics of a (loose) specification as a set of models. The proof system should be designed such that properties which can be proved about a given specification should hold for all its models. This paper shows why it is an interesting challenge to develop a proof system which are able to do this.

1 Introduction

Formal specification languages have properties not usually found in programming languages. One of these is the possibility of specifying constructs that denote a choice. Such 'loose specification' arises because a specification generally needs to be stated at a higher level of abstraction than that of the final implementation. When loose specification is used, the question of how to interpret this looseness is often ignored. However, this interpretation is important, especially if a specification is to be proven to implement another specification. The implementation relation relies on the interpretation of looseness. Thus, this interpretation is especially interesting in connection with the proof rules for the specification language. However, the implementation relation and the proof rules have not yet been formulated for the entire standard VDM-SL language.

Work on the provision of a basic proof theory for reasoning about specifications and developments in VDM has been done by researchers in the UK and Australia (to appear in [Bicarregui&93] and in [Fitzgerald&93]). The extension of this to give a proof theory for the full standard language VDM-SL is an area of the author's research. This paper will focus on one aspect: proof rules for explicit definitions.

It is natural that implicit function and operation definitions can contain looseness. However, in VDM-SL it is also possible to let explicit function and operation definitions be loosely specified (see e.g. [Larsen&89], and [Larsen92]). In some other specification languages, e.g. VVSL [Middelburg90], this is disallowed. It is a matter of taste whether one wishes to include such a style of specification in a language. However, we think that it is important to investigate the consequences of such a decision in the proof rules. In RSL [RAISE94], looseness in explicit definitions is interpreted as nondeterminism and not as underdetermined which is done inside functions in VDM-SL[1]. Underdeterminedness can be obtained by means of axioms in RSL, but these simply correspond to a more general form of implicit definitions than the pre-post style used in VDM-SL. Thus, the problems dealt with in this paper does not appear in RSL. This kind of looseness is also avoided in Z [Hayes93].

To sum up, we can say that, since explicit expressions in VDM-SL can be loose, we need to investigate how this can be reflected in the proof rules for VDM-SL. In this paper we will present different ways of treating such looseness and indicate their limitations. Prior to presenting the different possible approaches we explain the semantics which have been chosen for looseness in VDM-SL.

2 The Semantics of Looseness in VDM-SL

There are (at least) two different ways of interpreting loose specification. In VDM-SL we have termed these: 'underdeterminedness'[2] (allowing several different deterministic implementations) and 'nondeterminism' (allowing non-deterministic implementations). The difference between the two lies in the time at which the looseness is resolved. If a loosely specified construct is interpreted as underdetermined, it is decided by the implementer at implementation time which functionality to use. Since this choice is static the final implementation becomes deterministic. However, if a loosely specified construct is interpreted as nondeterministic, it is possible to delay this choice until execution time. In this way the actual functionality is chosen dynamically at run-time. This means that the final implementation may be nondeterministic. Ideally, a specifier would like to be able to choose freely between these different interpretations for all functions and operations.

In VDM-SL we have chosen to interpret function definitions as underdetermined, while operation definitions are interpreted as nondeterministic[3]. The difference between functions and operations is that operations may operate on a (specified) state space, while functions may not refer to the state. Thus, functions are applicative while operations may be imperative. Both expressions and pattern matchings can be loosely specified in VDM-SL. Thus, when there is looseness in an expression or a pattern, its interpretation depends upon whether it is used inside a function or an operation.

Concerning the proof rules, clearly the underdetermined interpretation gives rise to most problems, because two loose expression can be proved to be equal

---

[1] The distinction between these is further described in Section 2.

[2] In the literature 'underdeterminedness' has also been called 'under-specification'.

[3] The complexity of the semantics with an arbitrary combination of loose specification is given in [Wieth89].

under certain conditions. Two loose expressions which are interpreted in a nondeterministic way can never be proved to be equal. Thus, the proof rules we will derive in the remaining part of this paper will reflect the underdetermined semantics of looseness to illustrate how the hardest problem can be dealt with.

3 The naïve approach

In [Jones&91],p.267 a naïve approach for treating proof rules for looseness in expressions is presented. A general let-be-such-that expression like:

let $x : A$ be st $P(x)$ in $E(x)$

can contain looseness, because $P(x)$ does not necessarily restrict x to be a unique element from A. When such an expression is used in a specification it can be translated into:

$$\boxed{\text{letbe-def}_1} \frac{\exists\, x : A \cdot P(x)}{(\text{let } x : A \text{ be st } P(x) \text{ in } E(x)) = E(\varepsilon x : A \cdot P(x))}$$

Here the usual choice operator from first order logic is used. In [Jones&91] two extra axioms are defined for the choice operator:

$$\boxed{\varepsilon\text{-def}} \frac{\exists\, x : A \cdot P(x)}{P(\varepsilon x : A \cdot P(x))}$$

$$\boxed{\varepsilon\text{-form}} \frac{\exists\, x : A \cdot P(x)}{\varepsilon x : A \cdot P(x) : A}$$

As a consequence of the "ε-form" and the "=-self-I" rule[4] the following can be proved:.

$$\boxed{\varepsilon\text{-deterministic}} \frac{\exists\, x : A \cdot P(x)}{\varepsilon x : A \cdot P(x) = \varepsilon x : A \cdot P(x)}$$

However, if for example two functions f and g are defined with the same loose expression, models will exist where they yield different results. Let us consider a simple example which can be used to illustrate this[5]:

$f : () \rightarrow \mathbb{N}$

$f() \triangleq$
    let $x : \mathbb{N}$ be st $x \in \{1, 2\}$ in x

---

[4] $\boxed{\text{=-self-I}} \dfrac{a : A}{a = a}$

[5] These two functions can be slightly more elegantly described in VDM-SL by using the "be-such-that" expression as a set binding (and then not having a type binding at all). However, at this point we abstract away from this because the let-be-such-that expressions used in [Jones&91] always are typed in this way.

$g : () \rightarrow \mathbb{N}$

$g\,() \triangleq$
  let $x : \mathbb{N}$ be st $x \in \{1, 2\}$ in x

With the three proof rules defined above and a rule for function unfolding it is possible to derive for instance that $f() = g()$ which do not hold in all models. Thus, this model can describe looseness appropriately for one function alone, but cannot deal with combinations of loose functions.

4 Tagging with static context information

To repair an example like the one mentioned in the previous section, one can consider tagging the choice expression with the origin of the expression which contains the looseness. In this way it cannot be derived that $f() = g()$. However, it is not sufficient simply to tag an expression with the name of the function in which it is used, because the same syntactic expression can be used several times and it may not denote the same value in all models[6]. Thus, for each expression in a VDM-SL specification a unique identification must be present and used for tagging the corresponding choice expression.

The "letbe-def$_1$" rule above would now look something like:

$$\text{letbe-def}_2 \quad \frac{\exists x : A \cdot P(x)}{(\text{let } x : A \text{ be st } P(x) \text{ in } E(e))_{\mathcal{POS}} = E(\varepsilon x : A \cdot P(x)_{\mathcal{POS}})}$$

where $\mathcal{POS}$ indicates the position of the let-be-such-that expression in the concrete specification. Since the position of the body of the example functions f and g are different, it will neither be possible to prove that $f() = g()$ or $f() \neq g()$. This corresponds to the standard semantics because neither of these propositions holds in all models. However, if we modify f slightly we get another problem:

$f' : \mathbb{B} \rightarrow \mathbb{N}$

$f'\,(b) \triangleq$
  let $x : \mathbb{N}$ be st $x \in \{1, 2\}$ in x

Even though that the argument b is not used in the body of the function it will not hold in all models that $f'(\text{true}) = f'(\text{false})$[7], but this can be proved with the "letbe-def$_2$" rule defined above. Thus, this approach can deal with combinations of parameterless loose functions, but it cannot correctly cope with loose functions which have parameters.

---

[6]An example of this could be an expression like: (let $x : \mathbb{N}$ be st $x \in \{1, 2\}$ in x) + (let $x : \mathbb{N}$ be st $x \in \{1, 2\}$ in x) which also has a model where it denotes 3.

[7]Two of the models will map true and false to the same value (either 1 or 2) while the two other models will map true and false to different values.

5   Tagging with dynamic context information

To repair the problems with simply using static context information, one can add the dynamic dependencies, i.e. the parameters of the function in which the expression occur.

The "letbe-def$_2$" rule above would now look something like:

$$\text{letbe-def}_3 \quad \frac{\exists x : A \cdot P(x)}{(\text{let } x : A \text{ be st } P(x) \text{ in } E(e))_{(\mathcal{POS},[\text{args}])} = E(\varepsilon x : A \cdot P(x)_{(\mathcal{POS},[\text{args}])})}$$

With this rule one will neither be able to prove $f'(\text{true}) = f'(\text{false})$ nor $f'(\text{true}) \neq f'(\text{false})$ which is correct because they do not hold in all models.

Thus, this approach can deal with combinations of arbitrary loose functions which have parameters. Therefore, one can now try to investigate how proof rules can be derived for the most general expressions with arbitrary patterns. This will be presented in the form of skeletons which can be used as a basis for an automatic translation for each component of a given specification to its corresponding proof rules.

5.1   General rules for loose values

However, before we look at this, we first present three other rules for ε values which are more directly applicable than the "ε-def" and "ε-form" rules above[8]:

$$\varepsilon\text{-I} \quad \frac{\forall e : A \cdot (P(e) \Rightarrow Q(e)), \exists e : A \cdot P(e)}{Q(\varepsilon x : A \cdot P(x)_{\text{any tagging}})}$$

$$\varepsilon\text{-E} \quad \frac{a : A, P(a), \exists! x : A \cdot P(x)}{(\varepsilon x : A \cdot P(x)_{\text{any tagging}}) = a}$$

$$\varepsilon\text{-difference} \quad \frac{\exists x : A \cdot P(x), \exists x : A \cdot Q(x), \neg \exists x : A \cdot P(x) \wedge Q(x)}{\varepsilon x : A \cdot P(x)_{Tag_1} \neq \varepsilon x : A \cdot Q(x)_{Tag_2}}$$

The first of these rules simply says that if some property, Q, holds for all elements in the loose value, the property will also hold for the loose value[9]. The second rule says that if the loose value has only one possible value, then that is going to be the value of the choice expression. Finally the third rule says that if two choice values have disjoint predicates these choice values will be different in all models.

---

[8]In [Fitzgerald93] it is shown that these rules follow from a version of the "ε-def" and the ε-form" which are extended with tags

[9]The existential quantification assumption is needed because a loose value must at least have one possibility to choose from.

These rules can be formulated slightly more elegantly by using a set notation (allowing infinite sets[10]) instead:

$$\varepsilon\text{-I} \quad \frac{\forall e \in s \cdot (P(e) \;\Rightarrow\; Q(e)), \exists e : A \cdot P(e)}{Q(\varepsilon x \in \{e \mid e \in s \cdot P(x)\}_{\text{any tagging}})}$$

$$\varepsilon\text{-E} \quad \frac{a : A}{(\varepsilon x \in \{a\}_{\text{any tagging}}) = a}$$

$$\varepsilon\text{-difference} \quad \frac{s_1 \cap s_2 = \{\,\}}{(\varepsilon id_1 \in s_1)_{Tag_1} \neq (\varepsilon id_2 \in s_2)_{Tag_2}}$$

Instead of a type and a predicate we have here used a set notation because the predicate simply is used to create a subtype of the given type. The main advantage is that the notation from set theory simplify the appearance[11] of the assumptions in both the "ε-E" rule and the "ε-difference" rule.

Below we will use the set notation consequently[12].

5.2 Let expressions

Let us now consider a specification which contains an ordinary let expression with a general pattern (which can be loose):

let $pat = defexpr$ in $inexpr$

then one can produce a proof rule following a skeleton like:

$$\text{let-def} \quad \frac{\exists \text{patids} : \text{types inferred} \cdot pat' = defexpr}{\begin{array}{c}(\text{let } pat = defexpr \text{ in } inexpr)_{(\mathcal{POS},[args])} = \\ \varepsilon id \in \{inexpr \mid \text{patids} : \text{types inferred} \cdot pat' = defexpr\}_{(\mathcal{POS},[args])}\end{array}}$$

where "patids" will be the pattern identifiers which can be extracted from the pattern, pat, and "types inferred" will be the corresponding types which can be inferred from a static semantics analysis[13]. pat' is an expression which in the concrete syntax is identical to the pattern pat except that possible "don't care" patterns have been replaced with new and unused identifiers (which then

---

[10]In model-theoretic terms this simply correspond to the carrier sets of domains from the domain universe of VDM-SL where an ordering also is present.

[11]The existence of a single value satisfying a given predicate can be expressed as a singleton set.

[12]Alternatively we could have used the subtype notation from [Jones&91] (which we have used so far) or the domain notation from the domain universe.

[13]Here the "possibly well-formedness" (see [Bruun&91]) check will be performed on the $defexpr$ to derive its possible type. This derived type is then used to derive the type of the individual pattern identifiers which is inferred to be used here. Here it is important to make sure that the inferred types are sufficiently fine-grained, such that $defexpr$ is defined for all possible values from the inferred types.

also are used in the list of pattern identifiers in the existential quantification). Notice that under "normal" circumstances, i.e. where *pat* is not a loose pattern (contains neither a set union pattern nor a sequence concatenation pattern) this choice value can be reduced by the ε-E rule right away.

A simple example

Let us take a simple example which can be used to illustrate the let-def skeleton:

$$h : (\mathbb{N} \times \mathbb{N}) \rightarrow \mathbb{N}$$
$$h \, (pair) \; \underline{\triangle}$$
$$\quad \text{let } mk\text{-}(n, m) = pair \text{ in } n + m$$

would give rise to a proof rule like:

$$\boxed{\text{let-def(h)}_1} \; \frac{\exists \, n : \mathbb{N}, m : \mathbb{N} \cdot mk\text{-}(n, m) = pair}{(\text{let } mk\text{-}(n, m) = pair \text{ in } n + m)_{(\mathcal{POS},[pair])} = \varepsilon id \in \{n + m \mid n : \mathbb{N}, m : \mathbb{N} \cdot mk\text{-}(n, m) = pair\}_{(\mathcal{POS},[pair])}}$$

where the loose value can be reduced because it only contains a set comprehension expression which is simply a singleton set.

Below we present an example of a proof which uses this proof rule:

```
from n' : N, m' : N
1     n' + m' : N                                                            add-lem(h)
2     mk-(n', m') : (N × N)                                            two-tuple-form(h)
3     ∃ n : N, m : N · mk-(n, m) = mk-(n', m')                      ∃-equal-lem(h)
4     h(mk-(n', m')) = (let mk-(n, m) = mk-(n', m') in n + m)_(POS,[mk-(n',m')])h-defn₁(2)
5=4   εid ∈ {n + m | n : N, m : N · mk-(n, m) = mk-(n', m')}_(POS,[mk-(n',m')])
                                                                      let-def(h)₁(3,4)
6=4   ε ∈ {n' + m'}                                                setcomp-sin-lem(5=4)
infer h(mk-(n', m')) = n' + m'                                        ε-E(1,6=4)
```

Notice that the proof is displayed in the 'natural deduction' style except that a simplification resembling [Dijkstra&90] is used. The simplification we have used is that when a justified expression is an equality and one wish to rewrite the right-hand-side of it this can be done by adding an equal sign and a line number (where the equality come from) and then simply write the new right-hand-side. This simplification is very handy when the *lhs* and/or the *rhs* become large.

In the proof above the following extra rules and lemmas are used:

$$\boxed{\text{add-lem}} \; \frac{a : \mathbb{N}, b : \mathbb{N}}{a + b : \mathbb{N}}$$

This lemma simply says that adding two natural numbers give a new natural number.

$$\boxed{\text{two-tuple-form}} \quad \frac{a : A, b : B}{mk\text{-}(a, b) : (A \times B)}$$

This rule is simply a formation rule for two-tuples.

$$\boxed{\exists\text{-equal-lem}} \quad \frac{a : A, b : B}{\exists\, mk\text{-}(x, y) : (A \times B) \cdot mk\text{-}(a, b) = mk\text{-}(x, y)}$$

This lemma explains that knowledge about existence of two specific values can be used to introduce an existential quantification with equality.

$$\boxed{\text{h-defn}_1} \quad \frac{pair : (\mathbb{N} \times \mathbb{N})}{h(pair) = (\text{let } mk\text{-}(n, m) = pair \text{ in } n + m)_{(\mathcal{POS},[pair])}}$$

This rule corresponds to the translation for the explicit function definition for h.

$$\boxed{\text{setcomp-sin-lem}} \quad \frac{a : A, b : B, f(a, b) : C}{\{f(a', b') \mid a' : A, b' : B \cdot a = a' \wedge b = b'\} = \{f(a, b)\}}$$

This lemma simply says that a set comprehension which uniquely describes the member value by equality is a singleton set.

To prove the lemmas we appeal to the basic theories of LPF, type constructors and basic types.

A more complicated example

Let us now take a more complicated example which can be used to illustrate the let-def skeleton:

$$h : \mathbb{N}^+ \to \mathbb{N}^*$$
$$h\,(l) \stackrel{\triangle}{=}$$
$$\text{let } l' \frown [\text{-}] \frown l'' = l \text{ in } l'' \frown l'$$

This function removes an arbitrary element from a finite non-empty sequence of natural numbers and shift the preceding and succeeding sequences around. It would give rise to a proof rule like:

$$\boxed{\text{let-def(h)}_2} \quad \frac{\exists\, l' : \mathbb{N}^*, l'' : \mathbb{N}^*, id : \mathbb{N} \cdot l' \frown [id] \frown l'' = l}{\begin{array}{c} (\text{let } l' \frown [\text{-}] \frown l'' = l \text{ in } l'' \frown l')_{(\mathcal{POS},[l])} = \\ \varepsilon id \in \{l'' \frown l' \mid l' : \mathbb{N}^*, l'' : \mathbb{N}^*, id : \mathbb{N} \cdot l' \frown [id] \frown l'' = l\}_{(\mathcal{POS},[l])} \end{array}}$$

where the loose value cannot directly be reduced to a singleton set because looseness is present.
Below we present an example of a proof which uses this proof rule:

from $list : \mathbb{N}^+$

1	$\exists\, l' : \mathbb{N}^*, l'' : \mathbb{N}^*, id : \mathbb{N} \cdot l' \frown [id] \frown l'' = list$	seq-conc-lem(h)
2	$h(list) = (\text{let } l' \frown [\text{-}] \frown l'' = list \text{ in } l'' \frown l')_{(\mathcal{POS},[list])}$	h-defn$_2$(h)
3=2	$\varepsilon id \in \{l'' \frown l' \mid l' : \mathbb{N}^*, l'' : \mathbb{N}^*, id : \mathbb{N} \cdot l' \frown [id] \frown l'' = list\}_{(\mathcal{POS},[list])}$	let-def$_2$(h)(1,2)
4	$\forall l \in \{l'' \frown l' \mid l' : \mathbb{N}^*, l'' : \mathbb{N}^*, id : \mathbb{N} \cdot l' \frown [id] \frown l'' = list\} \cdot$	
	$\quad$ elems $l \subseteq$ elems $list$	elems-conc-lem(h)

infer elems $h(list) \subseteq$ elems $list$ $\qquad\qquad$ ε-I(1,4,3=2)

Where the following extra rules and lemmas are used:

$$\boxed{\text{seq-conc-lem}} \quad \frac{l : A^+}{\exists\, l_1 : A^*, l_2 : A^*, a : A \cdot l_1 \frown [a] \frown l_2 = l}$$

This lemma simply says that if one has a non-empty sequence there exists an element which can be used to split the sequence into two potentially empty sequences (and this element).

$$\boxed{\text{h-defn}_2} \quad \frac{l : \mathbb{N}^+}{h(l) = (\text{let } l' \frown [\text{-}] \frown l'' = l \text{ in } l'' \frown l')_{(\mathcal{POS},[mk\text{-}(n',m')])}}$$

This rule corresponds to the translation for the explicit function definition for h.

$$\boxed{\text{elems-conc-lem}} \quad \frac{list : A^+}{\forall l \in \{l'' \frown l' \mid l' : \mathbb{N}^*, l'' : \mathbb{N}^*, id : \mathbb{N} \cdot l' \frown [id] \frown l'' = list\} \cdot}$$
$$\text{elems } l \subseteq \text{elems } list$$

This lemma relies on the intuitive fact that if an element is removed from a sequence, the elements of the new sequence will be a subset of the elements of the original sequence.

The principle which is used in the skeleton for the let-def rule can be applied for other constructs which introduce looseness explicitly. Below we list the corresponding skeletons for let-be-such-that expressions, cases expressions and quantified expressions, where the most general form for patterns are taken into account in all cases.

5.3 Let-be-such-that expressions

Let us now consider a specification which contains a let-be-such-that expression with a general pattern (which can be loose):

let $pat : type$ **be** **st** $predexpr$ **in** $inexpr$

then one can produce a proof rule following a skeleton like:

$$\text{letbe-def} \quad \frac{\exists\, patids : types\ inferred \cdot predexpr}{(\textbf{let } pat : type \textbf{ be st } predexpr \textbf{ in } inexpr)_{(\mathcal{POS},[args])} =}{\varepsilon id \in \{inexpr \mid patids : types\ inferred \cdot predexpr\}_{(\mathcal{POS},[args])}}$$

where "patids" will be the pattern identifiers which can be extracted from the pattern, *pat*, and "types inferred" will be the corresponding types which can be inferred from a static semantics analysis (here it is worth noticing that if no matching is possible an empty set (or type) will be inferred and thus it will be impossible to satisfy the assumption with the existential quantification).

5.4 Cases expressions

Let us now consider a specification which contains a cases expression with general patterns (which can be loose):

```
cases match :
    pat₁ → expr₁,
    pat₂ → expr₂,
    ... → ...,
    patₙ → exprₙ
end
```

Notice that the last pattern, pat_n, can be an **others** clause which corresponds semantically to a "don't care"-pattern[14].

Then one can produce two proof rules by means of the two following skeletons:

$$\text{cases-def1} \quad \frac{\exists\, patids_1 : types\ inferred \cdot pat_1' = match}{(\textbf{cases } match : pat_1 \to expr_1, \ldots, pat_n \to expr_n \textbf{ end})_{(\mathcal{POS},[args])} =}{\varepsilon id \in \{expr_1 \mid patids_1 : types\ inferred \cdot pat_1' = match\}_{(\mathcal{POS},[args])}}$$

where "patids₁" will be the pattern identifiers which can be extracted from the pattern, pat_1, and "types inferred" will be the corresponding types which can be inferred from a static semantics analysis. pat_1' is an expression which in the concrete syntax is identically to the pattern pat_1 except that possible "don't care" patterns have been replaced with new and unused identifiers (which then also are used in the list of pattern identifiers in the existential quantification).

$$\text{cases-def2} \quad \frac{\neg\,\exists\, patids_1 : types\ inferred \cdot pat_1' = match, ``1 \neq n"}{(\textbf{cases } match : pat_1 \to expr_1, \ldots, pat_n \to expr_n \textbf{ end })_{(\mathcal{POS},[args])} =}{(\textbf{cases } match : pat_2 \to expr_2, \ldots, pat_n \to expr_n \textbf{ end })_{(\mathcal{POS},[args])}}$$

where "patids₁" will be the pattern identifiers which can be extracted from the pattern, pat_1, and "types inferred" will be the corresponding types which can be inferred from a static semantics analysis. pat_1' is an expression which in the

---

[14] Here it is worth noticing that the semantics of VDM-SL is such that if no **others** clause is present the matching patterns should cover all possible matching values. The cases expression yield bottom for all values which do not match any of the patterns.

concrete syntax is identically to the pattern pat_1 except that possible "don't care" patterns have been replaced with new and unused identifiers (which then also are used in the list of pattern identifiers in the existential quantification). The quoted part with $1 \neq n$ in the hypothesis is simply intended to indicate that there must be more alternatives if this rule is to be applied.

5.5 Quantified expressions

Let us now consider a specification which contains a number of quantified expressions with a general pattern (which can be loose):

> quantifier $pat : type \cdot predexpr$

For such a quantified expression one can use a skeleton like:

$$\text{quantifier-def} \quad \frac{\text{quantifier } patids : \text{type inferred} \cdot predexpr : \mathbb{B}}{(\text{quantifier } pat : type \cdot predexpr)_{(\mathcal{POS},[args])} = (\text{quantifier } patids : \text{type inferred} \cdot predexpr)_{(\mathcal{POS},[args])}}$$

where "patids" will be the pattern identifiers which can be extracted from the pattern, pat, and "types inferred" will be the corresponding types which can be inferred from a static semantics analysis. The quantifier can either be a universal quantifier ($\forall$), a existential quantifier ($\exists$), or a unique existential quantifier ($\exists!$). Here it is worth noting that looseness in patterns in the model theory (potentially) correspond to several models. At first sight this may not correspond to ones intuition but considering the unique existential quantification it becomes clear that this is the most natural solution (see the example in the section about quantifiers in [Larsen92]).

5.6 Combining looseness

Having defined skeletons for expressions which can introduce explicit looseness it becomes interesting to investigate whether it is possible to define proof rules which enables one to combine expressions which contain looseness. Thereby one can achieve a ε-calculus which can be used to manipulate loose values. However, it turns out that there is a problem with creating tags for the new loose values. Below we illustrate how this approach have problems with such combinations.

Let us consider an example where looseness is combined:

> let $a : \mathbb{N}$ be st $a \in \{1, 2\}$ in
> let $b : \mathbb{N}$ be st $b \in \{3, a + 2\}$ in $a + b$

it would be desirable to be able to reduce such an expression to a choice value like: $(\varepsilon id \in \{4, 5, 6\})_{(\mathcal{POS},[args])}$ where the looseness has been propagated to the outermost level. However, doing such a propagation requires some way of keeping a record of the choices made underway (e.g. that a may be bound to either 1 or 2). The tagging with dynamic context information cannot cope with this.

In addition, one would like for example to be able to define skeletons for binary operators like:

$$\text{loose-bin-comb1} \frac{\forall\, id \in s \cdot id \text{ binoprt } id : A}{(\varepsilon id \in s)_t \text{ binoprt } (\varepsilon id \in s)_t = (\varepsilon id \in \{e \text{ binoprt } e \mid e \in s\})_t}$$

and

$$\text{loose-bin-comb2} \frac{t_1 \neq t_2, \forall\, id_1 \in s_1, id_2 \in s_2 \cdot id_1 \text{ binoprt } id_2 : A}{\begin{array}{c}(\varepsilon id_1 \in s_1)_{t_1} \text{ binoprt } (\varepsilon id_2 \in s_2)_{t_2} = \\ (\varepsilon id \in \{e_1 \text{ binoprt } e_2 \mid e_1 \in s_1, e_2 \in s_2\})_{Combine(t_1,t_2)}\end{array}}$$

where "binoprt" is an arbitrary binary (infix) operator. The first rule states that if two identical loose values are combined the choice must only be performed once. The second rule express that for two different loose values all possible combinations must be considered in the new loose value.

The problem about rules like these is that one would like to be able to combine the different tags such that the traditional rules from set theory still hold. Consider a small example making use of the definitions of f and g from Section 3:

$$3 \times f() + g()$$

According to the dynamic semantics for VDM-SL this expression may yield 4, 5, 7, or 8 in the different legal models. Notice however that it cannot yield 6. The problem is now to let the tags reflect the chosen model for each of the functions even if the expression is rewritten using traditional rules from set theory forming e.g. $2 \times f() + g() + f()$. This turns out to be impossible unless one focuses on which choices that are made during "evaluation" instead of on the actual result of an expression.

One could also consider letting the *Combine* function (used in "loose-bin-comb2") simply maintaining a set of tags. One could then disallow combining looseness of choice values which had common elements unless both choice values are singleton sets (i.e. choice values which already rely on a combination of the semantics of some construct with another construct). This would save the example above by disallowing the user to combine the result of using traditional rules from set theory. However, this idea also does not work in all cases. Consider an expression like:

$$f() + \text{if } f() = 1 \text{ then } 2 \text{ else } 1$$

In all models this expression denotes 3, but the idea about letting *Combine* maintain a set of tags would indicate that this expression yields either 2 or 4. The problem is that even though the choice value corresponding to the if-then-else expression only rely on $f()$ it is in fact not using the models for $f()$ in its returned value. Thus, we can conclude that examples can be found where even a set of tags is insufficient for *Combine* to become unique.

The approach which tags loose values with dynamic context information can deal with combinations of arbitrary loose functions which have parameters. One can define a number of skeletons which correctly model the semantics for loose

130

expressions. However, it is not suitable for combinations of loose expressions inside the same function. In the next section we will investigate whether an approach which maintains all possible binding environments (and uses these as tags) are more suited to deal with this combination of loose expressions.

6 Maintaining all possible binding environments

The underlying strategy behind this approach is to record all possible bindings in which an expression can be evaluated. When looseness is introduced by either an expression or a pattern it is spread to another expression. In the approaches presented above the value of the expression into which the looseness had spread was "calculated" with the different possible models for the looseness. The idea behind this approach is to keep the expression to which the looseness is spreading, and then additionally record the different possible bindings which the looseness corresponds to. Let us first illustrate this principle on a few examples:

let $a = 3$ in $a + 2$

For a simple example like this one would like to get something like:

$\varepsilon\ a + 2$ with $\{\{a_{(\mathcal{POS},[args])} \mapsto 3\}\}$

where the syntax of the loose values now first take the resulting expression followed by a new keyword, with, which again is followed by a set of possible binding environments (i.e. in this case a singleton set because no looseness is present). Notice that it is the pattern identifier a which is tagged. Let us now consider how it would look with a loose pattern:

let $l' \frown l'' = [1]$ in l'

Here one would would get:

$\varepsilon\ l'$ with $\{\{l'_{(\mathcal{POS},[args])} \mapsto [], l''_{(\mathcal{POS},[args])} \mapsto [1]\},$
$\{l'_{(\mathcal{POS},[args])} \mapsto [1], l''_{(\mathcal{POS},[args])} \mapsto []\}\}$

Let us now consider an example where looseness is combined (we take the example from page 11 again):

let $a : \mathrm{N}$ be st $a \in \{1, 2\}$ in
let $b : \mathrm{N}$ be st $b \in \{3, a + 2\}$ in $a + b$

Here one would first get:

ε let $b : \mathrm{N}$ be st $b \in \{3, a + 2\}$ in $a + b$ with $\{\{a_{(\mathcal{POS}_1,[args])} \mapsto 1\},$
$\{a_{(\mathcal{POS}_1,[args])} \mapsto 2\}\}$

and in the next step one would like to get:

$\varepsilon\ (\varepsilon\ a + b$ with $\{\{b_{(\mathcal{POS}_2,[args])} \mapsto 3\}, \{b_{(\mathcal{POS}_2,[args])} \mapsto a + 2\}\})$ with
$\{\{a_{(\mathcal{POS}_1,[args])} \mapsto 1\}, \{a_{(\mathcal{POS}_1,[args])} \mapsto 2\}\}$

which one would like to be able to reduce to:

$$\varepsilon \ a + b \ \text{with} \ \{\{a_{(\mathcal{POS}_1,[args])} \mapsto 1, b_{(\mathcal{POS}_2,[args])} \mapsto 3\},$$
$$\{a_{(\mathcal{POS}_1,[args])} \mapsto 2, b_{(\mathcal{POS}_2,[args])} \mapsto 3\},$$
$$\{a_{(\mathcal{POS}_1,[args])} \mapsto 2, b_{(\mathcal{POS}_2,[args])} \mapsto 4\}\}$$

This corresponds exactly to the desired result with the previous approach. In the same way this strategy can be used to the other examples of combining looseness which where mentioned in the previous section.

This completes the motivation for being interested in investigating how an approach which maintains all possible bindings is able to deal with looseness in explicit definitions. We will now try to explain how the corresponding proof rules will look and elaborate upon the limitation of this approach.

Let us now consider a specification which contains an ordinary let expression with a general pattern (which can be loose):

let $pat = defexpr$ in $inexpr$

then one can produce a proof rule following a skeleton like:

$$\text{let-def'} \quad \frac{\exists \, patids : \text{types inferred} \cdot pat' = defexpr}{\begin{array}{c}(\text{let } pat = defexpr \text{ in } inexpr)_{(\mathcal{POS},[args])} = \\ \varepsilon inexpr \text{ with } PatternMatch(pat_{(\mathcal{POS},[args])}, defexpr)\end{array}}$$

where *PatternMatch* is a function which given a pattern, *pat*, and an expression, *defexpr*, yields the set of all possible binding environments arising from such a matching, i.e. a set of maps from pattern identifiers (tagged with dynamic information) to their corresponding value. This function will be quite similar to the *EvalPattern* from [Larsen92] and to the *PatternMatch* function from [Lassen&91]. This function must also have access to the environment which currently is in context.

However, as it is visible in [Larsen92] *PatternMatch* may in general yield an infinite set of possible bindings. Thus, if one wanted to support such an approach with a tool it would probably be necessary to restrict its use to an executable subset (like the one used by the IFAD VDM-SL interpreter[15]). One could envisage a looseness analysis tool which given a specification and an arbitrary expression (using constructs from the specification) would yield a set of all possible results which the expression may evaluate to, and under which assumptions (which binding choices) each result is obtained. Possibly one could even let the expression be so general that it simply was symbolically executed. However, as the results of [Kneuper89] also show it is very difficult to reduce the produced symbolic expressions.

7 Turning an explicit definition into an implicit one

Another approach which one also might attempt is to transform an explicit definition into an implicit one which is semantically equivalent. The advantage

---

[15]See [Larsen&91], or [Lassen93].

about the implicit function definitions is that it simply describes the intended relationship between input and output. Thus, when looseness is present it will not be possible to say explicitly what the output will be, but simply what it will fulfill. The problem with looseness in explicitly definitions is exactly that such definitions in an explicitly manner yield a result and that such explicit loose definitions can be directly combined.

However, this is not always possible, because explicitly defined functions in VDM-SL are given a least fixed point semantics while implicitly defined functions are given an all fixed point semantics treating the definition as a kind of equation[16]. In this section we will try to indicate under which restrictions this idea can be used.

For total first order functions (which do not take other functions as arguments or returns other functions) the least fixed point is the only fixed point and thereby all such explicitly defined functions can be turned into an equivalent implicit function. However, partial functions (which may return bottom even for domain values which satisfy the pre-condition) cannot be transformed to an implicit equivalents. Implicitly defined functions cannot return bottom when the pre-condition is satisfied. Higher order explicitly defined total functions could in principle be turned into an implicit equivalent. However, this requires that the argument (or result) functions are total as well. Otherwise, the least fixed point is not the only fixed point.

8 Concluding Remarks

Looseness in explicit definitions has not previously been given a systematic and formal treatment in the form of proof rules reflecting the intended semantics. Thus, this is what we consider the main result of the work reported in this paper. Unfortunately, this research indicates that all the approaches have limitations (in particular if one wishes to provide tool support for it). However, even with these limitations we believe that the proof rules presented here is a step forward in obtaining proof rules for full VDM-SL.

We think that the proof rule skeletons shown in this paper are very complex in order to reflect the semantics of VDM-SL. However, we also believe that the extensive amount of tagging can be hidden for a user by a supporting verification tool. Such a tool can be used to keep track of all the tags and in this way ensure that the proof rules only are applied in a consistent way. An expert user should then be allowed to look at the tags during a proof to understand why certain rules cannot be used for a given derived expression. More work will be put into this in the future to investigate the possibilities of making such complicated proof rules usable by tool support.

Acknowledgements

We would like to thank Cliff Jones and Richard Moore for arranging a one-weeks visit to Manchester University in November 1992 where the core ideas of the research reported here was developed. Furthermore we would like to thank

---

[16]Since no functional is present they cannot be treated in a least fixed point manner.

the anonymous referees, Kees de Bruin, Bo Stig Hansen and especially John Fitzgerald for their influencing suggestions to improve this paper.

References

[Bicarregui&93] Juan Bicarregui, John Fitzgerald, Peter Lindsay, Richard Moore and Brian Ritchie. *Proof in VDM: A Practitioner's Guide*. Springer-Verlag, December 1993.

[Bruun&91] Hans Bruun, Flemming Damm and Bo Stig Hansen. An Approach to the Static Semantics of VDM-SL. In *VDM '91: Formal Software Development Methods*, VDM Europe, Springer-Verlag, October 1991.

[Dijkstra&90] Edsger W. Dijkstra, Carel S. Scholten. *Predicate Calculus and Program Semantics*, chapter 4, pages 21–29. Springer-Verlag, 1990.

[Fitzgerald&93] John Fitzgerald and Richard Moore. Experiences in Developing a Proof Theory for VDM Specifications. In *Proceedings of the International Workshop on Semantics of Specification Languages, Utrect, October 1993*, Springer Verlag, 1994. 17 pages.

[Fitzgerald93] John Fitzgerald. *Private Communication*. March 1993.

[Hayes93] Ian Hayes. *Private Communication*. June 1993.

[Jones&91] Cliff Jones, Kevin Jones, Peter Linsay and Richard Moore, editors. *mural: A Formal Development Support System*. Springer-Verlag, 1991. 421 pages.

[Kneuper89] Ralf Kneuper. *Symbolic Execution as a Tool for Validation of Specifications*. PhD thesis, Department of Computer Science, Univeristy of Manchester, 1989. 154 pages. Technical Report Series UMCS-89-7-1.

[Larsen&89] Peter Gorm Larsen, Michael Meincke Arentoft, Brian Monahan and Stephen Bear. Towards a Formal Semantics of The BSI/VDM Specification Language. In Ritter, editor, *Information Processing 89*, pages 95–100, IFIP, North-Holland, 1989.

[Larsen&91] Peter Gorm Larsen and Poul Bøgh Lassen. An Executable Subset of Meta-IV with Loose Specification. In *VDM '91: Formal Software Development Methods*, VDM Europe, Springer-Verlag, October 1991.

[Larsen92] Peter Gorm Larsen. *The Dynamic Semantics of the VDM Specification Language*. Technical Report, The Institute of Applied Computer Science, July 1992. 177 pages.

[Lassen&91] Poul Bøgh Lassen, Kees de Bruin and Peter Gorm Larsen. *The Dynamic Semantics of IFAD VDM-SL*. June 1993. Internal document (IFAD)

[Lassen93] Poul Bøgh Lassen. IFAD VDM-SL Toolbox. In J.C.P. Woodcock and P.G. Larsen, editors, *FME'93: Industrial-Strength Formal Methods*, page 681, Springer-Verlag, Berlin Heidelberg, April 1993. 1 page.

[**Middelburg90**] Kees Middelburg. *Syntax and Semantics of VVSL – A Language for Structured VDM Specifications*. PhD thesis, University of Amsterdam, 1989. 395 pages.

[**RAISE94**] Chris George and Søren Prehn. *The RAISE Justification Handbook*. *The BCS Practitioners Series*, To be published by Prentice-Hall, 1994. 205 pages.

[**Wieth89**] Morten Wieth. Loose Specification and its Semantics. In G.X. Ritter, editor, *Information Processing 89*, pages 1115–1120, IFIP, North-Holland, August 1989.

Loose Real-Time Communicating Agents

Hans Toetenel

Faculty of Technical Mathematics and Informatics
Delft University of Technology
Delft, The Netherlands

Abstract

This paper presents an overview of the semantics of MOSCA, a combination of VDM-SL, a synchronization language based on the CCS primitives and constructions to capture time-dependent behaviour. The paper suggests a practical *application* of semantic theories in combining two different semantic approaches in the area of specification languages: denotational semantics and structured operational semantics. The paper highlights in particular the interpretation of looseness of the VDM-SL semantics in the operational semantics of MOSCA. It is assumed that the reader is aquainted with both VDM-SL and CCS.

1 Introduction and Overview

MOSCA[1] ([17], [19], [18]) is an experimental specification language extending the Vienna Development Method specification language VDM-SL [2] ([5], [11]) in order to increase the applicability of the language in the area of distributed, parallel and real-time systems. VDM-SL alone is not adequate for these application area's since it lacks facilities to specify multiple treads of control while furthermore, it does not support the notion of time within specifications. The MOSCA specification language builds on VDM-SL and CCS [14]. The model-oriented specification language of VDM is embedded within MOSCA by acting as the process algebra's value manipulation language. The combination is further extended with capabilities to describe *time dependant behaviour*.

This paper presents a semantics that offers data-manipulating communicating processes which incorporates looseness and timing facilities. Section 2 summarizes the syntax of the notation.

A behaviour expression is not equivalent to a data manipulating expression with respect to its denotation. Data manipulating expressions denote numerical values, which e.g. result from a numerical computation, by evaluating the expression according to a fixed set of rules. The meaning of data manipulating expressions in MOSCA is fixed by a denotational semantics.

Behaviour expressions cannot be said to denote a numerical value that can be *computed* according to a set of rules. One particular semantic approach takes the view that a behaviour expression denotes a *state* from which possible

---

[1] MOSCA is an acronym for *Model-Oriented Specification of Communicating Agents*.

[2] The specification language for VDM for which a ISO standard is currently being developed (ISO SC22/WG19).

transitions to other states, dictated by a set of transition rules, are possible. These states and transitions form a transition system. This approach builds on the theory of structured operational semantics (SOS). Section 3 introduces the SOS semantics for the MOSCA notation. Section 4 summarizes the most important properties of the model of time in MOSCA, section 5 presents some examples of the effect of loose VDM-SL constructions in MOSCA and section 6 summarizes the results sofar and gives a brief view into the future.

2   The MOSCA language

A MOSCA specification describes four aspects of complete systems of communicating processes: their data-containment, their functional behaviour, their process-structure and their time characteristics. For a survey of the concrete and abstract syntaxes and the SOS semantics of the full MOSCA language the reader is referred to [18].

The MOSCA view of a system consists of a composition of agents and its behaviour is specified as a composition of behaviour expressions. The basic element in the MOSCA model of a system is an *agent*, the MOSCA equivalent of a *process*. The definition of an agent may contain local VDM-SL definitions for types, values, states, functions and operations. Its behaviour is specified by a sequence of *behaviour specifications*. Ports can be used for synchronization with or without value passing. The port specification defines the communication ports associated with the agent. For each port the capability, the direction of the dataflow, and the type of the values that might pass the ports is specified.

Construction	Typical Example
Type 0 AgentService	*Agent*
Type 1,2 AgentService	*Agent* $\langle v \rangle$
AgentIf	if *Condition* then *Agent_1* else *Agent_2*
AgentValueLet	let *pattern* = *expr* in *Agent*
AgentValueLetBe	let *pattern* $\in$ *Set* in *Agent*
AgentAgentLet	let *identifier* = *Bexpr* in *Agent*
Idle Prefix	idle $(5.0) \odot$ *Agent*
Timed syn Prefix	syn_act, $\star t \odot$ *Agent*
Timed in Prefix	in_act(*pattern*), $\star t \odot$ *Agent*
Timed out Prefix	$\overline{\text{out\_act}}$(*value*), $\star t \odot$ *Agent*
StateManipulation	σ(*statement*) $\odot$ *Agent*
Choice	*Agent_1* $\oplus$ *Agent_2*
Composition	*Agent_1* | *Agent_2*
Restriction	*Agent* \ \{*label1*, ..., *labeln*\}
Relabelling	*Agent*[$l1 \mapsto l'1, ..., ln \mapsto l'n$]
Null Agent	null

Figure 1: MOSCA behaviour expressions

The behaviour of an agent is fixed through a series of agent behaviour constructions, each consisting of an value pattern and a behaviour expression. The value pattern enables case analysis over the behaviour constructions by matching the pattern against the value bound to the valuepart.

The concrete representation of the MOSCA notation is inspired by Milner's notation [14] and the mathematical concrete syntax of VDM-SL. Notational differences between CCS and MOSCA are highlighted in figure 1. The core abstract syntax for behaviour expressions is found in the appendix. A sample of the concrete syntax of MOSCA is given in the next example.

Example 2.1 In specification 2.1 a buffer agent capable of holding a sequence of natural numbers is given a counting device that registers the maximum number of elements in the buffer during its lifetime. The agent *CBuffer* offers three ports: an input port and an output port for passing buffer values and one additional output port that yields the number indicating the maximum length of the buffer during its lifetime so far.

```
CBuffer ⟨ℕ* × ℕ⟩                                    2.1 Counting Buffer
ports in in   : ℕ
      out out : ℕ
      out cnt : ℕ

CBuffer ⟨mk-([], max)⟩ ≜
    in(x) ⊙ CBuffer ⟨([x], if max > 0 then max else 1)⟩
    ⊕ cnt(max) ⊙ CBuffer ⟨([], max)⟩
CBuffer ⟨mk-([x] ⌢ s, max)⟩ ≜ out(x) ⊙ CBuffer ⟨(s, max)⟩
    ⊕ in(y) ⊙ let newbuf = [x] ⌢ s ⌢ [y] in
                if len newbuf > max
                then CBuffer ⟨(newbuf, len newbuf)⟩
                else CBuffer ⟨(newbuf, max)⟩
    ⊕ cnt(max) ⊙ CBuffer ⟨([x] ⌢ s, max)⟩
```

The agent behaviour constructions for *CBuffer* use product patterns. The first behaviour construction shows that an empty *CBuffer* may accept an element for buffering, and may offer the length so far. In the second agent behaviour construction the value of the counter is set using an agent *if* construction. The body of the second behaviour contains an agent *let* construction introducing the name 'newbuf' as a shorthand for the result of the prefix 'in(y)'. An agent *if* expression is used to compute the correct buffer length, which is either the length of the previous buffer *max*, or the length of the new buffer contents *newbuf*. □

The model of time in MOSCA is centered around the following issues.

- There is no central clock, or any other ticking device that registers the current time.

- Passing of time is measured related to actions: from the moment an action can be taken, i.e. offered to the environment, to the moment the action is actually performed in a communication. The passed time is recorded in time variables associated with the involved action.

- Time progression results from taking idle actions. Time flows contineously. There are no time stops.

Time identifiers of timed prefix constructions may occur as free variable within the behaviour expression following the $\odot$ operator. Taking the action of the prefix construction substitutes the actual value of time variable t in each free occurrence of the identifier t within the behaviour expression in P. This approach is similar to β substitution within the various forms of the λ-calculi, where a λ-term $\lambda x.f$ computes a value by substituting an actual value v in each free occurrence of x in f. Thus in

$$\mathsf{act}, \star t \odot Bexpr$$

each free occurrence of t in $Bexpr$ is bound by $\star t$. Upon taking the action act the actual value of the time variable t is substituted in all free occurrences of t in $Bexpr$.

Time progression is due to the taking of $idle$ actions. E.g.

$$\mathsf{idle}(5.2) \odot P$$

specifies a prefix expression, in which taking the action causes the time to progress with the value 5.2. Time progression is strongly connected to the semantics of the prefix construction, choice and composition operator.

The domain $\mathbb{T}$ for the values of the idle actions is chosen to be $\mathbb{R}_0^+$, the set of real values greater or equal to zero. The set of reals creates a model that fits more closely to reality than e.g. $\mathbb{N}$, the natural numbers. A time action is not the same as the normal actions (which are fully controllable) since the latter ones may be prevented from happening by the environment and time progression can never be blocked. The parallel composition is synchronous with respect to time events. E.g. in

$$idle(6) \odot P \mid idle(8) \odot Q$$

time may progress e.g. with 2 time units, resulting in

$$idle(4) \odot P \mid idle(6) \odot Q.$$

However, time progression is asynchronous for the normal actions except communications between its different components. In

$$P \mid Q$$

P and Q can perform actions asynchronously until a synchronization between the two subcomponents is due. For a fully synchronous system one may take a discrete time domain (like with SCCS in [13]), since all subagents refer to the same global intuition of time (e.g. a global clock), and events happen at certain moments in time. In the asynchronous case, any two agents may perform actions at times that are not equal, but arbitrary close to each other. Hence a dense time domain is preferred.

Example 2.2 (timed buffer) The next example illustrates the application of timed prefixes. The buffer holds tuples (n, t) such that t equals the time value

---

$TBuffer \ \langle (\mathbb{N} \times \mathbb{T})^* \times \mathbb{T} \rangle$ | 2.2 Timed Buffer

ports in **in**   : $\mathbb{N}$
    out $\overline{\text{out}}$: $\mathbb{N} \times \mathbb{T}$
    syn **restart**

$TBuffer \ \langle (s, tval) \rangle \ \triangleq$
    if $s = [\,]$
    then $\textbf{in}(v), \star t \odot TBuffer \ \langle ([[v, t + tval)], t + tval) \rangle \ \oplus$
        $\textbf{restart} \odot TBuffer \ \langle ([\,], 0) \rangle$
    else $\textbf{in}(v), \star t \odot TBuffer \ \langle (s \ ^\frown [(v, t + tval)], t + tval) \rangle \ \oplus$
        $\overline{\text{out}}(\text{hd } s), \star t \odot Tbuffer \ \langle (\text{tl } s, t + tval) \rangle \ \oplus$
        $\textbf{restart} \odot TBuffer \ \langle ([\,], 0) \rangle$

---

measured from the moment in time the buffer was activated to the moment the value n was entered through the input action **in**.   □

3   MOSCA's labelled transition system

A summary of the semantic structure of MOSCA is presented in figure 2. The starting point for the semantics is a representation of a MOSCA specification in *core abstract syntactic form* (CAS), which is build from both agent constructs and value constructs. The core abstract syntax for agent definitions is presented in the appendix. The agent constructs are assembled into an environment, together with the value denotations for the value constructs. The initial behaviour expression, together with the environment form the basic state on which the structured operational semantics is defined. The semantic function VS first maps the MOSCA abstract value constructs to constructs within the VDM-SL CAS representation, followed by applying the specific VDM-SL semantic mapping to achieve appropriate value denotations.

The MOSCA structured operational semantics is based on PLOTKIN'S SOS model and exhibits three particular properties, i.e.

- the state domain of the lts holds a notion called environment, capturing bindings from identifiers to both semantic value denotations and syntactic agent definitions;

- the label domain holds values from (i) the set of visual ports (as usual), (ii) values of the semantic domain VAL of VDM-SL and (iii) values of the semantic domain $TIME$;

- the transition relation reflects the looseness that is an inherent quality of the value specifications of MOSCA. To this end the transition rules are defined over states constructed as *sets of state items*.

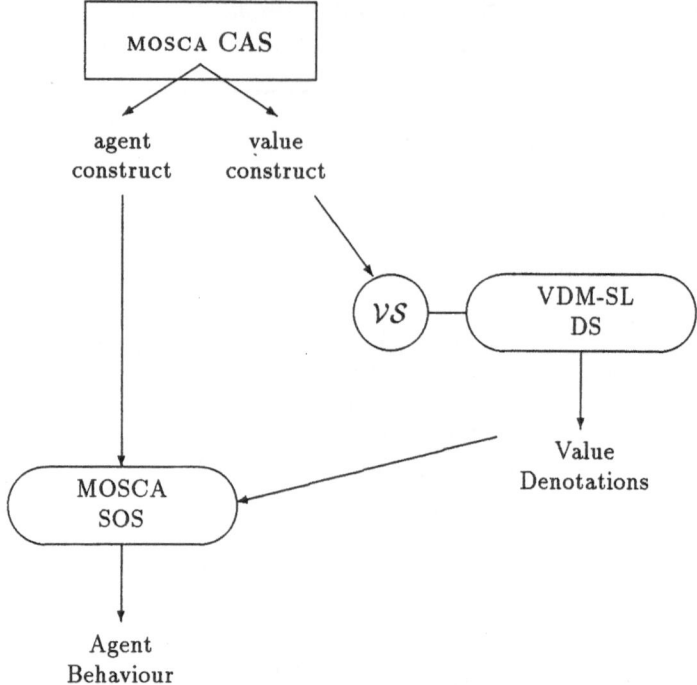

Figure 2: Semantic structure of MOSCA

The state space becomes infinite. Although the infinity aspect has difficult
theoretical properties (e.g. see [10] for an analysis concerning TCCS) the lts
offers a base for the operational description of the behaviour of agents.

3.1 The state space

The labelled transition system lts is a triple

$$\langle (P \times \rho)\text{-set}, Act, \longrightarrow \rangle$$

where P ranges over behaviour expressions, ρ ranges over environment expressions and $\longrightarrow$ is a relation

$$(P \times \rho)\text{-set} \times Act \times (P \times \rho)\text{-set}.$$

An environment ρ captures the set of definitions in which behaviour expressions
execute. These definitions include all data definitions like types, values and
functions, agent definitions, the set of local bindings resulting from value let
constructions, pattern matching etc. A transition state, or short ts, is an
element of the domain

$$TS = (Bexpr \times Eexpr)\text{-set}$$

A single element of a transition state is further referenced by the notion *state item*. *Bexpr* is the domain of behaviour expressions for agents. The structure of the environment *Eexpr* in a state item matches the composition and choice structure of the behaviour expressions. The environment has a double nature. It records

1. all possible value bindings, i.e. bindings between identifiers and *semantic* denotations of value constructions such as types, functions, values, operations and states, and

2. all possible agent bindings, i.e. bindings between identifiers and *syntactic* representations of agent definitions.

The full definition of the environment and the details concerning its structure can be found in [18].

3.2 The action set *Act*

The action set *Act* for MOSCA is defined by

$$ExtActs = InActs \cup OutActs \cup SynActs \tag{1}$$

$$TimeActs = \{\tau(d) \mid d \in TIME\} \tag{2}$$

$$IntAct = \iota \tag{3}$$

$$Act = ExtActs \cup \overline{ExtActs} \cup TimeActs \cup IntAct \tag{4}$$

with the usual co-name operation. The input actions *InActs* are denoted by $c?val$ where c is the label of an input port, *val* a value denotation of the value domain *VAL*. Such a value is e.g. defined by $\mathcal{VS}[\![vexpr]\!]$. The output actions *OutActs* are denoted by $c!val$, where c is the label of an output port and *val* the denotation of a MOSCA value-expression. The synchronization actions *SynActs* are denoted by c, where c is the label of a synchronization port. The class of time actions *TimeActs* that contains the idle action specifiers $\tau(d)$. Each value of d specifies a denotation of a time value. E.g. the transition

$$\{(P,\rho)\} \xrightarrow{\tau(d)} \{(Q,\rho')\}$$

denotes that agent P will become Q after $d \in TIME$ units of time. The action label $\tau(d)$ is pure semantical, and reflects the syntactic idle action in a prefix construction.

The last action label is ι, labelling an internal action. In MOSCA processes may perform different internal actions: state manipulations, initiated by the MOSCA state manipulating prefix constructions, environment manipulation and synchronization.

There is no syntactic τ action, like in CCS, that models an internal action on the syntactic level. In MOSCA an internal action with very similar semantics is specifiable by taking e.g. a state manipulation with a dummy statement, or an idle action with delay 0.

3.3 The transition relation

The $\longrightarrow$ relation is defined implicitly as the least relation defined by a set of inference rules. The general form of the inference rules are more complex than in the structural operational semantics of CCS. This is caused by the state extension with environments and the interplay of the loose value semantics with the agent behaviour expressions.

A transition step is denoted with the notation $\{s\} \xrightarrow{a} \{s'\}$ with $a \in ExtActs \cup TimeActs$ or $\{s\} \Longrightarrow \{s'\}$ where $\Longrightarrow$ is an abbreviation for $\xrightarrow{\iota}$. s is called the *basis* of the transition step, a the action label and s' the *result* of the transition.

The semantic rules fall into different classes: the internal action rules, external action rules and timed action rules. The general form of these rules are presented in figure 3. I will shortly discuss the templates and give some

---

State Expansion $\dfrac{}{\{s\} \Longrightarrow S}$

Expansion Propagation $\dfrac{\{s\} \Longrightarrow S}{S' \cup \{s\} \Longrightarrow S' \cup S}$ (a) $\qquad$ $\dfrac{\{s\} \Longrightarrow S}{\{s'\} \Longrightarrow S'}$ (b)

Internal Action $\dfrac{}{\{s\} \Longrightarrow \{s'\}}$

Action State Reduction $\dfrac{\{s\} \xrightarrow{a} \{s'\}}{S \cup \{s\} \xrightarrow{a} \{s'\}}$

Standard Action $\dfrac{}{\{s\} \xrightarrow{a} \{s'\}}$ (a) $\qquad$ $\dfrac{\left[\{s\} \xrightarrow{a} \{s'\}\right]^{1,2}}{\{t\} \xrightarrow{b} \{t'\}}$ (b)

Idling State Reduction $\dfrac{\{s\} \xrightarrow{\tau(d)} \{s'\}}{S \cup \{s\} \xrightarrow{\tau(d)} \{s'\}}$

Idle Action $\dfrac{}{\{s\} \xrightarrow{\tau(d)} \{s'\}}$ (a) $\qquad$ $\dfrac{\left[\{s\} \xrightarrow{\tau(d)} \{s'\}\right]^{1,2}}{\{t\} \xrightarrow{\tau(d)} \{t'\}}$ (b)

Figure 3: Transition rule templates

examples of actual rules.

The first section of figure 3 contains internal action rule templates. The first template covers all state expansion rules. These rules all result in an augmented state in the sense that the number of state items is increased which in all cases is caused by the evaluation of loose value constructions.

Example 3.1 The evaluation of value constructions is captured in an internal action step. E.g. the rule for the agent value let expression is

$$\text{AVL} \quad \frac{}{\{(avl,\rho)\} \Longrightarrow Eval\_AVL(avl,\rho)}$$

where *avl* represents an agent value let expression and *Eval_AVL* is a semantic evaluation function that results in a set of state items that share the body of the let expression as continuation behaviour but hold different values in the environment part that resulted from loose value evaluations. Similar rules exists for AgentService, AgentIf, AgentAgentLet, AgentValueLetBe, Timed in Prefix, Timed out Prefix and StateManipulation constructions. □

The next two templates cover the propagation of state expansion. Template (a) states that whenever a state expansion is due to a single item, the state in which the item occurs can may be expanded also. Template (b) covers all rules for propagation of state expansion in relation to the basic operations prefix, choice, composition, relabelling and restriction. E.g. the **Choice Expansion** rule defines the effect of state expansion in the context of a choice expression.

$$\text{Choice Expansion} \quad \frac{\{(A_i,\rho)\} \Longrightarrow S}{\{(A_1 \oplus A_2,\rho)\} \Longrightarrow S} \quad i=1,2$$

The last template in the top section of figure 3 covers rules that describe pure internal behaviour. A typical example of a rule that matches the last template is the rule for the divergent agent.

$$\text{Divergent Internal} \quad \frac{}{\{(div,\rho)\} \Longrightarrow \{(div,\rho)\}}$$

Here *div* denotes the divergent agent. The rule states that the agent *div* may take internal actions continuesly.

The middle section of figure 3 contains external action rule templates. The first template covers all state reduction actions. It states that whenever a single state item has an action a, then the whole state has that same action. The next two templates cover all standard action rules. Template (a) covers the prefix rules and template (b) cover the rules for choice, composition, relabelling and restriction. The notational shorthand $[action]^{1,2}$ denotes one or two different actions.

The bottom section of figure 3 contains timed action rule templates. The first template defines state reduction through idling. Whenever a state item idles, then the whole state is reduced to the result of the idling action. The next two templates describe the effect of proper idling actions. Template (a) introduces idling and template (b) covers the rules for idling propagation. In the next section some examples of these templates are discussed.

4 Semantics of Time

The basic properties of the semantics of time are summarized below. They originate from the work on TCCS in e.g. [3], [15] and [20] and are adapted to the semantic setting of MOSCA.

1. **Maximal Progress** Whenever an agent can proceed by taking an internal action it will not wait.

$$\{s\} \Longrightarrow \{s'\} \Rightarrow \nexists d \in TIME \cdot \{s\} \xrightarrow{\tau(d)} \{s''\} \tag{5}$$

   Whenever an agent can proceed by taking an external action it will not wait.

$$\exists a \in ExtAct \cdot \{s\} \xrightarrow{a} \{s'\} \Rightarrow \nexists d \in TIME \cdot \{s\} \xrightarrow{\tau(d)} \{s''\} \tag{6}$$

2. **Time Determinacy** To ensure the progress of time each agent, even the null agent and divergent agent can take idle actions. When time goes, if an agent idles, it can never reach different states:

$$\{s\} \xrightarrow{\tau(d)} \{s'\} \wedge \{s\} \xrightarrow{\tau(d)} \{s''\} \Rightarrow \{s\} \equiv \{s''\} \tag{7}$$

   where $\equiv$ means state equality. Time determinacy results from the properties of idling in combination with and choice and composition. The divergent agent $\perp$ must be able to take idle actions as well. As time progression in compositions is synchronous, $P \mid \perp$ would not allow the time to proceed if $\perp$ would only take internal actions and no idle actions as well.

3. **Time Continuity** During idling no time moment may be passed without notice.

$$\{s\} \xrightarrow{\tau(d+e)} \{s''\} \Leftrightarrow \{s\} \xrightarrow{\tau(d)} \{s'\} \wedge \{s'\} \xrightarrow{\tau(e)} \{s''\} \tag{8}$$

   This property is enforced by rule **IPI** given below.

4. **Time persistency** By idling an agent will not loose the ability to perform an action that it is able to perform originally.

$$(\{s\} \xrightarrow{\tau(d)} \{s'\} \wedge \{s\} \xrightarrow{x} \{s''\}) \Rightarrow \{s'\} \xrightarrow{x} \{s''\} \tag{9}$$

These basic properties of time in MOSCA result fom the incorporation of idling in the semantic rules of prefix, choice, composition, the null agent and divergent agents. The null agent is inactive but can be engaged in idling, to enable time progression in compositions that involve a null agent. The divergent agent is either idling or busy with internal actions.

The semantic rules for prefix constructions form the basis for time handling in MOSCA. There are three groups or rules.

1. **Prefix with synchronization action** This group consist of two rules
SPA, **SPI**. Rule **SPA** states the effect of the synchronization action.
Rule **SPI** expresses the effect of waiting through internal idling on the
environment to synchronize.

$$\textbf{SPA} \quad \frac{}{\{(mk\text{-}Prefix(mk\text{-}SynAct(lab,\text{-}),P),\rho)\} \xrightarrow{lab} \{(P,\rho)\}}$$

$$\textbf{SPI} \quad \frac{}{\{(mk\text{-}Prefix(mk\text{-}SynAct(lab,tid),P),\rho)\} \xrightarrow{\tau(d)} \{(mk\text{-}Prefix(mk\text{-}SynAct(lab,tid),P),Env\_Update(\rho,tid,d)\}}$$

2. **Prefix with in or out action** This group contains three rules for both
kind of prefixes. The first two rules realize the action, the last defines the
idling capacity. The action rules for the in action are:

$$\textbf{IPA} \quad \frac{}{\{(ipa,\rho)\} \xrightarrow{x?val} \{bipa,\rho)\}}$$

$$\textbf{BIPA} \quad \frac{}{\{(bipa,\rho)\} \Longrightarrow Eval\_BIPA(bipa,\rho)}$$

Rule **IPA** is a standard action rule. It binds the communicated value
$val \in Val$ to a cas structure $bipa$, which is expanded in the second rule
through the evaluation function $Eval\_BIPA$. The function matches the
value val against the pattern p of the input prefix. The result is a set
of bindings that are each stored in a separated environment. The action
rules for the out action are:

$$\textbf{OPA} \quad \frac{}{\{(opa,\rho)\} \Longrightarrow Eval\_OPA(opa,\rho)}$$

$$\textbf{EOPA} \quad \frac{}{\{(eopa,\rho)\} \xrightarrow{x!val} \{(eopa.cont,\rho)\}}$$

First the expression fixing the output value is evaluated, resulting in a set
of denotations. Each denotation is stored into a **EOPA** cas structure.
The second rule is a standard action rule that transforms the output
action into its continuation behaviour expression. The rules for idling are
similar to **SPI**.

3. **Prefix with state manipulation action** State manipulation is associated with an internal action. As such, to enforce the maximal progress

property, state manipulation actions may not idle. There is no transition rule to enable a state manipulation action to idle.

4. **Prefix with idle action** This group consists of three rules. The first rule initiates the idling, the second rule describes idling in progress and the third rule describes the finalization of the idling action. E.g. the agent $idle(5) \odot P$ operating in an environment ρ is after an initial internal action transformed into a construction called a count-down timer that contains the semantic evaluation of the idle expression, in this case 5, and the continuation behaviour P. The effect of the Idle Prefix is captured in the following three rules.

$$\mathbf{IPS} \quad \frac{}{\{(mk\text{-}Prefix(mk\text{-}IdleAct(delay)), P), \rho)\} \Longrightarrow} \\ \{(mk\text{-}CDT(dv, P), \rho) \mid dv \in \mathcal{VS}[\![delay]\!](\rho)\}$$

The rule **IPS** (an example of a state expansion rule) transforms the Idle Prefix into a set of *count down timers*. The next two rules describe the behaviour of a countdown timer. A countdown timer CDT resembles a count-down counting device that holds a clock value cv and a continuation behaviour *agent*. Whenever cv, which holds values of the semantic domain $TIME$, reaches 0 the construction continues its behaviour like *agent*. Rule **IPI** describes the effect of a running countdown timer and rule **IPE** initiates the continuation behaviour.

$$\mathbf{IPI} \quad \frac{}{\{(mk\text{-}CDT(dv, P), \rho)\} \xrightarrow{\tau(d)} \{(mk\text{-}CDT(dv - d, P), \rho)\}} \quad (d \le dv)$$

$$\mathbf{IPE} \quad \frac{}{\{(mk\text{-}CDT(dv, P), \rho)\} \xrightarrow{\tau(dv)} \{(P, \rho')\}}$$

5 Examples of Loose Behaviour

Example 5.1 (loose value nondeterminism) Suppose we have the following schematic agent definition

$OneOrTheOther \; \langle \mathbb{B} \rangle$
ports syn a
　　　syn b

$OneOrTheOther \; \langle \text{true} \rangle \quad \triangleq \quad \text{a} \odot Bexpr1$
$OneOrTheOther \; \langle \text{false} \rangle \quad \triangleq \quad \text{b} \odot Bexpr2$

The behaviour of the agent is determined by the value of the value part. Whenever true it behaves like $a \odot Bexpr1$, otherwise it behaves like $b \odot Bexpr2$. The agent behaves deterministic. Suppose the agent is subject to an agent service in the context of the next behaviour expression.

$$\text{let } v : \mathbb{B} \text{ in } OneOrTheOther \langle v \rangle$$

The resulting behaviour expression is not deterministic. It's behaviour depends on the actual value of v, which can be either true or false. The evaluation of the let expression results in two environments, one containing the binding $v \mapsto$ true and the other containing $v \mapsto$ false. Again assuming an environment ρ, the singleton state

$$\{((\text{let } v : \mathbb{B} \text{ in } OneOrTheOther \langle v \rangle \,), \rho)\}$$

is transformed by value-evaluation through the rule **AVL** into

$$\{(OneOrTheOther \langle v \rangle \, , \rho \cup \{v \mapsto \text{true}\}),$$
$$(OneOrTheOther \langle v \rangle \, , \rho \cup \{v \mapsto \text{false}\})\}$$

in which each element in the set contains one specific enrichment of the original environment ρ. The evaluation of the agent service expression in the first state item through pattern matching by application of the appropiate state expansion rules results in

$$\{(a \odot Bexpr1, \rho \cup \{v \mapsto \text{true}\}),$$
$$(OneOrTheOther \langle v \rangle \, , \rho \cup \{v \mapsto \text{false}\})\}$$

that either could be followed by a state reduction on the a action, giving

$$\{Bexpr1, \rho)\}$$

or could be followed state expansion of the second agent service expression leading to

$$\{(a \odot Bexpr1, \rho),$$
$$(b \odot Bexpr_2, \rho)\}$$

which now could be followed by state reduction either on a or b. □

The behaviour of the agent value let-be expression can be viewed as the *merged behaviours* of all possible value let expressions with deterministic value binding. Which transitions will be selected in an implementation depends on reification of the value components in the behaviour expression. When, in the example, after reification the let-be expression is transformed e.g. into a deterministic let construction, the choice of transition-path is narrowed accordingly.

Example 5.2 (loose pattern matching on value parts) Whenever an agent is defined through a series of behaviour definitions, the possibility of loose behaviour occurs. In specification 5.1 the agent UpOrDown either increments its value part or decrements it. The patterns to select one of these two,

---

$UpOrDown \langle \mathbb{N} \rangle$ ports out $\overline{\textbf{next}}$: $\mathbb{N}$	5.1 non deterministic patterns

$UpOrDown \langle p \rangle \;\triangleq\; \overline{\textbf{next}}(p) \odot UpOrDown \langle p+1 \rangle$

$UpOrDown \langle q \rangle \;\triangleq\; \overline{\textbf{next}}(q) \odot UpOrDown \langle q-1 \rangle$

---

are equivalent. After all, both p and q match the whole set of natural numbers. The state $\{(UpOrDown \langle n \rangle, \rho)\}$ is first transformed into

$$\{(\overline{\textbf{next}}(p) \odot UpOrDown \langle p+1 \rangle, \rho \cup \{p \mapsto n\}),$$
$$(\overline{\textbf{next}}(q) \odot UpOrDown \langle q-1 \rangle, \rho \cup \{q \mapsto n\})\}$$

by application of the state expansion rule for agent service. The resulting state forms the basis for two different transitions on the same action $\overline{\textbf{next}}$. □

Example 5.3 (Loose Time Specification)
The time consumption of idle actions is specified by *time expressions*, i.e. value expressions that after evaluation result in a value belonging to the semantic domain *TIME*. Within these expressions looseness may occur due to loose value specification. Let $\mathbb{T} = Real_0^+$. Let P denote an agent defined in the environment ρ.

$$IdleAndThenP \;\triangleq\; \text{idle (let } tc : \mathbb{T} \text{ be s.t. } tc \leq 10.0 \text{ in } tc) \odot P$$

The agent $IdleAndThenP$ denotes a behaviour expression that will idle for tc time units and then become P. The value-let-be construction delivers environments consisting of one binding between tc and a time value

$$\{tc \mapsto bindval \mid bindval : \mathbb{R} \cdot bindval \geq 0 \wedge bindval \leq 10\}.$$

Each environment initiates a time consumption equal to the value bound to tc. By application of the state expansion rule **IPS** the idle prefix is transformed into a (infinite) set of count-down timers, each holding a specific value from the interval $[0, 10]$. □

6 Summing up

The work on MOSCA is inspired by many other approaches on combining value manipulation, behaviour and time. [18] contains an detailed overview of related work. In this context at least the following pioneering research should be mentioned: BJØRNER and JONES for their work on VDM ([2], [12]), HENNESSY for his work on denotational semantics for process algebras ([7], [8], [9]), MILNER for his work on CCS and scientists working on time extensions of process algebraic notations, including BAETEN and BERGSTRA ([1]), CHEN ET AL. ([3]), DANIELS ([4]), HANSSON ([6]), MOLLER ET AL. ([15]), WANG ([21]) and many others.

This work differs from the other approaches mainly in the definition of the semantics, by combining a denotational semantics with a operational semantics. The combination was chosen on practical reasons. The VDM-SL language has been given a full denotational semantics, whereas the TCCS notations has been given a SOS semantics. It is a open question whether a single denotational or SOS semantics can be given that covers both the VDM-SL and TCCS notations.

The work on MOSCA is just begun. The definition of the semantics forms a firm basis to address other topics of interest concerning the notation such as a logic and a proof system and matters concerning refinement of value-manipulation expressions and equivalences between behaviour expressions and their interrelationship. The current approach of the propagation of the VDM-SL looseness into the SOS semantics is somewhat different than the approach taken in [18]. In this paper the looseness is incorporated by modelling the state space of the lts through sets of *state items* over which transitions are defined. In [18] the looseness is realized by defining sets of *transitions* over single state items. The current approach reflects the distinction between external actions and internal actions due to environment expansion more clearly. E.g. value passing actions are here represented by two transitions, one to pass the semantic value and one to realize either the evaluation (output action) or pattern matching steps (input action). In the former approach these two transition steps were merged into one action. The paper has put the emphasis on the presentation of some aspects of handling looseness and timing facilities of MOSCA. A complete presentation of all rules and semantic domains and auxiliary functions was not possible due to space limitations.

Currently the main focus is on two related topics: tool development and analysis techniques. A rapid prototyper has been developed that generates ADA code from MOSCA specifications [16]. Next to the prototyper a state space analysis tool is being developed. State space analysis is a technique that can be successfully applied to safety and liveness problems. A serious problem remains the efficient generation of finite derived state spaces out of infinite full state spaces which is a current topic of research.

References

[1] J.C.M. Baeten and J.A. Bergstra. Real Time Process Algebra. *Formal Aspects of Computing*, 3:142–188, 1991.

[2] D. Bjørner and C.B. Jones. *Formal Specification & Software Development*. PHI. Prentice Hall, 1982.

[3] L. Chen, S. Anderson, and F. Moller. A Timed Calculus of Communicating Systems. Technical Report LFCS-90-127, University of Edinburgh, 1990.

[4] M. Daniels. Modelling Real-Time Behaviour wih an Interval Time Calculus. In J. Vytopil, editor, *Formal Techniques in Real-Time and Fault-Tolerant Systems*, volume 571 of *LNCS*, pages 53–72. Springer Verlag, 1992.

[5] J. Dawes. *The VDM-SL Reference Guide*. Pitman, 1991.

[6] H. Hansson and B. Jonsson. A Calculus for Communicating Systems with Time and Probabilities. In Larsen K.G. and A. Skou, editors, *2nd Nordic Workshop on Program Correctness*. The University of Aalborg, October 1990.

[7] M. Hennessy. Acceptance Trees. *Journal of the ACM*, 32(4):896–928, October 1985.

[8] M. Hennessy. Value-passing in process algebras (abstract). In J.C.M. Baeten and J.W. Klop, editors, *CONCUR'90: Theories of Concurrency: Unification and Extension*, volume 458 of *LNCS*, pages 31–32, Amsterdam, The Netherlands., August 1990. Springer Verlag.

[9] M. Hennessy. A Proof System for Communicating Processes with Value-Passing. *Formal Aspects of Computing, Springer Verlag*, 3(4):346–366, 1991.

[10] U. Holmer, K. Larsen, and Y Wang. Deciding Properties for Regular Real-Time Timed Processes. Technical report, Draft Article, University of Göteborg (S), Chalmers (S) and Aalborg (DK), April 1991.

[11] ISO SC22/WG19. *VDM Specification Language — Proto-Standard*, 1991. Draft dated 9th March.

[12] C.B. Jones. *Systematic Software Development Using VDM, 2-nd edition*. PHI. Prentice Hall, 1990.

[13] R. Milner. Calculi for Synchrony and Asynchrony. *TCS*, 25:267–310, 1983.

[14] R. Milner. *Communication and Concurrency*. PHI. Prentice Hall, 1989.

[15] F. Moller and C. Tofts. A Temporal Calculus of Communicating Systems. In J.C.M. Baeten and J.W. Klop, editors, *CONCUR'90: Theories of Concurrency: Unification and Extension*, volume 458 of *LNCS*, pages 401–415, Amsterdam, The Netherlands., August 1990. Springer Verlag.

[16] A. Ottens and W.J. Toetenel. Simulation of Mosca Specifications in Ada. In J. van Katwijk, editor, *Proceedings of the Ada-Europe'92 conference*, LNCS. Springer Verlag, 1992.

[17] W.J. Toetenel. Model-Oriented Specification of Communicating Agents. In J. van Leeuwen, editor, *Computing Science in the Netherlands, proceedings, part II*. SION, 1991.

[18] W.J. Toetenel. *Model Oriented Specification of Communicating Agents*. PhD thesis, Faculty of Technical Mathematics and Informatics, Delft University of Technology, 1992.

[19] W.J. Toetenel. VDM + CCS + TIME = MOSCA. In *Proceedings of the 18th workshop of IFIP/IFAC WRTP'92*. Brugge, 1992.

[20] Y. Wang. An Interleaving Model for Real Time Systems. In K.G. Larsen and A. Skou, editors, *2nd Nordic Workshop on Program Correctness*. The University of Aalborg, October 1990.

[21] Y. Wang. Real-Time Behaviour of Asynchronous Agents. In J.C.M. Baeten and J.W. Klop, editors, *CONCUR'90 Theories of Concurrency: Unification and Extension*, volume 458 of *LNCS*, pages 502–520. Springer Verlag, 1990.

Appendix: MOSCA abstract syntax for agents

$AgDef$ :: $vpart$: [$Type$]
              $ports$: $PortDef$
           $behaviour$: $AgBehaviour^*$
           $localdefs$: $Definitions$

$PortDef$ :: $ports$: $Id \xrightarrow{m} PortSignature$

$PortSignature = Cap \times [Type]$

$Cap = \text{SYN} \mid \text{IN} \mid \text{OUT}$

$AgBehaviour$ :: $pattern$: $[Pattern]$
                $body$: $BExpr$

$BExpr = AgentService \mid$
        $AgentIf \mid$
        $AgentLet \mid AgentLetBe \mid$
        $Prefix \mid$
        $Choice \mid Composition \mid$
        $Restriction \mid Relabelling \mid$
        $NullAgent$

$AgentService$ :: $name$: Id
                  val : $[Expr]$

$AgentIf$ :: $test$: $Expr$
        $cons$: $BExpr$
        $altn$: $BExpr$

$AgentLet = AgValLet \mid AgAgLet$

$AgValLet$ :: $locals$: $LocalDef$
            in : $BExpr$

$AgAgLet$ :: $agents$: $Id \xrightarrow{m} Agdef$
           in : $BExpr$

$AgentLetBe$ :: $bind$: $Bind$
             st : $[Expr]$
             in : $BExpr$

$Prefix$ :: act : $Action$
        res : $BExpr$

$Action = IdleAct \mid SynAct \mid$
        $InAct \mid OutAct \mid SM$

$IdleAct$ :: $delay$: $Expr$

$SynAct$ :: $label$: Id
        $tvar$: Id

$InAct$ :: $label$: Id
        $pattern$: $Pattern$
        $dexpr$: $Expr$
        $tvar$: Id

$OutAct$ :: $label$: Id
        $result$: $Expr$
        $dexpr$: $Expr$
        $tvar$: Id

SM :: $effect$: $Statement$
      $dexpr$: $Expr$
      $tvar$: Id

$Choice$ :: lop : $BExpr$
        rop : $BExpr$

$Composition$ :: lop : $BExpr$
            rop : $BExpr$

$Restriction$ :: lop : $BExpr$
           rop : $Id\text{-set}$

$Relabelling$ :: lop : $BExpr$
           rop : $Id \xrightarrow{m} Id$

$NullAgent$ :: val : null

CDT :: $clockvalue$: $TIME$
        $agent$: $Bexpr$

$BIPA$ :: $cont$: $Bexpr$
        $pattern$: $Pattern$
        $matchval$: VAL
        $delay$: $Expr$
        $tvar$: Id

$EOPA$ :: $cont$: $Bexpr$
        $label$: Id
        $value$: VAL
        $delay$: $Expr$
        $tvar$: Id

A Timed Specification Language for Concurrent Reactive Systems

Michael Schenke

Universität Oldenburg, FB10

D-26111 Oldenburg, Germany

Abstract

In this paper we present a simple real-time specification language SL^{time}, for which we define a semantics based on timing diagrams. An example of a specification will illustrate the meaning of the single parts of SL^{time}. The aim of our approach is to develop and prove correct programs in an occam dialect PL^{time} which contains timing operators and concurrency with synchronous communication. This happens by *stepwise refinement* or *transformation* as originally advocated by Dijkstra and Wirth. We shall give the example of two rules for correct transformations. They will be applied to the example of a railway crossing.

1 Introduction

For systems with time restrictions a variety of specification formalisms have been developed, among them process algebraic approaches [1],[7], the duration calculus [3], generalised Hoare triples and metrical temporal logic [6]. However, it remains a difficult task to design correct implementations from such specifications. In the following we describe a simple specification language SL^{time}, which is particularly suited for the development of occam-like programs in a language called PL^{time} [5], which contains timing operators and concurrency with synchronous communication.

The basic idea is to embed the specification and programming languages into a common superset MIX of so-called mixed terms where specification and program notation can be mixed freely. The semantics of mixed terms is a further development of the readiness semantics [8], [10]. So one can observe whether a channel is communicating or ready to communicate or not at all available for communication. The semantic domain is made into a partial order that is defined by a relation "implements" in the sense that the implementing process is more deterministic. Then programs can be developed and proven correct by stepwise refinement or transformation and the task of designing PL^{time} programs conceptually boils down to transforming a given subset of the semantic domain, initially from a specification, into a new subset implementing it and after several steps finally into one that is expressible in the restricted set of operators offered by the programming language. Since each transformation step is proven correct, the final program implements the specification.

Our work originates from the ESPRIT Basic Research Action ProCoS (provably correct systems). There during the last years a method for this aim has been worked out for systems without time restrictions. [2] gives an overview over what has been achieved. In this paper we show how SL^{time} enriches the untimed formalism with time. The aim of ProCoS is to develop proven correct programs and to construct a proven correct compiler. The semantics of MIX, of which the semantics for SL^{time} is an essential part, is prepared for a later implementation on a proven correct compiler by means of a calculus. As a result of the facts that our aim is to develop implementable programs and that this happens by transformations within a common semantics of programming and specification languages the semantics of SL^{time} has to be fairly elaborated. We shall present this semantics and the ideas that have lead to the design decisions in detail. We mention only two examples of subtle points that had to be taken into consideration in the design of SL^{time}:

1.) As a time domain we prefer a continuous set, e.g. the non negative reals. This seems closer to the needs of a specifier. At some stage of the transformation process of course the step from continuous requirements imposed by the external world to the possible discrete models that are implementable in a computer has to be made. This has to be considered already in the design of the semantics.

2.) During the transformation process the programmer should have the choice to develop a sequential or a parallel program. The semantics of the specification language must be flexible enough to enable a refinement in either direction but hide the details from the specifier.

Finally we are going to show some transformation rules.

[14] is a preliminary version in which the task of developing sequential programs has been tackled. [13] is another attempt to design a specification language that is appropriate for the ProCoS purposes.

2 Syntax of the Specification Language SL^{time}

The syntax of SL^{time} is given by the following BNF style production rules:

$specification$ ::= spec $basic\_item^*$ end

$basic\_item$ ::= $typed\_interface\_component$
$|$ $trace\_assertion$
$|$ $local\_variable$ $|$ $communication\_assertion$
$|$ $time\_restriction$

$typed\_interface\_component$ ::= $kind$ $name^+$ of $type$

$kind$ ::= input $|$ output $|$ read $|$ write

$trace\_assertion$ ::= trace $\left[a\_name\ \text{on}\right]$ cs in pref re

$local\_variable$ ::= var v_name^+ of $type$ $\left[\ \text{init}\ value^+\right]$

$communication\_assertion$ ::= com $\left[a\_name\ \text{on}\right]$ ch $\left[\text{read}\ vs\right]$ $\left[\text{write}\ vs\right]$ $\left[\text{when}\ when\_predicate\right]$ $\left[\text{then}\ then\_predicate\right]$

$time\_restriction$ ::= wait between cs and cs min r
$|$ wait between ch and ch max r until cs

Here ch, cs and vs refer to interface channels, sets of interface channels and sets of local variables, re denotes a regular expression over the alphabet cs of channels preceding it with pref being its prefix and r is an element of the time domain, $^+$ stands for a non empty list and [...] denote optional syntax parts. For the *when* and *then* predicates a simple assertional language is used. But the syntactical details are not explained here. Since we did not want to deviate too much from the untimed language [10] in order to retain as many transformation rules as possible, this syntax coincides with the untimed language except for the time restrictions. Every specification S can be arranged into the following format:

$$S \equiv \Delta\ TA\ V\ CA\ TR$$

We use Δ, TA, V, CA, TR to refer to the interface, the trace assertions, the local variables with their optional initialisation, the communication assertions and the time restrictions of S. This arrangement reflects one point of the ProCoS specification language, the separation of control structure (TA), data flow (V, CA) and timing requirements (TR). The trace assertions serve as a synchronisation skeleton that denotes the possible sequencing of the channels that interact with the system's environment. For each single channel the communication assertions restrict the possibly communicated values. Each write variable can be written on by only one channel. In the time restriction part upper and lower bounds for the time between communications are given. In the next section the informal meaning of the components of SL^{time} will be given along with a detailed example. The formal semantics will be given and explained later.

The set of all channels in Δ will be abbreviated by $Chans(\Delta)$. $Vars(\Delta)$ will denote the set of all variables in Δ.

3   An Example: The Railway Crossing

The parts of an SL^{time} specification will be explained by means of a well known example, namely a variation of the railway crossing [17].

We consider a segment of a railway with several tracks each having a fixed direction along which the trains run. The tracks cross an ordinary road and the crossing is guarded by barriers and lamps. On each track i there is a sensor SA_i in a distance of 3000 meters before the crossing and a sensor SB_i at the end of the crossing. These sensors can be used to determine when trains enter and exit the supervised section. They give a signal $Enter_i$ or $Exit_i$ on a synchronous channel, when a wheel of a train is detected. We assume that the speed of a particular train is constant between the sensors.

The task is to design a program which controls the barriers and lamps. A barrier j is activated by sending signals Up_j and $Down_j$ along synchronous channels. Barriers may fail, and to detect a failure we have input channels $Doneup_j$ and $Donedown_j$ coming from sensors at barrier j and indicating the completion of an opening or closure operation. We assume that if the barrier does not fail then the opening or closure operation takes at most 4 seconds. If a barrier j fails this is indicated by a signal $Hold_j$ to lamp j. Such a lamp can be set to three positions: off (no train is detected), slow (a train is approaching, the lamp is slowly flashing, 1 sec on and 1 sec off) and hold (stop signal for the crossing in case of a failing barrier) by sending signals Off_j, $Slow_j$, $Hold_j$ to the lamps. The flashing is triggered by signals $FlOn_j$ and $FlOff_j$. We assume that the lamps never fail.

The control program has to obey to the following requirements:

R1) If there will be a train in the crossing section in less than 30s then a barrier which is not in failure mode should be down.

R2) If there will be a train in the crossing section in less than 40s and barrier j is not in failure mode then lamp j should be slow.

R3) If lamp j is off then no failure is detected for barrier j.

R4) If the barriers are up in some point of time they should be up in a period of 15s around that time. (This enables some cars to pass.)

R5) The barriers should begin opening within 1s after the last train has left, unless they are broken.

These timings and the distance of the sensors imply assumptions on the speed of trains that are used later.

3.1 Interface

This part of a specification lists the communication channels of the system with their direction (input or output) and value type. For the railway crossing the interface is given by

input	$Enter_i$, $Exit_i$, $Doneup_j$, $Donedown_j$	of signal
output	Up_j, $Down_j$, Off_j, $Slow_j$, $Hold_j$, $FlOn_j$, $FlOff_j$	of signal

with $i \in \{1, ..., n\}$, if n tracks are available, and $j \in \{1, 2\}$ for both sides of the railway. The type signal denotes a set with one element only which just indicates that a communication takes place.

3.2 Trace Part

The trace part specifies the sequencing constraints on the channels whereas the communicated values are ignored. This is done by stating one or more *trace assertions*, each one consisting of an alphabet, corresponding to a subset *cs* of channels, and a regular expression *re* over these channels. The regular expression describes sequencing constraints on the channels mentioned in *cs*. By stating several such trace assertions, we can specify different aspects of the intended system behaviour in a modular fashion. The informal semantics of this part of a specification is that the described behaviour must satisfy the sequencing constraints of all trace assertions simultaneously.

For the railway crossing the trace part is given by

trace $lamp_j$ on Off_j, $Slow_j$, $Hold_j$, $FlOn_j$, $FlOff_j$
in pref $(Slow_j.(FlOn_j.FlOff_j)^*.Off_j)^*.(Hold_j +$
$Slow_j.(FlOn_j.FlOff_j)^*.Hold_j + Slow_j.(FlOn_j.FlOff_j)^*.FlOn_j.Hold_j)$

trace $barrier_j$ on Up_j, $Down_j$, $Doneup_j$, $Donedown_j$, $Hold_j$
in pref $(Down_j.Donedown_j.Up_j.Doneup_j)^*.Down_j.$
$(Hold_j + Donedown_j.Up_j.Hold_j)$

trace $close_j$ on $Down_j$, $Doneup_j$, $Enter_1, ..., Enter_n$
in pref $((\sum_{i=1}^{n} Enter_i)^+.Down_j.(\sum_{i=1}^{n} Enter_i)^*.Doneup_j)^*$

trace $flash_j$ on $Slow_j$, Off_j, $Enter_1, ..., Enter_n$
in pref $((\sum_{i=1}^{n} Enter_i)^+.Slow_j.(\sum_{i=1}^{n} Enter_i)^*.Off_j)^*$

for each $j \in \{1, 2\}$. The first kind of trace assertions describes the behaviour of lamp j. The last alternative reflects the fact that the interrupt signal $Hold_j$ can happen at any time. By the second kind barrier j is described with $Hold_j$ possibly being issued after Up_j or $Down_j$ (if $Doneup_j$ or $Donedown_j$ has not been issued in time). Each single wheel issues an $Enter_i$, $Exit_i$ signal. The regular expressions simply say that, whenever barrier j is up (lamp j is off), at least one wheel must cross an entering sensor to issue a $Down_j$ (a $Slow_j$) signal again. The exit of a train is not monitored here but will be guarded by a local variable.

3.3 State Part

This part describes what the exact values are that can be exchanged over the interface channels. To this end local state variables may be introduced. These variables constitute the state space of the specification. In the communication assertions the values and channels are linked together.

The only local variables that are needed in the example are $wheels_i$ which monitor the number of wheels between the two sensors responsible for track i:

> **var** $wheels_i$ **of** *integer* init 0.

In a communication assertion for a single channel at first the read and write variables are given. The *when* predicate describes when the channel is enabled for communication. It may use the local variables as free variables. The *then* predicate describes the communication value and the effect of this communication on the state variables. It may additionally use a distinguished free variable @ch for the communicated value and primed versions of the write variables. As in the specification language Z [16] a primed variable v' refers to the value of the variable v at the end of the communication. A *true* in the *when* predicate shows that the communication is never forbidden by the state part, a *true* in the *then* predicate shows that the effect of the communication is unimportant. We further assume that each channel is attributed exactly one communication assertion but drop those in which *then* and *when* predicates are *true*.

For the railway crossing we use the following communication assertions

> **com** $Enter_i$ **write** $wheels_i$
> **when** *true* **then** $wheels_i' = wheels_i + 1$
>
> **com** $Exit_i$ **write** $wheels_i$
> **when** $wheels_i > 0$ **then** $wheels_i' = wheels_i - 1$
>
> **com** Up_j **read** $wheels_1, ..., wheels_n$
> **when** $\sum_{i=1}^n wheels_i = 0$ **then** *true*
>
> **com** Off_j **read** $wheels_1, ..., wheels_n$
> **when** $\sum_{i=1}^n wheels_i = 0$ **then** *true*

for each $i \in \{1, ..., n\}$ (first two assertions) and $j \in \{1, 2\}$ (last two assertions). By the first two communication assertions it is assured that each wheel is counted separately for each track on entering and leaving. The last two assertions ensure that the barriers can be opened and the lamps can be switched off only if there is no train (no wheel) on any track between the sensors.

3.4 Time Restrictions

In the time restriction part two kinds of restrictions can be specified. In both cases there are made statements about the readiness for communication via some channels which is feasable in the framework of the readiness semantics. Firstly lower bounds are expressed by the syntactical construct

> **wait between** cs_1 **and** cs_2 **min** r

meaning that the process after a communication on a channel in the set cs_1 cannot communicate via any channel from cs_2 for $r \, (\in \mathbb{R}^+)$ time units.

Secondly upper bounds of the syntactical form

$$\texttt{wait between } ch_1 \texttt{ and } ch_2 \texttt{ max } r \texttt{ until } cs$$

mean that whenever a communication via ch_1 happens the process must become ready to communicate via ch_2 within time r. Readiness of ch_2 must remain until a communication on ch_2 or some $ch_3 \in cs$ will take place. But also a preemption by ch_3 is possible before r time units have elapsed. The idea of this operator is the following: Since our systems communicate synchronously they cannot force the environment to communicate on ch_2 after a communication via ch_1. We can only claim readiness for the system itself and we must say how long readiness is maintained. So readiness is withdrawn (or not even established), as soon as one of the $ch \in cs$ is communicated on.

By this it is possible to model timeouts: Often then the elements of cs are inputs and ch_2 is an output. If no signal from cs has been received before time r, the system is ready to issue a signal on ch_2 that indicates an exception.

In our example we have the following time restrictions:

```
wait between FlOn_j and FlOff_j max 1 until {Off_j, Hold_j}
wait between FlOn_j and FlOff_j min 1−δ_1
wait between FlOff_j and FlOn_j max 1 until {Off_j, Hold_j}
wait between FlOff_j and FlOn_j min 1−δ_2
wait between Up_j and Hold_j max 4 until {Doneup_j}
wait between Up_j and Hold_j min 4−ε_1
wait between Down_j and Hold_j max 4 until {Donedown_j}
wait between Down_j and Hold_j min 4−ε_2
wait between Doneup_j and Down_j min 15
```

The first two pairs of restrictions describe the flashing of lamp j in the slow position. Each second the lamp is switched until an *Off* or *Hold* signal arrives and preempts the next flashing action. We cannot claim that the switching happens exactly each second. That would be unimplementable. A logical choice for the parameters δ_i which reflect this fact will be mentioned later. In the next two pairs of restrictions the necessity to issue the emergency *Hold* signal is modelled. For instance the fifth statement is a typical example for a timeout: four seconds after the barrier starts to move upwards (signal *Up*), issue the emergency signal (*Hold*), unless you are preempted by a *Doneup* signal. The last restriction ensures requirement R4.

3.5 Liveness

One of the main assumptions in the timed version of the programming language is the existence of a scheduler that guarantees progress in the following sense:

If all communication partners are ready for a communication via some channel ch for some time that is depending on the channel, then some communication has to take place (though not necessarily on ch).

This is weaker than the maximal progress assumption which is normally considered in semantics. The fact that we do not suppose immediate communication, if all partners are ready, reflects two properties of the underlying hardware. The first is the already mentioned step from continuous to discrete time, which evokes a certain granularity effect of discretisation, and secondly there is a certain unsynchrony between an internal clock and time in the environment (clock-drift). Thus we do not require synchronisation to happen exactly at some point of time but allow that it happens within some interval bounded by a so-called latency function.

At some stage of the transformation internal communication of a processor will be visible to the environment as non readiness of channels. So if we allow arbitraryly long internal communication we cannot prove that the system is making any progress at all. Hence we assume that there is some bound for the duration of uninterrupted internal communication. Of course it must be checked that a given implementation obeys to this bound. Schedulers that are similar to the ones needed here are described in [4],[11] by the duration calculus.

So we have the following five ingredients that allow us to model liveness: the behaviour of the environment, the scheduler, the time bound for internal communication, the upper bound timing restrictions and for each channel ch a duration time, namely the amount of time that is at most needed for a communication via ch.

In our example we assume the environment to be constantly ready for an observation of a lamp action, the upper bound timing restrictions provide readiness of the system. So the scheduler can actually enforce some action to happen. Only by these arguments the requirements can be proven to be fulfilled.

Definition:
a.) The *duration* is a function $dur : Chans(\Delta) \to \mathbb{R}^+$.
b.) The *latency* is a function $lat : Chans(\Delta) \to \mathbb{R}^+$.

The existence of a latency between readiness for communication and actual communication often leads to additional requirements that have to be taken into consideration. In the railway crossing for example the speed v of the train has to obey to the inequalities $v < d/lat(Down_j)$ and $v < d/lat(Slow_j)$, where d is the minimal distance between wheels. In practice these requirements are fulfilled, but otherwise we could not prevent that the wheels enter so quickly after each other that the control program has no chance to issue the $Down_j$ and $Slow_j$ signals.

A sufficient choice for the parameter δ_1 in the railway crossing would be $lat(FlOff_j)$.

4   The Semantic Model

The semantics of specifications will be defined by means of timing diagrams, i.e. by functions from the time domain $\mathbb{R}_0^+$, the non negative reals, to the channel state for each channel and the variable state for each global variable in the interface. This semantics is a further development of the readiness semantics [8], [10]. But in the present semantics there are no ready sets. Readiness of a channel to communicate (or non-readiness) will be indicated by two special values in the timing diagrams instead. Hence the channel state for a channel ch of type ty_{ch} can range in the set $State(ch) =_{df} \{\texttt{idle}, \texttt{ready}\} \cup ty_{ch}$, where $\texttt{idle}$ models a channel not being ready for a communication, $\texttt{ready}$ models a channel being ready, and elements of ty_{ch} denote a communication being performed and which value is communicated. Here $\texttt{idle}$ and $\texttt{ready}$ are completely new symbols not contained in any of the types. The variable state for a variable v of type ty_v is simply an element of ty_v.

Definition: 1.) A *timing diagram* is

a.) a function $td(ch)$ from $\mathbb{R}_0^+$ into a set $State(ch)$ for some channel ch, provided there is a finite partition $\{I_n\}$ of $\mathbb{R}_0^+$ such that $td(ch)$ is constant on each I_n and the image of $td(ch)$ is in $\{\texttt{idle},\texttt{ready}\}$ almost everywhere (this means that communications are points) or

b.) a function $td(v)$ from $\mathbb{R}_0^+$ into a set ty_v for some variable v, if there is a finite partition $\{I_n\}$ of $\mathbb{R}_0^+$ such that $td(v)$ is constant on each I_n.

2.) Let ch be a channel. A $t \in \mathbb{R}_0^+$ with $td(ch)(t) \in ty_{ch}$ is called a *communication point* of ch. The set of all communication points of ch, of a set of channels M is denoted by $com(ch)$ or $com(M) =_{df} \bigcup_{ch \in M} com(ch)$.

Each timing diagram models one concrete possible observation of the evolution of the channel state or the variable state over time. The timing diagrams are total functions. This indicates that the system controls the behaviour of the channels at every time instant in $\mathbb{R}_0^+$ and that there is no termination, because the specified systems are used for modeling constant and reliable communication with the environment. Such systems must not terminate. Communication points of a channel ch are those points of time, at which some communication via ch begins. By definition each channel has only finitely many communication points. In order to avoid Zeno behaviours, i.e. behaviours, where infinitely many communications can happen within a finite time, we put a quite technical restriction on the set of discontinuity points which is not explained here.

If there is no danger of mixing up the symbols we shall write $ch(t)$, $v(t)$ instead of $td(ch)(t)$ or $td(v)(t)$. Furthermore $td(M)$ denotes $\{td(m) \mid m \in M\}$, if M is a set of channels and variables, $td(\Delta)$ will abbreviate $td(Chans(\Delta)) \cup td(Vars(\Delta))$.

For a $ch \in Chans(\Delta)$ and an interval $I \subseteq \mathbb{R}_0^+$ let

$$ch \; idle\_on \; I \Leftrightarrow_{df} \forall t \in I : ch(t) = \texttt{idle} \text{ and}$$
$$ch \; ready\_on \; I \Leftrightarrow_{df} \forall t \in I : ch(t) = \texttt{ready}$$

In our model all communications via channels need some time. During that time no other communication is possible or carried out. This is represented by a short idle interval after each communication point. The possible behaviours of the system are taken from the following set:

Definition: For a given interface $\Delta = ch_1, ..., ch_m, v_1, ..., v_n$ with channels ch_i and variables v_j let the behaviour set $Beh(\Delta)$ consist of all pairs of the form $(\Delta, td(\Delta))$, which are *communication_idle*.

A pair $(\Delta, td(\Delta))$ is *communication_idle*, if $\forall t \in com(ch) \exists \delta : ch \; idle\_on \; (t, t+\delta]$

5 The Formal Semantics of SL^{time}

Each specification will be interpreted as a set, each of whose elements describes some possible behaviour of the system. A system P will implement another system Q, if its semantics is contained in the semantics of Q. Since the semantics is a set of possible behaviours, this means that the degree of nondeterminism has been reduced. As a consequence the sets that serve as a semantics for specifications are defined as large as possible without getting to contradictions (Superfluous elements can be dropped during the refinement). Thus in general it is possible to find different implementations for one specification, e.g. the choice between parallel or sequential implementation can be left open. In the whole section we fix an interface Δ. In order to make the formal semantics more easily understandable we provide a compositional semantics.

For a set TA of trace assertions we first calculate a regular language in a natural way: Let the $ta \in TA$ have the form $ta = \text{trace } \alpha_{ta} \text{ in pref } re_{ta}$. Then let

$$\mathcal{L}[\![\Delta, TA]\!] =_{df} \{ w \in Chans(\Delta)^* \mid \bigwedge_{ta \in TA} w \downarrow \alpha_{ta} \in \mathcal{L}[\![\text{pref } re_{ta}]\!] \} .$$

Thus a word w of channels is in $\mathcal{L}[\![\Delta, TA]\!]$ if for each trace assertion ta the projection of w onto the alphabet α_{ta} is in the language $\mathcal{L}[\![\text{pref } re_{ta}]\!]$ denoted by the regular expression $\text{pref } re_{ta}$. The semantics of trace assertions depends only on this regular language. The advantage is that during the transformations trace assertions can be exchanged, if the regular language remains the same.

Sometimes there is the need to refer to the sequence of the messages that are communicated via the channels of Δ. Since each timing diagram has only finitely many communication points, so has the finite set of channels of Δ. So the following definition leads to finite sets and sequences.

Definition: For a fixed pair $(\Delta, td(\Delta)) \in Beh(\Delta)$ let the *trace* be defined by
$tr(\Delta, td(\Delta)) =_{df} \{(ch, t, m) \mid m = ch(t) \in ty_{ch}\}$.
(The value m is communicated via ch at time t.)
Let the *uninterpreted trace* be defined by $chan(tr(\Delta, td(\Delta))) =_{df}$
$\{ch_1...ch_n \mid \exists t_1, ..t_n, m_1, .., m_n : i \le j \Rightarrow t_i \le t_j \wedge tr(\Delta, td(\Delta)) = \{(ch_i, t_i, m_i)\} \}$.

Note that normally the uninterpreted trace of a pair $(\Delta, td(\Delta)) \in Beh(\Delta)$ will have only one element. Only if there are points of time when two or more communications happen exactly simultaneously these communications are recorded in the trace in every possible order.

Definition: The semantics of the set TA of trace assertions is given by
$[\![(\Delta, TA)]\!] =_{df} \{(\Delta, td(\Delta)) \in Beh(\Delta) \mid compatible\_with(TA) \wedge extendable\_in(TA)\}$.

1.) $compatible\_with(TA) \Leftrightarrow_{df} chan(tr(\Delta, td(\Delta))) \bigcap \mathcal{L}[\![\Delta, TA]\!] \ne \emptyset$.
Let for example $tr(\Delta, td(\Delta)) = \{(a, 1, m_1), (b, 1, m_2)\}$. Then it is
$chan(tr(\Delta, td(\Delta))) = \{ab, ba\}$. This is compatible with the trace assertion
$\text{trace } \{a, b\} \text{ in pref } ab$.

2.) $extendable\_in(TA) \Leftrightarrow_{df} \forall ch \in Chans(\Delta), tr \in chan(tr(\Delta, td(\Delta))) \bigcap$
$\mathcal{L}[\![\Delta, TA]\!] : (tr.ch \in \mathcal{L}[\![\Delta, TA]\!] \Leftrightarrow \exists t \in \mathbb{R}_0^+ : ch \text{ ready\_on } [t, \infty))$.
Extendability expresses that after some trace an arbitrary channel ch finally is ready, iff the trace assertions allow the extension of the trace by ch.

In the semantics of communication assertions, we for each $ca \in CA$ consider the *when* predicate wh_{ca} and the *then* predicate th_{ca} as functions into the Boolean domain and thus evaluate v, the list of free variables, at appropriate times:
$\quad when_{ca}\text{-}is\_true\_at(t) \Leftrightarrow_{df} (wh_{ca})[v(t)/v]$.
$\quad then_{ca}\text{-}is\_true\_at(t, u) \Leftrightarrow_{df} (th_{ca})[v(u)/v', v(t)/v, ch_{ca}(t)/@ch_{ca}]$.

Definition: 1.) Let $ca = \text{com } ch_{ca} \text{ read } R_{ca} \text{ write } W_{ca} \text{ when } wh_{ca} \text{ then } th_{ca}$ be a communication assertion. Then we define
$[\![(\Delta, ca)]\!] =_{df} \{(\Delta, td(\Delta)) \mid$
$\quad \forall t \in \mathbb{R}_0^+ : ch_{ca}(t) = \text{ready} \Rightarrow when_{ca}\text{-}is\_true\_at(t) \wedge$
$\quad \forall t \in com(ch_{ca}) : (when_{ca}\text{-}is\_true\_at(t) \wedge \exists u \in (t, t + dur(ch_{ca}))] :$

$then_{ca\_is\_true\_at}(t, u) \wedge ch_{ca}\ idle\_on\ (t, u]\ )\}$.

2.) $[(\Delta, CA)] =_{df} \bigcap_{ca \in CA} [(\Delta, ca)]$ for a set CA of communication assertions.

Thus a communication is only possible, if the *when* predicate evaluates to true. A communication at time t is visible as an idle interval $(t, u]$ which must not last longer than the maximal possible duration $dur(ch_{ca})$. At the end of this interval the *then* predicate is established and links the initial and final values of the variables together.

The following time restriction defines lower bounds on execution times. After a communication on a channel from a set cs_1 there is no communication possible on any channel from the set cs_2 for r time units.

Definition: For the time restriction $trest =$ wait between cs_1 and cs_2 min r let $[trest] =_{df} \{(\Delta, td(\Delta)) \mid \forall t \in com(cs_1),\ ch \in cs_2 : ch\ idle\_on\ [t, t+r)\ \}$.

In order to give a semantics to upper bound time restrictions, we use the following auxilliary function, which is a version of the weak "until" from temporal logic: Beginning from time t a communication via ch is constantly enabled until a communication via some channel from the channel set cs takes place.

Definition: Let $cs \subseteq Chans(\Delta)$, $ch \in Chans(\Delta)$, $t \in \mathbb{R}_0^+$. Then we define the Boolean function $(ch\ \text{until}\ cs)(t) \Leftrightarrow_{df}$
$ch\ ready\_on\ [t, \infty) \vee (\exists ch_1 \in cs, u > t : u \in com(ch_1) \wedge ch\ ready\_on\ [t, u))$.

Definition: For the time restriction
$trest =$ wait between ch_1 and ch_2 max r until cs let
$[trest] =_{df} \{(\Delta, td(\Delta)) \mid \forall t \in com(ch_1) :$
$((\exists ch \in cs : preemption\_by(ch)) \vee (ch_2\ \text{until}\ cs \cup \{ch_2\})(t + r - lat(ch_2))\}$
with $preemption\_by(ch) \Leftrightarrow \exists u \in [t, t+r) : u \in com(ch)$.

The first case describes premature preemption, otherwise after a communication on channel ch_1 a communication on channel ch_2 must constantly be possible after $r - lat(ch_2)$ time units, unless ch_2 happens or some action from the preemption set cs. The reason for claiming readiness after $r - lat(ch_2)$ time units is that, if the environment is constantly willing to communicate on ch_2, the scheduler will enforce progress at time r at the latest. Note that we do not claim $ch_2 \in cs$. So a preemption by ch_2 is not necessarily possible.

Definition: $[(\Delta, TR)] =_{df} \bigcap_{trest \in TR} [trest]$ for a set TR of time restrictions.

Definition: For the specification $S =$ spec Δ TA V CA TR end let the *formal semantics* be given by
$[S] =_{df} [(\Delta, TA)] \cap [(\Delta, CA)] \cap [(\Delta, TR)]$.

Example: Under the given assumptions on the environment by means of this semantics it is possible to show that the railway crossing obeys to the requirements R1-R5. However, the duration calculus [3] which has been developed in ProCoS particularly for such situations would fulfil this task much more elegantly. Neither proof can be shown here. For a worst case estimation we need two data from [17]: The *Enter* sensor has a distance of 3000 m before the crossing and the maximal speed of a train is 30 m/s.

R1: The worst case is that an *Up* signal is issued exactly when a train enters.

So the barriers have to open and to close again. Then the time bounds are:
until issue of *Doneup* at most 4 sec (otherwise the timeout issues a *Hold*),
until readiness of *Down* 15 sec (last time restriction and semantics of trace assertions),
until issue of *Down* at most *lat(Down)* sec (due to the scheduler),
until issue of *Donedown* at most 4 sec (otherwise the timeout issues a *Hold*).
This amounts to $23+lat(Down) < 24$ sec in which the fastest train (30 m/s) covers 720m and hence reaches the crossing not before (3000-720)/30 sec = 76 sec. This proves R1.

R2: If the lamp is in a flashing state it cannot be switched off (fourth communication assertion). So the worst case is that an *Off* has just been issued. Then we have to wait for the *Slow* signal at most $dur(Off) + lat(Slow)$ sec, the time needed until the end of the *Off* plus the time for the scheduler to enforce the *Slow* signal. These time estimations are even easier to fulfil than for R1.

R3: This is clear since the trace assertions prohibit an *Off* and a *Hold* at the same time.

R4: This is a consequence of the fifth time restriction.

R5: When the last wheel exits, the signal *Up* is not longer prohibited by the third communication assertion. The last signal governing the barrier must have been *Donedown* which is also a consequence of the estimation for R1. Hence the *Up* is enabled and the scheduler forces it to happen within $lat(Up) < 1$ sec.

6   Implementation Relation and Transformation Rules

There is a unique way of definig a semantics for the superset MIX of SL^{time} and PL^{time}, such that the restriction to SL^{time} coincides with the semantics outlined here and the restriction to PL^{time} coincides with the semantics from [5]. Details have to be skipped here.

The following definition of the implementation relation within MIX captures the idea that implementation should be considered a reduction in the degree of non determinism (or in the amount of possibly observable behaviours). Basically it is inclusion for subsets of $Beh(\Delta)$, the behaviour set.

Definition: For a fixed interface Δ a mixed term M_1 *implements* a mixed term M_2, iff $[\![M_1]\!] \subseteq [\![M_2]\!]$ holds.

The main problem concerning implementation that excedes the difficulties of the untimed case is the interplay between trace assertions and time restrictions in particular how both have to be distributed to the single processors. The communication assertions are no problem in this connection, because it is clear to which processor each communication assertion belongs. (That is why in the following we can neglect the communication part.) In the untimed case several rules have been developed how to cope with trace assertions and communication assertions alone [10],[9]. In [14] rules are given for the development of sequential programs, but the specifications must fulfil very restrictive preconditions. In order just to give a glimpse of what transformation rules are good for in the present situation with time and parallelism we are going to show two rules that deal with the problem how to distribute time restrictions to processors. A typical problem is illustrated by the following

Example: *Assumption:* We have the specification with

> trace a, b in pref $a.b$
> trace a, c in pref $a.c$
> wait between a and b max r until $\emptyset$.

Aim: We should like to implement each trace assertion on an own processor, attribute the time restriction to the first trace assertion and use the methods from [10], [14] to develop a sequential program for each processor combined by the parallel operator PAR from PL^{time}.

Problem: The a would be shared between processors and must be visible at the interface, but occam has only synchronous point to point communication. (Hence in the PAR operator, unlike in the trace assertions, shared symbols refer to internal channels.)

Way Out: We add a parallel component $PC(a)$ whose only purpose is to communicate with the environment via a. It is triggered by internal actions (called a'_1, a''_1, a'_2, a''_2). Each a'_i denotes an input from some processor i. It indicates that the processor is waiting for a communication with the environment via a. Each a''_i is output to the processor i. It informs the processor that the communication via a has taken place. The sequence of the a'_i in $PC(a)$ (below) is arbitrary, since each processor has to be ready.

(Intermediate) Result: We get a mixed term with an aplication of the operator PAR that implements the given specification:

> $PAR[Spec_1, Spec_2, PC(a)]$ with
>
> $Spec_1 = $ trace a'_1, a''_1, b in pref $a'_1.a''_1.b$
>   wait between a''_1 and b max $\bar{r}$ until $\emptyset$,
>
> $Spec_2 = $ trace a'_2, a''_2, c in pref $a'_2.a''_2.c$,
>
> $PC(a) = $ trace $a'_1, a''_1, a'_2, a''_2, a$ in pref $(a'_1.a'_2.a.a''_1.a''_2)^*$

with $\bar{r} = r - lat(a''_1)$. Now the rules from [14], [10] can be applied to $Spec_1$. $\square$

A generalisation is handled in the following

Rule1: (Distribution of upper bound timings with synchronisation on the start action)

Assumption: The trace assertions and time restrictions have the form

> $ta_i = $ trace α_i in pref re_i
> $tr_{ij} = $ wait between a_{ij} and b_{ij} max r_{ij} until M_{ij}

with $i \in \{1, ..., m\}$ and $j \subset \{1, ..., n(i)\}$ where it is allowed that for some i there is no tr_{ij}. We suppose (*) and (**):

$$(*) \; \forall i, j : \{a_{ij}, b_{ij}\} \cup M_{ij} \subseteq \alpha_i \wedge (**) \bigcup_{i \neq j}(\alpha_i \cap \alpha_j) \subseteq \{a_{ij} \mid i = 1, ..., m, \; j = 1, ..., n(i)\}$$

Explanation: (*) says that each time restriction belongs in a natural way to some trace assertion. This is not a severe claim. Such a situation can always be established. More restrictive is (**) which says that the actions a_{ij} which start the time restrictions are the only actions that are shared by different trace assertions.

Again we want to implement each trace assertion on one processor and for this purpose we introduce new primed and doubly primed internal channels. Let $\bigcup_{i \neq j}(\alpha_i \cap \alpha_j) = \{\overline{a}_1, ..., \overline{a}_k\}$. For a fixed a in this set let $I(a) =_{df} \{i \mid a \in \alpha_i\}$. By just adding syntactically indices and primes we attribute to a new channels: $ch'(a) =_{df} \{a'_i \mid i \in I(a)\}$ and $ch''(a) =_{df} \{a''_i \mid i \in I(a)\}$. Let $s'(a)$, $s''(a)$ be arbitrary but fixed sequences of all elements of $ch'(a)$ and $ch''(a)$.

(Intermediate) Result: We get a mixed term that implements the given specification:

$$PAR[Spec_1, ..., Spec_m, PC(\overline{a}_1), ..., PC(\overline{a}_k)] \quad \text{with}$$

$Spec_i = \text{trace } \alpha_i[\overline{a}'_1, \overline{a}''_1/\overline{a}_1, ..., \overline{a}'_k, \overline{a}''_k/\overline{a}_k] \text{ in pref } re_i[\overline{a}'_1.\overline{a}''_1/\overline{a}_1, ..., \overline{a}'_k.\overline{a}''_k/\overline{a}_k],$
$\qquad tr_{ij}[a''_{ij}/a_{ij}, \overline{r_{ij}}/r_{ij}] \quad (\text{with } \overline{r_{ij}} = r_{ij} - \sum_{k \in I(a_{ij})}(dur(a''_k) + lat(a''_k)))$

$PC(\overline{a}_i) = \text{trace } ch'(\overline{a}_i) \cup ch''(\overline{a}_i) \cup \{\overline{a}_i\} \text{ in pref } (s'(\overline{a}_i).\overline{a}_i.s''(\overline{a}_i))^*.$ ☐

Example: *Assumption:* We have the specification with

> trace a_1, b_1, e in pref $a_1^*.e.b_1$
> trace a_2, b_2, e in pref $a_2^*.e.b_2$
> wait between a_1 and e max r_1 until $\emptyset$.
> wait between a_2 and e max r_2 until $\emptyset$.

Aim: Again we want to implement both trace assertions on a separate processor and distribute the time restrictions to the trace assertions. (But e would be shared.)

Way Out: We add a parallel component $PS(e)$ which communicates with the environment via e and is triggered by internal actions $(e_1^{ir}, e_1^{al}, e_1, e_2^{ir}, e_2^{al}, e_2)$.

(Intermediate) Result: We get a mixed term that implements the given specification:

$$PAR[Spec_1, Spec_2, PS(e)] \quad \text{with}$$

$Spec_1 = \text{trace } a_1, b_1, e_1^{ir}, e_1^{al}, e_1 \text{ in pref } a_1^*.(e_1^{ir} + e_1^{al}).e_1.b_1$
$\qquad\qquad$ wait between a_1 and e_1^{al} max r'_1 until $\emptyset$,

$Spec_2 = \text{trace } a_2, b_2, e_2^{ir}, e_2^{al}, e_2 \text{ in pref } a_2^*.(e_2^{ir} + e_2^{al}).e_2.b_2$
$\qquad\qquad$ wait between a_2 and e_2^{al} max r'_2 until $\emptyset$,

$PS(e) = \text{trace } e, e_1^{ir}, e_1^{al}, e_1, e_2^{ir}, e_2^{al}, e_2 \text{ in pref } (e_1^{al}.e_2^{ir}.e.e_1.e_2 + e_2^{al}.e_1^{ir}.e.e_1.e_2)^*$

with $r'_i = r_i - lat(a''_i)$.

Explanation: The e_1^{al} (al for alarm) shows that in the first processor the upper bound time of the time restriction becomes urgent and the e must be issued. Then the other component has to be informed about this. That is done in $PS(e)$ by the e_2^{ir} (ir for interrupt). Here it is essential that the second processor is ready to accept the interrupt (almost) immediately. Otherwise the time bounds might be violated. Then an external communication via e is possible and after the communication each processor including the one that has issued the alarm is informed about that (by the e_i). Likewise the second summand is explained. The traces in $PS(e)$ must start with the alarm followed by the interrupt. Now the rules from [14] and [10] can be applied. ☐

Rule2: (Distribution of upper bound timings with synchronisation on the end action)

Assumption: The trace assertions and time restrictions have the form

$ta_i = $ trace α_i in pref re_i

$tr_{ij} = $ wait between a_{ij} and b max r_{ij} until M_{ij} (always the same b)

with $i \in \{1, ..., m\}$ and $j \in \{1, ..., n(i)\}$. Again some i may have no tr_{ij}. We suppose

$$(*) \quad \forall i, j : \{a_{ij}, b\} \cup M_{ij} \subseteq \alpha_i \wedge \quad (**) \quad \bigcup_{i \neq j}(\alpha_i \cap \alpha_j) \subseteq \{b\}$$

and additionally whenever some a_{ij} has been issued the automaton defined by the trace assertions must be ready to accept b and the *when* predicate for b must constantly be fulfilled.

Explanation: Again we claim that each time restriction belongs in a natural way to some trace assertion and that the action b which ends the time restrictions is the only action that can be shared by different trace assertions. Since we can imagine b as an emergency exception that we want to happen, if no preemption has taken place, it is vital that the communication via b is not prevented by the internal state longer than necessary. This motivates that b must always be able to happen. Then we can estimate the duration of the internal communications. W.l.o.g. let $b \in \bigcap_{i=1}^{l} \alpha_i$ but in no other α_i and the trace assertions for which b appears as an exception in a time restriction are numbered $1, ..., k$. (Hence it is $k \leq l$.)

(Intermediate) Result: We get a mixed term that implements the given specification:

PAR$[Spec_1, ..., Spec_m, PS(b)]$ with

$Spec_i = $ trace $\alpha_i[b_i^{ir}, b_i^{al}, b_i/b]$ in pref $re_i[(b_i^{ir} + b_i^{al}).b_i/b]$
    wait between a_{ij} and b_i^{al} max r'_{ij} until M_{ij}

$PS(b) = $ trace $\{b_1, ..., b_l\} \cup \{b_1^{al}, ..., b_k^{al}\} \cup \{b_1^{ir}, ..., b_l^{ir}\} \cup \{b\}$
    in pref $(\sum_{i=1}^{k} b_i^{al}.b_1^{ir}...b_{i-1}^{ir}.b_{i+1}^{ir}...b_l^{ir}.b.b_1...b_l)^*$

with $r'_{ij} = r_{ij} - (dur(b_i^{al}) + lat(b_i^{al})) - \sum_{j=1, j \neq i}^{l}(dur(b_j^{ir}) + lat(b_j^{ir}))$.

Explanation: The initial b_i^{al} in a summand of $PS(b)$ shows that in the i-th processor (with $1 \leq i \leq k$ since the other ones cannot issue an alarm) the upper bound time of some time restriction belonging to it becomes urgent and the b must be issued. Then all other components have to be informed about this. That is done by the b_j^{ir} (with $j \neq i$). Then a communication via b is possible and after the communication each processor including the one that has issued the alarm is informed about that. In the trace assertions with $1 \leq i \leq k$ the possibilities of issuing an alarm and of receiving an interrupt must be recorded. Hence there each b has to be replaced by $(b_i^{al} + b_i^{ir}).b_i$, where the b_i only shows that b has been communicated. (In addition to the formally stated rule the alternative b_i^{ir} can be dropped in a trace assertion, if there is no other processor that can issue an alarm. For $k + 1 \leq i \leq l$ the b has to be replaced by $b_i^{ir}.b_i$ only).   □

Together with the rules from [14] and the timed equivalents for some rules in [10] a lot of standard examples can be proven correct, the above railway crossing, the watchdog timer ([6]) or the gas burner ([11],[2]). The rules cannot be proven here because of lack of space.

Example: In the railroad crossing the second rule applies to the third and fourth pairs of time restrictions. The other ones do not pose a problem, because they are not shared between trace assertions. Here we have b equal to $Hold_j$ with $k = 1$ and $l = 2$. Hence we have to introduce the new parallel component

$$PS(Hold_j) = \mathtt{trace}\ \{Hold_j, Hold_{j1}^{al}, Hold_{j2}^{ir}, Hold_{j1}, Hold_{j2}\}$$
$$\mathtt{in\ pref}\ (Hold_{j1}^{al}.Hold_{j2}^{ir}.Hold_j.Hold_{j1}.Hold_{j2})^*$$

In the trace assertions governing the behaviour of barrier j the $Hold_j$ is replaced by $Hold_{j1}^{al}.Hold_{j1}$, the first being output and the second being input. An alternative $Hold_{j1}^{ir}.Hold_{j1}$ is not necessary, because no other trace assertion is accompanied by a time restriction with $Hold_j$ as exception. In the trace assertions governing the behaviour of lamp j the $Hold_j$ is replaced by $Hold_{j2}^{ir}.Hold_{j2}$, both being input. In the time restrictions belonging to barrier j (the fifth until eighth) the $Hold_j$ is replaced by $Hold_{j1}^{al}$ and the time bound by $4 - (dur(Hold_{j1}^{al}) + lat(Hold_{j1}^{al})) - (dur(Hold_{j2}^{ir}) + lat(Hold_{j2}^{ir}))$. In the time restrictions belonging to lamp j (the first until fourth) the $Hold_j$ is replaced by $Hold_{j2}^{ir}$. Now there is a clear division into trace assertions and accompanying time restrictions. So the rules from [14] and [10] can be applied. □

7 Conclusions, Final Remarks, Future Work

The present paper bridges the gap between two well established subjects of computer science, the duration calculus (DC for short) and occam.

The DC is well-known as a powerful means for describing timing requirements of a system. The DC formulae are interpreted over timing diagrams and one can consider these formulae as a shorthand for sets of timing diagrams. So there is a natural implementation relation between DC formulae and SL^{time} specifications. For the railway crossing the ProCoS methodology means to formulate the requirements R1-R5 in DC and show that the specification given in this paper implies them. By means of the DC then other properties of the crossing could be proven, for example that whenever a train is passing the road the barriers are closed (,or the lamps are in $Hold$ position). For further connections between the duration calculus and the ideas shown in this paper and for further case studies compare [4],[11],[15].

From requirements of a system (like R1-R5) and the DC formulae expressing them, however, it is by no means clear, how a suitable occam-program should look like. That is where the intermediate step comes in, the specification language SL^{time} which can be seen as the main supporting pillar of the bridge between DC and occam. The target language PL^{time} is basically occam but provided with a semantics that also is based on timing diagrams. For the untimed versions of SL and PL a lot of transformation rules have been developed [10]. In the presence of time there exist new ones which could not have been formulated in untimed SL. Two of these are shown in the paper.

So all three languages stand on a uniform basis and hence allow a development method of proven correct software by refinement. For this software even a proven correct compiler is being constructed by the ProCoS team in Kiel.

Future work will consist in a continuation of work at the development method, aiming at a possibly complete transformation calculus. The whole approach should be tested by major case studies. An example of a complete transformation from DC to occam (PL^{time}), the gas burner from [11], can be found in [15]. Also an implementation of the transformation rules is being realised presently at Oldenburg.

Acknowledgements. The author wishes to express his gratefulness to Michael R. Hansen and Ernst-Rüdiger Olderog for the numerous helpful and detailed discussions.

References

[1] J.C.M.Baeten, J.A.Bergstra. Real time process algebra. Formal Aspects of Computing 3(2), 1991, 142-188.

[2] J.Bowen, M.Fränzle, E.-R.Olderog, A.P.Ravn. Developing Correct Systems, 5th EuroMicro Workshop on Real-Time Systems, Oulu, Finland 1993, (IEEE Computer Society Press) 176-187.

[3] Zhou Chaochen, C.A.R.Hoare, A.P.Ravn. A Calculus of Durations. IPL 40(5), 1992, 269-276.

[4] Zhou Chaochen, M.R.Hansen, A.P.Ravn, H.Rischel. Duration Specifications for Shared Processors. FTRTFT Nijmegen 1992, LNCS 571, 21-32.

[5] M.Fränzle. Proposal for a Programming Language Core for ProCoS II, ProCoS Project Document [MF 11/2], Universität Kiel.

[6] J.J.M.Hooman. Specification and Compositional Verification of Real-Time Systems. LNCS 558 (1991).

[7] X.Nicollin, J.Sifakis, S.Yovine. From ATP to Timed Graphs and Hybrid Systems. REX 1991, LNCS 600, 549-572.

[8] E.-R.Olderog, C.A.R.Hoare. Specification-oriented semantics for communicating processes. Acta Inform. 23 (1986), 9-66.

[9] E.-R.Olderog. Interfaces between Languages for Communicating Systems. ICALP 1992, LNCS 623, 641-655, invited paper.

[10] E.-R. Olderog,S. Rössig, J.Sander, M. Schenke. ProCoS at Oldenburg: The Interface between Specification Language and occam-like Programming Language. Technical Report Bericht 3/92, Univ. Oldenburg 1992.

[11] A.P.Ravn, H.Rischel, K.M.Hansen. Specifying and Verifying Requirements of Real-Time Systems. Transactions on Software Engineering, vol 19,1 (1993) 41-55.

[12] S. Rössig, M. Schenke. Specification and stepwise development of communicating systems. VDM'91, LNCS 551 (1991), 148-163.

[13] M.Schenke. Predicative Specification of Timed Processes. REX 1991, LNCS 600, 603-617.

[14] M.Schenke. Refinement Proves the Correctness of Timing Constraints. ProCoS Project Document [OLD MS 4/1], Universität Oldenburg , 1992.

[15] M.Schenke. Specification and Transformation of a Gas Burner. ProCoS Project Document [OLD MS 10/1], Universität Oldenburg , 1993.

[16] J.M. Spivey. The Z Notation: A Reference Manual. Prentice Hall, 1989.

[17] E.Zijlstra. The railroad crossing. Deliverable, Esprit project DESCARTES, Foxboro, The Netherlands, 1988.

Multiparadigm
Specification Languages:
a First Attempt at Foundations[*]

Egidio Astesiano   and   Maura Cerioli

DISI–Dipartimento di Informatica e Scienze dell'Informazione,

Università di Genova, Viale Benedetto XV,

6132 Genova, Italy,

e-mail: {astes,cerioli}@disi.unige.it

Abstract

This paper is a first attempt at a formal foundation of specification languages allowing their basic modules to be defined in several formalisms. More precisely a rigorous notion of a compositional tool for importing/exporting specifications between two instances of one specification metalanguage on different basic algebraic frameworks is proposed.

Adopting the notion of institution as a synonym for formalism, we introduce and develop the concept of *simulation* of an institution by another. Then we deal with the simulation of basic and structured specifications, introducing the concept of *simulation independent metalanguage*, a generalization of institution independent languages, which allows "putting together theories *from different formalisms* to make specifications". Since simulation generalizes the notion of implementation and allows relating implementations in different formalisms, a third dimension is added to the well known horizontal and vertical compositions of specifications, typical of Clear and ASL.

1 Motivations

Most software systems needed to solve concrete problems are far too large to be handled by human minds without the support of a rigorous methodology. Formal specifications, providing tools for modularity and refinement (see e.g. [9, 13]), facilitate reuse and maintenance of produced software.

As a result both of theoretical investigations and of preliminary attempts at applications, the nature of the algebras, the logics used to define the classes of admissible realizations of a data type and even the notion of signature have been changed, w.r.t. the pioneering papers of the ADJ group, more or less recently, producing a considerable proliferation of specification formalisms. Indeed this work has grown out of the experience of the first author who has been

---

[*]This work has been partially supported by Esprit-BRA W.G. n.6071 COMPASS, Progetto Finalizzato Sistemi Informatici e Calcolo Parallelo of C.N.R. (Italy), MURST-40% Modelli della computazione e dei linguaggi di programmazione

involved with his group in various formal specification projects, where different formalisms, like partial conditional logic, order-sorted logic, first-order structures have been used, depending on the target application.

From a pragmatic point of view, the existence of a number of different formalisms is pretty reasonable, because each one of them may be the more comfortable to work within, depending on the problem under examination, the field tradition, the available tools and (not least) the personal taste. However, from the point of view of a specification language user, the ability of supporting modularity and refinement is essential in order to allow reuse of specifications. Thus it is important (not to say crucial) to assemble, possibly at different levels of implementative detail, specification modules in different formalisms. Rephrasing the title of a landmark paper by Burstall and Goguen [3], the issue is "putting together theories *from different formalism* to make specifications".

This paper presents a formal approach to this translation problem, showing how it deals with modularity and refinement. It is worth noting that, in order to support the stepwise refinement, we regard specifications as classes of *possibly non-isomorphic* models, so that, by fixing implementative details at the different design levels, the model class is restricted, until only one model (up to isomorphisms) remains, that is the required realization. Thus we consider specification languages based on this loose approach (see e.g. ASL [15], or CLEAR [4]) more than languages where specifications describe (the isomorphism class of) one model (see e.g. VDM [10], Z [16], OBJ [8]).

Adopting the notion of institution, developed by Burstall and Goguen (see e.g. [6]) in order to define the semantics of the CLEAR language, as a rigorous counterpart of the notion of formalism, we use the concept of simulation (see e.g. [1, 5] of an institution by another (section 2): if μ is a simulation of $\mathcal{I}$ by $\mathcal{I}'$, then $\mathcal{I}'$ has at least the same expressive power as $\mathcal{I}$ and moreover μ indicates how $\mathcal{I}$ can be translated into $\mathcal{I}'$. Intuitively a simulation μ of $\mathcal{I}$ by $\mathcal{I}'$ codes the syntax of $\mathcal{I}$, i.e. the signatures and the sentences, into the syntax of $\mathcal{I}'$ in a consistent way w.r.t. the semantics, in the sense that a class of models in $\mathcal{I}'$ is chosen to represent the models of $\mathcal{I}$. Particularly interesting are *logical* simulations, that are those for which the class of models in $\mathcal{I}'$ chosen to represent the models of $\mathcal{I}$ are the model class of a set of $\mathcal{I}'$ sentences, because for such simulations there is an immediate correspondence between the basic specifications (i.e. the model classes of sets of sentences) of the two frames.

Then the basic notion of simulation between institutions is extended to deal with simple and structured specifications. In particular using any simulation of a framework $\mathcal{I}$ by another $\mathcal{I}'$, every specification language defined on $\mathcal{I}$ is allowed to import, in a rigorous way, specifications defined for the $\mathcal{I}'$ paradigm. However this capability is in some sense rough, as the structure of the imported specification, if any, is lost by the importing process. In order to improve the import process, the first step is using, instead of two generic languages on $\mathcal{I}$ and $\mathcal{I}'$, instances of one common metalanguage whose semantics is uniformly defined for both frameworks so that preserving the structure has a formal meaning; for this aim the notion of institution independent metalanguage by Sannella and Tarlecki (see e.g. [14]) is perfectly fitting. However institution independence is not sufficient for every translation to be compatible with the structure of the language and has to be refined to that of *(logical) simulation independent operation* (section 3), which is the basis for (logical) simulation independent metalanguages. Such metalanguages can structure specifications defined in several frameworks, provided that the translations of these input specifications into a common framework are given by means of (logical) simulations of the original paradigms by the new chosen one. Although this approach is very promising, non every detail has been fixed yet and in particular it is still under investigation which can be the most suitable set of (logical) simulation independent operators, depending on the actual specification languages used in practice.

Finally, in connection with the refinement problem, it is shown how simulation adds a third dimension to the well known horizontal and vertical composition of implementations, thus allowing the composition of software modules not only from different formalisms, but also at different levels of abstraction.

The concept of simulation plays a central role in the Ph.D. thesis [5], where many applications are explored and an exhaustive comparison with related works is made. In [1] it is shown how simulations may provide a tool for comparing frameworks and translating deductive systems. In the present paper, corresponding roughly to chapter 5 in [5], the emphasis is on multiparadigm specification languages.

Following the suggestions of the referees, all technical details have been summarized in an appendix, keeping the exposition at a semiformal level.

2   The concept of simulation

To introduce the concept of simulation (see e.g. [1]) and the corresponding notation from an intuitive point of view, we begin with an informal example, which is the reduction of partial algebra logic with ground conditional formulas built on existential equations ($t = t'$ holds iff t and t' denote the same element), from now on $\mathcal{PAR}$, to the conditional fragment of typed logic, from now on $\mathcal{TL}$, making explicit the definedness of elements, by definedness predicates; this technique has been used in practice in order to make deduction for partial specifications by tools defined for the total case, as in [12] (and analogously for the homogeneous total frame, see e.g. [11]).

Example 2.1 Let us fix a many-sorted signature Σ with sorts S and function symbols F. We define the translation of Σ into a typed logic signature $\Phi(\Sigma)$, by setting $\Phi(\Sigma) = (S, F, P')$, where P' contains only the typing predicates and a binary relation, playing the role of existential equality, i.e. $P'_s = \{D_s\}$ $P'_{ss} = \{\_eq_e\_\}$, where the symbol $\_$ denotes the place of the arguments in an infix notation, and $P'_w = \emptyset$ for all $w \notin \{s, ss\}$.

Any partial conditional equation over Σ can be translated into a total equivalent one over $\Phi(\Sigma)$; indeed it is sufficient to substitute the predicate eq_e for the existential equality. Thus let us consider a partial positive conditional formula $\xi = (t_1 = t'_1 \wedge \ldots \wedge t_n = t'_n \supset t = t')$ over Σ and define $\alpha_\Sigma(\xi) = (t_1 \, eq_e \, t'_1 \wedge \ldots \wedge t_n \, eq_e \, t'_n \supset t \, eq_e \, t')$.

To illustrate in which sense $\alpha_\Sigma(\xi)$ is equivalent to ξ, a class $dom(\mu)_\Sigma$ of total algebras with predicates (first-order structures) is chosen, which soundly represents the partial algebras and s.t. a total algebra satisfies $\alpha_\Sigma(\xi)$ iff the partial algebra represented by it satisfies ξ. Informally, the idea is to distinguish any carrier of a total algebra in two parts, the "defined" elements and the junk, by means of the definedness predicates and to impose that the predicate eq_e corresponds to the restriction of the (usual) equality to the defined part; moreover, as in the partial frame functions are *strict*, i.e. the definedness of a function application result implies the definedness of each argument. More formally a total algebra A' is a sound representation of a partial algebra A, we write $A = \beta_\Sigma(A')$, iff both $a\,eq_e^{A'}\,b$ is equivalent to $\{D_s^{A'}(a), D_s^{A'}(b), a = b\}$ for all elements a and b and every sort s, and $D_s^{A'}(f^{A'}(a_1,\ldots,a_n))$ implies $D_{s_i}^{A'}(a_i)$ for all $i = 1,\ldots,n$, for every function symbol $f \in F_{s_1\ldots s_n,s}$. If A' satisfies this condition, then A is the partial algebra whose carrier of sort s is $D_s^{A'}$ and f^A is the restriction of $f^{A'}$ to $s_1^A \times \ldots \times s_n^A$ for every functions symbol f. It is easy to check that A' satisfies $\alpha_\Sigma(\xi)$ iff A satisfies ξ. Note that total algebras differing only on elements which do not satisfy the definedness predicates represent the same partial algebra.

Thus, for every many-sorted signature Σ a typed logic signature $\Phi(\Sigma)$ and two functions are defined: α_Σ, which translates many sorted positive conditional sentences on Σ into Horn-Clauses on $\Phi(\Sigma)$ built on definedness and existential equality predicates, and β_Σ, which partially translates total first-order structures on $\Phi(\Sigma)$ into partial algebras on Σ and is surjective, as it is immediate to check.

Since the change of notation, via signature morphisms, has a great relevance in the algebraic approach and in particular for specification languages, being used for example to bind the actual to the formal parameters in parameterized specifications and to "put theories together to make specifications", we have to investigate the compatibility between the coding functions α_Σ and β_Σ defined for any signature Σ and the changes of notation.

Let $\bar\sigma: \Sigma_1 \to \Sigma_2$ be a morphism of many-sorted signatures, i.e. a pair of functions $\sigma: S_1 \to S_2$, renaming the sorts, and $\phi: F_1 \to F_2$ translating function symbols in a consistent way w.r.t. the sort renaming (i.e. if $f: s_1 \times \ldots \times s_n \to s$, then $\phi(f): \sigma(s_1) \times \ldots \times \sigma(s_n) \to \sigma(s)$). Then $\bar\sigma$ naturally induces a typed logic signature morphism (σ, ϕ, π) from $\Phi(\Sigma_1)$ into $\Phi(\Sigma_2)$, defined by $\pi(D_s) = D_{\sigma(s)}$ and $\pi(eq_e) = eq_e$ for any $s \in S$. It is easy to check that the translation of sentences is compatible with signature morphisms, i.e. that $\Sigma_1(\bar\sigma(\xi)) = \Phi(\bar\sigma)(\Sigma_1(\xi))$, where the application of a signature morphism to a sentence is the usual renaming of function (and predicate) symbols.

Instead the partiality of the translation of algebras makes the compatibility between the algebra translations and signature morphisms delicate. Indeed it is intuitive to expect that the translation along a signature morphism of a total algebra simulating a partial algebra simulates the translation of that partial algebra; more formally, recalling that algebras are translated along signature morphisms in a countervariant direction into their *reduct*, we have that if $A' \in dom(\mu)_{\Sigma_2}$, then $A'_{|\Phi(\bar\sigma)} \in dom(\mu)_{\Sigma_1}$ and $(\beta_{\Sigma_2}(A'))_{|\bar\sigma} = \beta_{\Sigma_1}(A'_{|\Phi(\bar\sigma)})$. But it may be that $A' \notin dom(\mu)_{\Sigma_1}$ only because the interpretation of one function symbol f in A' is non-strict and that such an f is dropped by $\Phi(\bar\sigma)$, so that $A'_{|\Phi(\bar\sigma)} \in dom(\mu)_{\Sigma_1}$ and hence the converse of the first implication does not hold. Therefore we have a weaker condition (called *partial-naturality*) for algebras than the one for sentences.

Generalizing this example, we have that every framework consists of a category **Sign** of *signatures* (representing the symbols for types, operations and such, together with the admissible changes of notation) and, for every signature Σ, of a set of *sentences* $Sen(\Sigma)$ and of a category $Mod(\Sigma)$ of *models*; $Mod(\Sigma)$ and $Sen(\Sigma)$ are related by the *validity relation* $\models_\Sigma$: $A \models_\Sigma \xi$ states that the model A satisfies the sentence ξ. It is important to notice that the validity relation is invariant under change of notation, i.e. the reduct of a model along a signature morfism satisfies a formula iff the model satisfies the translation of the formula along the same signature morfism. This notion of logical framework is formalized by the *institutions* by Goguen and Burstall (see e.g. [6]), whose definition is recalled in appendix.

Let us abstract from the above construction the general aspects of the coding of a *new* formalism $\mathcal{I}$ into an *old* one $\mathcal{I}'$, as in the example the "new" partial framework was reduced the the "old" total; a *simulation* $\mu: \mathcal{I} \to \mathcal{I}'$ consists og:

- of a translation $\Phi: \mathbf{Sign} \to \mathbf{Sign}'$ of the new signatures in terms of the old ones;

- a translation $\alpha_\Sigma: Sen(\Sigma) \to Sen'(\Phi(\Sigma))$, for every signature Σ, coding the new sentences into the old ones on the corresponding signature;

- a partial surjective mapping $\beta_\Sigma: Mod'(\Phi(\Sigma)) \to Mod(\Sigma)$, for every signature Σ, of the old models into the new ones on the corresponding signature.

Moreover the translation of sentences has to be *natural* w.r.t. the signature morphisms, i.e. the following diagram commutes for every $\sigma: \Sigma \to \Sigma'$:

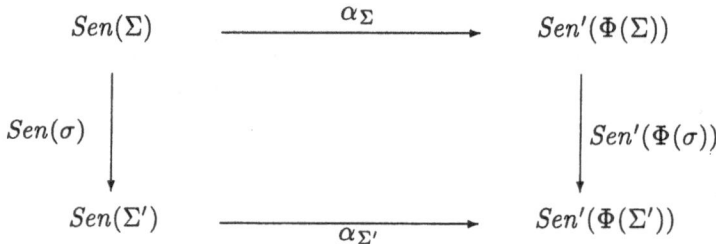

Analogously the translation of models has to be *partially-natural* w.r.t. the signature morphisms, i.e. if the lower path of the following diagram exists, then the upper path exists too and they are equal for every $\sigma: \Sigma \to \Sigma'$:

$$
\begin{array}{ccc}
Mod'(\Phi(\Sigma)) & \xrightarrow{\ \beta_\Sigma\ } & Mod(\Sigma) \\[1em]
\Big\uparrow{\scriptstyle Mod'(\Phi(\sigma))} & & \Big\uparrow{\scriptstyle Mod(\sigma)} \\[1em]
Mod'(\Phi(\Sigma')) & \xrightarrow[\ \beta_{\Sigma'}\ ]{} & Mod(\Sigma')
\end{array}
$$

This scheme generalizes to the frame of institutions by lifting maps to the proper categorical objects, taking care of the delicate points due to the partiality of model translation, and requiring that the only non-categorical structure, i.e. the validity relation, is preserved (see Def. A.2).

3 Simulations and modularity

In order to support stepwise refinement, it seems crucial that a specification is the collection of its possible realizations, i.e. of algebras satisfying appropriate requirements, expressed at the first stage by axioms in the framework and then by more general properties. Indeed such realizations are non-necessarily isomorphic, so that more decisional details can be fixed at every refinement step, restricting the class of possible models toward a completely determined model, hopefully defined in a (pseudo)executable language. Thus, as the modularity principle requires the ability of "putting together" specifications by means of structuring operations, we want to extend the capabilities of specification languages by allowing the different specifications that have to be composed to be defined in different frameworks. Therefore simulations, dealing only with the basic objects of a frame (i.e. signatures, sentences and models) have to be extended to work on specifications, i.e. classes of models, and the compatibility with structuring operations has to be investigated.

3.1 Basic Specifications

Informally a specification is the collection of the admissible models of a data type; formally it is completely determined by a class of algebras over one signature. Thus for every institution $\mathcal{I} = (\textbf{Sign}, Sen, Mod, \models)$, a *specification functor* $Spec_{\mathcal{I}} : \textbf{Sign} \rightarrow \textbf{Cat}^{\textbf{Op}}$ is defined, associating each signature Σ with the power set of its model class, i.e. $Spec_{\mathcal{I}}(\Sigma) = \wp(|Mod(\Sigma)|)$.

It is worth noting that the above construction is a particular case of building a new kind of objects starting from the ones explicitly given in the definition of institution, like models, signatures and so on. In the next subsection we will face the problem from a more general point of view.

Having built a new kind of objects, a new component of the simulation dealing with them has to be defined and is called from now on γ, possibly decorated. As the construction of specifications relies on algebras, the modularity principle requires that γ is analogously based on β, i.e. that if $\gamma(sp)$ is defined, then $\gamma(sp) = \beta(sp)$, where $\beta(sp) = \{\beta(A) \mid A \in sp\}$; but it is not obvious which specifications have to be translated.

The minimal requirement that has to be imposed so that $\gamma(sp)$ is defined is that every model $A \in sp$ belongs to the domain of the simulation, because this condition guarantees that the validity relation extended to specifications is reflected. Indeed, defining $sp \models \phi$ iff $A \models \phi$ for all $A \in sp$, it is always true that $sp' \models' \alpha(\phi)$ implies $\beta(sp') \models \phi$, because if $A' \models' \alpha(\phi)$, then $\beta(A') \models \phi$ for any A' s.t. $\beta(A')$ is defined, by definition of simulation. But in general $\beta(sp') \models \phi$ does not imply $sp' \models' \alpha(\phi)$, because A' may exist s.t. $A' \not\models' \alpha(\phi)$ and $\beta(A')$ is not defined, so that the condition of validity preservation by simulation does not apply. Of course the totality of β over sp', which is not necessary in the general case, in many significant cases is needed.

174

Besides requiring β to be total on sp, many other conditions can be imposed in order that a specification translation fits special purposes. This lack of canonicity leads to define, for every simulation $\mu: \mathcal{I} \to \mathcal{I}'$, a *specification extension* of μ to be any partially-natural transformation $\delta: Spec_{\mathcal{I}'} \cdot \Phi \to Spec_{\mathcal{I}}$ s.t. if $\delta(sp)$ is defined then $sp \subseteq dom(\beta)$ and $\delta(sp) = \beta_\Sigma(sp)$.

Among the many possible specification extensions, a particular role is played by the *maximal* specification extension γ of μ (one for each signature Σ), defined by:

if $sp \subseteq dom(\mu)_\Sigma$, then $\gamma_\Sigma(sp) = \beta_\Sigma(sp)$, else $\gamma_\Sigma(sp)$ is undefined.

Since β is surjective on models, there exists at least one $sp' \in Spec_{\mathcal{I}'}(\Phi(\Sigma))$ for each $sp \in Spec_{\mathcal{I}}(\Sigma)$ s.t. $\gamma_\Sigma(sp') = sp$. Such an sp' consists of $\{A' \mid \beta_\Sigma(A') \in sp\}$. This formalizes the intuitive idea that an institution is simulated by another one if each of its specifications is "implemented" by at least one specification of the other institution.

Using simulations, then, specifications can be imported/exported between institutions; thus every specification language L defined for a frame represented by an institution $\mathcal{I}$ can be enriched by constructs of the form

import sp via μ

where sp is a specification in an institution $\mathcal{I}'$ (possibly defined using another language L') and μ is a simulation from $\mathcal{I}$ into $\mathcal{I}'$. This capability is reminiscent of the feature common to most programming environment, allowing a program in a language to use an external module defined in another language.

Let us analyze a standard example of use of such an "import" feature: the specification of the natural numbers with sum and product is enriched by a *predecessor* operation. Let us consider how this can be realized in different formalisms. First of all consider the usual specification of natural numbers in a total many-sorted paradigm.

```
spec Nat =
    sorts   N
    opns    z: → N
            s: N → N
            _ + _: N × N → N
            _ * _: N × N → N
    axioms  x + z = x
            x + s(y) = s(x + y)
            x * z = z
            x * s(y) = x + (x * y)
```

Now suppose that this specification has to be enriched by a *partial* predecessor operation; as the chosen paradigm is *total*, we have to deal with the elements obtained as application of the predecessor operation to zero and to erroneous terms. There are two possibilities, neither of them pleasant: either no axioms are imposed on the errors, so that in most models, and in particular in the initial one, several distinguished "junk" elements are present, or many axioms have to be given in order to propagate the error, making the specification innecessarily long, and moreover this propagation is incompatible with the original specification, against every modularity principle. Consider indeed the following naive enrichment of the specification Nat.

```
spec Nat⊥ =   enrich  Nat  by
    opns    err: → N
            p: N → N
    axioms  p(s(x)) = x
            p(z) = err
    –       error propagation axioms
            s(err) = err
            p(err) = err
            x + err = err
            err + x = err
            x * err = err
            err * x = err
```

It is easy to check that from $err * x = err$ and $x * z = z$, $err = z$ follows, and then, by the error propagation axioms, every term is identified with err, so that the unique (up to isomorphism) term-generated model of the specification is the trivial one. To avoid this problem the unique possibility is introducing an "ok" predicate, false on the errors, and restricting the application of the original axioms to the "ok" elements, by conditional axioms (see e.g. [7]), so that the "parameter" Nat is changed by its enrichment.

But there is an obvious embedding ϵ of total into partial algebras that can be formalized as a simulation, so that the Nat specification can be translated along ϵ and then easily enriched in the partial framework with the successor operation.

The simulation ϵ consists of the identity translation $\bar{\Phi}$ of signatures, the identity translation $\bar{\alpha}$ of sentences and the embedding $\bar{\beta}$ of the partial algebras satisfying the family of *total axioms* $D_s(f(x_1,\ldots,x_n))$, one for each operation symbol $f: s_1 \times \ldots \times s_n \to s$ of the signature, where the x_i are distinct variables of sort s_i, respectively. As it is immediate to check, the partial algebras satisfying such axioms are all and only the total algebras on the same signature, so that $\bar{\beta}$ is well defined and surjective.

Now, using the "import_along_a_simulation" feature, we can easily define the required enrichment.

```
spec NatP =   enrich  import Nat along ε by
    opns    p: N → N
    axioms  p(s(x)) = x
```

Although, as the above example shows, the capability of importing specifications along simulations is a first step toward assembling specifications from different paradigms, it is quite unsatisfactory, because the possible structure of the imported specification is lost, as in the above example the axiomatic characterization of Nat. In order to get a more powerful kind of import, the structuring operations available in either language should be translated into the other language and the simulation used to import actual specifications should be compatible with such a structure.

3.2   Structured Specifications

In order to attain the capability of translating structured specifications along simulations in a way that the structure is preserved, the languages in the two frameworks should be instances of one common metalanguage, so that the intuitive meaning of "preserving the structure" can be rigorously formalized. Thus we need an *institution independent* metalanguage (see e.g. [14]). The sorts of this metalanguage may be both *basic*, i.e. implicitly defined by the concept of institution, like the sort of signatures, of algebras and so on, and *derived*, i.e. built from the basic ones using categorical and set-theoretic concepts, like the specifications which come from the algebras applying the powerset functor. Analogously the operations of this metalanguage are defined only involving the usual categorical and set-theoretic language, so that the interpretation of sorts and operations in any institution is standard.

Let us start with a few examples of institution independent operations, imported more or less from [14] and generalizing some ASL constructs.

models is the basic operation of every formalism, usually implicit; it takes in input a theory (Σ, Γ) and yields the class of models of Γ, i.e. $models(\Sigma, \Gamma) = \{A \mid A \in Mod(\Sigma), A \models \Gamma\}$; for example $models(Nat)$ denotes the variety of total algebras satisfying the axioms on $+$ and $*$. Note that the semantics of *models* can be defined for any institution, as it only involves the notion of validity, that is one of the institution ingredients.

$\_+\_$ takes in input two specifications on the same signature and yields the specification whose models are models of both, i.e. $sp + sp' = \{A \mid A \in sp \text{ and } A \in sp'\}$. In standard frameworks, where signatures consist of sorts, (predicates) and operations and signature morphisms are changes of notation, this operation allows the implementations of different operations to be independently developed, getting several specifications on one signature, eachone with a subset of the operations axiomatically described and the remaining free (without conditions imposed on them) and then, summing the subspecifications, one specification is obtained where all operations are axiomatized.

translate _ by _ in _ takes in input a Σ-specification sp, a signature morphism $\sigma: \Sigma \to \Sigma'$ and a Σ'-specification sp' and yields the subclass of sp' models whose σ-reduct is in sp, i.e.

$$translate \ sp \ by \ \sigma \ in \ sp' = \{A' \mid A' \in sp', Mod(\sigma)(A') \in sp\};$$

In standard frameworks the *translate* operation is used both to rename the operation symbols (by a bijective σ) and to embed a specification in another with larger signature, so that parts of a big specification can be developed on smaller signatures and then lifted by *translate* to the original signature so that the $+$ operation applies.

derive _ by _ takes in input a Σ'-specification sp' and a signature morphism $\sigma: \Sigma \to \Sigma'$ and yields the class of σ-reducts of sp' models, i.e.

$$derive \ sp' \ by \ \sigma = \{Mod(\sigma)(A') \mid A' \in sp'\}.$$

In standard frameworks the *derive* operation is used to hide implementative parts (if σ is a non-surjective embedding, then the sorts and/or operations in $\Sigma' - \Sigma$ concur to build the Σ-models, but become invisible in the reducts $Mod(\sigma)(A')$).

Using these operations more familiar operations can be defined, for example

enrich sp **by sorts** S' **opns** Op' **axioms** Ax'

for a specification sp on the signature (S, Op), corresponds to *translate sp by ι in sp'*, where $sp' = models((S \cup S', Op \cup Op'), Ax')$ and ι is the embedding of (S, Op) into $(S \cup S', Op \cup Op')$.

Let us consider again the example of natural numbers from the previous section. The specification **import** Nat **along** ϵ can now be more formally expressed by $\bar{\beta}^{-1}(models(Nat))$; but also the theory Nat can be translated along the simulation ϵ, as we will see in the sequel, by a theory extension Θ and hence we have an *a priori* different specification $models(\Theta(Nat))$. Obviously the latter possibility is easier to deal with, because it is a basic specification, so that, for example, deductive tools can be used for rapid prototyping.

Thus it would be interesting to have conditions guaranteeing that $\bar{\beta}^{-1}(models(Nat)) = models(\Theta(Nat))$; for this aim we can play with the choice of theory and specification extensions. Let us consider as specification extension the maximal one; for every logical simulation $\mu = (\Phi, \alpha, \beta)$, and hence in particular for ϵ, there are two standard possibilities for the definition of the theory extension:

- any theory (Σ, Γ) in the domain is translated by the *complete theory extension* $\Psi^{\bullet}$ into the theory $(\Phi(\Sigma), (\alpha(\Gamma) \cup th(\mu, \Sigma))^{\bullet})$ in the codomain, where $th(\mu, \Sigma)$ is a set of sentences defining the domain of μ and $\_^{\bullet}$ denotes the validity closure, i.e. $\Delta^{\bullet} = \{\epsilon \mid A \models \epsilon \text{ for all } A \models \Delta\}$;

- any theory (Σ, Γ) in the domain is translated by the *trivial theory extension* Ψ into the theory $(\Phi(\Sigma), \alpha(\Gamma))$ in the codomain (this choice is available for non-logical simulations as well).

With the trivial theory extension $models(\Psi(Nat))$ has many non-total models, and hence $\bar{\beta}^{-1}(models(Nat)) \neq models(\Psi(Nat))$, while it is easy to check that with the complete theory extension $\bar{\beta}^{-1}(models(Nat)) = models(\Psi^{\bullet}(Nat))$.

In general it can be proved that this property holds for any logical simulation, i.e. that given a logical simulation $\mu = (\Phi, \alpha, \beta)$, for every theory th in the domain of μ translating specifications along the maximal specification extension and theories along the complete theory extension $models(th) = \gamma(models(\Psi^{\bullet}(th)))$.

This last property can be seen as an instantiation of a general property, quite reminiscent of the homomorphism condition, that can be rephrased for every institution independent operation (see Def. A.5); for example for the $+$ operation it becomes $\beta(sp + sp') = \beta(sp) + \beta(sp')$, for the *translate* it becomes $\beta(translate\ sp\ by\ \Phi(\sigma)\ in\ sp') = translate\ \beta(sp)\ by\ \sigma\ in\ \beta(sp')$ and so on.

If, for an institution independent operation op, this generalized homomorphism condition is satisfied by every (logical) simulation, then we call op *(logical) simulation independent*. In our opinion simulation independent operations are the crucial point in building a specification language allowing the basic modules to be defined in different frameworks, as they guarantee that the composition of specifications is well behaving w.r.t. their translation between frameworks. In particular this condition suffices for the interpretation of every (closed) term of the specification language in the domain of the simulation

178

to be translated in the interpretation of the same term in the codomain, so that structured proofs are preserved, the expressive power of the language is unaffected, and the import mechanism can be seen as an easier way for defining specifications. Thus if the language enjoys the property that every closed term can be reduced to a basic specification, i.e. to an axiomatic description, (as many languages do), then simulation independency guarantees that the imported specification can be reduced to basic specifications as well.

It can be directly checked that with the complete theory extension and the maximal specification extension the *models*, *translate _ by _ in _* and *derive _ by _* operations are logical simulation independent.

It is worth noting that the *_+_* operation is not logical simulation independent w.r.t. this choice of extensions. Indeed a model A may exists in $\gamma(sp) + \gamma(sp')$ for which a $B \in sp$ and a $B' \in sp'$ exist s.t. $\beta(B) = A = \beta(B')$, but both $B \notin sp$ and $B' \notin sp'$ and more in general there does not exist a $C \in sp + sp'$ s.t. $\beta(C) = A$, so that $A \notin \gamma(sp + sp')$. As the *_+_* operation is very useful for the modular approach to the specification of complex data types, it can be interesting to change the notion of specification extension, by allowing only specifications closed w.r.t. the simulation, i.e. those sp s.t. $A \in sp$ and $\beta(A) = \beta(B)$ imply $B \in sp$, to be mapped. In the sequel such a specification extension will be called *closed* and denoted by $\gamma^\bullet$. With this definition the *_+_* operation becomes logical simulation independent, and so are the *models* and the *translate _ by _ in _*; but the *derive _ by _* is not, as in general it does not preserve the closure w.r.t. simulation, so that the result of *derive sp by* $\mu(\sigma)$ cannot be translated, although sp can be and hence the homomorphism condition is lost.

4 Simulations and the third dimension of implementation

In the literature a concept of implementation is largely used in different contexts, which is based on the idea of *refinement*. So a specification sp_2 implements a specifications sp_1, denoted by $sp_1 \rightsquigarrow sp_2$, iff in sp_2 more details have been fixed and hence sp_2 has less models than sp_1, i.e. $sp_2 \subseteq sp_1$ (see e.g. [15, 17]); this concept may also be extended to functions on specifications, by saying that a function f *implements* a function g iff for every possible argument sp we have $g(sp) \rightsquigarrow f(sp)$, and hence to parameterized specifications, viewed as denotation of functions. For an introductory exposition of the subject see e.g. section 8.1 of [17].

A relevant result (see fact. 8.1.1 of [17]) is the double composability law of implementation for specification-building operations monotonic w.r.t. the set-inclusion: in the "vertical" sense we have that if $sp \rightsquigarrow sp_1$ and $sp_1 \rightsquigarrow sp_2$, then $sp \rightsquigarrow sp_2$, by the transitivity of the subset relation, while in the "horizontal" sense we have that if a parameterized specification p_2 implements another parameterized specification p_1 of the same type, and if an actual parameter sp for p_1 is implemented by a specification sp_1, then $p_1(sp) \rightsquigarrow p_2(sp_1)$.

Since every specification extension is monotonic w.r.t. the set inclusion for all simulations μ, the implementation relation is translated by simulation from the old to the new frame, whatever notion of specification extension is chosen. Moreover if closed specification extension is chosen, then it is also preserved in the opposite direction; in this case the restriction of the old implementation relation to the domain of $\gamma^\bullet$ coincides with the new implementation relation (see the appendix for the formal statement).

Using simulations the concept of implementation is generalized, involving models in two institutions: given a simulation $\mu: \mathcal{I} \to \mathcal{I}'$ and two specification $sp \in Spec_\mathcal{I}(\Sigma)$ and $sp' \in Spec_{\mathcal{I}'}(\mu(\Sigma))$, we say that sp is μ-*implemented* by sp', denoted by $sp \overset{\mu}{\leadsto} sp'$, iff it is implemented in the standard sense by the translation of sp' along μ. This generalizes in the obvious way to functions and parameterized specifications (see Def. A.9).

Note that in the particular case that $\mathcal{I} = \mathcal{I}'$ and μ is the identity, $\overset{\mu}{\leadsto}$ coincides with $\leadsto$ and hence every result for $\overset{\mu}{\leadsto}$ applies also to $\leadsto$.

The vertical and horizontal composability for the usual implementation relation can be generalized to deal with simulations, in the sense that the implementation along the composition of two simulations is the composition of the implementation along the two given simulations and that all monotonic functions satisfy the "horizontal" composition w.r.t. the relation $\overset{\mu}{\leadsto}$, too.

Thus a more suggestive diagram than the usual one can be proposed, where every path is an implementation (possibly via simulation) arrow and three dimensions are present: horizontally and vertically moving within an institution, while along the third dimension different institutions are connected.

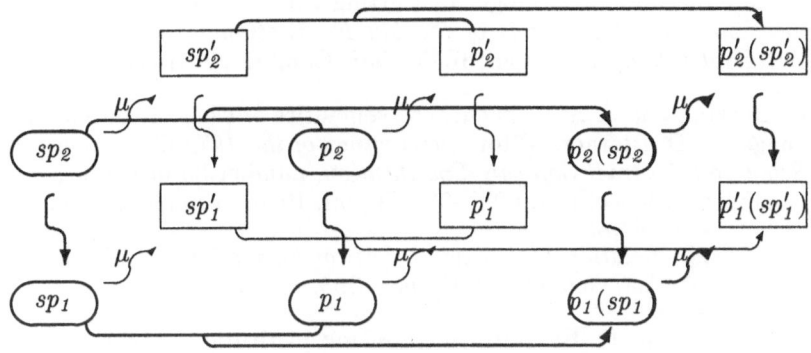

It is worth noting the difference between this approach and the one in [2]. Indeed here implementation is defined as a relation between specifications in different institutions, while in [2] an institution is proposed whose sentences represent the implementation inside a basic institution.

Conclusions

We have presented a preliminary attempt to state the foundation for specification metalanguages allowing their specification to be defined in different formalisms. In particular it has been shown how, using simulation in order to translate modules from one framework into another one, specifications can be declared "external" by a language and imported from a different paradigm.

The issue becomes more complex if we want to preserve the structure of the imported specification; indeed, for the problem to be meaningful, the importing and exporting languages have to be instances of one metalanguage and the extension of simulations to the language metasorts have to be carefully tailored to fit the operations. Although it is not difficult to find extensions working for a significant subset of the most common specification building operations, a completely satisfactory choice is missing and this point is still under investigation.

Acknowledgments. We wish to thank Joseph Goguen and Josè Meseguer for their patient attention, encouragement and useful criticism.

References

[1] E. Astesiano and M. Cerioli. Relationships between logical frames. In *Recent Trends in Data Type Specification*, number 655 in Lecture Notes in Computer Science, pages 126–143, Berlin, 1993. Springer Verlag.

[2] C. Beierle and A. Voss. Viewing implementations as an institution. In D. Pitt, A. Poigné, and D. Rydeheard, editors, *Proceedings of Category Theory and Computer Science*, number 283 in Lecture Notes in Computer Science, pages 196–218, Berlin, 1987. Springer Verlag.

[3] R. Burstall and J. A. Goguen. Putting theories together to make specifications. In *Proceedings of the 5th International Joint Conference on Artificial Intelligence*, pages 1045–1058, Cambridge, 1977.

[4] R. Burstall and J. A. Goguen. The semantics of clear, a specification language. In D. Bjørner, editor, *Proceedings of the 1979 Copenhagen Winter School on Abstract Software Specification*, number 86 in Lecture Notes in Computer Science, pages 292–332, Berlin, 1980. Springer Verlag.

[5] M. Cerioli. *Relationships between Logical Formalisms*. PhD thesis, Universities of Pisa, Genova and Udine, 1993.

[6] J. Goguen and R. Burstall. Introducing institutions. In E. Clarke and D. Kozen, editors, *Logics of Programs Workshop*, number 164 in Lecture Notes in Computer Science, pages 221–256, Berlin, 1984. Springer Verlag.

[7] J. Goguen, J. Thatcher, and Wagner. An initial algebra approach to the specification, correctness, and implementation of abstract data types. In R. Yeh, editor, *Current Trends in Programming Methodology*, pages 80–149. Prentice-Hall, 1976.

[8] J. Goguen and T. Winkler. Introducing OBJ3. Technical Report SRI-CSL-88-9, Computer Science Lab., SRI International, 1988.

[9] C. Hoare. Proof of correctness of data representation. *Acta Informatica*, 1:271–281, 1972.

[10] C. Jones. *Systematic Software Development using VDM*. Prentice Hall International, 1990.

[11] V. Manca, A. Salibra, and G. Scollo. Equational type logic. *Theoretical Computer Science*, 77:131–159, 1990. Special Issue dedicated to AMAST'89.

[12] M. Navarro, P. Nivela, F. Orejas, and A. Sanchez. On translating partial to total specifications with applications to theorem proving for partial specifications. Technical Report LSI-89-21, Universitat Politecnica de Catalunya, 1990.

[13] D. Parnas. A technique for software module specification. *Communications of A.C.M.*, 15, 1972.

[14] D. Sannella and A. Tarlecki. Specifications in an arbitrary institution. *Information and Computation*, 76:165–210, 1988.

[15] D. Sannella and M. Wirsing. A kernel language for algebraic specification and implementation. In M. Karpinski, editor, *International Conference on Foundations of Computation*, number 158 in Lecture Notes in Computer Science, pages 413–427, Berlin, 1983. Springer Verlag.

[16] J. Spivey. *The Z Notation: a Reference Manual*. Prentice-Hall, New-York, 1989.

[17] M. Wirsing. Algebraic specification. In *Handbook of Theoretical Computer Science*. North Holland, 1990.

A Formal Foundations

In this appendix we collect the formal definitions of the concepts and the rigorous statements of results informally presented in the paper.

A.1 Institutions and simulations

We recall first the notion of institution.

Def. A.1 [[6] def.14] An *institution* $\mathcal{I}$ consists of a category **Sign** of *signatures*, a functor $Sen:$ **Sign** $\to$ **Set** giving the set of *sentences* over a given signature, a functor $Mod:$ **Sign** $\to$ **Cat**^{Op} giving the category (sometimes called the *variety*) of *models* of a given signature (the arrows in $Mod(\Sigma)$ are called the *model morphisms*) and a satisfaction relation[1]

$$\models \subseteq |Mod(\Sigma)| \times Sen(\Sigma)$$

for each Σ in **Sign**, sometimes denoted $\models_\Sigma$, such that for each morphism $\phi: \Sigma_1 \to \Sigma_2$ in **Sign**, the *Satisfaction Condition*

$$M' \models Sen(\phi)(\xi) \iff Mod(\phi)(M') \models \xi$$

holds for each M' in $|Mod(\Sigma_2)|$ and each ξ in $Sen(\Sigma_1)$. □

---

[1] for any category $\mathbf{C}$ we denote by $|\mathbf{C}|$ the class of the objects of $\mathbf{C}$.

Since models are partially mapped, the usual notion of natural transformation is insufficient to describe the translation of the (*old*) model functor and we have to explicitly deal with the *partiality* of each component of this "partially"-natural transformation.

Def. A.2 Let $\mathcal{I} = (\mathbf{Sign}, Sen, Mod, \models)$ and $\mathcal{I}' = (\mathbf{Sign}', Sen', Mod', \models')$ be institutions. Then a *simulation* $\mu\colon \mathcal{I} \to \mathcal{I}'$ consists of

- a functor $\Phi\colon \mathbf{Sign} \to \mathbf{Sign}'$;

- a natural transformation $\alpha\colon Sen \to Sen' \cdot \Phi$,

- a surjective *partially-natural* transformation $\beta\colon Mod' \cdot \Phi \to Mod$, that is a family of functors $\beta_\Sigma\colon dom(\mu)_\Sigma \to Mod(\Sigma)$, where $dom(\mu)_\Sigma$ is a (non-necessarily full) subcategory of $Mod'(\Phi(\Sigma))$, s.t. β_Σ is surjective on $|Mod(\Sigma)|$ and the family is partially-natural, i.e. for any signature morphism $\sigma \in \mathbf{Sign}(\Sigma_1, \Sigma_2)$

$$Mod'(\Phi(\sigma))(dom(\beta)_{\Sigma_2}) \subseteq dom(\beta)_{\Sigma_1}$$

and $Mod(\sigma) \cdot \beta_{\Sigma_2}$ is the restriction of $\beta_{\Sigma_1} \cdot Mod'(\Phi(\sigma))$ to $dom(\mu)_{\Sigma_2}$;

s.t. the following *satisfaction condition* holds:

$$A \models \alpha_\Sigma(\xi) \iff \beta_\Sigma(A) \models \xi$$

for all $A \in |dom(\mu)_\Sigma|$ and all $\xi \in Sen(\Sigma)$.

If for every $\Sigma \in |\mathbf{Sign}|$ a set $th(\Sigma, \mu)$ of $\mathcal{I}'$-sentences on $\Phi(\Sigma)$ exists s.t. the class of algebras satisfying $th(\Sigma, \mu)$ is the object class of $dom(\mu)_\Sigma$ and $dom(\mu)_\Sigma$ is a full sub-category of $Mod'(\Phi(\sigma))$, then μ is called *logical*. □

It is easy to check that $\mu^\natural\colon \mathcal{PAR} \to \mathcal{TL}$, whose components were informally sketched in example 2.1, is a simulation, that is logical if open formulas are considered in $\mathcal{TL}$.

A.2 Simulating Specifications

Def. A.3 Let $\mathcal{I} = (\mathbf{Sign}, Sen, Mod, \models)$ be an institution. The *specification functor*, $Spec_\mathcal{I}\colon \mathbf{Sign} \to \mathbf{Cat}^{\mathbf{Op}}$ is the composition of Mod with the power functor, i.e.

- $Spec_\mathcal{I}(\Sigma)$ is the partially ordered category w.r.t. the class inclusion having as objects $\wp(|Mod(\Sigma)|)$, for all $\Sigma \in |\mathbf{Sign}|$;

- $Spec_\mathcal{I}(\sigma)(sp) = \{Mod(\sigma)(A) \mid A \in sp\}$ for all $\sigma \in \mathbf{Sign}(\Sigma_1, \Sigma_2)$ and all $sp \in Spec_\mathcal{I}(\Sigma_2)$. □

Def. A.4 Let $\mu\colon \mathcal{I} \to \mathcal{I}'$ be a simulation. A *specification extension* of μ is any partially-natural transformation $\alpha\colon Spec_{\mathcal{I}'} \cdot \mu \to Spec_\mathcal{I}$ s.t. if $\alpha(sp)$ is defined then $sp \subseteq dom(\beta)$ and $\alpha(sp) = \beta_\Sigma(sp)$.

The *maximal specification extension* γ of μ is defined by: if $sp \subseteq dom(\beta)$, then $\gamma_\Sigma(sp) = \beta_\Sigma(sp)$, else $\gamma_\Sigma(sp)$ is undefined. If no ambiguity arises γ_Σ will be denoted by γ or, simply, by μ. □

While it is clear what a metalanguage based on a categorical and set-theoretical language is, the only way to define it completely formally seems to be explicitly enumerating which sorts and operations are allowed; thus we limit ourselves to a semi-formal level and propose a scheme of construction of a generic metalanguage using as paradigmatic examples the operations of [14].

A.2.1 A building scheme for an institution independent language.

Let X be a set of variables[2], which will be evaluated in $|\mathbf{Sign}|$ for all institutions $\mathcal{I} = (\mathbf{Sign}, Sen, Mod, \models)$.

- Starting from the elements of X a set MS of *metasorts* is built, only using categorical and set-theoretical concepts; for example for any $\Sigma_1, \Sigma_2 \in X$ consider the metasort $Sign(\Sigma_1, \Sigma_2)$ of signature morphisms from Σ_1 into Σ_1.

- A set MF of metaoperations of arity in MS is built, only using categorical and set-theoretical concepts; for example for any $\Sigma \in X$ consider the metaoperation $models \colon \wp \cdot Sen(\Sigma) \to Spec(\Sigma)$, associating with any set of sentences the class of its models.

- Let us fix an institution $\mathcal{I} = (\mathbf{Sign}, Sen, Mod, \models)$ and a valuation $V \colon X \to |\mathbf{Sign}|$; with each symbol of MS and each operation symbol in MF the corresponding standard interpretation is associated; for example $(Sign(\Sigma_1, \Sigma_2))^{\mathcal{I},V} = \mathbf{Sign}(V(\Sigma_1), V(\Sigma_2))$ and $(s_i^{\mathcal{I},V} \colon \wp(Sen(V(\Sigma))) \to Spec_{\mathcal{I}}(V(\Sigma))$ on Ax yields $\{A \mid A \models \alpha, \text{ for all } \alpha \in Ax\}$. $\qquad \Box$

For each new sort we need to know the way it has to be translated w.r.t. a generic simulation μ, as we have seen in the case of specifications, where specification extensions had been defined to translate them. Analogously to the definition of the metalanguage, in order to define the new components of simulations we start from symbols to denote the components dealing with signatures, sentences and models, which will be evaluated to the components of the simulation, and use them to formally define an extension of a generic simulation by means of the categorical and set-theoretic metalanguage. The only requirement made for the choice of the extensions is that the composition of the (chosen) extensions of two composable simulations is the extension of the composition itself.

In the sequel both the symbol for the extension of metasort s of a simulation and its evaluation on a concrete simulation will be denoted by μ^s.

A.2.2 Simulating Structured Specifications

With the help of a metalanguage, institutions are provided of algebraic structure; thus we are looking for conditions guaranteeing that the simulation extensions are behaving like homomorphisms of this new structure. As the extensions of a simulation for the derived metasorts can be partial or countervariant, the standard formulation of many-sorted homomorphisms, $h_s(op^{\mathcal{I}}(a_1, \ldots, a_n)) =$

---

[2]Since in any significant example we have seen, the language is based only on metavariables of sort *signatures*, we use a set of variables for sake of simplicity; but there are no problems using a family of variable sets indexed on the basic elements of institutions.

$op^{\mathcal{I}'}(h_{s_1}(a_1), \ldots, h_{s_n}(a_n))$, has to be worked out carefully. It is easier starting from the following equivalent formulation of the homomorphism condition:

$$a'_1 = h_{s_1}(a_1) \wedge \ldots \wedge a'_n = h_{s_n}(a_n) \supset h_s(op^{\mathcal{I}}(a_1, \ldots, a_n)) = op^{\mathcal{I}'}(a'_1, \ldots, a'_n);$$

indeed it is sufficient to modify the premises, allowing that, depending on the co/counter-variance of the s component of the homomorphism, either $a'_i = h_{s_i}(a_i)$, or $a_i = h_{s_i}(a'_i)$ are used.

Def. A.5 Let $\mu: \mathcal{I} \to \mathcal{I}'$ be a simulation and $L = (MS, MF)$ be an institution independent metalanguage on variables X. Then μ is an L-*homomorphism* iff a_i related by μ to a'_i implies $op^{\mathcal{I},V}(a_1, \ldots, a_n)$ related by μ to $op^{\mathcal{I}',\mu \cdot V}(a'_1, \ldots, a'_n)$, where two elements a and a' of the same metasort s are related by μ iff one of them is the image of the other one along the extension μ^s, for all valuations $V: X \to |\mathbf{Sign}|$ and all $op \in MF_{s_1 \ldots s_n, s}$.

Let L be an institution independent metalanguage and M be a class of simulations. Then L is *M-independent* iff μ is an L-homomorphism for each $\mu \in M$ and it is *(logical) simulation independent* iff μ is an L-homomorphism for all (logical) simulations μ. $\square$

It is easy to check that L-homomorphisms are well behaving w.r.t. the composition of simulations, the union and the operational closure of languages.

A.3 Implementation and Simulation

Def. A.6

- A specification sp_2 *implements* a specifications sp_1, denoted by $sp_1 \rightsquigarrow sp_2$, iff both sp_1 and sp_2 are on the same signature and $sp_2 \subseteq sp_1$.

- Let $f, g: Spec_{\mathcal{I}} \to Spec_{\mathcal{I}}$ be functions on specifications; then f *implements* g, denoted by $g \rightsquigarrow f$ iff $g(sp) \rightsquigarrow f(sp)$ for all specifications sp.

- Let $p_1 = \lambda X : \Sigma_{Par}.sp_1(\_)$ and $p_2 = \lambda X : \Sigma_{Par}.sp_2(\_)$ be terms of the same sort on some (institution independent) metalanguage; then p_2 *implements* p_1, denoted by $p_1 \rightsquigarrow p_2$, iff $sp_1[sp] \rightsquigarrow sp_2[sp]$ for all specifications sp. $\square$

Prop. A.7 Let sp, sp_1 and sp_2 be specifications and p_1, p_2 be parameterized specifications in a metalanguage whose specification-building operations are monotonic w.r.t. the set-inclusion.

1. If $sp \rightsquigarrow sp_1$ and $sp_1 \rightsquigarrow sp_2$, then $sp \rightsquigarrow sp_2$;

2. If $sp \rightsquigarrow sp_1$, $p_1 \rightsquigarrow p_2$ and sp is an actual parameter of p_1 (i.e. $p_1(sp)$ is defined), then $p_1(sp) \rightsquigarrow p_2(sp_1)$.

Proof. See fact. 8.1.1 of [17]. $\square$

Prop. A.8 Let $\mu: \mathcal{I} \to \mathcal{I}'$ be a simulation, sp'_1 and sp'_2 belong to $Spec_{\mathcal{I}'}(\mu(\Sigma))$ s.t. both $sp'_1, sp'_2 \subseteq dom(\beta)$; if $sp'_1 \rightsquigarrow sp'_2$, then $\gamma(sp'_1) \rightsquigarrow \gamma(sp'_2)$. Moreover if $\gamma^\bullet(sp'_1)$ and $\gamma^\bullet(sp'_2)$ are defined, then $sp'_1 \rightsquigarrow sp'_2$ iff $\gamma^\bullet(sp'_1) \rightsquigarrow \gamma^\bullet(sp'_2)$.

Proof. If $sp'_1 \rightsquigarrow sp'_2$, then $sp'_2 \subseteq sp'_1$ and hence $\gamma(sp'_1) \rightsquigarrow \gamma(sp'_2)$, as

$$\gamma(sp'_2) = \beta(sp'_2) \subseteq \beta(sp'_1) = \gamma(sp'_1).$$

Let us assume that $\gamma^{\bullet}(sp'_1)$ and $\gamma^{\bullet}(sp'_2)$ are defined; then, analogously to the previous point, $sp'_1 \rightsquigarrow sp'_2$ implies $\gamma^{\bullet}(sp'_1) \rightsquigarrow \gamma^{\bullet}(sp'_2)$. Vice versa if $\gamma^{\bullet}(sp'_1) \rightsquigarrow \gamma^{\bullet}(sp'_2)$, then $\beta^{-1}(\gamma^{\bullet}(sp'_2)) \subseteq \beta^{-1}(\gamma^{\bullet}(sp'_1))$, i.e., by the condition of definedness of $\gamma^{\bullet}$, $sp'_1 \rightsquigarrow sp'_2$, as

$$sp'_2 = \beta^{-1}(\gamma^{\bullet}(sp'_2)) \subseteq \beta^{-1}(\gamma^{\bullet}(sp'_1)) = sp'_1. \quad \square$$

Def. A.9 Let $\mu: \mathcal{I} \to \mathcal{I}'$ be a simulation, $sp \in Spec_{\mathcal{I}}(\Sigma)$, $sp' \in Spec_{\mathcal{I}'}(\mu(\Sigma))$; then sp is μ-*implemented* by sp', denoted by $sp \overset{\mu}{\rightsquigarrow} sp'$, iff $sp' \subseteq dom(\beta)$ and $\beta(sp') \subseteq sp$, i.e. iff $\gamma(sp')$ is defined and $sp \rightsquigarrow \gamma(sp')$.

Let $f: Spec_{\mathcal{I}}(\Sigma_1) \to Spec_{\mathcal{I}}(\Sigma_2)$ and $f': Spec_{\mathcal{I}'}(\mu(\Sigma_1)) \to Spec_{\mathcal{I}'}(\mu(\Sigma_2))$ be functions; then f is μ-*implemented* by f', denoted by $f \overset{\mu}{\rightsquigarrow} f'$, iff $f(sp) \overset{\mu}{\rightsquigarrow} f'(\beta^{-1}(sp))$ for all $sp \in Spec_{\mathcal{I}}(\Sigma)$.

Let $p_1 = \lambda X : \Sigma_{Par}.sp_1(\_)$ and $p_2 = \lambda X : \Sigma_{Par}.sp_2(\_)$ be terms of the same sort on some institution independent metalanguage; then p_1 is μ-*implemented* by p_2, denoted by $p_1 \overset{\mu}{\rightsquigarrow} p_2$, iff $p_1{}^{\mathcal{I},V} \overset{\mu}{\rightsquigarrow} p_2{}^{\mathcal{I}',\mu \cdot V}$ for all valuations V for the free variables of p_1 and p_2 in $\mathcal{I}$. $\qquad \square$

Prop. A.10 Let $\mathcal{I}$, $\mathcal{I}'$ and $\mathcal{I}''$ be institutions, $\mu: \mathcal{I} \to \mathcal{I}'$ and $\nu: \mathcal{I}' \to \mathcal{I}''$ be simulations. The following conditions hold:

1. $sp \overset{\mu}{\rightsquigarrow} sp'$ and $sp' \overset{\nu}{\rightsquigarrow} sp''$ implies $sp \overset{\nu \cdot \mu}{\rightsquigarrow} sp''$ for all $sp \in Spec_{\mathcal{I}}(\Sigma)$, all $sp' \in Spec_{\mathcal{I}'}(\mu(\Sigma))$ and all $sp'' \in Spec_{\mathcal{I}''}(\nu(\mu(\Sigma)))$.

2. $sp \overset{\mu}{\rightsquigarrow} sp'$ and $f \overset{\mu}{\rightsquigarrow} f'$ implies $f(sp) \overset{\mu}{\rightsquigarrow} f'(sp')$ for all $sp \in Spec_{\mathcal{I}}(\Sigma_1)$, all $sp' \in Spec_{\mathcal{I}'}(\mu(\Sigma_1))$ all monotonic $f: Spec_{\mathcal{I}}(\Sigma_1) \to Spec_{\mathcal{I}}(\Sigma_2)$ and $f': Spec_{\mathcal{I}'}(\mu(\Sigma_1)) \to Spec_{\mathcal{I}'}(\mu(\Sigma_2))$.

Proof.

1. Since $sp' \subseteq dom(\beta)$ and $\beta'(sp'') \subseteq sp'$, $sp'' \subseteq dom(\nu \cdot \mu)$. Moreover if $sp' \overset{\nu}{\rightsquigarrow} sp''$, then $\beta'_{\Phi(\Sigma)}(sp'') \subseteq sp'$, and if $sp \overset{\mu}{\rightsquigarrow} sp'$, then $\beta_{\Sigma}(sp') \subseteq sp$, so that $\beta_{\Sigma}(\beta'_{\Phi(\Sigma)}(sp'')) \subseteq sp$, i.e. $sp \overset{\nu \cdot \mu}{\rightsquigarrow} sp''$.

2. By definition of $\overset{\mu}{\rightsquigarrow}$, it is sufficient to show that $\beta_{\Sigma}(f'(sp')) \subseteq f(sp)$. By definition of $\overset{\mu}{\rightsquigarrow}$, $f \overset{\mu}{\rightsquigarrow} f'$ implies that $f'(\beta_{\Sigma}{}^{-1}(sp_1)) \overset{\mu}{\rightsquigarrow} f(sp_1)$, so that $\beta_{\Sigma}(f'(\beta_{\Sigma}{}^{-1}(sp_1)) \subseteq f(sp_1)$ for all $sp_1 \in Spec_{\mathcal{I}}(\Sigma_1)$; thus, for $sp_1 = \beta_{\Sigma}(sp')$, $\beta_{\Sigma}(f'(\beta_{\Sigma}{}^{-1}(\beta_{\Sigma}(sp'))) \subseteq f(\beta_{\Sigma}(sp'))$. Since $sp \overset{\mu}{\rightsquigarrow} sp'$, $sp' \subseteq dom(\beta)$ and hence $sp' \subseteq \beta_{\Sigma}{}^{-1}(\beta_{\Sigma}(sp'))$, so that, as f' is monotonic, $f'(sp') \subseteq f'(\beta_{\Sigma}{}^{-1}(\beta_{\Sigma}(sp')))$. Finally from $sp \overset{\mu}{\rightsquigarrow} sp'$, i.e. $\beta_{\Sigma}(sp') \subseteq sp$, and from the monotony of f, the thesis follows. $\qquad \square$

The Semantics of Extended ML: A Gentle Introduction

Stefan Kahrs[*]

Laboratory for Foundations of Computer Science, Edinburgh University
Edinburgh, Scotland

Donald Sannella[†]

Laboratory for Foundations of Computer Science, Edinburgh University
Edinburgh, Scotland

Andrzej Tarlecki[‡]

Institute of Informatics, Warsaw University, and
Institute of Computer Science, Polish Academy of Sciences,
Warsaw, Poland

Abstract

Extended ML (EML) is a framework for the formal development of modular Standard ML (SML) software systems. Development commences with a specification of the behaviour required and proceeds via a sequence of partial solutions until a complete solution, an executable SML program, is obtained. All stages in this development process are expressed in the EML specification language, an extension of SML with axioms for describing properties of module components.

This is a report on the current state of the semantics of the EML specification language as it nears completion. EML is unusual in being built around a "real" programming language having a formal semantics. Interesting and complex problems arise both from the nature of this relationship and from interactions between the features of the language.

1 Introduction

Extended ML (EML) is a framework for the formal development of modular Standard ML (SML) software systems which are correct with respect to a specification of their required behaviour. The long-term goal of work on EML is to provide a practical framework for formal development together with an integrated suite of computer-based specification and development support tools and complete mathematical foundations to substantiate claims of correctness. A short-term subgoal is to complete the formal definition of the semantics of the

---

[*]This research was supported by SERC grants GR/E78463, GR/H73103 and GR/J07303.

[†]This research was supported by SERC grants GR/E78463, GR/J07693, a SERC Advanced Fellowship, and the COMPASS Basic Research working group.

[‡]This research was supported by SERC grants GR/H76739 and GR/E78463, an EC-funded COST fellowship, and KBN grant PB 1247/P3/93/04.

EML specification language [14], in order to provide a basis for further research on foundations and tools. This paper is a report on the current state of this definition as it nears completion.

SML is a widely-used functional programming language. Apart from useful features it shares with a number of similar languages (a flexible type system with polymorphic types, function definition by patterns, etc.) it has two special characteristics which make it very well-suited to the enterprise mentioned above. First, it provides state-of-the-art modularisation facilities for building large software systems by defining and combining self-contained generic program units. Such facilities seem to be a prerequisite for the use of formal development methods on examples of significant size. The main emphasis of EML is on development "in the large", relying heavily on linguistic support from the SML module facilities and incorporating ideas from foundational work on specification and formal development of modular systems [37], [33], [30], [36]. Second, the syntax and semantics of SML is formally defined [22]. This makes it possible (at least in principle) to reason formally about the behaviour of SML programs, as required for proofs of correctness with respect to a specification of requirements. The size and complexity of the semantics is such that fully formal use of it, e.g. to prove correctness of an optimizing transformation, would be quite a difficult task. Nevertheless, the semantics is small and elegant enough that such use seems not to be completely out of the question.

The idea of building a fully-fledged specification and formal development framework around a "real" programming language seems to be novel to EML. Somewhat related is work on the Anna language for annotating Ada programs with assertions concerning their intended behaviour [19]; but this is not intended for formal development of software from specifications (although see [17]), and as far as we are aware there is no formal semantics of Anna nor any intention to formally relate Anna to the semantics of Ada [2]. Similar comments apply to Larch [10], which has been used in connection with various programming languages. Attempts to apply Larch to the specification of SML modules have recently begun [39], but this work is still at an early stage and many problems remain to be solved. Real programming languages are inevitably complex, and any serious attempt to give a formal treatment of such a language and a development framework based on it is an ambitious goal bringing a host of problems which do not arise when considering toy programming languages or when considering specification and formal development in abstract terms.

Another novelty of this work is in its treatment of the specification of a number of "difficult" facets of computation, all of which arise in SML. These include polymorphic types, higher-order functions, exceptions and non-termination. In spite of the fact that these are common features of modern programming languages, they are rarely addressed by approaches to specification. There have been attempts to treat each of these features in isolation, but not in combination with one another. It is precisely in the interaction between such features that some of the most difficult issues arise.

The structure of the paper is as follows. Section 2 gives a short introduction to the main features of SML and EML in order to set the scene for the rest of the paper. We have resisted the temptation to dwell at length on aspects of EML which are not directly relevant to the topic at hand; for more information, see the papers cited in Section 2. Section 3 discusses the way in which EML relates to and extends SML. Section 4 is an overview of the semantics of EML which attempts to give the reader an overall impression of its structure without the need to study the details of [14], while touching on the ideas behind many of the most interesting and important points. Section 5 concludes with some remarks about the trials and tribulations involved in writing such a semantics.

2 An overview of EML

The main aim of this section is to provide enough background concerning EML to make the paper self-contained. The first subsection is a summary of the features of the SML programming language, which is the target of EML formal program development and on which EML is based. The next subsection gives an overview of the EML language and formal development framework. A small example is given to demonstrate some of the features of the language, and a final subsection summarizes the main features of the logic used to write axioms.

2.1 SML

The following is necessarily very brief. Readers with no prior knowledge of SML or related languages (Hope, Haskell, etc.) will probably find it necessary to consult e.g. [11] or [24].

SML consists of two sub-languages: the *core* language and the *module* language. The core language provides constructs for programming "in the small" by defining a collection of types and values (including functions) of those types. The module language provides constructs for programming "in the large" by defining and combining a number of self-contained program units coded using the core. To a large extent, these sub-languages can be understood separately from each other, both because the dependency is only one-way (modules contain core constructs, but not vice versa) and because the constructs available in the module language are applicable to the organization of declarations of any kind. SML is an interactive language in which top-level declarations are typechecked, compiled and evaluated one at a time.

The SML core language is a strongly typed functional programming language with a flexible type system including polymorphic types, disjoint union, product and (higher-order) function types, recursive types, and user-defined abstract and concrete types. Conceptually, all values in SML (except those of certain special built-in types, such as **real** and function types) are represented as finite ground terms built from uninterpreted *constructors*. A function is defined by a sequence of equations, each of which specifies the value of the function over some subset of the set of possible argument values. This subset is described by a *pattern* (a term containing constructors and variables only, without repeated variables) on the left-hand side of the equation, which serves both for case selection and variable binding. Certain types are designated by SML as *equality types*; roughly, these are types whose definitions do not involve abstract types or function types. The built-in equality function = has type ''a * ''a -> bool; the type variable ''a can only be instantiated to equality types (in contrast to 'a which can be instantiated to any type), preventing values of non-equality types from being tested for equality. Exceptions (possibly carrying values) may be raised by built-in functions (e.g. division by zero) or by user code. Once raised, an exception propagates until it is trapped by a surrounding handler or reaches top level. Typed references are available with dereferencing and assignment operations. Input/output is handled via streams; input streams are associated with producers (e.g. a keyboard or a file) and output streams are associated with consumers.

The SML module language provides mechanisms that allow large SML programs to be structured into self-contained program units with explicit interfaces. Under this scheme, interfaces (*signatures*) and their implementations (*structures*) are defined separately. Structures contain definitions of types, values and exceptions, and may also contain definitions of lower-level structures (*substructures*). Signatures may be attached to structures; this imposes a requirement for the structure to *match* that signature, meaning that the structure must define types, values, exceptions and substructures with the names indicated by the signature, and the types of values and exceptions as well as the signatures of substructures must correspond to those given in the signature. *Functors* are "parameterized" structures; the application of a functor to a structure yields a structure. A functor has an input signature describing structures to which it may be applied, and an output signature describing the structure which results from such an application. It is possible, and sometimes necessary to allow interaction between different parts of a program, to declare that certain substructures (or just certain types) are identical or *shared*. Structures and functors are referred to collectively as *modules*.

Signatures serve both to impose constraints on the bodies of modules and to restrict the information which is made available externally about the components of module bodies. Roughly speaking, only the information that is explicitly recorded in the signature(s) of a module is available externally. (In fact, this statement is not accurate for SML, but it *is* accurate in the context of EML. See Section 3 for more on this point.) Such information hiding is vital to allow parts of a large software system to be developed and maintained independently.

2.2   EML

EML is a vehicle for the formal development of programs from specifications by means of individually-verified steps. EML is called a *wide-spectrum* language [4] since it allows all stages in the formal development process to be expressed in a single formalism, from the initial high-level specification to the final program itself and including intermediate stages in which specification and program are intermingled. The target of the formal development process is a modular program in SML, and thus (a large subset of) SML is an executable sub-language of EML. Earlier stages in the development of such a program are incomplete modular programs in which some parts are only specified by means of axioms rather than defined in an executable fashion by means of SML code.

Syntactically, the main difference between SML and EML is that EML permits axioms to be included in signatures and in module bodies. Including axioms in signatures allows properties to be specified which are required to hold of any structure matching that signature. The general idea is similar to that of providing *types* of values in signatures in addition to their *names*; the difference is that types (and sharing constraints) can be checked mechanically, while checking that axioms are satisfied requires the use of a theorem prover (and human ingenuity). One reason for including types of values in an SML signature is to provide enough information about the module it describes to enable subsequent code which refers to it to be typechecked and compiled without making reference to the details of the code in the module body. This is essential for purposes of separate compilation. Similarly, a reason for including axioms in an EML signature is to provide enough information about the module it describes to enable *properties* of such subsequent code to be *proved* without reference to the module body. This separation of an interface from its implementation permits different implementations (satisfying the axioms in the interface) to be developed and used later without affecting the correctness of the rest of the system, and enables implementations for different modules to be developed independently.

Axioms in module bodies may be used to describe components for which executable definitions (in the form of SML code) are not yet available. Syntactically, one gives a declaration containing the place-holder expression "?", followed by axioms referring to the undefined object. For example:

```
val x:int = ?
axiom x>7 andalso isprime x
```

Module bodies containing axioms may be regarded as unfinished or incomplete *abstract programs* in which some decisions have already been taken but others, such as choice of algorithms, remain open. The intention is that at a later stage in the development of the program, the question mark will be replaced by code that satisfies the axioms. In the first version of a module declaration, a question mark may be used as a place-holder for the entire module body.

In EML, each structure comes equipped with a signature (this is optional in SML) containing the information which is available externally concerning the structure body. As in SML, the body is required to match this signature. In addition to the name/type matching required in SML, the body must be *correct*: the axioms in the signature must be satisfied by any model of the body (that is, by any structure containing the code in the structure body and satisfying any axioms it includes). Obviously, a proof is generally required to establish correctness. Following ideas concerning the use of axioms to specify encapsulated abstractions (see e.g. [26], [9], [32]), the axioms in the signature need not actually be satisfied "literally": it is enough if they are satisfied "up to behavioural equivalence". Briefly, this means that for any model of the structure, there must be some structure satisfying the axioms in the signature from which the model cannot be distinguished by performing computations that yield observable results (i.e. results of base types such as bool). Similar remarks apply to functor declarations, which must contain both an input signature (also required in SML) and an output signature (optional in SML); in this case, all models of the functor body which extend "literal" models of the input signature are required to satisfy the output signature up to behavioural equivalence. See Section 4.3 for some further details, and see [34] for more on the role of behavioural equivalence in the context of EML.

Formal development of a system begins with an initial high-level specification of the problem to be solved, in the form of an EML module declaration having a question mark in place of its body. If the module is parameterized (i.e., is a functor) the input signature specifies the facilities (types, values, exceptions, and structures) to be taken as given, in addition to the built-ins of SML. The output signature of the module specifies the additional facilities required. These signatures will normally contain axioms. At later stages of development, this module declaration will be refined by providing it with a body which is correct in the sense described above. This may contain axioms, and may make reference to further structures or functors that are themselves not yet defined in an executable fashion. The development process is finished once all functor and structure bodies on which the original "goal" module depends are *complete*, meaning that all question marks and axioms in module bodies have been replaced by executable SML code. At this point, erasing all axioms from signatures (or, much more usefully, regarding them as complete and formally checked documentation) yields an executable SML program. This is correct with respect to the initial specification since correctness is maintained by each development step.[1]

The EML formal development methodology defines a number of ways of gradually refining an unfinished module declaration towards a complete and correct version. A common way to proceed is to decompose the problem into simpler problems by specifying a number of new modules and defining the module at hand as a composition of these. The task of providing a body for each of these new modules becomes a refinement task in its own right which can be tackled separately from the others. Such steps give rise to proof obligations which must be proved in order to ensure that correctness is preserved; these proof obligations can be generated mechanically from the "before" and "after" versions of the module at hand. See [34], [35], [15] and [28] for further details, and see [34], [27] and [29] for examples of EML-style formal software development.

2.3   An example in EML

The example in Figure 1 illustrates some of the language features of EML. It is an implementation of evaluation for a rewrite system, based on some simple abstract properties one would expect for arbitrary rewrite systems, (enriched) λ-calculi, etc. This takes the form of a functor, where properties required of the argument and properties of the result are specified by EML axioms. The functor itself is coded in the executable subset of EML, so this is an example of what might emerge from a formal development which began with a specification of the problem consisting of the same functor with its body replaced by the place-holder "?".

The idea of the example is as follows. Rewrite systems operate on some set of terms; each term is either a normal form (NF) or contains a redex that can be contracted. A (one-step) strategy picks a redex in a term and returns the redex together with the context of its occurrence in the term, given as a function. The functor Reduce provides a function eval which repeatedly contracts redexes selected by the given strategy until a term in normal form is obtained. A copy of the argument structure L is included as a substructure T of the result in order to provide convenient access to the type of terms. T inherits the signature of L (TERMSIG).

---

[1]To be completely accurate, it must be mentioned that the compilation of the resulting program is not guaranteed to terminate: EML copes gracefully with non-terminating functions, as explained below, but not with non-terminating *declarations*. The guarantee of correctness is subject to this proviso.

```
signature TERMSIG =
    sig
        type term
        val contract: term -> term
        val NF: term -> bool
        axiom forall t => (NF t) proper
        val strategy: term -> term * (term -> term)
        exception noredex
        axiom forall t =>
            if NF t then (strategy t) raises noredex
            else ((strategy t) proper andalso
                    let val (u,f) = strategy t
                    in f u == t andalso
                        (f (contract u)) proper
                    end)
    end;

signature EVAL =
    sig
        structure T: TERMSIG
        val eval: T.term -> T.term
        axiom forall t =>
            (eval t) terminates implies T.NF(eval t)
    end;

functor Reduce (L: TERMSIG) :
    sig include EVAL; sharing L=T end =
    struct structure T = L
            fun eval t =
                if L.NF t then t
                else let val (redex,context) = L.strategy t
                    in eval (context (L.contract redex))
                    end
    end;
```

Figure 1: An example: evaluation for a rewrite system

The signature **TERMSIG** imposes certain requirements on the behaviour of **NF** and **strategy**: the axiom **forall t => (NF t) proper** is true if the evaluation of **NF t** neither fails to terminate nor raises an exception; for **strategy** there are even stronger conditions, for example that the redex created by **strategy** can be properly contracted, and that **strategy t** raises an exception if and only if **t** is in normal form. Typical for EML is here the mixture of logical connectives and programming language constructs.

The functor **Reduce** gives us an evaluation function **eval**, as specified in the "included" signature **EVAL**, for any rewrite system matching **TERMSIG**. From the interface of **TERMSIG** and the implementation of **eval** we can show that it will never raise an exception (although it may fail to terminate). The sharing equation, an SML feature, is needed to ensure that the type **T.term** used in the type of **eval** is the same as the type **L.term** provided by the argument of **Reduce**, so evaluation is for the kind of terms defined by the argument and not for some other kind of terms. It also makes **eval** applicable to terms other than the ones that can be built using structure **T** only. This is quite desirable, as structure **T** contains no functions for building terms, except by contraction of other terms; normally, the argument of **Reduce** (or structures on which it depends) will contain such functions, in addition to those required by **TERMSIG**.

2.4 The language of EML axioms

The syntax used to write axioms in the above example should have been sufficiently self-explanatory to make the intended meaning clear. However, the logical system used is not a conventional one; it is necessarily much more complex than (for example) many-sorted equational logic or first-order predicate logic because of the need to deal with all the features of SML programs. For example, consider an equation asserting that the values of two expressions, *exp* and *exp'*, are equal. What if either *exp* or *exp'* (or both) fail to terminate? What if one raises an exception (or in the terminology of the SML definition, evaluates to a *packet*)? What if *exp* and *exp'* are of a function type? And in the case of universally and existentially quantified formulae, what is the meaning of quantification over a polymorphic type?

The syntax of EML axioms is designed to be a natural extension of the syntax of EML boolean expressions, with the meaning of the new constructs chosen to be as simple and natural as possible under the circumstances. We have attempted to maximize expressive power, and to avoid making certain common specification idioms unduly awkward to write.

Any expression of type **bool** may be used as an axiom in EML. Such use amounts to an assertion that the expression evaluates[2] to the value **true** rather than evaluating to the value **false**, or evaluating to a packet, or failing to terminate. Hence, the basic connectives are those of SML: **andalso**, **orelse**, and **not**, with the additional connective **implies**. The first two of these have the same "sequential" interpretation as they do in SML (and analogously for **implies**), so for example the expression **true orelse** *exp* evaluates to **true** even if *exp* produces a packet or fails to terminate.

A "logical" equality predicate **==** complements the "computational" equality **=** provided by SML. The expression *exp==exp'* is well-formed whenever *exp* and

---

[2] Actually, *verificates* — see Section 4.3.

exp' have the same type, in contrast to $exp=exp'$ which requires this to be an equality type. Logical equality is extensional equality in "logical-relation style" [23] on function types, meaning that if f, f' are both of type $\tau \to \tau'$ then $f==f'$ is defined as

```
forall (x:τ,x':τ) => x==x' implies (f x)==(f' x')
```

— see below for the meaning of quantification. It is also "extensional" for packets and non-termination: $exp==exp$ is **true** even if exp produces a packet or fails to terminate. For any expression exp, additional atomic formulae are:

exp **terminates**, which is **true** if exp produces a normal value or a packet, and **false** if it fails to terminate;

exp **proper**, which is **true** if exp produces a normal value, and **false** if it produces a packet or fails to terminate; and

exp **raises** $excon$,[3] which is **true** if exp raises the exception $excon$ and **false** if it produces a normal value or raises a different exception. If exp fails to terminate then so does exp **raises** $excon$.

Universal and existential quantification is provided over all SML types; function types are included here so this gives a form of higher-order logic, although since quantification ranges over values that are *expressible* in SML, it is not true higher-order quantification. The meaning of quantification over polymorphic types is a tricky issue. An easy choice would be to require explicit quantification of type variables, as in System F [8], but this seems contrary to the spirit of SML in which all such quantification is implicit. The best balance seems to be struck by viewing a quantified formula as having a defined value only if it has that value for all instances (including polymorphic instances) of the type of the bound variable. More explicitly, this amounts to the following four cases:

- In order for **forall** $x:\tau$ => exp to be **true**, the expression $exp[x := v]$ must be **true** for every expressible value v of every instance of τ.

- In order for **exists** $x:\tau$ => exp to be **true**, there must be an expressible value v of type τ such that $exp[x := v]$ is **true**. (Note that this is stronger than requiring such a v of some instance of τ.)

- In order for **forall** $x:\tau$ => exp to be **false**, there must be an expressible value v of type τ such that $exp[x := v]$ is **false**.

- In order for **exists** $x:\tau$ => exp to be **false**, the expression $exp[x := v]$ must be **false** for every expressible value v of every instance of τ.

Note that the third and fourth cases above are obtained from the second and first cases respectively using the de Morgan laws ($\forall x.\varphi = \neg\exists x.\neg\varphi$, and $\exists x.\varphi = \neg\forall x.\neg\varphi$). The value of a quantified expression is left undefined if none of the above applies, so for example **forall** $x:\tau$ => exp has no value if $exp[x := v]$ is **false** for some expressible value v of some instance of τ, but there is no expressible value v of type τ itself such that $exp[x := v]$ is **false**.

An example of a formula involving polymorphic quantification that is **true** for some type instances but **false** for others is the following:

---

[3]In fact, this is a special case of a slightly more general form.

```
forall (x,xs) => [x] @ xs == xs @ [x]
```

where `@` is concatenation of lists and `[x]` is a singleton list containing `x`. One might expect the value of this formula to be **false**, since this is what happens when (for example) `x:int` and `xs:int list`. But when `x:unit` (the type having just one value, written `()`) and `xs:unit list`, the value of the formula is **true** since lists of type `unit list` are uniquely determined by their length. As a consequence, this formula has no value whatsoever. Fortunately, such odd examples occur rarely. A positive example of a polymorphic formula that holds is

```
forall xs => exists ys => xs @ ys == ys @ xs
```

because for any list type, the empty list has the property required for `ys`. The type quantification is left implicit.

A similar but slightly different semantics for quantifiers is considered by Kazmierczak in [16].

Datatype declarations in SML can be seen as carrying logical content. For example, consider the declaration:

```
datatype t = c1 | c2 of int
```

Apart from declaring a new type `t` which is different from all previously-defined types, a constant value `c1:t` and a function value `c2:int->t`, this makes the following assertions (the terminology is due to [5]):

"No junk": The only values of type `t` are `c1` and `(c2 n)` for integer values n:

```
forall x:t => (x == c1 orelse exists n:int => x == c2 n)
```

"No confusion": The values produced by different constructors are different, and each constructor function is injective and total:

```
forall n:int => not(c1 == c2 n)
forall (n:int,n':int) => (c2 n == c2 n' implies n == n')
forall n:int => c2 n proper
```

"No junk" corresponds to an induction principle for the new datatype; in the case of recursive datatype declarations, this is necessarily a higher-order formula. Both conditions are necessary for the use of constructors in patterns. EML provides a new form of declaration which has syntax similar to that of datatype declarations, but which only asserts "no junk":

```
spantype ''a set = empty | singleton of ''a
                         | union of ''a set * ''a set
```

Here we are specifying that all sets are either empty, or singletons, or unions of such sets, but we are not saying (for example) whether union is commutative or not; if such a property is required, an axiom can be added to impose it. In this paper, the term "axiom" refers to spantypes (although they are syntactically quite different from axioms) as well as to ordinary axioms.

3   The relationship between SML and EML

The EML language was very deliberately designed as a language for specifying modular SML software systems. In contrast to much related work, the intention was *not* to create a completely general-purpose specification language. One of the main guiding principles of the design was to make EML a *minimal* extension to SML. The addition of axioms was clearly necessary to enable module properties to be specified, but we have attempted to keep the syntax of axioms simple and have resisted the temptation to add features or to repair minor defects in the design of SML. For example, EML does not include parameterised specifications (functions from signatures to signatures), despite the fact that these are commonly provided by other specification languages. We have not yet seen a compelling need to add parameterised specifications to EML. In fact, it has become clear to us [30] that what is really important in formal software development is the ability to specify parameterised program modules (i.e. SML functors), and EML already has this facility: one uses an EML functor declaration having a question mark in place of a body.

There are at least four senses in which EML is a minimal extension of SML. First, the syntax of EML minimally extends the syntax of SML. As already stated, the main syntactic extension is the addition of axioms. Second, the semantics of EML is based directly on the semantics of SML, as will be explained in detail in the next section. This is to ensure consistency with SML "by construction" — the fact that significant portions of the two semantic definitions are identical would make a proof of consistency considerably simpler than otherwise. Our initial attempts to give a semantics of EML took quite a different and much more "algebraic" route [31]; we have temporarily abandoned this approach, in part because of the difficulty of ensuring consistency with the existing definition of SML (but see [16]). A third and related point is that the extension to the semantics of SML is such that the semantics of the SML fragment of EML is preserved, making EML a "conservative" extension of SML. This is vital to ensure that the end-product of EML formal development can be compiled and run using existing implementations of SML without modification. Finally, we have attempted to preserve the *spirit* of SML in the extensions insofar as this is possible. This is a necessarily vague statement, but there was already an example of this in Section 2.4 where we eschew the use of explicit quantification of type variables in axioms because such quantification is always left implicit in SML.

In spite of the above, EML is not quite an extension of SML; it is an extension of a large subset of SML. This subset is obtained by excluding the imperative features of SML (references, assignment, and so-called imperative type variables) and input/output, by requiring structure declarations and functor declarations to include explicit signatures, and by adopting a more restrictive view of the role of signatures as interfaces. The first restriction is made for the sake of simplicity, and for philosophical reasons which will be familiar to advocates of functional programming [3]. The second restriction seems appropriate in a specification and formal development framework in which signatures play a central role, in contrast to a programming language where the need to supply explicit signatures may be viewed as an unnecessary inconvenience. The only structure declarations that are exempt from this restriction are those in which the signature is already available from the structure used in the body of the declaration, as in the case of the structure declaration in the body of **Reduce** in Figure 1. The final restriction is to enforce the principle that only the information which is explicitly recorded in the signature(s) of a module is available externally, as mentioned in Section 2.1. This is necessary since the SML module system does not otherwise fully insulate the clients of a module from choices in the representation of types in the body, and therefore does not properly support separate development of the components of a modular system. See [34] for more on the methodological technicalities behind this restriction.[4] None of these changes makes EML incompatible with SML, as any program in the SML fragment of EML (which therefore satisfies these restrictions) is a well-formed SML program. However, certain SML programs cannot be developed using EML.

There is one additional restriction imposed by EML which causes certain pathological but well-formed SML programs to be regarded as incorrect. This is demonstrated by the following example:

```
signature SIG =
    sig
        type t
        local val x:t in end
    end;

structure S:SIG =
    struct
        datatype t = foo of t
    end
```

This is well-formed according to SML but fails to *verificate* in EML because S.t is a type with no values! (Recall that values in SML are represented as finite ground terms built from constructors; since the only constructor for type S.t is S.foo:S.t->S.t, there are no finite ground terms of type S.t.) The point here is that **local val x:t in end** in SIG imposes a logical constraint, namely that t has at least one value, which is disregarded by SML but cannot be correctly disregarded by EML. Apart from this minor restriction and the restrictions mentioned above, EML does not limit the freedom of the SML programmer in the sense that well-formed SML programs satisfying these restrictions (even "ugly" ones) are also well-formed according to EML. Of course, it is clear that it will be easier to reason about the correctness of some SML programs than others, in EML or any other framework.

Compatibility between SML and EML is a more delicate matter than simply insuring compatibility for the SML fragment of EML. For example, the dynamic semantics of EML (see Section 4.2), which defines the result of evaluating EML "code" insofar as this is possible, raises the exception **NoCode** when producing a result would involve evaluating a specification construct such as a quantifier or question mark. Refinement steps involve the replacement of question marks by expressions. This would lead one to expect that successive refinement steps should cause the dynamic semantics to raise **NoCode** exceptions less frequently,

---

[4]The original design of the SML module system [20] proposed an additional kind of structure, a so-called *abstraction*, for which the stricter interpretation of signatures taken in EML would apply. This was unfortunately not included in SML as defined in [22] although some SML implementations provide it as a non-standard extension [1].

198

without affecting the "ordinary" values produced. In order to achieve this, it is essential to define **NoCode** as a special exception which cannot be trapped by any surrounding handler. Consider the following (contrived) refinement example:

```
val x = (? handle _ => 2)   ~~>   val x = (1 handle _ => 2)
```

In SML, *exp* **handle** _ => 2 evaluates to 2 if *exp* raises any exception. If this were the case in EML, then the above refinement would change the result of evaluating **x** from 2 to 1. By treating **NoCode** as a special non-trappable exception (which involves a change to the dynamic semantics of the SML fragment of EML!) the result changes from [**NoCode**] to 1, as desired.

By way of disclaimer, it should be noted that the assertions above concerning such matters as compatibility between the semantics of SML and EML should be formally regarded as conjectures which we strongly believe to be true but which have not yet been formally proved; the same goes for similar assertions in the remainder of the paper.

4   An Overview of the EML semantics

As mentioned earlier, one of the most important features of SML is that it has a fully formal definition (modulo some minor faults [13]). Not only is its syntax formally defined, which is quite common, but also the meaning of SML programs is determined unambiguously by a formal mathematical semantics [22], [21]. This is given in the form of so-called *natural semantics* [12] (or structural operational semantics [25]) via deduction rules which determine a meaning for each SML phrase. We will present a number of such rules below, hopefully giving the reader the flavour of the entire semantics.

The semantics of SML consists of some two hundred rules, grouped to reflect both the structure of the language and the envisaged phases of program interpretation. Thus, on one hand, the semantics of SML divides into the semantics for the core layer of the language and the semantics for its module system. Then, the semantics for the core and the semantics for modules are split into two parts: the *static semantics*, which describes the type-checking phase of program interpretation, and the *dynamic semantics*, which describes the actual evaluation of programs. In addition, the *derived forms* of the language are described by translation to phrases of the *bare language*.

The dependencies between various parts of the semantics are kept to a minimum, to facilitate understanding of the quite complex language definition. As expected, the static semantics for modules relies on the static semantics for the core. Similarly for the dynamic semantics: the dynamic semantics for modules relies on the dynamic semantics for the core. However, no part of the semantics for the core depends on the semantics for modules, and the static semantics and the dynamic semantics are independent[5]. All the parts are joined at the top level, where the overall semantics for SML *programs* involves both type-checking (the static semantics) and evaluation (the dynamic semantics).

---

[5]Although this statement is technically accurate, a successful "run" of the static semantics is needed to ensure that the dynamic semantics yields expected meanings. In this sense the dynamic semantics depends on the static semantics. A precise statement of this "soundness" property may be found in [38].

The semantics of EML inherits its basic form and structure from the semantics of SML. It is given as a natural semantics and consists of a number of deduction rules grouped to reflect the structure of the language and the various aspects of the interpretation of EML phrases. As in the SML semantics, the semantics for EML core and modules are given separately, each of them incorporating static semantics and dynamic semantics. The meaning of the derived forms of EML is given by translation to the bare language — the description of this translation is considerably more detailed than the corresponding part of the SML semantics, since we have decided to capture formally all the technicalities, whereas the definition of SML relies on a somewhat informal English description.

In addition we also have a *verification semantics* for EML, again split into the verification semantics for the core and for modules. In a way, the verification semantics for EML modules is the essence of Extended ML. It is here that the correctness of modules w.r.t. their interfaces is formally defined. We consider a (well-typed) EML program to be *correct* if the verification semantics produces a meaning for it. If the verification semantics *fails* for this program, that is, no verification meaning for the program may be derived, the program is considered incorrect. Incorrect programs may still be "run" (according to their dynamic semantics) — but the results are not guaranteed to meet the requirements expressed in the module interfaces.

The dependencies between the various parts of the EML semantics are somewhat more complicated than in SML. As in SML, the semantics for modules depends on the semantics for the core, while the semantics for the core does not depend on the semantics for modules. The static semantics and the dynamic semantics are independent. However, the new part of the semantics, the verification semantics, depends on both the static and the dynamic semantics. As explained in Section 2.4, the interpretation of axioms depends on typing information (for example, the type of the bound variable must be known to interpret the meaning of a universally quantified formula) — hence the dependency on the static semantics. The dependency on the dynamic semantics results from the need to interpret axioms describing evaluation properties of expressions (for example, stating that an expression terminates). We should hasten to add that neither the static nor the dynamic semantics depends on the verification semantics, as should be expected. Finally, as for SML, all the parts of the semantics are joined at the top level, where the overall semantics of EML "programs" is given.

In the rest of this section we present fundamental ideas important for each part of the semantics — see [14] for the complete semantics. We skim through the static and the dynamic semantics, as the issues involved there are much the same as in the semantics of SML — we hope, however, to give the flavour of these parts. More attention is paid to the verification semantics, as this is the really new (and most interesting) part of EML.

4.1 Static semantics

The static semantics of EML describes the process of static *elaboration* of EML phrases. This includes, for example, checking that all the objects used have been declared in the current environment and, most significantly, that phrases are *well-typed*.

Perhaps most typically, the rules of the static semantics for expressions allow one to derive judgements of the form $C \vdash exp \Rightarrow \tau$. This is to be read: in the context C, the expression exp can elaborate to the type τ (or exp can have type τ). Here, contexts are triples, where the most essential component is a *static environment* storing typing information about the objects declared in the current environment. We have $C \vdash$ [1] $\Rightarrow$ int list and $C \vdash$ [] $\Rightarrow$ int list (for any[6] context C). Note, however, that we also have $C \vdash$ [] $\Rightarrow \alpha$ list, where α list is the type of lists over arbitrary type α. The *polymorphic generalisation* of this type is written as $\forall \alpha. \alpha$ list. It is formed when an expression of type α list is bound to an identifier (provided α is not fixed by the context). $\forall \alpha. \alpha$ list may be instantiated to any type of the form τ list.

Declarations are slightly more complicated: the static semantics elaborates a declaration to a static environment, containing typing information about the objects introduced by the declaration. The corresponding judgements are of the form $C \vdash dec \Rightarrow E$, and for example we have $C \vdash$ val a = 5 $\Rightarrow$ $\{a \mapsto \text{int}\}$. Examples involving function declarations are no more complicated: we have $C \vdash$ val f = fn x => [x] $\Rightarrow \{f \mapsto \text{int} \to \text{int list}\}$, as well as $C \vdash$ val f = fn x => [x] $\Rightarrow \{f \mapsto \forall \alpha. \alpha \to \alpha \text{ list}\}$.

The judgements mentioned above may be formally derived using the rules of the static semantics. A typical example of such a rule, involving the elaboration of both declarations and expressions, is the following rule for expressions with local declarations (this is a simplified version of the rule!):

$$\frac{C \vdash dec \Rightarrow E \qquad C \oplus E \vdash exp \Rightarrow \tau}{C \vdash \text{let } dec \text{ in } exp \text{ end} \Rightarrow \tau}$$

This is to be read: if in the context C the declaration *dec* elaborates to the static environment E and in the context C extended by the static environment E the expression *exp* elaborates to the type τ, then in the context C the expression let *dec* in *exp* end elaborates to the type τ. Notice that the result of the elaboration of *dec* does not appear in the overall result. For example, using this rule we can derive $C \vdash$ let val f = fn x => [x] in f 5 end $\Rightarrow$ int list (for any context C).

The static semantics for modules proceeds in much the same way as that for the core, but the semantic values built are more complex. For example, structure expressions elaborate to static environments, which store typing information about the objects declared within the structure, together with a unique name attached to the structure to keep track of sharing. The corresponding judgements have the form $B \vdash strexp \Rightarrow (m, E)$, where B is a *static basis*, containing a context and a set N of *structure names*, like m, used so far. Here is a typical rule, for the encapsulation of a structure-level declaration of objects to form a new structure:

$$\frac{B \vdash strdec \Rightarrow E \qquad m \notin (N \text{ of } B) \cup \text{names } E}{B \vdash \text{struct } strdec \text{ end} \Rightarrow (m, E)}$$

The hints above on the static semantics apply to SML as well as to EML. However, as mentioned before, there are some differences. For example (cf.

---

[6]We tacitly assume that contexts, environments, etc., used in the small running examples throughout this section map the built-in type constructors and values of EML to their expected meanings, as described in the initial basis for SML, cf. [22].

Section 3) we have designed typing for EML modules to be stricter than for SML, and this change is properly reflected by the static semantics for EML modules. Let us consider a simple structure declaration:

```
structure S: sig type t; val c:t end =
       struct type t = int; val c = 17 end
```

In SML, the signature constraint in this particular example has *no effect*: the static environment assigned to the structure identifier S maps t and c to int. A signature constraint in SML, if present, is used only to check that the structure matches the signature and to hide auxiliary structure components. In EML, signature constraints have an additional purpose: they also hide information about structure components — only the information provided in the signature can be exploited when using the structure. In particular, in the above example, the EML static semantics binds S to a static environment which maps t and c to a new, otherwise unknown type. Consequently, in the context of the above structure binding, in EML we cannot form expressions like S.c+2 — this is not well-typed in EML (but it is well-typed in SML). This behaviour of EML is compatible with SML in the sense that every successful elaboration in EML will also succeed in SML.

Another difference is that in EML we have a new part of the semantics, the verification semantics, which relies on the type information gathered during static elaboration. We need some mechanism to export this information from the static to the verification semantics of EML, also covering cases in which the intermediate types for some parts of EML phrases do not appear in the overall result, as for example the type of f in the elaboration of let val f = fn x => [x] in f 5 end, which we considered earlier. This is done by requiring that all the types used in a static elaboration of a phrase are accumulated in an additional component of the result of elaboration: a tree of *type guesses*. One can think of this as an annotation of the entire parse tree for the phrase with results of the static analysis. The presence of type guesses somewhat complicates both the form of judgements and the rules of the static semantics. For instance, the above rule for expressions with local declarations in fact looks as follows[7]:

$$\frac{C \vdash dec \Rightarrow E, \gamma \qquad C \oplus E \vdash exp \Rightarrow \tau, \gamma' \qquad \text{tynames}\, \tau \subseteq T \text{ of } C}{C \vdash \text{let } dec \text{ in } exp \text{ end} \Rightarrow \tau, \gamma \cdot \gamma'}$$

Here, the tree of type guesses γ accumulates the types used in the elaboration of *dec* to the static environment E in the context C, γ' accumulates the types used in the elaboration of *exp* to the type τ in the context $C \oplus E$, and consequently $\gamma \cdot \gamma'$ accumulates the types used in the elaboration of let *dec* in *exp* end to the type τ in the context C.

An additional problem is that the static semantics may "choose" different types for some parts of a phrase without affecting the overall result (the differences would be visible in the tree of intermediate type guesses though).

---

[7]The third premise, which requires that the type of *exp* does not use any new type names not mentioned in the original context, is not present in the corresponding rule of the SML definition. The type system is unsound without this requirement, because type names introduced by different let expressions can accidentally become equal. This was an oversight in the definition of SML [22] which was not fixed in [21].

As mentioned above, the type of `fn x => [x]` may be either `int → int list` or $\alpha \to \alpha$ `list` (among others). Moreover, since `f 5` elaborates to `int list` both in the context assigning `int → int list` to `f` and in the context assigning $\forall \alpha. \alpha \to \alpha$ `list` to `f`, the elaboration of `let val f = fn x => [x] in f 5 end` may proceed either via the judgement $C \vdash$ `val f = fn x => [x]` $\Rightarrow \{$ `f` $\mapsto$ `int → int list`$\}$, or via $C \vdash$ `val f = fn x => [x]` $\Rightarrow \{$ `f` $\mapsto \forall \alpha. \alpha \to \alpha$ `list`$\}$, in each case yielding $C \vdash$ `let val f = fn x => [x] in f 5 end` $\Rightarrow$ `int list`, but with different intermediate type guesses. The type chosen for `f` may influence the result of the verification semantics (well, not in this trivial case, but for example if `f` was involved in an axiom like `forall (x, y) => f x = f y`, which unexpectedly happens to be true if `f` is typed as `unit → unit list` — see Section 2.4). To resolve the potential ambiguity, we have to decide which of the possible types should be "exported". The obvious choice is the most general, *principal* type [6] ($\forall \alpha. \alpha \to \alpha$ `list` for `f` here), and so an appropriate principality requirement is imposed on type guesses, much as in the SML static semantics for modules the principality requirement is imposed on signatures. The existence of principal types and signatures is a fundamental property of the SML type system (see [21] for a precise statement and proof) which is retained by EML.

The requirement of principality is essentially an infinitary condition which states that *any* type that can be used in the static elaboration of a phrase is an instance of the principal type the elaboration is required to choose. In the semantics of SML it is imposed for example in the following rule:

$$\frac{C \text{ of } B \vdash dec \Rightarrow E \quad E \text{ principal for } dec \text{ in } (C \text{ of } B)}{B \vdash dec \Rightarrow E}$$

which states that if a declaration *dec* elaborates as a core declaration to a static environment E that is moreover principal for *dec* in the given context, then *dec*, as a structure-level declaration, elaborates to E (notice the crucial distinction between the elaboration of *dec* as a core declaration and as a structure-level declaration). Infinitary requirements of this kind, hidden behind somewhat informal (but precise enough) English descriptions, occur in a very few places in the semantics of SML. They are, however, rather more common in the semantics of EML; for example, they naturally arise in the semantics of quantifiers or extensional equality, see Section 2.4. We have decided to make such requirements explicit and formalise the use of infinitary conditions via *higher-order rules*. For instance, the above SML rule may be expressed as follows:

$$\frac{C \text{ of } B \vdash dec \Rightarrow E \quad \dfrac{C \text{ of } B \vdash dec \Rightarrow E'}{E \succ E'}}{B \vdash dec \Rightarrow E}$$

Here, the second premise is a rule, which is true as a premise if it is admissible as a rule. The meta-variable E' is scoped at this premise, making it universally quantified for the local rule. Thus, the premise requires each E' to which *dec* may elaborate to be an instance of E. Consequently, the new rule means exactly the same as its original version quoted above from the semantics of SML.

Actually, the semantics of EML uses here yet a different rule, which imposes the principality requirement not just on the resulting static environment, but on the entire elaboration as accumulated in the tree of type guesses:

$$\frac{C \text{ of } B \vdash dec \Rightarrow E, \gamma \qquad N = \text{names}\, \gamma \setminus N \text{ of } B \qquad \dfrac{C \text{ of } B \vdash dec \Rightarrow E', \gamma'}{(N)\gamma \succ \gamma'}}{B \vdash dec \Rightarrow E, \gamma}$$

The last premise of this rule requires that any tree of type guesses corresponding to an elaboration of *dec* in the given context may be obtained from the tree of type guesses γ by instantiating new type variables introduced in the corresponding elaboration of *dec*. As explained above, this requirement, stronger than just principality of the resulting environment, is necessary for the semantics of EML.

Higher-order rules, which come with an additional scoping mechanism for meta-variables, considerably increase the expressive power of the formalism. They have to be used with care, as the formalism no longer guarantees that the rules inductively define all the true judgement of the semantics. In particular, "impredicative" dependencies between premises and conclusions in higher-order rules must be avoided.

4.2 Dynamic semantics

The dynamic semantics of SML, as for any other programming language, is the key part of its description. After all, the main reason for writing programs is in order to evaluate them, and this is what the dynamic semantics describes. One might think, however, that a dynamic semantics for a program development framework like EML is somewhat pointless: the dynamic semantics for the programs produced by formal development is provided by the definition of SML, and can be used to evaluate them. One reason to nevertheless provide a separate dynamic semantics for EML is that the verification semantics, the main part of the EML semantics, relies on the dynamic semantics, for example to determine the value of the **terminates** predicate — hence, the dynamic semantics is needed here for the sake of completeness of the formal definition of EML. Another important reason is that we want to formally define a basis for early practical experiments with incomplete programs. EML programs, even those which are incomplete and contain specification constructs, are viewed as "partially executable". The idea is that any such program should be executable insofar as this is possible, and that evaluation should proceed as in SML for the parts which contain only SML code. The dynamic semantics of EML formalises this.

The dynamic semantics describes the *evaluation* of language phrases. In particular, for expressions, the dynamic semantics allows one to derive judgements of the form[8] $E \vdash exp \Rightarrow v$, stating that in the (dynamic) *environment* E, the expression *exp* evaluates[9] to the value v, where environments store the values of objects currently defined. For example, we have $\{a \mapsto 27\} \vdash a*37 \Rightarrow 999$. Environments are built by declarations, with corresponding judgements of the form $E \vdash dec \Rightarrow E'$ expressing the fact that in the environment E the declaration *dec* evaluates to the environment E', which stores the values of objects

---

[8] This is an approximation used here for presentation purposes only; more details will be provided below.

[9] $E \vdash exp \Rightarrow v$ literally means that in E, exp can evaluate to v, but since evaluation is deterministic, v is uniquely determined (if it exists).

declared in *dec*. For instance, we have $E \vdash$ val a = 27 $\Rightarrow \{a \mapsto 27\}$ (for any environment E). Formally, judgements are derived using the rules of the dynamic semantics, with a typical example being the following rule for expressions with local declarations:

$$\frac{E \vdash dec \Rightarrow E' \qquad E + E' \vdash exp \Rightarrow v}{E \vdash \text{let } dec \text{ in } exp \text{ end} \Rightarrow v}$$

Using this rule, we can for example derive directly from the judgements above that $E \vdash$ let val a = 27 in a * 37 end $\Rightarrow$ 999.

Evaluation of expressions involving functions is just as simple. One has to remember though that values of function types are not functions in the usual sense but rather *closures*, which result from the encapsulation of expressions defining function bodies [18]. Closures are expanded when applied to arguments, and a rather elaborate scheme of self-expansion is used to model recursion (see [22] for details). The possibility of non-termination is reflected by the fact that using the rules of the dynamic semantics one cannot derive values for all the expressions of the language. For example, there is no value v for which the judgement $E \vdash$ let fun loop() = loop() in loop() end $\Rightarrow v$ can be derived, as expected.

Another complication arises from the fact that SML (and hence EML) expressions may raise exceptions. In this case, the result of evaluation is a *packet* (an exception name possibly together with a value). Consequently, the formal judgements of the dynamic semantics for expressions may also have the form $E \vdash exp \Rightarrow p$ (in the environment E the expression exp evaluates to the packet p). To express the two possibilities jointly, we write $E \vdash exp \Rightarrow v/p$, and use the semantic rules to determine which form is derivable for a particular expression. The possibility of a phrase raising an exception is often left implicit in the semantic rules, relying on the so-called "exception convention" to ensure that packets are propagated by the rules of the dynamic semantics. Thus, the above rule for expressions with local declarations induces implicitly, by the exception convention, the following rule:

$$\frac{E \vdash dec \Rightarrow E' \qquad E + E' \vdash exp \Rightarrow p}{E \vdash \text{let } dec \text{ in } exp \text{ end} \Rightarrow p} \ .$$

(and similarly for packets arising from evaluation of *dec*). Of course, some semantic rules must be exempted from the exception convention. Most notably, the rules that describe how exceptions may be trapped (how packets may be handled) deal with packets explicitly.

Another aspect of dealing with exceptions is that the set of exception names used is determined dynamically — a new exception name is generated each time an exception declaration is evaluated (this new exception name is used as the meaning of the exception identifier declared). Consequently, the set of exception names generated so far must be stored. In SML this set is one of the components of the current *state* — and since its other components are used to describe the imperative features of SML programs, this is the only component of states in the dynamic semantics of EML (apart from the *specification flag*, see below). This means that states are necessary in EML, and the real form of semantic judgements describing evaluation of expressions is $s, E \vdash exp \Rightarrow v/p, s'$ (in the state s and the environment E, the expression exp evaluates to the value

v or packet p with the resulting state s'). The so-called "state convention" allows one to formulate many rules without mentioning states explicitly, using the order of premises to determine how states resulting from evaluation of one phrase are passed to another. Thus, in particular, the above rule for expressions with local declarations expands to the following:

$$\frac{s, E \vdash dec \Rightarrow E', s' \qquad s', E + E' \vdash exp \Rightarrow v, s''}{s, E \vdash \texttt{let } dec \texttt{ in } exp \texttt{ end} \Rightarrow v, s''}$$

The rules resulting from the use of the exception convention are affected similarly.

The above remarks apply to SML as well as to EML — the overall ideas on how programs are evaluated are the same. What is new in EML is that it contains some phrases which, intuitively, cannot be evaluated. Typical examples here are objects defined by declarations where no code is provided (the lack of code being represented by ?) or phrases containing constructs for building formulae, such as ==, terminates, or forall. Even though the dynamic semantics of EML simply skips axioms, these non-executable constructs may be encountered in evaluation of EML expressions. When this is the case, a special exception NoCode is raised. NoCode cannot be handled explicitly in programs, as explained in Section 3. However, to enable execution of completed parts of EML programs, NoCode is trapped by the dynamic semantics of EML at the declaration level and a special value Incomplete is used to mark its presence in the evaluation of an object declaration. An attempt to use the value Incomplete causes NoCode to be raised again. Here are a few examples:

$$E \vdash (\texttt{fn x : int => x - 1}) \texttt{ == } (\texttt{fn x : int => x + 1}) \Rightarrow [\texttt{NoCode}]$$
$$E \vdash \texttt{val x : int = ?} \Rightarrow \{\texttt{x} \mapsto \texttt{Incomplete}\}$$
$$\{\texttt{x} \mapsto \texttt{Incomplete}\} \vdash \texttt{x + 27} \Rightarrow [\texttt{NoCode}]$$
$$\{\texttt{x} \mapsto \texttt{Incomplete}, \texttt{y} \mapsto \texttt{Incomplete}\} \vdash \texttt{27 * 3} \Rightarrow 81$$
$$E \vdash \texttt{let val x : int = ?; val y = x + 1; val a = 27 in a * 3 end} \Rightarrow 81$$

This yields a rather subtle difference between the dynamic semantics of EML and both the dynamic semantics of SML (which simply does not deal with these special new constructs of EML) and the verification semantics of EML (where, in a sense, these constructs are properly dealt with). To make this explicit, we have added to EML states a new component, a *specification flag*, which is raised by the dynamic semantics whenever one of these special new constructs is encountered. When the specification flag is not raised during the evaluation of a phrase, the results provided by the dynamic semantics of EML coincide with the results of the dynamic semantics of SML[10] as well as with the results of the verification semantics for the core of EML (see Section 4.3 below). However, when the specification flag is raised, then the dynamic semantics of SML cannot yield a result, and the verification semantics of EML may yield a different result (or fail to yield a result at all).

The dynamic semantics for EML modules follows the dynamic semantics for SML modules in the same manner as the dynamic semantics for the EML core sketched above follows the dynamic semantics for the SML core. Thus, in

---

[10] Somewhat informally, we mean here the semantics of SML literally applied to EML phrases, hence in particular with no rules applicable for the special new constructs of EML.

particular, EML structure expressions evaluate to environments, but evaluation need not terminate and may modify the state. Moreover, evaluation proceeds in a *basis*, a "richer" environment which apart from the values of objects stored as in the dynamic environment for the core may also store functors and signatures. The corresponding judgements have the form $s, B \vdash strexp \Rightarrow E, s'$. The specific EML constructs are treated as sketched above: axioms are disregarded, evaluation of non-executable expressions raises the `NoCode` exception and may result in the value `Incomplete` being stored in the environment. In particular, environments resulting from evaluation of EML structures may contain objects with `Incomplete` stored as their value.

4.3   Verification semantics

Although we provide a dynamic semantics for EML, the main stress in a framework like EML is not so much on running programs (their dynamic evaluation) but rather on the verification of correctness assertions that are present in EML phrases. Consequently, we view the verification semantics as the main part of the formal description of EML. The essence of this semantics is to check whether structures and functors *match* their signatures, which in particular means that they satisfy the axioms given in the signatures. This is described by the verification semantics for EML modules. Verification of an EML phrase does not result in a binary statement saying whether the phrase is correct or not. Some more detailed information about the contribution of the phrase to the meaning of the whole program must be determined as well. We will say that the verification semantics describes how EML phrases *verificate*[11] to semantic objects.

One crucial idea of the EML methodology is that not only should developed modules be correct w.r.t. their specifications, but also this should follow solely from properties stated in module interfaces. Consequently, the verification semantics must express the information hiding implicit in this EML understanding of the role of module interfaces. Incompleteness of information is represented by the fact that EML module phrases verificate to sets of semantic objects, rather than just to a single semantic object as in the dynamic semantics. For instance, in a given basis, EML structure expressions verificate to sets of environments[12], with the corresponding formal judgements having the form $B \vdash strexp \Rightarrow \mathcal{E}$. Typically, in a complete EML structure expression (containing only SML code) without substructures, the resulting set of environments will contain exactly one element: the environment determined by the SML code. But there are several reasons why this set might not be a singleton. Most obviously, there may be unresolved choices within *strexp*. For example, a structure-level declaration like `val a : int = ?` results in a set of environments, each mapping `a` to a different integer. Then, inconsistency within *strexp* may cause the resulting set to be empty. For example, an axiom like `axiom a>5 andalso a<3` results in the

---

[11] An obvious alternative is "verify", but this carries connotations we would like to avoid.

[12] To be quite precise, we should point out that just as in the dynamic semantics of EML it was necessary to consider environments together with state s, in the verification semantics of EML structure expressions verificate to sets of elements that are pairs of an environment and a state. Fortunately, this does not bring much additional complication, and for the purposes of the presentation here we disregard states in the further discussion of the verification semantics.

empty set of environments. Notice, however, that this is different from a failure to verificate at all! Finally, and perhaps most crucially for the methodological aspects of the verification of EML programs, if *strexp* contains a substructure or uses another structure then the interface attached to it is used to filter the information available, hiding the more detailed information given in its body. Consequently, the "verification meaning" of the structure is the set of environments matching its interface, rather than the particular environment given by its body.

This last point is perhaps best explained by looking at the verification of a single structure declaration **structure S** : *sigexp* = *strexp*. To verificate this, one proceeds as follows (we leave the basis in which the verification takes place implicit):

1. First, verificate the signature expression *sigexp*, obtaining a *verification interface* Σ. This stores the names of objects specified in the signature together with static information about them. Moreover, axioms given in the signature are stored in an appropriate form — see below for more details.

2. Then, verificate the structure expression *strexp*, obtaining a set of environments $\mathcal{E}$ as discussed above.

3. The next step is where the real verification takes place: check that each environment $E \in \mathcal{E}$ matches the interface Σ. This involves checking whether the axioms incorporated in Σ are satisfied by E. Section 2.4 presents the particular forms of axioms and their intended meaning, which we return to below.

4. The result is the set of all environments binding **S** to an environment that matches the interface Σ. Notice that this "includes" but is in general larger than the set $\mathcal{E}$ of environments obtained from the verification of *strexp*.

If any of the above steps fails (this may happen in step 2, for example if *strexp* contains an incorrect substructure declaration, or in step 3, if the verification requirement formulated there does not hold) then the structure declaration **structure S** : *sigexp* = *strexp* is incorrect and hence its verification fails as well. This is different, however, from the case in which the result is the empty set. The latter is possible when *sigexp* is inconsistent, and hence *strexp* (which satisfies it) is inconsistent as well.

Here is (a simplified version of) the rule which embodies the above verification procedure:

$$\frac{B \vdash sigexp \Rightarrow \Sigma \qquad B \vdash strexp \Rightarrow \mathcal{E} \qquad \text{for each } E \in \mathcal{E}, \ E \text{ matches } \Sigma}{B \vdash \textbf{structure S} : sigexp = strexp \Rightarrow \{ \{S \mapsto E'\} \mid E' \text{ matches } \Sigma\}}$$

A few comments are necessary here. First, we omit a formal definition of the condition stating that an environment matches an interface. Second, for the presentation here we have used an *ad hoc* (but self-explanatory) notation to present a rule with an infinite set of premises, where moreover the number of these depends on a semantic object mentioned in another premise. The formal semantics uses a higher-order rule to express this more precisely. Finally, this is a very simplified version of a rule that does not actually appear in the semantics, but may be derived using more elementary rules for structure bindings and for structure declarations.

To take a simple example, consider the following structure declaration:

```
structure S: sig val a: int; axiom a>0 andalso a<5 end =
    struct val a: int = ?; axiom a>1 andalso a<4 end
```

The verification of the structure expression in this declaration results in the set of environments $\{E_2, E_3\}$ where we write E_i for $\{a \mapsto i\}$. It is then checked that each of these environments does indeed match the interface, and in particular satisfies the axiom given there. The resulting set of environments assigning an interpretation for the structure S contains not only $\{S \mapsto E_2\}$ and $\{S \mapsto E_3\}$, but also $\{S \mapsto E_1\}$ and $\{S \mapsto E_4\}$, since the set of environments matching the interface is exactly $\{E_1, E_2, E_3, E_4\}$.

If we modify the interface as follows:

```
structure S: sig val a: int; axiom a>0 andlalso a<3 end =
    struct val a: int = ?; axiom a>1 andalso a<4 end
```

then the check that each of the environments resulting from the verification of the structure expression (E_2 and E_3) matches the interface fails (since E_3 does not satisfy the modified axiom). Thus, the verification of this structure declaration fails. Intuitively, the structure declaration is incorrect.

Summing up, the outcome of a successful verification of a structure-level declaration is a set of environments, each expressing a possible meaning of the declared objects. Further verification proceeds for each of these possibilities separately, as expressed by the following rule for sequential composition of structure-level declarations (again, a very simplified version is used, with an *ad hoc* notation to represent dependencies between objects):

$$\frac{B \vdash strdec_1 \Rightarrow \mathcal{E}_1 \qquad \text{for each } E \in \mathcal{E}_1, \ B \oplus E \vdash strdec_2 \Rightarrow \mathcal{E}_2[E]}{B \vdash strdec_1 ; strdec_2 \Rightarrow \{E_1 + E_2 \mid E_1 \in \mathcal{E}_1, E_2 \in \mathcal{E}_2[E_1]\}}$$

The above rule appropriately respects the dependencies between consecutive structure declarations. Consider the following example:

```
structure S: sig val a: bool end =
    struct val a: bool = ? end;
structure T: sig val b: bool; axiom b = S.a end =
    struct val b: bool = S.a end
```

The verification of these two declarations will result in the set of environments containing $\{S \mapsto S_t, T \mapsto T_t\}$ and $\{S \mapsto S_f, T \mapsto T_f\}$, where $S_t = \{a \mapsto \mathtt{true}\}$, $T_t = \{b \mapsto \mathtt{true}\}$, $S_f = \{a \mapsto \mathtt{false}\}$ and $T_f = \{b \mapsto \mathtt{false}\}$. However, the resulting set of environments does not contain for example $\{S \mapsto S_t, T \mapsto T_f\}$ even though the interface for S does not determine the value of a (nor does the structure body in this case). The point is that the verification of the declaration of T proceeds in the context of an arbitrary but fixed interpretation for S.a, for each of the open possibilities separately.

On the other hand, removing the explicit information about the dependency from the interface for T changes the result:

```
structure S: sig val a: bool end =
    struct val a: bool = ? end;
structure T': sig val b: bool end =
    struct val b: bool = S.a end
```

Now, the result of the verification of these two declarations will consist of four environments: $\{S \mapsto S_t, T' \mapsto T_t\}$ and $\{S \mapsto S_f, T' \mapsto T_f\}$ as before, but also $\{S \mapsto S_t, T' \mapsto T_f\}$ and $\{S \mapsto S_f, T' \mapsto T_t\}$. Even though the verification of the structure expression in the declaration of T' results in the set of only two environments (as before), this information is filtered out by the interface provided in the binding. Consequently, a further declaration

```
structure U: sig val c: bool; axiom c = S.a end =
    struct val c: bool = T'.b end
```

is incorrect and does not verificate.

All the small examples above were extremely simple and an intuitive understanding of EML axioms as presented in Section 2.4 was sufficient to interpret them. In general, however, the situation may be much more complex, and matching an EML structure against an EML signature involves a number of rather subtle points. Perhaps the most obvious is the fact that the axioms in the signature must be interpreted relative to the type instantiation determined by the structure. For example, in

```
signature A = sig type t
                  axiom exists x:t => true
              end
```

the axiom requires the type t to be non-empty and its satisfaction depends on the particular realisation of t in the structure we match against A.

Another important point is that signatures in both SML and EML allow the use of hidden functions and hidden types. For the dynamic semantics hidden objects are of no concern, but they do matter in the verification semantics, because their interpretation may influence the verification of axioms. For example, a structure matching the following signature

```
signature B = sig local val b: int
                        axiom b>0
                  in val c: int
                        axiom c>b+1
                  end
              end
```

need not include a value b (but has to include an integer value c, of course). However, to successfully verificate the axiom c>b+1, such a value b has to be guessed so that both the "hidden" axiom b>0 and then the "visible" axiom c>b+1 are satisfied (in this example, this would not be possible unless the value of c is greater than 2). In a certain sense, the hidden declarations are existentially quantified (see [7]). To take appropriate care of such cases the axioms in verification interfaces are stored in a rather more elaborate form of *generalised axioms*.

The above presentation of the verification of structure declarations extends to the verification of functor declarations in the obvious way.

In this sketch of the verification semantics for EML modules we have entirely omitted the issue of behavioural equivalence mentioned in Section 2.2. Unfortunately, we have not yet put the relevant technicalities into the current version of the semantics. However, we do not anticipate major problems with this. First, a concept of behavioural equivalence between EML structures (environments) will be needed. In any basis, this will be defined to require that any well-formed expression (possibly built in the context of an additional declaration of a local structure) of observable type has the same value in behaviourally equivalent structures. The appropriate set of observable types to choose seems to be the set of all equality types (for the verification of functor bodies, the types in parameter interfaces, which may be instantiated by equality types, should also be treated as observable). Then, the only further change in the verification semantics for structure declarations will be to replace the requirement that all environments resulting from the verification of a structure expression match the structure interface by the requirement that each of these environments is behaviourally equivalent to an environment which matches the interface.

The verification semantics for the EML core is quite similar to its dynamic semantics. The basic ideas are the same, and for example expressions verificate to values or to packets (since exceptions may be raised), possibly changing the current state. This is captured by judgements of the form $s, M \vdash exp \Rightarrow v/p, s'$, where M is a *model*, a richer context in which the EML core phrases are verificated. Similarly for declarations, where judgements have the form $s, M \vdash dec \Rightarrow E, s$. In contrast to the verification semantics for modules, the verification of EML core phrases yields single objects, as in the dynamic semantics. There are, however, some crucial differences.

First, the specification constructs added in EML, such as ==, **terminates**, **forall**, are now viewed as special operators with their own verification rules (recall that an attempt to evaluate them in the dynamic semantics simply raises **NoCode**, a special exception reserved for this purpose). The rules of the verification semantics capture the meaning of these constructs as sketched in Section 2.4. It is important to realise that in most cases verification of these constructs depends in an essential way on static information inherited from the static semantics and incorporated in models.

Then, in contrast to the dynamic semantics, axioms are not ignored. When the verification semantics encounters an axiom declaration, it attempts to verificate the axiom body and proceeds further only if the result obtained is the value **true**. Otherwise, verification fails. This does not necessarily mean that the structure declaration in which this axiom occurs is incorrect. Rather, it implies only that a particular choice of resolving all the open possibilities in the structure body, the choice currently under consideration by the verification semantics, is not successful and does not yield a realisation of the structure satisfying this axiom. The crucial point which makes this work is the interpretation of question marks. In the verification semantics for the EML core the interpretation of question marks is provided by an extra component of the model. These question mark interpretations are guessed in an arbitrary way by the verification semantics for modules at the point where a core declaration is viewed as a structure-level declaration. Only those environments resulting from a successful verification of the declaration for some guess of the interpretation of question marks contribute to the result of the verification of this declaration at the structure level. This is captured by the verification rule given below, again in a somewhat simplified form. Rather informally, we write $M[B, QI]$ for the model obtained by extracting the appropriate components of the verification basis B and adding the question mark interpretation QI.

$$\overline{B \vdash dec \Rightarrow \{E \mid \text{for some } QI, M[B, QI] \vdash dec \Rightarrow E\}}$$

As in the static semantics (see the rule imposing principality discussed in Section 4.1) the declaration dec is viewed here as a core declaration in the judgement $M[B, QI] \vdash dec \Rightarrow E$, and as a structure-level declaration in $B \vdash dec \Rightarrow \{E \mid \ldots\}$.

Here is a simple example of a structure expression:

```
struct
    val a: int = ?
    axiom a>5 andalso a<8
    val b = a+2
end
```

(The question mark in the declaration of a should perhaps be indexed to avoid potential confusion with other question marks elsewhere.) The verification semantics for the declaration enclosed in struct ... end tries to verificate its enclosed sequence of core declarations for each possible interpretation of the question mark, one interpretation $\{? \mapsto i\}$ for each integer i. It is clear that the verification succeeds only for the interpretations $\{? \mapsto 6\}$ and $\{? \mapsto 7\}$, yielding environments $E_6 = \{a \mapsto 6, b \mapsto 8\}$ and $E_7 = \{a \mapsto 7, b \mapsto 9\}$ respectively. The result of the verification of the declaration is thus $\{E_6, E_7\}$, and this set of environments is taken as the result of verification of the entire structure expression.

In the same way as our quantification is based on expressible values (see Section 2.4) question marks interpretations QI map question marks to expressions, not to values. In this way ill-formed values are avoided, and moreover, the interpretation of each question mark may depend on the context in which it appears. The latter point means that in the verification of a function declaration like

```
fun f x = let val c = ? in g c end
```

question mark interpretations may replace the ? by expressions containing free occurrences of x.

The treatment of question marks in type expressions is somewhat different. The static semantics guarantees that whatever replacement a question mark interpretation provides (preserving certain attributes), the *success* of static analysis, and hence well-formedness of the program, is not affected. However, the exact *results* of static analysis are affected, and this has to be taken into account in the verification semantics, by interpreting the types derived during static analysis with respect to some *realisation*. Realisations are functions on semantic objects that assign concrete types to formal type parameters.

5   Final remarks

We have tried in this paper to provide a readable exposition of the semantics of EML, a framework for formal specification and development of SML programs. We have not discussed here in any detail the methodological assumptions and theoretical underpinnings underlying the design of this framework — these have been presented elsewhere. We have also refrained from discussing merits of the design of the SML programming language.

Work on the EML semantics is nearly finished: the complete formal definition [14] is at the proof-reading stage. Because the definition is still subject to change, there is a small possibility that some of the details in the above presentation will turn out to be slightly inaccurate with respect to the final version. But we are confident that the basic principles presented in this paper are correct and stable, and accurately reflect the intentions incorporated in the design of the framework.

The problems we are wrestling with are those inherent in the enterprise of engineering a sizable completely formal definition of a realistic, practically useful formalism. All the different aspects of this formalism interact with each other, and their mutual relationship is a delicate matter which has to be handled with care and extreme attention to detail. We should perhaps quote here the example of the formal definition of SML on which we build. The original definition of SML went through three major revisions before it was finally officially published as [22]. As a result of the study of the semantics by a larger body of users, this was then followed by a number of subsequent changes included in [21]. And even now, some inaccuracies, weak points and minor mistakes in the definition are still being discovered [13]. Nevertheless, as a whole, the SML semantics is considered (certainly by us) to be an excellent example of the precise definition of a realistic programming language, with very few practical examples of formal design achieving a comparable level of accuracy and mathematical precision.

Thus, the main problems with producing the formal definition of EML are the problems of size, necessarily involving a struggle with many tedious details. We have tried to illustrate this point in the paper. This does not mean that all the issues addressed in the semantics are mathematically trivial: on the contrary, in our view some of the specific decision in the semantics, especially those related to the formal definition of the logic of axioms, are of independent interest, and deserve further separate study.

The next major step, once the semantics is finished, is to develop a sound proof theory, which would provide the user with some formal proof rules and proof tactics to verify the correctness conditions arising in the process of program development. Given the complexity of SML and hence of EML, it may be difficult to come up with appropriate proof rules. Furthermore, checking the formal soundness of these rules w.r.t. the semantics given will be a formidable task on its own.

Defining the formal semantics of a framework like EML, or indeed of a programming language like SML, is not a futile exercise. Most obviously, it provides a common unambiguous reference for all the users of the formalism. Perhaps even more importantly, such a semantics constitutes a basis for all further work on the framework: sound development methodologies, proof techniques, support tools (including the compiler for the programming language) must all be based on and checked against precise semantics if they are to be trustworthy in practical applications. Defining the formal semantics of a language involves taking a very close look at all the details of the language and of the complex interactions between its features. Such a detailed examination of a language is a good way (perhaps the only way) of uncovering both major and minor problems that would otherwise escape notice.

Acknowledgements: Thanks to Fabio da Silva for early collaboration on the static and dynamic semantics of EML and to Edmund Kazmierczak and anonymous referees for helpful comments on a draft of this paper. We owe special thanks to Robin Milner, Mads Tofte and Robert Harper for their work on the semantics of SML, without which the research described here would not have been possible.

References

[1] A. Appel and D. MacQueen. Standard ML of New Jersey, version 0.93. AT&T Bell Laboratories (1993).

[2] E. Astesiano *et al.* The draft formal definition of ANSI-MIL/STD 1815A Ada. Deliverable 7 of the CEC-MAP project (1986).

[3] J. Backus. Can programming be liberated from the von Neumann style? A functional style and its algebra of programs. **Comm. of the Assoc. for Computing Machinery** 21(8):613–641 (1978).

[4] F.L. Bauer, R. Berghammer, M. Broy, W. Dosch, F. Geiselbrechtinger, R. Gnatz, E. Hangel, W. Hesse, B. Krieg-Brückner, A. Laut, T. Matzner, B. Möller, F. Nickl, H. Partsch, P. Pepper, K. Samelson, M. Wirsing, and H. Wössner. **The Munich Project CIP, Vol. 1: The Wide Spectrum Language CIP-L**. Springer LNCS 183 (1985).

[5] R. Burstall and J. Goguen. An informal introduction to specifications using Clear. In: **The Correctness Problem in Computer Science** (R. Boyer and J.S. Moore, eds.), 185–213. Academic Press (1981).

[6] L. Damas and R. Milner. Principle type schemes for functional programs. **Proc. 9th Annual ACM Symp. on Principles of Programming Languages**, 207–212 (1982).

[7] J. Farrés-Casals. Verification in ASL and Related Specification Languages. Ph.D. thesis; Report CST-92-92, Univ. of Edinburgh (1992).

[8] J.-Y. Girard, Y. Lafont and P. Taylor. **Proofs and Types**. Cambridge University Press (1989).

[9] J. Goguen and J. Meseguer. Universal realization, persistent interconnection and implementation of abstract modules. **Proc. 9th Intl. Colloq. on Automata, Languages and Programming**, Aarhus. Springer LNCS 140, 265–281 (1982).

214

[10] J. Guttag and J. Horning. Report on the Larch shared language. **Science of Computer Programming** 6(2):103–134 (1986).

[11] R. Harper. Introduction to Standard ML (revised edition). Report ECS-LFCS-86-14, Univ. of Edinburgh (1989).

[12] G. Kahn. Natural semantics. In: **Programming of Future Generation Computers** (K. Fuchi and M. Nivat, eds.), 237–258. North-Holland (1988).

[13] S. Kahrs. Mistakes and ambiguities in the definition of Standard ML. Report ECS-LFCS-93-257, Univ. of Edinburgh (1993).

[14] S. Kahrs, D. Sannella and A. Tarlecki. The definition of Extended ML. Draft report, Univ. of Edinburgh (1993).

[15] E. Kazmierczak. Modularizing the specification of a small database system in Extended ML. **Formal Aspects of Computer Science** 4(1):100-142 (1992).

[16] E. Kazmierczak. Model theory for Extended ML. Draft report, Univ. of Edinburgh (1992).

[17] B. Krieg-Brückner. PROgram development by SPECification and TRAnsformation. **Technique et Science Informatiques** (1990).

[18] P. Landin. The mechanical evaluation of expressions. **Computer Journal** 6:308–320 (1964).

[19] D.C. Luckham, F.W. von Henke, B. Krieg-Brückner and O. Owe. **Anna, a Language for Annotating Ada Programs: Reference Manual**. Springer LNCS 260 (1987).

[20] D. MacQueen. Modules for Standard ML. In: Report ECS-LFCS-86-2, Univ. of Edinburgh (1986).

[21] R. Milner and M. Tofte. **Commentary on Standard ML**. MIT Press (1991).

[22] R. Milner, M. Tofte and R. Harper. **The Definition of Standard ML**. MIT Press (1990).

[23] J. Mitchell. Type systems for programming languages. In **Handbook of Theoretical Computer Science, Vol. B** (J. van Leeuwen, ed.). North Holland (1990).

[24] L. Paulson. **ML for the Working Programmer**. Cambridge Univ. Press (1991).

[25] G. Plotkin. A structural approach to operational semantics. Report DAIMI FN-19, Aarhus University (1981).

[26] H. Reichel. Behavioural equivalence: a unifying concept for initial and final specification methods. **Proc. 3rd Hungarian Computer Science Conference**, 27–39 (1981).

[27] D. Sannella. Formal program development in Extended ML for the working programmer. **Proc. 3rd BCS/FACS Workshop on Refinement**, Hursley Park. Springer Workshops in Computing, 99–130 (1991).

[28] D. Sannella. Static and logical correctness conditions in formal development of modular programs. Draft report, Univ. of Edinburgh (1993).

[29] D. Sannella and F. da Silva. Case studies in Extended ML. Draft report, Univ. of Edinburgh (1993).

[30] D. Sannella, S. Sokołowski and A. Tarlecki. Toward formal development of programs from algebraic specifications: parameterisation revisited. **Acta Informatica** 29:689–736 (1992).

[31] D. Sannella and A. Tarlecki. Extended ML: an institution-independent framework for formal program development. **Proc. Workshop on Category Theory and Computer Programming**, Guildford. Springer LNCS 240, 364–389 (1986).

[32] D. Sannella and A. Tarlecki. On observational equivalence and algebraic specification. **Journal of Computer and System Sciences** 34:150–178 (1987).

[33] D. Sannella and A. Tarlecki. Toward formal development of programs from algebraic specifications: implementations revisited. **Acta Informatica** 25:233–281 (1988).

[34] D. Sannella and A. Tarlecki. Toward formal development of ML programs: foundations and methodology. **Proc. Joint Conf. on Theory and Practice of Software Development**, Barcelona. Springer LNCS 352, 375–389 (1989).

[35] D. Sannella and A. Tarlecki. Extended ML: past, present and future. **Proc. 7th Workshop on Specification of Abstract Data Types**, Wusterhausen. Springer LNCS 534, 297–322 (1991).

[36] D. Sannella and A. Tarlecki. Toward formal development of programs from algebraic specifications: model-theoretic foundations. **Proc. Intl. Colloq. on Automata, Languages and Programming**, Vienna. Springer LNCS 623, 656–671 (1992).

[37] O. Schoett. Data Abstraction and the Correctness of Modular Programming. Ph.D. thesis; Report CST-42-87, Univ. of Edinburgh (1987).

[38] M. Tofte. Operational Semantics and Polymorphic Type Inference. Ph.D. thesis; Report CST-52-88, Univ. of Edinburgh (1988).

[39] J. Wing, E. Rollins and A. Zaremski. Thoughts on a Larch/ML and a new application for LP. Report CMU-CS-92-135, Carnegie Mellon University (1992).

Type-checking Revisited: Modular Error-handling

T.B. Dinesh*

Department of Software Technology, CWI

Amsterdam, The Netherlands

e-mail: `dinesh@cwi.nl`

Abstract

Static-semantics determines the validity of a program, while a type-checker provides more specific type error information. Type-checkers are specified based on the static semantics specification, for the purpose of identifying and presenting type errors in invalid programs.

We discuss a style of algebraically specifying the static semantics of a language which facilitates automatic generation of a type-checker and a language specific error reporter. Such a specification can also be extended in a modular manner to yield human-readable error messages.

1   An Introduction

Static-semantics of a language determines the validity of a program written in that language. Type-checking of a program, to be useful in practice, should not only indicate whether a given program is valid or not, but also summarize the type errors and show the location of the erroneous constructs which caused the errors. Thus, specifying a type-checker that is useful in practice results in (textually) modifying the specification of static semantics to "knit" in the reporting of the nature and location of type errors. Knitting such reporting information about the details of type-checking into the specification of static semantics is a lot of work and is error prone.

We discuss different styles of specifying type-checkers and present a specification style which facilitates the generation of an error reporting tool that automatically locates the erroneous constructs. This specification style advocates the concise and abstract specification of static semantics. A significant advantage of this style is that error handling (providing a summary of type errors) need not be knit in the type-checker specification, but can be specified as a modular extension to the static semantics.

To illustrate our specification style, we use the toy language Pico [1]. Pico programs consists of declarations followed by statements. The syntax and a brief description of Pico can be found in the appendix. The small size of Pico allows us to discuss different styles used in the specifications in detail.

In Section 2, we briefly discuss algebraic specifications and term rewriting systems, and introduce the specification formalism used in this paper. In Section 3 we examine a "classical" style of specifying static semantics of Pico [1,

---

*Supported by the European Communities, ESPRIT project 5399: Compiler Generation for Parallel Machines — COMPARE

Chapter 9], and how it is modified to serve as a useful type-checker in practice. Then we introduce an alternative style that helps achieve this automatically. In Section 4 we illustrate the general notion of *origin tracking* which facilitates automatic generation an error reporter. In Section 5 we discuss *tokenization*, to assure sufficient origins, since the standard notion of *origin tracking* is insufficient for our case. In Section 6 we discuss some related work.

2 Algebraic specifications and term rewriting systems

Algebraic specifications are typically used as formalisms to specify abstract data types. An abstract data type (ADT) is an isomorphism class of many-sorted *algebras*. A many-sorted algebra is a collection of *carrier sets* and associated *functions*. In an algebraic specification formalism, the properties of the data type to be specified have to be expressed in terms of *equations*.

An interesting consequence of algebraic specifications is that they can be executed if they can be interpreted as *term rewriting systems* (TRS). For a specification to be a TRS, it must obey two rules:

- No variable may occur on the right-hand side of an equation which does not occur on the left-hand side.

- The left-hand side of an equation cannot be a sole variable.

In such a specification (TRS), an equation $s = t$ is interpreted as a rewrite rule $s \rightarrow t$, meaning that s can be rewritten to t. A term is said to be in its *normal form* if it cannot be further rewritten. A term containing variables is called *open*, otherwise it is called a *ground term*. A *substitution* assigns values (terms) to the variables in term. An *instantiation* of an open term is obtained by substituting, for each of its variables, an assigned value.

If $s = t$ is an equation in ASF, it is interpreted as a reduction rule $s \rightarrow t$. If s^σ is an instantiation of s using substitution σ, then $s^\sigma \rightarrow t^\sigma$ is called a basic reduction step. In this reduction step s^σ is called a *redex* (for reducible expression). A term with a hole, i.e., an unknown subterm is referred to as a *context* and is denoted as $C[]$. Applying a rewrite rule $r : s \rightarrow t$ in a context C using the substitution σ is denoted by $C[s^\sigma] \rightarrow_r C[t^\sigma]$. Also, t^σ is often referred to as contractum and $C[t^\sigma]$ as the reduct.

2.1 ASF+SDF

ASF is an algebraic specification formalism that allows modular construction of specifications [1]. A *basic* ASF module consists of

- A set of *sorts* and *function* declarations. Together these constitute the so called *signature* of the module. Sorts are names of the carrier sets and functions correspond to functions in the algebra described by the module.

- A set of *Variable declarations*, which together with the signature define a language of terms.

- A set of *equations* over the terms.

SDF, Syntax Definition Formalism, has been developed [11] to support the definition of lexical, context-free and abstract syntax. The ASF and the SDF formalisms have been combined into one algebraic specification formalism called ASF+SDF.

Specifying in the ASF+SDF formalism is supported by the ASF+SDF *Meta environment* [13]. This system is able to generate parsers and implementations based on rewrite rules from ASF+SDF specifications, thus allowing the execution of ASF+SDF specifications.

An important feature of the ASF+SDF formalism is the existence of list functions and list variables. As an example, suppose we would like to have a function [] for the empty set, [E1] for a set with one element, [E1, E2] for a set with two elements, and so on.

The way to define this in ASF+SDF is as follows:

sorts ELEMENT SET
context-free functions
    "[" {ELEMENT ","}∗ "]"   → SET

The asterisk * says that we want zero or more ELEMENTs, while the comma says that they should be separated by commas. Thus, a set consists of ELEMENTs, separated by commas and the set itself is delimited by [and].

In order to define equations over list functions, we need list variables:

variables
    $Elts$ [*123*]   → {ELEMENT ","}∗
    i → ELEMENT
equations
    [eq1] $[Elts_1, i, Elts_2, i, Elts_3] = [Elts_1, i, Elts_2, Elts_3]$

$Elts_1$, $Elts_2$, and $Elts_3$ are list variables, ranging over list of zero or more ELEMENTs separated by commas.

Here we have specified in one single equation that elements of sets do not have multiplicity: any set containing element i at least two times is equal to the set containing one occurrence less of i.

3   Type-checker specifications

We first introduce, what we refer to as the classical style of specifying static-semantics (type-checker[1]). After discussing its problems, in Section 3.2, we introduce what we refer to as our style which introduces types (abstract values) to value domains in the language and interprets the language constructs at type level ([14] used this style for type-checking expressions in Algol).

---

[1] We use the phrases "static-semantics" and "type-checker" inter-changeably when the specification of static-semantics is executable, although the error-handling capabilities of such a specification would be trivial.

3.1 Classical style

A straight-forward specification of a type-checker for Pico was done using a type-environment (sort TENV, see Appendix A), which is a table used to maintain the associations between identifiers and their type declarations [1, Chapter 9]. The type-checking was specified as shown in the module below. The function tc returns a BOOL result. Checking the statement series using the type-environment results in BOOL, and checking if two types are same results in BOOL. Extracting the type of an expression using the type-environment results in TYPE (either **natural** or **string**).

module Pico-typecheck-old
imports Pico-syntax Type-environments
exports
  context-free functions

tc(PROGRAM)	$\rightarrow$ BOOL
tenv(DECLS)	$\rightarrow$ TENV
TENV "[" SERIES "]"	$\rightarrow$ BOOL
TENV "." EXP	$\rightarrow$ TYPE
compatible(TYPE, TYPE)	$\rightarrow$ BOOL

equations

$$[\text{Tc1a}] \quad \frac{\text{tenv}(D)[S] = \text{true}}{\text{tc(begin } D\ S \text{ end)} = \text{true}}$$

$$[\text{Tc1b}] \quad \frac{\text{tenv}(D)[S] \neq \text{true}}{\text{tc(begin } D\ S \text{ end)} = \text{false}}$$

$$[\text{Tc2}] \quad \frac{Tenv[Stat] = \text{true}, Tenv[Stat\text{-}list] = \text{true}}{Tenv[Stat;Stat\text{-}list] = \text{true}}$$

$$[\text{Tc3}] \quad Tenv[] = \text{true}$$

$$[\text{Tc4}] \quad \frac{\text{compatible}(Tenv\ .\ Id, Tenv\ .\ Exp) = \text{true}}{Tenv[Id := Exp] = \text{true}}$$

$$[\text{Tc5}] \quad \frac{Tenv\ .\ Exp = \text{natural}, Tenv[S_1] = \text{true}, Tenv[S_2] = \text{true}}{Tenv[\text{if } Exp \text{ then } S_1 \text{ else } S_2 \text{ fi}] = \text{true}}$$

$$[\text{Tc6}] \quad \frac{Tenv\ .\ Exp = \text{natural}, Tenv[S] = \text{true}}{Tenv[\text{while } Exp \text{ do } S \text{ od}] = \text{true}}$$

$$[\text{Tc7}] \quad \frac{Tenv\ .\ Exp_1 = \text{natural}, Tenv\ .\ Exp_2 = \text{natural}}{Tenv\ .\ Exp_1 + Exp_2 = \text{natural}}$$

$$[\text{Tc8}] \quad \frac{Tenv\ .\ Exp_1 = \text{natural}, Tenv\ .\ Exp_2 = \text{natural}}{Tenv\ .\ Exp_1 - Exp_2 = \text{natural}}$$

$$[\text{Tc9}] \quad \frac{Tenv\ .\ Exp_1 = \text{string}, Tenv\ .\ Exp_2 = \text{string}}{Tenv\ .\ Exp_1 \parallel Exp_2 = \text{string}}$$

$$[\text{Tc10}] \quad [Idt*,Id : Type,Idt*']\ .\ Id = Type$$

[Tc11] *Tenv . Nat-con* = natural
[Tc12] *Tenv . Str-con* = string

[TcTv] tenv(declare *Idt*;) = [*Idt*]

[TcCa] compatible(natural, natural) = true
[TcCb] compatible(string, string) = true

Let us consider the equations [Tc1a] and [Tc1b] in this specification. The equation [Tc1a] specifies that type-checking a program is "true" if type-checking the statements using the type-environment obtained from the declarations results in "true". However, equation [Tc1b] specifies that if type-checking statements is *not* "true", then the result is "false". Equations such as [Tc1b] are solely used in initial algebra specifications to avoid non-standard values[2]. In this case, the goal was that the result of type-checking be the standard values of sort BOOL ("true" or "false").

The problem with this specification is that generating error messages (which was ignored in the above specification) requires modification of the specification to handle alternate cases and to keep track of errors (as well as error propagation).

For example, to specify error handling for Pico, we would need to modify [Tc1a] and [Tc1b] to account for errors. From [12], we could extract the following style of specification, that addressed error handling while type-checking Pico.

$$[\text{Tc1}] \quad \frac{\text{tenv}(D) = Tenv : Error_1, \; Tenv[S] = Error_2}{\text{tc(begin } D \; S \text{ end)} = Error_1 \; \& \; Error_2}$$

Note that the result of function `tc` is a conjunction of error messages. The result of some functions involved in type-checking (e.g., tenv) should now be a pair consisting of a value component (like before) with an additional error component that is to be propagated.

3.2 Our style

In a specification of a type-checker, it is desirable to specify only the cases for which the program is considered valid while the erroneous constructs be identified automatically. It is tempting to use partial algebra semantics, which gives "run-time" errors, say by identifying the non-standard values as "undefined". This approach, however, is not what is desired for type-checking a program, since checking a program as "undefined" does not help identify the type error. While type-checking a program, we want to know *what* went wrong (i.e., why it did not type-check as "true") and *where* it went wrong. Let us first concentrate on extracting the "why" information and then discuss how the "where" information can be extracted (Section 5).

---

[2] *Non-standard* values are introduced when a new function is defined over an existing sort without giving sufficient equations (i.e., not "sufficiently complete") to simplify expressions containing that function. In initial algebra semantics, the definition of such a function introduces new elements for the "undefined cases" (in a partial algebra sense). These additional elements, are known as "non-standard values".

Our first observation is that, by avoiding conditions in the equations, [Tc1a] and [Tc1b] merges to equation [Tc1]:

[Tc1] tc(begin D S end) = tenv $(D)[S]$

Thus avoiding conditions results in the reduction of the term to something "smaller", although it may not reduce to "true". Observing equation [Tc2] above (module Pico-typecheck-old) suggests that the condition could be avoided if Booleans provided for an operation where "true" is the identity. Thus we could use the conjunction operation "&" and rewrite the equation:

[Tc2] $Tenv[Stat; Stat\text{-}list] = Tenv[Stat] \& Tenv[Stat\text{-}list]$

The next step is to eliminate conditions in equations [Tc4] — [Tc6]. This requires distribution of the type-environment over the components of a statement, which results in transforming the statements to an abstract representation (see equations [Tc16] — [Tc19] below in module Pico-typecheck-new). It is then simple to identify the correct abstract statements. We could thus *inject*[3] statements as non-standard values of Booleans, which means that the type incorrect statements will be non-standard values of sort Booleans.

The need for the compatible predicate (discussion in [1, Section 9.2]) in the specification above is basically to avoid accidentally equating the "undeclared variable" cases as type correct. However, this accident is naturally avoided here since the abstract representations have to be explicitly identified as correct.

Note that we are distributing type-environments over the components of expressions, the result of which should be sort TYPE. Thus we need to inject TYPEs into EXPs. Also, we can keep the specification simple by generalizing the assignment statement to EXP := EXP. This extension to the syntax is only available in type-check modules and does not affect the syntax of the language Pico itself.

In the following specification statements and expressions evaluate to their abstract values. When the tc function is applied to a program, it either evaluates to true (indicating a type-correct program) or it reduces to a normal form which is a conjunction of type incorrect statements in their abstract form (all expressions in them are also reduced to their normal form).

---

[3]The ASF+SDF formalism provides the facility to *inject* one sort into another. This can be simulated in other formalisms by introducing explicit *injection functions*. E.g., instead of injecting statements into Booleans, we could specify a function bool(STATEMENT) → BOOL which acts as an abstraction function that represents statements in Booleans.

module Pico-typecheck-new
imports Pico-syntax Type-environments
exports
  context-free functions

tc(PROGRAM)	→ BOOL
tenv(DECLS)	→ TENV
TENV "[" SERIES "]"	→ BOOL
TENV "." EXP	→ TYPE
EXP ":=" EXP	→ STATEMENT
STATEMENT	→ BOOL
TYPE	→ EXP

equations

[Tc1] $tc(\text{begin } D\ S \text{ end}) = tenv(D)[S]$

[Tc2] $Tenv[Stat;Stat\text{-}list] = Tenv[Stat] \ \& \ Tenv[Stat\text{-}list]$

[Tc3] $Tenv[] = \text{true}$

[Tc4] $Tenv[Id := Exp] = Tenv\ .\ Id := Tenv\ .\ Exp$

[Tc5] $Tenv[\text{if } Exp \text{ then } S_1 \text{ else } S_2 \text{ fi}] =$
     $\text{if } Tenv\ .\ Exp \text{ then else fi } \& \ Tenv[S_1] \ \& \ Tenv[S_2]$

[Tc6] $Tenv[\text{while } Exp \text{ do } S \text{ od}] = \text{while } Tenv\ .\ Exp \text{ do od } \& \ Tenv[S]$

[Tc7] $Tenv\ .\ Exp_1 + Exp_2 = Tenv\ .\ Exp_1 + Tenv\ .\ Exp_2$

[Tc8] $Tenv\ .\ Exp_1 - Exp_2 = Tenv\ .\ Exp_1 - Tenv\ .\ Exp_2$

[Tc9] $Tenv\ .\ Exp_1 \ ||\ Exp_2 = Tenv\ .\ Exp_1 \ ||\ Tenv\ .\ Exp_2$

[Tc10a] $[Idt*,Id : Type,Idt*']\ .\ Id = Type$
[Tc10b] $Tenv\ .\ Type = Type$

[Tc11] $Nat\text{-}con = \text{natural}$
[Tc12] $Str\text{-}con = \text{string}$

[Tc13] natural + natural = natural
[Tc14] natural − natural = natural
[Tc15] string || string = string

[Tc16] natural := natural = true
[Tc17] string := string = true
[Tc18] if natural then else fi = true
[Tc19] while natural do od = true

[TcTv] $tenv(\text{declare } Idt*;) = [Idt*]$

The techniques used in the above specification are to:

- Avoid conditions in the equations.
- Distribute the type-environment over statements (equations [Tc2]–[Tc6]).
- Distribute the type-environment over expressions ([Tc7]–[Tc9]).

- Evaluate the expressions at an abstract (type) level ([Tc13]–[Tc15]).
- Identify the abstract type-correct statements ([Tc16]–[Tc19]).
- Extended syntax in order to generalize, when needed.
- Change the constants to their abstract representation ([Tc11]–[Tc12]).

The equations [Tc13]–[Tc19] are the crux of this style of specification. The other equations help transform the source program into its abstract form. The equations [Tc13]–[Tc19] identify the type-correct constructs, while anything that is not reducible by these equations become *structured error* messages.

Thus, the result of applying the tc function for the program

```
begin
  declare x : natural,
          s : string;
  x := 10;
  while x do
    x := x - s;
    s := s || "#"
  od
end
```

is

```
natural := natural - string
```

This structured error message indicates the following: (1) the program has a type error (did not evaluate to true) (2) the error is in an assignment statement (3) the type of the left-hand side of the assignment is incompatible with the right-hand side and (4) the right argument for a subtraction operation has string operand.

This error information can easily be further processed by a separate module which issues human-readable error messages. For instance, by applying "readable-msg" to the result of "tc": readable-msg(tc(*Program*)).

For the structured error above, all or some of the 4 error indications can be used to generate human readable error messages (for details see [7]). The equations below rewrite the above message to error indication 4.

[E1]   readable-msg($Exp := Exp'$) = msg($Exp :=$ simplify(Exp'))

[E2]   msg($Exp := Type$) = cannot assign(:=) $Type$ to Exp

[E3]   msg($Exp := Exp_1\ Op\ Exp_2$) = msg($Exp_1\ Op\ Exp_2$)

[E4]   msg($Exp_1 -$ string) = right argument for (-) has string operand

The obvious lack of information in such a message, however, is an indication of where in the source program the errors are located. It is mandatory to have information on location of errors in large programs. Generation of this information is often done by keeping track of line numbers in the input program. We claim that error location information can be automatically generated by a programming environment generator and discuss how this is done currently in the ASF+SDF system in Section 5.

224

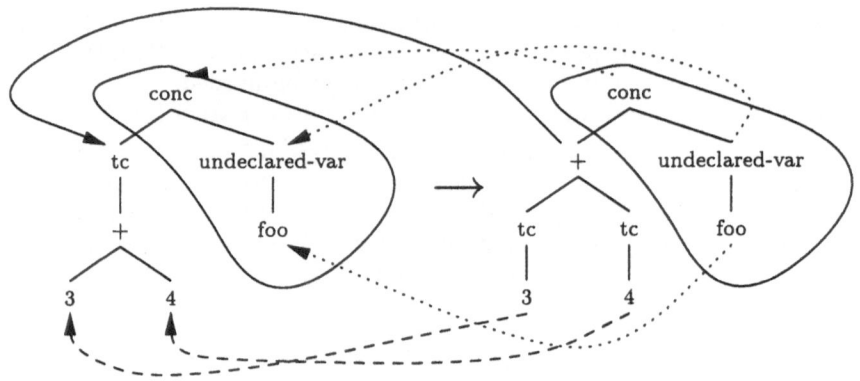

Rewrite rule:	$tc(E_1 + E_2) \rightarrow tc(E_1) + tc(E_2)$
Substitution:	$\{E_1 \mapsto 3,\ E_2 \mapsto 4\}$
Context:	$conc(\Box, undeclared\text{-}var(foo))$

Dashed arrows:	Origins for Common Variables
Dotted arrows:	Context Origins
Solid arrow:	Origin for Redex-Contractum.

Figure 1: Origins established for one rewrite step.

4 Origin Tracking

Origin tracking is a generic technique for relating parts of intermediate terms, which occur during term rewriting, to parts of the initial term. It automatically maintains certain forms of relations between the source and result that can be exploited for generating an error reporter, by using the specification style presented in Section 3.2.

Figure 1 illustrates some origin relations established in one rewrite rule. Such single step origins are composed to yield origin relations from intermediate terms to initial term. For a detailed description of origin tracking and its applications, the reader is referred to [5].

Figure 2 shows the use of origin tracking in the ASF+SDF system [13], to find the location of erroneous constructs in a CLaX program [7]. Here, function "errors" is applied to a CLaX program in the large window. The resulting type errors are displayed in the small window. These error messages, albeit useful, provide no information regarding the specific constructs of the program that caused it or the position where it originated. Origin tracking in the system provides one with the ability to identify the culprit program constructs by clicking on the desired error and requesting the system to show its origin. Label "step" is defined twice in the program (but a label should be defined uniquely) and in small window there is an error message that indicates this. By selecting this error message and asking the system to show origins both occurrences of the label **step** that caused this error are high-lighted by the system.

Figure 2: Example of a generated environment using origin tracking.

5   On identifying error locations

To explain the idea of automating the process of error location identification, we will consider the origin tracking mechanism and modify our specification so that enough origins can be tracked to determine complete information on where the errors are located.

We consider equation [Tc11] from the Pico-typecheck-old specification for our discussion.

[Tc11]   *Tenv . Nat-con* = natural

If we look at this equation for relationships between the left hand side and right hand side, we can hardly see any other than the obvious one indicated by the = symbol (the Redex-Contractum case [5]). Since the possible terms which match the left side are not program terms (Pico syntax terms), there would be no (transitive) relation from the reduct to any program term.

Now let us compare [Tc11] from the module Pico-typecheck-old to the equations [Tc10b] and [Tc11] from module Pico-typecheck-new.

226

[Tc10b]   *Tenv . Type = Type*

The equation [Tc10b] suggests not only a relationship indicated by the = symbol (as in Redex-contractum case), but also one about the variable *Type*; the variable *Type* on left-hand side and right-hand side are the same (the Common Variables case [5]). Thus, when this rule is used to rewrite a term, the reduct term could be related to its redex in two ways. First, the Redex-Contractum case, is similar to that for [Tc11] of Pico-typecheck-old and would not lead to relating the reduct to a source program sub-term for our specification. But the second, the Common Variables case could be useful since *Type* on the left-hand side could be a subterm of the source program. In our case **natural** and **string** are two words that can be found in the program source. The second relation could thus help the system in tracking the reduct to a part of the source program; e.g., if the word **natural** has origin to a subterm of the source program (in our case a constant of type natural).

Next we can consider the case of constants of type natural that equation [Tc11], of Pico-typecheck-old, was used for by considering [Tc11] of module Pico-typecheck-new.

[Tc11]   *Nat-con* = natural

It is now easy to observe that the necessary relation between a constant and its reduct the word **natural** (type name in our case) exists as desired (the Redex-Contractum case). Handling the constants like this (equations [Tc11] and [Tc12] of module Pico-typecheck-new) seems to provide enough information to the system to show automatically the error location information if a constant is involved in causing the error message.

Another situation that is somewhat similar to the case of constants is the lexicals of the syntax constructors — e.g., the need to know which ":=" or "-" in the source program appeared in error message discussed earlier. The specification of the module Pico-syntax abstracts away such tokens, i.e., the origin relation for equation [Tc8] in Pico-typecheck-new is (no relations for the - token):

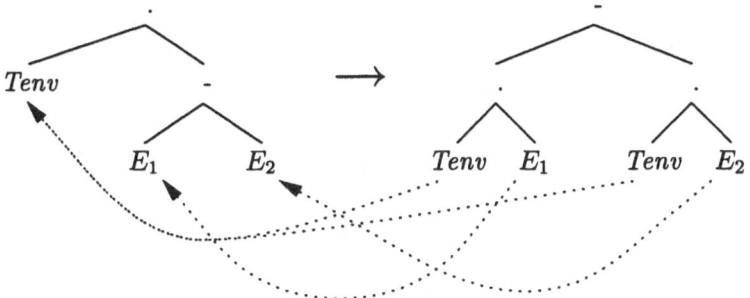

We therefore need to adapt our specification in such a way that meaningful origins result for this case. An immediate result of this is that the syntax could be defined slightly differently so that the rest comes for free. The following modification to the syntax, effectively re-does the implicit structure of operations and statements without asking for changes in the specification of the type-checker. Thus replacing module Pico-syntax by module Pico-syntax-new, which uses the module Pico-tokens shown below, provides us with enough of the location information for tracking the origin of error messages.

module Pico-tokens
exports
  sorts AOP SOP IF THEN ELSE FI WHILE DO OD ASGN
  context-free functions

"+"	→ AOP	if	→ IF	while	→ WHILE
"−"	→ AOP	then	→ THEN	do	→ DO
"||"	→ SOP	else	→ ELSE	od	→ OD
":="	→ ASGN	fi	→ FI		

By using the above module Pico-tokens, the context-free functions in module Pico-syntax can be written differently using the sort names in module Pico-tokens. For example, the function

    EXP "+" EXP → EXP {**left**}

can be written instead as

    EXP AOP EXP → EXP {**left**}

The origin relations for equation [Tc8] now become:

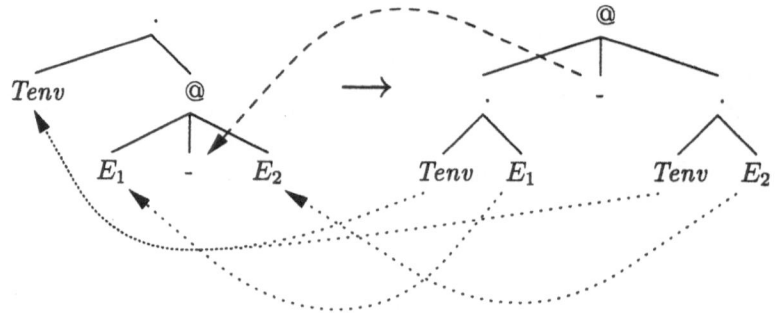

where the @ is a nameless abstract function.

Some of the concrete syntax is converted to abstract syntax for the program constructs, which can now be handled by the origin-tracking mechanism to indicate the location of the error. The rest of the specification need not be altered in any manner.

We note that it is undesirable to force this *tokenization* on the specifier. But on the brighter side, we also observed that such tokenization does not call for modification of the rest of the specification. Thus, tokenization could be automatically performed by the system and hidden from the user (specifier).

6   Related work

Methods to handle exceptional states in algebraic specification is a much discussed subject [9], however type errors encountered during type-checking are not exceptions of this nature. Order-sorted algebras [8] allow errors to be dealt in separate sorts. This by itself does not help modularization, whereas our recommended style could be used in that context. Thus specifiers of type-checkers need not be bothered about building the error propagation machinery from the start.

In Section 3 we compared our style of specification in detail to what we called the classical style including adaptations it needed for error-handling [12]. To give an indication of the conciseness of our style, we compare the number of lines (rounded to 2 significant digits) of ASF+SDF type-checker specifications for Pico [12], CLaX [7] (a subset of Pascal) and Pascal [2].

	syntax	type checker		style used
		static semantics	+ error handling	
Pico	30	35	+ 50 = 85	ours
Pico	30	35+85=120		classical ([12])
CLaX	280	650	+250 = 900	ours ([7])
Pascal	300	2500		classical ([2])

Although measuring number of lines is a vague estimate, we can conclude that the effectiveness of our style dramatically increases with the size of the language.

Jan Heering [10] has experimented with using higher-order algebraic specifications and uses an abstract interpretation style to specify a type-checker for Pico. This necessitated defining origin-tracking for higher-order TRS [4]. The general idea of using an abstract interpretation style for specifying type-checkers itself is not new [14] and is likely used by many people. Also, this style appears to be a natural by-product when the static semantics is semi-automatically derived from the dynamic semantics [6].

Alternative methods to get an effect similar to that of tokenization are of interest. A notion of *syntax directed* origins discussed in [3] appears to provide origin information needed for the cases of interest here.

GNU Emacs [15] and various workbenches extract the line number from a compiler error message and highlight that line in an editor window. In our case, error reporting is language specific and highlighting does not indicate an entire line for some error, but only the offending program constructs.

7 Concluding Remarks

The style of type-checking illustrated in this paper concentrates on specifying only the necessary information, while still providing reasonably good error messages. The style described makes use of the so called non-standard values of an initial algebra specification to generate errors. The result of type-checking is to effectively form a conjunction of the abstract meanings of statements of the language. All type correct statements evaluate to "true" while an incorrect statement reduces to a structured error. This together with origin tracking automatically provides information on the location of errors in the source program. The structured errors can be used by a separate module to generate human-readable error messages.

The advocated specification style also allows type-checking over effectively incomplete programs [7]. Incomplete programs can be written in the ASF+SDF system using meta-variables in the input term.

It is an interesting exercise to adopt this style for languages with polymorphic types or to define a notion of origin tracking for systems that are not term rewriting systems.

Acknowledgements: I thank Arie van Deursen, Jan Heering, Paul Klint and Susan Uskudarli for many discussions, and comments on earlier drafts of the paper. Arie also helped with many figures in the paper.

References

[1] J.A. Bergstra, J. Heering, and P. Klint, editors. *Algebraic Specification*. ACM Press Frontier Series. The ACM Press in co-operation with Addison-Wesley, 1989.

[2] A. van Deursen. An algebraic specification for the static semantics of Pascal. Report CS-R9129, Centrum voor Wiskunde en Informatica (CWI), Amsterdam, 1991. Extended abstract in: *Conference Proceedings of Computing Science in the Netherlands CSN'91*, pages 150-164. Available by *ftp* from ftp.cwi.nl:/pub/gipe as Deu91.ps.Z.

[3] A. van Deursen. Origin tracking in primitive recursive schemes. Technical report, Centrum voor Wiskunde en Informatica (CWI), 1993. To appear.

[4] A. van Deursen and T. B. Dinesh. Origin-tracking for higher-order term rewriting systems. In *An International Workshop on Higher-Order Algebra, Logic and Term Rewriting*, 1993.

[5] A. van Deursen, P. Klint, and F. Tip. Origin tracking. *Journal of Symbolic Computation*, 15:523–545, 1993. Special Issue on Automatic Programming.

[6] T. B. Dinesh. Interactive specification of static semantics from dynamic semantics. Technical report, Centrum voor Wiskunde en Informatica (CWI), 1994. To Appear.

[7] T.B. Dinesh and F. Tip. Animators and error reporters for generated programming environments. Report CS-R9253, Centrum voor Wiskunde en Informatica (CWI), Amsterdam, 1992. Available by *ftp* from ftp.cwi.nl:/pub/gipe as DT92.ps.Z.

[8] J. Goguen, C. Kirchner, H. Kirchner, A. Mégrelis, J. Meseguer, and T. Winkler. An introduction to OBJ3. In S. Kaplan and J.-P. Jouannaud, editors, *Proceedings of the First International Workshop on Conditional Term Rewriting Systems*, volume 308 of *Lecture Notes in Computer Science*, pages 258–263. Springer-Verlag, 1988.

[9] J. A. Goguen. Abstract errors for abstract data types. In E.J. Neuhold, editor, *Formal descriptions of programming concepts*, pages 491–525. North-Holland, 1978.

[10] J. Heering. Second-order algebraic specification of static semantics. Report CS-R9254, Centrum voor Wiskunde en Informatica (CWI), Amsterdam, 1992. Available by *ftp* from ftp.cwi.nl:/pub/gipe as Hee92b.ps.Z.

[11] J. Heering, P.R.H. Hendriks, P. Klint, and J. Rekers. The syntax definition formalism SDF - reference manual. *SIGPLAN Notices*, 24(11):43–75, 1989.

[12] P. Klint. Error handling in algebraic specifications. Unpublished, April 1991.

[13] P. Klint. A meta-environment for generating programming environments. *ACM Transactions on Software Engineering Methodology*, 2(2):176–201, 1993.

[14] P. Naur. Checking of operand types in algol compilers. *BIT*, 5:151–163, 1965.

[15] R. Stallman. *GNU Emacs Manual*. Free Software Foundation, 675 Mass Ave., Cambridge, MA, USA, emacs version 18 edition, 1991. For unix users.

A Pico Language

A Pico program consists of declarations followed by statements and is defined in Chapter 9 of [1]. All variables are declared to be either of type natural or of type string. Statements may be assignment statements, if-statements and while-statements. Expressions may be a single identifier, addition or subtraction of natural numbers, or concatenation of strings.

The imported modules define the lexical identifiers, constants for natural numbers and strings used in the language. The variables defined in this module are used (since they are exported) in the equations of modules that import Pico-syntax (e.g., Pico-typecheck modules).

module Pico-syntax
imports Layout Identifiers Integers Strings Booleans

exports
   sorts PROGRAM DECLS ID-TYPE SERIES STATEMENT EXP TYPE
   context-free functions

begin DECLS SERIES end	→ PROGRAM
declare {ID-TYPE ","}* ";"	→ DECLS
ID ":" TYPE	→ ID-TYPE
{STATEMENT ";"}*	→ SERIES
ID ":=" EXP	→ STATEMENT
if EXP then SERIES else SERIES fi	→ STATEMENT
while EXP do SERIES od	→ STATEMENT
natural	→ TYPE
string	→ TYPE
EXP "+" EXP	→ EXP {**left**}
EXP "−" EXP	→ EXP {**left**}
EXP "||" EXP	→ EXP {**left**}
ID	→ EXP
NAT-CON	→ EXP
STR-CON	→ EXP
"(" EXP ")"	→ EXP {**bracket**}

   variables

D	→ DECLS
Idt "*" [']*	→ {ID-TYPE ","}*
S [12]*	→ SERIES
$Stat$	→ STATEMENT
$Stat\text{-}list$	→ {STATEMENT ";"}+
Exp [12']*	→ EXP
$Type$	→ TYPE

Specifying a type-checker for Pico is done using a table for type-environments TENV. Table is simply defined as a list with identifier-type pairs.

module Type-environments
imports Pico-syntax

exports
   sorts TENV
   context-free functions
      "[" {ID-TYPE ","}* "]"   → TENV
   variables
      $Tenv$ → TENV

Proof Theory for μCRL:
A Language for Processes with Data*

Jan Friso Groote

Department of Philosophy, Utrecht University

Utrecht, The Netherlands

Alban Ponse

Dep. of Mathematics and Computer Science, University of Amsterdam

Amsterdam, The Netherlands

Abstract

A simple specification language, called μCRL (*micro Common Representation Language*), is introduced. It consists of process algebra extended with abstract data types. The language μCRL is designed such that it contains only basic constructs with a straightforward semantics. It has been developed under the assumption that an extensive and mathematically precise study of these constructs and their interaction will yield fundamental insights that are are essential to an analytical approach of well-known and much richer specification languages. To this end, a simple property language is defined in which basic properties of processes, data and the process/data relationship can be expressed in a formal way. Next a proof system is defined for this property language, comprising a rule for induction, the Recursive Specification Principle, and process algebra axioms. The proof theory thus obtained is designed such that automatic proof checking is feasible. It is illustrated with a case study of a counter.

1 Introduction

To guarantee the reliability of software for distributed systems, the need is felt to have more and better means for structural analysis than the contemporary ones. Simulation is effective on large specifications of systems, but it only serves to show that a system is erroneous and it is not very well suited to show a system correct. Most advanced analysis techniques, for instance those that depend on complete explorations of state spaces, are generally only applicable to very small distributed systems. The reason for this is that contemporary state space explorations seldom use the structure present in specifications and therefore the state spaces tend to become very large (see e.g. [16, 21]). Here we are interested in studying the structure that results from the separation between data and processes.

To this purpose we have defined the language μCRL [12]. This is a simple language that comprises a straightforward mechanism to specify abstract data

---

*The work reported herein was supported by the European Communities under RACE project no. 1046, Specification and Programming Environment for Communication Software (SPECS).

types using plain equations. Furthermore, it consists of elementary process constructors, taken from process algebra [1]. The language is so simple that its semantics is clear. Yet the language is sufficiently expressive to describe large classes of distributed systems. Therefore μCRL is well-suited for further investigations into the process/data relationship.

In order to express and formally prove properties about distributed systems, a proof theory has been developed for μCRL [13]. This proof theory, introduced and illustrated in the present paper, is intended to enable very precise proofs of the correctness of distributed systems and programs. It is well-known that even the slightest error in a program may have serious consequences. Human-made proofs of the correctness of programs are not necessarily correct. If the proofs are sufficiently precise, they can be checked using an appropriate computer program. This increases the reliability of proofs considerably. For μCRL, proof checking by computer has been done and is described in [20].

The language μCRL and its proof theory have been used in several case studies, and have led to a new stream of research. In the last section an overview is given of the current state of the art. The conclusion that we draw from the current developments around μCRL is that it pays off to restrict oneself to a simple core language. Using μCRL we have gained insight in the process data relationship and we have proved distributed systems correct that were outside the scope of process-algebraic techniques a few years ago.

Acknowledgements. We thank Jan Springintveld for his comments regarding this paper. Furthermore, we thank all those, of which we only mention Jan Bergstra, who have contributed to μCRL and its proof theory via comments and discussion.

2 The specification language μCRL

In μCRL data are specified by equational specifications: one can declare sorts and functions working upon these sorts, and describe the meaning of these functions by equational axioms. Processes are described in the style of CCS [18], CSP [14] or ACP [1], where the particular process syntax has been taken from ACP. Starting point is a set of uninterpreted actions that may be parameterised by data. These actions can represent all kinds of real world activities, depending on the usage of the language. Here we do not introduce the syntax of μCRL in detail, but sketch it by an example (that is used to illustrate the proof system). Consider the μCRL specification E in Table 1. It introduces some μCRL keywords, generally printed in boldface. The sort **Booleans** with constants (**func**) t and f are obligatory in any μCRL specification. A second data type *Nat* with some functions is specified, where most functions are defined in the **rewrite** section, using the variables declared in **var**. The atomic actions in E are *inc*(rease)and *dec*(rease). Finally two process specifications occur (after **proc**). First the process *Counter(t)* for any closed data term t over *Nat* is defined. The behaviour of eg. *Counter(0)* is defined by the process term $inc \cdot Counter(S(0)) + \delta \triangleleft is\text{-}zero(0) \triangleright dec \cdot Counter(P(0))$. Here the $\cdot$ represents *sequential composition* and the $+$ represents *choice*. The ternary operator $.\triangleleft.\triangleright.$ is called the *conditional*; it must be read as then-if-else. Precedence of the operators is $\cdot, .\triangleleft.\triangleright., +$. In the case of *Counter(0)* the positive consequence of the

sort	**Bool**
func	t, f :$\rightarrow$ **Bool**
sort	Nat
func	$0 :\rightarrow Nat$
	$S, P : Nat \rightarrow Nat$
	$add : Nat \times Nat \rightarrow Nat$
	$is\text{-}zero : Nat \rightarrow$ **Bool**
var	$x, y : Nat$
rew	$P(0) = 0$
	$P(S(x)) = x$
	$add(x, 0) = x$
	$add(x, S(y)) = S(add(x, y))$
	$is\text{-}zero(0) = $ t
	$is\text{-}zero(S(x)) = $ f
act	$inc \;\; dec$
proc	$Counter(x{:}Nat) = inc \cdot Counter(S(x)) +$
	$\qquad\qquad\qquad\qquad\quad \delta \triangleleft is\text{-}zero(x) \triangleright dec \cdot Counter(P(x))$
	$X = inc \cdot (X \parallel dec)$

Table 1: An example of a μCRL specification

conditional is the constant δ, *inaction* or *deadlock*, which by definition is a process term. As δ is redundant in a + context, the process $Counter(0)$ can only perform an *inc* action and evolve into $Counter(S(0))$. In turn, $Counter(S(0))$ can perform an *inc* action and further behave as $Counter(S(S(0)))$, or a *dec* action and evolve into $Counter(P(S(0)))$ (which behaves just as $Counter(0)$ by the second **rew**rite rule of E). It is not hard to see that $Counter(0)$ indeed models a "counter". Then the process X is defined. It is not parameterised, and behaves as follows: first *inc* is executed, and then behaviour is conform $X \parallel dec$, the *parallel composition* of X and *dec*, which in turn represents an interleaved execution of both components.

The proof theory to be introduced now gives the means to *formally prove* (respecting the standard semantics) that the process $Counter(0)$ is *equal to* (bisimilar with) the process $Counter(0) \parallel Counter(0)$, in fact stating that two counters in parallel behave as one counter. Furthermore, it can also be proved that $Counter(0) = X$. Both identities illustrate that proving properties of parallel processes may be reducible to proving properties of process descriptions in which no parallel operators occur, and in which control is partly encoded by simple data parameterisation. This is an important feature of the μCRL proof theory.

There are a few other constructs in μCRL that have not been used in the example. Actions may, just as processes, be parameterised. The *label* of an action is simply its name without its possible parameter instantiation. For instance an action $send(0)$ has $send$ as its label. There is a *sum operator*, written as $\sum_{d:D}(p)$ which says that the process p may be executed for each possible value for the variable d of data type D. It is generally used to describe input actions of a process. There are a *left merge operator*, written as $\parallel$, and a *communication merge operator*, written as $\mid$, that are auxiliary and which are used for calculation with parallel processes. The process $p \parallel q$ expresses that p and q run in parallel, but the first step must come from p. The process $p \mid q$ expresses that p and q run in parallel, but the first actions of p and q must communicate (explained below). Furthermore, there is a *hiding operator*, τ_I, an *encapsulation operator*, ∂_H, and a *renaming operator*, ρ_R. The process $\rho_R(p)$ behaves as p, except that the labels of all actions are renamed according to the function R. The process $\tau_I(p)$ behaves as p, except that all actions in p of which the labels occur also in the set I are renamed to the specially dedicated internal action τ. The process $\partial_H(p)$ behaves as p, except that all actions of which the labels occur in the set H are blocked. There is one other unmentioned feature, which is the way communication is declared. If actions a and b must communicate into c, then this is expressed by specifying

$$\textbf{comm} \quad a \mid b = c.$$

This also specifies that possible parameterised occurrences of a and b communicate if they have equal instantiations. For instance $a(0) \mid b(0) = c(0)$.

For a complete specification of the language μCRL see [13], where the language, its static semantics, its operational semantics and some useful subsets of the language are completely formally described.

3 A property language for μCRL

A language is introduced in which simple properties of specifications can be formally expressed. These properties consist of identities between data or process terms, linked together with propositional connectives.

In order to express properties that a specification may have we use *(data) variables* over the sorts declared, and *(process) variables*. We further introduce *substitutions* to extract the precise instances we are interested in. Because properties always refer to a particular specification and because we are dealing with names in a very precise and restrictive way, we define both these concepts relative to the signature of a specification.

Definition 3.1 (*Data and process variables*). Let E be a specification. A finite set V_d containing elements of the form $\langle d{:}D \rangle$ with d some name is called a *set of data variables over* E iff the name D is declared as a sort in E, d is not a constant, or an unparameterised action or process from E, and for each sort name $D' \not\equiv D$ of E it holds that $\langle d{:}D' \rangle \notin V_d$. If we are not interested in the sort of d, we just say that d is 'a variable from V_d'.

Given a set V_d of data variables over E, a finite set V_p of names is called a set of *process variables over* E *and* V_d iff non of its elements occur as a variable in V_d.

We generally use triples E, V_d, V_p, meaning that E is a (well-formed) specification, V_d is a set of data variables over E, and V_p is a set of process variables over E and V_d. Given E, V_d, V_p, we define many sorted terms that may contain variables. We distinguish two kinds of such terms: data terms and process terms.

Definition 3.2 (*Data terms and process terms*). A *data term over* E, V_d, V_p is either a constant from E, a variable from V_d, or an application of a function from E to data terms over E, V_d, V_p of the appropriate sort. A data term is called *closed* iff it does not contain any variables from V_d. Note that for data terms the actual contents of V_p is not relevant.

A *process term over* E, V_d, V_p is defined inductively:

- $p \circ q$ with $\circ \in \{+, \cdot, \|, \|\!\|, \|, \triangleleft t \triangleright\}$ and t a data term over E, V_d, V_p of sort **Bool**, is a *process term over* E, V_d, V_p if both p and q are,

- $\sum_{d:D}(p)$ is a *process term over* E, V_d, V_p if p is a process term over

$$E, (V_d \setminus \{\langle d{:}n \rangle \mid n \text{ a sort name}\}) \cup \{\langle d{:}D \rangle\}, V_p \setminus \{d\},$$

- $C_{\{n_1,\ldots,n_m\}}(p)$ with $C \in \{\partial, \tau\}$ is a *process term over* E, V_d, V_p if p is, and the n_i are labels of actions from E,

- $\rho_{\{n_1 \to n'_1, \ldots, n_m \to n'_m\}}(p)$ is a *process term over* E, V_d, V_p if p is, and the n_i are labels of actions from E such that if n_i is an action from E then so is n'_i, and if $n_i{:}S_1 \times \ldots \times S_k$ is an action declaration in E then so is $n'_i{:}S_1 \times \ldots \times S_k$,

- δ and τ are *process terms over* E, V_d, V_p,

- n is a *process term over* E, V_d, V_p if n is an action or a process from E or if $n \in V_p$,

- $n(t_1, \ldots, t_m)$ is a *process term over* E, V_d, V_p if either E contains an action declaration of the form $n{:}S_1 \times \ldots \times S_m$ or a process declaration of the form $n(x_1{:}S_1, \ldots, x_m{:}S_m) = q$ and any t_i is a data term over E, V_d, V_p of sort S_i.

A process term is *closed* iff it does not contain any variables from V_d or V_p.

Definition 3.3. A *property over* E, V_d, V_p is defined inductively in the following way:

- $\mathcal{F}$ ("Falsum") is a *property over* E, V_d, V_p,

- $t = u$ is a *property over* E, V_d, V_p iff

  - either t and u are data terms over E, V_d, V_p that are of the same sort,
  - or t and u are process terms over E, V_d, V_p,

- $\neg(\phi)$ is a *property over* E, V_d, V_p iff ϕ is a property over E, V_d, V_p,

- $(\phi \circ \psi)$ with $\circ \in \{\vee, \wedge, \to, \leftrightarrow\}$ is a *property over* E, V_d, V_p iff both ϕ and ψ are.

In properties we omit brackets according to the convention that $=$ binds stronger than any of the logical operators $\neg, \vee, \wedge, \rightarrow, \leftrightarrow$, that $\neg$ binds stronger than any of the logical binary operators, and that $\vee, \wedge$ bind stronger than $\rightarrow, \leftrightarrow$.

Now a *property formula*, the basic means to express that some specification has some property, simply consist of a property that has as an attribute the originating specification and variable sets:

$$\phi \text{ from } E, V_d, V_p$$

with ϕ a property over E, V_d, V_p. A property formula ϕ **from** E, V_d, V_p is called *closed* iff ϕ contains neither variables from V_d, nor process variables from V_p.

We have introduced more logical symbols than strictly necessary for expressing the properties we are interested in. We regard the symbols $\rightarrow$ and $\mathcal{F}$ as basic, and use the other symbols as abbreviations in the usual way (cf. [7], and recall that $\neg\phi$ abbreviates $\phi \rightarrow \mathcal{F}$).

4 Logical deductions

A proof system over this property language is defined. This system is given in a natural deduction format because this is close to intuitive reasoning. It contains so called 'logical' axioms and rules, suitable to derive the fundamental properties induced by the equality relation $=$ and by the propositional connectives. Our set-up is based on [22].

A deduction can be seen as a tree of which each node is labelled with a property formula (and possibly the name of a rule which has been applied to obtain the property formula). The leaves of the tree are the *assumptions* (also called hypotheses) of the deduction. We use symbols $\mathcal{D}$, possibly subscripted, for arbitrary deductions. We write

$$\mathcal{D}$$
$$\psi \text{ from } E, V_d, V_p$$

to indicate that $\mathcal{D}$ has *conclusion* ψ **from** E, V_d, V_p (so the occurrence ψ **from** E, V_d, V_p is part of $\mathcal{D}$ itself). We use the notation $[\phi$ **from** $E, V_d, V_p]$ for a possibly empty set of occurrences of a property formula ϕ **from** E, V_d, V_p in a deduction, thus

$$[\phi \text{ from } E, V_d, V_p]$$
$$\mathcal{D}$$

is a deduction $\mathcal{D}$ with a set $[\phi$ **from** $E, V_d, V_p]$ of assumptions in $\mathcal{D}$. As a rule we assume that $[\phi$ **from** $E, V_d, V_p]$ refers to *all* assumptions of the form ϕ **from** E, V_d, V_p in $\mathcal{D}$.

We define logical deductions inductively.

Definition 4.1. The single-node tree with as label a property formula ϕ **from** E, V_d, V_p is a deduction from the open assumption ϕ **from** E, V_d, V_p. There are no cancelled assumptions.

Let $\mathcal{D}_1, \mathcal{D}_2$ be deductions. A new deduction can be constructed according to the rules in Table 2. These rules are subject to the following restrictions:

1. In applications of the introduction rule $\rightarrow$I and the rule RAA (Reductio Ad Absurdum) *all* open assumptions of the form indicated by [...] are cancelled.

2. In applications of $\rightarrow$I, RAA, the reflexivity rule REFL, the variable rule VAR and the substitution rule SUB, the conclusion should be a property formula.

3. In applications of SUB the variable x may not be free in any (uncancelled) hypothesis of $\mathcal{D}_1$.

4. Each application of VAR is restricted to one of the following two cases:

   (a) $V_d \subseteq V_d'$ or $V_d' \subseteq V_d$, and $V_p = V_p'$,
   (b) $V_p \subseteq V_p'$ or $V_p' \subseteq V_p$, and $V_d = V_d'$.

$$\frac{\begin{array}{c}[\phi \textbf{ from } E, V_d, V_p]\\ \mathcal{D}_1\\ \psi \textbf{ from } E, V_d, V_p\end{array}}{\phi \rightarrow \psi \textbf{ from } E, V_d, V_p}\ \rightarrow\text{I}$$

$$\frac{\begin{array}{cc}\mathcal{D}_1 & \mathcal{D}_2\\ \phi \textbf{ from } E, V_d, V_p & \phi \rightarrow \psi \textbf{ from } E, V_d, V_p\end{array}}{\psi \textbf{ from } E, V_d, V_p}\ \rightarrow\text{E}$$

$$\frac{\begin{array}{c}[\neg\phi \textbf{ from } E, V_d, V_p]\\ \mathcal{D}_1\\ \mathcal{F} \textbf{ from } E, V_d, V_p\end{array}}{\phi \textbf{ from } E, V_d, V_p}\ \text{RAA} \qquad \frac{}{t = t \textbf{ from } E, V_d, V_p}\ \text{REFL}$$

$$\frac{\begin{array}{cc}\mathcal{D}_1 & \mathcal{D}_2\\ \phi[t/x] \textbf{ from } E, V_d, V_p & t = u \textbf{ from } E, V_d, V_p\end{array}}{\phi[u/x] \textbf{ from } E, V_d, V_p}\ \text{REPL}$$

$$\frac{\begin{array}{c}\mathcal{D}_1\\ \phi \textbf{ from } E, V_d, V_p\end{array}}{\phi[t/x] \textbf{ from } E, V_d, V_p}\ \text{SUB} \qquad \frac{\begin{array}{c}\mathcal{D}_1\\ \phi \textbf{ from } E, V_d, V_p\end{array}}{\phi \textbf{ from } E, V_d', V_p'}\ \text{VAR}$$

Table 2: Rules for logical deductions

The notation $u[t/x]$ means that t is substituted for x in u. The definition of this notion is fully standard, but care must be taken that the types of t and x are the same, and no name clashes occur with data variables bound by the Σ operator. A full definition is given in [13]. The reflexivity rule REFL has an empty premiss, and is therefore called an 'axiom'. The rule VAR is a structural rule that allows (restricted) replacement of variable sets. In the next section we introduce axioms that specify the minimal variable sets involved. With VAR we can obtain variable sets that are suitable for further derivations.

In most deductions the form of the property formulas itself already determines which rule is being applied. Therefore we often omit the names of the rules in deductions. A method that helps to grasp the structure of a given deduction is to number the occurrences of assumptions which are being cancelled, and to repeat the number near the node where the cancellation takes place. Assumptions which are cancelled simultaneously may be given the same number. However, the numbering of discharged assumptions is redundant: by definition any assumption is cancelled at the earliest opportunity.

Example 4.2. Let ϕ from E, V_d, V_p and ψ from E, V_d, V_p be two property formulas. We derive

$$
\frac{\dfrac{\phi \text{ from } E, V_d, V_p \;\; {}^{(1)}}{\psi \to \phi \text{ from } E, V_d, V_p} \;\; {\to}\text{I}}{\phi \to (\psi \to \phi) \text{ from } E, V_d, V_p} \;\; {\to}\text{I, [1]}
$$

Here the [1] in '$\to$I, [1]' indicates that the assumption "ϕ from E, V_d, V_p $^{(1)}$" is cancelled.

Definition 4.3 (*Derivability*). Let Γ be a set of property formulas. We write

$$\Gamma \vdash \phi \text{ from } E, V_d, V_p$$

iff there is a deduction with all uncancelled assumptions in Γ that has conclusion ϕ from E, V_d, V_p. In this case we say that there is a *proof* of ϕ from E, V_d, V_p from Γ. If $\Gamma = \emptyset$ the conclusion is called *logically valid*.

We adopt the following two conventions. If in a derivation only property formulas over fixed E, V_d, V_p are considered, we often leave out the additions 'from E, V_d, V_p'. Furthermore, a proved result may be further used as a single step in future deductions.

The following lemma provides some standard results (among which the congruence properties of $=$).

Lemma 4.4. *Let E, V_d, V_p be given. It holds that*

1. $\vdash \phi \to (\psi \to \phi)$,
2. $\{t = u\} \vdash u = t$,
3. $\{v = t,\; t = u\} \vdash v = u$,
4. $\{t = u\} \vdash w[t/z] = w[u/z]$,
5. $\{\phi \to \psi,\; \psi \to \chi\} \vdash \phi \to \chi$,
6. $\{\phi \to \psi\} \vdash \neg\psi \to \neg\phi$,
7. $\{\phi \to \psi,\; \neg\phi \to \psi\} \vdash \psi$

where in 4 it is assumed that w is a (process or data) term over E, V_d, V_p and $[t/z], [u/z]$ are substitutions over E, V_d, V_p.

For readability we further introduce the notations

$$\bigvee_{i \in I} \phi_i \text{ from } E, V_d, V_p \quad \text{and} \quad \bigwedge_{i \in I} \phi_i \text{ from } E, V_d, V_p$$

for iterated finite disjunctions and conjunctions, respectively. We adopt the usual convention that $\bigvee_{i \in \emptyset} \phi_i$ from $E, V_d, V_p \stackrel{def}{=} \mathcal{F}$ from E, V_d, V_p.

5   Modules for μCRL

As μCRL is based on ACP [1] we follow its methodology and consider 'building blocks' of axioms and rules that describe a feature of concurrency in a certain semantical setting. We call such building blocks *modules*. If $M_1, \ldots, M_n$ are modules, then the notation

$$M_1 + \cdots + M_n + \Gamma \vdash \phi \text{ from } E, V_d, V_p$$

expresses that with the axioms and rules from $M_1, \ldots, M_n$ we can derive ϕ **from** E, V_d, V_p with all uncancelled assumptions in some set Γ of property formulas.

The module BOOL.   Concerning the standard sort **Bool** we define two axioms, corresponding with the demand that any model of a specification E is *boolean preserving* ([12]):

$$\frac{}{\neg(\mathsf{t} = \mathsf{f}) \text{ from } E, \emptyset, \emptyset} \text{ Bool1}$$

$$\frac{}{\neg(b = \mathsf{t}) \rightarrow b = \mathsf{f} \text{ from } E, \{\langle b{:}\mathbf{Bool}\rangle\}, \emptyset} \text{ Bool2.}$$

The axiom Bool1 states that the Booleans t and f are considered different in our proof system, and the axiom Bool2 expresses that there are at most two Boolean values, represented by t and f. The two axioms Bool1 and Bool2 form the module BOOL. The following lemma states that the reverse implication in Bool2 is derivable.

Lemma 5.1. *For any specification E it holds that*

$$\text{BOOL} \vdash b = \mathsf{f} \rightarrow \neg(b = \mathsf{t}) \text{ from } E, \{\langle b{:}\mathbf{Bool}\rangle\}, \emptyset.$$

The module FACT.   The basic identities on data terms are those declared in a specification E. Assume $t = u$ occurs as an axiom in E, i.e. $t = u$ is preceded by the keyword **rew**. Then we have an axiom

$$\frac{}{t = u \text{ from } E, V_d, \emptyset} \text{ FACT}$$

where V_d is the set of data variables occurring in t and u. Note that the module consisting of all the FACTs from E is implicitly present in the E occurring in property formulas. Therefore we generally do not mention FACT before the turnstyle, although it may have been used.

The module IND(C). In μCRL it is required that any model for the data part is minimal. In the proof theory this can be captured via induction. Therefore we introduce an induction rule. The induction rule that is given here, is a simplified variant of the induction rule provided in [13]. Both rules are not very satisfactory. In order to nicely formulate an induction rule, we need higher order variables (ranging over property formulas). And in order to use the induction principle for a wide range of purposes, such as simultaneous induction, property formulas should have quantifiers that bind variables.

We start with a preparatory definition.

Definition 5.2 (*Constructors*). Let E be a specification, S the name of a sort occurring in E, and C a subset of the function declarations occurring in E. We say that C is a *constructor set of the sort S* iff all functions in C have target sort S, and any closed data term of sort S can be proved equal to a data term that is obtained from applications of the functions in C and terms not of sort S only.

In general it is not possible to prove that a given set is a constructor set within our framework. Reasons for this are that we can neither express 'existential' properties of data terms, nor that a term is obtained from application of a constructor function. Therefore such a proof must be given on a meta-level (structural induction on closed terms).

Assume that for given E, V_d, V_p we have that $\{\langle x{:}S\rangle\} \subseteq V_d$.

$$C \stackrel{def}{=} \{f_j{:}S_1^j \times \ldots \times S_{l_j}^j \to S \mid 1 \le j \le k \,,\, k > 0 \,,\, l_j \ge 0\}$$

be a constructor set of the sort S of cardinality k. We introduce the following induction rule IND(C) that is parameterised by the constructor set C. The induction takes place on the variable x.

$$\mathcal{D}_j$$

$$\frac{(\bigwedge_{\sigma \in I_j} \sigma(\phi)) \to \phi[f_j(z_1^j, \ldots, z_{l_j}^j)/x] \text{ from } E, V_d \cup \{\langle z_n^j{:}S_n^j\rangle \mid 1 \le n \le l_j\}, V_p}{\phi \text{ from } E, V_d, V_p} \quad 1 \le j \le k$$

where for each $1 \le j \le k$ the index set I_j is a set of substitutions over $E, V_d \cup \{\langle z_n^j{:}S_n^j\rangle \mid 1 \le n \le l_j\}, V_p$ satisfying:

$$\sigma \in I_j \iff \sigma \text{ is the identity, except that it maps } x \text{ to}$$
$$\text{some element from } \{z_n^j \mid 1 \le n \le l_j\}.$$

Note that it is required that in IND(C) all the variables $x, z_1^j, \ldots, z_{l_j}^j$ are pairwise different for all appropriate j.

The module REC. This module is the first of a series that can be used to derive identities between process terms using the originating specification and standard process algebra axioms and rules.

Let for some given E it be the case that $n = p$ is a process declaration in E (i.e. the last keyword preceding $n = p$ is **proc**). Then we have an axiom

$$\frac{}{n = p \text{ from } E, \emptyset, \emptyset} \text{ REC}$$

If $n(x_1{:}S_1,\ldots,x_k{:}S_k) = p$ is a process declaration in E, then we have an axiom

$$\frac{\rule{7cm}{0.4pt}}{n(x_1,\ldots,x_k) = p \textbf{ from } E, \{\langle x_1{:}S_1\rangle,\ldots,\langle x_k{:}S_k\rangle\}, \emptyset} \text{ REC}$$

Like in the case of FACT we adopt the convention not to denote the module REC before the turnstyle.

The modules pCRL and μCRL. Let E be a specification. For any equation ϕ displayed in Table 3,4 and 5 we have an axiom

$$\frac{\rule{5cm}{0.4pt}}{\phi \textbf{ from } E, V_d, V_p} \textit{ name of } \phi$$

where V_d and V_p are the sets of variables occurring in ϕ. In these tables x, y are process variables and p, q are process terms in which the variable d may occur. The letters $t_1,\ldots,t_n$ and $u_1,\ldots,u_m$ stand for data terms, and $\bar{t}$ for a sequence of data terms. c, c' represent δ, τ or range over (declared) actions $a(t_1,\ldots,t_n)$, where $a(t_1,\ldots,t_n)$ represents a if $n = 0$. $\tilde{\gamma}$ is the pre-communication function such that $\tilde{\gamma}(a,b) = c$ if a rule **comm** $a\,|\,b = c$ appears in the specification E. Otherwise $\tilde{\gamma}(a,b) = \delta$. γ is the symmetrical closure of γ.

A1	$x + y = y + x$	SUM1	$\sum_{d:D}(x) = x$
A2	$x + (y + z) = (x + y) + z$	SUM2	$\sum_{d:D}(p) = \sum_{e:D}(p[e/d])$
A3	$x + x = x$		provided e not free in p
A4	$(x + y) \cdot z = x \cdot z + y \cdot z$	SUM3	$\sum_{d:D}(p) = \sum_{d:D}(p) + p$
A5	$(x \cdot y) \cdot z = x \cdot (y \cdot z)$	SUM4	$\sum_{d:D}(p + q) = \sum_{d:D}(p) + \sum_{d:D}(q)$
A6	$x + \delta = x$	SUM5	$\sum_{d:D}(p \cdot x) = \sum_{d:D}(p) \cdot x$
A7	$\delta \cdot x = \delta$	SUM11	$(\forall d \in D \; p = q) \rightarrow$
			$\qquad\qquad \sum_{d:D}(p) = \sum_{d:D}(q)$

Table 3: Axioms for pCRL

Interesting are the SUM axioms that appeared first in [13]. SUM1 says that we may omit the Σ operator in $\sum_{d:D}(x)$ as d does not occur in variable x. SUM2 expresses a form of α-conversion. This axiom is superfluous, because it is derivable by definition of substitution [13]. SUM3 says that for each term $\sum_{d:D}(p)$ we may extract a copy of p where the variable d may occur unbounded in p. Although no completeness result for these axioms does exist, they appeared fully adequate for all calculations that we have encountered up till now.

The axioms in Table 3, together with Bool1, Bool2, C1 and C2 are called the pCRL (pico CRL, [4]) axioms. The axioms of pCRL together with the axioms in Table 4 and 5 are called the μCRL axioms.

SUM6	$\sum_{d:D}(p \parallel\!\!\!\!\parallel z) = \sum_{d:D}(p) \parallel\!\!\!\!\parallel z$		CF	$a(t_1,\ldots,t_n) \mid b(u_1,\ldots,u_m)$
SUM7	$\sum_{d:D}(p \mid z) = \sum_{d:D}(p) \mid z$			
SUM8	$\sum_{d:D}(\partial_H(p(d))) = \partial_H(\sum_{d:D}(p))$		$=$	$\left\{ \begin{array}{l} \gamma(a,b)(t_1,\ldots,t_n) \text{ if} \\ \quad n = m,\ t_i = u_i, \\ \quad \gamma(a,b) \text{ defined} \\ \delta \qquad\qquad \text{otherwise} \end{array} \right.$
SUM9	$\sum_{d:D}(\tau_I(p(d))) = \tau_I(\sum_{d:D}(p))$			
SUM10	$\sum_{d:D}(\rho_R(p(d))) = \rho_R(\sum_{d:D}(p))$			
			CD1	$\delta \mid x = \delta$
			CD2	$x \mid \delta = \delta$
CM1	$x \parallel y = x \parallel\!\!\!\!\parallel y + y \parallel\!\!\!\!\parallel x + x \mid y$		CT1	$\tau \mid x = \delta$
CM2	$c \parallel\!\!\!\!\parallel x = c{\cdot}x$		CT2	$x \mid \tau = \delta$
CM3	$c{\cdot}x \parallel\!\!\!\!\parallel y = c{\cdot}(x \parallel y)$			
CM4	$(x + y) \parallel\!\!\!\!\parallel z = x \parallel\!\!\!\!\parallel z + y \parallel\!\!\!\!\parallel z$		DD	$\partial_H(\delta) = \delta$
CM5	$c{\cdot}x \mid c' = (c \mid c'){\cdot}x$		DT	$\partial_H(\tau) = \tau$
CM6	$c \mid c'{\cdot}x = (c \mid c'){\cdot}x$		D1	$\partial_H(a(\bar{t})) = a(\bar{t})$ if $a \notin H$
CM7	$c{\cdot}x \mid c'{\cdot}y = (c \mid c'){\cdot}(x \parallel y)$		D2	$\partial_H(a(\bar{t})) = \delta$ if $a \in H$
CM8	$(x + y) \mid z = x \mid z + y \mid z$		D3	$\partial_H(x + y) = \partial_H(x) + \partial_H(y)$
CM9	$x \mid (y + z) = x \mid y + x \mid z$		D4	$\partial_H(x{\cdot}y) = \partial_H(x){\cdot}\partial_H(y)$

Table 4: Primary μCRL-axioms

TID	$\tau_I(\delta) = \delta$		RD	$\rho_R(\delta) = \delta$
TIT	$\tau_I(\tau) = \tau$		RT	$\rho_R(\tau) = \tau$
TI1	$\tau_I(a(\bar{t})) = a(\bar{t})$	if $a \notin I$	R1	$\rho_R(a(\bar{t})) = R(a)(\bar{t})$
TI2	$\tau_I(a(\bar{t})) = \tau$	if $a \in I$		
TI3	$\tau_I(x + y) = \tau_I(x) + \tau_I(y)$		R3	$\rho_R(x + y) = \rho_R(x) + \rho_R(y)$
TI4	$\tau_I(x{\cdot}y) = \tau_I(x){\cdot}\tau_I(y)$		R4	$\rho_R(x{\cdot}y) = \rho_R(x){\cdot}\rho_R(y)$

Table 5: More μCRL-axioms

The module COND. We define for any specification E two axioms characterising the behaviour of the conditional [15]:

$$\frac{\rule{4cm}{0.4pt}}{x \triangleleft t \triangleright y = x \text{ from } E, \emptyset, \{x, y\}} \text{ C1} \qquad \frac{\rule{4cm}{0.4pt}}{x \triangleleft f \triangleright y = y \text{ from } E, \emptyset, \{x, y\}} \text{ C2.}$$

These two axioms form the module COND. The following lemma describes two basic properties that can be proved using the module COND. Both these results will be used later in the paper.

Lemma 5.3. *Let* E, V_d, V_p *be such that* $\langle b{:}\mathbf{Bool} \rangle \in V_d$ *and* $\{x, y, z\} \subseteq V_p$. *Then*

1. $\mu\text{CRL} \vdash x + x \triangleleft b \triangleright \delta = x \text{ from } E, V_d, V_p$,

2. $\text{BOOL} + \text{COND} \vdash (b = t \rightarrow x = y) \rightarrow (x \triangleleft b \triangleright z = y \triangleleft b \triangleright z) \text{ from } E, V_d, V_p$.

The module RSP. In order to derive identities between infinite processes we introduce (an extended version of) the Recursive Specification Principle (RSP, see eg. [1]).

The idea of RSP is that if two (different) process terms both satisfy some 'process-equation', then those process terms are considered equal. In general we use a system of such equations, each of which must contain at its left-hand side a (possibly parameterised) fresh identifier and at its right-hand side a 'process term' that may contain the new identifiers. These identifiers may be parameterised with data. We introduce a mechanism that defines substitution of parameterised process terms in a system of process-equations. The soundness of RSP depends on the guardedness of the system of process-equations used. In the following we make all these notions precise, and introduce the rule RSP.

Let E, V_d, V_p be given and let $n_1, \ldots, n_m$ be m different fresh identifiers. We call a system G of m equations $G_1, \ldots, G_m$ a system of *process-equations* over E, V_d, V_p if each equation G_i has at its left-hand side an expression of the form n_i or of the form

$$n_i(x_{i1}, \ldots, x_{im_i})$$

where any x_{ij} is a data variable from V_d. Moreover, the right hand side of each equation G_i may only contain free variables x_{ij} and the new, properly typed identifiers n_i or $n_i(t_{i1}, \ldots, t_{im_i})$ for $1 \leq i \leq m$ and $1 \leq j \leq m_i$.

Next we introduce a substitution mechanism for a system $G = G_1, \ldots, G_m$ of process-equations over E, V_d, V_p. Abbreviating the (possible) variables of n_i by $\bar{x}_i$, we define

$$G_i[\lambda \bar{x}_i.p(\bar{x}_i)/n_i]$$

as the equation obtained by substituting $\lambda \bar{x}_i.p(\bar{x}_i)$ for the n_i-occurrences in G_i, and then repeatedly performing β-conversion on the respective arguments of the process name n_i. For any identifier without arguments only the substitution of p is performed.

The rule RSP is restricted to systems of process-equations that are (syntactically) guarded. In [5] a stronger variant of RSP, called CL-RSP, is introduced. This notion uses the notion of convergent linear process operators, which is necessary to handle internal actions conveniently. But for the example in this paper the current version of RSP suffices.

Definition 5.4 (*Guardedness of G*). A term p is a *guard* iff:

- $p \equiv \delta$, or

- $p \equiv n(t_1, \ldots, t_n)$ or $p \equiv n$ and n is an action label, or

- $p \equiv q_1 \circ q_2$ with $\circ \in \{+, \lessdot t \rhd\}$ and q_1 and q_2 are guards, or

- $p \equiv q_1 \circ q_2$ with $\circ \in \{\cdot, \|, \|\!\!\lfloor\,\}$ and q_1 or q_2 are guards, or

- $p \equiv q_1 \mid q_2$, or

- $p \equiv \sum_{x:S}(q_1)$ and q_1 is a guard, or

- $p \equiv C_S(q_1)$ with $C \in \{\partial, \rho\}$ and S being a set of labels, and q_1 is a guard.

Let G be a system of process-equations and let N be the left-hand side of one of the equations of G. We say that N is *guarded* in r, where r is a subterm of one of the right-hand sides of G, iff

- $r \equiv q_1 \circ q_2$ with $\circ \in \{+, \|, \|\!\!\lfloor, \mid, \lessdot t \rhd\}$, and N is guarded in q_1 and q_2,

- $r \equiv q_1 \cdot q_2$ with N is guarded in q_1, and q_1 is a guard or N is guarded in q_2,

- $r \equiv \Sigma_{x:S} q_1$ and N is guarded in q_1,

- $r \equiv C_S(q_1)$ with $C \in \{\partial, \rho\}$ and S being a set of labels (or in the case of ρ a renaming function), and N is guarded in q_1,

- $r \equiv \delta$ or $r \equiv \tau$,

- $r \equiv n'$ for a *name* n' and $N \not\equiv n'$,

- $r \equiv n'(u_1, \ldots, u_{m'})$ and $N \not\equiv n'(x_{i1}, \ldots, x_{im_i})$.

If N is not guarded in r we say that N appears *unguarded* in r.

The *Identifier Dependency Graph* of G, notation $IDG(G)$, is constructed as follows:

- each fully instantiated left-hand side of the equations of G is a node,

- if $N = r \in G$, M appears unguarded in r, N' is obtained by instantiating N via a closed substitution σ, and M' is obtained by instantiating M via σ (where variables in M bound in r are supposed to be different from those in N), then there is an edge $N' \to M'$.

We call G *guarded* iff $IDG(G)$ is well founded, i.e. does not contain an infinite path.

Given a guarded system $G_1, \ldots, G_m$ of m process-equations over E, V_d, V_p, we define the following rule RSP:

$$
\cfrac{\overset{\mathcal{D}_{1i}}{G_i[\lambda \bar{x}_j.p_j(\bar{x}_j)/n_j]_{j=1}^m \text{ from } E, V_d, V_p} \qquad \overset{\mathcal{D}_{2i}}{G_i[\lambda \bar{x}_j.q_j(\bar{x}_j)/n_j]_{j=1}^m \text{ from } E, V_d, V_p}}{p_k(\bar{x}_k) = q_k(\bar{x}_k) \text{ from } E, V_d, V_p \quad (1 \le k \le m)} \; 1 \le i \le m
$$

where

- for $1 \leq i \leq m$ the $p_i(\bar{x}_i)$ and $q_i(\bar{x}_i)$ are process terms over E, V_d, V_p,

- the notation $[\ldots]_{j=1}^m$ abbreviates the m given, simultaneous substitutions.

6 An example: proving some properties of counters

In this section we first illustrate the μCRL proof theory by proving some properties of the specification given in Table 1. As formal proofs (i.e. deductions) of non-trivial facts are often hard to read, and may take in our case a larger space than available on one page, we will not give these. Instead we only write down the essential steps of a proof, trusting that the suggestion of a formal proof is sufficiently clear. Furthermore we will often represent proofs in a linear style: in a context where E, V_d, V_p are fixed, we write $t = u$ if this identity can be obtained by applications of reflexivity, symmetry or substitutivity (see Lemma 4.4.2+4), or via the rule SUB (so no variables that occur free in an open assumption are instantiated). Moreover, based on the transitivity of $=$, proved in Lemma 4.4.3, we write $t_1 = t_2 = \ldots = t_n$ to represent a proof with conclusion $t_1 = t_n$. For convenience we sometimes write names of axioms or identities above the $=$.

The following results are about the specification in Table 1. Note that it is not hard to check that

$$C \overset{def}{=} \{0: \to Nat, S:Nat \to Nat\}$$

is a set of constructors of sort Nat. First we prove the following relation between the parallel operator and the addition operator add on the data type Nat.

Theorem 6.1. *Two counters in parallel behave as one counter with the contents added. Let $V_d = \{\langle b:Nat \rangle, \langle c:Nat \rangle\}$. Then*

$$\mu\text{CRL} + \text{IND}(C) + \text{RSP} \vdash$$

$$Counter(b) \parallel Counter(c) = Counter(add(b,c)) \quad \text{from } E, V_d, \emptyset.$$

Proof. The main step in the proof is an application of RSP. First we define the guarded system G as follows:

$$n(b,c) = \; inc \cdot n(S(b),c) + inc \cdot n(S(c),b) + \\ \delta \triangleleft is\text{-}zero(b) \triangleright dec \cdot n(P(b),c) + \delta \triangleleft is\text{-}zero(c) \triangleright dec \cdot n(P(c),b).$$

We prove $G[\lambda b, c. Counter(b) \parallel Counter(c)/n]$ from $E, V_d, \emptyset$ and $G[\lambda b, c. Counter(add(b,c))/n]$ from $E, V_d, \emptyset$. Then by RSP the theorem follows in a straightforward way.

First we show $G[\lambda b, c.Counter(b) \parallel Counter(c)/n]$. This is a straightforward expansion.

$$Counter(b) \parallel Counter(c) \stackrel{\text{expansion}}{=}$$

$inc \cdot (Counter(S(b)) \parallel Counter(c))) +$
$(\delta \lhd \textit{is-zero}(b) \rhd dec \cdot Counter(P(b))) \parallel\!\!\!\parallel Counter(c) +$
$inc \cdot (Counter(S(c)) \parallel Counter(b))) +$
$(\delta \lhd \textit{is-zero}(c) \rhd dec \cdot Counter(P(c))) \parallel\!\!\!\parallel Counter(b)$
$= inc \cdot (Counter(S(b)) \parallel Counter(c))) +$
$\quad \delta \lhd \textit{is-zero}(b) \rhd dec \cdot (Counter(P(b)) \parallel Counter(c)) +$
$\quad inc \cdot (Counter(S(c)) \parallel Counter(b)) +$
$\quad \delta \lhd \textit{is-zero}(c) \rhd dec \cdot (Counter(P(c)) \parallel Counter(b)).$

Now we show $G[\lambda b, c.Counter(add(b, c))/n]$.

$$Counter(add(b, c)) \stackrel{\text{expansion}}{=}$$

$inc \cdot Counter(S(add(b, c))) +$
$\delta \lhd \textit{is-zero}(add(b, c)) \rhd dec \cdot Counter(P(add(b, c)))$
$=$
$\quad inc \cdot Counter(add(S(b), c)) + inc \cdot Counter(add(S(c), b) +$
$\quad \delta \lhd \textit{is-zero}(b) \rhd dec \cdot Counter(add(P(b), c)) +$
$\quad \delta \lhd \textit{is-zero}(c) \rhd dec \cdot Counter(add(P(c), b))$

by the property $add(S(b), c) = add(S(c), b) = S(add(b, c))$ (by IND(C)), Lemma 5.3, BOOL, COND and $\textit{is-zero}(c) = f \rightarrow P(add(b, c)) = add(P(c), b)$ (and the symmetric variant). $\qquad\square$

Corollary 6.2. *Let* $V_d = \{\langle a:Nat\rangle, \langle b:Nat\rangle, \langle c:Nat\rangle\}$. *Then*

$\mu CRL + IND(C) + RSP \vdash$

$(Counter(a) \parallel Counter(b)) = (Counter(b) \parallel Counter(a))$ and

$(Counter(a) \parallel Counter(b)) \parallel Counter(c) =$
$\quad Counter(a) \parallel (Counter(b) \parallel Counter(c))$ **from** $E, V_d, \emptyset$.

Proof. By commutativity and associativity of the addition operator add (standard) and Theorem 6.1. $\qquad\square$

We conclude with the following theorem, stating that the process specified by $Counter(0)$ satisfies a standard definition (see [1]).

Theorem 6.3. *The process* $Counter(0)$ **from** E *satisfies*

$\mu CRL + IND(C) + RSP \vdash Counter(0) = X$ **from** $E, \emptyset, \emptyset$.

Proof. With some intermediate results and RSP we can prove

$Counter(S(b)) = Counter(b) \parallel dec.$

Hence $inc \cdot Counter(S(0)) = inc \cdot (Counter(0) \parallel dec)$ by the congruence properties of '=' and instantiation. Using the definitions we obtain

$Counter(0) = X.$

$\qquad\square$

7 Conclusion

The major advantage of a formal language and a formal proof system is also its major drawback, because one fixes beforehand all allowed means for expressing oneself and for providing proofs. When designing a proof system it is very hard to foresee how it will be used and whether it is appropriate for that usage. We think that experience is the key to an appropriately designed formal system. Thus we have developed the proof system simultaneously with its application to small examples. From these initial examples we concluded that the property language as defined in this document was adequate. But when applying the proof system to larger examples, as described below, we felt that existential and universal quantification would be convenient in the property language. Moreover, quantification should not be restricted to first order quantification over processes and data terms, but also range over higher order objects such as functions (see for instance the sum elimination lemma in [10] that can be more elegantly expressed using higher order quantification). Another problem that we did not foresee is that the hiding-, encapsulation- and renaming operators rename actions independently of their data parameter. Up till now this is satisfactory when writing down specifications, but it causes problems when providing proofs (see [17]).

Despite the problems sketched above we are rather satisfied with the language μCRL, the property language and its proof system. This is a consequence of the developments sketched below. On all fronts we have made considerable advances during the last two years and there is no sign that this will change in the future. As regards the further developments of the proof system, we have clear guidelines for extending the property language, which we expect to be heavily influenced by the lambda-calculus based languages used in contemporary theorem provers [8]. The major problem will be to keep the proof system concise, and yet sufficiently expressive to handle the next generation of proofs.

- First the developments around μCRL have led to some theoretical results. The expressive power of μCRL has been investigated in [19]. Subsets of μCRL have been identified that can generate primitive recursive and recursive transition systems. In [4] the status of invariants in process algebra has been cleared up. It is concluded that invariants are theoretically superfluous, but practically useful. In [4] derived rules are provided that enable to calculate in process algebra with the explicit use of invariants.

  In [2] a version of process algebra with data has been provided where the variable binding of the Σ operator has been avoided by explicitly using combinators. In [9] a version of μCRL extended with time is given.

- Second, μCRL, and in particular its proof theory have led to a yet rather small class of precise logical correctness proofs of distributed systems. In [17] Milner's scheduler provided in [18] is re-verified. It is concluded that the proof in [18] is indeed very precise, but contains a lot of meta notation and reasoning. Furthermore, a condition, namely that a scheduler should always consist of more than one cycler has been forgotten. This is exactly the kind of mistake that we want to eradicate, so we see this as an assuring result. In [11] a bounded retransmission protocol is verified. In [5, 6] sliding window protocols are verified. The last two verifications are particularly interesting because sliding window protocols were generally considered too hard for process-algebraic techniques. Finally, we mention [10] where a bakery protocol is proven correct. In this document many elementary results about calculations with processes and data have been established, among which the fundamental sum elimination lemma.

The techniques for process-algebraic verifications are developed further by studying more examples that lead to the identification of systematic approaches for providing proofs. The first result of this kind is the above mentioned work on invariants in process algebra [4]. As stated earlier, this article concludes that invariants are theoretically superfluous, but do allow a separation of concerns, which is badly needed in calculations that require many pages. In [5] a technique using *cones* and *foci* has been identified, which is crucial in [6]. It is expected that, when the complexity and size of distributed systems that are proven correct increase, more of these general methods are identified.

- Third, as a result of the very precise logical nature of μCRL and its proof system, proof checking turns out to be possible. The general method for doing so in the proof system Coq [8] is outlined in [20]. The first larger example of a proof that was verified in this way is the alternating bit protocol as proved correct in [1]. This is described in [3]. The above mentioned proofs in [11] and [17] have been computer checked, too.

From these experiments we draw the simple conclusion that proof checking by computer is feasible, but, due to the rather large number of applications of axioms in a verification, it is still a lot of work. We can also conclude that proof checking is useful. In the case studies mentioned above more or less serious mistakes in the proofs have been detected, and minor improvements of the proven theorems have been made.

Currently, we see as the most important issue of research that proof checking must be made more efficient. We believe that the best methods for doing so is via (higher order) rewriting and more advanced matching techniques.

References

[1] J.C.M. Baeten and W.P. Weijland. *Process Algebra*. Cambridge Tracts in Theoretical Computer Science 18. Cambridge University Press, 1990.

[2] J.A. Bergstra, I. Bethke, and A. Ponse. Process algebra with combinators. Report P9319, Programming Research Group, University of Amsterdam, 1993.

[3] M.A. Bezem and J.F. Groote. A formal verification of the alternating bit protocol in the calculus of constructions. Technical Report Logic Group Preprint Series No. 88, Utrecht University, March 1993.

[4] M.A. Bezem and J.F. Groote. Invariants in process algebra with data. Technical Report Logic Group Preprint Series No. 98, Utrecht University, September 1993.

[5] M.A. Bezem and J.F. Groote. A correctness proof of a one bit sliding window protocol in μCRL. To appear as technical report, Logic Group Preprint Series, Utrecht University, 1993.

[6] M.A. Bezem and J.F. Groote. A correctness proof of a sliding window protocol in μCRL. To appear as technical report, Logic Group Preprint Series, Utrecht University, 1993.

[7] D. van Dalen. *Logic and Structure*. Springer-Verlag, 1983.

[8] G. Dowek, A. Felty, H. Herbelin, G. Huet, C. Murthy, C. Parent, C. Paulin-Mohring, and B. Werner. The Coq proof assistant user's guide. Version 5.8. Technical report, INRIA – Rocquencourt, May 1993.

[9] W.J. Fokkink. A simple specification language combining processes, time and data. Technical Report CS-R9132, CWI, Amsterdam, 1991.

[10] J.F. Groote and H. Korver. A correctness proof of the bakery protocol in μ-CRL. Technical Report 80, Logic Group Preprint Series, Utrecht University, 1992.

[11] J.F. Groote and J.C. van de Pol. A bounded retransmission protocol for large data packets. To appear as Technical Report, Logic Group Preprint Series, Utrecht University, 1993.

[12] J.F. Groote and A. Ponse. The syntax and semantics of μCRL. Report CS-R9076, CWI, Amsterdam, 1990.

[13] J.F. Groote and A. Ponse. Proof theory for μCRL. Report CS-R9138, CWI, 1991.

[14] C.A.R. Hoare. *Communicating Sequential Processes*. Prentice-Hall International, Englewood Cliffs, 1985.

[15] C.A.R. Hoare, I.J. Hayes, He Jifeng, C.C. Morgan, A.W. Roscoe, J.W. Sanders, I.H. Sorensen, J.M. Spivey, and B.A. Sufrin. Laws of programming. *Communications of the ACM*, 30(8):672–686, August 1987.

[16] G.J. Holzmann. *Design and Validation of Computer Protocols*. Prentice-Hall International, 1991.

[17] H. Korver and J. Springintveld. A computer-checked verification of Milner's scheduler. Technical report, CWI, Amsterdam, 1993. To Appear.

[18] R. Milner. *Communication and Concurrency*. Prentice-Hall International, Englewood Cliffs, 1989.

[19] A. Ponse. Computable processes and bisimulation equivalence. Report CS-R9207, CWI, Amsterdam, January 1992.

[20] M.P.A. Sellink. Verifying process algebra proofs in type theory. Technical Report Logic Group Preprint Series No. 87, Utrecht University, March 1993.

[21] R. de Simone and D. Vergamini. Aboard AUTO. Technical Report 111, INRIA, Centre Sophia-Antipolis, Valbonne Cedex, 1989.

[22] A.S. Troelstra and D. van Dalen. *Constructivism in Mathematics, An Introduction (vol I)*. North-Holland, 1988.

Case Study: Stepwise Development of a Communication Processor using Trace Logic*

Stephan Kleuker**

Fachbereich Informatik

Universität Oldenburg

26111 Oldenburg, Germany

Abstract

This paper shows a stepwise development of a complex parallel system. Both the initial requirements and the subsequent design stages are formulated in trace logic and so every proof of correctness boils down to reasoning about trace predicates. The relation between trace logic and a program language is shown by a transformation from trace logic into a program specification language, called SL. The advantage is that a large set of verified SL-specifications can be automatically transformed into correct OCCAM programs. In contrast to trace logic, SL-specifications describe the process behaviour in more detail.

Keywords: formal program development, specification and verification, parallel algorithms

1   Introduction

The aim of this case study is to show a formal development of a complex parallel system beginning with an informal description and finishing with an implementation in OCCAM. The development combines three different, but related specification techniques: trace logic, a specification language SL with state and trace part, and OCCAM programs. The emphasis in this paper is to explain the main steps of the development and motivate the choice of the different specification techniques.

Our example is taken from [1] where the implementation of a *communication processor* (abbreviated CP) is described. This processor is a result of the DOOM[1] project and is successfully realized in hardware. A CP is part of a network NW through which many parallel working processors $P_1, \ldots, P_n$ can exchange data. This scenario is sketched in figure 1 where processors $P_1, \ldots, P_n$ want to communicate with each other. The idea is to decompose NW into subprocesses so that each P_i owns a communication processor, CP_i (see later, e.g. 2).

In contrast to [1] we concentrate on a stepwise development of the CP from a formalization of the requirements to a distributed implementation. The requirements and the first specifications are formalized in *trace logic* which is a

---

*This research was partially supported by the German Ministry of Research and Technologies (BMFT) as part of the project KORSO (Korrekte Software) under grant no. 01 IS 203 N.

**E-mail: Stephan.Kleuker@informatik.uni-oldenburg.de, Tel: +49-441-798-3124

[1]Decentralized Object Oriented Machine, ESPRIT project 415-A

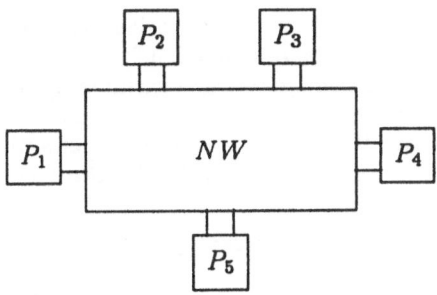

Figure1: overview of system

well studied logic [7, 12] for specifying communicating synchronized systems. Trace logic describes a system as a process that can engage in traces of communications. Such communications are: a processor sends a message and a processor receives a message. Each process can be refined into a distributed system consisting of a set of smaller processes. In a later design stages we transform the purely trace based specification into a specification where both traces and states are used. For this a specification language SL^2 [6] is used. For SL verified transformation rules have been developed that produce correct OCCAM [4] programs.

This paper is structured as follows. The next section is a short introduction into trace logic. The third section begins with a description of the CP. The informal description leads to formal requirements. It will be proved for each decomposition step that the resulting specification fulfills these requirements. The final specification will be transformed to SL and an OCCAM-program. It should be possible to transfer the ideas of this paper of a stepwise design process to other specification languages [2, 11].

2 Specification in Trace Logic

We consider processes that can communicate with each other along directed channels. Formally, a *communication* is a pair (c, v) of a channel name c and a communicated value (*message*) v. We follow the predicative approach as advocated by Hehner [3] and specify processes by predicates describing their observables. We begin with a simple approach where traces are the only observables. A *trace* is a sequence of communications with finite length. We use trace logic, a first order predicate logic with two sorts, traces and integers. Processes are specified by so called *trace predicates*, i.e. predicates with only one free variable, the trace variable tr.

We use the following notations in predicates. The empty trace is denoted by ε. The function $|.|$ gives the *length* of a trace, i.e. $|(c, 1).(d, 2)| = 2$. The *projection* operator $. \downarrow .$ projects a trace on a set of channels or messages or communications, i.e. $((c, 1).(d, 2)) \downarrow \{c\} = (c, 1)$. The function $chan(.)$ reduces a given trace to a trace of used *channel words*, i.e $chan((c, 1).(d, 2)) = c.d$.

$P[t/tr]$ denotes the predicate P where the trace expression t is substituted for all occurrences of tr in P.

^2SL was developed in the ESPRIT project ProCoS (Provable Correct Systems), ESPRIT BRA 3104

All Channels of a process P are summarized in the set $Chan(P)$. The parallel composition of processes is defined using a synchronization operator SYN. The resulting process has a free trace variable tr, too. A communication over a channel between a sender and a receiver can only happen if both processes are ready to communicate. If some processes are synchronized, a process P will not care for channels that are not in $Chan(P)$. So the synchronization operator SYN can be defined as follows.

Definition : Let $P_1, \ldots, P_k$ be trace predicates, then is defined for the process $SYN[P_1, \ldots, P_k]$:

$$\forall t \bullet (SYN[P_1, \ldots, P_k][t/tr] \Leftrightarrow \bigwedge_{i=1}^{k} P_i[[(t \downarrow Chan(P_i))/tr])$$

3 Case Study

3.1 Task of the Case Study

We consider processors of two parts, of a *data processing element* (abbreviated DPE) where the internal computation of the processor happens and where data for other processors are produced, and of a CP where the whole exchange of messages is managed. Every processor owns a local storage, no global storage is existent. The CP receives messages from and sends messages to his connected DPE and to other connected CPs of neighbour processors. The transitive closure of all connections between all CPs is a complete network, so each CP can communicate with each other CP.

As it is not possible in general that every CP is connected directly with each other CP, the CP must also have the ability to forward messages to his neighbours. Every message contains a part determining the destination processor. The situation is sketched in the following picture 2. Note that connections between the processes are only sketched and will be examined later. The dashed box summarizes the CPs into one process called *network*. Every CP has a certain routing information that tells which CPs of its neighbours are possible receivers for a message with a certain destination. This information ensures that every message is transmitted over a shortest path from sender to receiver. The aim of this case study is to specify a deadlock free and starvation free CP that transmits produced messages from sender to receiver.

3.2 Requirements for a CP

Let n be the number of processors given. Each Processor P_i consists of a local data processing element DPE_i and a local communication processor CP_i. We use a protocol where the receiver asks the sender for messages for the exchange of data. If the sender holds a message that can be transmitted in the direction of the receiver, this message is transmitted, otherwise the sender answers with a *negative synchronization message* (abbreviated NSM). This protocol is realized by four channels between DPE_i and CP_i and four channels between each connected CP.

- $ireq_i$:(input request) DPE_i asks CP_i on this channel if there is a message for it. This is only a signal, no other information is sent.

- in_i : CP_i answers the request of the DPE_i on this channel.

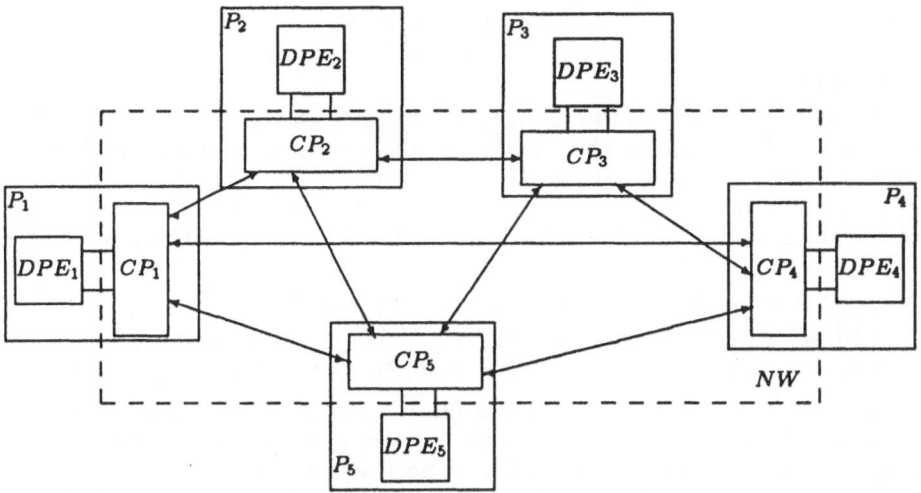

Figure2: Example for a network of CPs

- $oreq_i$:(output request) Here, CP_i asks DPE_i with this signal if it wants to give out a message.

- out_i : This cannel is used by DPE_i to answer the request of CP_i.

For an external observer it is only important that messages given to NW arrive at the destination processor. The whole system is a process

$$SYSTEM = SYN[DPE_1, \ldots, DPE_n, NW]$$

We can group all CPs together and synchronize them to a network $NW = SYN[CP_1, \ldots, CP_n]$.

Messages range over the domain Msg. Two types of messages exist as mentioned in the short description of the communication protocol. A predicate $pos(x)$ is fulfilled by a message x when x is a 'real' message (no NSM). It is assumed that every real message is unique. Let $\mathcal{N} = \{1, \ldots, n\}$ be the set of processor indices.

We specify the requirements now. Starvation freedom is formalized as follows. Every message that is received by a CP is transmitted in finite number of output communications where real messages are transmitted to its destination. The result of the function $dest : Msg \rightarrow \mathcal{N}$ is for a message x the index of the destination processor.

(k_i ($i \in \{1, \ldots, 4\}$) are parameters given by the system structure and have to be chosen dependent on n and the connectivity (number of connections per each CP).)

$(R1)\ \forall t\ \forall t' \bullet ((SYSTEM[(t.(out_i, x).t')/tr] \wedge k_1 < |t' \downarrow IN_{pos}| \wedge dest(x) = j)$
$\Rightarrow (\exists t'', t''' \bullet\ t' = t''.(in_j, x).t'''))$

with $IN_{pos} = \{(in_i, y) | 1 \leq i \leq n \wedge pos(y) \wedge y \in Msg\}$

IN_{pos} is the set of all real input communications to DPEs. So, if a trace $t.(out_i, x).t'$ happens in $SYSTEM$, where (out_i, x) is an output from a DPE to a CP, and there are more than k_1 inputs to DPEs in t' and the message x has the destination j then it is required that there is a communication in t' that x is given to DPE_j.

Deadlock freedom is formalized as follows. If a message exists that is given to NW and has not arrived by a DPE then there is always a possibility that this message reaches its destination. The set $M(t)$ contains all messages that were given to NW in trace t and not taken out. It is required for every extension of t that each message of $M(t)$ has reached or has the possibility to reach a DPEs.

$$M(t) = \{x|pos(x) \wedge |t \downarrow OUT(x)| = 1 \wedge |t \downarrow IN(x)| = 0\}$$
with $OUT(x) = \{(out_i, x)|1 \leq i \leq n\}$, $IN(x) = \{(in_i, x)|1 \leq i \leq n\}$

(R2) $\forall t \bullet (SYSTEM[t/tr] \Rightarrow (\forall x \in M(t) \, \exists t' \bullet SYSTEM[(t.t'.(in_i, x))/tr]))$

The distinction between $(R1)$ and $(R2)$ is that $(R2)$ allows in contrast to $(R1)$ that for a system which produces always new messages some messages may stay infinitely long inside NW. If no new messages are produced $(R2)$ requires that all messages in NW are given out in the next steps, but $(R1)$ allows that the system can stop with real messages left in NW.

The next six requirements are typical for systems that transmit messages.

- New messages will be produced by DPEs only. If a message is given to a DPE it was produced by another DPE earlier.

  $(R3)\forall t \bullet (SYSTEM[(t.(in_i, x))/tr] \wedge pos(x) \Rightarrow |t \downarrow OUT(x)| = 1)$

- Messages will be received by no other DPE than the destination DPE.

  $(R4)\forall t \bullet (SYSTEM[(t.(in_i, x))/tr] \Rightarrow dest(x) = i)$

- Messages will not be doubled.

  $(R5)\forall t \bullet (SYSTEM[(t.(in_i, x))/tr] \Rightarrow t \downarrow IN(x) = \varepsilon)$

- There is always the possibility that each DPE will be asked infinitely often if it wishes to give a message to NW. In a trace section with a certain number of requests of DPEs every DPE is asked.

  $(R6)(\forall t \bullet (SYSTEM[t/tr]$

  $$\Rightarrow (\exists t' \bullet SYSTEM[t.t'/tr] \wedge \bigwedge_{i=1}^{n} 1 \leq |t' \downarrow \{oreq_i\}|)))$$

  $\wedge(\forall t, t' \bullet ((SYSTEM[(t.t')/tr] \wedge k_2 \leq |t' \downarrow OREQ|)$

  $$\Rightarrow (\bigwedge_{i=1}^{n} 1 \leq |t' \downarrow \{oreq_i\}|)))$$

  with $OREQ = \{oreq_i|1 \leq i \leq n\}$

- If DPE_i asks for a message and there is a real message that could be given to DPE_i in the next communication (the difference between received messages with destination i and outputs with destination i is larger than zero) then a real message is given out with destination DPE_i.

$(R7) \forall t \bullet ((SYSTEM[(t.(in_i, y))/tr]$

$\qquad \wedge \, 0 < |t \downarrow \{(out_j, x) | 1 \le j \le n \wedge pos(x) \wedge dest(x) = i\}|$

$\qquad\qquad -|t \downarrow \{(in_i, x) | pos(x)\}|) \Rightarrow pos(y))$

- Every request is answered after a finite number of answer communications.

$(R8)(\forall t, t' \bullet ((SYSTEM[(t.ireq_i.t')/tr] \wedge k_3 \le |t' \downarrow IN|)$

$\qquad\qquad \Rightarrow (\exists tt, tt' \bullet \, t' = tt.(in_i, x).tt')))$

$\qquad \wedge \, (\forall t, t' \bullet ((SYSTEM[(t.oreq_i.t')/tr] \wedge k_3 \le |t' \downarrow OUT|)$

$\qquad\qquad \Rightarrow (\exists tt, tt' \bullet \, t' = tt.(out_i, x).tt')))$

with $IN = \{in_i | 1 \le i \le n\}$, $OUT = \{out_i | 1 \le i \le n\}$

We also need the following assumption for each DPE. If the CP has a message for the connected DPE, the DPE will be ready to ask for such a message after a finite number of internal communications of the DPE. The assumption (ASS) requires that, if it is possible for NW to give a message to a DPE then the DPE makes maximal k_4 steps before it takes over the message. The first line means that $SYSTEM$ has worked of the trace t and that it is possible for the subprocess NW to answer a request of DPE_i with a real message. The next line focusses on the extension of t w.r.t. DPE_i. This extension consists only of a finite number of internal actions before DPE_i takes over the message.

$(ASS) \; \forall t, i \bullet (SYSTEM[t/tr] \wedge NW[((t \downarrow Chan(NW)).ireq_i.(in_i, x))/tr] \wedge pos(x))$

$\qquad \Rightarrow (\forall t' \bullet ((P_i[((t \downarrow Chan(DPE_i)).t')/tr])$

$\qquad\qquad \Rightarrow (\exists t'' \bullet (t' \downarrow (Chan(DPE_i) \cap Chan(NW)) = \varepsilon \wedge |t'| < k_4)$

$\qquad\qquad\qquad \vee (t' \downarrow (Chan(DPE_i) \cap Chan(NW)) = ireq_i \wedge |t'| \le k_4)$

$\qquad\qquad\qquad \vee \, t' \downarrow (Chan(DPE_i) \cap Chan(NW)) = ireq_i.(in_i, x).t''))))$

If a trace t happens in $SYSTEM$ that can be extended with an input to DPE_i ($ireq_i.(in_i, x)$) from NW then DPE_i continues after t with less than k_4 internal actions or the last action was the input or the input happened in the continuation t' of t.

If this assumption is not fulfilled by a DPE then the following statements do not hold.

3.3 Stepwise Development of a CP

Now three stages are introduced in which the CPs are specified at increasingly detailed levels. In stage 1 we specify the process NW only. In stage 2 NW is split into the n CPs. In stage 3 every CP is split into further subprocesses.

The following trace predicates use sometimes regular expressions as abbreviations. The standard notion with '+' for choice and '*' for Kleene star is used. $\mathcal{L}[re]$ is the language that is described by the regular expression re. The function $pref(.)$ delivers for a given language its prefix-closure.

3.3.1 Stage 1: Observable Communications

The process NW is specified as a conjunction of subpredicates. Every subpredicate will be introduced and discussed. This first stage is a straightforward transformation of the given requirements. This specification is a starting point

258

of our decomposition process and shows how to get a specification that fulfills the requirements. We want to specify an implementable system, so the storage place of NW is limited to a finite number of messages and other parameters are introduced dependent of the number of processors n. The first two predicates refer to the mentioned communication protocol. NW always starts with a request and accepts the answer next. These loops of requests and answers with different DPEs can be mixed.

$$(P1) = \bigwedge_{i=1}^{n} chan(tr \downarrow \{oreq_i, out_i\}) \in pref(\mathcal{L}[\![(oreq_i.out_i)^*]\!])$$

The same loop of requests and answers is possible for requests started by a DPE.

$$(P2) = \bigwedge_{i=1}^{n} chan(tr \downarrow \{ireq_i, in_i\}) \in pref(\mathcal{L}[\![(ireq_i.in_i)^*]\!])$$

A message (out_i, x) that was given to NW leaves NW in a finite number (g_1) of real output communications $((in_j, x))$. $((P3)$ directly implies that the requirement $(R1)$ is fulfilled.)

$$(P3) = \forall t, t' \bullet ((tr = t.(out_i, x).t' \wedge g_1 \le |t' \downarrow IN_{pos}| \wedge dest(x) = j)$$
$$\Rightarrow (\exists tt, tt' \bullet t' = tt.(in_j, x).tt'))$$

If NW transmits a real message to DPE_i then it was given to NW by another DPE first, its destination is i and it was not an input to a DPE earlier (implies $(R3), (R4), (R5)$).

$$(P4) = \forall t, t' \bullet ((tr = t.(in_i, x).t' \wedge pos(x))$$
$$\Rightarrow (\exists tt, tt' \bullet t = tt.(out_j, x).tt' \wedge dest(x) = i \wedge t \downarrow IN(x) = \varepsilon))$$

All DPEs are fairly asked if they want to give a message to NW. If a trace part includes more than g_2 output requests then each DPE is asked at least one time (e.g., g_2 must be grater than n). At the beginning every DPE is asked one time. So, the number of output requests must be the number of different output requests (implies $(R6)$).

$$(P5) = \forall t, t', t'' \bullet$$
$$(((tr = t.t'.t'' \wedge g_2 \le |t' \downarrow OREQ|) \Rightarrow (\bigwedge_{i=1}^{n} 1 \le |t' \downarrow \{oreq_i\}|))$$
$$\wedge (|tr \downarrow OREQ| \le n \Rightarrow |tr \downarrow OREQ| = |\{i| \ tr \downarrow \{oreq_i\} \neq \varepsilon\}|))$$

If DPE_i requests for a message and a message with destination i exists in NW (the number of messages NW received with destination i is greater than the number of real messages given to i) then a real message is given to DPE_i (implies $(R7)$).

$$(P6) = \forall t, t' \bullet ((tr = t.(in_i, y).t'$$
$$\wedge 0 < |t \downarrow \{(out_j, x)|1 \le j \le n \wedge pos(x) \wedge dest(x) = i\}|$$
$$- |t \downarrow \{(in_i, x)|pos(x)\}|) \Rightarrow pos(y))$$

A request for a message of a DPE is answered in a finite number (g_3) of answer communications (implies $(R8)$).

$$(P7) = \forall t, t' \bullet ((tr = t.ireq_i.t' \wedge g_3 \le |t' \downarrow IN|)$$
$$\Rightarrow (\exists tt, tt' \bullet t' = tt.(in_i, x).tt'))$$

A DPE is asked for a message only if the number of messages that were received and not given out is not greater than the number of storage places (g_4).

$(P8) = \forall t, t' \bullet (tr = t.oreq_i.t' \Rightarrow (|t \downarrow OUT_{pos}| - |t \downarrow IN_{pos}| < g_4))$

with $OUT_{pos} = \{(out_i, x) | 1 \leq i \leq n \wedge pos(x)\}$, the set of made receives in NW

The DPEs can be specified as follows. The third line ensures that a request is answered in the next h communications.

$DPE_i = (chan(tr) \downarrow \{oreq_i, out_i\}) \in pref(\mathcal{L}[(oreq_i.out_i)^*])$

$\wedge (chan(tr) \downarrow \{ireq_i, in_i\}) \in pref(\mathcal{L}[(ireq_i.in_i)^*])$

$\wedge (\forall t, t' \bullet ((tr = t.oreq_i.t' \wedge h \leq |t'|) \Rightarrow (\exists tt, tt' \bullet t' = tt.(out_i, x).tt')))$

$\wedge$ (internal actions)

Note that the DPEs do the real work, so their communication behaviour can be described only, the real work is hidden in the predicate (internal actions). Every DPE fulfills the assumption (ASS).

Definition:

$$NW_1 = \bigwedge_{i=1}^{8} (Pi) \qquad\qquad SYSTEM_1 = SYN[NW_1, DPE_1, \ldots, DPE_n]$$

Theorem 1: $SYSTEM_1$ fulfills the requirements $(R1) - (R8)$ (with appropriate choice of the parameters)

Proof: Most requirements correspond directly to a subpredicate. So $(R1)$ can be easily shown by substituting $SYSTEM$ by $(P3)$. It is important for $(R2)$ that (ASS) holds, so the destination processor asks for each message. These requests are answered in a finite number of steps $((P2)$ and $(P7))$. $(P6)$ ensures that messages are transmitted if possible. So it is guaranteed that messages left in NW are given to their destination processor for every possible extension of a trace. Full proofs are given in [5].

3.3.2 Stage 2: Class Climbing

NW is split into the real n CPs. Now deadlocks can arise when two CPs with a full storage want to exchange all messages with each other. Note that deadlocks are no problem in stage 1 because only one process (NW) decides what happens. We use an algorithm called *class climbing* that was introduced in [1] to avoid deadlocks. Class climbing is explained briefly now. The idea is to embed a large acyclic graph into the given network.

A network can be seen as a directed graph where the processors are the vertices and every edge is a connection between a sender and a receiver. This graph is called G'. Deadlocks can only arise because of existing cycles in G'. Note that we have a complete network, so there are cycles.

Let G be an acyclic directed graph whose undirected version is equal to the undirected version of G'. The idea is to take a finite number of versions of G and to connect them in a way which is presented next, to a new directed, acyclic graph which can be represented in the given processors. Messages are transmitted only in the direction of the edges of the new graph.

So, let d be the maximum of the shortest distances between any two CPs in the network. Every message is augmented by a dynamic information, a so called *class*, taking values between 0 and d. A version of G exists for each class in the large acyclic graph. The class of a newly produced message is 0. The same class can be assigned to different messages. CPs ask their neighbours for messages of a certain class. For a request from CP_j to CP_i for class c the following rules are established. Only messages which are transmitted can change their class.

- If (i, j) is an edge in G and CP_i has a message of class c that can be transmitted to CP_j then the oldest possible message (the message of class c that arrived first an can be transmitted to CP_j) is taken. The message stays in the same class.

- If (i, j) is not an edge in G and CP_i has a message of class $c - 1$ that can be transmitted to CP_j then the oldest possible message of this kind is taken. The message changes its class from $c - 1$ to c (class climbing).

- If none of the first two rules can be taken then an NSM is sent from CP_i to CP_j.

The idea is sketched in the following picture 3. G' is the underlying graph of a network. G is one possible directed acyclic graph that fits the above requirements. The large acyclic graph which is embedded in the processors is H. The vertices B_0, B_1, B_2 (one index for each class) of H are represented in the processors which stands for vertice B in G'.

A message x can be transported from A to C by the following steps:

A generates x. The class of x is 0. B asks A for a message of class 1. (A, B) is not an edge in G, so x is transported from A to B and its class changes to 1. The step from B to C is comparable to the step from A to B. Finally, x arrives at C within class 2. x has used the vertices A_0, B_1 and C_2 in H. (If D has asked A for a message of class 1 then x would have used the vertices A_0, D_1 and C_1 to arrive in class 1 at C.)

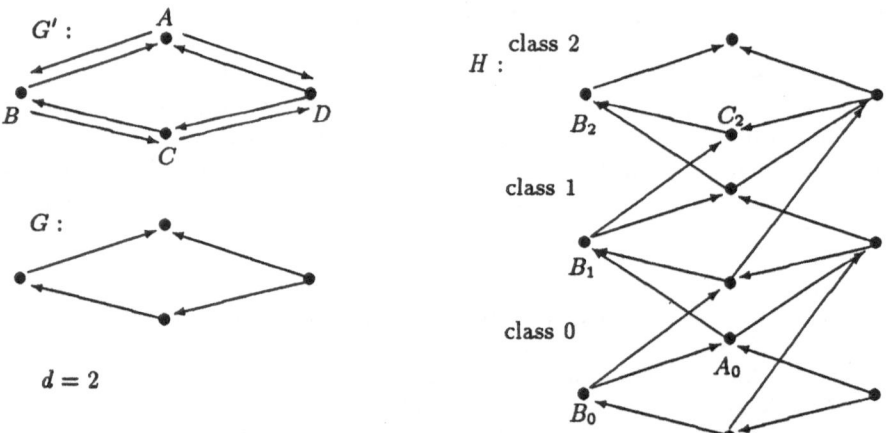

Figure3: Graph of a network and the embedded acyclic graph

Theorem 2:[1] If every CP has a storage place for at least one message for each class and if every CP asks each of its neighbours for each class observing fairness then the explained algorithm guarantees deadlock- and starvation freedom.

We have to specify now class climbing in trace logic. There are two channels between two CPs where one can be sender and the other receiver of a message.

- req_{k-l}: CP_k asks CP_l on this channel for messages.

- ch_{k-l}: CP_l answers requests of CP_k on this channel (note that the index is $k - l$ but l is the sender and k the receiver).

Channels between CP_i and DPE_i are taken from stage 1. We need the following functions to represent class climbing in trace logic. A function cl : $Msg \rightarrow \{0, \ldots, d\}$ which changes its values if a communication of a CP happens is introduced for each CP to transform the idea of class climbing into trace logic. (It is obvious in every part of this work to which CP $cl(.)$ refers, so an index is left out.) The function $cl(.)$ gives the current class of a message with regard to a CP. The function $cl(.)$ can change one value if a communication happens. If a new message x arrives from the connected DPE the value of $cl(x)$ changes from undefined to zero and if a message is received from a neighbour and the CP has asked for message of class c before the value of $cl(x)$ changes from undefined to c.

The acyclic Graph G is stored in a function $g : \mathcal{N} \times \mathcal{N} \rightarrow Bool$, where $g(i,j)$ is true iff (i,j) is an edge in G.

The following subpredicates are used to specify CP_i (only the main ones are formalized here, for the remaining see [5]):

- The first predicates deal with the correct handling of requests and answers. (not formalized here)

- Requests from neighbours and DPE_i are answered in a finite number of answer communications. (not formalized here)

- All neighbours are asked for messages of each class fairly. (not formalized here)

- There are h_3 storage places for messages of each class. A request for a class c can be started if less than h_3 storage places are covered by messages or reserved for other requests. $(PC8)$ is important for requests for class zero because neighbours and the DPE are related. We have to add the number of messages of class zero received by DPE_i and neighbours and of reserved storage places for messages of class zero for DPE_i and neighbours and to subtract the number of messages of class zero that were given to other processors. If the calculated value is less than h_3 a reservation for class zero is possible. The next five functions allow us to formulate the predicates in an easier way: $get_{CP_i}(t, c)$ is the number of messages of class c that were received in trace t. $get_{DPE_i}(t)$ is the number of messages that were produced by DPE_i and sent to CP_i. $reserve_{CP_i}(t, c)$ is the number of reservations of class c in trace t that have not been answered yet. $reserve_{DPE_i}(t)$ is one if there is a not answered reservation for the DPE else zero. $away_i(t, c)$ is the number of messages of class c in trace t that were given out to other CPs or to DPE_i. ($A_i = \{c_{i_1}, \ldots, c_{i_{m_i}}\} \subseteq \{1, \ldots, n\}$ is the set of indices of the neighbours of CP_i, $|A_i| = m_i$.)

$$get_{CP_i}(t, c) = \mid t \downarrow \{(ch_{i-y}, x) \mid y \in A_i \wedge pos(x) \wedge cl(x) = c\} \mid$$

$$get_{DPE_i}(t) = \mid t \downarrow \{(out_i, x) \mid pos(x)\} \mid$$

$$reserve_{CP_i}(t, c) = |\{y \mid y \in A_i \wedge (\exists s \bullet t \downarrow \{req_{i-y}, ch_{i-y}\} = s.(req_{i-y}, c))\}|$$

$$reserve_{DPE_i}(t) = \mid \{s \mid t \downarrow \{oreq_i, out_i\} = s.oreq_i\} \mid$$

262

$$away_i(t,c) = |\ t \downarrow \{(ch_{y-i}, x)|y \in \mathcal{A}_i \wedge pos(x) \wedge cl(x) = c\}\ |$$
$$+|\ t \downarrow \{(in_i, x)|pos(x) \wedge cl(x) = c\}\ |$$

$$(PC8) = \bigwedge_{j=1}^{m_i} (\forall t, t' \bullet ((tr = t.(req_{i-ci_j}, 0).t' \vee tr = t.oreq_i.t')$$
$$\Rightarrow h_3 > (get_{CP_i}(t, 0) + get_{DPE_i}(t) + reserve_{CP_i}(t, 0)$$
$$+reserve_{DPE_i}(t)) - away_i(t, 0)))$$

The neighbours are important only for starting requests for other classes than zero ($(PC9)$) because DPE_i only produces messages of class zero.

$$(PC9) = \bigwedge_{c=1}^{d} (\bigwedge_{j=1}^{m_i} (\forall t, t' \bullet (tr = t.(req_{i-ci_j}, c).t'$$
$$\Rightarrow h_3 > get_{CP_i}(t, c) + reserve_{CP_i}(t, c) - away_i(t, c))))$$

- A message is sent to DPE_i only if it was received before and its destination is i. (not formalized here)

- If it is possible to answer a request with a real message then a real message is transmitted. We use the following shorthands: $received_i(c, j, t)$ is the number of messages of class c that were received in trace t and could be given in the next transmission to CP_j. $out_i(c, j, t)$ is the number of the same messages that left CP_i. $L_i(j) \subseteq \mathcal{A}_i$ is the set of indices of neighbours to which a message with destination j could be sent.

$$received_i(c, j, t) = |\ t \downarrow \{(ch_{i-k}, y)|k \in \mathcal{A}_i \wedge pos(y) \wedge cl(y) = c$$
$$\wedge j \in L_i(dest(y))\}\ |$$
$$out_i(c, j, t) = |t \downarrow \{(ch_{k-i}, y)|k \in \mathcal{A}_i \wedge pos(y) \wedge cl(y) = c \wedge j \in L_i(dest(y))\}|$$

The next four predicates represent four cases of requests that have to be answered with a real message. The first predicate stands for requests of DPE_i. If DPE_i has asked for a message of class c that has not been answered yet and the number of messages with destination i received by CP_i is greater than the number of messages of class c given to DPE_i then the request is answered with a real message.

$$(PC11) = \forall t, t', t'' \bullet ((tr = t.(in_i, x).t' \wedge t \downarrow \{ireq_i\} = t''.(ireq_i, c)$$
$$\wedge 0 < |\ t \downarrow \{(ch_{i-j}, y)|j \in \mathcal{A}_i \wedge pos(y) \wedge dest(y) = i\}\ |$$
$$-|\ t \downarrow \{(in_i, y)\ |pos(y)\}|) \Rightarrow pos(x))$$

The second predicate stands for a request for a class greater than zero and an existing edge between sender and receiver in G, the third for a request for a class greater than one and no existing edge, and the fourth for requests for class zero and an existing edge or for class one and no existing edge. (The four cases are needed to distinguish between DPE and connected CPs and between requests for a class c that have to be answered with a message of class c or class $c-1$ because of the principles of class climbing.)

$$(PC12) = \forall t, t', t'' \bullet ((tr = t.(ch_{j-i}, x).t' \wedge t \downarrow \{req_{j-i}\} = t''.(req_{j-i}, c)$$
$$\wedge c > 0 \wedge g(i, j) \wedge 0 < received_i(c, j, t) - out_i(c, j, t)) \Rightarrow pos(x))$$

$(PC13) = \forall t, t', t'' \bullet ((tr = t.(ch_{j-i}, x).t' \wedge t \downarrow \{req_{j-i}\} = t''.(req_{j-i}, c)$
$\qquad \wedge c > 1 \wedge \neg g(i,j) \wedge 0 < received_i(c-1, j, t) - out_i(c-1, j, t)) \Rightarrow pos(x))$
$(PC14) = \forall t, t', t'' \bullet ((tr = t.(ch_{j-i}, x).t'$
$\qquad \wedge ((t \downarrow \{req_{j-i}\} = t''.(req_{j-i}, 0) \wedge g(i,j))$
$\qquad\qquad \vee (t \downarrow \{req_{j-i}\} = t'.(req_{j-i}, 1) \wedge \neg g(i,j)))$
$\qquad \wedge 0 < received_i(0, j, t) + |t \downarrow \{(out_i, y)|pos(y)\}| - out_i(0, j, t))$
$\qquad\qquad \Rightarrow pos(x))$

- If a real message x is sent from CP_i to CP_j then the rules of class climbing are used. We have to ensure that CP_j is on the shortest way to the destination of x, that x was received first, that x is an answer to a request and has the right class and that there is no message of the same class that can also be sent to CP_j and that waits longer than x. (not formalized here)

- A new message which is received from DPE_i gets the class zero. (not formalized here)

- CP_i alternates between input and output actions. (not formalized here)

Definition: $CP_i = \bigwedge\limits_{j=1}^{17} PCj$
$$SYSTEM_2 = SYN[DPE_1, \ldots, DPE_n, CP_1, \ldots, CP_n]$$
Theorem 3: $SYSTEM_2$ fulfills the requirements $(R1) - (R8)$

3.3.3   Stage 3: Buffer Management

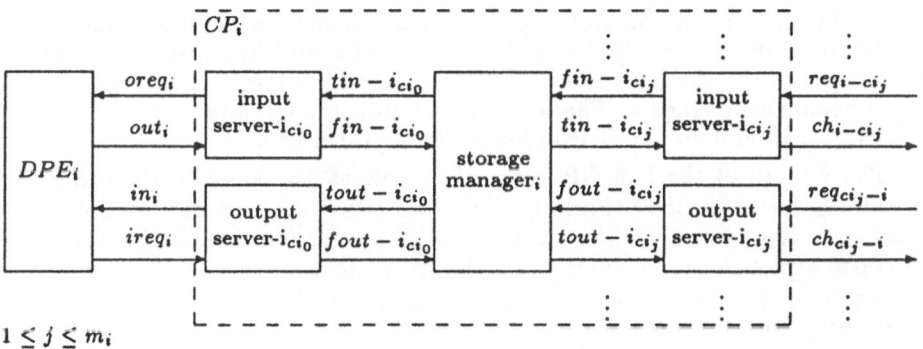

$1 \leq j \leq m_i$

Figure4: Decomposition of a CP

At this stage every CP consists of three kinds of processes.

- One *input server* (abbreviated IS) exists for each neighbour. The IS starts requests to a connected CP and receives the answer. The IS asks the storage manager (see below) at first which request shall be made and transmits the received answer to the storage manager.

- One *output server* (abbreviated OS) exists for each neighbour. The OS receives requests from the IS of a connected CP. The OS answers the request with real messages or NSMs. The OS exchanges informations with the storage manager and knows how many messages of a certain class are in the storage manager that can be given out through this OS.

- One *storage manager* (abbreviated SM) exists for each CP. The SM is responsible to manage the whole storage and to provide the connected server with the right information. Messages that were received by an IS are stored in the SM. If a new message arrives or a message leaves the SM every OS that could transmit this message is informed about the action. The informations for the OS is the class of the message that has arrived at or has left the CP. The SM asks in a fair way every OS if they want to get a message. If an OS wants a message it is given to him in the next step.

The communication protocol uses the following loop. An IS asks its SM for a class number. The SM reserves a storage place of a special class and sends its number to the IS. If no reservation is possible a cancel message is sent. Otherwise, the IS sends a request with the received class number to the connected OS of a neighbour CP. The OS receives the request. If the connected SM asks whether the OS wants a message then if there is a possible message in the SM the OS sends a request for message to the SM. If there is no possible answer an NSM is sent to the IS. If there is a possible message then this message is transmitted from SM to OS and is given in the next step to the connected IS. The IS sends the answer after receiving it to its connected SM. Now, the loop can start again.

For CP_i let m_i be the number of connected neighbours. $\mathcal{A}_i = \{ci_1, \ldots, ci_{m_i}\}$ is the set of indices of CPs that are connected to CP_i.

The channel names that we use for the connections between SM, IS and OS can be taken from the previous figure 4. (*fin* means 'from input server', *tin* means 'to input server', *tout* and *fout* means 'to' and 'from output server'.) The names of the channels that connect two CPs and the CPs with the DPEs are the same as in stage 2. The connection between a CP and its DPE are also built by an IS and an OS. The index of these processes is ci_0.

The j-th IS of the i-th CP is specified now as an example, the other IS, OS and SM are specified similarly. The IS starts with a request to SM for a class number and receives the answer next. If the answer is negative then the IS starts again at the beginning else the IS sends a request to the connected OS, receives the answer and transmits the answer to the SM. This leads to the following predicate.

$$(PI1) = chan(tr) \in pref(\mathcal{L}[\![((fin - i_{ci_j}.tin - i_{ci_j}.(\varepsilon + req_{i-ci_j}.ch_{i-ci_j}.\ fin - i_{ci_j}))^*]\!])$$

The connected OS is asked for class c only if the class was transmitted by the SM before.

$$(PI2) = \forall t, t' \bullet (tr = t.(req_{i-ci_j}, c).t' \Rightarrow (\exists t'' \bullet t = t''.(tin - i_{ci_j}, c)))$$

The IS asks the SM for a class at the beginning of a request loop, after transmitting the received answer of the connected OS to the SM and after receiving a *cancel*-message from the SM.

$$(PI3) = \forall t, t' \bullet (tr = t.(fin - i_{ci_j}, req).t'$$
$$\Rightarrow (t = \varepsilon$$
$$\vee(\exists t'' \bullet t = t''.(fin - i_{ci_j}, x) \wedge x \neq request)$$
$$\vee(\exists t'' \bullet t = t''.(tin - i_{ci_j}, cancel))))$$

If the IS receives an answer from the OS then the answer is given to the SM. If the answer is a real message then this message is sent else the number of the last requested class c is sent as message $free(c)$ to release the reserved storage place.

$$(PI4) = \forall t, t' \bullet (tr = t.(ch_{i-ci_j}, x).t'$$
$$\Rightarrow (t' = \varepsilon$$
$$\vee(\exists t'' \bullet t' = (fin - i_{ci_j}, x).t'' \wedge pos(x))$$
$$\vee(\exists t'', t''' \bullet t \downarrow \{tin - i_{ci_j}\} = t''.(tin - i_{ci_j}, c)$$
$$\wedge t' = (fin - i_{ci_j}, free(c)).t''' \wedge \neg pos(x))))$$

The channels of the IS that are connected to the DPE must be renamed from req_{i-ci_o} in $oreq_i$ and from ch_{i-ci_o} in out_i.

Definition: The IS are defined by $IS - i_{ci_j} = \bigwedge\limits_{k=1}^{4} (PIk)$

$$i \in \mathcal{N}, j \in \{0, \ldots, m_i\}$$

The output server ($OS - i_{ci_j}$) and storage manager ($SM - i$) can be specified in the same way.

Definition: The specified processes are composed as follows.
$SYSTEM_3 =$
$SYN[IS - 1_{cl_0}, \ldots, IS - 1_{cl_{m_1}}, OS - 1_{cl_0}, \ldots, OS - 1_{cl_{m_1}}, SM - 1, DPE_1, \ldots$

$$\vdots$$

$IS - n_{cn_0}, \ldots, IS - n_{cn_{m_n}}, OS - n_{cn_0}, \ldots, OS - n_{cn_{m_n}}, SM - n, DPE_n]$

Theorem 4: $SYSTEM_3$ fulfills the requirements $(R1) - (R8)$

3.4 Transformation of Trace Logic Specifications into SL-Specifications

Trace Logic is used so far as a well known specification language that is easy to understand and where refinement steps are easy to describe. With the aim to reach a distributed system we transform trace predicates into a language SL [6, 8] because it is possible to transform a large set of SL-specifications into OCCAM-like programs automatically. Other SL-specifications can be transformed by verified transformation rules into OCCAM-like programs. If we start from a verified specification and use verified transformation rules we will gain a verified program.

3.4.1 A Short Description of SL

The specification of a single process in SL consists of a trace part and a state part. More precisely, the syntax of a single process P is as follows.

P = **spec**
     dir_{ch_i} ch_i **of** ty_{ch_i} with $1 \leq i \leq r$ (A)
     trace a_{ta_i} **in** re_{ta_i} with $1 \leq i \leq s$ (B)
     var x_i **of** ty_{x_i} [**init** $init_{x_i}$]   with $1 \leq i \leq t$ (C)

266

```
      com ch_{ca_i} read R_{ca_i} write W_{ca_i}              with 1 ≤ i ≤ r   (D)
                 when wh_{ca_i} then th_{ca_i}
  end
where r, s, t ≥ 0
```

The parts $(A), (B), (C)$ and (D) of the specifications are explained in the following example.

Example: We describe a buffer with capacity one. The buffer reads in an integer x and gives out x in the next step. This happens in an infinite loop. The value of x is stored in the local variable *store*.

```
buffer = spec
            input in of int                                        (A)
            output out of int                                      (A)
            trace in, out in pref((in.out)*)                       (B)
            var store of int                                       (C)
            com in write{store} when true then store'=@in          (D)
            com out read{store} when true then @out=store          (D)
         end
```

- (A): This part describes the channels or *interface* of P. $dir_{ch_i} \in \{input, output\}$ is the direction, ch_i the name, and ty_{ch_i} the type of the messages that are transmitted of the channel. $Chan(P)$ is the set of all channels of P.

  in is an input and *out* an output channel in the example.

- (B): The *trace assertions* describe the set of possible communication sequences. $a_{ta_i} \subseteq Chan(P)$ is the set of related channels and re_{ta_i} a regular expression. A trace t is possible iff for every trace assertion the following holds: $\forall i \in \{1, \ldots, s\} : chan(t) \downarrow a_{ta_i} \in \mathcal{L}[\![re_{ta_i}]\!]$

  The trace assertion of the example allows only prefixes of traces of the following kind: $in.out.in.out....$

- (C): The variable list contains all local variables of P. It consists of name (x_i), type (ty_{x_i}) and an optional initialization ([init $init_{x_i}$]) of the variables. $Var(P)$ is the set of all variables of P.

  The local variable *store* is used for storing the value of the input in the example.

- (D): The *communication assertions* describe when a communication ca_i can happen and the state after the execution of ca_i. $R_{ca_i} \subseteq Var(P)$ is the set of read-only variables. $W_{ca_i} \subseteq Var(P)$ is the set of variables that can be read and changed. $R_{ca_i} \cap W_{ca_i} = \emptyset$ is required. wh_{ca_i}, the when-predicate, is an enabling predicate. A communication can only happen if wh_{ca_i} can be fulfilled. The free variables $free(wh_{ca_i})$ are a subset of R_{ca_i}. The then-predicate th_{ca_i} describes the final state change of the execution of the communication. $free(th_{ca_i}) \subseteq R_{ca_i} \cup W_{ca_i} \cup W'_{ca_i} \cup \{@ch_{ca_i}\}$. $W'_{ca_i} = \{x' | x \in W_{ca_i}\}$ is the set of variables of W_{ca_i} decorated with a prime. A primed variable stands for the value after and a not primed variable for the value before the communication is executed. We use channel names prefixed by the symbol @ as variables referring to the communication values on this channels. Predicates of the form com c when true then true can be left out.

The first communication assertion of the example ensures that the input value is stored and the second describes that the last input value is the output.

Note that a communication can only happen if it is possible w.r.t. both communication and trace assertions.

The semantics of an SL-specification requires a new kind of predicate with two important free variables. The free variable tr is a trace variable with the same meaning as in trace logic predicates. The communications that can happen after the trace tr are summed up in the free variable Rdy, the *ready set*. This set describes the progress properties of the system. Let $[\![S]\!]$ denote the predicate that describes the semantics of the SL-specification S.

Here we give only a description of parts of SL that are interesting for this paper. A complete description of SL is given in [8]. E.g, the following valuations fulfills the SL-predicate of our example:

$tr = \varepsilon \wedge Rdy = \{in\}$, $tr = (in, 1) \wedge Rdy = \{out\}$,
$tr = (in, 1).(out, 1) \wedge Rdy = \{in\}$

SL-specifications can be composed by a synchronization operator SYN. The semantics of SYN is the same as the semantics of the SYN-operator for trace logic predicates except that now also the ready sets have to be taken into account.

3.4.2 The Idea of Transformation

The relationship between SL and trace logic is given by the following definition.

Definition: Let P be a trace predicate and S a SL-specification. S is *generated* by P (abbreviated $S =< P >$), iff

$$\forall t, R \bullet ([\![S]\!][t/tr, R/Rdy] \Leftrightarrow P[t/tr] \wedge R = \{ch | \exists m \bullet P[(t.(ch, m))/tr]\})$$

Trace predicates are transformed by the following idea to get a generated SL-specification. We start with the empty specification S = spec { used channels } end. We take the first subpredicate of the trace predicate and formulate an SL-part that is generated by the first subpredicate. This is done for each subpredicate taking the previous ones into account. We gain a generated specification of P after transforming the last subpredicate. So it is easy to transform stepwise every part of a large conjunction and to prove that the specification is generated by the given predicate.

We illustrate this idea by transforming the first trace predicates of the IS. ($PI1$) is transformed into a trace assertion.

> trace $fin - i_{ci_j}, tin - i_{ci_j}, req_{i-ci_j}, ch_{i-ci_j}$
>   in pref$((fin - i_{ci_j}.tin - i_{ci_j}.(\varepsilon + req_{i-ci_j}.ch_{i-ci_j}.fin - i_{ci_j}))^*$)

We use two variables cl and $unused$ to transform ($PI2$). The class number that was given to the IS by the SM in the last step is stored in cl. The variable $unused$ indicates whether the value of cl was given to the connected OS or not.

> var cl of class   /* class = 0..d */
> var $unused$ of bool init false

com $tin - i_{ci_j}$ write$\{cl, unused\}$
 when true
 then $(@tin - i_{ci_j} \neq cancel \Rightarrow cl' = @tin - i_{ci_j} \wedge unused')$
 $\wedge (@tin - i_{ci_j} = cancel \Rightarrow \neg unused' \wedge cl' = cl)$
com req_{i-ci_j} read$\{cl\}$ write$\{unused\}$
 when $unused$
 then $@req_{i-ci_j} = cl \wedge \neg unused')$

The predicates $(PI3)$ and $(PI4)$ are transformed in the same way. The list of variables and the communication assertions have to be expanded.

Theorem 5: Input-Server$_{ci_j}$-SL = $<$ Input-Server$_{ci_j}$ $>$

3.5 Transformation into OCCAM programs

We can use the transformation rules of [8, 9, 10] to obtain a OCCAM-like program implementing that specification from a specification as the above one. Every transformation rule is proved to be correct, so it is sure that we get a verified program.

This idea can only be sketched here. The trace assertion with the regular expression $(f.t.(\varepsilon + r.c.f))^*$ of the input server leads to the following program skeleton:

```
WHILE (wh_f,SEQ[ trans(f);
                trans(t);
                IF[ wh_f → SKIP
                    wh_r → SEQ[ impl(th_r); trans(c); trans(f) ]
            ]  ]          )
```

Here the following abbreviations are used: $f \equiv fin - i_{ci_j}, t \equiv tin - i_{ci_j}, r \equiv req_{i-ci_j}, c \equiv ch_{i-ci_j}$, impl$(th_{ch})$ means the implementation of the then-predicate of the channel ch, trans(ch) means for an input channel ch IF$[wh_{ch} \rightarrow$ impl$(th_{ch})]$ and for an output channel ch IF$[wh_{ch}$ & ch?@ch $\rightarrow$ impl$(th_{ch})]$. It is important for the transformation that $wh_f \wedge wh_r$ is never true.

The loop shows that the process starts with a trace $f.t$. If wh_f is fulfilled after that then the loop starts again (the input server must not start a request). If wh_r is fulfilled then the trace $r.c.f$ is executed and the loop starts again. This is the same description for the loop as the explanation to $(PI1)$ (see section 3.3.3).

4 Conclusions and Final Remarks

This paper shows the possibility of specifying a complex process system in trace logic and how such a specification can be used to obtain verified programs. The advantage of trace logic is that requirements and specifications and so the correctness proofs are all handled in the same logic.

Another advantage of trace logic specifications is that it is easy to transform them into a program specification language such as SL. The transformation follows the idea to transform every subpredicate stepwise to get the generated program specification.

The idea is then to transform a verified specification by verified transformation steps into a program [9, 10]. The aim to get such transformation rules and to get a possibility of automatic transforming are studied in the projects ProCoS and KORSO.

Finally, this paper shows how a specification language can be applied to a realistic example. This might be a starting point of a discussion which specification technique is appropriate for what kind of practical problem.

In contrast to the original work [1] no optimization of the usage of storage places is considered here, but this could be done by a little change of stage 3 which would lead to a new stage 4.

Acknowledgements. The author thanks Ernst-Rüdiger Olderog, Michael R. Hansen and Werner Damm for numerous helpful and detailed discussions.

References

[1] J.K. Annot, R.A.H van Twist, A Novel Deadlock Free and Starvation Free Packet Switching Communication Processor, LNCS 258, pp68-85,1987

[2] K.M. Chandy, J. Misra, Parallel Program design - A Foundation, Addison-Wesley, 1988

[3] E.C.R. Hehner, Predicative Programming, Comm. ACM 27 (2), 1984

[4] Inmos Limited, OCCAM 2 Reference Manual, Prentice Hall International Series in Computer Science, 1988

[5] S. Kleuker, KORSO Fallstudie: Spezifikation eines Kommunikationsprozessors, internal paper (german) , Univ. Oldenburg, 1993

[6] E.-R. Olderog, Towards a Design Calculus for Communicating Programs, LNCS 527, pp61-77, 1991

[7] E.-R. Olderog, Nets, Terms and Formulas: Three Views of Concurrent Processes and their Relationship, Cambridge University Press, 1991

[8] E.-R. Olderog, S. Rössig, J. Sander, M. Schenke, ProCoS at Oldenburg: The Interface between Specification Language and OCCAM-like Programming Language. Technical Report Bericht 3/92, Univ. Oldenburg, Fachbereich Informatik, 1992.

[9] S. Rössig, Transformation of SL_0 Specifications into PL Programs, ProCoS Document OLD SR 1/4, 1990

[10] S. Rössig, M. Schenke, Specification and Stepwise Development of Communicating Systems, LNCS 551, pp149-163, 1991

[11] J.M. Spivey, The Z Notation: A Reference Manual, Prentice Hall, 1989

[12] J. Zwiers, Compositionality, Concurrency and Partial Correctness - Proof Theories for Networks of Processes and Their Relationship, LNCS 321, 1989

Rendez-Vous with Bundle Event Structures

Bart Botma

Dept. of Computer Science, University of Twente

Enschede, The Netherlands

Abstract

Event structure models have been used to give a non-interleaving semantics to various process algebras such as CSP, ACP, CCS, LOTOS. In this paper we extend the *Bundle Event Structure* ($\mathcal{BES}$) model to be able to give a semantics to Full LOTOS. We add *data* and we introduce a new relation called *rendezvous* to deal with process recursion.

The addition of data forces us to introduce *environments* passed with the computation of labelled posets. Unfortunately, by adding *Abstract Data Types* to describe the data we introduce the semi-computability problem of algebraic specifications w.r.t. equality.

The addition of a new relation called *rendezvous* complies with lazy evaluation, which entails simulations of possibly infinite bundle event structures. But *Goal Oriented Execution* techniques are required to reduce the synchronization constraints.

1   Framework

Unlike formal description techniques based on the state representation of a system (Finite State Machines[1], Petri Nets[2, 3], Estelle[4]) *LOTOS* describes a system by defining the temporal relations between externally observable events at so-called event gates. LOTOS is thereby based on process-algebraic methods which were introduced by Milner's work on CCS[5]. CCS models concurrent system behaviour by arbitrary interleaving, i.e. the following rule is part of the CCS axioms (LOTOS notation):

$$a \mathrel{|||} b \; = \; a;b \mathrel{[]} b;a$$

This axiom characterizes the interleaving semantics of the parallel operator by expressing the independence of the events a and b as a choice between their interleavings. Interleaving semantics is well studied and has attractive proof techniques and axiomatizations.

Interleaving semantics is based on an abstraction with several characteristics[6]:

- It considers the system as a whole, i.e. it looks only at the global state of a system, thereby disregarding its distributed nature.

- It is observational in nature; it considers what can globally be observed, not how the system is designed. Aspects like independence or distribution of actions are therefore not reflected in the semantics.

- It abstracts from time aspects like the duration of an event.

Interleaving semantics is mainly observational in nature and abstracts away from intensional aspects such as causality and concurrency. In the literature, several models have been proposed which respect concurrency. In [7] it is argued that *Petri Nets* are less suitable for an adequate description of the causal relations between events in a distributed system, unless the nets are used as occurrence nets[8]. But such nets, just like prime event structures[9] lack the more advanced operational semantics of other event-based models, such as stable event structures[10] and bundle event structures[12, 7]. In [6, 13] several event-based models are compared.

Event structures, introduced by Winskel[10], are a natural domain for modelling concurrency. Semantics however, is a relative notion in this context, because each event structure model carries with it its own semantics. Usually, the semantics of event structure models is defined in terms of families of (labelled) partially ordered sets (lposets). The aim of a partial order semantics is to model the behaviour of processes in such a way as to respect both concurrency and nondeterminism. Event-based models satisfy these requirements by using (indivisible) events to model the small pieces of behaviour and relations between events to model causality, conflict and independence. Concurrency is respected by the fact that system runs are only partially, not totally, ordered. This "bare" semantics is inappropriate, because from a designer point of view these lposets lack an intuitive structure. Therefore in [12] Langerak advocated the use of an "intuitive" intermediate model which on one hand formalizes a non-interleaving semantics for Basic LOTOS, but on the other hand still has an lposets semantics. This Bundle Event Structure ($\mathcal{BES}$) model has been used to define a non-interleaving semantics for basic LOTOS [12, 14].

Bundle Event Structures are attractive from a graphical point of view and several equivalence laws have already been defined. The model has already been used in the study of architectural problems [15], probabilistic process algebras [16], and tool support has demonstrated the usefulness and merits of the model [17].

In this paper we focus on two orthogonal aspects of LOTOS which were not elaborated in the original Bundle Event Structure model: data and (a pragmatic view of) recursive behaviour. The reader unfamiliar with the Bundle Event Structure model is urged to take a look at Appendix A, which explains and extends some of the work on the Bundle Event Structure model.

2 Data

Basic LOTOS, i.e. LOTOS without data, is a powerful process algebra on its own, and often usable basic LOTOS specifications can obtained by the naive projection which removes all data from a full LOTOS specification, resulting in a ϕ-simulation equivalent specification [18]. In this section we will show that data can be incorporated into the Bundle Event Structure model.

Let T be the conditional theory derived from the *Abstract Data Type* part of a LOTOS specification S [1]. Let $\mathcal{E} = (E, \leadsto, \mapsto)$ be a Bundle Event Structure.

---

[1]In T we identify types by *Typ*, variables by *Var*, operations by *Ope* and well-formed

Data is added to $\mathcal{E}$ by tupling events in E with the LOTOS gate identifier, with **offers**, as with LOTOS attributes to events, and **predicates**, as with LOTOS behaviour guards. An offer can either be a send offer, e.g. the !5 in the event $(g!5)$, or a receive offer, e.g. the $?x : Int$ in the event $(g?x : Int)$. Predicates act as guard on each event, such that $(g?x : Int[\{x < 5\}])$ is interpreted as an event $(g?x : Int)$ provided the condition $\{x < 5\}$ holds within the conditional theory T. Predicates may contain free variables, in which case the used decision algorithm must find a (most general) unifier for the predicates to hold [19, 20, 21]. Thus, each event e becomes a four tuple $e^{\otimes} = \langle e, g, \bar{d}, \bar{p} \rangle$, marking it as an event e on gate g with offers $\bar{d}$ and predicates $\bar{p}$.

Definition 2.1 (Bundle Event Structure)
The *Bundle Event Structure* $\mathcal{E}^{\otimes}$ is now a three tuple $(E^{\otimes}, \rightsquigarrow, \mapsto)$ with:

o $E^{\otimes} \subseteq E \times Act \times \overline{Off} \times \overline{Pre}$, a set of *events* E, tupled with *event offers* from $\overline{Off}$ on gates in Act with *predicates* from $\overline{Pre}$, where:

   $E \subseteq Evt$, the *events*

   $Act = \{\mathbf{i}\} \cup \{g : g \text{ a label/gate in } S\}$

   $\overline{Off} \subseteq (!Exp|?\,Var : Typ)^{*}$, the *event offers*

   $\overline{Pre} \subseteq (Exp = Exp)^{*}$, the *predicates*

o $\mapsto \subseteq (2^{E^{\otimes}} \times E^{\otimes})$, the *bundle set*
o $\rightsquigarrow \subseteq (E^{\otimes} \times E^{\otimes})$, the *(asymmetric) conflict relation*

such that the following properties hold:

P1: $X^{\otimes} \mapsto e^{\otimes} \Rightarrow \forall e_1^{\otimes}, e_2^{\otimes} \in X^{\otimes} : (\, e_1^{\otimes} \neq e_2^{\otimes} \Rightarrow e_1^{\otimes} \rightsquigarrow e_2^{\otimes}\,)$
P2: $\rightsquigarrow$ is irreflexive, i.e. $\forall e_1^{\otimes}, e_2^{\otimes} \in E^{\otimes} : (\, e_1^{\otimes} \rightsquigarrow e_2^{\otimes} \Rightarrow e_1^{\otimes} \neq e_2^{\otimes}\,)$

The labelling function $l : Evt \rightarrow Act$ of the original BES model is made implicit by Act in $E^{\otimes}$.

Example 2.2 (Conflicts)
The concept of conflict must be adapted, because even though the two events in the following event structure are independent, t.i. no conflict nor bundle relations, they inherit the semantic conflict between their guard predicates:

   $g!x[x = 5]$ ●   ● $g!x[x \neq 5]$

Example 2.3 (Environments)
Values obtained by input offers must somehow be passed to the subsequent behaviour. We have chosen not to do this through bundles, because that way we would have to save the causal history of each event. Instead, we will introduce *environments* which collect the data history only. In the following Bundle Event Structure, the event $h!x$ inherits the (data) environment from either the $g?x : Int, [\{x = 5\}]$ event or the $g?x : Int, [\{x \neq 5\}]$ event (if we abstract from event identities we may write $g!x[\{x = 5\}]$ instead of $\langle e, g, !x, \{x = 5\}\rangle$, etc):

---

formulas over Var and Ope by Exp. Predicates, Pre, are equalities between two well-formed formula in Exp (with = TRUE optional) with boolean value. Equalities over (open) formulas are semi-computable, t.i. the decision algorithm returns TRUE, FALSE or UNKNOWN. In the latter case the algorithm fails to find a unifier which proves the equality.

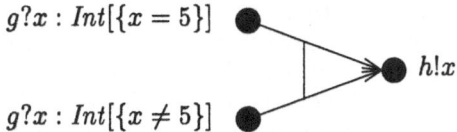

The transition system is defined is terms of families of (labelled) partially ordered sets. The first step is to define a system run, or *proving sequence*.

Definition 2.4 (Proving Sequence)
Let $\mathcal{E}^{\otimes} = (E^{\otimes}, \leadsto, \mapsto)$ be a Bundle Event Structure. A *proving sequence* is a sequence $e_1^{\otimes}, \ldots, e_n^{\otimes}$ of events, satisfying:

1. $X^{\otimes} \mapsto e_i^{\otimes} \implies \{e_1^{\otimes}, \ldots, e_{n-1}^{\otimes}\} \cap X^{\otimes} \neq \emptyset$
2. $e_i^{\otimes} \leadsto e_j^{\otimes} \implies i < j$
3. $\bigcup_i \{\overline{p}_i | e_i^{\otimes} = \langle e_i, -, -, \overline{p}_i \rangle\} \not\vdash_T$ FALSE

Definition 2.5 (Proving Sequence)
A set $C^{\otimes} \subseteq E^{\otimes}$ is called a configuration if there is a proving sequence $e_1^{\otimes}, \ldots, e_n^{\otimes}$ such that: $C^{\otimes} = \{e_1^{\otimes}, \ldots, e_n^{\otimes}\}$.

A definitions of *lposet* (a proving sequence with causal history) and *remainder* (of a system $\mathcal{E}^{\otimes}$ after a configuration $C^{\otimes}$, notation $\mathcal{E}^{\otimes}[C^{\otimes}]$) can easily be adapted [12] (see also Appendix A). In the definition of *transition*, the environments play an essential rôle. A *(data) environment* is a (finite) collection of predicates with binds some of the variables to (open) terms, e.g. $\{x = 5, x = z\}$ is an environment which binds the variable x to the ground term 5 and to the unbound variable z (see also Section 3).

Definition 2.6 (Data Environment)
A *(data) environment* P is a (finite) set of predicates, $P \subseteq Pre$. A variable $v \in Var$ is *bound* (or non-free) in P if it can be mapped to a ground term in P, otherwise it is called *free* (or un-bound) in P.

In the presence of predicates with free variables, no sufficient restrictions on the Abstract Data Types have been found to guarantee correctness and termination of the decision procedure w.r.t. equality. Experiments with narrowing techniques have demonstrated that this is often not an issue [21].

Definition 2.7 (Lposet Transition)
The full bundle event structure $\mathcal{E}^{\otimes}$ in a (data) environment P has a (lposet) transition $\langle \mathcal{E}^{\otimes}, \overline{C}^{\otimes}, \mathcal{E}^{\otimes\prime} \rangle$, or $\mathcal{E}^{\otimes}(P) \xrightarrow{\overline{C}^{\otimes}} \mathcal{E}^{\otimes\prime}(P')$ iff $\overline{C}^{\otimes}$ is a lposet of $\mathcal{E}^{\otimes}$, $\mathcal{E}^{\otimes\prime} = \mathcal{E}^{\otimes}[C^{\otimes}]$, and $P' = P \cup \bigcup_i \{\overline{p}_i | \langle e_i, -, -, \overline{p}_i \rangle \in C^{\otimes}\} \not\vdash$ FALSE. A *transition system* can now be defined in terms of states and transitions[22].

In [6] it is shown that with an asymmetric conflict relation it is not sufficient to define the semantics of Bundle Event Structures in terms of families of configurations. In the above definition of (lposet) transition system this is acknowledged by using the $\overline{C}^{\otimes}$ in stead of $C^{\otimes}$ in the transition relation. Note however, that $C^{\otimes}$ is sufficient to compute the remainder after $\overline{C}^{\otimes}$.

Example 2.8 (Configurations versus Lposets)
That configurations are not expressive enough can be seen by the following
example: given the LOTOS behaviour $(a; \textbf{exit} \; [> b; \textbf{exit})$, the configuration
$\{b, \textbf{exit}\}$ is not maximal, because the event a can be added. The poset $\{b, \textbf{exit}\}$
with $b \prec_{\{b,\textbf{exit}\}} \textbf{exit}$ should be considered maximal because here the adding
of the event a violates the causal ordering w.r.t. b. Note that the family of
configurations of $(a; \textbf{exit} \; [> b; \textbf{exit})$ is the same as that of $(a; \textbf{exit} \; ||| \; b; \textbf{exit})$.

As proof of the pudding we have defined a mapping from LOTOS behaviour expressions with data to Bundle Event Structures. The most interesting operator
is the parallel operator, because with this operator the event offers participate
in the synchronization (see also Section 3 where we approach the synchronization of the parallel operator in a completely different way). Synchronization
can give 3 different kinds of interaction types between offers:

behaviour A	behaviour B	interaction	predicate
$g!E_1$	$g!E_2$	value matching	$E_1 = E_2$
$g!E$	$g?x : t$	value passing	$x = E$
$g?x : t$	$g?y : t$	value generation	$x = y = v$, some $v \in t$

Each of these interactions creates new predicates with the events. In the
next section these new predicates are made explicit by the *rendezvous* relation.
The mappings of **choice, enabling, disabling, guards, local-definitions,
action-prefix, inaction** and **termination** have also been extended to incorporate data interactions.

3   Behaviour

In non-interleaving semantics the problem with infinite behaviour stems from
the synchronizations between two possibly infinite behaviours. In this section
we will introduce a new relation called *rendezvous* for synchronizations which
allows us to formulate a (labelled) poset transition system for full LOTOS.

The standard LOTOS semantics is defined in terms of (structured) labelled
transition systems[14], or $\mathcal{LTS}$ for short. Given two LOTOS behaviour expressions B and C, we write $B =_{\mathcal{LTS}} C$, or $B = C$ for short, iff B may be replaced
by C and vice versa in all LOTOS contexts without changing its meaning. B
and C are then said to be *weak bisimulation congruent*. We have already seen
one of these congruences, $(a \; ||| \; b = a; b \; [] \; b; a)$. But here we are interested in
yet another of these laws, the *expansion theorem*[14] for the parallel operator,
which looks like:

$$
\begin{aligned}
B \; |[A]| \; C = \quad &[] \; \{b_i; (B_i \; |[A]| \; C) \mid name(b_i) \notin A, i \in I\} \\
&[] \; [] \; \{c_j; (B \; |[A]| \; C_j) \mid name(c_j) \notin A, j \in J\} \\
&[] \; [] \; \{a; (B_i \; |[A]| \; C_j) \mid a = b_i = c_j, name(a) \in A, i \in I, j \in J\}
\end{aligned}
$$

if all $b_i (i \in I), c_j (j \in J)$ are of the form $g!E_1 \ldots E_n$

The congruence $(a \; ||| \; b = a; b \; [] \; b; a)$ is a special case of the expansion theorem
with $B = (a; \textbf{stop})$, $C = (b; \textbf{stop})$ and $A = \emptyset$. Since $A = \emptyset$, only the first two
expansion clauses apply.

In simulators this congruence is used to expand (in)finite behaviours with synchronizations to action prefix behaviours. Unfortunately, this congruence does not hold in a non-interleaving semantics. The reason why is the same as for the special case of this congruence: it introduces a causal ordering between events which we just want to avoid in a non-interleaving semantics. How to deal with infinite behaviours if we can not use expansion congruences?

Infinite behaviour originates in process recursion. Therefore, one solution would be to move to domain theory. We can define a complete partial order on Bundle Event Structures, and use fixpoint approximations to get solutions of recursively defined equations. Langerak followed this path in his thesis [6], and several others have done the same for other event structure models (e.g. [10]).

The importance of this result is that it gives us a recipe for obtaining progressively better (finite) approximations of the (possibly infinite) solution. Yet, the ordering $\trianglelefteq$ in [6] is non-trivial, and the relation between different approximations is unclear: what is the relation between one approximation and the next one? The $\trianglelefteq$ does not provide an answer other then that the next approximation is "better". There is no easy way given a system run in a certain approximation to derive a new system run in the next approximation other than to recompute everything. From a pragmatic point of view, this is not acceptable.

An other path followed by Latella [23] is to restrict the specification language such that a less powerful model than BES can be used which allows for "unrollings" of recursive behaviours. His model *recBES* turns out to be at least as powerful as Finite State Automata, but extension of this work to full LOTOS seems somewhat problematic.

Our solution is to look at how simulators traditionally cope with infinite behaviours. In the realm of interleaving semantics, the above expansion theorem gives a strong hold. Since basically the only difference between non-interleaving and interleaving semantics originates in the treatment of the parallel operator, it is in that area that we must look for alternative formulations which would allow for some sort of (lazy) expansion. Most LOTOS operators comply with lazy expansion. Of course, as always, the one exception is the LOTOS parallel operator, which shouldn't surprise anyone because only with this operator do the non-interleaving and interleaving semantics diverge. The standard event structure approach to synchronization is elegant yet straightforward: remove it. That is, events which must synchronize are mapped by the model onto a single new event. We call this approach straightforward because this naturally only works with finite Bundle Event Structures (remember that every approximation is a *finite* structure). However, if we look at the LOTOS parallel operator, we recognize that it supports multi-way synchronization. That is, both sides must synchronize on all events in the synchronization set, and both sides may represent infinite behaviour. This is too strong a notion, because in this form it can only be incorporated into event structure formalisms with fixed point theories. Therefore, an additional level between LOTOS on the one hand and Bundle Event Structures on the other must be defined, which supports a gradual shift from LOTOS towards Bundle Event Structures. Our solution is to introduce a new relation called *rendezvous*, which acts like a one-way synchronization relation. As we will see, this allows for local changes to be made which do not affect the whole behaviour. Take the following example, a `two slot buffer`.

```
specification two_slot_buffer[input,output]:noexit

behaviour

    hide middle in
      buffer[input,middle]
        |[middle]|
      buffer[middle,output]

where
    process buffer[input,output]:noexit:=
      input ?x:nat; output !x;
      buffer[input,output]
    endproc

endspec
```

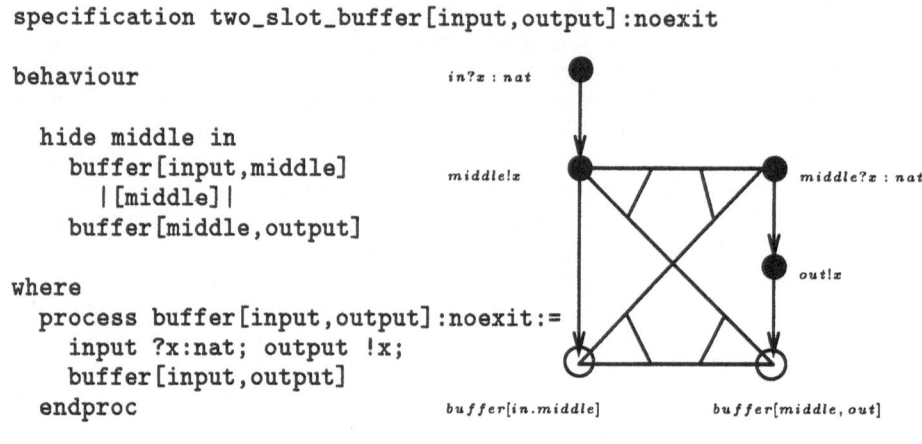

Figure 1: A two-slot-buffer in LOTOS and as BES

In the above visualization we delay the synchronization requirements by using four *rendezvous* relations. These relations provide an abstract view of an infinite relation in which the abstract **buffer** events are expanded. The synchronization requirements are caused by the synchronization requirement |[**middle**]| of the parallel operator between the two buffer processes which we display by two abstract events which represent their unevaluated behaviours. This *abstract view* of the **two slot buffer** already shows some details of the otherwise infinite bundle event structure. But after the single event **in?x:Any** occurs, no other events can happen without interfering with a rendezvous relations between an abstract event and a non-abstract event. How to continue at this point? Expansion does not resolve the rendezvous constraints. Fortunately, at this point we can prove that although the **middle** events are both in a rendezvous relation with an abstract **buffer** event, they can never synchronize with any of these events after expansion. Thus the expansion may proceed by synchronizing the two **middle** events (thereby ignoring the abstract events in the rendezvous relations). And so on.

It is a two step approach. First, we replace the LOTOS parallel operator in the Bundle Event Structure domain by *rendezvous* relations. In the second step, we prune the resulting Bundle Event Structure based on configurations, or system runs. This last step is somewhat under-specified because in this step several strategies can be employed. Currently, we are investigating one of these strategies based on *Goal Oriented Execution*[24, 25]. After pruning, we obtain a Bundle Event Structure in which the *init* events (see [6]) are no longer contained in a rendezvous relation with an infinite rendezvous set (see definition 3.3). Then we can employ the expansion as explained informally above.

The shift towards a relational model for the synchronization operator (in contrast with the original model which completely removes the synchronization information from the Bundle Event Structure by mapping synchronization events onto a single new event) is an essential step for lazy evaluation. But it can also be used for reach-ability analysis and subsequent optimizations of synchronization. It also allows for local changes which do not affect the whole behaviour.

The novel concept in the process domain is therefore the introduction of the rendezvous ($\Vdash$) relation in the Bundle Event Structure model which complies with lazy evaluation.

Definition 3.1 ("Full" Bundle Event Structure)

The *Bundle Event Structure* $\mathcal{E}^{\otimes}$ is now a four tuple $(E^{\otimes}, \rightsquigarrow, \mapsto, \Vdash)$ with:

- o $E^{\otimes} \subseteq E \times Act \times \overline{Off} \times \overline{Pre}$, a set of *events* E, tupled with *event offers* from $\overline{Off}$ on gates in Act with *predicates* from $\overline{Pre}$, where:

    $E \subseteq Evt$, the *events*

    $Act = \{i\} \cup \{g : g \text{ a label/gate in } S\}$

    $\overline{Off} \subseteq (!Exp|?Var : Typ)^*$, the *event offers*

    $\overline{Pre} \subseteq (Exp = Exp)^*$, the *predicates*

- o $\mapsto \subseteq (2^{E^{\otimes}} \times E^{\otimes})$, the *bundle set*
- o $\rightsquigarrow \subseteq (E^{\otimes} \times E^{\otimes})$, the *(asymmetric) conflict relation*
- o $\Vdash \subseteq (2^{E^{\otimes}} \times E^{\otimes})$, the *rendezvous set*

such that the following properties hold:

P1: $X^{\otimes} \mapsto e^{\otimes} \Rightarrow \forall e_1^{\otimes}, e_2^{\otimes} \in X^{\otimes} : (e_1^{\otimes} \neq e_2^{\otimes} \Rightarrow e_1^{\otimes} \rightsquigarrow e_2^{\otimes})$
P2: $\rightsquigarrow$ is irreflexive, i.e. $\forall e_1^{\otimes}, e_2^{\otimes} \in E^{\otimes} : (e_1^{\otimes} \rightsquigarrow e_2^{\otimes} \Rightarrow e_1^{\otimes} \neq e_2^{\otimes})$

The rendezvous relation complies with lazy evaluation because there is no longer a mapping of all synchronization events onto a single event, as in the original Bundle Event Structure model. Instead, such events are gathered in a rendezvous relation. As relations can typically be subjected to delayed evaluation, process recursion with synchronization can now be adequately modelled (we get a computational model for expansion, e.g. the enabling operator with value passing can be mapped to a rendezvous relation over the exit events on the left hand side with the *init* events on the right hand side, modulo event renamings).

Corollary 3.2 (Flattening)

We can always remove the rendezvous relation by a process called *flattening*. Flattening is a process with takes a rendezvous relation and removes it by generating all possible synchronizations thereby creating the same event structure as generated directly by the [] mapping in the original model. But as in the original model, this works only for finite (approximations of) event structures. In our case, we can use the same goal oriented techniques to reduce the synchronization contraints of a rendezvous relation, hopefully yielding a finite (sub-)event structure from which we can remove the rendezvous relation by the flattening process. This flattening process is loosely demonstrated by the following examples (event subscripts mark the origins of the events).

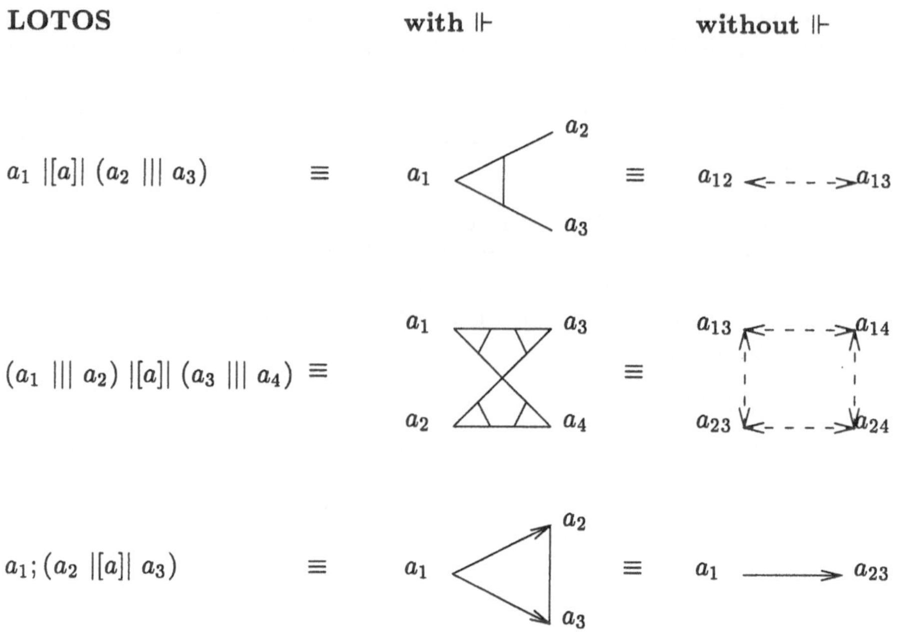

LOTOS	with ⊩	without ⊩

$a_1 \,|[a]|\,(a_2 \,|||\, a_3)$ $\quad\equiv\quad$ $a_1 \overset{a_2}{\underset{a_3}{<}}$ $\quad\equiv\quad$ $a_{12} \;\dashleftarrow\!-\!-\!\dashrightarrow\; a_{13}$

$(a_1 \,|||\, a_2)\,|[a]|\,(a_3 \,|||\, a_4) \equiv$ $\quad$ (diagram: a_1, a_3 top; a_2, a_4 bottom with crossing bundles) $\quad\equiv\quad$ $a_{13} \dashleftrightarrow a_{14}$, $a_{23} \dashleftrightarrow a_{24}$ (conflict box)

$a_1;(a_2 \,|[a]|\, a_3)$ $\quad\equiv\quad$ $a_1 \overset{a_2}{\underset{a_3}{\triangleleft}}$ $\quad\equiv\quad$ $a_1 \longrightarrow a_{23}$

In $a_1 \,|[a]|\,(a_2 \,|||\, a_3)$, the a_1 on the left hand side must either synchronize with the right hand a_2 or a_3. The flattening maps these two possibilities to a_{12} and a_{13} which must therefore be in mutual conflict.

Similar to the first one, $(a_1 \,|||\, a_2)\,|[a]|\,(a_3 \,|||\, a_4)$ now gives two events on both sides. The flattening gives a nice conflict box where either a_{13} and a_{24} may happen, or a_{14} and a_{23}, but no other combinations.

In $a_1;(a_2 \,|[a]|\, a_3)$, a_1 must precede both a_2 and a_3. But a_2 and a_3 must occur simultaneously because of the rendezvous relation. In the flattening this results in a single bundle from a_1 to the combined event a_{23}.

Figure 2: Flattening of rendezvous relations

The semantics of "Full" Bundle Event Structures is defined in terms of families of partially ordered sets. The ordering relation is defined over the events in $E^{\otimes}$. Therefore we need some new notion of "atomic" event, because the rendezvous relation which has been added to the model requires that two event occur simultaneously.

Definition 3.3 (Rendezvous Set)
A *rendezvous set* $\widehat{e}^{\otimes}$ is a minimal event set satisfying the rendezvous (or synchronization) restrictions: $\forall e^{\otimes} \in \widehat{e}^{\otimes} : X^{\otimes} \Vdash e^{\otimes} \Rightarrow \widehat{e}^{\otimes} \cap X^{\otimes} \neq \emptyset$.

Rendezvous sets play the rôle of atomic events ($\forall e_1^{\otimes}, e_2^{\otimes} \in \widehat{e}^{\otimes} : l(e_1^{\otimes}) = l(e_2^{\otimes})$). In [12], all events in a rendezvous set are mapped onto a single interaction event. Following is a reformulation and extension of [12] in terms of rendezvous sets and event interactions.

Definition 3.4 (Interaction Restriction)
The *interaction restriction* generated by the rendezvous set $\widehat{e}^\otimes$, notation $\overline{p}(\widehat{e}^\otimes)$, is defined as the union of the event predicates and the event interaction restrictions:
$\overline{p}(\widehat{e}^\otimes) = P \cup \text{MATCH} \cup \text{PASS} \cup \text{GEN}$ where:

$$
\begin{aligned}
\text{P} &= \bigcup_i \{\overline{p}_i | \langle e_i, -, -, \overline{p}_i \rangle \in \widehat{e}^\otimes\} \\
\text{MATCH} &= \bigcup_{i,j,k} \{E_k = E'_k | \langle e_i, g, \ldots !E_k \ldots, - \rangle, \langle e_j, g, \ldots !E'_k \ldots, - \rangle \in \widehat{e}^\otimes\} \\
\text{PASS} &= \bigcup_{i,j,k} \{x_k = E'_k | \langle e_i, g, \ldots ?x_k : t \ldots, - \rangle, \langle e_j, g, \ldots !E'_k \ldots, - \rangle \in \widehat{e}^\otimes\} \\
\text{GEN} &= \bigcup_{i,j,k} \{x_k = x'_k | \langle e_i, g, \ldots ?x_k : t \ldots, - \rangle, \langle e_j, g, \ldots ?x'_k : t \ldots, - \rangle \in \widehat{e}^\otimes\}
\end{aligned}
$$

Definition 3.5 (Rendezvous Set Enabling)
A rendezvous set $\widehat{e}^\otimes$ is *enabled* if $\overline{p}(\widehat{e}^\otimes) \nvdash \text{FALSE}$. The predicates $\overline{p}(\widehat{e})$ are evaluated in the (conditional) theory T derived from the Abstract Data Type part of the LOTOS specification (see Section 2).

In practice the decision procedure for $\overline{p}(\widehat{e}^\otimes) \nvdash \text{FALSE}$ might not yield a free variable substitution function ρ such that $\rho(\overline{p}(\widehat{e}^\otimes)) \vdash \text{TRUE}$, because equality in the most general sense is often not decidable within T [26]. But as said before, in practice this is often not an issue.

A *proving sequence* is a finite sequence of distinct rendezvous sets which is used to describe the dynamical behaviour of a system. Although a proving sequence itself is (partially) ordered, the events in a rendezvous set are unordered, because there can not be $\mapsto$ or $\rightsquigarrow$ relations between events in a rendezvous set (for the proof of this you need the mapping $[\![\,]\!][6]$). This reliefs us of the obligation to introduce equivalence classes for each possible successive numbering of events in proving sequences.

Definition 3.6 (Proving Sequence)
Let $\mathcal{E}^\otimes = (E^\otimes, \mapsto, \rightsquigarrow, \Vdash)$ be a "Full" Bundle Event Structure. A *proving sequence* is sequence of rendezvous sets $\widehat{e}^\otimes_1, \ldots, \widehat{e}^\otimes_n$ satisfying [2]:

1. $\widehat{e}^\otimes_i \cap \widehat{e}^\otimes_j = \emptyset, i \neq j$
2. $\widehat{e}^\otimes_1 \cup \cdots \cup \widehat{e}^\otimes_n$ is conflict-free
3. $X \mapsto e^\otimes_i \Longrightarrow \{e^\otimes_1, \ldots, e^\otimes_{i-1}\} \cap X^\otimes \neq \emptyset$
4. $e^\otimes_i \rightsquigarrow e^\otimes_j \Longrightarrow i < j$
5. $\bigcup_i \overline{p}(\widehat{e}^\otimes_i) \nvdash \text{FALSE}$

If $\widehat{e}^\otimes_1, \ldots, \widehat{e}^\otimes_n$ is a proving sequence, then $C^\otimes = \bigcup \widehat{e}^\otimes_1 \ldots \widehat{e}^\otimes_n$ is called a *configuration*. $C^\otimes$ can be identified as the flattening of all constituent rendezvous sets, $C^\otimes = \{e^\otimes_1, \ldots, e^\otimes_{\sum_{i=1}^n |\widehat{e}^\otimes_i|}\}, e^\otimes_{(\sum_{i=1}^{k-1}|\widehat{e}^\otimes_i|)+1} \cdots e^\otimes_{\sum_{i=1}^k |\widehat{e}^\otimes_i|} \in \widehat{e}^\otimes_k, 1 \leq k \leq n$. Proving sequences can be seen as (partial) system runs. After a proving sequence has occurred a new "Full" Bundle Event Structure emerges. This new system is called the *remainder*.

---

[2]We number the events in $\widehat{e}^\otimes_1, \ldots, \widehat{e}^\otimes_n$ successively.

Definition 3.7 (Remainder)
Let $\widehat{e}_1^{\otimes}, \ldots, \widehat{e}_n^{\otimes}$ be a proving sequence, $C^{\otimes}$ its corresponding configuration, $C^{\otimes}(= \{e_1^{\otimes}, \ldots, e_{\sum_{i=1}^{n} |\widehat{e}_i^{\otimes}|}^{\otimes}\})$. The *remainder* of $\mathcal{E}^{\otimes}$ after $C^{\otimes}$, notation $\mathcal{E}^{\otimes}[C^{\otimes}]$, is defined as follows:
$\mathcal{E}^{\otimes}[C^{\otimes}] = (E^{\otimes'}, \mapsto', \leadsto', \Vdash')$ where

$\circ \quad E^{\otimes'} \quad = \quad E^{\otimes} - C^{\otimes}$

$\circ \quad \mapsto' \quad = \quad \mapsto -\{(X^{\otimes}, e^{\otimes}) \mid X^{\otimes} \mapsto e^{\otimes} \wedge X^{\otimes} \cap C^{\otimes} \neq \emptyset\}$

$\circ \quad \leadsto' \quad = \quad (\leadsto \cap (E^{\otimes'} \times E^{\otimes'})) \cup$
$\qquad\qquad\qquad \{\{\} \mapsto e_1^{\otimes} \mid e_1^{\otimes} \in E^{\otimes'} \wedge \exists e_2^{\otimes} \in C^{\otimes} : e_1^{\otimes} \leadsto e_2^{\otimes}\}$

$\circ \quad \Vdash' \quad = \quad \Vdash \cap (E^{\otimes'} \times E^{\otimes'})$

Example 3.8 (Rendezvous with Remainder)
Given $(g!1 \;|||\; g!2 \;|||\; g!3) \;|[g]|\; (g?x : int \;|||\; g?y : int)$, we get for $\Vdash$:

$\begin{array}{ll}
(g!1, g!2, g!3) & \Vdash g?x : Int \\
(g!1, g!2, g!3) & \Vdash g?y : Int \\
(g?x : Int, g?y : Int) & \Vdash g!1 \\
(g?x : Int, g?y : Int) & \Vdash g!2 \\
(g?x : Int, g?y : Int) & \Vdash g!3
\end{array}$

The remainder of $\Vdash$ after the rendezvous set $\{g!1, g?x : Int\}$ is given by:

$\begin{array}{ll}
(g!2, g!3) & \Vdash g?y : Int \\
(g?y : Int) & \Vdash g!2 \\
(g?y : Int) & \Vdash g!3
\end{array}$

Unlike [12], we need some notion of current state w.r.t. data values for the open variables. In the above example, the rendezvous set $\{g!1, g?x : Int\}$ binds x to 1. This binding information must be preserved and passed onto the remaining bundle event structure.

Definition 3.9 (Data Environment)
A *(data) environment* for a "Full" Bundle Event Structure $\mathcal{E}^{\otimes} = (E^{\otimes}, \mapsto, \leadsto, \Vdash)$ is a list of predicates P which must be fulfilled for each event $e^{\otimes} \in E^{\otimes}$. In other words, the transition relation is decorated with a (global) guarding predicate list [3].

Definition 3.10 (Precedence Relation)
The precedence relation $\prec_{C^{\otimes}} \subseteq E^{\otimes} \times E^{\otimes}$ between rendezvous sets is defined by: $\widehat{e}_1 \prec_{C^{\otimes}} \widehat{e}_2^{\otimes}$ iff $\exists e_1^{\otimes} \in \widehat{e}^{\otimes}, e_2^{\otimes} \in \widehat{e}_2^{\otimes}, X^{\otimes} \subseteq E^{\otimes} : (e_1^{\otimes} \in X^{\otimes} \wedge X^{\otimes} \mapsto e_2^{\otimes}) \vee (e_1^{\otimes} \leadsto e_2^{\otimes})$. The relation $\leq_{C^{\otimes}}$ is defined as $\leq_{C^{\otimes}} = \prec_{C^{\otimes}}^{*}$, i.e. the reflexive and transitive closure of $\prec_{C^{\otimes}}$.

---

[3]This adheres more to the notion of states and transitions then intended. Unfortunately, taking the constraints directly into account seems not feasible at this stage.

Definition 3.11 (Labelled Partially Ordered Set)
Let $C^\otimes$ be a configuration of a Bundle Event Structure $\mathcal{E}^\otimes$. Then $\mathcal{E}^\otimes$ has a *labelled partially ordered set* or lposet corresponding to $C^\otimes$, notation $\overline{C}^\otimes$, defined as $\overline{C}^\otimes = (C^\otimes, \leq_{C^\otimes})$.

Now we are ready to define the lposet transition system. This is done in terms of states ("Full" Bundle Event Structures) and transitions (lposets) between states.

Definition 3.12 (Lposet Transition)
Let $\widehat{e}_1^\otimes, \ldots, \widehat{e}_n^\otimes$ be a proving sequence, $C^\otimes = \{e_1^\otimes, \ldots, e_{\sum_{i=1}^n |\widehat{e}_i^\otimes|}^\otimes\})$. We say

$\mathcal{E}^\otimes$ has a $\langle \mathcal{E}^\otimes, \overline{C}^\otimes, \mathcal{E}^{\otimes\prime} \rangle$ *transition* in a data environment P iff $(\mathcal{E}^\otimes(P)) \xrightarrow{\overline{C}^\otimes} (\mathcal{E}^{\otimes\prime}(P'))$, $\mathcal{E}^{\otimes\prime} = \mathcal{E}^\otimes[C^\otimes]$, and $P' = P \cup \bigcup_i \overline{p}(\widehat{e}_i^\otimes)$.

Definition 3.13 (Active Lposet Transition)
Let $\widehat{e}_1^\otimes, \ldots, \widehat{e}_n^\otimes$ be a proving sequence, $C^\otimes = \{e_1^\otimes, \ldots, e_{\sum_{i=1}^n |\widehat{e}_i^\otimes|}^\otimes\})$. A transition $\langle \mathcal{E}^\otimes, \overline{C}^\otimes, \mathcal{E}^{\otimes\prime} \rangle$ is *active* in a data environment P iff $\mathcal{E}^\otimes(P) \xrightarrow{\overline{C}^\otimes}$ and $P \cup \bigcup_i \overline{p}(\widehat{e}_i^\otimes) \nvdash \mathsf{FALSE}$.

The *concurrent transition system* is defined in terms of a partial *residual operation* over the transitions[22].

Definition 3.14 (Concurrent Transition System)
Let $\mathcal{E}^\otimes$ be a b.e.s., the *concurrent transition system* corresponding to $\mathcal{E}^\otimes$ in a data environment P is given by the tuple $\langle Sta, Tra \rangle$ where

- $Sta \stackrel{def}{=} \{\mathcal{E}^\otimes[C^\otimes] \mid (\mathcal{E}^\otimes(P)) \xrightarrow{\overline{C}^\otimes}\}$, is the set of *states*
- $Tra \stackrel{def}{=} \{\langle \mathcal{S}, \overline{C}^\otimes, \mathcal{S}' \rangle \in Sta \times \mathbf{Pos} \times Sta \mid (\mathcal{S}(P)) \xrightarrow{\overline{C}^\otimes} (\mathcal{S}'(P))\}$, is the set of active transitions, where $\mathbf{Pos}$ is the category of partially ordered rendezvous sets.

This gives us a full featured concurrent transition system for LOTOS in terms of our new model, with both data and a new relation called *rendezvous*.

4 Conclusions

In Section 2 we have extended the Bundle Event Structure model with data. This was a two step approach. First, from the *Abstract Data Types* in the LOTOS specification we derived a conditional theory T in which we evaluate our predicates (see [19, 20, 21]). Second, we extended the Bundle Event Structure model. The new Bundle Event Structure model has events augmented with LOTOS *actions*, with *event offers*, and with *predicates*. In order to define a *transition system* for this new model, we needed to introduce *environments* in which the interaction restrictions are collected. These environments are then passed onto subsequent behaviour. We did not show the mapping from LOTOS to our new Bundle Event Structure model. This mapping can easily be derived from the original mapping in [12, 6], given the above formalizations.

282

In Section 3 we have extended the Bundle Event Structure model with a *rendezvous* relation. Unfortunately, this is only part of the solution of how to deal with process recursion, or more specifically, process recursion in the presence of synchronizations. It is not an easy problem to solve in the realm of non-interleaving semantics, as opposed to the interleaving semantics counter part, and we do not propose here to have the answer to it. But we made a first step, and our current research on how to prune the *rendezvous* relations does seem promising. The intermediate level of abstraction provided us with more structural information then the "bare" event structure on the lowest level of abstraction. The flattening examples imply that we do not use the rendezvous relation to extend the intrinsic expressivity of the event structure model (it remains an intermediate model).

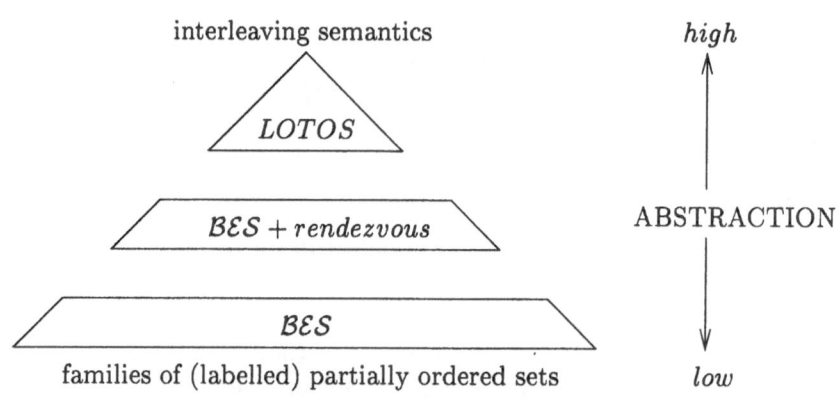

Figure 3: Abstraction levels

In this paper we have extend the *Bundle Event Structure* model with data. The presence of data in process algebras in general makes the underlying transition systems often infinite. As a result verification tools can only be used to give partial results by using finite approximation, or alternatively, by using some symbolic finite representation in which case narrowing techniques can provide more complete results (e.g. *SMILE* [21]).

We have also chosen a non-interleaving semantics. When considering timing aspects of systems it becomes clear that there is a significant difference between sequential and concurrent execution: $(a \mid\mid\mid b)$ and $(a;b \mathrel{[]} b;a)$. Yet in an interleaving framework, both systems are equal. The introduction of the *rendezvous* relation is a first step towards a non-interleaving semantics for full LOTOS.

Acknowledgements

I thank Rom Langerak for his guidance and early remarks on this paper, Pim Kars for his useful comments, and all members of the TIOS group for the pleasant atmosphere at work.

A   Bundle Event Structure model revisited

Definition 3.1 (Bundle Event Structure)

The *Bundle Event Structure* model is one the newer formalisms to compete in the realm of true-concurrency semantics models for process algebraic languages [10, 27, 7, 28, 12, 6, 13]. The following is based on [6] and extended to incorporate the data and rendezvous extensions.

A system modelled by a *Bundle Event Structure*, or $\mathcal{BES}$ for short, has the following ingredients:

Labelled events.
A Bundle Event Structure has a set of *events* $E^{\otimes}$; an event models the execution or occurrence of an *action* from a set of actions *Act*. The action that an event represents is given by an implicit *labelling function* $l : E^{\otimes} \to Act$. Different events can model executions of the same action; l is generally neither injective nor surjective. In Section 2 we have extended to notion of event to include the *gate identifier*, the *event offers* and the *predicates*. The denotation of an event is irrelevant and only serves to distinguish the event from other events. Only actions can be observed and not the events themselves. This means that in fact we consider event structures modulo event renaming; this allows for a LOTOS notation of events such as $g?x : Int[x < 5]$ in stead of $\langle e, g, ?x : Int, \{x < 5\}\rangle$.

We suppose that there is an infinite ("large enough") universe *Evt* of events.

Conflicts
We introduce a new relation between events, the *asymmetric conflict* relation $\rightsquigarrow$, with $\rightsquigarrow \subseteq E^{\otimes} \times E^{\otimes}$. Contrary to the # conflict relation in other models we do not require this relation to be symmetric, so if $e_1^{\otimes} \rightsquigarrow e_2^{\otimes}$ we do not require $e_2^{\otimes} \rightsquigarrow e_1^{\otimes}$ (we do allow $e_2^{\otimes} \rightsquigarrow e_1^{\otimes}$, so the relation is not antisymmetric !).

This relation can be considered to be a mixture of conflict and precedence. The intuitive meaning of $e_1^{\otimes} \rightsquigarrow e_2^{\otimes}$ is :

o if $e_2^{\otimes}$ occurs when $e_1^{\otimes}$ has not yet occurred, then $e_1^{\otimes}$ cannot happen anymore (as if it were the case that $e_1^{\otimes} \# e_2^{\otimes}$).

o if both $e_1^{\otimes}$ and $e_2^{\otimes}$ occur in a run, then $e_1^{\otimes}$ causally precedes $e_2^{\otimes}$ (as if it were the case that $\{e_1^{\otimes}\} \mapsto e_2^{\otimes}$)

The (asymmetric) conflict relation is irreflexive, therefore there are no selfconflicting events in this model. Impossible events (evens that can not happen which are not the same as self-conflicting events) are modelled by an empty bundle pointing towards the event (we use an irreflexive asymmetric conflict relation). They can be used to mark deadlock situations.

Bundles
This is the novel concept of the original Bundle Event Structure model. A bundle is a pair $(X^{\otimes}, e^{\otimes})$, with $X^{\otimes} \subseteq E^{\otimes}$, $e^{\otimes} \in E^{\otimes}$; notation $X^{\otimes} \mapsto e^{\otimes}$. The interpretation is that $X^{\otimes}$ is a set of causal conditions for $e^{\otimes}$, in the following sense: if $e^{\otimes}$ happens, at least one of the events in $X^{\otimes}$ has to have happened already. So an event $e^{\otimes}$ is enabled if for each bundle $X^{\otimes} \mapsto e^{\otimes}$, some $e^{\otimes'} \in X^{\otimes}$ has happened.

We want our event structures to be "stable" in the sense of [10] : given a run, the causal dependency between the events in the run should not be ambiguous. Suppose we would have a bundle $\{e_1^\otimes, e_2^\otimes\} \mapsto e^\otimes$ and $e_1^\otimes$, $e_2^\otimes$ and $e^\otimes$ would all occur in a certain run. Then we would not know whether $e^\otimes$ had been caused by $e_1^\otimes$ or $e_2^\otimes$. In order to avoid this we demand that for each bundle $X^\otimes \mapsto e^\otimes$, all events in $X^\otimes$ are pairwise in conflict, so if $e^\otimes$ happens, exactly one event in $X^\otimes$ has happened already. In this way we avoid causal ambiguity.

Note that we do allow $X^\otimes$ to be the empty set. If we have a bundle $\emptyset \mapsto e^\otimes$ then we call this an *empty* bundle and we call $e^\otimes$ an *impossible* event; impossible events can never happen. In this sense impossible events are similar to the self-conflicting events in flow event structures. However, it is always possible to remove impossible events. Impossible events (and empty bundles) therefore do not enhance the expressivity of Bundle Event Structures; they are just technically convenient in expressing some operations in a concise way.

Rendezvous.

A *rendezvous* relation $X^\otimes \Vdash e^\otimes$ is a binary relation between a single event $e^\otimes$ and an event set $X^\otimes$ such that at least one of the events in $X^\otimes$ must happen at the same time (synchronize) with the event $e^\otimes$. By turning the multi-way synchronization operator of LOTOS into a set of rendezvous relations in the Bundle Event Structure domain we allow for local changes to the synchronization restrictions to be made which do not affect the complete behaviour. Although only one event in $X^\otimes$ may synchronize with $e^\otimes$, different events in $X^\otimes$ do not, as is the case with bundles, exclude each other.

A *"Full" Bundle Event Structure* $\mathcal{E}^\otimes$ is a four tuple $(E^\otimes, \leadsto, \mapsto, \Vdash)$ with:

- $E^\otimes \subseteq E \times Act \times \overline{Off} \times \overline{Pre}$, An event models the execution (or occurrence) of an *action* from a set of actions Act. Events carry with them both their offers and their predicates.
- $\mapsto \subseteq (2^{E^\otimes} \times E^\otimes)$, the *bundle set*. The interpretation of the bundle $(X^\otimes \mapsto e^\otimes)$ is that $X^\otimes$ is the set of causal conditions for $e^\otimes$, in the following sense: if $e^\otimes$ happens, exactly one of the event in $X^\otimes$ has to have happened already. This is enforced by the first property: $X^\otimes \mapsto e^\otimes \Rightarrow \forall e_1^\otimes, e_2^\otimes \in X : (e_1^\otimes \neq e_2^\otimes \Rightarrow e_1^\otimes \leadsto e_2^\otimes)$.
- $\leadsto \subseteq (E^\otimes \times E^\otimes)$, the *(asymmetric) conflict relation*. The interpretation of the conflict $(e_1^\otimes \leadsto e_2^\otimes)$ is that if both $e_1^\otimes$ and $e_2^\otimes$ occur in a run, then $e_1^\otimes$ causally precedes $e_2^\otimes$, and if $e_2^\otimes$ occurs when $e_1^\otimes$ has not yet occurred, then $e_1^\otimes$ cannot happen anymore. The conflict relation is irreflexive, which is enforced by the second property: $\forall e_1^\otimes, e_2^\otimes \in E^\otimes : (e_1^\otimes \leadsto e_2^\otimes \Rightarrow e_1^\otimes \neq e_2^\otimes)$.
- $\Vdash \subseteq (2^{E^\otimes} \times E^\otimes)$, the *rendezvous relation*. The interpretation of the rendezvous $(X^\otimes \Vdash e^\otimes)$ is that if $e^\otimes$ occurs in a run, exactly one of the events in $X^\otimes$ must happen also, and within the same synchronization as $e^\otimes$. That is, such paired events rendezvous in a single interaction.

We represent a Bundle Event Structure graphically in the following way [28, 29, 30]. Events are drawn as dots; near the dot we sometimes give the event name and/or the action (and offers/predicates). Asymmetrical conflicts are indicated by dotted arrows. A bundle $X^\otimes \mapsto e^\otimes$ is indicated by drawing an arrow from each element of $X^\otimes$ to $e^\otimes$ and connecting all the arrows by small lines. Here we adopt that representation, and extend it a little to incorporate both the rendezvous relation and the data extensions ($\mapsto$ and $\Vdash$ relations are represented as hyper arcs, t.i. multi source arcs). Event identity is preserved by the graphical dot.

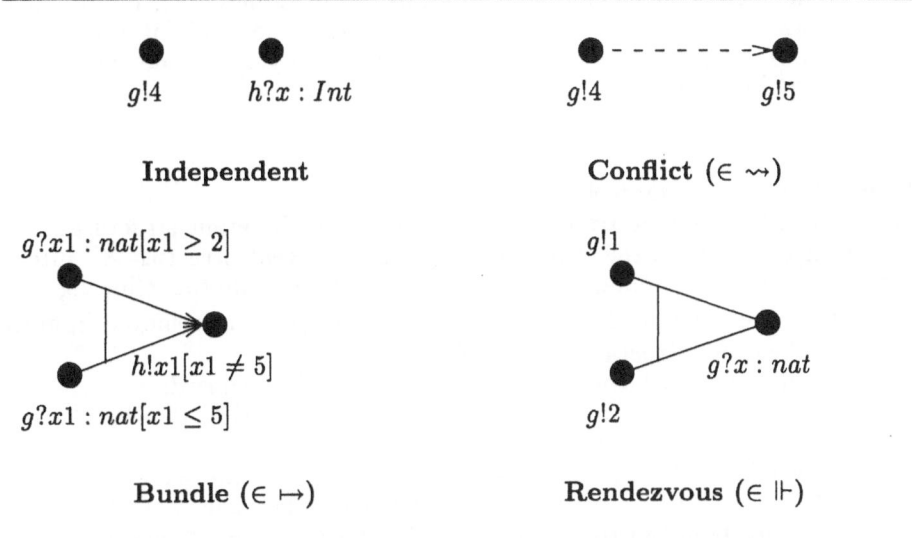

Figure 4: Graphical representation of the relations

Definition 3.3 (Rendezvous set)
Each event participating in a rendezvous relation must find one partner to synchronize with. The minimal condition is essential because it allows for multiple events from the same rendezvous relation to participate in a rendezvous set provided all these events have found different partners to synchronize with.

Definition 3.4 (Interaction restriction)
P denotes the collection of predicates of all events in $\widehat{e}^{\otimes}$, MATCH the collection of all synchronization constraints w.r.t. value matching, t.i. both events carry send offers, PASS the collection of all synchronization constraints w.r.t. value passing, t.i. one events carries a send offer whereas the other carries the receive offer, and finally GEN denotes the collection of all synchronization constraints w.r.t. value generation, t.i. both events carry receive offers.

Definition 3.6 (Proving sequence)

1. Each event may be contained in one rendezvous set only. This ensures that each event can happen only once.
2. Two events $e_1^{\otimes}$ and $e_2^{\otimes}$ are said to be in conflict if both $e_1^{\otimes} \rightsquigarrow e_2^{\otimes}$ and $e_2^{\otimes} \rightsquigarrow e_1^{\otimes}$. A event set $E^{\otimes}$ is conflict-free if no two events in $E^{\otimes}$ are in conflict. Obviously, $\widehat{e}_1^{\otimes} \cup \cdots \cup \widehat{e}_n^{\otimes}$ must be conflict-free.
3. For each bundle $X^{\otimes} \mapsto e^{\otimes}$, at least one event in $X^{\otimes}$ must have happened before $e^{\otimes}$ may happen. This is ensured by this second requirement $X^{\otimes} \mapsto e_i^{\otimes} \implies \{e_1^{\otimes}, \ldots, e_{i-1}^{\otimes}\} \cap X^{\otimes} \neq \emptyset$.

4. The conflict relation is asymmetrical, t.i. if $e_1^\otimes \leadsto e_2^\otimes$ and $e_2^\otimes$ happens, than $e_1^\otimes$ can not happen anymore. But if $e_1^\otimes$ happens, than $e_2^\otimes$ can still happen. This is enforced by the fourth requirement $e_i^\otimes \leadsto e_j^\otimes \Longrightarrow i < j$.

5. The interaction restrictions are taken into account by the fifth requirement. These predicates may contain free variables. Therefore, there exists a substitution for the free variables if and only if the evaluation of the predicates in the (conditional) theory T does not yield false: $\bigcup_i \bar{p}(\hat{e}_i^\otimes) \not\vdash \text{FALSE}$.

Definition 3.7 (Remainder)

We would like to define transition relations on bundle event structures. For this we need to define the remainder of a Bundle Event Structure $\mathcal{E}^\otimes$ after a configuration $C^\otimes$. To obtain this remainder, we have to do the following:

- After the events in $C^\otimes$ have happened, they should be removed from the bundle event structure: $E^{\otimes'} = E^\otimes - C^\otimes$.
- All bundles which contain events in $C^\otimes$ must be removed:
  $\mapsto' = \mapsto - \{(X^\otimes, e^\otimes) \mid X^\otimes \mapsto e^\otimes \wedge X^\otimes \cap C^\otimes \neq \emptyset \}$. Note that if $X^\otimes \mapsto e^\otimes$ and $e^\otimes \in C^\otimes$ then $X^\otimes \cap C^\otimes \neq \emptyset$.
- All conflicts which contain events in $C^\otimes$ must be removed:
  $\leadsto' = (\leadsto \cap (E^{\otimes'} \times E^{\otimes'}))$, but we must add impossible events (by means of empty bundles) to all events $e_1^\otimes$ if $e_1^\otimes \leadsto e_2^\otimes$ and $e_2^\otimes$ has happened: $\{\{\} \mapsto e_1^\otimes \mid e_1^\otimes \in E^{\otimes'} \wedge \exists e_2^\otimes \in C^\otimes : e_1^\otimes \leadsto e_2^\otimes\}$.
- All events in $C^\otimes$ must be removed from the rendezvous relation:
  $\Vdash' = \Vdash \cap (E^{\otimes'} \times E^{\otimes'})$.

Definition 3.10 (Precedence relation)

If we add to a configuration the information on causal ordering we obtain a labelled partially ordered set (see e.g. [13]). Lposets form the basic underlying semantics for event structures in the sense that all other semantics can be defined on top of lposet semantics.

The precedence relation is a binary relation between rendezvous sets. Given two rendezvous sets $\hat{e}_1^\otimes$ and $\hat{e}_2^\otimes$ in a single configuration $C^\otimes$, then $\hat{e}_1^\otimes \prec_{C^\otimes} \hat{e}_2^\otimes$ if either there exists an event $e_1^\otimes$ in $\hat{e}_1^\otimes$, and an event $e_2^\otimes$ in $\hat{e}_2^\otimes$ with a bundle between $e_1^\otimes$ and $e_2^\otimes$ (causal dependence): $e_1^\otimes \in X^\otimes \wedge X^\otimes \mapsto e_2^\otimes$, or, there exists a asymmetric conflict relation between $e_1^\otimes$ and $e_2^\otimes$: $e_1^\otimes \leadsto e_2^\otimes$. Note that since both $e_1^\otimes$ and $e_2^\otimes$ are present in the configuration $C^\otimes$, $e_1^\otimes$ must causally precede $e_2^\otimes$.

Definition 3.12 (Lposet transition)

Clearly, we must have a proving sequence $\hat{e}_1^\otimes, \ldots, \hat{e}_n^\otimes$ with configuration $C^\otimes$ of $\mathcal{E}^\otimes$. And, the interaction restrictions, $\bigcup_i \bar{p}(\hat{e}_i^\otimes)$, together with P, the environment, must not yield FALSE. The two other requirement determine the result of $\mathcal{E}^\otimes$ resp. P after the transition has occurred. $\mathcal{E}^\otimes$ transforms itself into its remainder, $\mathcal{E}^{\otimes'} = \mathcal{E}^\otimes[C^\otimes]$, and the new environment now also contains the interaction restrictions, $P' = P \cup \bigcup_i \bar{p}(\hat{e}_i^\otimes)$. For $\mathcal{E}^\otimes$ to have a transition

$\mathcal{E}^{\otimes} \xrightarrow{\overline{C}^{\otimes}} \mathcal{E}^{\otimes\prime}$, it is clear that:

- $C^{\otimes}$ must be a configuration of $\mathcal{E}^{\otimes}$
- $\overline{C}^{\otimes}$ must be the corresponding lposet of $C^{\otimes}$
- $\mathcal{E}^{\otimes}$ transforms itself into its remainder: $\mathcal{E}^{\otimes\prime} = \mathcal{E}^{\otimes}[C^{\otimes}]$

See also [22] on how to derive a *transition system*.

References

[1] G.V. Bochmann, A general transition model for protocol and communication services, IEEE Transactions on Communications, vol 28, nr 4, April 1980

[2] M. Diaz, Modelling and analysis of communication and cooperation protocols using Petri Net based models, In C. Sunshine, editor, Protocol Specification, Testing and Verification, II, Amsterdam, 1983

[3] U. Goltz, A. Rensink, Finite Petri Nets as Models for Recursive Causal Behaviour, Arbeitspapiere der GMD 604, Germany, 1991

[4] ISO 86b, Information processing systems, Estelle

[5] R. Milner, A Calculus of Communicating Systems, LNCS 92, Springer-Verlag, 1980

[6] R. Langerak, Transformations and Semantics for LOTOS, PhD. Thesis, University of Twente, The Netherlands, 1992

[7] G. Boudol, I. Castellani. Flow Models of Distributed Computations: Event Structures and Nets, INRIA Research Report 1482, Sophia Antipolis, France, 1991

[8] M. Nielsen, G. Plotkin, G. Winskel, Petri nets, event structures and domains, Theoretical Computer Science 13, 1981

[9] F.W. Vaandrager, A simple definition for parallel composition of prime event structures, Report ACMCS-R8903, Centre for Mathematics and Computer Science, Amsterdam, The Netherlands, 1989

[10] G. Winskel, An Introduction to Event Structures, LNCS 354, pp.364-397, Springer Verlag, 1989

[11] G. Winskel, Event structures semantics for CCS and related languages, Proc. 9th ICALP, LNCS 140, pp. 561-576, 1982

[12] R. Langerak, Bundle Event Structures, Fifth International Conference on Formal Description Techniques, Perros-Guirec, France, 1992

[13] A. Rensink, *Posets for Configurations!*, Memoranda Informatica 91-20, december 1991, CONCUR, 1992

[14] ISO 8807, Information processing systems, LOTOS - A formal description technique based on the temporal ordering of observational behaviour,

[15] J. Schot, The role of Architectural Semantics in the formal approach of Distributed Systems Design, PhD. Thesis, University of Twente, The Netherlands, 1992

[16] J.P. Katoen, R. Langerak, D. Latella, Modelling Systems by Probabilistic Process Algebra, An Event Structures Approach, Forte, Boston, USA, 1993

[17] B. Botma, Protocol Visualization, A (Bundle) Event Structure Approach, Memoranda Informatica, University of Twente, The Netherlands, 1992

[18] E. Madelaine, LOTOS to basic LOTOS projections, Reference Lo/WP2-/T2.2/INRIA/N004, Deliverable LOTOSPHERE project (#2304), June 1990

[19] J.M. Hullot, Canonical forms and unification, Proc. 5th Conference on Automated Deduction, Springer-Verlag, 1980

[20] H. Hussmann, Unification in conditional-equational theories, EUROCAL 204, Springer-Verlag, 1985

[21] H. Eertink, D. Wolz, Symbolic execution of LOTOS specifications, Fifth International Conference on Formal Description Techniques, Perros-Guirec, France, 1992

[22] E.W. Stark, Concurrent transition systems, Theoretical Computer Science, 64, pages 221-269, 1989

[23] D. Latella, Recursive Bundle Event Structures, Memoranda Informatica 93-27, University of Twente, The Netherlands, 1993

[24] M. Haj-Hussein, L. Logrippo, J. Sincennes, Goal-Oriented Execution for LOTOS, Fifth International Conference on Formal Description Techniques, FORTE92, Lanion, France, 1992

[25] H. Brinksma, H. Eertink, Goal-driven LOTOS execution, Protocol Specification, Testing and Verification, PSTV XIII Liege, Belgium, 1993

[26] B. Botma, A Meta-level Solution for Recursion, Protocol Simulation with Bundle Event Structures, Memoranda Informatica, University of Twente, The Netherlands, 1993

[27] G. Boudol, I. Castellani. Flow Models of Distributed Computations: Three Equivalent Semantics for CCS, INRIA Research Report 1484, Sophia Antipolis, France, 1991

[28] R. Langerak, Event Structures for the Design and Transformation in LO-TOS, In K. Parker, G. Rose, editors, Fourth International Conference on Formal Description Techniques, pages 271-287, Sydney, Australia, 1991

[29] D.H. New, Protocol Visualization, Ph.D. Thesis, University of Delaware, 1991

[30] F.N. Paulish, W.F. Tichy, EDGE: And Extendible Graph Editor, Software-Practice and Experience, vol. 20(S1), june 1990

Syntactic Action Refinement in Presence of Multiway Synchronization

Djamel-Eddine Saïdouni and Jean-Pierre Courtiat

LAAS-CNRS 7, av. du Colonel Roche

31077 Toulouse France

Abstract

This paper deals with the action refinement problem in process algebra, which consists in replacing actions at a given level of abstraction by processes at a lower level. We show how the problem may be dealt with in presence of multiway synchronization and illustrate our approach by applying it to a language derived from the standardized Formal Description Technique LOTOS [12]. Two solutions are proposed : the first solution does not make any a priori assumption about action atomicity, and the second solution corresponds to a slight modification of the first one, which shows how action atomicity may still be preserved in presence of action refinement.

1   Introduction

Looking at several ongoing works on action refinement, we can classify the approaches undertaken in two main categories: (i) either action refinement is performed on a wide spectrum specification language for distributed systems like CCS, ACP, LOTOS or even Petri nets [1, 11, 7, 8, 15] (ii) or action refinement is performed on a semantic domain for concurrent systems like Event Structures or Causal Trees [17, 6].

Clearly, our work belongs to the first category for which we can further distinguish two ways of performing action refinement: (i) either action refinement is performed by means of syntactical substitution, i.e. substituting a process for any action to be refined , (ii) or refinement is performed by means of a new operator of the language.

Performing action refinement by means of syntactical substitution (referred to as a syntactic refinement in the sequel) appears to be very natural and interesting, as it permits to formalize the design trajectory of a system, in which the specification provided for each design step is fully consistent with the initial specification [13].

As already shown in [5], performing syntactic action refinement implies to carefully address the synchronisation issue, which is far from being obvious when multiway synchronization is to be dealt with. In [5], we have proposed a solution for the action refinement problem in LOTOS based on the introduction of a new operator, namely refinement operator ρ, whose operational semantics has been provided within the causality-based framework initially introduced in [3]. Also, in [7], Degano and Gorrieri have defined an action refinement operator, and within the context of an interleaving semantics, they did succeed, by means of some semantical level treatment, to escape from the synchronization problem. However, both solutions, as proposed in [5] and [7], are not satisfactory from a practical point of view, as they do not permit to perform actually syntactic substitution of actions by processes along a design trajectory and until the final implementation stage. Finally, note that in [8], Engberg, Nielsen and Larsen propose a syntactic action refinement solution but they avoid the synchronization problem by imposing that no communication is possible in their language.

In conclusion of this discussion, we can say that any general solution for performing syntactic refinement should address the synchronization issue. It is our belief that resolving this issue is crucial in order to actually put action refinement to work in practice.

For formalizing the general solution proposed in this paper, we have chosen a language derived from Basic LOTOS [12]. In consequence, it is assumed that the reader has a basic knowledge of Basic LOTOS (see [2] for an introducing tutorial on LOTOS). The paper is organized into four main sections: in a first section, we discuss the problems induced by the multiway synchronization and present step by step the intuition behind our proposal; in a second section, we formalize the proposed refinement approach by applying it to a language derived from Basic LOTOS; in a third section, we discuss the action atomicity issue and show how this assumption may be dealt with in our approach; finally, in a conclusion section, we relate our proposal to ongoing works on action refinement.

2 Action refinement and synchronization

Let us first consider process $E \equiv a; stop|[a]|a; stop$. This process may offer action a leading to transition $E \xrightarrow{a} stop|[a]|stop$. If one wants to perform the refinement of action a by some process $P \equiv b; c; exit$ (we note this refinement by $\rho(a, P, E)$), it appears to be intuitive to proceed in the following way:

1. to replace (syntactically) action a by process P within process E

2. to use the Basic LOTOS enabling operator $>>$ instead of the prefixing operator ;

3. to replace, within the synchronization gate list of the parallel operator, action a by process P actions.

This results in $\rho(a, P, E) \equiv (b; c; exit) >> stop|[b, c]|(b; c; exit) >> stop$.
Interpreting the refined action as a process leads therefore to the following transitions:
$\rho(a, P, E) \xrightarrow{b} \xrightarrow{c} \xrightarrow{i} \xrightarrow{i} stop|[b, c]|stop$, the two internal action occurrences being the consequence of process P termination. But, unfortunately, things are not always so simple, as deadlocks may be induced when considering the model branching structure [8]. This may be shown by the following example:
let $P \equiv b; exit[]b; b; exit$; then, performing the refinement in the same way as previously, results in:

$\rho(a, P, E) \equiv (\mathbf{b}; exit[]b; b; exit) >> stop|[b]|(b; exit[]\mathbf{b}; b; exit) >> stop.$ It should be clear, that the following transitions are now possible (selecting the bold b for synchronization):

$\rho(a, P, E) \xrightarrow{b} \xrightarrow{i} stop|[b]|(b; exit) >> stop$ which corresponds to a deadlock state, where execution of part of process P is pending forever. Thus, due the combination of both synchronization and nondeterminism, the result is clearly not the expected one. Before developing our approach for addressing the action refinement issue in presence of synchronisations, we will first try to study more into details the reasons which led to this problem.

Assuming a design methodology like the one defined within the LotoSphere project [13], let us consider the LOTOS specification of some intermediate design along the design trajectory, and let $Design(N)$ be the name given to this specification. Actions defined in $Design(N)$ represent in fact abstractions of some behaviors which are not interesting at the abstraction level associated with this stage of the design trajectory. Performing a new design step by action refinement, consists therefore in exhibiting the behavior associated with some action, let us say a, of $Design(N)$; then, action a is to be replaced by some process, let us say P, in the new specification, $Design(N + 1)$. It is exactly what we proposed to do before, and we saw a problem in presence of both synchronisation and non-determinism. The reason of this problem is just the following: performing such a syntactic substitution (substituting process P for action a) led us to forgetting about the origin of the actions of P, i.e. action a of specification $Design(N)$.

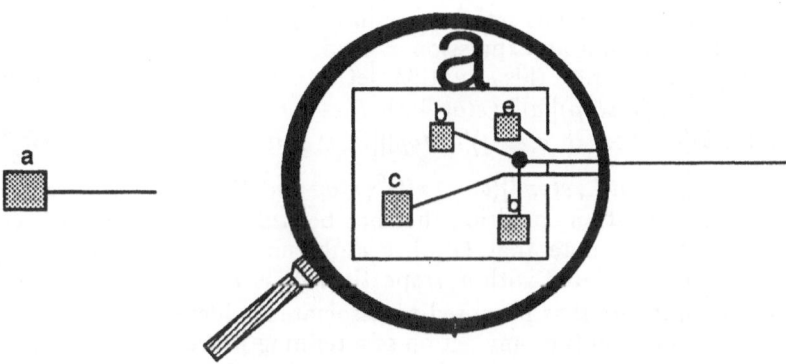

Figure 1: Actions are Abstractions of Processes

This remark is the keypoint of our proposal, which will be formalized in the next section. To be able to keep track of the origin of the processes present in a specification, we introduce the following abstraction operator : $\langle P \rangle^a$ means that action a is an abstraction of process P, or conversely that process P is the refinement of action a; we will show how to deal with this new information, i.e. action a which is the origin of process P, to resolve the problems induced by the presence of both synchronisation and non-determinism. As $\langle P \rangle^a$ is understood as action a abstracting process P, we will use the classical action prefixing operator, instead of the enabling operator, for expressing the sequential composition of $\langle P \rangle^a$ with some process Q (i.e. $\langle P \rangle^a; Q$).

To look at the problems induced by both synchronization and non determinism, let us consider again the last example, using abstraction operator $\langle P \rangle^a$: then, let $\rho(a, P, E) \equiv G|[a]|H \equiv \langle b; exit[\,]b; b; exit \rangle^a; stop|[a]|\langle b; exit[\,]b; b; exit \rangle^a; stop$ [1].

A necessary condition for ensuring that the synchronization may be performed as required, is that the refinement residues of action a are equal for both G and H after the occurrence of each action of refining process P (such an action is referred to as a sub-action of a). Thus, let $G \xrightarrow{(b)^a} G' \equiv \langle exit \rangle^a; stop$, where $\langle b \rangle^a$ is action b of process P which is itself the refinement of previous action a, then the refinement residue of a in G', noted $G'[a]$, is $exit$. In a similar way, let us consider the possible derivations for process H with respect to action $\langle b \rangle^a$, i.e. $H \xrightarrow{(b)^a} H'$; imposing that $G'[a] \equiv H'[a]$, as previously mentionned, then $H \xrightarrow{(b)^a} H' \equiv \langle exit \rangle^a; stop$ is the unique possible derivation for H; then, finally, $\rho(a, P, E) \xrightarrow{(b)^a} \langle exit \rangle^a; stop|[a]|\langle exit \rangle^a; stop$.

The reason for not modifying the synchronisation gate list within the parallel operator is to make it possible to refine actions within some process E by processes containing themselves actions already present in the initial process E. For instance, let us consider the following process:

$E \equiv (a; stop|||b; stop)|[a]|a; stop$, with $P \equiv b; c; exit$; then, $\rho(a, P, E) \equiv ((\langle b; c; exit \rangle^a; stop|||b; stop)|[a]|(\langle b; c; exit \rangle^a; stop)$; the synchronization on b deals therefore only with the occurrence of b which is a consequence of the refinement of action a by process P, and not with the occurrence of action b already present in the specification of process E.

However, this solution is not satisfactory in the general case, as the presence of several a actions within an expression E leads to an ambiguity for refinement residue $E[a]$. To illustrate this situation, let us consider the following example: Let $E \equiv (a; stop|||a; stop)|[a]|a; stop$ with $P \equiv b; c; exit$; then $\rho(a, P, E) \equiv G|[a]|H \equiv (\langle b; c; exit \rangle^a; stop|||\langle b; c; exit \rangle^a; stop)|[a]|\langle b; c; exit \rangle^a; stop$.

If $G \xrightarrow{(b)^a} G' \equiv \langle c; exit \rangle^a; stop|||\langle b; c; exit \rangle^a; stop$ and $H \xrightarrow{(b)^a} H' \equiv \langle c; exit \rangle^a; stop$ then the synchronization condition that has been defined previously is $G'[a] \equiv H'[a]$. It is easy to note that $G'[a]$ is ambiguous, because two refinement residues may be associated with a, respectively $c; exit$ and $b; c; exit$.

To solve this problem, it is proposed to associate an identifier with the occurrence of any sub-action (i.e. any action of a refining process), and to propagate this identifier to the refinement residue generated by the sub-action occurrence. In order to be consistent, we assume that a special identifier $\bot$ is associated with each refinement residue for which no action has yet occurred (in other words, the refinement residue is still in its initial state). Applying this approach to the previous example leads to the following derivations:

$G \xrightarrow{(b)^a_x} G' \equiv \langle c; exit \rangle^a_x; stop|||\langle b; c; exit \rangle^a_\bot; stop$, and $H \xrightarrow{(b)^a_y} H' \equiv \langle c; exit \rangle^a_y; stop$.

The synchronization condition may then be stated as $G'[x] \equiv H'[y]$. After the synchronization, identifiers x and y should be unified (by substituting z for both x and y), as the synchronization characterizes the occurrence of only one

---

[1]Note that the synchronization gate within the E parallel operator is still a after the refinement of a by $b; exit[\,]b; b; exit$

action. The following derivation can then be obtained:

$$\rho(a, P, E) \xrightarrow{(b)_{\perp}^{a}} \xrightarrow{(c)_{\perp}^{a}} \xrightarrow{(i)_{\perp}^{a}} (stop|||\langle b; c; exit\rangle_{\perp}^{a}; stop)|[a]|stop$$

Unfortunately, this solution is still not satisfactory in the general case. To be convinced, let us consider the following example:

$E \equiv (a; stop|||a; stop)|[a]|(a; stop|||a; stop)$ with $P \equiv b; c; exit$. Then

$\rho(a, P, E) \equiv$

$(\langle b; c; exit\rangle_{\perp}^{a}; stop|||\langle b; c; exit\rangle_{\perp}^{a}; stop)|[a]|(\langle b; c; exit\rangle_{\perp}^{a}; stop|||\langle b; c; exit\rangle_{\perp}^{a}; stop)$

Applying the synchronization condition established before, the following derivations are possible:

$$\rho(a, P, E) \xrightarrow{(b)_{x}^{a}} \xrightarrow{(b)_{y}^{a}} I|[a]|J \equiv$$

$(\langle c; exit\rangle_{x}^{a}; stop|||\langle c; exit\rangle_{y}^{a}; stop)|[a]|(\langle c; exit\rangle_{x}^{a}; stop|||\langle c; exit\rangle_{y}^{a}; stop).$

The occurrence of sub-action $\langle b\rangle_{x}^{a}$ (respectively $\langle b\rangle_{y}^{a}$) has led to the refinement residues $c; exit$ (respectively $c; exit$). Applying again the synchronization condition leads to the following possible derivations:

$I \xrightarrow{(c)_{u}^{a}} I' \equiv (\langle exit\rangle_{u}^{a}; stop|||\langle c; exit\rangle_{y}^{a}; stop)$, and

$J \xrightarrow{(c)_{v}^{a}} J' \equiv (\langle c; exit\rangle_{x}^{a}; stop|||\langle exit\rangle_{v}^{a}; stop)$

One can note that $I'[u] \equiv J'[v]$, making it possible to synchronize I and J in the following way:

$I|[a]|J \xrightarrow{(c)_{w}^{a}} (\langle exit\rangle_{w}^{a}; stop|||\langle c; exit\rangle_{y}^{a}; stop)|[a]|(\langle c; exit\rangle_{x}^{a}; stop|||\langle exit\rangle_{w}^{a}; stop).$

This synchronization is not correct, because we mismatched the refinement residues. To avoid this problem, we add identifiers to the transition derivations to ensure that only the residues generated by the same sub-action occurrence are allowed to proceed their synchronization. The derivations are now (look at the purpose of new identifiers x and y):

$I \xrightarrow{x(c)_{u}^{a}} I' \equiv (\langle exit\rangle_{u}^{a}; stop|||\langle c; exit\rangle_{y}^{a}; stop)$, and

$J \xrightarrow{y(c)_{v}^{a}} J' \equiv (\langle c; exit\rangle_{x}^{a}; stop|||\langle exit\rangle_{v}^{a}; stop).$

As expected, the synchronization cannot take place, as $x \neq y$.

The solution as presented at this stage of the discussion is indeed correct, and leads to the expected multiway synchronizations in presence of syntactic action refinements. This approach is formalized in the next section.

3 Formalization

This section is made up of three paragraphs: in a first paragraph, we define the language on which action refinement will be performed; then, in a second paragraph, we develop the operational semantics of this language using the SOS style; finally, in a last paragraph, we characterize a strong bisimulation.

3.1 The Language

For formalizing our approach, we have considered a language derived from Basic LOTOS which embodies the main features encountered in most concurrent

294

languages. The operators are the following:

- ; is the action prefix operator

- [] is the choice operator

- $|[L]|$ is the general parallel operator, where L represents the finite synchronization gate list

- *hide L in E* is the LOTOS hiding operator, where L represents the finite list of gates which will be hidden in E

- $recX.E$ is the fixed-point recursive operator of CCS

- $\langle P \rangle_x^a$ is our abstraction operator, where a is the abstraction of process P.

Let $\mathcal{G}$ be a finite set of *gates*, where L stands for an arbitrary finite subset of $\mathcal{G}$. Let also $Act = \mathcal{G} \cup \{i\}$ be the usual set of actions, where $i \overset{def}{\notin} \mathcal{G}$. The LOTOS successful termination action being noted δ, let $\mathcal{G}^\delta = \mathcal{G} \cup \{\delta\}$ be the set of the observable actions, and let $Act^\delta = Act \cup \{\delta\}$ be the set of all actions, ranged over by $a, b, \cdots$. Let furthermore $\mathcal{I}$ be a denumerable set of action identifiers ranged over by $\cdots, x, y, z, \perp \overset{def}{\notin} \mathcal{I}$ be a special identifier, and $\mathcal{I}^\perp$ denote $\mathcal{I} \cup \{\perp\}$. Finally, let Var be a denumerable set of variables, ranged over by $\cdots, X, Y, Z$. The syntax of the language may then be characterized by the following BNF-like syntax:

$E ::= stop \mid exit \mid a; E \mid \langle E \rangle_x^a; E' \mid E[]E' \mid E|[L]|E' \mid hide\ L\ in\ E \mid recX.E$

Terms generated by this syntax are called *behavior expressions*. Let $\mathcal{A}$, ranged over by $E, F, \cdots$, denote the set of all behavior expressions.

An occurrence of variable X is said to be *bound* in E iff it is in a term $recX.E'$ in E, otherwise it is said to be *free*. E is said to be a closed behavior expression if the set of the free variables in E is empty. Let $\mathcal{A}_0$, ranged over by $P, Q, \cdots$, denote the set of all closed behavior expressions, or shortly *"behaviors"*. [2]

Sets $\mathcal{L}$ and $\mathcal{L}_0$ are defined as the subsets of $\mathcal{A}$ and $\mathcal{A}_0$ respectively, whose terms are generated by the following BNF syntax (the same syntax as previously, but without the abstraction operator):

$E ::= stop \mid exit \mid a; E \mid E[]E' \mid E|[L]|E' \mid hide\ L\ in\ E \mid recX.E$ [3]

Definition 1 *Let E be a behavior expression; the set of the free action identifiers in E is defined by induction on the structure of E as follows:*

- $\Phi(stop) = \emptyset$ $\Phi(exit) = \emptyset$ $\Phi(a; E) = \emptyset$ $\Phi(recX.E) = \emptyset$
- $\Phi(hide\ L\ in\ E) = \Phi(E)$ $\Phi(E\ []\ F) = \Phi(E) \cup \Phi(F)$

- $\Phi(E\ |[L]|\ F) = \Phi(E) \cup \Phi(F)$ $\Phi(\langle E \rangle_x^a; F) = \begin{cases} \emptyset & \text{if } x = \perp \\ \{x\} & \text{otherwise} \end{cases}$

Action identifiers belonging to $\Phi(E)$ are said to be free in E.

---

[2] In order to avoid excessive use of parentheses, the usual priority order for the above operators is assumed. Symbols $|||$ and $||$ denote particular cases of the general parallel composition operator $\_|[L]|\_$, respectively when $L = \emptyset$ and $L = \mathcal{G}$.

[3] Without any loss of generality with respect to the purpose of the paper, we will consider in the sequel only closed behavior expressions.

For instance, let $E \equiv \langle \cdots \rangle_x^a; \ stop \ ||| \ \langle \cdots \rangle_y^b \ ; \ b; \ stop$, then, by construction, $\Phi(E) = \{x, y\}$.

A renaming function is defined below in order to substitute an identifier for another, as it will be required later when defining the language operational semantics.

Definition 2 *The renaming function is defined recursively on the structure of the behaviour expressions as follows:*

- $y/x stop \equiv stop$
- $y/x exit \equiv exit$
- $y/x(a; E) \equiv a; E$
- $y/x(recX.E) \equiv recX.E$
- $y/x(hide \ L \ in \ E) \equiv hide \ L \ in \ y/xE$
- $y/x(E \ [] \ F) \equiv y/xE \ [] \ y/xF$
- $y/x(E \ |[L]| \ F) \equiv y/xE \ |[L]| \ y/xF$
- $y/x(\langle E \rangle_z^a; F) \equiv \begin{cases} \langle E \rangle_z^a; F & \text{if } z = \bot \text{ or } z \neq x \\ \langle E \rangle_y^a; F & \text{otherwise} \end{cases}$

We proceed by defining formally the action refinement function [4].

Definition 3 *An action refinement function $\rho : Act \times \mathcal{L}_0^* \times \mathcal{A}_0 \longrightarrow \mathcal{A}_0$ is defined recursively on $\mathcal{A}_0$ terms, where $\mathcal{L}_0^* \subseteq \mathcal{L}_0$ is the set of finite behavior expressions, as follows:*

(r1) $\rho(a, P, stop) \equiv stop$

(r2) $\rho(a, P, exit) \equiv exit$

(r3) $\rho(a, P, b; E) \equiv b; \rho(a, P, E) \ if \ a \neq b$

(r4) $\rho(a, P, a; E) \equiv \langle P \rangle_\bot^a; \rho(a, P, E)$

(r5) $\rho(a, P, \langle E \rangle_x^b; F) \equiv \langle \rho(a, P, E) \rangle_x^b; \rho(a, P, F)$

(r6) $\rho(a, P, hide \ L \ in \ E) \equiv \begin{cases} hide \ L \ in \ \rho(a, P, E) & \text{if } a \notin L \\ hide \ L \ in \ E & \text{otherwise} \end{cases}$

(r7) $\rho(a, P, E[]F) \equiv \rho(a, P, E)[]\rho(a, P, F)$

(r8) $\rho(a, P, E|[L]|F) \equiv \rho(a, P, E)|[L]|\rho(a, P, F)$

(r9) $\rho(a, P, recX.E) \equiv recX.\rho(a, P, E)$

Only rules **(r4)**, **(r5)**, **(r6)** and **(r8)** require a short explanation.

Rule **(r4)** states that the refinement of action a by process P in process $a; E$ leads to process $\langle P \rangle_\bot^a; \rho(a, P, E)$; one can note that the identifier associated with P is equal to $\bot$; this expresses the fact that process P is still in its initial state (no sub-action of a, i.e. no action of P has yet occurred).

Rule **(r5)** deals with a multilevel refinement, which consists in refining an action within a process, which is already the refinement of another action.

Rule **(r6)** states that hidden actions cannot be refined; this restriction is consistent with most action refinement approaches described in the literature. However, from a theoretical point of view, it seems that our approach could be extended for refining hidden actions.

---

[4] For simplifying the presentation, and whenever there is no danger of confusion, we adopt the following notation conventions:

1. $\Phi(E)$ is shortly noted as E,

2. the braces of identifier unary sets are omitted

Following this convention, $y \notin E \backslash x$ is a shorthand notation for $y \notin \Phi(E) \backslash \{x\}$ where $\backslash$ denotes the usual set substraction operation.

Rule (r8) shows all the interest of action refinement in practice, as ρ distributes over the parallel operator; in other words, this means, that, when starting from some initial specification, it is possible to derive an implementation by stepwise refinement, where each parallel operator argument is executed on a distinct locality.

3.2 Operational semantics

Definition 4 *Transition relation* $\longrightarrow \subseteq A_0 \times \mathcal{I}^\perp \times Act^\delta \times Act^\delta \times \mathcal{I}^\perp \times A_0$ *is defined as the least relation satisfying the following rules:*

(1) $$\frac{}{exit \xrightarrow{\perp (\delta)^\delta_\perp} stop}$$

(2) $$\frac{}{a;E \xrightarrow{\perp (a)^a_\perp} E}$$

(3.a) $$\frac{E \xrightarrow{x (c)^b_y} E'}{(E)^a_z;F \xrightarrow{x (c)^a_z} (E')^a_z;F} \quad \text{for any } t \in \mathcal{I}$$

(3.b) $$\frac{E \xrightarrow{x (\delta)^b_y} E'}{(E)^a_z;F \xrightarrow{x (i)^a_z} F}$$

(4) $$\frac{E \xrightarrow{x (b)^a_y} E'}{E[]F \xrightarrow{x (b)^a_y} E' \qquad F[]E \xrightarrow{x (b)^a_y} E'}$$

(5.a) $$\frac{E \xrightarrow{x (b)^a_\perp} E'}{E|[L]|F \xrightarrow{x (b)^a_\perp} E'|[L]|F \qquad F|[L]|E \xrightarrow{x (b)^a_\perp} F|[L]|E' \text{ if } a \notin L^\delta}$$

(5.b) $$\frac{E \xrightarrow{x (b)^a_y} E'}{E|[L]|F \xrightarrow{x (b)^a_z} z/yE'|[L]|F \qquad F|[L]|E \xrightarrow{x (b)^a_z} F|[L]|z/yE' \text{ if } a \notin L^\delta \text{ and } y \neq \perp}$$
$$\text{for any } z \notin F \cup E' \backslash y \cup \{\perp\}$$

(5.c) $$\frac{E \xrightarrow{x (b)^a_\perp} E' \qquad F \xrightarrow{x (b)^a_\perp} F'}{E|[L]|F \xrightarrow{x (b)^a_\perp} E'|[L]|F' \text{ if } a \in L^\delta}$$

(5.d) $$\frac{E \xrightarrow{x (b)^a_y} E' \qquad F \xrightarrow{x (b)^a_z} F'}{E|[L]|F \xrightarrow{x (b)^a_t} t/yE'|[L]|t/zF' \text{ if } a \in L^\delta \text{ if } a \in L^\delta , y,z \neq \perp \text{ and } E'(y) \doteq F'(z)}$$
$$\text{for any } t \notin E' \backslash y \cup F' \backslash z \cup \{\perp\}$$

(6) $$\frac{E \xrightarrow{x (b)^a_y} E'}{hide \ L \ in \ E \xrightarrow{x (i)^a_y} hide \ L \ in \ E' \text{ if } a \in L \qquad hide \ L \ in \ E \xrightarrow{x (b)^a_y} hide \ L \ in \ E' \text{ if } a \notin L}$$

(7) $$\frac{[(recX.E)/X]E \xrightarrow{x (b)^a_y} E'}{recX.E \xrightarrow{x (b)^a_y} E'}$$

Rules (1) and (2) mean that when an action occurrence comes from a process which is not itself the refinement of another action, then both sub-action identifiers are $\perp$, because there are no refinement residue neither before nor after the sub-action occurrence (note that in this case, the sub-action is in fact an action).

Rule (3.a) characterizes multilevel refinement; it states that if a refinement residue E of action a offers sub-action c ($c \neq \delta$) of action b, which is itself a sub-action of action a, then c is considered as sub-action of a.

Rule (3.b) expresses the successful termination of a refinement residue; it states that if refinement residue E of action a offers δ, then δ enables process F after the occurrence of an internal action (see the semantics of the enabling operator in Basic LOTOS); the presence of the $\perp$ identifier is a consequence of the termination of the refinement residue.

Rule **(4)** corresponds to the classical semantics of the choice operator; it expresses the fact that $E[]F$ behaves either like E or F.

Rules **(5.a)** and **(5.b)** express the semantics of the parallel operator without synchronization; it corresponds to the case where sub-action b offered by E is a sub-action of a, with a not belonging to L^δ; rule **(5.a)** corresponds to the special case where b is the last sub-action of a; this restriction does not apply to rule **(5.b)**, which includes an additional identifier renaming, as identifier y, chosen within the context of E', may already be a free identifier in F; for illustrating this last point, let us consider the following example:

$G \equiv E|||F$ such that $E \equiv \langle b; exit \rangle_x^a; stop$, and $F \equiv \langle c; d; exit \rangle_y^e; stop$.

One possible derivation from E is $E \xrightarrow{x\langle b \rangle_y^a} \langle exit \rangle_y^a; stop$.

As there is no relationship between a and e, then another identifier must be substituted for y, as illustrated in the next derivation:

$G \xrightarrow{x\langle b \rangle_z^a} \langle exit \rangle_z^a; stop|||\langle c; d; exit \rangle_y^e; stop$ with $z \neq y$.

Rules **(5.c)** and **(5.d)** express the semantics of the parallel operator with synchronization; it corresponds to the case where sub-action b offered by E is a sub-action of a, with a belonging to L^δ; both rules enforce that the sub-actions to be synchronized should have the same refinement history (see the use of the x identifier for the offering of both sub-actions); rule **(5.c)** corresponds to the special case where b is the last sub-action of a; this restriction does not apply to rule **(5.b)**, which includes an additional identifier renaming, for the same reason as for rule **(5.b)**. Note furthermore that the same t has been substituted for both y and z, in order to characterize that the synchronization has led to the occurrence of just one (sub-)action. The synchronization condition introduced in the previous section, i.e. $E'[y] \equiv F'[z]$, has been slightly modified, i.e., $E'[y] \doteq F'[z]$, in order to account for multilevel refinement. A detailed explanation of this synchronization condition will be provided after the formal definition of $\doteq$ relation.

Rule **(6)** expresses the *hide* operator semantics; note that if $a \in L$, then $x = y = \perp$ and $a = b$ as the hidden actions are not allowed to be refined according to definition 3.

Rule **(7)** expresses the recursion semantics, and it is completely similar with the one of CCS (and Basic LOTOS).

Finally, we can conclude the presentation of the operational semantics by an important remark: for $\mathcal{L}_0$ behavior expressions, only rules **(1)**, **(2)**, **(4)**, **(5.a)**, **(5.c)**, **(6)** and **(7)** are applicable, and, in all derivations $E \xrightarrow{x\langle b \rangle_y^a} E'$, the following conditions are fulfilled: $x = y = \perp$ and $a = b$. This states that $\mathcal{A}_0$ behavior expressions are a strict extension of $\mathcal{L}_0$ behavior expressions, or in other words that our language is a strict extension of Basic LOTOS (just by extending the language with enabling, disabling and relabeling operators, which were not considered here for the sake of simplicity).

We conclude this paragraph, by introducing an equivalence relation between $\mathcal{A}_0$ behavior expressions which is useful when considering multi-level refinement.

Definition 5 $E \doteq F$ *if there is a bijection* $f : \Phi(E) \longrightarrow \Phi(F)$, *such that* $E \stackrel{1}{=} f(F)$ *where* $f(F)$ *is behaviour expression* F *in which all identifiers of* F *have been replaced by their corresponding ones in* E *according to bijection* f, *and where $\doteq$ is defined inductiveley on behaviour expressions as follows:*

- $E \equiv F \Rightarrow E \doteq F$
- $(\langle E \rangle_x^a; G \doteq \langle F \rangle_y^a; H) \Leftrightarrow ((x = y) \text{ and } (G \equiv H) \text{ and } (E \doteq F))$
- $(E[]F \doteq E'[]F') \Leftrightarrow ((E \doteq E') \text{ and } (F \doteq F'))$
- $(E|[L]|F \doteq E'|[L]|F') \Leftrightarrow ((E \doteq E') \text{ and } (F \doteq F'))$
- $(hide\ L\ in\ E \doteq hide\ L\ in\ F) \Leftrightarrow (E \doteq F)$

where $\equiv$ denotes the syntactic identity relation between behaviour expressions.

Lemma 1 $\doteq$ *is an equivalence relation (see proof in [16]).*

To motivate the purpose of this equivalence relation, let us consider the following example:
let $G \equiv a; stop|[a]|a; stop$ and let us assume that action a is to be refined by $P \equiv c; d; exit$; assume also that sub-action c of a is furthermore to be refined by process $Q \equiv e; f; exit$. The resulting process is therefore:
$G' \equiv E|[a]|F \equiv \langle\langle e; f; exit\rangle_\perp^c; d; exit\rangle_\perp^a; stop|[a]|\langle\langle e; f; exit\rangle_\perp^c; d; exit\rangle_\perp^a; stop$.

Possible derivations from E and F are $E \xrightarrow{\perp (e)_y^a} E' \equiv \langle\langle f; exit\rangle_x^c; d; exit\rangle_y^a; stop$

and $F \xrightarrow{\perp (e)_t^a} F' \equiv \langle\langle f; exit\rangle_z^c; d; exit\rangle_t^a; stop$. It is obvious that processes $E'[y] \equiv \langle f; exit\rangle_x^c; d; exit$, and $F'[t] \equiv \langle f; exit\rangle_z^c; d; exit$ are equivalent up to an identifier substitution. This is the purpose of relation $\doteq$.
In the sequel, we will restrict ourselves to well-formed terms, which are defined in the following way:

Definition 6 *Let WT be a set of a well-formed terms defined by:*
$WT = \{E \in \mathcal{A}_0\}$ *such that for some $G \in \mathcal{A}_0$ and for some*
$F \equiv \rho(\cdots(\rho(\ ,\ ,G)\cdots)$, *there exists a derivation $F \to \cdots \to E$.*

3.3 Strong bisimulation

Definition 7 *Let $\mathbf{R} \subseteq \mathcal{A}_0 \times \mathcal{A}_0$ be a binary relation between behaviors. Then, let $\mathbf{F} : Rel(\mathcal{A}_0) \longrightarrow Rel(\mathcal{A}_0)$ be a function defined as follows:*
$\langle P, Q \rangle \in \mathbf{F}(\mathbf{R})$ *if:*

1. *whenever $P \xrightarrow{x (b)_y^a} P'$ with $a, b \in Act^\delta$, there exists $Q \xrightarrow{x' (b)_{y'}^{a'}} Q'$ such that $\langle P', Q' \rangle \in \mathbf{R}$, and*

2. *whenever $Q \xrightarrow{x (b)_y^a} Q'$ with $a, b \in Act^\delta$, there exists $P \xrightarrow{x' (b)_{y'}^{a'}} P'$ such that $\langle P', Q' \rangle \in \mathbf{R}$*

$\mathbf{R}$ *is called a strong bisimulation iff $\mathbf{R} \subseteq \mathbf{F}(\mathbf{R})$. If $\langle P, Q \rangle \in \mathbf{R}$ for some strong bisimulation $\mathbf{R}$, then P and Q are said to be strong bisimilar, in symbols $P \sim Q$ [5]. As usual, this may be expressed as: $\sim = \bigcup\{S : S$ is a strong bisimulation$\}$*

---

[5] As it may be seen, the bisimulation deals only with the external behavior, as characterized by the sub-action occurrences; in particular, the definition does not need to take into account

Proposition 1 *Let* $\mathbf{R} \subseteq \mathcal{A}_0 \times \mathcal{A}_0$ *be a strong bisimulation. Then* $\langle P, Q \rangle \in \mathbf{F(R)}$ *implies:*

1. *whenever* $P \xrightarrow{a} P'$, $a \in Act^\delta$, *there exists* $Q \xrightarrow{a} Q'$ *such that* $\langle P', Q' \rangle \in \mathbf{R}$, *and*

2. *whenever* $Q \xrightarrow{a} Q'$, $a \in Act^\delta$, *there exists* $P \xrightarrow{a} P'$ *such that* $\langle P', Q' \rangle \in \mathbf{R}$

Proof By hypothesis, $\mathbf{R}$ is a strong bisimulation, then $\mathbf{R} \subseteq \mathbf{F(R)}$ which implies that $\langle P, Q \rangle \in \mathbf{F(R)}$ then (1) and (2).

Proposition 2 *Relation* $\sim$ *has the following properties (similar proof as in [14]):*

1. $\sim$ *is the largest strong bisimulation.*

2. $\sim$ *is an equivalence relation.*

Lemma 2 $\doteq$ *is a strong bisimulation (see proof in [16]).*

As it can be noted, the choice of the identifiers is not unique; lemma 2 shows also that if we construct the behavior expression classes with respect to equivalence relation $\doteq$, then all behavior expressions within a class are strong equivalent. This remark leads us to defining a *strong equivalence up to* $\sim$ in the same way as it has been defined in [14]. Consequently, we shall often write $P \, \mathbf{S} \, Q$ to mean $\langle P, Q \rangle \in \mathbf{S}$, for any binary relation $\mathbf{S}$. Note also that $\sim \mathbf{S} \sim$ is a composition of binary relations: $P \sim \mathbf{S} \sim Q$ means therefore that for some P' and Q', we have $P \sim P'$, $P' \, \mathbf{S} \, Q'$ and $Q' \sim Q$.

Definition 8 *S is a strong bisimulation up to* $\sim$, *if* $P \, S \, Q$ *implies,*

1. *whenever* $P \xrightarrow{a} P'$, $a \in Act^\delta$, *there exists* $Q \xrightarrow{a} Q'$ *such that* $P' \sim S \sim Q'$, *and*

2. *whenever* $Q \xrightarrow{a} Q'$, $a \in Act^\delta$, *there exists* $P \xrightarrow{a} P'$ *such that* $P' \sim S \sim Q'$.

Lemma 3 *If* $\mathbf{S}$ *is a strong bisimulation up to* $\sim$, *then* $\sim \mathbf{S} \sim$ *is a strong bisimulation (similar proof as in [14]).*

Proposition 3 *Let P and Q be two behaviors, and let furthermore P' and Q' be two other behaviors, such that $P \doteq P'$ and $Q \doteq Q'$; then P and Q are strong bisimilar, if there is a relation $\mathbf{S}$, such that $\langle P', Q' \rangle \in \mathbf{S}$, satisfying, for any $\langle P_1, Q_1 \rangle \in \mathbf{S}$:*

1. *whenever* $P_1 \xrightarrow{a} P'_1$, $a \in Act^\delta$, *there is* $Q_1 \xrightarrow{a} Q'_1$ *such that for some* $P"_1 \doteq P'_1$ *and* $Q"_1 \doteq Q'_1$, $\langle P"_1, Q"_1 \rangle \in \mathbf{S}$, *and*

---

which actions have been refined; for that reason, the notation $\xrightarrow{b}$ will be used, whenever there is no danger of confusion, to denote $\xrightarrow{x\,(b)\,^a_y}$ for some action a and some identifiers x and y.

2. *whenever* $Q_1 \xrightarrow{a} Q'_1$, $a \in Act^\delta$, *there is* $P_1 \xrightarrow{a} P'_1$ *such that for some* $P"_1 \doteq P'_1$ *and* $Q"_1 \doteq Q'_1$, $\langle P"_1, Q"_1 \rangle \in \mathbf{S}$.

Proof Because $\doteq$ is a strong bisimulation.

This proposition is very useful in practice, it states that, for testing the strong bisimilarity between two behaviors P and Q, it is not necessary to find a relation R which contains $\langle P, Q \rangle$ and which satisfies definition 7; it is possible to decide the bisimilarity between P and Q, by means of a relation S such that for all $\langle P_1, Q_1 \rangle$ and $\langle P_2, Q_2 \rangle$ in S, we have $P_1 \not\equiv P_2$ and $Q_1 \not\equiv Q_2$.

Lemma 4 *For any behavior expressions* P_1, P_2, P_3 *such that* $P_1 \doteq P_2 \doteq P_3$, *any action* a *and any identifiers* x, y, *then*

$$\langle P_1 \rangle_x^a; stop \sim \langle P_2 \rangle_y^a; stop \,|[a]|\, \langle P_3 \rangle_y^a; stop$$

(see proof in [16]).

Corollary 1 *For any behavior expression* P, *any action* a *and any identifiers* x, y,

$$\langle P \rangle_x^a; stop \sim \langle P \rangle_y^a; stop \,|[a]|\, \langle P \rangle_y^a; stop$$

Proof Derives directly from lemma 4.

This corollary shows the consistency of the action refinement with respect to the synchronization and therefore proves that the informal statement made at the end of section 2 ("the solution ... is indeed correct") is indeed correct.

4 Dealing with Action Atomicity

In the previous section, no hypothesis has been made on action atomicity. In fact, actions were considered as non atomic as it may easily be seen with the following example:

let $E \equiv \langle c; d; exit \rangle_\bot^a; stop|||b; stop$, then by means of rule **(5.a)** the following derivation is possible: $E \xrightarrow{\bot(c)_x^a} \xrightarrow{\bot(b)_\bot^b} \langle d; exit \rangle_x^a; stop|||stop$, which means that action b has occurred after the occurrence of a part of action a (i.e., sub-action c), but before the successful termination of the process refining action a . This consideration is useful in causality-based semantics [3, 5], when one wants to express that concurrent actions do not have any causal relationship among them. On the contrary, in interleaving-based semantics, actions should be considered as atomic. It is therefore important to show how this atomicity assumption may be taken into account in our approach, in order to stress that the refinement solution proposed does not depend on any particular concurrency semantics.

In order to ensure action atomicity within some specification E, it is necessary and sufficient to ensure that there exists at most one refining process which has not yet terminated in E; this condition is formally stated by $card(\Phi(E)) \leq 1$.

To ensure this condition, a new transition relation $\longrightarrow_a \subseteq \mathcal{A}_0 \times \mathcal{I}^\bot \times Act^\delta \times Act^\delta \times \mathcal{I}^\bot \times \mathcal{A}_0$ is defined as the least relation satisfying rules **(1')**, **(2')**, **(3.a')**, **(3.b')**, **(4')**, **(5.c')**, **(5.d')**, **(6')** and **(7')** (which are respectively rules **(1)**, **(2)**,

(3.a), (3.b), (4), (5.c), (5.d), (6) and (7), in which $\longrightarrow$ has been replaced by $\longrightarrow_a$), and rules (5.a') and (5.b') defined as:

(5.a')
$$\frac{E \xrightarrow{x^{(b)}{}^a_\perp} E'}{E\|[L]\|F \xrightarrow{x^{(b)}{}^a_\perp} E'\|[L]\|F \qquad F\|[L]\|E \xrightarrow{x^{(b)}{}^a_\perp} F\|[L]\|E' \text{ if } a \notin L^\delta \text{ and } \Phi(F)=\emptyset}$$

(5.b')
$$\frac{E \xrightarrow{x^{(b)}{}^a_y} E'}{E\|[L]\|F \xrightarrow{x^{(b)}{}^a_z} z/y E'\|[L]\|F \qquad F\|[L]\|E \xrightarrow{x^{(b)}{}^a_z} F\|[L]\|z/y E' \text{ if } a \notin L^\delta \ y\neq\perp \text{ and } \Phi(F)=\emptyset}$$
for any $z \notin F \cup E' \backslash y \cup \{\perp\}$

Let us now consider the previous example,

$E \xrightarrow{\perp^{(c)}{}^a_x} E' \equiv G\|\|H \equiv \xrightarrow{\perp^{(b)}{}^b_\perp} \langle d; exit\rangle^a_x; stop\|\|stop$. Transition $E' \xrightarrow{\perp^{(b)}{}^a_\perp}$ is denied because $\Phi(G) \equiv \{x\}$ which is different from $\emptyset$, thus the unique derivations from this state are:

$$E' \xrightarrow{x^{(d)}{}^a_y}_a \xrightarrow{y^{(i)}{}^a_\perp}_a stop\|\|b; stop \xrightarrow{\perp^{(b)}{}^b_\perp}_a stop\|\|stop$$

Using transition relation $\longrightarrow_a$ instead of transition relation $\longrightarrow$, the properties introduced in the previous section for the non-atomicity assumption can easily be proven to be correct for the atomicity assumption.

5 Conclusion and Related Works

Before assessing the proposed approach, let us first relate it to some of the most relevant works of the litterature.

In [1], Aceto & Hennessy define action refinement on a CCS-like process algebra with an approach making it possible to treat refinement as a syntactical substitution. We do not agree however with the way refinement is considered in presence of synchronization. To illustrate this, let us consider process $E \equiv a.nil|\bar{a}.nil$; then E behaves either like $a.nil$ or $\bar{a}.nil$ independentely, or a synchronization may occur and then E behaves like $\tau.nil$. Assuming now that action a be refined in process $P \equiv b.c.nil$, then, following [1], the following derivation is possible:

$$\rho(a, P, E) \equiv b.c.nil|\bar{b}.\bar{c} \xrightarrow{b} c|\bar{b}\bar{c} \xrightarrow{\bar{b}} c|\bar{c} \xrightarrow{\tau} nil|nil$$

This implies that $\rho(a, P, E)$ may perform a part of P, a part of $\overline{P}$, as well as a synchronization between parts of P and $\overline{P}$. In our approach however, the behavior of $\rho(a, P, E)$ should be either P or $\overline{P}$ in absence of any synchronization, or $\tau.\tau.nil$ when synchronizing peer actions of P and $\overline{P}$. This way to proceed appears to much more natural that [1] approach, as the semantics of a actions is preserved.

In [8], Engberger, Nielsen & Larsen have developped a refinement approach for a language without communication. The underlying semantics is a pomset notation (semiwords) and refinement is considered as a syntactical substitution. Applying our abstraction operator within their framework should permit to take synchronization into account.

In [7], Degano & Gorrieri have studied atomic action refinement on a CSP-like language within an interleaving-based semantics. As we have done in [5], refinement is performed at a semantic level, which makes it possible to escape from the synchronization problem, but which has a number of limitations from a practical point of view. Because the assumptions made for action refinement (like the action atomicity, the termination of the refining process, $\cdots$), used in [7], are also satisfied in our approach, we believe that a denotation by atomic trees can be generalized to their language extended by the abstraction operator. In [6], Darondeau & Degano propose an action refinement approach for causal trees. Within this context, they prove that their causal branching congruence is preserved under action refinement. Considering an action refinement operator in LOTOS, see [5], a branching causality-based bisimulation has been proven to be preserved under action refinement; we conjecture that a branching causality-based bisimulation is still preserved under action refinement for LOTOS extended by the abstraction operator.

Finally in [10], Gorrieri, Marchetti & Montanari define a notion of abstraction for CCS where actions are considered as atomic, and a relation between high-level and low-level CCS specifications (before and after refinement) is established. In their approach, derivation $F \overset{u_1}{\leadsto} I_1 \cdots \overset{u_n}{\leadsto} F_2$ at a low abstraction level has an equivalent conterpart $F \overset{u_1 \cdots u_n}{\longrightarrow} {}^n F_2$ at a higher level. This can be interpreted in our semantics by $\Phi(F_i) = \emptyset$ and $card(\Phi(I_j)) = 1$. Then, by means of the atomic action semantics presented in the paper, the same abstraction notion can now be defined for languages having a multiway synchronization operator.

Main contribution of the paper is related with the definition of an abstraction operator for languages like CCS or LOTOS. On a language very similar to Basic LOTOS, we have defined an operational semantics of the language in the SOS style. Applying the proposed approach, we have shown how to perform a syntactic refinement in presence of multiway synchronization and how to deal with the action atomicity assumption. This approach, which is a continuation of previous works dealing with stepwise refinement of formal specifications [4, 5], seems therefore particularily attractive, as it permits to give a formal background for an action refinement approach.

Direction of future work includes an extension of the proposed approach to full LOTOS taking into account value passing; an interesting way to proceed seems to adapt to the present work the proposal of Giannotti & Latella [9] dealing with gate splitting in LOTOS specifications.

References

[1] L. Aceto, M. Hennessy, Adding action refinement to finite algebra, In M Rodriguez, J Leach Albert, B Monien, editor, Automata, Languages and programming, 18th International Colloquium, volume 510 of LNCS, pages 506 - 519. Springer-Verlag, 1991.

[2] T. Bolognesi, E. Brinksma, Introduction to the ISO Specification Language LOTOS, Computer Networks and ISDN Systems (North-Holland), No. 14, 1987, pp. 25-59.

[3] R. Coelho Da Costa, J.P. Courtiat, A true concurrency semantics for LOTOS, In Proceedings of the IFIP TC6/WG6.1 5th Int. Conf. on Formal

Description Techniques (FORTE'92), North-Holland, 1992.

[4] J.P. Courtiat, D.E. Saïdouni, A Case Study in Protocol Design, In E. Brinksma , T. Bolognesi and C.A. Vissers, editors, Third LotoSphere Workshop & Seminar, Pise, Italy, September 1992.

[5] J.P. Courtiat, D.E. Saïdouni, Action Refinement in LOTOS, In Proceedings of the 13th IFIP Symposium on Protocol Specification, Testing and Verification. (PSTV 93), North-Holland, 1994.

[6] P. Darondeau, P. Degano, About semantic action refinement, Fundamenta Informaticae, XIV:221-234, 1991.

[7] P. Degano, R. Gorrieri, Atomic refinement in process description languages, In A. Tarlecki. editor, Mathematical Foundations of Computer Science, volume 520 of LNCS, pages 121-130. Springer-Verlag, 1991.

[8] U. Engberg, M. Nielsen, K.S. Larsen, Fully abstract models for a process language with refinement, In J.W. de Bakker, W.P. de Roever and G. Rozenberg, editors, Linear Time, Branching Time and Partial Order in Logics and Models for Concurrency, volume 354 of LNCS, pages 523-548. Springer-Verlag, 1989.

[9] F. Giannotti, D. Latella, Gate Splitting in LOTOS Specifications Using Abstract Interpretation, TAPSOFT'93, volume 668 of LNCS, pages 437-452, Springer-Verlag, 1993.

[10] R. Gorrieri, S. Marchetti, U. Montanari, A^2CCS: Atomic Action for CCS, TCS 72:203-223, 1990.

[11] A. Kiehn, E. Best, R. Devillers and L. Pomello, Concurrent bisimulations in Petri nets, Acta Informatica, 28:231-264, 1991.

[12] LOTOS, A Formal Description Technique Based on the Ordering of Observational Behaviour, ISO IS 8807, Novembre, 1988.

[13] Proceeding of the Third LotoSphere Workshop & Seminar, E Brinksma , T. Bolognesi and C.A. Vissers, editors, Pise, Italy, September 1992.

[14] R. Milner, Communication and Concurrency, C.A.R. Hoare Series Editor. Prentice Hall, 1989.

[15] G. Rozenberg, M. Nielsen, K.S. Thiagarajan, Elementary transition systems and refinement, Acta Informatica, 29: 555-578, 1992.

[16] D.E. Saïdouni, J.P. Courtiat, Syntactic Action Refinement in Presence of Multiway Synchronization, Research Report 93129, LAAS-CNRS, April 1993, (extended version of the paper with proofs).

[17] R.J. van Glabbeek, Comparative Concurrency Semantics and Refinement of Actions, PhD thesis, Vrije Universiteit Te Amsterdam, 1990.

From Implicit via Inductive to Explicit Definitions

Gerard R. Renardel de Lavalette

Department of Computing Science, University of Groningen

P.O. Box 800, 9700 AV Groningen, The Netherlands

E-mail: grl@cs.rug.nl

Abstract

This paper reports on a method to provide general implicit descriptions with a sound logical semantics. This method has been applied in the specification languages COLD and VVSL.

1 Introduction

Besides precision through formality, another desired feature of specification and design languages is generality. It should be possible for the user of such a language to create abstract and high-level descriptions, e.g. when the overall structure of the system or model at hand is to be formulated. During the subsequent development process, ranging from detailed specifications based on the overall specification to the implementation (possibly via transformations), abstraction and generality will give way to concrete and explicit formulations.

1.1 Definitions

Here we consider definitions in the light of generality. In high-level and general descriptions, many definitions are implicit: an object or a collection of objects is often not explicitly defined, but only described in terms of itself. A standard example here is the characterisation of the collection N of natural numbers in terms of 0 and S (successor) by

$$0 \in N \land \forall x (x \in N \rightarrow Sx \in N). \tag{1}$$

Another more telling example is the description of the collection $\mathcal{F}(C)$ of finite sets of objects of a collection C:

$$\emptyset \in \mathcal{F}(C) \ \land \ \forall x \in C(\{x\} \in \mathcal{F}(C)) \ \land \ \forall XY \in \mathcal{F}(C)(X \cup Y \in \mathcal{F}(C)) \tag{2}$$

Here we assume the usual explicit definitions $\emptyset$, $\{.\}$ and $\cup$ in terms of $\in$ to be given beforehand, together with the extensionality property $\forall XY(\forall a(a \in X \leftrightarrow a \in Y) \leftrightarrow X = Y)$. When we compare (2) with the more common definition (using the insertion function $i : C \times \mathcal{F}(C) \rightarrow \mathcal{F}(C)$):

$$\emptyset \in \mathcal{F}(C) \land \forall x \in C \forall X \in \mathcal{F}(C)(i(x, X) \in \mathcal{F}(C)) \tag{3}$$

which is usual in algebraic specifications and declarative programming, we have the opinion that (3) is more biased to implementation (e.g. by term rewriting) and hence less abstract than (2). In section 4, we shall come back to this example when we give an inductive definition of the cardinality function which runs parallel to (2).

In (1) and (2), the intention is to characterise N resp. $\mathcal{F}(C)$ as the smallest collection satisfying the description. This intended meaning is obtained when (1) and (2) are considered as inductive definitions. In this paper, we study the mechanisms involved in this interpretation of implicit definitions.

1.2 COLD and VVSL

The method of making implicit definitions explicit by considering them as inductive definitions has been used in the logical semantics of the wide spectrum languages COLD and VVSL. COLD (Common Object-oriented Language for Design) is developed at Philips Research Eindhoven, mainly by Hans Jonkers. We refer to [3] for the formal definition of the kernel language COLD-K and its semantics and to [2] for a textbook on formal specification and design based on COLD. VVSL (for VIP VDM Specification Language) is a specification language designed by Kees Middelburg in the ESPRIT project VIP (VDM Interfaces for the PCTE). VVSL is based on VDM, temporal logic and the modularisation and parametrisation mechanisms of COLD-K. See [8], [9].

The definition of the logical semantics of COLD and VVSL uses MPL_ω (Many-sorted Partial infinitary Logic). This is an extension of classical first-order logic with sorts, definedness predicates $\downarrow_S$ for every sort S ($t \downarrow_S$ means: t is a defined term of sort S), partial functions (i.e. $f(x)\downarrow$ does not hold automatically), descriptions $\iota x : S(A)$ (meaning: the unique x of sort S satisfying A if such an x exists, otherwise undefined) and countably infinite conjunctions $\bigwedge_n A_n$ and disjunctions $\bigvee_n A_n$. MPL_ω is a definitional extension of $L_{\omega_1 \omega}$ (first-order logic with $\bigwedge_n A_n$ and $\bigvee_n A_n$; see [5], [7]) and shares with it a Completeness Theorem and the Interpolation Property. See [6] for more information on MPL_ω. In this paper, we work with logics like MPL_ω: as we shall see further on, infinite disjunctions are used to make inductive definitions

1.3 Inductive and explicit definitions

In section 1.1 we mentioned that implicit definitions like (1) can be considered as inductive definitions, viz.

$$N \text{ is the smallest predicate satisfying } N(0) \wedge \forall x (N(x) \rightarrow N(x+1)). \quad (4)$$

But this is only one way to present inductive definitions, another is to define N as the least fixpoint $\mu\Phi$ of a monotonic operator Φ on predicates: the definition then reads

$$N =_{\text{def}} \mu(\lambda P.\{x | x = 0 \vee \exists y (x = y + 1 \wedge P(y))\}). \quad (5)$$

Definition (5) is, in some sense, more explicit than (4), and it is straightforward to define its semantics in logical terms if the logic used allows the definition of least fixpoints of predicate operators. This is e.g. the case for the logic MPL_μ, a forerunner of MPL_ω introduced in [4] for the definition of the semantics of a fragment of COLD. (N.B. MPL_μ is called MPL in [4], but the latter name is used to denote the finitary fragment of MPL_ω in subsequent publications, e.g. [11].)

On the other hand, definitions of type (5) have the disadvantage that they are harder to read and more difficult to devise. This makes it interesting to consider the following question: how to define the logical semantics of definitions like (4)?

In second-order logics with enough comprehension, this is no problem: predicate definitions of the form

P is the smallest predicate satisfying $A(P)$

can be made explicit by $Px \leftrightarrow \exists X(Xx \wedge \forall Y(A(Y) \rightarrow \forall y(Xy \rightarrow Yy)))$. However, second-order logic was thought to be far too heavy and not well enough understood to provide the logical semantics of specification languages. As to COLD-K, this led to considering weaker extensions of first-order logic such as MPL_μ and MPL_ω of which the second one has been chosen, for the following reasons:

- the Interpolation Property, desirable for an adequate sementics of modularisation and parametrisation, holds for MPL_ω and not for MPL_μ (see [10]);

- fixpoints $\mu\Phi$ of continuous predicate functions Φ can be expressed explicitly in MPL_ω as follows: $\mu\Phi = \bigvee_n A_n$ with $A_0 = \bot, A_{n+1} = \Phi(A_n)$.

So the problem is solved if we can find a method to transform formulae as in (4) into predicate operators as in (5). The rest of this paper is devoted to finding and elaborating such a method.

2 Preliminaries

In the rest of this paper, we consider the situation from two perspectives: set theory and logic. The logic we have in mind is MPL_ω, but for simplicity we restrict it most of the time to $L_{\omega_1\omega}$ (first-order logic with equality and countably infinite conjunctions and disjunctions; no sorts, no partiality, no descriptions). We shall use a definitional extension $\mathcal{L}$ in which the following are present:

- term substitution $[x := t]A$;

- predicate variables $X, Y, \ldots$, all assumed to be unary (for the sake of simplicity), with the equivalent notations Xt and $t \in X$;

- defined predicates $\{x|A\}$, with the meaning given by $t \in \{x|A\} \equiv \{x|A\}(t) \equiv [x := t]A$;

- predicate substitution of the defined predicate D for the predicate variable X in the formula A denoted by $[X := D]A$;

- predicate substitution $[X^+ := D]$ and $[X^- := D]$, which only act on the positive resp. negative occurrences of X;

- predicate functions $\Lambda X.A$ and predicate operators $\Lambda X.\{x|A\}$, with the meaning given by $(\Lambda X.A)D = [X := D]A, (\Lambda X.\{x|A\})D = \{x|[X := D]A\}$.

$\mathcal{L}$ will sometimes be used to denote the collection of formulae of the language of $\mathcal{L}$; $\mathcal{L}(X)$ is the subset of $\mathcal{L}$ of formulae containing no predicate variables besides X, and $\mathcal{L}(X, x)$ the subset of $\mathcal{L}(X)$ of formulae containing no individual variables besides x.

For reasoning in the realm of sets we fix a universe U, so elements are elements of U and sets are subsets of U. γ is the first cardinal larger than the cardinality of U. We define x^c, the complement of x, by $x^c =_{def} \{y \in U | y \neq x\}$ for elements x. Operators Φ between sets are called *monotonic* if $\forall XY(X \subseteq Y \Rightarrow \Phi X \subseteq \Phi Y)$ and *continuous* if $X_1 \subseteq X_2 \subseteq X_3 \ldots$ implies $\Phi(\bigcup\{X_n | n \in \omega\}) = \bigcup\{\Phi(X_n) | n \in \omega\}$; Φ is a *closure operator* if it is monotonic and projective, i.e. $\Phi \circ \Phi = \Phi$. A *condition* C is a subset of $\wp(U)$; the notations $X \in C$ and $C(X)$ have the same meaning. C is called $\bigcap$-*closed* if, for all conditions $C' \subseteq \wp(U)$, we have $\forall X \in C'(C(X)) \Rightarrow C(\bigcap C')$.

The link between the set-theoretic and the logical perspective is provided by interpretation of expressions of the language $\mathcal{L}$ in a model with U as its universe. The details of this are fairly standard and will not be given here. We only observe that defined predicates are interpreted by sets, predicate functions by conditions and predicate operators by operators between sets. For the rest of this paper, we assume some interpretation I of $\mathcal{L}$ into U to be given; it is clear that I is completely determined by its effect on the nonlogical constants (function and predicate symbols) of $\mathcal{L}$. A set X is called $\mathcal{L}$-*definable* or *elementary* (modulo I) if there is a formula A with $X = I(\{x|A\})$; similar for conditions and operators. So the interpretation by I of the nonlogical constants act as a parameter in this definability notion.

3 Implicit definition of predicates

3.1 What are inductive definitions?

In [1], Aczel defines the notion of *inductive definition* of a set X by

$$X \text{ is the smallest set closed under a collection of rules } R; \tag{6}$$

rules are of the form $Y \to y$, where Y is a set and y an element; a set Z is closed under rule $Y \to y$ iff $Y \subseteq Z \Rightarrow y \in Z$ holds. (6) is a good definition, for

$$X = \bigcap\{Z | \forall r \in R(Z \text{ is closed under } r)\}; \tag{7}$$

this follows from the fact that the condition C_R with $C_R(Z) = \forall r \in R(Z$ is closed under $r)$ is $\bigcap$-closed. This observation suggests an alternative and more abstract notion of inductive definition:

$$X \text{ is the smallest set satisfying the } \bigcap\text{-closed condition } C;$$

this is also a good definition, for

$$X = \bigcap\{Z | C(Z)\}. \tag{8}$$

We observe that (7) and (8) are examples of *impredicative* definitions: X is defined in terms of the collection of subsets of U, to which X itself belongs.

For the case of (7), there is a well-known method (named after its inventor S.C. Kleene) to obtain a more 'constructive' definition of X in stages: it is the construction of the least fixpoint $\mu\Phi$ of the monotonic set operator $\Phi = \Phi_R$, defined by $\Phi_R(Z) = Z \cup \{y \mid$ there is a rule $Y \to y$ in R with $Y \subseteq Z\}$. The definition reads (α, β range over the ordinals):

$$\mu\Phi = \bigcup\{\Phi^\alpha \mid \alpha < \gamma\}, \text{ where } \Phi^\alpha =_{\text{def}} \bigcup\{\Phi^\beta \mid \beta < \alpha\};$$

then $\mu(\Phi_R) = \bigcap\{Z \mid C(Z)\}$ (for a proof and more information we refer to [1], section 1.3, and [6], section 4.1). If Φ is continuous, then we can stop the definition of $\mu\Phi$ at ω, and $X = \bigcup\{\Phi^n \mid n \in \omega\}$; then we have a genuinely predicative definition of X which can be finitely approximated. If Φ happens to be a closure operator then the construction becomes trivial, for $\mu\Phi = \Phi^1 = \Phi(\emptyset)$, so only one step suffices.

In the next subsection, we try to answer the following question: is it possible to generalize the transition from C_R to Φ_R to arbitrary $\bigcap$-closed conditions?

3.2 A syntactical trick

Let us have a closer look at the two inductive definitions (4) and (5) of N given in 1.3, but now in a slightly different formulation,

N is the smallest predicate X satisfying $C_N(X)$,
$\qquad$ where $C_N(X) =_{\text{def}} X(0) \wedge \forall x(X(x) \to X(x+1))$;

$N =_{\text{def}} \mu(\lambda X.\{x \mid B_N(X, x)\})$,
$\qquad$ where $B_N(X, x) =_{\text{def}} (x = 0 \vee \exists y(x = y + 1 \wedge X(y)))$.

To find out how B_N can be obtained from C_N, we rewrite C_N to

$$\neg(\neg X(0) \vee \exists y(X(y) \wedge \neg X(y+1))),$$

and now it is not hard to see that B_N can be obtained from C_N by replacing the positive occurrences of X by $x^c (= \{z \mid z \neq x\})$ and dropping the leftmost negation sign:

$$\neg x^c(0) \vee \exists y(X(y) \wedge \neg x^c(y+1)),$$

and this is equivalent to B_N! We capture this transformation of C_N into $\Lambda X.\{x \mid B_N(X, x)\}$ in the following definition:

$$\Delta X.C =_{\text{def}} \Lambda X.\{x \mid \neg[X^+ := x^c]C\}.$$

Now, $N, \Delta X.C_N = \Phi_N$ and $\mu(\Delta X.C_N) = N$, but can this be generalized? Let us therefore consider the transition from the condition C to the predicate operator $\Delta X.C$ in a set-theoretic setting.

3.3 From conditions to operations

We start with the following diagram summarizing the situation described in section 3.1:

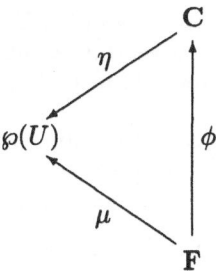

with the definitions

$$\mathbf{F} =_{\text{def}} \{\Phi : \wp(U) \to \wp(U)|\Phi \text{ monotonic }\}$$

$$\mathbf{C} =_{\text{def}} \{C \subseteq \wp(U)|C \text{ is } \bigcap -\text{closed}\}$$

$\eta : \mathbf{C} \to \wp(U)$ is defined by $\eta(C) = \bigcap\{X|C(X)\}$

$\mu : \mathbf{F} \to \wp(U)$ is defined by $\mu(\Phi) = \bigcap\{X|\Phi(X) \subseteq X\}$

$\phi : \mathbf{F} \to \mathbf{C}$ is defined by $\phi(\Phi) = \{X|\Phi(X) \subseteq X\}$

One easily verifies that ϕ is well-defined and that $\phi(\Phi_R) = C_R$ (with Φ_R, C_R as in 3.1). We have the following facts:

$$\mu(\Phi) = \bigcup\{\Phi^\alpha|\alpha < \gamma\}$$
$$\eta \circ \phi = \mu$$

What we are looking for is a right inverse $\psi : \mathbf{C} \to \mathbf{F}$ of ϕ, for then the diagram commutes (since $\mu \circ \psi = \eta \circ \phi \circ \psi = \eta$). A possible definition is

$$\psi(C)(X) = \bigcap\{Y \supseteq X|C(Y)\}.$$

Then ψ is well-defined and $\phi \circ \psi = id_C$, for $\phi(\psi(C)) = \{X|\psi(C)(X) \subseteq X\} = \{X|\bigcap\{Y \supseteq X|C(Y)\} \subseteq X\} = \{X|\{Y \supseteq X|C(Y)\} = X\} = \{X|C(X)\} = C$; for the fourth equality we used that $C(\bigcap\{Y \supseteq X|C(Y)\})$ holds, as a consequence of the $\bigcap$-closedness of C.

At first sight it seems that this ψ works; there are, however, two objections. Firstly, ψ has a nonelementary definition which has no counterpart in $\mathcal{L}$. Secondly, $\psi(C)$ appears to be a closure operator, since $X \subseteq \bigcap\{Y \supseteq X|C(Y)\} = \psi(C)(X)$ and $\psi(C)(\psi(C)(X)) = \psi(C)(\bigcap\{Y \supseteq X|C(Y)\}) = \bigcap\{Z \supseteq \bigcap\{Y \subseteq X|C(Y)\}|C(Z)\} = \bigcap\{Y \supseteq X|C(Y)\} = \psi(C)(X)$, where the $\bigcap$-closedness of C is used for the third equality. As a consequence, $\eta(C) = \psi(\mathbf{C})(\emptyset)$ so all induction steps are absorbed in the definition of $\psi(C)$.

So this direct transition from $\mathbf{C}$ to $\mathbf{F}$ does not work, and we try it indirectly. The syntactical trick of 3.2 suggests to consider conditions C as the diagonal of binary relations $D = D(X, Y)$, i.e. $C(X) = D(X, X)$. We therefore define $\mathbf{D}$ as the collection of binary relations on sets which are antimonotonic in their first argument and both monotonic and $\bigcap$-closed in their second argument, so

$$\mathbf{D} = \{D \subseteq \wp(U)^2|\forall X X'Y Y'(D(X, Y) \wedge X' \subseteq X \wedge Y \subseteq Y' \to D(X', Y'))$$

$$\text{and } \forall X \forall C \subseteq \wp(U)(\forall Y \in C D(X, Y) \to D(X, \bigcap C))\}.$$

The diagonalizing mapping $\delta : \mathbf{D} \to \mathbf{C}$ defined by $\delta(D)(X) \leftrightarrow D(X,X)$ maps $\mathbf{D}$ into $\mathbf{C}$, for $D(X,X)$ is $\bigcap$-closed if $D \in \mathbf{D}$: to see this, assume $\forall X \in C\, D(X,X)$, then $\forall X \in C\, D(\bigcap C, X)$ (for $D(X,Y)$ is antimonotonic in X), hence $D(\bigcap C, \bigcap C)$ (for $D(X,Y)$ is $\bigcap$-closed in Y).

A mapping $\alpha : \mathbf{F} \to \mathbf{D}$ which commutes with ϕ and δ is straightforward: put $\alpha(\Phi)(X,Y) \leftrightarrow \Phi(X) \subseteq Y$. For the other way round, we find inspiration in the definition of $\Delta X.A$ presented in the previous section, and we put

$$\beta : \mathbf{D} \to \mathbf{F} \text{ is defined by } \beta(D)(X) = \{x | \neg D(X, x^c)\}.$$

This turns out to work, for we have

Lemma.
i) $\alpha \circ \beta = id_{\mathbf{D}}$;
ii) $\beta \circ \alpha = id_{\mathbf{F}}$;
iii) $\phi \circ \beta = \delta$.

Proof.
i) $\alpha(\beta(D))(X,Y) \Leftrightarrow \beta(D)(X) \subseteq Y \Leftrightarrow \{x | \neg D(X, x^c)\} \subseteq Y \Leftrightarrow \forall x (D(\neg X, x^c) \to x \in Y) \Leftrightarrow \forall x \notin Y\, D(X, x^c) \Leftrightarrow D(X, \bigcap \{x^c | x \notin Y\}) \Leftrightarrow D(X,Y)$.
ii) $\beta(\alpha(\Phi))(X) = \{x | \neg \alpha(\Phi)(X, x^c)\} = \{x | \neg(\Phi(X) \subseteq x^c)\} = \{x | x \in \Phi(X)\} = \Phi(X)$.
iii) $\phi \circ \beta = \delta \circ \alpha \circ \beta = \delta \circ id_{\mathbf{D}} = \delta$. $\qquad\square$

We observe that α and β have elementary definitions. What is still missing is a mapping from $\mathbf{C}$ to $\mathbf{D}$ which commutes with δ and has an elementary definition. We do not intend to give such a mapping here: presumably it does not exist in this set-theoretic context. However, we can get quite close to this by defining a subset $\mathbf{S}$ of $\mathcal{L}$-formulae which can be seen as representations of elementary conditions in $\mathbf{D}$. This is done as follows: define $\mathbf{S}$ and the mappings ρ and σ by

$$\mathbf{S} =_{\text{def}} \{A \in \mathcal{L}(X) | Y \text{ not in } A, I(\Lambda XY.[X^+ := Y]A) \in \mathbf{D}\}$$
$$\rho : \mathbf{S} \to \mathbf{C} \text{ is defined by } \rho(A) = I(\Lambda X.A)$$
$$\sigma : \mathbf{S} \to \mathbf{D} \text{ is defined by } \sigma(A) = I(\Lambda XY.[X^+ := Y]A)$$

It is evident that $\delta \circ \sigma = \rho$, so ρ is well-defined and we have the following commuting diagram (where $*$ indicates the non-elementary mappings):

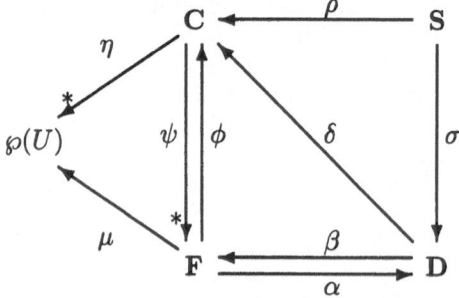

We summarize the upshot of this section in a theorem:

Theorem.
For every condition $C = \rho(A)$ in the range of ρ, an elementary monotonic operator $\Phi = \beta(\sigma(A)) = I(\Delta X.A)$ can be found which satisfies $\mu\Phi = \eta C$.

3.4   Syntactical conditions

In this section we return to the logical perspective and establish some syntactically defined subsets of $\mathbf{S}$. Since $[X^+ := Y]A$ (Y not in A) is always antimonotonic in X and monotonic in Y, we have

$$\mathbf{S} = \{A \epsilon \mathcal{L}(X) | I(\Lambda XY.[X^+ := Y]A) \text{ is } \cap\text{-closed in its second argument}\}$$

Lemma. $\mathbf{S}$ contains all formulae of the form

$$\bigwedge \forall (A \to X(t)) \qquad (X \text{ not negatively in } A),$$

i.e. all (finite or infinite) conjunctions of universally quantified formulae of the form $A \to X(t)$ where X does not occur negatively in A.

Proof. This is a consequence of

$$X(t) \epsilon \mathbf{S}$$

$$A_1, A_2, \ldots \epsilon \mathbf{S} \Rightarrow \bigwedge_n A_n \mathbf{S}$$

$$A \epsilon \mathbf{S}, X \text{ not negatively in } B \Rightarrow (B \to A) \epsilon \mathbf{S}$$

$$A \epsilon S \Rightarrow \forall x A \epsilon \mathbf{S}.$$

□

The previous lemma describes a collection of formulae for which the first part of the method works: going from a formula A defining a $\cap$-closed condition $I(\Lambda X.A) \epsilon C$ to an operator $I(\Delta X.A)$ whose fixpoint equals the smallest set satisfying $I(\Lambda X.A)$. The second step is the restriction to $\mathcal{L}$-definable fixpoints, which is accomplished if the operator $I(\Delta X.A)$ is continuous, for then the fixpoint is reached in a countable number of steps (viz. ω) and hence definable by an infinite disjunction in $\mathcal{L}$. So we define

$$\delta X.A = \bigvee_n B_n, \text{ where } B_0 = \bot, B_{n+1} = (\Delta X.A)(B_n)$$

$$\mathbf{Cts} = \{A \epsilon \mathcal{L}(X, x) | I(\Lambda X.\{x | A\}) \text{ is continuous}\}$$

$$\mathbf{Adm} = \{A \epsilon \mathbf{S} | \neg [X^+ := x^c] A \epsilon \mathbf{Cts}\}$$

and we have: if $A \epsilon \mathbf{Adm}$, then

$\delta X.A$ is the smallest predicate satisfying A,

i.e. $[X := \delta X.A]A$ and $(A \to \delta X.A \subseteq X)$. $\qquad\qquad$ (9)

Lemma. $\mathbf{Cts}$ contains all formulae of the form

$$\bigvee \exists (A \wedge X(t_1) \wedge \ldots \wedge X(t_n)) \qquad (X \text{ not in } A),$$

i.e. all (finite or infinite) disjunctions of existentially quantified formulae $A_1 \wedge \ldots \wedge A_n$, where A_i is of the form $X(t)$ or does not contain X.

Proof. This is a consequence of the following closure properties:

$$X(t) \epsilon \mathbf{Cts}$$

$$A \epsilon \mathbf{Cts} \text{ if } X \text{ not in } A$$

$$A_1, A_2, \ldots \epsilon \mathbf{Cts} \Rightarrow \bigvee_n A_n \epsilon \mathbf{Cts}$$

$$A, B \epsilon \mathbf{Cts} \Rightarrow A \wedge B \epsilon \mathbf{Cts}$$

$$A \epsilon \mathbf{Cts} \Rightarrow \exists y A \epsilon \mathbf{Cts}$$

□

Now we define the class of formulae for which the full method works:

Definition. A *Horn formula* in X is a formula of the form

$$\bigwedge \forall (A \wedge X(s_1) \wedge \ldots \wedge X(s_n) \to X(t)) \qquad (X \text{ not in } A),$$

i.e. a (finite or infinite) conjunction of universally quantified formulae of the form $A_1 \wedge \ldots \wedge A_m \to X(t)$ $(m \geq 0)$, where A_i is of the form $X(s)$ or does not contain X. The collection of all Horn formulae in X is denoted $\mathbf{Horn}(X)$.

Lemma. $\mathbf{Horn}(X) \subseteq \mathbf{Adm}$.

Proof. $\mathbf{Horn}(X) \subseteq \mathbf{S}$ is evident; if $A \in \mathbf{Horn}$ then $\neg[X^+ := x^c]A \in \mathbf{Cts}$ by previous lemma. So $A \in \mathbf{Adm}$. $\qquad\qquad\qquad\qquad\qquad\qquad\qquad\qquad\qquad \square$

Theorem. If A is a Horn formula in X, then $\delta X.A$ is the predicate inductively defined by A, hence satisfies (9).

4   Implicit definitions of functions

For implicitly defined *functions* the story is somewhat more complicated. We need a logical language with definedness predicate and with descriptions (viz. the description of MPL_ω in section 1.2). The method now proceeds by first going from functions f (which, for simplicity, we assume to be unary) to functional predicates $\mathbf{F}$ with $f(x) = y \Leftrightarrow F(x, y)$, then making the definition of F explicit by δF, followed by going back from the predicate $\delta F.A$ to the function $\delta f.A$ using descriptions: $\delta f.A = \lambda x.\iota y.(\delta F.A)$. There is complication, however: the condition needed for the expected property

> $\delta f.A$ is the smallest partial function satisfying A,
> i.e. $[f := \delta f.A]A$ and $(A \to \delta f.A \subseteq f)$

to hold, has two parts. The first part is as for predicates and can be approximated with a syntactical criterion $\mathbf{Horn}(f)$, requiring A to be a conjunction of universally quantified formulae of the form $A_1 \wedge \ldots \wedge A_m \wedge s \downarrow \to (f(s) \hookrightarrow t)$ where A_i is atomic or does not contain f and with f not in s. Here $\hookrightarrow$ is a directed weakening of equality:

$$(a \hookrightarrow b) \text{ is defined by } \forall x(x = b \to x = a) \quad (\equiv (b \downarrow \to a = b)).$$

The intended meaning of $a \hookrightarrow b$ can be paraphrased as: a is defined as b, or: a rewrites/reduces to b. (In COLD-K and VVSL, $=$ is written for $\hookrightarrow$). The second part of the condition, however, has to do with the functionality of the predicate used to define $\delta f.A$ and this functionality requirement eludes syntactical characterisation. See [11] for more details.

We give two examples. For the first, we assume that m, n range over the natural numbers. Now

$$\forall n(0 + n \hookrightarrow n) \wedge \forall mn(S(m) + n \hookrightarrow S(m + n)) \qquad (10)$$

inductively defines $+$ (addition) in terms of 0 and S (although (10) does not belong to $\mathbf{Horn}(+)$ properly, but it can easily be brought into that form). The functionality requirement involved here follows from the properties of 0 and S.

The second example is related to $\mathcal{F}(C)$, defined in (2). Then the cardinality function $|.| : \mathcal{F}(C) \to I\!N$, can be defined implicitly by

$$|\emptyset| \hookrightarrow 0 \wedge \forall c \epsilon C(|c| \hookrightarrow 1) \wedge \forall XY(|X \cup Y| \hookrightarrow |X| + |Y| - |X \cap Y|) \qquad (11)$$

and this yields a cardinality function with all the desired properties.

5 Final remarks

5.1 Closure properties of Adm

Adm is *not* closed under $\equiv$, so formulae equivalent to an element of **Horn** are not always in **Adm**; however, if $A \equiv B$ are both element of **Adm** then $\delta X.A \equiv \delta X.B$. On the other hand, **Adm** is closed under a stronger equivalence $\equiv_X$, defined by

$$A \equiv_X B \quad =_{\text{def}} \quad [X^+ := Y]A \equiv [X^+ := Y]B \qquad (Y \text{ not in } A, B).$$

5.2 Conclusion

We described and provided the foundations for a method which turns a large class of implicit descriptions of predicates and functions into explicit definitions in a logical language with infinite conjunctions and disjunctions. This method is applied in the definition of the logical semantics of COLD-K ([3]) and VVSL ([9]); as a consequence, these languages support the use of fairly easy readable implicit descriptions, appropriate for abstract and high-level specifications and designs. This was illustrated with the example of finite sets and the cardinality function (see (2) and (11)).

5.3 Acknowledgement

Karst Koymans (University of Utrecht) is gratefully acknowledged for pointing out clearly the relevance of the set-theoretic perspective in these matters.

References

[1] P. Aczel, *An introduction to inductive definitions*, in: *Handbook of Mathematical Logic* (J. Barwise ed.), North-Holland (1977) 739 - 782

[2] L.M.G. Feijs, H.B.M. Jonkers, *Formal Specification and Design*, Cambridge University Press, 1992

[3] L.M.G. Feijs, H.B.M. Jonkers, C.P.J. Koymans, G.R. Renardel de Lavalette, *Formal definition of the design language COLD-K (Preliminary version)*, Technical Report, ESPRIT project 432, Doc.Nr. METEOR/t7/PRLE/7 (1987) (Revised version in 1989.)

[4] H.B.M. Jonkers, C.P.J. Koymans, G.R. Renardel de Lavalette, *A semantic framework for the COLD-family of languages*, Technical Report, ESPRIT project 432, Doc.Nr. METEOR/t2/PRLE/1 (1986); also appeared

as Logic Group Preprint Series No. 9, Department of Philosophy, University of Utrecht (1986)

[5] C. Karp, *Languages with Expressions of Infinite Length*, North-Holland (1964)

[6] C.P.J. Koymans, G.R. Renardel de Lavalette, *The logic MPL$_\omega$*, in: *Algebraic methods: Theory, Tools and Applications* (M. Wirsing, J.A. Bergstra, eds.) Springer Lecture Notes in Computer Science 394, Springer-Verlag (1989) 247 - 282

[7] E.G.K. Lopez-Escobar, *An interpolation theorem for denumerably long sentences*, Fundamenta Mathematicae 57 (1965) 253 - 272

[8] C.A. Middelburg, *VVSL: a language for structured VDM specifications*, Formal Aspects of Computing 1 (1989) 115 - 135

[9] C.A. Middelburg, *Syntax and semantics of VVSL, a language for structured VDM specifications*, Ph.D. thesis, University of Amsterdam (1990)

[10] G.R. Renardel de Lavalette, *Modularisation, Parametrisation, Interpolation*, Journal of Information Processing and Cybernetics EIK 25 (1989) 283 - 292

[11] G.R. Renardel de Lavalette, *The static part of the design language COLD-K*, this volume.

Verifying Process Algebra Proofs in Type Theory

M. P. A. Sellink

Department of Philosophy, Utrecht University

Utrecht, The Netherlands

Abstract

In this paper we study automatic verification of proofs in process algebra. Formulas of process algebra are represented by types in typed λ-calculus. Inhabitants (terms) of these types represent proofs. The specific typed λ-calculus we use is the *Calculus of Inductive Constructions* as implemented in the interactive proof construction program Coq.

Introduction

Automatic verification will, as we expect, have a beneficial influence on the application of process theory. We believe that it is the only way to reach an acceptable level of correctness of proofs for programs and protocols of realistic size.

Automatic verification of propositions of process theories is not new. Already in the 80's Rance Cleaveland and Prakash Panangaden [4] gave an implementation of Milner's *Calculus of Communicating Systems* (CCS) [13] in NuPrl [5]. They constructed a model of CCS in non-well-founded set theory $ZFC^- + AFA$ (*ZFC* where the foundation-axiom is replaced by the anti-foundation-axiom *AFA*) and then implemented $ZFC^- + AFA$ in NuPrl.

In 1991, Urban Engberg, Peter Grønning and Leslie Lamport published a paper on mechanical verification of concurrent systems. They started from the *Temporal Logic of Actions* (TLA) which is a logic for specifying and reasoning about concurrent systems. They made use of the verification system LP [8]. In order to avoid errors in the encoding of TLA-expressions into LP, a translator from TLA to LP is written.

As more recent work we can mention [15]. It uses results about I/O automata [12] to extract a set of proof obligations. The verification is done in LP.

We adopt the algebraic approach of Jan Bergstra and Jan Willem Klop [2]. This approach is known as *Algebra of Communicating Processes* (ACP). Jan Friso Groote and Alban Ponse developed a formal language [9] and an accompanying proof theory [10] for ACP (+ data). The formal language is called μCRL. This paper builds upon the proof theory for μCRL, which was designed to facilitate automatic proof verification.

We indicate how μCRL properties can be transformed to types, how μCRL axioms can be represented, how the logical deduction rules are treated, and so on. There are numerous ways to do this things. At this stage the best (correct, efficient) way to follow is not yet fully clear to us. This paper must be seen as a first attempt.

Proofs for Milner's Scheduler and the good old alternating bit protocol are computer-checked using the representation introduced here [12, 3]. Recently, Jaco van de Pol checked a μCRL proof of the Bounded Retransmission Protocol (BRP). Different from [12] and [3] the BRP proof was checked by building large tacticals that automatically rewrite the huge μCRL process terms into some kind of normal form. This seems to save a lot of work.

This paper is organised as follows. In Section 1 we give a short, informal introduction to type theory. μCRL and its proof theory are briefly explained in Section 2. In Section 3 we explain how we represent notions of μCRL by types. Section 4 discusses the correctness of the representation with respect to the rules of the proof theory for μCRL and the correspondence with type theory. Finally, some examples of μCRL axioms are given in an appendix.

Acknowledgements. First of all I would like to thank Christine Paulin-Mohring for her hospitality during my visit to Lyon and answering my questions about Coq.

This paper benefited much from discussions with Marc Bezem, Jan Friso Groote, Jaco van de Pol and Jan Springintveld.

1   Type theory

Types (also called *sorts*) are frequently used in mathematics, logic and computer science. We just mention many sorted predicate logic. In strongly typed programming languages, every expression has a type. Primitive expressions, such as variables, have a type by declaration. These declarations usually classify the variables. Such classes (INTEGER, REAL, CHAR,...) are called *types*. 'x is of type A' is denoted as $x : A$. In Subsection 1.2 we treat type forming connectives more extensively. For the moment we just mention that $A \to B$ is a type if A and B are types.

In the λ-*calculus* [1] types are used to restrict application: a term F may only be applied to a term x if the types of F and x satisfy some restriction. More specifically, $Fx : B$ if $F : A \to B$ and $x : A$. (This is formalised in the inference rule *App* of Table 1.) Expressions of the form $b : B$ are called *statements*. The naive interpretation of a statement is a set theoretic one. This means that types are interpreted as sets and $b : B$ is interpreted as $b \in B$ (b is an element of set B). The type $A \to B$ is interpreted as the set of functions from A to B. When b is an element of B (that possibly contains x), then $\lambda x : A \cdot b$ is the function from A to B that maps a to $b[x := a]$ for all $a \in A$.

1.1   The Curry-Howard-interpretation

The λ-calculus consists of two basic operations on terms, *application* and *abstraction*, both with their corresponding typing rules. These rules are exposed in Table 1. The set Γ is called the *context*. It is a sequence of *statements* of the form $x_i : A_i$ with all the x_i's mutually distinct variables. The types A_i in Γ represent the assumptions (declarations) that are made. The axiom Ax encodes the idea that the statements of the context are assumptions.

$$\frac{}{\Gamma \vdash x : A} \; Ax \quad \langle x : A \rangle \in \Gamma$$

$$\frac{\Gamma \vdash F : A \to B \quad \Gamma \vdash x : A}{\Gamma \vdash Fx : B} \; App$$

$$\frac{\Gamma, x : A \vdash b : B}{\Gamma \vdash \lambda x : A . b : A \to B} \; Abs$$

Table 1: Rules of inference

Curry and Howard introduced another interpretation of the statement $b : B$, often referred to as 'propositions as types'. In this interpretation the type B represents a proposition instead of a set and b represents a proof of that proposition B. In this case the arrow is interpreted as the logical implication. *App* is understood as 'Fx proves B when F proves $A \to B$ and x proves A'. *Abs* is understood as '$\lambda x : A . b$ proves $A \to B$ when b proves B'. $\lambda x : A . b$ builds the proof $b[x := a]$ of B from the proof a of A. This is exactly the intuitionistic idea that a proof of $A \to B$ is an object that transforms a proof of A into a proof of B. In the Curry-Howard interpretation the application rule *App* corresponds to the arrow-elimination rule $(\to E)$ of propositional logic, and the abstraction rule *Abs* rule corresponds to the arrow-introduction rule $(\to I)$.

We give an example of the Curry-Howard interpretation. We omit brackets according to the convention that $A \to B \to C$ stands for $A \to (B \to C)$ and xyz stands for $(xy)z$. When $\Gamma \stackrel{\text{def}}{=} \langle x : A \to B \to C , y : A \to B , z : A \rangle$ then we have the following derivation

$$\cfrac{\cfrac{\cfrac{\overline{\Gamma \vdash x : A \to B \to C}\ Ax \quad \overline{\Gamma \vdash z : A}\ Ax}{\Gamma \vdash xz : B \to C}\ App \quad \cfrac{\overline{\Gamma \vdash y : A \to B}\ Ax \quad \overline{\Gamma \vdash z : A}\ Ax}{\Gamma \vdash yz : B}\ App}{\Gamma \vdash xz(yz) : C}\ App}{\cfrac{\cfrac{\langle x : A \to B \to C\ ,\ y : A \to B \rangle \vdash \lambda z.\, xz(yz) : A \to C}{\langle x : A \to B \to C \rangle \vdash \lambda yz.\, xz(yz) : (A \to B) \to A \to C}\ Abs}{\langle\ \rangle \vdash \lambda xyz.\, xz(yz) : (A \to B \to C) \to (A \to B) \to A \to C}\ Abs}\ Abs$$

proving the well-known tautology $(A \to B \to C) \to (A \to B) \to A \to C$.

The typed λ-calculus given by the inference rules of Table 1 is known as $\lambda^\to$ in the literature. In the following subsections we will extend $\lambda^\to$ in order to improve the expressive power of the system.

1.2 The type forming connectives $\to$ and Π

In the preceding subsection we already mentioned that $A \to B$ is a type whenever A and B are. In Backus-Naur-form we could express this as follows:

$$\mathbb{T} ::= \mathbb{C} \mid \mathbb{T} \to \mathbb{T}$$

$\mathbb{T}$ stands for the set of all possible types. $\mathbb{C}$ is a set of constants.

In the previous subsection we explained that for instance $B \to A$ is provable in context $\langle x : A \rangle$. In fact we also have the 'meta assumption' that A and B are propositions. One can introduce a constant $*^p \in \mathbb{C}$ representing the set of all propositions. This enables us to declare the assumption that A is a proposition by $\langle A : *^p \rangle$. Now it is no longer a meta assumption. For instance the proposition $B \to A$ is not provable in context $\langle x : A \rangle$ but in context $\langle A : *^p\ ,\ B : *^p\ ,\ x : A \rangle$. Similarly we can define a constant $*^s$ representing the set of all sets.

$x : A$ and $A : *^s$ is interpreted as x is an element of set A
$x : A$ and $A : *^p$ is interpreted as x is a proof of proposition A

A is called a *type* and x is called a *term* of type A. The following example illustrates that the rules of Table 1 are not satisfactory anymore when $*^p$ and $*^s$ are added to the system.

Example 1.1. Consider the context $\Gamma \equiv \langle B : *^p\ ,\ A : *^p\ ,\ x : A \rangle$. This must be understood as 'Let A and B are propositions and x a proof of A', then

$$\cfrac{\cfrac{\cfrac{\overline{\Gamma \vdash x : A}\ Ax}{\langle B : *^p\ ,\ A : *^p \rangle \vdash \lambda x{:}A.\, x : A \to A}\ Abs}{\langle B : *^p \rangle \vdash \lambda A{:}*^p.\, \lambda x{:}A.\, x : *^p \to A \to A}\ Abs \quad \cfrac{\overline{\langle B : *^p \rangle \vdash B : *^p}\ Ax}{}}{\langle B : *^p \rangle \vdash \lambda x{:}B.\, x : A \to A}\ App$$

Something is going wrong here: $\lambda x : B.\, x$ should not be a proof of $A \to A$. When we replace $*^p$ by $*^s$ in this example then exactly the same problem arises: $\lambda x : B . x$ should not be a mapping from A to A. Apparently it is not correct to say that the type of $\lambda A : * . \lambda x : A . x$ is $* \rightarrow A \rightarrow A$ (where $*$ ranges over $\{*^p, *^s\}$).

The problem is caused by the fact that the variable from which has been abstracted, occurs in the type of the term. In this example: A occurs in $A \rightarrow A$. This was not the case when we abstracted from x. What we need is another type forming operation, which allows the dependence of $A \rightarrow A$ on A. For this new operation the symbol Π is used, so:

$$\lambda A : *^p . \lambda x : A . x : \Pi A : *^p . A \rightarrow A$$

We have to modify our set $\mathbb{T}$ of all possible types. The basic types A and B have become type variables (i.e. abstractions from A and B are allowed) but $*^p$ and $*^s$ remain constants for no abstractions from $*^p$ or $*^s$ are allowed. Furthermore we have to add the new type forming operator Π.

$$\mathbb{T} ::= \mathbb{V} \mid \mathbb{C} \mid \mathbb{T} \rightarrow \mathbb{T} \mid \Pi \mathbb{V} : \mathbb{T} . \mathbb{T}$$

From now on the set $\mathbb{T}$ is only a set of *pseudo types*. For instance $\Pi v : v . t$ with $v \in \mathbb{V}$ and $t \in \mathbb{T}$ is a type that one would like to exclude. Such types will be called *illegal*.

Note that the choice of Π is a natural choice when we interpret types as sets again. $F : \Pi x : A . B(x)$ is an object that gives an element $F \, a : B(a)$ when applied to element $a : A$. Such object can be identified with an element of the product of sets $B(x)$ with x ranging over set A, usually denoted by

$$\prod_{x \in A} B(x)$$

The interpretation of the type forming operator Π in the case of 'propositions as types' is well illustrated by the term $I_{poly} \equiv \lambda A : *^p . \lambda x : A . x$. This term constructs a proof of $A \rightarrow A$ from an arbitrary proposition A. In other words: it is a proof of $\forall A . A \rightarrow A$. This suggests that in the Curry-Howard interpretation Π should be read as $\forall$.

Another observation is that a function from A to B is in fact a tuple $(\ldots, b_x, \ldots)$ with x ranging over A. This tuple is an element of

$$\prod_{x \in A} B$$

where x is a variable that does not occur free in B. (The product of A copies of the same set B.) Therefore, $A \rightarrow B$ is nothing more than a special case of $\Pi x : A . B$. From now on the type $A \rightarrow B$ is just an abbreviation of $\Pi x : A . B$ with the bound variable x not occurring free in B. The rules given in Table 1 are replaced by the more general rules given in Table 2. Note that ΠE (resp. ΠI) generalises $\rightarrow E$ (resp. $\rightarrow I$) as $B[x := a] \equiv B$ whenever x does not occur free in B.

So far we are able to build objects of the form $\lambda term.term$ $(I_A \equiv \lambda x : A . x)$ as well as objects of the form $\lambda type.term$ $(I_{poly} \equiv \lambda A : *^p . I_A)$. Under the

$$\frac{}{\Gamma \vdash x : A} \, Ax \quad \langle x : A \rangle \in \Gamma$$

$$\frac{\Gamma \vdash F : \Pi x {:} A . B \quad \Gamma \vdash a : A}{\Gamma \vdash Fa : B[x := a]} \, \Pi E$$

$$\frac{\Gamma, x : A \vdash b : B}{\Gamma \vdash \lambda x {:} A . b : \Pi x {:} A . B} \, \Pi I$$

Table 2: Π-introduction and Π-elimination

Curry-Howard-interpretation this corresponds to second order propositional logic. Since we are also interested in predicate logic we need the facility to build objects of the form $\lambda term.type$. Defining a predicate over some set A, corresponds to permitting dependency of propositions on specific elements of A. When $P(x) : *^p$ for some $x : A$ and $A : *^s$ then $\lambda x : A . P(x)$ is of the form $\lambda term.type$. However, building $\lambda x : A . P(x)$ by using ΠI of Table 2 is not possible because $\Pi x : A . *^p$ ($\equiv A \to *^p$) which should be the type of $\lambda x : A . P(x)$ is not allowed since $x \notin \mathbb{V}$. (x is not a *type* variable.) This problem is solved when we extend $\mathbb{T}$ with elements of the form $\lambda \mathbb{V} {:} \mathbb{T} . \mathbb{T}$ and $\mathbb{T} \, \mathbb{T}$. Both *types* and *terms* then can come from the same set $\mathbb{T}$. Types and terms are not mixed up, because types have type $*^p$ or $*^s$. The system we defined by the rules of Table 2 together with the modification that both terms and types come from the set

$$\mathbb{T} ::= \mathbb{C} \mid \mathbb{V} \mid \mathbb{T} \, \mathbb{T} \mid \lambda \mathbb{V} {:} \mathbb{T} . \mathbb{T} \mid \Pi \mathbb{V} {:} \mathbb{T} . \mathbb{T},$$

and the context does not contain illegal types, will be denoted by us as λLC. (L stands for Logic.) When $*^p$ and $*^s$ are identified in λLC then we obtain the *Calculus of Constructions* (λC) [6].

1.3 The calculus of inductive constructions

The *Calculus of Inductive Constructions* (λIC) is an extension of λLC. The main difference between λIC and λLC is the presence of so called *inductive types* in λIC. We illustrate the motivations for extending λLC with inductive types by an example.

Example 1.2. Assume that we want to have a type *nat*, representing the natural numbers. The first (naive) suggestion is to declare $nat : *^s$, $O : nat$ and $S : nat \to nat$. Now $\underline{n} \stackrel{\text{def}}{=} \underbrace{S(\cdots(S \, O) \cdots)}_{n}$ represent $n \in \mathbb{N}$. The problem with this implementation is that the numbers are too passive. It is impossible to construct for instance a term *sum* satisfying the property

$$sum \; \underline{n} \; \underline{m} =_\beta \underline{n+m} \qquad \text{for all } n, m \in \mathbb{N}$$

This problem can be solved by using the following impredicative definition for the natural numbers.

$$
\begin{aligned}
nat &\equiv \Pi X{:}*^s \,.\, X \to (X \to X) \to X \\
O &\equiv \lambda X{:}*^s \,.\, \lambda x{:}X \,.\, \lambda f{:}X \to X \,.\, x \\
S &\equiv \lambda n{:}nat \,.\, \lambda X{:}*^s \,.\, \lambda x{:}X \,.\, \lambda f{:}X \to X \,.\, f(n \; X \; x \; f)
\end{aligned}
$$

Obviously we have that $O : nat$ and $S : nat \to nat$ again. In this case

$$\underline{n} \overset{\text{def}}{=} \lambda X{:}*^s \,.\, \lambda x{:}X \,.\, \lambda f{:}X \to X \,.\, \underbrace{f(\cdots(f \; x)\cdots)}_{n}$$

Note that $S \; \underline{n} =_\beta \underline{n+1}$. ($\underline{n}$ is called a *Church numeral*.) It is easy to verify that

$$sum \equiv \lambda n{:}nat \,.\, \lambda m{:}nat \,.\, \lambda X{:}*^s \,.\, \lambda x{:}X \,.\, \lambda f{:}X \to X \,.\, n \; X \; (m \; X \; x \; f) \; f$$

satisfies $sum \; \underline{n} \; \underline{m} =_\beta \underline{n+m}$ for all $n, m \in \mathbb{N}$.

Although the latter encoding is considerably better than the first one, it still has some serious disadvantages:

- We don't have a proof for the induction principle on the natural numbers. Consequently we can not prove properties like $\Pi x : nat \,.\, less \; x \; (S \; x)$ although we can prove $less \; \underline{n} \; (S \; \underline{n})$ for every $n \in \mathbb{N}$.
  ($less : nat \to nat \to *^p$ represents the $<$-relation.)

- We are not able to prove $\underline{0} \neq \underline{1}$

- Any predecessor function takes at least linear time. (The predecessor of $\underline{n+1}$ is computed in at least n steps.)

All these problems can be solved by extending the system with inductive types. The extension is too complicated to be explained here in detail. We only illustrate the basic idea by some representative examples.

Definition 1.3. *The set* $\mathbb{T}$ *of pseudo types is defined by the following abstract syntax:*

$$
\begin{aligned}
\mathbb{T} \quad ::= \quad & \mathbb{C} \mid \mathbb{V} \mid \mathbb{T} \, \mathbb{T} \mid \lambda \mathbb{V}{:}\mathbb{T} . \mathbb{T} \mid \Pi \mathbb{V}{:}\mathbb{T} . \mathbb{T} \mid \mathsf{Ind}(\mathbb{V} : \mathbb{T})\{\mathbb{T} \mid \cdots \mid \mathbb{T}\} \mid \\
& \mathsf{Constr}(\mathbb{N}, \mathbb{T}) \mid \mathsf{Elim}(\mathbb{T}, \mathbb{T})\{\mathbb{T} \mid \cdots \mid \mathbb{T}\}
\end{aligned}
$$

Note that λIC *consists of extra typing rules for* Ind-*types,* Constr-*types and* Elim-*types. All these rules can be found in* [15]. *We do not expose them here. Types of the form* $\mathsf{Ind}(\mathbb{V} : \mathbb{T})\{\mathbb{T} \mid \cdots \mid \mathbb{T}\}$ *are called inductive types.*

For instance

$$\mathsf{Ind}(X : *^s)\{X \mid X \to X\}$$

is an inductive type. X is a bound variable in this type. This inductive type should be understood as 'the smallest set X that is closed under two constructors, one of type X and one of type $X \to X$. More general $\mathsf{Ind}(X : A)\{C_1 \mid \cdots \mid C_p\}$ is the smallest set (weakest proposition) of type A that is closed under its p constructors, that have types $C_1, \ldots, C_p$. Under suitable conditions (that are satisfied in all our examples of inductive types) this smallest set does exist. $\mathsf{Constr}(i, \mathsf{Ind}(X : A)\{C_1 \mid \cdots \mid C_p\})$ of type $C_i[X := \mathsf{Ind}(X : A)\{C_1 \mid \cdots \mid C_p\}]$ stands for the i-th constructor of $\mathsf{Ind}(X : A)\{C_1 \mid \cdots \mid C_p\}$. $(1 \leq i \leq p)$. Together with an inductive type comes a computational device: ι-reduction. All together, we have the following inductive encoding for the natural numbers.

Example 1.4. Encoding of the natural numbers in λIC.

$$
\begin{array}{llll}
nat & \equiv \mathsf{Ind}(X : *^s)\{X \mid X \to X\} & : & *^s \\
O & \equiv \mathsf{Constr}(1, nat) & : & X \quad [X := nat] \quad \equiv nat \\
S & \equiv \mathsf{Constr}(2, nat) & : & X \to X[X := nat] \quad \equiv nat \to nat
\end{array}
$$

Example 1.5. Let $\Gamma \equiv \langle A : *^p \,, B : *^p \rangle$. Another interesting inductive type, definable in context Γ, is

$$\mathsf{Ind}(X : *^p)\{A \to X \mid B \to X\}$$

It is natural to abbreviate this term with $or(A, B)$ because it is true (inhabited) whenever A or B is true (inhabited). This follows directly from the typing rule for *constr*-terms [15]:

$$
\begin{array}{llll}
\mathsf{Constr}(1, or(A, B)) & : & A \to X[X := or(A, B)] & \equiv A \to or(A, B) \\
\mathsf{Constr}(2, or(A, B)) & : & B \to X[X := or(A, B)] & \equiv B \to or(A, B)
\end{array}
$$

It is perfectly allowed to construct a polymorphic 'or' via λ-abstractions:

$$or \equiv \lambda A{:}*^p . \lambda B{:}*^p . or(A, B)$$

For the construction of inhabitants of the induction principles ($or(A, B)$ is the *weakest* proposition which is true when A and B are true, *nat* is the *smallest* set containing all elements that can be constructed from O and S, ect.) we need terms of the form $\mathsf{Elim}(\mathbb{T}, \mathbb{T})\{\mathbb{T} \mid \cdots \mid \mathbb{T}\}$. The induction principles are obtained by abstracting from the free variables in such Elim-terms (see examples). In general the term $\mathsf{Elim}(a, B)\{f_1 \mid \cdots \mid f_p\}$ is not legal. One of the constraints is that the type A of a must be of the form $I\ t_1 \cdots t_m$ for some inductive type I. The type of f_i must be F_i, where F_i is derived from the i-th constructor of I as explained in [15] (for all $1 \leq i \leq p$, $p \geq 0$ is the number of constructors of I). When $\mathsf{Elim}(a, B)\{f_1 \mid \cdots \mid f_p\}$ is constructed from a then the inductive type I is eliminated. This explains the name Elim. When a is build from the i-th constructor of I, then the type of $\mathsf{Elim}(a, B)\{f_1 \mid \cdots \mid f_p\}$ is an application of f_i. We restrict ourselves to some examples.

Example 1.6. Define $sum \equiv \lambda n : nat. \lambda m : nat. \mathsf{Elim}(n, nat)\{m \mid \lambda y : nat. S\}$ then

$$sum \; \underline{n} \; \underline{m} =_\beta \underline{n+m}$$

where $\underline{n}$ abbreviates $\underbrace{S(\cdots(S\; O)\cdots)}_{n}$. The term sum is a recursively defined sum. Its reduction behaviour is as follows:

$$
\begin{aligned}
sum\; O\; m \quad &\twoheadrightarrow_\iota \quad m \\
sum\; (S\; n)\; m \quad &\twoheadrightarrow_\iota \quad (\lambda y : nat. S)\; n\; (sum\; n\; m) \quad \twoheadrightarrow_\beta \quad S\; (sum\; n\; m)
\end{aligned}
$$

More generally, when $b : B$ and $f : nat \to B \to B$, then

$$
\begin{aligned}
\mathsf{Elim}(O, B)\{b \mid f\} \quad &\twoheadrightarrow_\iota \quad b \\
\mathsf{Elim}(S\; n, B)\{b \mid f\} \quad &\twoheadrightarrow_\iota \quad f\; n\; \mathsf{Elim}(n, B)\{b \mid f\}
\end{aligned}
$$

Example 1.7. Assume
$\langle P : nat \to *^p \;, \; f_O : (P\; O) \;, \; f_S : \Pi x : nat. (P\; x) \to (P(S\; x)) \rangle \subseteq \Gamma$ then

$$\Gamma \vdash \mathsf{Elim}(n, P)\{f_O \mid f_S\} : (P\; n)$$

An inhabitant of the induction principle on nat is constructible now by simple λ-abstractions.

The false proposition ($\bot$) and the true proposition ($\top$) are also representable by inductive types. $\bot$ can be represented by an inductive type without any constructors (a term of type $\bot$ can not be constructed).

$$
\begin{aligned}
\bot \quad &\equiv \quad \mathsf{Ind}(X : *^p)\{\;\} \quad : \quad *^p \\
& \quad \mathsf{Elim}(f, P)\{\;\} \quad : \quad P \qquad \qquad \text{for all } f : \bot \text{ and } P : *^p
\end{aligned}
$$

The accompanying induction principle $\Pi P : *^p . \bot \to P$, which is inhabited by $\lambda P : *^p . \lambda f : \bot . \mathsf{Elim}(f, P)\{\;\}$, expresses that $\bot$ is the weakest proposition. The dual thing to say is that $\top$ is the strongest proposition. In formula:

$$\Pi P : *^p . P \to \top. \tag{1}$$

However, the inductive types can only express minimality, so (1) does not correspond to any induction principle. We only can say that $\top$ is the *least* proposition satisfying the property 'being true'.

$$
\begin{aligned}
\top \quad &\equiv \quad \mathsf{Ind}(X : *^p)\{X\} \quad : \quad *^p \\
\mathbb{I} \quad &\equiv \quad \mathsf{Constr}(1, \top) \quad : \quad X[X := \top] \equiv \top \\
& \quad \mathsf{Elim}(t, P)\{x\} \quad : \quad P \qquad \qquad \text{for all } P : *^p, x : P \text{ and } t : \top
\end{aligned}
$$

which leads to the induction principle $\Pi P : *^p . P \to (\top \to P)$ inhabited by the term $\lambda P : *^p . \lambda x : P . \lambda t : \top . \mathsf{Elim}(t, P)\{x\}$. Note that (1) is inhabited by $\lambda P : *^p . \lambda x : P . \mathbb{I}$.

2 The specification language μCRL

The syntax and semantics of μCRL are described in the style of ACP, which stands for Algebra of Communicating Processes [2]. We give a brief overview of the most important features.

2.1 Specifications in μCRL

The specification language μCRL is based on CRL (*Common Representation Language*). It has been developed by J.F. Groote and A. Ponse in 1990. The language μCRL consists of process algebra extended with abstract data types.

Assume a set $\mathcal{N}$ of so called *names*. These names are used to denote sorts, variables, functions, processes and labels of actions. An element of $\mathcal{N}$ is a word over an alphabet not containing the following symbols:

$$\mathcal{F} \ + \ \| \ \mathbb{L} \ | \ \lhd \ \rhd \ \cdot \ \partial \ \delta \ \tau \ \rho \ \sum \ \sqrt{} \ \times \ \to \ : \ = \ , \ ) \ (\ \} \ \{$$

Moreover, $\mathcal{N}$ does not contain "a space", "a newline" and the reserved keywords **sort, proc, var, act, func, comm, rew** and **from**.

In μCRL *data terms* and *process terms* are distinguished. In Backus-Naur notation the definition of process terms is as follows:

Definition 2.1. *An expression p is called a process term iff p has the following syntax:*

$$p \ ::= \ (p+p) \mid (p \cdot p) \mid (p \parallel p) \mid (p \mathbb{L} p) \mid (p \mid p) \mid (p \lhd t \rhd p) \mid$$
$$\sum(d : D, p) \mid \partial(\{n_1, \ldots, n_m\}, p) \mid \tau(\{n_1, \ldots, n_m\}, p) \mid$$
$$\rho(\{n_1 \to n_1', \ldots, n_m \to n_m'\}, p) \mid \delta \mid \tau \mid n(t_1, \ldots, t_k).$$

where $k \geq 0$, $n, n_i, n_i' \in \mathcal{N}$. The t, t_i stand for data terms (explained later), d is a variable and D denotes a sort name. Brackets are omitted according to

sort	Bool		
	D		
func	$true, false$	$: \to$ **Bool**	
act	r_1, r_2, c_2, s_2, s_3	$: D$	
proc	$B_{12} = \Sigma(d : D, r_1(d) \cdot s_2(d)) \cdot B_{12}$		B12
	$B_{23} = \Sigma(d : D, r_2(d) \cdot s_3(d)) \cdot B_{23}$		B23
	$B_{123} = \tau(\{c_2\}, \partial(\{r_2, s_2\}, B_{12} \parallel B_{23}))$		B123
comm	$r_2 \mid s_2 = c_2$		

Table 3: The μCRL specification *BUFFER*.

the convention that $\cdot$ binds strongest, the conditional construct binds stronger than the parallel operators which in turn bind stronger than $+$. We briefly describe the behaviour of the different processes.

- $p + q$ behaves like p or like q.

- $p \cdot q$ behaves like q after p.

- $p \parallel q$ denotes the interleaving of p and q, except that actions of both arguments may communicate if explicitly allowed in a communication specification.

- $p \parallel\!\!\!\!\_ \, q$ behaves like $p \parallel q$ except that the first step must originate from p.

- $p \mid q$ behaves like $p \parallel q$ except that the first step is a communication action between p and q.

- $p \triangleleft t \triangleright q$ behaves like p when t evaluates to *true* and as q when t evaluates to *false*.

- $\sum(d : D, p(d))$ behaves like $p(d_1) + p(d_2) + \cdots$, where $p(d)$ denotes a process term which possibly contains d and $D = \{d_1, d_2, \ldots\}$.

- $\partial(\{n_1, \ldots, n_m\}, p)$ renames n_i to δ.

- $\tau(\{n_1, \ldots, n_m\}, p)$ renames n_i to τ.

- $\rho(\{n_1 \twoheadrightarrow n'_1, \ldots, n_m \twoheadrightarrow n'_m\}, p)$ renames n_i to n'_i.

- δ describes the process that cannot do anything, in particular it cannot terminate.

- τ represents internal activity that cannot be observed.

- $n(t_1, \ldots, t_k)$ stands for an action or process with k parameters.

The syntax of *specifications in μCRL* is illustrated in Tables 3 and 4. For details we refer to [10].

2.2 Data- and process variables

In order to express general properties that a specification may have μCRL consists of two kinds of *variables*.

Definition 2.2. *A finite set V_d containing elements of the form $\langle d : D \rangle$ with d some name is called a set of data variables over E iff*

1. *the name D is declared as a sort in E,*

2. *d is not a constant, or an unparameterised action or process from E,*

3. *for each sort $D' \not\equiv D$ of E it holds that $\langle d : D' \rangle \not\subseteq V_d$.*

Let V_d be a set of data variables over E.

Definition 2.3. *A finite set V_p of names is called a set of process variables over E and V_d iff none of its elements occur as a variable in V_d.*

sort	Bool	
	D	
	bag	
var	b_1, b_2	: Bool
	b, c	: bag
	d, e	: D
func	$true, false$	: $\rightarrow$ Bool
	if_bool	: Bool $\times$ Bool $\times$ Bool$\rightarrow$Bool
	if_bag	: Bool $\times$ bag $\times$ $bag$$\rightarrow$$bag$
	eq	: $D \times D$$\rightarrow$Bool
	$\varnothing$	: $\rightarrow bag$
	$test$	: $D \times bag$$\rightarrow$Bool
	in, rem	: $D \times bag$$\rightarrow$$bag$
	con	: $bag \times bag$$\rightarrow$$bag$
act	r, s	: D
rew	$if\_bool(true, b_1, b_2) = b_1$	IF1
	$if\_bool(false, b_1, b_2) = b_2$	IF2
	$if\_bag(true, b, c) = b$	IF3
	$if\_bag(false, b, c) = c$	IF4
	$eq(d, d) = true$	EQ
	$test(d, \varnothing) = false$	BAG1
	$test(d, in(e, b)) = if\_bool(eq(d, e), true, test(d, b))$	BAG2
	$in(d, in(e, b)) = in(e, in(d, b))$	BAG3
	$rem(d, \varnothing) = \varnothing$	BAG4
	$rem(d, in(e, b)) = if\_bag(eq(d, e), b, in(e, rem(d, b)))$	BAG5
	$con(\varnothing, b) = b$	BAG6
	$con(in(d, b), c) = in(d, con(b, c))$	BAG7
proc	$Bag(x : bag) = \Sigma(d : D, r(d) \cdot Bag(in(d, x))) +$	
	$\Sigma(d : D, s(d) \cdot Bag(rem(d, x)) \triangleleft test(d, x) \triangleright \delta)$	BAG

Table 4: The μCRL specification BAG.

We write E, V_d, V_p when E is a *well-formed specification* [10] with data variables V_d and process variables V_p.

Definition 2.4. *A data term over* E, V_d, V_p *is either a constant from* E, *a variable from* V_d *or an application of a function from* E *to data terms over* E, V_d, V_p *of the appropriate sort. A data term is called closed iff it does not contain any variables from* V_d.

Definition 2.5. *A process term over* E, V_d, V_p *is defined inductively over the syntax given in Definition 2.1*

- $p \circ q$ *with* $\circ \in \{+, \cdot, \|, \|\!\!\|, |, \triangleleft t \triangleright\}$ *and* t *a data term over* E, V_d, V_p *of sort* **Bool**, *is a process term over* E, V_d, V_p *if both* p *and* q *are,*

- $\Sigma(d : D, p)$ is a process term over E, V_d, V_p if p is a process term over

$$E, (V_d \setminus \{\langle d : n \rangle | n \in \mathcal{N}\}) \cup \{\langle d : D \rangle\}, V_p \setminus \{d\},$$

- $C(\{n_1, \ldots, n_k\}, p)$ with $C \in \{\partial, \tau\}$ is a process term over E, V_d, V_p if p is, and the n_i are labels of actions from E,

- $\rho(\{n_1 \rightarrow n_1', \ldots, n_m \rightarrow n_m'\}, p)$ is a process term over E, V_d, V_p if p is, and the n_i are labels of actions from E such that if $n_i : S_1 \times \cdots \times S_k$ is an action declaration in E then so is $n_i' : S_1 \times \cdots \times S_k$,

- δ and τ are process terms over E, V_d, V_p, from E or if $n \in V_p$,

- $n(t_1, \ldots, t_k)$ is a process term over E, V_d, V_p if either E contains an action declaration of the form $n : S_1 \times \cdots \times S_k$ or a process declaration of the form $n(x_1 : S_1, \ldots, x_k : S_k) = q$ and any t_i is a data term over E, V_d, V_p of sort S_i,

A process term is called closed iff it does not contain any variables from $V_d \cup V_p$.

Note: $k = 0$ is allowed in Definition 2.1 and Definition 2.5.

Definition 2.6. A formula over E, V_d, V_p is defined inductively in the following way:

- $\mathcal{F}$ is a formula over E, V_d, V_p.

- $t_1 = t_2$ is a formula over E, V_d, V_p iff

  - either t_1 and t_2 are data terms over E, V_d, V_p that are of the same sort,

  - or t_1 and t_2 are process terms over E, V_d, V_p.

- $\phi \rightarrow \psi$ is a formula over E, V_d, V_p iff both ϕ and ψ are formulas over E, V_d, V_p.

ϕ is a formula over E, V_d, V_p will be denoted as

$$\phi \quad \text{from} \quad E, V_d, V_p$$

The following abbreviations are used:

$$\neg\phi \stackrel{\text{def}}{=} \phi \rightarrow \mathcal{F},$$
$$\phi \vee \psi \stackrel{\text{def}}{=} (\neg\phi) \rightarrow \psi,$$
$$\phi \wedge \psi \stackrel{\text{def}}{=} \neg(\phi \rightarrow \neg\psi),$$

2.3 The accompanying proof theory

The proof theory for μCRL is given in a natural deduction format. A deduction is seen as a tree of which each node is labelled with a formula. The leaves of the tree are the *hypotheses* of the deduction.

Natural deductions are defined in a recursive way:

Definition 2.7. $\mathcal{D}$ is called a *logical deduction* if

- $\mathcal{D}$ is a single node tree with as label a formula

$$\phi \quad \text{from } E, V_d, V_p.$$

- $\mathcal{D}$ is constructed out of natural deductions $\mathcal{D}_1$ and $\mathcal{D}_2$ using the rules given in Table 5 under the following restrictions:

  - In applications of the rule $(\rightarrow I)$ and the rule *RAA* (Reductio Ad Absurdum) all open assumptions of the form indicated by $[\ldots]$ are cancelled.

  - In applications of $(\rightarrow I)$, *RAA*, *REFL*, *VAR* and *SUB* the conclusion must be a formula.

  - In applications of *SUB* the variable x may not be free in any hypothesis of $\mathcal{D}_1$.

  - Each application of *VAR* is restricted to one of the following cases:
    * $V_d \subseteq V_d'$ or $V_d' \subseteq V_d$, and $V_p = V_p'$.
    * $V_p \subseteq V_p'$ or $V_p' \subseteq V_p$, and $V_d = V_d'$.

Instantiations of the rule

$$\frac{}{\phi \quad \text{from } E, V_d, V_p} \text{ name of } \phi$$

are given in so called *modules*. These modules are 'building blocks' consisting of axioms and rules that describe a feature of concurrency in a certain semantical setting. Examples of modules are the *A*-axioms and the *CM*-axioms given in the appendix. More modules can be found in [11].

3 The representation of a μCRL specification

In this section we describe the encoding of process algebra notions in λIC. Every μCRL formula ϕ is mapped to a type $t : *^p$ of λIC. We write $[\![\phi]\!]$ for the type that represents ϕ. Instead of constructing a μCRL proof tree for formula ϕ we construct a λIC-term $p : [\![\phi]\!]$ in order to prove ϕ. For the construction of p we make use of the interactive proof construction program Coq [7], which is based on λIC. We frequently use the higher order features of λIC. Consequently we actually work in a much stronger and more expressive formalism than μCRL. This raises two problems. First, we would like to be able to prove that $[\![\phi]\!]$ is inhabited whenever there is a proof tree for ϕ. This

$$
\begin{array}{l}
[\phi \quad \text{from } E, V_d, V_p] \\
\qquad \mathcal{D}_1 \\
\dfrac{\psi \quad \text{from } E, V_d, V_p}{\phi \!\to\! \psi \quad \text{from } E, V_d, V_p}\,(\to\! I)
\end{array}
\qquad
\dfrac{\rule{0pt}{1.2em}}{\phi \quad \text{from } E, V_d, V_p}\ \text{name of } \phi
$$

$$
\dfrac{\begin{array}{cc} \mathcal{D}_1 & \mathcal{D}_2 \\ \phi \quad \text{from } E, V_d, V_p & \phi \!\to\! \psi \quad \text{from } E, V_d, V_p \end{array}}{\psi \quad \text{from } E, V_d, V_p}\,(\to\! E)
$$

$$
\begin{array}{l}
[\neg\phi \quad \text{from } E, V_d, V_p] \\
\qquad \mathcal{D}_1 \\
\dfrac{\mathcal{F} \quad \text{from } E, V_d, V_p}{\phi \quad \text{from } E, V_d, V_p}\,RAA
\end{array}
\qquad
\dfrac{\rule{0pt}{1.2em}}{t = t \quad \text{from } E, V_d, V_p}\,REFL
$$

$$
\dfrac{\begin{array}{cc} \mathcal{D}_1 & \mathcal{D}_2 \\ \phi[t/x] \quad \text{from } E, V_d, V_p & t = u \quad \text{from } E, V_d, V_p \end{array}}{\phi[u/x] \quad \text{from } E, V_d, V_p}\,REPL
$$

$$
\dfrac{\begin{array}{c} \mathcal{D}_1 \\ \phi \quad \text{from } E, V_d, V_p \end{array}}{\phi[t/x] \quad \text{from } E, V_d, V_p}\,SUB
\qquad
\dfrac{\begin{array}{c} \mathcal{D}_1 \\ \phi \quad \text{from } E, V_d, V_p \end{array}}{\phi \quad \text{from } E, V_d', V_p'}\,VAR
$$

Table 5: Rules for logical deductions

appears to be unproblematic since λIC is so much stronger than μCRL. The second problem, which is the converse of the first, is not so easily solved by handwaving. The question is the following: if a type of λIC encodes a formula of μCRL, is this formula then necessarily also a theorem of μCRL? One could weaken this question as follows: if a theorem of λIC encodes a formula of μCRL, is this formula true in the preferred semantic of μCRL (e.g. weak bisimulation semantics [...])? We need at least a positive answer to the weaker question (which of course would follow from a positive answer to the stronger question). In this paper we leave these questions aside, since we first want to explore whether our type theoretic approach is at all feasible, trusting that both questions have positive answers. If not in general, then at least under suitable conditions that can be met.

In the sequel we define a context $\Gamma(E, V_d, V_p)$ such that for all ϕ

$$
\phi \quad \text{from } E, V_d, V_p \implies \Gamma(E, V_d, V_p) \vdash [\![\phi]\!] : *^P. \tag{2}
$$

$\Gamma(E, V_d, V_p)$ contains statements that represent the information of μCRL specification E as well as statements (e.g. $[\![A3]\!] : [\![x + x = x]\!]$) representing the information given in the modules. The μCRL notions *sort, function, process* and *formula* are all represented in λIC by types. We write $[\![O]\!]$ for the type that represents the μCRL notion O.

3.1 Representing sorts and functions as types

We want to build a context $\Gamma(E, V_d, V_p)$ in which all the information of μCRL specification E is encoded. The first step in the construction of $\Gamma(E, V_d, V_p)$ is the encoding of the sorts and functions of E. The sorts and functions (including constants) can be represented in a straightforward way. Consider for instance the μCRL specification *BUFFER*, given in Table 3. The sorts and functions of this specification can be encoded as

$$\langle\, [\![\mathbf{Bool}]\!]\,,\ [\![D]\!] : *^s\,,\ [\![true]\!],\ [\![false]\!] : [\![\mathbf{Bool}]\!]\,\rangle \tag{3}$$

Functions which have a cartesian product as domain (like $test : D \times bag \twoheadrightarrow \mathbf{Bool}$ in μCRL specification *BAG*) can be represented by identifying $A \times B \twoheadrightarrow C$ with $A \twoheadrightarrow (B \twoheadrightarrow C)$. So,

$$[\![test]\!] : [\![D]\!] \to [\![bag]\!] \to [\![\mathbf{Bool}]\!]$$

The μCRL symbol $\twoheadrightarrow$, standing for functional implication here, is identified with the arrow of λIC. An alternative would be to define

$$[\![test]\!] : [\![\times]\!]\,[\![D]\!]\,[\![bag]\!] \to [\![\mathbf{Bool}]\!]$$

where $[\![\times]\!]$ abbreviates $\lambda A : *^s . \lambda B : *^s . \mathsf{Ind}(X : *^s)\{A \to B \to X\}$. We prefer the first option. Encoding the cartesian product as an inductive type would force us to work with pairs and projections, which can be quite tedious.

In μCRL one has the option to assume a module IND. This module facilitates the construction of proofs by induction. For instance a proof for $P(x)$, $x \in \mathbb{N}$, can be constructed from a proof for $P(O)$ and a proof of $\forall y.P(y) \to P(S(y))$. The set $\{O, S\}$ must be a so called *set of constructors* for $\mathbb{N}$. The property of 'being a set of constructors' can only be proved on a meta-level.

Examples of sets of constructors are $\{\varnothing, in\}$ which is a set of constructors for *bag* (see specification *BAG* on page 12) and $\{true, false\}$ which is a set of constructors for $\mathbf{Bool}$.

The meta result that $\{true, false\}$ is a set of constructors for $\mathbf{Bool}$ can be encoded by using an inductive type. $[\![\mathbf{Bool}]\!]$, $[\![true]\!]$ and $[\![false]\!]$ are removed from (3) in that case and defined as abbreviations for the following terms.

$$[\![\mathbf{Bool}]\!] \stackrel{\mathrm{def}}{=} \mathsf{Ind}(X : *^s)\{X \mid X\}$$
$$[\![true]\!] \stackrel{\mathrm{def}}{=} \mathsf{Constr}(1, [\![\mathbf{Bool}]\!])$$
$$[\![false]\!] \stackrel{\mathrm{def}}{=} \mathsf{Constr}(2, [\![\mathbf{Bool}]\!])$$

3.2 Representing the rewrite rules as types

Rewrite rules of a μCRL specification are of the form $d_1 = d_2$ where d_1 and d_2 are data terms of the same sort, say D. This can be encoded by adding a term p of type $[\![d_1 = d_2]\!]$ to $\Gamma(E, V_d, V_p)$. (p represents a proof for $d_1 = d_2$.) Assume that we already have representations $[\![d_1]\!]$, $[\![d_2]\!]$ and $[\![D]\!]$ for d_1, d_2

and D, then $d_1 = d_2$ can be represented by $[\![=_D]\!] [\![d_1]\!] [\![d_2]\!]$ for some suitable term $[\![=_D]\!]$, of type $[\![D]\!] \rightarrow [\![D]\!] \rightarrow *^p$, representing equality on D. The representation $[\![=_D]\!]$ for equality on D must be correct with respect to the rules *REFL* and *REPL* of Table 5.

Given a type $A : *^s$ and a type $a : A$ then we can define the predicate 'being equal to a' as an inductive type for it is the *weakest* predicate that holds in a. When we abstract from $a : A$ and from $A : *^s$ afterwards then we get a polymorphic equality. In formula:

$$[\![=]\!] \overset{\text{def}}{=} \lambda A:*^s . \lambda a:A . \mathsf{Ind}(X : A \rightarrow *^p)\{X\ a\} : \Pi A:*^s . A \rightarrow A \rightarrow *^p.$$

Now we can define $[\![=_D]\!] \equiv [\![=]\!] [\![D]\!]$. This inductively defined equality is equivalent to *Leibniz equality* (identity of indiscernibles) which is easy to formulate in type theory:

$$\mathcal{L} \overset{\text{def}}{=} \lambda A:*^s . \lambda a,b:A . \Pi P:A \rightarrow *^p . (P\ a) \rightarrow (P\ b)$$

It is a trivial exercise to construct a proof of $([\![=]\!]\ A\ a\ b)$ from a proof of $(\mathcal{L}\ A\ a\ b)$ and vice versa.

The correctness with respect to the *REFL* rule follows directly from the typing rule for Constr-terms:

$$\mathsf{Constr}(1, [\![=]\!] [\![D]\!] [\![d]\!]) : X\ [\![d]\!] [X := [\![=]\!] [\![D]\!] [\![d]\!]] \equiv [\![=]\!] [\![D]\!] [\![d]\!] [\![d]\!].$$

In Section 4 the correctness of our representation with respect to the rules in Table 5 is explained in more detail.

3.3 The representation of the actions as types

We introduce the following denotation.

$$\mathcal{A}^E_{\delta,\tau} \overset{\text{def}}{=} \{a \mid a \text{ is an atomic action of } E\} \cup \{\delta, \tau\}.$$

Our first idea was to define a variable $[\![\mathcal{A}^E_{\delta,\tau}]\!] : *^s$ representing the set of all actions. An action declaration

act $\quad a : D_1 \times \cdots \times D_k$

could in that case be represented by adding

$$[\![a]\!] : [\![D_1]\!] \rightarrow \cdots \rightarrow [\![D_k]\!] \rightarrow [\![\mathcal{A}^E_{\delta,\tau}]\!]$$

to $\Gamma(E, V_d, V_p)$. This way we do not encode that $\mathcal{A}^E_{\delta,\tau}$ is the least set containing the actions of specification E and hence we can not prove that $a_1 \neq a_2$ when a_1 and a_2 are actions of E. However, such proofs turned out to be very useful at several places. For instance the construction of a λ-term *in_list* of type $[\![\mathcal{A}^E_{\delta,\tau}]\!] \rightarrow (list\,[\![\mathcal{A}^E_{\delta,\tau}]\!]) \rightarrow *^p$ which represents the membership relation is difficult without such proofs.

Of course we can simply posit that $a_1 \neq a_2$ by adding a term of type $[a_1 \neq a_2]$ to your context (where $[a_1 \neq a_2]$ is some proper representation of $a_1 \neq a_2$), but this quadratic in the number of actions and can be quite a lot of boring work in large examples. This motivates our choice to represent the actions by an inductive type.

Representing $\mathcal{A}^E_{\delta,\tau}$ by an inductive type is realised by saying that $[\mathcal{A}^E_{\delta,\tau}]$ is the smallest set X closed under certain constructors and adding a constructor for every action of your μCRL specification. The action a above is represented by a constructor of type $[D_1] \to \cdots \to [D_k] \to X$. In formula:

$$[\mathcal{A}^E_{\delta,\tau}] \equiv \mathsf{Ind}(X : *^s)\{\cdots | [D_1] \to \cdots \to [D_k] \to X | \cdots\}$$

It is convenient to omit the data part at this stage. In fact we represent the set of action-*names* instead of the set of actions. The data is added later when we interpret our action as a process (see Subsection 3.4).

Let $\{a_1, \ldots, a_n\}$ be the set of action-names of specification E, then

$$[\mathcal{A}^E_{\delta,\tau}] \overset{\text{def}}{=} \mathsf{Ind}(X : *^s)\{\underbrace{X | \cdots | X}_{n+2}\}$$

$$[a_i] \overset{\text{def}}{=} \mathsf{Constr}(i, [\mathcal{A}^E_{\delta,\tau}]) \qquad \text{for } i = 1, \ldots, n$$

$[\delta] \overset{\text{def}}{=} \mathsf{Constr}(n+1, [\mathcal{A}^E_{\delta,\tau}])$ represents δ and $[\tau] \overset{\text{def}}{=} \mathsf{Constr}(n+2, [\mathcal{A}^E_{\delta,\tau}])$ represents τ. Now we can prove $[a_1 \neq a_2]$ when $[a_1 \neq a_2]$ stands for $[=] [\mathcal{A}^E_{\delta,\tau}] [a_1] [a_2] \to \bot$. Define $P_i \equiv \lambda a : [\mathcal{A}^E_{\delta,\tau}] . \mathsf{Elim}(a, *^p)\{C_1, \ldots, C_n\}$ where $C_i \equiv \top$ and $C_j \equiv \bot$ for all $j \neq i$. Now

$$\lambda H : [=] [\mathcal{A}^E_{\delta,\tau}] [a_i] [a_j] . \mathsf{Elim}(H, P_i)\{\mathbb{I}\} : [a_i \neq a_j]$$

for all $j \neq i$ and for all $i = 1, \ldots, n$.

3.4 The representation of the processes as types

We write $\mathcal{P}^E$ for the set of processes generated by specification E. Examples of elements of $\mathcal{P}^{BAG}$ are

$r(e) + Bag(in(d, \varnothing))$
$r(d)^\omega$
$s(d) \lhd test(e, \varnothing) \rhd \delta$.

$r(d)^\omega$ is the unique process satisfying $X = r(d) \cdot X$. It seems natural to implement the processes as an inductive set: $\mathcal{P}^E$ is the smallest set such that $x + y \in \mathcal{P}^E$, $x \cdot y \in \mathcal{P}^E$, etc. if $x, y \in \mathcal{P}^E$. (One has to add a constructor that constructs infinite processes from their defining equations and a constructor that interprets actions as processes.)

However, the set $\mathcal{P}^E$ is not a *free structure*, i.e. two processes that are built from different constructors are not necessarily different (e.g. $(z \cdot z) + (z \cdot z) =$

$(z \cdot z)$ by the idempotency rule A3 of Table 6). Consequently we can not use the inductive type $[\![=]\!]$ that we used for equality on data terms for equality on inductively defined processes. Example 3.1 shows how to construct a proof of $\perp$ when $[\![=]\!]$ is used for equality on inductively defined processes.

Example 3.1. Let

$$[\![\mathcal{P}^E]\!] \equiv \mathsf{Ind}(X : *^s)\{X \to X \to X | X \to X \to X | \cdots\}$$
$$[\![+]\!] \equiv \mathsf{Constr}(1, [\![\mathcal{P}^E]\!])$$
$$[\![\cdot]\!] \equiv \mathsf{Constr}(2, [\![\mathcal{P}^E]\!])$$

Assume $z \in \mathcal{P}^E$ and define F of type $[\![\mathcal{P}^E]\!] \to *^p$ as follows:

$$F \equiv \lambda p \colon [\![\mathcal{P}^E]\!] . \mathsf{Elim}(p, *^p)\{$$
$$\lambda q_1 \colon [\![\mathcal{P}^E]\!] . \lambda Q_1 \colon *^p . \lambda q_2 \colon [\![\mathcal{P}^E]\!] . \lambda Q_2 \colon *^p . \perp \mid$$
$$\lambda q_1 \colon [\![\mathcal{P}^E]\!] . \lambda Q_1 \colon *^p . \lambda q_2 \colon [\![\mathcal{P}^E]\!] . \lambda Q_2 \colon *^p . \top \mid \cdots \}$$

Now, $F [\![(z \cdot z) + (z \cdot z)]\!] \twoheadrightarrow_\beta \perp$ and $F [\![z \cdot z]\!] \twoheadrightarrow_\beta \top$. When we combine this with the inhabitant $[\![A3]\!]$ of type $\Pi x \colon [\![\mathcal{P}^E]\!] . [\![=]\!] [\![\mathcal{P}^E]\!] x \, ([\![+]\!] \, x \, x)$ then we find

$$\mathsf{Elim}([\![A3]\!] \, [\![z \cdot z]\!], F)\{\mathbb{I}\} : \perp$$

This problem can be solved by using another encoding for equality on processes. Another way (followed by us) to solve the problem is using a non-inductive type for the representation of $\mathcal{P}^E$ (*ia* stands for *interpretation action*):

$$[\![\mathcal{P}^E]\!] \quad : \quad *^s$$
$$[\![+]\!], [\![\cdot]\!], [\![\parallel]\!], [\![L]\!], [\![\mid]\!] \quad : \quad [\![\mathcal{P}^E]\!] \to [\![\mathcal{P}^E]\!] \to [\![\mathcal{P}^E]\!]$$
$$[\![\triangleleft \triangleright]\!] \quad : \quad [\![\mathcal{P}^E]\!] \to [\![\mathbf{Bool}]\!] \to [\![\mathcal{P}^E]\!] \to [\![\mathcal{P}^E]\!]$$
$$[\![\Sigma]\!] \quad : \quad \Pi D \colon *^s . (D \to [\![\mathcal{P}^E]\!]) \to [\![\mathcal{P}^E]\!]$$
$$ia \quad : \quad \Pi D \colon *^s . [\![A^E_{\delta, \tau}]\!] \to D \to [\![\mathcal{P}^E]\!]$$

An advantage of this approach is that we can use $[\![=]\!]$ for equality on processes. The μCRL rule *REPL*, which is used very frequently in derivations, is easier to handle when $[\![=]\!]$ is used.

Processes can be labelled with several data elements. A process $p(d_1, d_2)$ labelled with data elements $d_1 \in D_1$ and $d_2 \in D_2$ can be represented by a term $[\![p]\!] : [\![D_1]\!] \to [\![D_2]\!] \to [\![\mathcal{P}^E]\!]$. This way, it is not so easy to quantify over all processes in a satisfying way. For instance, let $\varphi(p(d_1, \ldots, d_k), d_1, \ldots, d_k)$ be a property depending on a process $p(d_1, \ldots, d_k)$ and its data elements $d_1, \ldots, d_k$, then it is difficult to express something like 'for any collection of data sets $D_1, \ldots, D_k$ and for any process $p : D_1 \times \cdots \times D_k$ and for any $d_1 \in D_1, \ldots, d_k \in D_k . \varphi(p(d_1, \ldots, d_k), d_1, \ldots, d_k)$ holds'. When every process is parameterised with exactly *one* data element then this can be expressed by

$$\Pi D \colon *^s . \Pi p \colon D \to [\![\mathcal{P}^E]\!] . \Pi d \colon D . [\![\varphi(p(d), d)]\!] .$$

Such quantification is used by the representation of the *Recursive Specification Principle* RSP (not explained here). *At most one* data set is achieved by using $[\times]$ in cases where more then one data set is involved. *At least one* data set is achieved by introducing a dummy data set

$$\Im \;\equiv\; \mathsf{Ind}(X : *^s)\{X\}$$
$$i \;\equiv\; \mathsf{Constr}(1, \Im)$$

for unlabelled processes.

The encoding of a process declaration is best explained by examples:

proc $X = a \cdot X$ *P1*

        $Y(d_1, d_2 : D) = Y(d_1, d_2) \lhd (d_1 = d_2) \rhd \delta$ *P2*

is encoded by adding to $\Gamma(E, V_d, V_p)$:

$$[X] \;:\; \Im \to [\mathcal{P}^E]$$
$$[Y] \;:\; ([\times]\,[D]\,[D]) \to [\mathcal{P}^E]$$
$$[P1] \;:\; [=]\,[\mathcal{P}^E]\,([X]\,i)\,([\cdot]\,(ia\,\Im\,[a]\,i)\,([X]\,i))$$
$$[P2] \;:\; \Pi d\!:\! [\times]\,[D]\,[D]\,.\, [=]\,[\mathcal{P}^E]\,([Y]\,d)\,([\lhd\,\rhd]\,([Y]\,d)$$
$$([=]\,[D]\,(\pi_1\,d)\,(\pi_2\,d))\,(ia\,\Im\,[\delta]\,i))$$

where π_1 and π_2 are the projection functions by $[\times]$ as given in [8].

3.5   The representation of μCRL formulae

Now that we have defined $[d]$ for data term d as well as $[p]$ for process term p, we can define how we represent the μCRL formulae.

Definition 3.2. *Let p_1, p_2 be process terms and d_1, d_2 be data terms of sort D. Furthermore let ϕ_1, ϕ_2 be μCRL formulae.*

$$[\mathcal{F}] \;\overset{\text{def}}{=}\; \bot$$
$$[d_1 = d_2] \;\overset{\text{def}}{=}\; [=]\,[D]\,[d_1]\,[d_2]$$
$$[p_1 = p_2] \;\overset{\text{def}}{=}\; [=]\,[\mathcal{P}^E]\,[p_1]\,[p_2]$$
$$[\phi_1 \rightarrowtail \phi_2] \;\overset{\text{def}}{=}\; [\phi_1] \to [\phi_2]$$

Consequently $[\neg\phi] \equiv [\phi \rightarrowtail \mathcal{F}] \equiv [\phi] \to [\mathcal{F}] \equiv [\phi] \to \bot$ *etc.*

Note that we identify $\to$ and $\rightarrowtail$ again. This time the symbol $\rightarrowtail$ stands for logical implication (instead of functional implication). The identification of both arrows is not correct now because $\rightarrowtail$ is a *classical* implication. We repair this 'mistake' by adding

$$Cl : \Pi P\!:\!*^P . (or\; P\; (P \to \bot))$$

to our context $\Gamma(E, V_d, V_p)$. A more rigorous way to overcome the problem of different meanings of logical symbols is the following strategy:

See $\to$ as a formalisation of the meta-implication $\implies$, and Π as a formalisation of meta-quantification.

We explain this by an example. The μCRL rule $\to E$ contains meta-implications. It can be rewritten as

$$\phi \text{ from } E, V_d, V_p \implies \phi \to \psi \text{ from } E, V_d, V_p \implies \psi \text{ from } E, V_d, V_p$$

This rule is schematic in ϕ and ψ (meta-quantification). Encode this rule by declaring

$$[\![\to E]\!] : \Pi p, q{:}\mathbf{F} . p \to ([\![\to]\!] \ p \ q) \to q$$

where $[\![\to]\!]$ is a variable of type $\mathbf{F} \to \mathbf{F} \to \mathbf{F}$ that represents $\to$ and $\mathbf{F}$ is a new sort that represents the set of μCRL formulae. Similarly

$$[\![\to I]\!] : \Pi p, q{:}\mathbf{F} . (p \to q) \to ([\![\to]\!] \ p \ q).$$

A drawback of this method is the amount of encoding. It is not yet clear to us how useful such an approach would be in practice. Some experiments in this direction are running in Utrecht at this moment. Formal correctness is of course what one should aim for, but one should realise that although our method is not (yet) proven correct, in practice we detect the errors in a hand-made proof by using this method.

3.6   The representation of the communication function γ

Assume the following communication declarations in the specification E.

comm $\quad \alpha_1^1 \mid \alpha_1^2 = \alpha_1^3$

$$\vdots$$

$$\alpha_r^1 \mid \alpha_r^2 = \alpha_r^3$$

where α_j^i ranges over the set of atomic actions $\{a_1, \ldots, a_m\}$. This communication declaration defines the communication function

$$\gamma : \mathcal{A}_{\delta,\tau}^E \times \mathcal{A}_{\delta,\tau}^E \longrightarrow \mathcal{A}_\delta^E$$

that maps (α_i^1, α_i^2) to α_i^3 for all $i = 1, \ldots, r$ and (a, a') to δ otherwise. We can represent γ by $[\![\gamma]\!]$ of type $[\![\mathcal{A}_{\delta,\tau}^E]\!] \to [\![\mathcal{A}_{\delta,\tau}^E]\!] \to [\![\mathcal{A}_{\delta,\tau}^E]\!]$ which is defined as follows:

$$\lambda a, b : [\![\mathcal{A}_{\delta,\tau}^E]\!] . \mathsf{Elim}(a, [\![\mathcal{A}_{\delta,\tau}^E]\!])$$
$$\{\mathsf{Elim}(b, [\![\mathcal{A}_{\delta,\tau}^E]\!])\{ \, [\![\gamma(a_1, a_1)]\!] \mid \cdots \mid [\![\gamma(a_1, a_n)]\!] \mid [\![\delta]\!] \mid [\![\delta]\!] \, \}$$

$$\vdots$$

$$\mid \mathsf{Elim}(b, [\![\mathcal{A}_{\delta,\tau}^E]\!])\{ \, [\![\gamma(a_n, a_1)]\!] \mid \cdots \mid [\![\gamma(a_n, a_n)]\!] \mid [\![\delta]\!] \mid [\![\delta]\!] \, \}$$
$$\mid [\![\delta]\!]$$
$$\mid [\![\delta]\!] \}$$

Now $[\![\gamma]\!] \ [\![a]\!] \ [\![b]\!] \ \twoheadrightarrow_\beta [\![\gamma(a, b)]\!]$ for all $a, b \in \mathcal{A}_\delta^E$.

4 The rules for logical deduction

Notation: When x is a variable and $\phi(x)$ is a property that possibly contains x, then we write $\Lambda x.\phi(x)$ for the function that maps x to $\phi(x)$.
Furthermore $[\![\Lambda x.\phi(x)]\!]$ stands for $\lambda [\![x]\!] : [\![\mathcal{P}^E]\!] . [\![\phi(x)]\!]$ when x is a process variable and for $\lambda [\![x]\!] : [\![D]\!] . [\![\phi(x)]\!]$ when x is a data variable of sort D.

We somewhat informally show by induction over the structure of the μCRL derivation of ϕ that we have property (2).

- The rule $(\rightarrow I)$ of Table 5 corresponds with the ΠI rule of λIC. Assume that
  $\Gamma(E, V_d, V_p), x : [\![\phi]\!] \vdash p(x) : [\![\psi]\!]$ for some term $p(x)$ representing a proof of ψ possibly using a proof x of hypothesis ϕ, then

  $$\Gamma(E, V_d, V_p) \vdash \lambda x : [\![\phi]\!] . p(x) : [\![\phi]\!] \rightarrow [\![\psi]\!]$$

  so $[\![\phi \rightarrow \psi]\!]$ is provable in context $\Gamma(E, V_d, V_p)$.

- Similar, the rule $(\rightarrow E)$ corresponds with ΠE.

- Let $\aleph$ be the name of a μCRL axiom ϕ given in some module, then

  $$\frac{\qquad\qquad}{\phi \text{ from } E, V_d, V_p}\;\aleph$$

  according to Table 5. Now $\Gamma(E, V_d, V_p) \vdash [\![\aleph]\!] : [\![\phi]\!]$ because $[\![\aleph]\!] : [\![\phi]\!] \in \Gamma(E, V_d, V_p)$ by definition.

- The μCRL formula $\mathcal{F}$ is represented by $\bot$ (Definition 3.2), so assume that

  $$\Gamma(E, V_d, V_p), H : [\![\neg\phi]\!] \vdash f : \bot .$$

Now $\mathsf{Elim}(f, [\![\phi]\!])\{\ \}$ is a proof of $[\![\phi]\!]$. The cancellation of $\neg\phi$ makes RAA a classical rule. In general the term f can contain a free variable of type $[\![\neg\phi]\!]$. In that case we do not have

$$\Gamma(E, V_d, V_p) \vdash \mathsf{Elim}(f, [\![\phi]\!])\{\ \} : [\![\phi]\!] .$$

However, we use $\mathcal{C}\ell : \Pi P :*^p . (or\ P\ (P \rightarrow \bot))$ to form

$$
\begin{aligned}
M \quad\equiv\quad & \lambda P :*^p . \lambda H :(P \rightarrow \bot) \rightarrow \bot . \\
& \mathsf{Elim}(\mathcal{C}\ell\ P, P)\{\lambda x : P . x \mid \lambda x : P \rightarrow \bot . \mathsf{Elim}(H\ x, P)\{\ \}\}
\end{aligned}
$$

of type $\Pi P :*^p . ((P \rightarrow \bot) \rightarrow \bot) \rightarrow P$. Now we can use

$$M [\![\phi]\!] (\lambda H : [\![\neg\phi]\!] . f)$$

instead of $\mathsf{Elim}(f, [\![\phi]\!])\{\ \}$ as a proof for $[\![\phi]\!]$. The λ-abstraction from H binds all the free occurrences of H in f and hence

$$\Gamma(E, V_d, V_p) \vdash M [\![\phi]\!] (\lambda H : [\![\neg\phi]\!] . f) : [\![\phi]\!] .$$

- Assume that t is a data term (of some sort D declared in specification E) or a process term. Then

$$\Gamma(E, V_d, V_p) \vdash \mathsf{Constr}(1, [\![=]\!] [\![D]\!] [\![t]\!]) : [\![t = t]\!].$$

Analogously, when t is a process term then

$$\Gamma(E, V_d, V_p) \vdash \mathsf{Constr}(1, [\![=]\!] [\![\mathcal{P}^E]\!] [\![t]\!]) : [\![t = t]\!].$$

This corresponds with the rule *REFL* of Table 5.

- Assume that $\Gamma(E, V_d, V_p) \vdash H : [\![\phi(t_1)]\!]$. When we have a proof e of type $[\![t_1 = t_2]\!]$ then

$$\Gamma(E, V_d, V_p) \vdash \mathsf{Elim}(e, [\![\Lambda x.\phi(x)]\!])\{H\} : [\![\phi(t_2)]\!]$$

($[\![\Lambda x.\phi(x)]\!] [\![t]\!] \equiv [\![\phi(t)]\!]$ for all terms t.) This corresponds with rule *REPL* of Table 5.

- Assume that $\Gamma(E, V_d, V_p), [\![x]\!] : [\![D]\!] \vdash p([\![x]\!]) : [\![\phi(x)]\!]$. Now $\Gamma(E, V_d, V_p) \vdash \lambda [\![x]\!] : [\![D]\!] . p([\![x]\!]) : \Pi [\![x]\!] : [\![D]\!] . [\![\phi(x)]\!]$. Let $[\![d]\!] : [\![D]\!]$ then $[\![\phi(x)]\!] [[\![x]\!] := [\![d]\!]] \equiv [\![\phi(d)]\!]$. From ΠE it follows that

$$\Gamma(E, V_d, V_p) \vdash p([\![d]\!]) : [\![\phi(d)]\!].$$

This corresponds with rule *SUB* of Table 5.

- The rule *VAR* is covered by Ax of Table 2.

Appendix

The A-axiom describe the behaviour of the operators $\cdot$ and $+$ and the *CM*-axioms describe the behaviour of the parallel operators. All these axiom are standard in ACP.

References

[1] H.P. Barendregt. Lambda calculi with types. In S. Abramsky, D.M. Gabbay, and T.S.E. Maibaum, editors, *Handbook of Logic in Computer Science*, pages 117–309. Oxford University Press, Oxford, 1992.

[2] J.A. Bergstra and J.W. Klop. The algebra of recursively defined processes and the algebra of regular processes. In *Proceedings 11th ICALP*, Antwerp, volume 172 of *Lecture Notes in Computer Science*, pages 82–95. Springer-Verlag, 1984.

A1:	$x + y = y + x$	**from** $E, \varnothing, \{x, y\}$
A2:	$x + (y + z) = (x + y) + x$	**from** $E, \varnothing, \{x, y, z\}$
A3:	$x + x = x$	**from** $E, \varnothing, \{x, y, z\}$
A4:	$(x + y) \cdot z = x \cdot z + y \cdot z$	**from** $E, \varnothing, \{x, y, z\}$
A5:	$(x \cdot y) \cdot z = x \cdot (y \cdot z)$	**from** $E, \varnothing, \{x, y, z\}$
A6:	$x + \delta = x$	**from** $E, \varnothing, \{x\}$
A7:	$\delta \cdot x = \delta$	**from** $E, \varnothing, \{x\}$

Table 6: The A-axioms of ACP. $a, b \in \mathcal{A}^E_{\delta, \tau}$.

CM1:	$x \parallel y = x \, \lfloor\!\lfloor \, y + y \, \lfloor\!\lfloor \, x + x \mid y$	**from** $E, \varnothing, \{x, y\}$
CM2:	$a \, \lfloor\!\lfloor \, x = a \cdot x$	**from** $E, \varnothing, \{x, y\}$
CM3:	$a \cdot x \, \lfloor\!\lfloor \, y = a \cdot (x \parallel y)x$	**from** $E, \varnothing, \{x, y\}$
CM4:	$x + y \, \lfloor\!\lfloor \, z = x \, \lfloor\!\lfloor \, z + y \, \lfloor\!\lfloor \, z$	**from** $E, \varnothing, \{x, y, z\}$
CM5:	$a \cdot x \mid b = (a \mid b) \cdot x$	**from** $E, \varnothing, \{x\}$
CM6:	$a \mid b \cdot x \, \lfloor\!\lfloor \, y = (a \mid b) \cdot x$	**from** $E, \varnothing, \{x\}$
CM7:	$a \cdot x \mid b \cdot y = (a \mid b) \cdot (x \parallel y)$	**from** $E, \varnothing, \{x, y\}$
CM8:	$(x + y) \mid z = x \mid z + y \mid z$	**from** $E, \varnothing, \{x\}$
CM9:	$x \mid (y + z) = x \mid y + x \mid z$	**from** $E, \varnothing, \{x\}$

Table 7: The CM-axioms of ACP. $a, b \in \mathcal{A}^E_{\delta, \tau}$.

[3] M.A. Bezem and J.F. Groote. A formal verification of the alternating bit protocol in the calculus of constructions. Technical Report 88, Logic Group Preprint Series, Utrecht University, March 1993.

[4] R. Cleaveland and P. Panangaden. Type theory and concurrency. *International Journal of Parallel Programming*, 17:153–206, 1988.

[5] R.L. Constable, S.F. Allen, H.M. Bromley, W.R. Cleaveland, J.F. Cremer, R.W. Harper, D.J. Howe, T.B. Knoblock, N.P. Mendler, P. Panangaden, J.T. Sasaki, and S.F. Smith. *Implementing Mathematics with the NuPrl Development System*. Prentice-Hall, inc., Englewood Cliffs, New Jersey, first edition, 1986.

[6] T. Coquand and G. Huet. The calculus of constructions. *Information and Control*, 76:95–120, 1988.

[7] G. Dowek, A. Felty, H. Herbelin, G. Huet, C. Murthy, C. Parent, C. Paulin-Mohring, and B. Werner. The Coq proof assistant user's guide. Version 5.8. Technical report, INRIA – Rocquencourt, May 1993.

[8] S.J. Garland and J.V. Guttag. An overview of LP, the Larch prover. In N. Dershowitz, editor, *Proceedings of the 3rd International Conference on Rewriting Techniques and Applications*, volume 355 of *Lecture Notes in Computer Science*, pages 137–155. Springer-Verlag, 1989.

[9] J.F. Groote and A. Ponse. The syntax and semantics of μCRL. Technical Report CS-R9076, CWI, Amsterdam, December 1990.

[10] J.F. Groote and A. Ponse. Proof theory for μCRL. Technical Report CS-R9138, CWI, Amsterdam, August 1991.

[11] H. Korver and J. Springintveld. A computer-checked verification of Milner's scheduler. 1993. to appear.

[12] N.A. Lynch and M.R. Tuttle. Hierarchical correctness proofs for distributed algorithms. Technical Report MIT/LCS/TR-387, MIT Laboratory of Computer Science, April 1987.

[13] R. Milner. *A Calculus of Communicating Systems*, volume 92. Springer-Verlag, Berlin, 1980.

[14] C. Paulin-Mohring. Inductive definitions in the system Coq. Rules and properties. In M. Bezem and J.F. Groote, editors, *Proceedings of the 1st International Conference on Typed Lambda Calculi and Applications, TLCA '93*, Utrecht, The Netherlands, volume 664 of *Lecture Notes in Computer Science*, pages 328–345. Springer-Verlag, 1993.

[15] J.F. Søgaard-Andersen, S.J. Garland, J.V. Guttag, N.A. Lynch, and A. Pogosyants. Computer-assisted simulation proofs. February 1993.

Reasoning about Dynamic Features in Specification Languages

– A Modal view on Creation and Modification –

Rix Groenboom
Gerard R. Renardel de Lavalette

Department of Computing Science, University of Groningen
P.O. Box 800, 9700 AV Groningen, The Netherlands.
E-mail: {rix,grl}@cs.rug.nl.

Abstract

Using algebras over some signature to model the notion of state is quite common in specification languages. Some specification formalisms, e.g. COLD and Evolving Algebras, also allow for the dynamic change of states. Two kinds of elementary procedures are used: creation (of a new object) and modification (of a function or predicate at some point).

In this paper we present and investigate **MLCM** (Modal Logic of Creation and Modification), a multimodal predicate logic for reasoning over programs built up from such procedures. **MLCM** deviates from traditional dynamic predicate logic in two respects: creation is added as a primitive program construct and assignment (to variables) is replaced by assignment to constants and parametrized assignment to function and predicate symbols.

We present a definition of syntax, semantics and axiomatisation of **MLCM** and establish completeness for the repetition-free fragment via a traditional Henkin construction.

1   Introduction

The idea that algebraic methods admit a clear and precise description of abstract data types, already expressed and exemplified in [11], has been incorporated in many specification languages and related formalisms. Another advantage of algebraic specifications is also exploited in many places, viz. executability via rewriting.

In this paper, we consider an extension of this algebraic paradigm with a dynamical aspect: algebras (containing functions and predicates) are considered as states, and so-called *procedures* may change such algebras, leading to new ones (with the same signature). This extended paradigm can be found at the core of, e.g., the specification language COLD and the specification formalism of *Evolving Algebras*. We introduce and study the multimodal logic **MLCM** (Modal Logic of Creation and Modification), a variant of dynamic logic intended to capture the ideas behind COLD and Evolving Algebras.

New in this paper are the following:

- a nontrivial variant of dynamic logic for reasoning over programs involving object creation and function and predicate modification (**MLCM**);

- a semantics for this logic which is different from the semantics for dynamic logic;

- a partial completeness result.

1.1 Survey of the rest of this paper

In section 2, we give some background information about COLD, Evolving Algebras and dynamic logic. We then present **PL** in section 3, a one-sorted predicate logic, serving as the basis for **MLCM**. **PL** has a slightly non-standard semantics: quantification is defined over existing objects of the sort, and functions and predicates are evaluated on equivalence classes (completeness is shown in Appendix A). **PL** and its semantics prelude on the logic **MLCM**, the modal extension of **PL**, the subject of section 4. We give its semantics, axiomatisation and present a partial completeness result (for the fragment without the repetition construct, in Appendix B). We end with conclusions and suggestions for further research in section 5.

1.2 Acknowledgements

This research is the spin-off of the 'Dynamic logic and Relational calculus' group. The authors are indebted to Rutger Dijkstra, Dirk Roorda, Erik Saaman and Jan Terlouw, the other members of the group, for their frequent and constructive suggestions and criticism.

2 Background

In this section we shortly discuss some formalisms that inspired us to the development of **MLCM**. First we sketch COLD and Evolving Algebra, two specification formalisms where the need for a reasoning system about programs involving certain modification constructs was felt. Then we give a survey of dynamic logic which allows reasoning over programs with assignments and show the need for a variant of dynamic logic.

2.1 COLD

The wide-spectrum specification language COLD (Common Object-oriented Language for Design) is developed at Philips Research Eindhoven in several ESPRIT-projects, during the last ten years. The main ideas for the language originate from Hans Jonkers. The formal definition of COLD-K and its semantics have has been given in 1987 in [6]. The semantics is based on the many sorted partial infinitary logic MPL_ω, see [16]. The textbook [5] gives a good introduction into COLD-K, the kernel language of COLD.

For state-based specifications COLD has so-called *classes*. A class is a sort of abstract machine with states and nondeterministic procedures. A state is associated with an algebra, containing sorts, predicates and functions. The procedures that operate on these states may modify the state by extending the sorts and changing the functions and predicates of the state.

To illustrate the operations of creation and modification, we give the signature of a state-based specification of memory cells:

```
CLASS cell-class

SORT  Nat
      Cell

FUNC  0          : -> Nat
      s          : Nat -> Nat
      val        : Cell -> Nat

PROC  create     : -> Cell
      store      : Cell x Nat ->
```

The intuition behind this is: a memory cell can contain a natural number, its value. For natural numbers we have a constant function 0 and the successor function s. The procedures that change the state of the class are: create and store. With the procedure create we make a new memory cell, with store we update the value of a cell.

To specifiy the behaviour of create in COLD we want to write (among other things) that it returns a cell when applied. This is done as follows:

```
[ LET c:Cell; c:=create] (EXIST x:Cell (x=c))
```

We shall see that **MLCM** gives the possibility to reason about these kind of procedures, in such a way that we may infer:

$\vdash \quad [NEWc]\exists x : \text{Cell}(x = c)$

$\vdash \quad \forall x : \text{Cell}, y : \text{Nat}\big([\text{store}(x,y)](\text{val}(x) = y)\big)$

A general COLD specification contains besides a signature definition also axioms that the functions and procedures must satisfy. It is also possible to give implementations of the specified procedures in terms of dynamic logic. So the behaviour of create may be specified by:

```
AXIOM < create > TRUE
AXIOM [ LET c:Cell; c:= create]
           ( c! AND (PREV NOT c!) AND
             FORALL d:Cell ( (PREV NOT d!) => d=c ) )
```

The first axiom ensures termination, the second expresses that c was not defined in the previous state but has come into existence in the current state, and that it is the only new object.

2.2 Evolving algebras

Evolving algebras have been introduced by Gurevich in [8] and [9], and applied for the specification of several programming languages like Occam [10] and Prolog [1, 2].

The basic idea of evolving algebras is that computational processes change dynamically over time. In evolving algebras, states are represented as many-sorted first-order structures S with universes and functions. States can change under the influence of application of *transaction rules*. Adopting the notation as given in [2], these are rules of the form:

```
if B then U1 and U2 and ... and Un.
```

Here each `Ui` is an *update*:

```
F(E1, ..., Ej) := E0
```

B is a boolean expression, F is a function, and each Ei is an expression in the signature of the structure S.

To modify universes (i.e. to let them grow by creating new objects), there are updates of the form:

```
extend A by E1,..., Em with U1 and U2 and ... and Un end.
```

The updates Uj depend on Ei's, setting the values of some functions on newly created elements Ei of A. Typically the universes are initially empty.

Normally the updates are executed in parallel, but to execute updates sequentially, one may write:

```
seq U1 and U2 and ... and Um endseq
```

We mention in passing that this last construct can also be expressed in COLD, as well as the `let` and `if ... then ... else ...` constructs mentioned in [2].

To come back on the memory cell example, a way for specifing that a new memeory cell will initially be 0 we can give the following rule:

```
let rule = (extend Cell by c with val(c) := 0)
```

After execution of `rule` one would like to prove that

$$\vdash \quad [\text{rule}]\exists x : \text{Cell}(x = c \land \text{val}(x) = 0)$$

and this is the type of reasoning that we want to cover in **MLCM**.

2.3 Dynamic logic

Dynamic logic originates from V. Pratt (see [17]), after a suggestion of his student R. Moore in 1974. D. Harel has made many contributions to the subject, especially the version with first-order quantification (see [12]). The original idea was to express Hoare triples in a modal setting: the Hoare triple $A\{\alpha\}B$ (if A holds before executing statement α then B holds afterwards) is expressed in dynamic logic as $A \rightarrow [\alpha]B$. In terms of Dijkstra's wp-calculus ([4]), $[\alpha]A$ corresponds with $wlp.\alpha.A$, the weakest liberal precondition needed to guarantee that A holds after every possible execution of α (here *liberal* refers to the fact that termination of α is not required).

Dynamic logic is a formalism for expressing and reasoning with assertions about programs. In its usual first-order setting, programs are built up from assignments to variables ($x := t$) and guards ($A?$), using the program constructs ; (sequential composition), ∪ (nondeterministic choice) and * (repetition). As a consequence, variables play the double role of both logical and programming variable in dynamic logic. These roles will be separated in **MLCM**.

A second, and more important shortcoming (at least for our purposes sketched above) of dynamic logic is that is not possible to make assertions about function modification, like:

$$\forall x : \texttt{Cell}, y : \texttt{Nat}([\texttt{store}(x,y)](\texttt{val}(x) = y)$$

The axiomatisation of the behaviour of programs makes it possible to use e.g. tactical theorem provers to support proving of properties about programs. The system KIV (Karlsruhe Interactive Verifier, see [14] for a general description of the system) is an interactive system designed for formal reasoning about imperative Pascal-like programs. The KIV system uses a variant of dynamic logic, as presented by Goldblatt ([7]) in combination with tactical theorem proving. A description of this KIV logic, which uses an approximation of the infinitary rules for proving repetition by induction, can be found in [13].

3 PL: Predicate Logic

As mentioned earlier, we present the logic **MLCM** in two stages. Here we introduce the predicate logic **PL**, with a somewhat unusual semantics, prepared for extending it to the semantics of the full language **MLCM**. In fact, **PL** is the *local* logic of **MLCM**, i.e. the logic of (the algebra of) a single state. The uncommon feature of the semantics of **PL** is that functions and predicates are defined on equivalence classes instead of individual objects; moreover, functions are partial. The extension to **MLCM** follows in the next section.

3.1 The language and notation

The language of **PL** is defined by:

VAR	x	(a countably infinite collection of variables)
FUNC	f	(function symbols, with arity ≥ 0)
PRED	p	(predicate symbols, with arity ≥ 0)
TERM	t	$::= \uparrow \mid x \mid f(t_1, \ldots, t_n)$
FORM	A	$::= (t = t) \mid p(t_1, \ldots, t_n) \mid A \wedge A \mid \neg A \mid \forall x A$

The formulae $\top, \bot, A \vee B, A \to B, A \leftrightarrow B$ and $\exists x A$ are defined as usual. The symbol $\uparrow$ denotes the undefined object. We also define a unary *definedness* predicate $\cdot\downarrow$ and *weak equality* $\cdot \simeq \cdot$ (also called equivalence or partial equality):

$$
\begin{aligned}
t\downarrow \quad &=_{\text{def}} \quad (t = t) \\
s \simeq t \quad &=_{\text{def}} \quad (s\downarrow \vee\, t\downarrow) \to s = t
\end{aligned}
$$

The notions of free and bound variables of a formula are defined as usual. The same holds for *substitution*, denoted as $[t/x]s$ and $[t/x]A$ which can be read as 'substitute t for variable x in s resp. A'. A formula without free variables is called a *sentence*.

3.2 Axiomatisation of PL

PL is axiomatized as follows (for the sake of simplicity, we assume here and later that functions and predicates are unary):

Taut	All tautologies of propositional logic
MP	$A, A \to B \Rightarrow B$
Eq	$x \simeq y \to y \simeq x$
	$x \simeq y \land y \simeq z \to x \simeq z$
	$x \simeq y \to fx \simeq fy$
	$x \simeq y \to (px \leftrightarrow py)$
Undef	$\neg(\uparrow\downarrow)$
Quan	$(x\downarrow \to A) \Rightarrow \forall x A$
	$(\forall x A \land x\downarrow) \to A$
Subst	$A \Rightarrow [t/x]A$

In this axiomatisation, the expressions containing $\Rightarrow$ are rules, the others are axioms.

$\Gamma \vdash A$ (A is derivable from Γ), is defined inductively as usual: all $A \in \Gamma$ and all instances of axioms are derivable from Γ, and if all premises of a rule are derivable from Γ then so is the conclusion. A collection of formulae Γ is called *consistent* iff $\Gamma \nvdash \perp$.

Let x be not free in Γ. Observe that we do *not* have $\Gamma \vdash A \Leftrightarrow \Gamma \vdash \forall x A$ for x not free in Γ, i.e. a counterexample is $\Gamma = \emptyset, A = x\downarrow$. But we do have, again for x not free in Γ:

$$\Gamma \vdash A(x) \quad \Leftrightarrow \quad \Gamma \vdash (\forall x A(x)) \land A(\uparrow) \tag{1}$$
$$\Gamma \vdash \forall x A(x) \quad \Leftrightarrow \quad \Gamma \vdash x\downarrow \to A(x) \tag{2}$$

3.3 Semantics of PL

The semantics for **PL** is slightly nonstandard and has the following characterics. The universe U is divided in equivalence classes, and each function and predicate is defined on equivalence classes. One special object $\star$ plays the role of the undefined object.

More formally: a model M for **PL** is a quadruple $M = <U, \sim, F, P>$, where

- U is the *pre-universe*, elements $u \in U$ are called pre-objects, and $\star \in U$ is the *undefined object*;

- $\sim$ is an equivalence relation on U;

- $F = \{\underline{f} | f \in \text{FUNC}\}$ with $\underline{f} : U_\sim^n \to U_\sim$ (n the arity of f);

- $P = \{\underline{p} | p \in \text{PRED}\}$ with $\underline{p} \subseteq U_\sim^n$ (n the arity of p).

Here (and later) we use the following definitions:

$\tilde{u}$	$=_{\text{def}}$	$\{u' \| u' \sim u\}$	(the objects of the universe)
$U_\sim$	$=_{\text{def}}$	$\{\tilde{u} \| u \in U\}$	(the universe of M)
$U_\sim^+$	$=_{\text{def}}$	$U_\sim \setminus \{\tilde{\star}\}$	(the universe with only existing objects)

346

Assignments $a \in \text{ASS} = \text{VAR} \to U$ and pointwise modification $a[x \mapsto u]$ (where $x \in \text{VAR}, u \in U$) of an assignment are defined as usual.

Now we can define the interpretation $[\![t]\!]_{M,a}$ of a term t and $M, a \models A$ of a formula A in model M under assignment a. The interpretation function has the following type $[\![\,.\,]\!] : \text{TERM} \to U_\sim$. We use $\tilde{a}(x)$ to denote $\{u | u \sim a(x)\}$. We recursively define:

$$
\begin{aligned}
[\![\uparrow]\!]_{M,a} &= \tilde{\star} \\
[\![x]\!]_{M,a} &= \tilde{a}(x) \\
[\![ft]\!]_{M,a} &= \underline{f}([\![t]\!]_{M,a}) \\
M, a \models pt &=_{\text{def}} [\![t]\!]_{M,a} \in \underline{p} \\
M, a \models (s = t) &=_{\text{def}} [\![s]\!]_{M,a} = [\![t]\!]_{M,a} \neq \tilde{\star} \\
M, a \models \neg A &=_{\text{def}} \text{not } (M, a \models A) \\
M, a \models A \wedge B &=_{\text{def}} M, a \models A \text{ and } M, a \models B \\
M, a \models \forall x A &=_{\text{def}} \textbf{forall } u \in (U \setminus \tilde{\star})\ (M, a[x \mapsto u] \models A) \\
M \models A &=_{\text{def}} \textbf{forall } a \in \text{ASS}(M, a \models A) \\
\Gamma \models A &=_{\text{def}} \textbf{forall } M(\textbf{forall } B \in \Gamma(M \models B) \Rightarrow M \models A) \\
\models A &=_{\text{def}} \textbf{forall } M(M \models A)
\end{aligned}
$$

In this definition, Γ stands for a set of sentences. It is obvious that, for *sentences* A we have that $M, a \models A$ and $M \models A$ are equivalent. Observe the difference between $M \models A(x)$ and $M \models \forall x A(x)$:

- $M \models A(x)$ means: all objects of M satisfy A;
- $M \models \forall x A(x)$ means: all *existing* objects of M satisfy A.

However, we do have the following equivalences, cf. (1) and (2):

$$M \models A(x) \quad \Leftrightarrow \quad M \models (\forall x A(x)) \wedge A(\uparrow) \tag{3}$$
$$M \models \forall x A(x) \quad \Leftrightarrow \quad M \models x{\downarrow} \to A(x) \tag{4}$$

Equivalences (1), (2), (3) and (4) enable us to reduce formulae to sentences with the same derivability and semantical properties.

3.4 Soundness and completeness

Soundness ($\Gamma \vdash A \Rightarrow \Gamma \models A$) is proved straightforwardly with induction over the definition of derivability. For the substitution rule, the following property is needed:

$$
\begin{aligned}
[\![[t/x]s]\!]_{M,a} &= [\![s]\!]_{M,a[x \mapsto [\![t]\!]_{M,a}]} \\
M, a \models [t/x]A &\Leftrightarrow M, a[x \mapsto [\![t]\!]_{M,a}] \models A
\end{aligned}
$$

This is proved with induction over s and A, respectively. Completeness ($\Gamma \models A \Rightarrow \Gamma \vdash A$) is obtained by adapting the Henkin construction. For a sketch of this proof see Appendix A.

4 MLCM: Modal Logic of Creation and Modification

The logic **MLCM** is an extension of **PL**, obtained by adding formulae $[\alpha]A$, where α is a program expression. For the composition of complex program expressions the same operations are used as in dynamic logic (see 2.3).

New in **MLCM** are the three atomic program statements:

- NEWc (creating a new object and letting the constant c refer to it);

- $f(t_1, \ldots, t_n) := t$ (changing the value of function f on the arguments $t_1, \ldots, t_n$ to the value of t);

- $p(t_1, \ldots, t_n) :\leftrightarrow A$ (changing the value of predicate p on the arguments $t_1, \ldots, t_n$ to the truth value of A).

The second of these (function modification) is related to the assignment statement $x := t$ in dynamic logic, but there are two differences.

First, the simple assignment can be modeled in **MLCM** by changing the value of a *constant* (i.e. a function with zero arguments), not a variable. In other words, program variables are treated as constant names, not as logical variables. This leads to a clear separation between *logical* variables and *programming* variables.

Secondly, **MLCM** allows for parametrized assignments by changing functions with positive arity.

The syntax of **MLCM** reads:

VAR	x	(a countably infinite collection of variables)
FUNC	f	(function symbols, with arity ≥ 0)
PRED	p	(predicate symbols, with arity ≥ 0)
TERM	$t ::=$	$\uparrow \mid x \mid f(t_1, \ldots, t_n)$
PROG	$\alpha ::=$	NEW$c \mid f(t_1, \ldots, t_n) := t \mid p(t_1, \ldots, t_n) :\leftrightarrow A \mid$
		$A? \mid \alpha; \alpha \mid \alpha \cup \alpha \mid \alpha^*$
FORM	$A ::=$	$(t = t) \mid p(t_1, \ldots, t_n) \mid A \wedge A \mid \neg A \mid \forall x A \mid [\alpha] A$

Here, c stands for constant symbols, i.e. function symbols with arity 0. We have the standard abbreviations for $\top, \bot, A \vee B, A \rightarrow B, A \leftrightarrow B, \exists x A$ and $<\alpha> A$.

4.1 Semantics of MLCM

The definition of the semantics of **MLCM** has two steps. First we define the notion of *structure*, a kind of proto-model in which terms and formulae of **MLCM** can be interpreted. Then we restrict this notion to *models* by imposing requirements on the accessibility relations corresponding to the program statements: the interpretation of formulae is used in the formulation of these requirements.

A *structure* is a triple $M = <U, W, R>$, where

- U is the *global* pre-universe with $\star \in U$;

- $W \neq \emptyset$ is the collection of *worlds*: they are triples $w = <\sim_w, F_w, P_w>$ such that $<U, \sim_w, F_w, P_w>$ is a model of **PL**. Thus $F_w = \{f_w | f \epsilon \text{FUNC}\}$ and $P_w = \{p_w | p \epsilon \text{PRED}\}$;

- $R = \{R_{\alpha,a} | \alpha \in \text{PROG}, a \in \text{ASS}\}$ is a collection of binary relations on W.

We define:

$$u_w \quad =_{\text{def}} \quad \{u' \mid u' \sim_w u\}$$
$$U_w \quad =_{\text{def}} \quad \{u_w \mid u \in U\}$$
$$U_w^+ \quad =_{\text{def}} \quad U_w \setminus \{\star_w\}$$

Let $[\![t]\!]_{w,a}$, the interpretation of term t in world w with assignment a, be defined by:

$$[\![\uparrow]\!]_{w,a} \quad = \quad \star_w$$
$$[\![x]\!]_{w,a} \quad = \quad (a(x))_w$$
$$[\![ft]\!]_{w,a} \quad = \quad f_w([\![t]\!]_{w,a})$$

We let f_w and p_w range of F_w resp. P_w.

For $w, a \models A$, the interpretation of formula A in world w with assignment a, we have

$$
\begin{array}{lll}
w, a \models pt & =_{\text{def}} & [\![t]\!]_{w,a} \in p_w \\
w, a \models (s = t) & =_{\text{def}} & [\![s]\!]_{w,a} = [\![t]\!]_{w,a} \neq \star_w \\
w, a \models \neg A & =_{\text{def}} & \text{not } (w, a \models A) \\
w, a \models A \wedge B & =_{\text{def}} & w, a \models A \text{ and } w, a \models B \\
w, a \models \forall x A & =_{\text{def}} & \text{forall } u \in (U \setminus \star_w)(w, a[x \mapsto u] \models A) \\
w, a \models [\alpha]A & =_{\text{def}} & \text{forall } w' \in W(wR_{\alpha,a}w' \Rightarrow w', a \models A) \\
w \models A & =_{\text{def}} & \text{forall } a \in \text{ASS}(w, a \models A) \\
\Gamma \models A & =_{\text{def}} & \text{forall } w \in W(\text{forall } B \in \Gamma(w \models B) \Rightarrow w \models A) \\
\models A & =_{\text{def}} & \text{forall } w \in W(w \models A)
\end{array}
$$

A structure is called a *model* if it satisfies a number of requirements for the relations $R_{a,a} \epsilon R$. We sketch the ideas before giving the formal definitions.

If $wR_{NEWc,a}w'$, then there is exactly one new existing object (i.e. a new equivalence class) in $U_{w'}$, to which c refers. When going from w to w', the behaviour of functions f is as follows: $f_{w'}$ behaves like f_w on 'old' objects, and for the unique new object $c_{w'}$ we have $f_{w'}c_{w'} = f_{w'}\star_{w'}$. For predicates, the situation is analogous: their extension is equal with respect to the 'old' universe, and $p_{w'}c_{w'}$ iff $p_{w'}\star_{w'}$.

If $wR_{f(s):=t,a}w'$, then the universe is unchanged, and so are all functions and predicates except f. Compared with f_w, $f_{w'}$ is changed in one point, viz. the value of s in w, which becomes the value of t in w. Observe that both s and t may contain f, so their value in w' may be different from that in w.

Similar observations can be made when $wR_{p(s):\leftrightarrow A,a}w'$ holds.

Now for the precise formulation:

- if $wR_{NEWc,a}w'$ then:

  - $U_w^+ = U_{w'}^+ \setminus \{c_{w'}\}$

  - $c_{w'} \in U_{w'}^+$

  - $f_{w'} = i \circ f_w \circ j$ **forall** $f \in \text{FUNC} \setminus \{c\}$

  - $p_{w'} = j^{-1}(p_w)$ **forall** $p \in \text{PRED}$

Here the functions $i : U_w \to U_{w'}$ and $j : U_{w'} \to U_w$ are defined by

$$
\begin{aligned}
i(u) &= u && \text{for } u \in U_w^+ \\
i(\star_w) &= \star_{w'} \\
j(u) &= u && \text{for } u \in U_w^+ \\
j(c_{w'}) &= \star_w \\
j(\star_{w'}) &= \star_w
\end{aligned}
$$

and $j^{-1}(p_w)$ means the image in $U_{w'}$ of the elements U_w for which p_w holds.

- if $wR_{f(s):=t,a}w'$ then:

  - $U_{w'} = U_w$
  - $f_{w'}(\llbracket s \rrbracket_{w,a}) = \llbracket t \rrbracket_{w,a}$
  - $f_{w'}v = f_w v$ **forall** $v \in U_w \setminus \{\llbracket s \rrbracket_{w,a}\}$
  - $g_w = g_{w'}$ **forall** $g \in \text{FUNC} \setminus \{f\}$
  - $p_w = p_{w'}$ **forall** $p \in \text{PRED}$

- if $wR_{p(s):\leftrightarrow A,a}w'$ then:

  - $U_{w'} = U_w$
  - $(\llbracket s \rrbracket_{w,a}) \in p_{w'}$ **iff** $w, a \models A$
  - $v \in p_{w'} \Leftrightarrow v \in p_w$ **forall** $v \in U_w \setminus \{\llbracket s \rrbracket_{w,a}\}$
  - $f_w = f_{w'}$ **forall** $f \in \text{FUNC}$
  - $q_w = q_{w'}$ **forall** $q \in \text{PRED} \setminus \{p\}$

- $R_{A?,a} = \{(w,w)|w, a \models A\}$

- $R_{\alpha;\beta,a} = R_{\alpha,a} \circ R_{\beta,a}$

- $R_{\alpha\cup\beta,a} = R_{\alpha,a} \cup R_{\beta,a}$

- $R_{\alpha^*,a} = R_{\alpha,a}^*$

4.2 Substitution

Substitution $[t/x]A$ of term t for x in A is not always defined in **MLCM**, only if no function symbols in t come into the scope of program statements that may change their meaning. So, e.g., $[c/x]([\text{NEW}c](x = y))$ nor $[fy/x]([f(s) := t](x = z))$ is defined. The clauses for the definition of substitution are as usual, except for formulae of the form $[\alpha]A$:

$$[t/x]([\alpha]A) = [[t/x]\alpha]([t/x]A)$$
$$\text{if } func(t) \cup mod(\alpha) = \emptyset \text{ or } x \text{ does not occur freely in } A$$

Here $func(t)$ is the set of function symbols occurring in t and $mod(\alpha)$, the collection of signature elements that are possibly modified by α, is defined by

$$
\begin{aligned}
mod(\text{NEW}c) &= \{c\} \\
mod(f(s) := t) &= \{f\} \\
mod(p(s) :\leftrightarrow A) &= \{p\} \\
mod(A?) &= \emptyset \\
mod(\alpha; \beta) &= mod(\alpha) \cup mod(\beta) \\
mod(\alpha \cup \beta) &= mod(\alpha) \cup mod(\beta) \\
mod(\alpha^*) &= mod(\alpha)
\end{aligned}
$$

4.3 Axiomatisation

MLCM is axiomatised as follows ($[\alpha]\Gamma$ stands for $\{[\alpha]A \mid A\epsilon\Gamma\}$):

PL   All axioms and rules of **PL** (with only those instances of the substitution rule for which the substitution is defined)

N $\Gamma \vdash A \Rightarrow [\alpha]\Gamma \vdash [\alpha]A$

C1 $x = y \rightarrow [\text{NEW}c](x = y \neq c)$

C2 $x \neq y \rightarrow [\text{NEW}c](x \neq y \lor x = c)$

C3 $px \rightarrow [\text{NEW}c]px$

C4 $\neg px \rightarrow [\text{NEW}c]\neg px$

C5 $[\text{NEW}c](c\!\downarrow \land fx \neq c \land fc \simeq f\!\uparrow \land (pc \leftrightarrow p\!\uparrow))$

FM1 $A \leftrightarrow [f(s) := t]A$ for all A not containing f

FM2 $s \simeq x \land t \simeq y \rightarrow [f(s) := t]fx \simeq y$

FM3 $s \not\simeq x \land fx \simeq y \rightarrow [f(s) := t]fx \simeq y$

PM1 $A \leftrightarrow [p(s) :\leftrightarrow C]A$ for all A not containing p

PM2 $s \simeq x \rightarrow (C \leftrightarrow [p(s) :\leftrightarrow C]px)$

PM3 $s \not\simeq x \rightarrow (px \leftrightarrow [p(s) :\leftrightarrow C]px)$

?AX $[A?]B \leftrightarrow (A \rightarrow B)$

;AX $[\alpha; \beta]A \leftrightarrow [\alpha][\beta]A$

∪AX $[\alpha \cup \beta]A \leftrightarrow ([\alpha]A \land [\beta]A)$

∗AX $[\alpha^*]A \leftrightarrow (A \land [\alpha][\alpha^*]A)$

INF $\{A \rightarrow [\alpha^n]B \mid n \in \mathbb{N}\} \Rightarrow A \rightarrow [\alpha^*]B$

Here, $[\alpha^n]$ is recursively defined as: $[\alpha^0] = [\top?]$ and $[\alpha^{n+1}] = [\alpha][\alpha^n]$.

4.4 Some consequences

Given this axiomatisation we can make the following observations.
The axiom rule [**N**] is used to derive:

Nec $A \Rightarrow [\alpha]A$ (Necessitation)

Distr $[\alpha](A \rightarrow B) \rightarrow ([\alpha]A \rightarrow [\alpha]B)$ (Distribution)

¿From the infinitary axiom INF, we have the following induction principle:

1 $[\alpha^*](A \to [\alpha]A) \to (A \to [\alpha^*]A)$

Furthermore, we have:

2 $x{\downarrow} \to [\text{NEW}c](x{\downarrow} \wedge x \neq c)$

3 $\neg x{\downarrow} \to [\text{NEW}c](\neg x{\downarrow} \vee x = c)$

4 $x \simeq y \to [\text{NEW}c](x \simeq y \vee (\neg x{\downarrow} \wedge y = c) \vee (\neg y{\downarrow} \wedge x = c))$

5 $x \not\simeq y \to [\text{NEW}c](x \not\simeq y \wedge (x = c \to y{\downarrow}) \wedge (y = c \to x{\downarrow}))$

6 $fx \simeq y \to [\text{NEW}c](fx \simeq y \vee (fx \simeq{\uparrow} \wedge y = c))$

7 $fx \not\simeq y \to [\text{NEW}c](fx \not\simeq y \wedge (y = c \to fx{\downarrow}))$

4.5 Soundness and completeness

Soundness is proved straightforwardly by checking that the requirements on the $R_{\alpha,a}$ are sufficient to make the axioms valid in all models. In Appendix B we sketch a partial completeness proof for the fragment of **MLCM** without the repetition construct *.

5   Concluding remarks

We presented a multimodal logic **MLCM** intended to formalise reasoning over evolving algebras and (partially) over procedures in COLD. The work is in progress and e.g. a full completeness has not been established yet, and is subject of further investigation (the problems lie in the combination of quantification and the repetition construct). Not all dynamic language constructs COLD are covered by **MLCM**, e.g., the operator PREV which refers to the previous state. It seems more than plausible that this can be modeled by keeping track of the history, i.e. the sequence of states on a computation path. The extension of **MPL**$_\omega$, the logic underlying COLD, to a modal framework is a (presumably straightforward) exercise.

The generality of arbitrary equivalence relations in the definition of universes from a pre-universe in the semantics of **MLCM** is not fully needed for the purpose of this theory: here it would suffice to work with universes where all equivalence classes are singletons, except the class containing $\star$, the undefined object. We did so with an eye on further generalisation.

For Evolving Algebras, a parallel function modification has to be introduced in the language. Then any specific evolving algebra description can easily be translated into an **MLCM** program. We hope to come back to these issues in subsequent publications.

Axiomatisation of the logic of COLD and Evolving Algebra clears the way for automated construction of proofs for these formalisms: the development of **MLCM** is only the first step towards such an axiomatisation. However, it is our intention to investigate the possibilities of theorem proving for **MLCM** and its variants. The work in the KIV project (see [14]) looks interesting in this perspective.

References

[1] E. Börger, A logical operational semantics for full prolog, In: *Proceedings CSL '89*, E. Börger, H. Kleine Büning and M.M. Richter (Eds.), LNCS 440, Springer Verlag, 1990, pp. 36 – 64.

[2] E. Börger and D. Rosenzweig, *The WAM – definition and Compiler Correctness*, Technical Report TR - 14/92, Department of Computer Science, University of Pisa, 1992.

[3] C.C. Chang and H.J. Keisler, *Model Theory*, North Holland, Second revised editon, 1990.

[4] E.W. Dijkstra and C.S. Scholten, *Predicate Calculus and Program Semantics*, Springer Verlag, 1990.

[5] L.M.G. Feijs and H.B.M. Jonkers, *Formal Specification and Design*, Cambridge Tracts in Theoretical Computer Science 35, 1992.

[6] L.M.G. Feijs, H.B.M. Jonkers, C.P.J. Koymans and G.R. Renardel de Lavalette, *Formal definition of the design language COLD-K (Preliminary version)*, ESPRIT document METEOR/t7/PRLE/7, April 1987 (Final version: August 1989).

[7] R. Goldblatt, *Axiomatising the logic of computer science*, LNCS 130, Springer Verlag, 1982.

[8] Y. Gurevich, Logic and the challenge of computer science, In: *Trends in Theoretical computer science*, E. Börger (ed.), Computer Science Press, 1988, pp. 1 – 57.

[9] Y. Gurevich, Evolving algebras; a tutorial introduction, Bulletin of the EATCS 43, Febr. 1991, pp. 264 – 284,

[10] Y. Gurevich and L. Moss, Algebraic operational semantics and Occam, In: *Peoceedings CSL '89*, E. Börger, H. Kleine Büning and M.M. Richter (Eds.), LNCS 440, Springer Verlag, 1990, pp. 176 – 192.

[11] J.V. Guttag and J.J. Horning, *The algebraic specification of abstract data types*, Acta Informatica 10, 1978, pp. 27 – 52.

[12] D. Harel, Dynamic Logic, In: *Handbook of Philosophical Logic, Vol. II*, D. Gabbay and F. Guenthner (eds.), D. Reidel Publishing Company, 1984, pp. 497 – 604.

[13] M. Heisel, W. Reif and W. Stephan, A dynamic logic for program verfication, In: *Logic at Botik 89*, A. Meyer, M. Taitslin (eds), LNCS 363, Springer Verlag, pp. 134 – 145.

[14] M. Heisel, W. Reif and W. Stephan, Tactical Theorem Proving in Program Verification, In: *Conference on Automated Deduction*, Siekmann (ed), LNAI, Spinger Verlag, 1990.

[15] L. Henkin, *The completeness of the first order functional calculus*, The Journal of Symbolic Logic 14, 1949, pp. 159 –166.

[16] C.P.J. Koymans and G.R. Renardel de Lavalette, The logic MPL$_\omega$, In: *Algebraic Methods: Theory, tools and applications*, M. Wirsing and J.A. Bergstra (eds.), LNCS 394, Springer Verlag, 1989, pp. 247 – 282.

[17] V.R. Pratt, *Semantical considerations on Floyd-Hoare logic*, Proc. 17th annual IEEE symp. on foundations of computer science, 1976, pp. 109 – 121.

Appendix A. Completeness of PL

In order to prove the completeness ($\Gamma \models A \Rightarrow \Gamma \vdash A$) of **PL**, we first use (1), (2), (3) and (4) of sections 3.2 and 3.3 to reduce formulae to sentences. Then we show that $\Gamma \models A \Rightarrow \Gamma \vdash A$ for (collections of) sentences Γ, A by constructing for every *consistent* collection of sentences Γ in $\mathcal{L}$ (the language of **PL**) a model M with $M \models \Gamma$. This is enough to obtain completeness: if $\Gamma \models A$ then $\Gamma \cup \{\neg A\}$ holds in no model and hence is inconsistent, so $\Gamma \vdash A$.

To obtain M, we slightly adapt the wellknown Henkin construction for ordinary predicate logic (see [15], a good exposition is in [3]). The general idea is to extend a consistent set of sentences Γ to Γ'' from which a model $H = H(\Gamma'')$ can be defined that satisfies:

$$H \models A \Leftrightarrow A \in \Gamma'' \tag{5}$$

Starting with a consistent set of sentences Γ, H is obtained in four steps:

- Let $\mathcal{C}$ be a countably infinite collection of fresh constants (i.e. not occurring in $\mathcal{L}$), the so-called *Henkin constants*. We extend $\mathcal{L}$, the language of **PL**, to $\mathcal{L}^+$ by adding all substitution instances of elements of $\mathcal{L}$ with Henkin constants. $\mathcal{C}^\dagger = \mathcal{C} \cup \{\dagger\}$ will become the pre-universe of our model.

  So ASS = VAR $\to \mathcal{C}^\dagger$, and $a \in$ ASS will be used as mappings transforming $\mathcal{L}^+$-formulae in $\mathcal{L}^+$-sentences (by substitution).

- Extend Γ to $\Gamma' \subseteq \mathcal{L}^+$, satisfying

  - Γ' is consistent;
  - Γ' contains *witnesses* for $\mathcal{L}^+$ in $\mathcal{C}$, i.e. for every $A \in \mathcal{L}^+$ with at most one free variable x, there is a $c \in \mathcal{C}$ with $\Gamma' \vdash (\exists x A) \to (c\!\downarrow \wedge [c/x]A)$.

  Observe that this last property is preserved under extension of Γ'.

- Extend Γ' to a maximally consistent $\Gamma'' \subseteq \mathcal{L}^+$, i.e. satisfying

  - if $\Delta \supseteq \Gamma''$ and Δ consistent, then $\Delta = \Gamma''$.

Now Γ'' satisfies:

$$\neg A \in \Gamma'' \quad \Leftrightarrow \quad A \notin \Gamma''$$
$$A \wedge B \in \Gamma'' \quad \Leftrightarrow \quad A \in \Gamma'' \text{ and } B \in \Gamma''$$
$$\exists x A \in \Gamma'' \quad \Leftrightarrow \quad \textbf{for some } c \in \mathcal{C} \text{ we have } (c\!\downarrow \wedge [c/x]A) \in \Gamma''$$

These three properties will be the induction steps in the proof of (5).

- Now, for any maximally consistent set with witnesses Γ, the Henkin model $H = H(\Gamma) =\ <\mathcal{C}^\uparrow, \sim, F, P>$ is defined as follows:

$$\sim = \{(c,d) \in \mathcal{C}^\uparrow \times \mathcal{C}^\uparrow | (c \simeq d) \in \Gamma\}$$
for all $f \in \text{FUNC}, v \in \mathcal{C}^\uparrow/\sim \quad \underline{f}v = \{d \in \mathcal{C}^\uparrow | (fc \simeq d) \in \Gamma, c \in v\}$
for all $p \in \text{PRED} \quad \underline{p} = \{d \in \mathcal{C}^\uparrow | pd \in \Gamma\}/\sim$

With this definition of H, we obtain (5) for atomic A:

$$a(s = t) \in \Gamma'' \quad \Leftrightarrow \quad H, a \models s = t$$
$$a(pt) \in \Gamma'' \quad \Leftrightarrow \quad H, a \models pt$$

which finishes the proof for (5).

Appendix B: Partial completeness of MLCM

In this section we sketch the proof of completeness of **MLCM** for the fragment without repetition. The argument runs via an extension of the Henkin construction given above. (Observe that the Henkin constants are *not* allowed as the main constant or function in creation or modification statements.) In order to deal with the modal operators, we add the following step to the model construction:

The Henkin model $H =\ <\mathcal{C}, W, R>$ is defined as follows.

- $W = \{\Gamma \mid \Gamma$ maximally consistent in $\mathcal{L}^+$ and has witnesses in $\mathcal{C}\}$;

- $\sim_\Gamma = \{(c,d) \in \mathcal{C}^\uparrow \times \mathcal{C}^\uparrow | (c \simeq d) \in \Gamma\}$;

- **for all** $f \in \text{FUNC}, v \in \mathcal{C}^\uparrow/\sim_\Gamma$ we have $f_\Gamma(v) = \{d \in \mathcal{C}^\uparrow | (fc \simeq d) \in \Gamma$ **for some** $c \in v\}$;

- **for all** $p \in \text{PRED}$ we have $p_\Gamma = \{d \in \mathcal{C}^\uparrow | pd \in \Gamma\}$

- **for all** $\alpha \in \text{PROG}, a \in \text{ASS}$ we have $R_{\alpha,a} =_{\text{def}} \{(\Gamma, \Gamma') \mid$ **forall** $A \in \mathcal{L}^+(a([\alpha]A) \in \Gamma \Rightarrow a(A) \in \Gamma')\}$

In order to show (cf. 5 in Appendix A)

$$\Gamma, a \models A \Leftrightarrow a(A) \in \Gamma$$

we proceed as in Appendix A. The base caes, $A = (s = t)$ and $A = pt$, are treated likewise. The same holds for the induction steps except for $A = [\alpha]B$. For this step, we need the following. For all sentences A we have:

$$[\alpha]A \in \Gamma \Leftrightarrow \text{ forall } \Gamma'(\Gamma R_{\alpha,a}\Gamma' \Rightarrow A \in \Gamma') \tag{6}$$

This is proved as follows.

$\Rightarrow$: directly by the definition of $R_{\alpha,a}$.

$\Leftarrow$: by contraposition. Let $[\alpha]A \notin \Gamma$; it suffices to construct a Γ' with $\Gamma R_{\alpha,a}\Gamma'$ and $A \notin \Gamma'$. So put

$$\Gamma'' = \{\neg A\} \cup \{B \mid [\alpha]B \in \Gamma\}.$$

We claim that Γ'' is consistent. To see this, assume the contrary, then we have $\{B \mid [\alpha]B\epsilon\Gamma\} \vdash A$ and (with [**N**]) $\{[\alpha]B \mid [\alpha]B \in \Gamma\} \vdash [\alpha]A$, so $\Gamma \vdash [\alpha]A$, i.e. contradiction. Now extend Γ'' to $\Gamma' \in W$. Then $\Gamma R_{\alpha,a}\Gamma'$ and $\neg A \in \Gamma'$, so $A \notin \Gamma'$. This ends the proof of (6).

The only thing we have to do yet is to show that H is not only a structure but also a model. This is done as follows: let $\Gamma R_{\alpha,a}\Gamma'$, then for all sentences A we have

$$[\alpha]A \in \Gamma \Rightarrow A \in \Gamma' \tag{7}$$

Using this and the properties of **MLCM** we must be able to conclude that $R_{\alpha,a}$ satisfies the requirements in the definition of the semantics. We consider several cases for α.

The case $\alpha = \text{NEW}c$: for the first two requirements we need

$$d \simeq e \in \Gamma \Leftrightarrow \tag{8}$$
$$(d \simeq e \in \Gamma' \text{ or } (d \simeq\uparrow \wedge e \simeq c) \in \Gamma' \text{ or } (e \simeq\uparrow \wedge d \simeq c) \in \Gamma'),$$

for then $U_{\Gamma'}$ is the extension of U_Γ with the object $c_{\Gamma'}$. Now (8) follows from (consequence **4**), (consequence **5**) and (7).

For the behaviour of functions (the third requirement) we need

$$fd \simeq e \in \Gamma' \Leftrightarrow (fd \simeq e \in \Gamma \text{ and } e \not\simeq c \in \Gamma') \tag{9}$$

for then we have that $f_{\Gamma'}c = f_{\Gamma'} \uparrow$ and $f_{\Gamma'}$ behaves like f_Γ elsewhere. Now (9) follows from (consequence **6**), (consequence **7**), $[\text{NEW}c]fx \not\simeq c$ and (7).

The behaviour of predicates (the fourth requirement) is treated likewise.

For $\alpha = (f(s) := t)$ the first requirement states that the universe does not change, and this follows from

$$d \simeq e \in \Gamma \Leftrightarrow d \simeq e \in \Gamma' \tag{10}$$

which is a consequence of [**FM1**] (reading $d \simeq e$ and $d \not\simeq e$ for A) and (7). One easily checks that [**FM 2**] and [**FM 3**] take care of the behaviour of f.

The case $\alpha = (p(s) :\leftrightarrow A)$ is treated likewise.

For $\alpha = A?$, $\alpha = \beta;\gamma$ or $\alpha = \beta \cup \gamma$ the proof is straightforward.

Author Index

Published in 1990–92

AI and Cognitive Science '89, Dublin City University, Eire, 14–15 September 1989
Alan F. Smeaton and Gabriel McDermott (Eds.)

Specification and Verification of Concurrent Systems, University of Stirling, Scotland, 6–8 July 1988
C. Rattray (Ed.)

Semantics for Concurrency, Proceedings of the International BCS-FACS Workshop, Sponsored by Logic for IT (S.E.R.C.), University of Leicester, UK, 23–25 July 1990
M. Z. Kwiatkowska, M. W. Shields and R. M. Thomas (Eds.)

Functional Programming, Glasgow 1989
Proceedings of the 1989 Glasgow Workshop, Fraserburgh, Scotland, 21–23 August 1989
Kei Davis and John Hughes (Eds.)

Persistent Object Systems, Proceedings of the Third International Workshop, Newcastle, Australia, 10–13 January 1989
John Rosenberg and David Koch (Eds.)

Z User Workshop, Oxford 1989, Proceedings of the Fourth Annual Z User Meeting, Oxford, 15 December 1989
J. E. Nicholls (Ed.)

Formal Methods for Trustworthy Computer Systems (FM89), Halifax, Canada, 23–27 July 1989
Dan Craigen (Editor) and Karen Summerskill (Assistant Editor)

Security and Persistence, Proceedings of the International Workshop on Computer Architectures to Support Security and Persistence of Information, Bremen, West Germany, 8–11 May 1990
John Rosenberg and J. Leslie Keedy (Eds.)

Women into Computing: Selected Papers 1988–1990
Gillian Lovegrove and Barbara Segal (Eds.)

3rd Refinement Workshop (organised by BCS-FACS, and sponsored by IBM UK Laboratories, Hursley Park and the Programming Research Group, University of Oxford), Hursley Park, 9–11 January 1990
Carroll Morgan and J. C. P. Woodcock (Eds.)

Designing Correct Circuits, Workshop jointly organised by the Universities of Oxford and Glasgow, Oxford, 26–28 September 1990
Geraint Jones and Mary Sheeran (Eds.)

Functional Programming, Glasgow 1990
Proceedings of the 1990 Glasgow Workshop on Functional Programming, Ullapool, Scotland, 13–15 August 1990
Simon L. Peyton Jones, Graham Hutton and Carsten Kehler Holst (Eds.)

4th Refinement Workshop, Proceedings of the 4th Refinement Workshop, organised by BCS-FACS, Cambridge, 9–11 January 1991
Joseph M. Morris and Roger C. Shaw (Eds.)

AI and Cognitive Science '90, University of Ulster at Jordanstown, 20–21 September 1990
Michael F. McTear and Norman Creaney (Eds.)

Software Re-use, Utrecht 1989, Proceedings of the Software Re-use Workshop, Utrecht, The Netherlands, 23–24 November 1989
Liesbeth Dusink and Patrick Hall (Eds.)

Z User Workshop, 1990, Proceedings of the Fifth Annual Z User Meeting, Oxford, 17–18 December 1990
J.E. Nicholls (Ed.)

IV Higher Order Workshop, Banff 1990
Proceedings of the IV Higher Order Workshop, Banff, Alberta, Canada, 10–14 September 1990
Graham Birtwistle (Ed.)

ALPUK91, Proceedings of the 3rd UK Annual Conference on Logic Programming, Edinburgh, 10–12 April 1991
Geraint A.Wiggins, Chris Mellish and Tim Duncan (Eds.)

Specifications of Database Systems
International Workshop on Specifications of Database Systems, Glasgow, 3–5 July 1991
David J. Harper and Moira C. Norrie (Eds.)

7th UK Computer and Telecommunications Performance Engineering Workshop
Edinburgh, 22–23 July 1991
J. Hillston, P.J.B. King and R.J. Pooley (Eds.)

Logic Program Synthesis and Transformation
Proceedings of LOPSTR 91, International Workshop on Logic Program Synthesis and Transformation, University of Manchester, 4–5 July 1991
T.P. Clement and K.-K. Lau (Eds.)

Declarative Programming, Sasbachwalden 1991
PHOENIX Seminar and Workshop on Declarative Programming, Sasbachwalden, Black Forest, Germany, 18–22 November 1991
John Darlington and Roland Dietrich (Eds.)

Building Interactive Systems:
Architectures and Tools
Philip Gray and Roger Took (Eds.)

Functional Programming, Glasgow 1991
Proceedings of the 1991 Glasgow Workshop on
Functional Programming, Portree, Isle of Skye,
12–14 August 1991
Rogardt Heldal, Carsten Kehler Holst and
Philip Wadler (Eds.)

Object Orientation in Z
Susan Stepney, Rosalind Barden and
David Cooper (Eds.)

Code Generation – Concepts, Tools, Techniques
Proceedings of the International Workshop on Code
Generation, Dagstuhl, Germany, 20–24 May 1991
Robert Giegerich and Susan L. Graham (Eds.)

Z User Workshop, York 1991, Proceedings of the
Sixth Annual Z User Meeting, York,
16–17 December 1991
J.E. Nicholls (Ed.)

Formal Aspects of Measurement
Proceedings of the BCS-FACS Workshop on
Formal Aspects of Measurement, South Bank
University, London, 5 May 1991
Tim Denvir, Ros Herman and R.W. Whitty (Eds.)

AI and Cognitive Science '91
University College, Cork, 19–20 September 1991
Humphrey Sorensen (Ed.)

5th Refinement Workshop, Proceedings of the 5th
Refinement Workshop, organised by BCS-FACS,
London, 8–10 January 1992
Cliff B. Jones, Roger C. Shaw and
Tim Denvir (Eds.)

Algebraic Methodology and Software
Technology (AMAST'91)
Proceedings of the Second International Conference
on Algebraic Methodology and Software
Technology, Iowa City, USA, 22–25 May 1991
M. Nivat, C. Rattray, T. Rus and G. Scollo (Eds.)

ALPUK92, Proceedings of the 4th UK
Conference on Logic Programming,
London, 30 March – 1 April 1992
Krysia Broda (Ed.)